The Dinner at Gonfarone's
Salomón de la Selva and
His Pan-American Project in Nueva York,
1915–1919

American Tropics: Towards a Literary Geography

American Tropics: Towards a Literary Geography

The term 'American Tropics' refers to a kind of extended Caribbean, an area which includes the southern USA, the Atlantic littoral of Central America, the Caribbean islands, and northern South America. European colonial powers fought intensively here against indigenous populations and against each other for control of land and resources. This area shares a history in which the dominant fact is the arrival of millions of white Europeans and black Africans; shares an environment which is tropical or sub-tropical; and shares a socio-economic model (the plantation) whose effects lasted well into the twentieth century. The approach taken by the series is geographical in the sense that the focus of each volume is on a *region*. Each region is a zone of encounter, bringing together sets of writing in different languages and styles, from different literary and cultural backgrounds, all of which have in common the attention paid to the same place.

The imaginative space of the American Tropics series therefore offers a differently centred literary history from those conventionally produced as US, Caribbean, or Latin American literature. The development of the discipline of cultural geography has encouraged more sophisticated analyses of notions of place and region, which this series brings to bear on its materials. The individual volumes therefore stand at an angle to national literary histories, offering a different perspective, with each volume contributing one piece of the jigsaw towards a completely new map of the literary history of the area.

Series Editors

Maria Cristina Fumagalli (Professor in the Department of Literature, Film, and Theatre Studies at the University of Essex)

Peter Hulme (Emeritus Professor in the Department of Literature, Film, and Theatre Studies at the University of Essex)

Jak Peake (Senior Lecturer in the Department of Literature, Film, and Theatre Studies at the University of Essex)

Owen Robinson (Senior Lecturer in the Department of Literature, Film, and Theatre Studies at the University of Essex)

Lesley Wylie (Associate Professor in the School of Modern Languages at the University of Leicester)

The Dinner at Gonfarone's

Salomón de la Selva and
His Pan-American Project in Nueva York,
1915–1919

PETER HULME

LIVERPOOL UNIVERSITY PRESS

First published 2019 by
Liverpool University Press
4 Cambridge Street
Liverpool
L69 7ZU

Copyright © 2019 Peter Hulme

The right of Peter Hulme to be identified as the author of this book has been asserted by him in accordance with the Copyright, Designs and Patents Act 1988.

All rights reserved. No part of this book may be reproduced, stored in a retrieval system, or transmitted, in any form or by any means, electronic, mechanical, photocopying, recording, or otherwise, without the prior written permission of the publisher.

British Library Cataloguing-in-Publication data
A British Library CIP record is available

ISBN 978-1-78694-200-5 cased

Typeset by Carnegie Book Production, Lancaster
Printed and bound in Poland by BooksFactory.co.uk

Jessie Rittenhouse, Edna St Vincent Millay, and Salomón de la Selva at the Pan-American Dinner in honour of Millay, Felix-Portland Hotel, Thursday, 27 December 1917. Photographer unknown.
Enclosed in a letter from Salomón de la Selva to Edna St Vincent Millay, 28 December 1917. Edna St. Vincent Millay Papers (MSS 32920), Library of Congress, Washington, DC.

For all my American friends

To the North I came, with a dream, with a song,
With a noise like the music of the rain in the Spring,
For I held the Vision and it ruled my tongue,
And North and South would hear me sing.

Salomón de la Selva,
from 'The Dreamer's Heart Knows Its Own Bitterness',
Tropical Town (1918)

Contents

List of Illustrations	xi
Notes on Translation, Usage, and Abbreviations	xiii
Introduction	1
1 Setting the Scene: New York in 1914	9
The Hispanic Presence	10
The Poetic Waters	19
Modernity and Modernism	26
2 American Geopolitics in the New Century (1898–1914)	33
The Famous States	34
Pan-Americanism	44
Roosevelt's Vision	49
The Shakespearean Allegory	56
3 The Changing of the Poetic Guard (1915)	75
Growing up in New York	77
Rubén Darío in Hospital	82
Befriending Pedro, Loving Edna	106
The First Dinner	127
4 New York through Spanish Eyes (1916)	136
Courting Archer	137
The Recently Married Poet	141
Edwin Markham on Staten Island	158
Wilson's Crime in Santo Domingo	164
A Tale from Faerieland	169
5 Goading the Bull Moose (1917)	178
Confronting Roosevelt	179
Mamita Schauffler	189

	Chicago	198
	Introducing Edna	202
6 The Pan-American Dream (1918)		208
	Is America Honest?	210
	Translating Poetry	217
	Tropical Town	237
	Falling in Love Again	252
	Fighting for England	257
7 The Last Dinner (1919)		277
	Nueva York	279
	A Soldier Returns	284
	The Dinner at Gonfarone's	291
	The Gulf of Misunderstanding	323
	Nicaragua Has Me	329
Aftermath		335
	Leaving New York	335
	In Mexico	342
	Later Life	345
	Taking Account	349
Biographies		354
Acknowledgements		366
Select Bibliography		369
Index		382

Illustrations

Frontispiece Jessie Rittenhouse, Edna St Vincent Millay, and Salomón de la Selva at the Pan-American Dinner in December 1917

1	Archer Milton Huntington	17
2	Hispanic Society of America	19
3	William Walker's entrance into Granada	37
4	The Butterick Building	78
5	Salomón de la Selva aged 16, probably on Staten Island	79
6	Rubén Darío in New York in 1915	89
7	Manuel Florentino Cestero	110
8	Jesusa Alfau Galván	114
9	Pedro Henríquez Ureña	115
10	José Santos Chocano drawn by Conrado Massaguer	127
11	Juan Ramón Jiménez painted by Joaquín Sorolla y Bastida	142
12	Martín Luis Guzmán	150
13	Edwin Markham	159
14	Fabio Fiallo	165
15	National Arts Club	182
16	'A 100 Per Cent Fighting Family'	195
17	Programme for the pan-American dinner in honour of Edna St Vincent Millay	206
18	Alfonso Guillén Zelaya	221
19	Thomas Walsh	241

20	Jeanne Robert Foster	253
21	Theresa Helburn	257
22	Salomón de la Selva enlists in the British Army	265
23	Salomón de la Selva in the uniform of the British Army	268
24	Salomón de la Selva and his platoon in Felixstowe, 1918	271
25	Marya Zaturenska	287
26	Muna Lee	288
27	W. Adolphe Roberts	292
28	Vennette Herron	295
29	José Castellot Batalla	310
30	Arturo Torres Rioseco	314
31	Carmen Torres Calderón de Pinillos	320
32	Graciela Mandujano	322
33	Jessie Rittenhouse	331

Notes on Translation, Usage, and Abbreviations

Unless otherwise mentioned, all translations are mine. The original (mostly Spanish) is sometimes given, when deemed of particular importance. It should be noted that most of Salomón de la Selva's words quoted in this book were written in English.

'America' is the continent and its adjective is 'American'. 'The USA' is the country and its adjective is 'US'.

I mostly eschew 'Latino' on the grounds that it wasn't often used in the years central to this study. 'Hispanic' is used frequently, partly because it encompasses Spanish as well as Spanish-American writers.

At the time, 'Pan-Americanism' and its cognates sometimes appeared with a hyphen, sometimes without, sometimes with upper-case initial for 'pan', sometimes not. Apart from quotations, I try to hold on to a distinction between official 'Pan-American(ism)' and more general and unofficial 'pan-American(ism)'.

Abbreviations to archives and manuscript collections are explained at first mention in the footnotes and in the first section of the *Select Bibliography*.

Introduction

At 8.30 on the evening of Saturday, 21 June 1919, 32 writers gathered in a private room at the restaurant in the Hotel Gonfarone, in Greenwich Village, New York, for a dinner to celebrate the publication of a book of poems by one of their number. After dinner there were readings by various guests; the party broke up in the early hours. Perhaps the only unusual aspect to the occasion is that it had been advertised as a 'pan-American' dinner. This book is an attempt to understand just what resonance the term pan-American had in literary circles in Manhattan at that time. One immediate key is found on the invitation list. The guests were divided more or less equally between US and Hispanic writers: the organiser was clearly making a point. That organiser was a young Nicaraguan poet called Salomón de la Selva, whose life in New York will here remain the touchstone. The pan-American literary project was to a large extent of de la Selva's making: he certainly tried his hardest to sustain it over the five years between 1915 and 1919, the period covered in these pages. That 1919 dinner was the final event in a sequence that began in 1915, book-ending a period that saw dramatic fluctuations in the literary, cultural, social, sexual, and political life of New York, which here forms the backdrop to the less recognised but persistent presence of Hispanic voices interpreting the capital of the twentieth century. Sometimes these Hispanic writers found themselves adrift in the alien yet strangely hypnotic world of New York, but they also often interacted with fellow-writers as they were drawn into de la Selva's ambitious imagining of a trans-American community of poets. During these five years de la Selva worked as a professional translator and spent ten months as a member of the British Army, but mostly he wrote. There survive from this period more than 200 poems, almost all in English, more than 50 translations of poems, from Spanish to English and vice versa, more than ten prose essays and reviews, and nearly 200 letters, some of them more than 20 pages long. The book that follows draws extensively on that material.

*

The main part of the book is organised chronologically. The scene-setting of Chapter 1 takes place in New York in 1914, just as the young poet is about to make his debut. Although the great influx of Spanish speakers into New York didn't happen until the 1920s, New York was already in significant ways a Hispanic city: a northern outpost of the largely Spanish-speaking and tropical world south of the border. The school de la Selva attended on Staten Island had a substantial number of pupils from Central and South America, and his early work, translating into Spanish for a fashion magazine, would have introduced him to other Spanish speakers. Already flourishing up in Washington Heights was the Hispanic Society of America, founded by Archer Huntington, which was gearing up to sponsor Hispanic writers and artists. Another stage awaiting de la Selva was the grand room at the National Arts Club, in the beautiful Samuel Tilden Mansion on Gramercy Park South where the new Poetry Society of America (PSA) had just started meeting. It was here that de la Selva would make his first contacts in the world of US poetry: Margaret Widdemer, Jessie Rittenhouse, Joyce and Aline Kilmer, Louis Untermeyer, Alan Seeger, Edwin Markham. Although these were the leading poets of their day in New York, their reputations would not survive the later canonisation of the high modernism whose early signs were just becoming apparent: Ezra Pound attended just one PSA meeting in 1911 before he decamped to London. But 1914 did see the arrival in New York of Rubén Darío, the high priest of *modernismo*, the Spanish-American predecessor of its Anglo namesake, whose persistent presence on the early fringes has tended to embarrass histories of modernism written in English. Chapter 1 takes the opportunity to recalibrate that relationship in order to provide a more welcoming environment in which to approach Salomón de la Selva's poetic practice.

Chapter 2 sketches the relevant geopolitical background: the relationship between the USA and the Spanish-speaking countries to its south between 1898 and 1914. The year 1898 had seen the USA defeat Spain and inherit the remnants of its empire. Puerto Rico became a US possession; Cuba was very much under US control, with the Guantánamo Bay naval base a key element in guarding the Atlantic route to and from the Panama Canal, which opened in 1914. Theodore Roosevelt's policies dominated these years, even after the end of his presidency in March 1909. By 1914, the governance of Nicaragua was overseen by US Marines; the Dominican Republic and Haiti would soon follow into US control. Increasingly, America was seen as divided into two, north and south, Anglo and Latin. The official ideology of Pan-Americanism was meant to soothe the division, but Latin Americans tended to prefer a Shakespearean allegory in which they were Ariel to the US Caliban. Salomón de la Selva refused to accept either version, although at times he must have felt as if he were one poet facing a continent divided against itself.

Chapters 3 to 7 then each cover a year from 1915 to 1919, tracing the development of de la Selva's project, with the occasional counterpoint of other Hispanic visitors to New York, most of whom he knew. Chapter 3 (1915) begins with the latter stages of Rubén Darío's visit to the city and one of his final pieces of writing, set in a hospital. Two of de la Selva's most important friendships began in this year: with the Dominican writer and polymath Pedro Henríquez Ureña and with the young sensation of US poetry, Edna St Vincent Millay. The letters de la Selva wrote to Millay form one of the most important threads running through *The Dinner at Gonfarone's*: he always opened his heart to Edna. The chapter ends with the first dinner in the sequence that would culminate at Gonfarone's.

One outcome of Darío's visit to New York was the Hispanic Society of America's sponsorship of the first translations into English of his poetry, undertaken by de la Selva and the US Hispanist Thomas Walsh, with whom de la Selva had a fraught relationship. This provides the opening section of Chapter 4 (1916), followed by a discussion of the experimental semi-epic which resulted from the visit to New York of the Spanish poet Juan Ramón Jiménez. Another thread of de la Selva's correspondence began this year, with Edwin Markham, probably the US poet who showed most interest in young Hispanic writers in the city, and whose own poem, 'The Man with the Hoe', provided a model for some, in particular the Puerto Rican, Luis Muñoz Marín, with whom de la Selva would strike up a close friendship. The Hispanic cause of the year, which would remain an issue throughout this period, was the US occupation of the Dominican Republic.

If Roosevelt was still the iconic US figure of these years, then 1917, the subject of Chapter 5, saw the iconic pan-American confrontation when Salomón de la Selva read his specially written poem denouncing US foreign policy in front of Roosevelt himself at a glittering National Arts Club dinner. It was de la Selva's finest public moment. That winter he was teaching at Williams College in Massachusetts, an appointment that led to another important female relationship, with Florence Schauffler, the mother of two of his students. Finally, at the end of the year he managed to organise a dinner at which seven Latin American poets could honour Edna Millay.

Once the USA had joined the war in Europe, de la Selva was determined to fight for France and civilisation, but that proved easier said than done. Chapter 6 (1918) deals with his busiest year to date, marked by the beginning (and end) of his project for a poetry magazine, the publication of his own first book of poems, and his enlistment in the British Army, which led to frustrating months in East Anglia, hoping in vain to be sent to the trenches. In retrospect, the poetry magazine—with translation from English to Spanish and vice versa—was a pioneering achievement, even if de la Selva had to do most of the translations himself. *Tropical Town*, too, although respectfully received, would have to wait more than half a century for proper recognition.

Back in New York, de la Selva organised a final pan-American event, the dinner at Gonfarone's, to celebrate the publication of his friend Adolphe Roberts's first book of poems. Chapter 7 (1919) offers a detailed look at the organisation of the dinner and at its guest list, taking the pulse of Nueva York, before ending with a long letter in which de la Selva announced a defining decision as to his poetic identity.

'Aftermath' then sketches de la Selva's withdrawal from New York, the writing of his second book *El soldado desconocido*, and—very briefly—the rest of his life, before ending with a few paragraphs about his own reflections on his pan-American project. 'Biographies' provides further information on what happened subsequently to figures significant for de la Selva's New York years.

*

The Dinner at Gonfarone's situates itself within the field of trans-American literary studies.[1] Since its origins in the eighteenth century, literary history has been tied to national history, either territorial or linguistic, often both. Various versions of 'world literature' hold out the promise of allowing us to understand cross-national transactions, but in practice their focus is too wide for significant detail to be visible. A trans-American lens is alert to literary work which appears at best interstitial to conventional historiography. So the American Tropics project takes as its geographical frame an area which includes the southern part of North America, the eastern part of Central America, the Caribbean islands, and the northern part of South America.[2] Within that frame, close attention can then be focused on a much

---

[1] See Kirsten Silva Gruesz, *Ambassadors of Culture: The Transamerican Origins of Latino Writing*, Princeton, NJ: Princeton University Press, 2002; and Laura Lomas, 'The Trans-American Literature of Empire and Revolution, 1880–1938', in *The Cambridge Companion to Latino/a Literature*, ed. John Morán González and Laura Lomas, New York: Cambridge University Press, 2016, pp. 17–35.

[2] See, for example, Maria Cristina Fumagalli, Peter Hulme, Owen Robinson, and Lesley Wylie, eds, *Surveying the American Tropics: A Literary Geography from New*

smaller region or place seen as a crucible or crossroads, looking in detail at the relationships within it. New York between 1915 and 1919 is suitable for such an analysis because of the number of writers from all parts of the American Tropics (and beyond) then residing in, visiting, and writing about the city. The presence of Salomón de la Selva's pan-American project provides a sharp focus for the resulting interaction of those writers with their surroundings and with each other. It constitutes a small but significant piece in an emerging new geography of American literary history.[3]

Salomón de la Selva (1893–1959) rarely now merits more than a footnote in literary histories of any stripe. Within that of Latin American literature, he is seen as a minor poet who bridges the gap between his eminent predecessor, Rubén Darío, and the vanguard generation led by César Vallejo: in this context he is best known as the author of *El soldado desconocido* [*The Unknown Soldier*], the only book of First World War poetry written in Spanish. The first Spanish-language version of the anthologies of 'new American poetry' appeared in 1926: de la Selva was the only Nicaraguan, with four poems from *El soldado desconocido*.[4] Then, 15 years later, the 1,134 pages of the ambitious *Laurel: Antología de la poesía moderna en lengua española* included the work of 30 poets, starting with Miguel de Unamuno and Rubén Darío; de la Selva had 17 poems, 11 of them from *El soldado desconocido*, compared with 18 by César Vallejo, 15 by Federico García Lorca, and four by Vicente Huidobro, although one was very long. This amounted to a canonisation of sorts for de la Selva—but it didn't last long.[5] Something

---

York to Rio, Liverpool: Liverpool University Press, 2013. The *American Tropics* book series grew out of a research project which ran from 2006 to 2011: <https://www1.essex.ac.uk/lifts/American_Tropics/> accessed December 2018.

[3] The book's longer time frame, 1898 to 1919, is exactly the period covered by Mike Wallace in *Greater Gotham: A History of New York City from 1898 to 1919*, New York: Oxford University Press, 2017, which provides an indispensable background.

[4] *Indice de la nueva poesía americana*, ed. Alberto Hidalgo, Vicente Huidobro, and Jorge Luis Borges, Mexico and Buenos Aires: Sociedad de Publicaciones El Inca, 1926: 'Remordimiento', 'Granadas', 'El Palomar', and 'La Bala' (pp. 247–49). It seems as if Hidalgo made the selection.

[5] *Laurel: Antología de la poesía moderna en lengua española*, Mexico City: Laberinto Editorial Seneca, 1941. The selection was made by Emilio Prados, Xavier Villaurrutia, Juan Gil-Albert, and Octavio Paz. Villaurrutia signed the Introduction. Pablo Neruda and Leon Felipe had asked to be excluded. Twenty years later Paz defended the inclusion of de la Selva: Octavio Paz, '*Laurel* y la poesía moderna', *Quimera*, 26 (1982), 10–19, and 27 (1982), 12–22 (at 13).

of a second coming was then initiated in 1980 by a short but influential essay by the Mexican poet and critic José Emilio Pacheco, identifying the countercurrent in twentieth-century Latin American poetry called 'antipoesía' or 'poesía conversacional' as having its origins in the reading of early twentieth-century US poetry by the Dominican critic Pedro Henríquez Ureña, and the adoption of its informality into poetry in Spanish by Salomón de la Selva, who was thereby recognised as a kind of cultural go-between, a translator of poetic modalities from one linguistic tradition to another.[6] Although Pacheco doesn't make the point, attention might then properly be directed at New York, where Henríquez Ureña and de la Selva lived and worked before both moving to Mexico City in the early 1920s. Soon after Pacheco's essay, de la Selva's work as a propagandist for the nationalist fighter Augusto Sandino in the late 1920s and early 1930s was recognised by the Sandinista government in Nicaragua, which sponsored new editions and fostered a wider interest at least at home in de la Selva's life and work.[7]

---

[6] José Emilio Pacheco, 'Nota sobre la vanguardia', *Casa de las Américas*, XX, no. 18 (1980), 103–07. See also Jorge Eduardo Arellano, 'Salomón de la Selva y "la otra vanguardia"', *Anales de literatura hispanoamericana*, 18 (1989), 99–103; and Steven F. White, 'Salomón de la Selva: poeta comprometido de la "otra" vanguardia', *Revista Iberoamericana*, 157 (October–December 1991), 915–21. Other studies of de la Selva's Spanish-language poetry of the 1920s include José Eduardo Serrato Córdova, 'Tres poetas centroamericanos en la vanguardia mexicana (1922-1948): Salomón de la Selva, Arqueles Vela y Luis Cardoza y Aragón', in *Tensiones de la modernidad: del modernismo al realismo*, ed. Valeria Grinberg Pla and Ricardo Roque Baldovinos, Guatemala: F & G Editores, 2009, pp. 191–212.

[7] New editions and collections included *El soldado desconocido* [1922], Managua: Editorial Nueva Nicaragua, 1982; *Sandino: Free Country or Death*, ed. Jorge Eduardo Arellano, Managua: Biblioteca Nacional de Nicaragua, 1984; and *La guerra de Sandino o el pueblo desnudo*, Managua: Editorial Nueva Nicaragua, 1985. There was also *Homenaje a Salomón de la Selva*, Managua: Biblioteca Banco de Nicaragua, 1976; *Siete Ensayos y un Poema sobre Salomón de la Selva*, Managua: Fundación Internacional Rubén Darío, 1993; and the large-scale if incomplete critical and biographical study: Jorge Eduardo Arellano, *Aventura y genio de Salomón de la Selva*, León: Alcaldía Municipal, 2003; followed more recently by the three-volume anthology: *Antología Mayor/I Poesías*, ed. Julio Valle-Castillo, Managua: Fundación UNO, 2007; *Antología Mayor/II Narrativa*, ed. Julio Valle-Castillo, Managua: Fundación UNO, 2007; *Antología Mayor/III Ensayos*, ed. Julio Valle-Castillo, Managua: Fundación UNO, 2009. See also Fernando Centeno Zapata, 'Salomón de la Selva: Precursor de las luchas sociales en Nicaragua' [1974], *Revista de temas nicaragüenses*, no. 82 (February 2015), 166–82. For a more sceptical view of de la Selva's political positioning, see Iván Molina Jiménez, 'Entre Sandino y Somoza: La trayectoria de Salomón de la Selva', *Secuencia*, 53 (2002), 139–61. On *El soldado desconocido*, see Ernesto Cardenal, 'Salomón de la Selva: El soldado desconocido', *Rueca*, V, no. 18 (1948), 12–19; and Steven F. White, 'Salomón

Until recently, the fact that he wrote poems in both English and Spanish tended to count against de la Selva: his work in English didn't contribute to Latin American literature but was ignored in studies of US writing, 'ethnic' or otherwise. A growing interest in the Hispanic heritage within the USA eventually resulted in the recovery of the achievement of de la Selva's first book, *Tropical Town and Other Poems* (1918), which was given a new edition in 1999 as part of the series Recovering the US Hispanic Literary Heritage, but he still didn't merit even a mention in the 2,489 pages of *The Norton Anthology of Latino Literature*.[8] Slowly, however, in recent years, a more complex picture of the poet has gradually begun to emerge, though there is still much confusion about even the basic facts of his biography and publications. However, some of his previously uncollected poems in English have recently been published, new studies have appeared in Nicaragua, and his pioneering rôle as a pan-Americanist has begun to be recognised.[9]

---

de la Selva: Testimonial Poetry and World War I', in his *Modern Nicaraguan Poetry: Dialogues with France and the United States*, Lewisburg, PA: Bucknell University Press, 1993, pp. 119–43.

[8] Salomón de la Selva, *Tropical Town and Other Poems*, ed., with an introduction, by Silvio Sirias, Houston, TX: Arte Público Press, 1999; and see Nicolás Urbina, 'Salomón de la Selva de la modernidad al neoclasisismo', *Hispanic Poetry Review*, 5, no. 2 (2006), 1–16; Hervé Le Corre, 'Un *passeur* encore méconnu: Salomón de la Selva (1893–1956)', in *América: Cahiers du CRICCAL, n°39, 2010. Transamériques. Les échanges culturels continentaux*, 11ᵉ Colloque international du CRICCAL, Paris, 16–18 October 2008, pp. 195–206; and David A. Colón's two essays, 'Deep Translation and Subversive Formalism: The Case of Salomón de la Selva's *Tropical Town, and Other Poems* (1918)', *Journal of Philosophy: A Cross-Disciplinary Inquiry*, 7, no. 17 (2012), 11–27, and 'Making It Nuevo: Latina/o Modernist Poetics Remake High Euro-American Modernism', in *The Cambridge History of Latina/o American Literature*, ed. John Morán González and Laura Lomas, New York: Cambridge University Press, 2018, pp. 353–70. The new edition led to the appearance of three of de la Selva's poems in *The New Anthology of American Poetry*, ed. Steven Gould Axelrod, Camille Roman, and Thomas J. Travisano, 3 vols., New Brunswick, NJ: Rutgers University Press, 2005, vol. 2, *Modernisms 1900–1950*, pp. 477–79 (marred by several errors in the brief biography). *The Norton Anthology of Latino Literature*, ed. Ilan Stavans, New York: W.W. Norton & Co., 2011. There is a cursory mention in *The Routledge Companion to Latino/a Literature*, ed. Suzanne Bost and Frances Aparicio, Abingdon: Routledge, 2013, as part of an essay on Central American writing in the USA (pp. 449–50).

[9] *An Unknown Songster Sings: Salomón de la Selva's Collected Poems, 1915–1958 = Un bardo desconocido canta: poemas recolectados de Salomón de la Selva, 1915–1958*, compilation, prologue, and annotation by Luis M. Bolaños-Salvatierra; translation by Luis M. Bolaños-Salvatierra, Guillermo Fernández-Ampié, and Moisés Elías Fuentes, Managua: Academia Nicaraguense de la Lengua, 2015; María Augusta Montealegre, *Ideas estéticas y políticas de las Vanguardias en Nicaragua (1918–1933)*, vol. 1, *Salomón*

Although not a biography as such, this present book does try to reconstruct a detailed picture of de la Selva over the years 1915 to 1919 in order to understand the complexities of a very early 'pan-American' life: a writer trying to live and love in two languages and two cultures, committed to both at a time when other forces were driving them apart. I'm suggesting that it is useful to remember de la Selva's pan-American poetry project as a significant ancestor of strands of contemporary writing situated close to the interface between English and Spanish: what is often now referred to as 'Latino' or 'Latinx' literature, written in English by writers with a Hispanic background such as Pedro Pietri, Julia Álvarez, Tato Laviera, and Junot Díaz. Long before these writers were born, Salomón de la Selva constructed and inhabited that project and *The Dinner at Gonfarone's* follows his movements and thinking and contacts as closely as possible in order to try to understand how he responded to the challenges that faced him. At the same time, the book is determined, as much as possible, not to read through the lens of hindsight. While what happened subsequently in the realms of political and literary history or in the personal lives of the book's protagonists can't simply be ignored, it is possible not to operate on the assumption that those subsequent events were inevitable and that later readings of the period have therefore produced unproblematic truths and canons cast in stone. Some effort is made, in other words, to recapture the sense of openness and possibility that characterised these years of vertiginous change in so many fields.

Finally, the book is also concerned to reconstruct the places associated with the pan-American project; hence what might seem to some readers the obsessive recounting of precise addresses. There is a rationale here. To the extent to which early twentieth-century Hispanic New York has been recognised, it has tended to be seen as an *area* of the city. The classic study is Konrad Berkovici's *Around the World in New York* (1924), which identified Little Spain, Little Hungary, Little Syria, as if the city were divided into units. The interest here in identifying the actual places where writers lived and where meetings took place is intended to demonstrate the pervasiveness of the presence of Hispanic writers in New York—Nueva York—during these years. Literary history is always also literary geography.

---

de la Selva, Managua: Academia de Geografía e Historia de Nicaragua, 2016 (her full doctoral thesis is 'Las ideas estéticas y políticas de las vanguardias en Nicaragua (1918-1933): Salomón de la Selva y el autodenominado Movimiento Nicaragüense de Vanguardia', University of Salamanca, 2015); Steven F. White, *Rubén Darío y Salomón de la Selva: Ecos de la muerte y la guerra*, León: Promotora Cultural Leonesa, 2016; and Jonathan Cohen, 'Remembering Salomón de la Selva—Pioneer Leader of Pan-American Poetry', *Review: Literature and Arts of the Americas*, 48, no. 2 (2015), 193-99.

Chapter One

Setting the Scene: New York in 1914

And a deep labyrinth, most intricate,
Through whose black vaults unwound the thread of Fate.[1]

The years covered by *The Dinner at Gonfarone's* were marked by the eruption in New York of all the signs of modernity. Telephones and motor cars became ubiquitous; skyscrapers rose higher and higher; campaigns for women's suffrage and for birth control gained traction, as did those for racial equality and workers' rights. After a slow start, the twentieth century was gathering pace, but while the 1920s were quickly seen as 'roaring', an epithet that has stuck, the previous decade has never been susceptible to easy definition; indeed, its first few years are sometimes regarded as the dregs of the nineteenth century. From a literary perspective, these years are conventionally cast as the calm before the storm of modernism associated with the *annus mirabilis* of 1922. In the chronological *A New Literary History of America*, almost all years have entries, but the second half of the second decade of the twentieth century includes only three: 1915 features for Robert Frost's return to the USA from England and the release of D. W. Griffiths's *The Birth of a Nation*, and 1917 for Albert C. Barnes's request to John Dewey to attend his seminar at Columbia.[2] *The Dinner at Gonfarone's* suggests that rather more of significance was going on at this time.

---

[1] From Salomón de la Selva, 'A Tale from Faerieland', *Tropical Town and Other Poems*, New York: John Lane Company, 1918, p. 88.

[2] *A New Literary History of America*, ed. Greil Marcus and Werner Sollors, Cambridge, MA: Belknap Press of Harvard University Press, 2009, pp. 531–45. For recognition of the cultural significance of this period, see Henry F. May, *The End of American Innocence: A Study of the First Years of Our Own Time, 1912–1917*, New York: Alfred A. Knopf, 1959; and Arthur Frank Wertheim, *The New York Little Renaissance: Iconoclasm, Modernism, and Nationalism in American Culture, 1908–1917*, New York: New York University Press, 1976.

The Hispanic Presence

By the end of 1914, there was already a substantial Hispanic population in New York, though the large influx which would help determine the later character of the city had yet to take place. Broadly speaking—and with the focus on writers—there had been two previous generations of Hispanic presence in New York, both dominated by Cubans, almost all of them agitating against Spanish control of their island. Some were well-to-do plantation owners who lived transnational lives, others were political exiles.[3] Félix Varela was perhaps the key figure in the first generation, José Martí definitely the central figure in the second; but as early as 1806 Francisco de Miranda's grand scheme to liberate Spanish America had been formed in New York: he was intercepted en route, but it wouldn't be the last such effort.[4] Early links between New York and Cuba were mostly commercial, but Varela had been sentenced to death for his advocacy of independence and the abolition of slavery: his New York-published magazine, *El Habanero* (1824–26) was written to be smuggled into Cuba—as it was, with some success.[5] The Cuban poet José María Heredia came briefly to the city too, and his work was translated by William Cullen Bryant, one of the two nineteenth-century US Hispanists—along with Henry Wadsworth Longfellow—whose Spanish interests included Hispanic America, possibly, in Bryant's case, as a result of having lodged for several years with a Spanish-Cuban family in New York.[6] Cuban planters favoured annexation

---

[3] See, in general, the essays in Edward J. Sullivan, ed., *Nueva York 1613–1945*, New York: The New-York Historical Society in association with Scala Publishers, 2010, particularly Mike Wallace, 'Nueva York: The Back Story' (pp. 18–81), Lisandro Pérez, 'Cubans in Nineteenth-Century New York: A Story of Sugar, War, and Revolution' (pp. 96–107), Carmen Boullosa, 'Notes on Writing in Spanish in New York' (pp. 122–35), and Katherine E. Manthorne, 'Painters, Politics, and Pastries: How New York Became a Cultural Crossroads of the Americas, 1848–99' (pp. 137–53); the essays in Claudio Iván Remeseira, ed., *Hispanic New York: A Sourcebook*, New York: Columbia University Press, 2010, particularly those by Gabriel Haslip-Viera, 'The Evolution of the Latino Community in New York City: Early Nineteenth Century to the 1990s' (pp. 33–55) and Dionisio Cañas, 'New York City: Center and Transit Point for Hispanic Cultural Nomadism' (pp. 245–99); and those in 'The Americas in New York: Writing and Arts in *La Gran Manzana*', *Review: Literature and Arts of the Americas*, 47, no. 2 (2014). See also Nancy Raquel Mirabal, *Suspect Freedoms: The Racial and Sexual Politics of Cubanidad in New York, 1823–1957*, New York: New York University Press, 2017.

[4] Wallace, 'Nueva York', pp. 26–27.

[5] Pérez, 'Cubans in Nineteenth-Century New York', p. 98.

[6] See Anna Brickhouse, '"A Story of the Island of Cuba": William Cullen Bryant and the Hispanophone Americas', *Nineteenth-Century Literature*, 56, no. 1 (2001),

by the USA, to which end Narciso López tried to launch an invasion from New York: his ships were seized by US authorities, though not before the free flag of Cuba had fluttered for the first time—in Lower Manhattan.[7] Further efforts from New Orleans only ended with López's capture and execution. The exiled Cubans' literary output was impressive too: a group including Miguel Teurbe Tolón—an editor on the *New York Herald*—put together the anthology of poems called *El laúd del desterrado* (1858).

As the Spanish-speaking community grew, Spanish-language magazines proliferated, now at least partly addressed to a *local* readership. *Noticioso de Ambos Mundos* (1836–43) was 'Dedicado a las artes, comercio, agricultura, política y bellas letras' [dedicated to the arts, business, agriculture, politics, and literature], a not uncommon range: its two worlds ['ambos mundos'] already not the old and the new, but North and South America. *El Mundo Nuevo* and its successor *América Ilustrada* (1872–75) had huge circulations across the whole continent.[8] The Colombian writer Rafael Pombo came to New York in 1855 as a diplomat, representing his country's interests in the negotiations over the isthmian traverse, and stayed for 17 years, living at Gramercy Park House, a hotel at Gramercy Park and East 20th Street. He undertook translations and adaptations, wrote poetry, and moved in US literary circles: he knew Bryant and translated 11 of his poems into Spanish. Like many Hispanic visitors he was alienated by the increasing commercialism of New York, but was there long enough to be impressed by other features of its modern life, not least the prodigious growth in print culture. He also wrote a scathing poem, seemingly not published at the time, about William Walker's filibustering exploits in Central America.[9] The Argentine intellectual and politician Domingo Faustino Sarmiento—later president of his country—also lived in New York between 1865 and 1868 and was mightily impressed by US technical achievements, such as the Croton aqueduct that brought fresh water into New York.[10]

The second generation began when the Cuban insurrection in 1868— and resulting ten-year struggle—led to a new wave of exiles, some merely

---

1–22; and Kirsten Silva Gruesz, *Ambassadors of Culture: The Transamerican Origins of Latino Writing*, Princeton, NJ: Princeton University Press, 2002, pp. 36–37, 52–56.

[7] Pérez, 'Cubans in Nineteenth-Century New York', p. 102.

[8] Gruesz, *Ambassadors of Culture*, pp. 190–96.

[9] See Gruesz's fascinating discussion of Pombo: *Ambassadors of Culture*, pp. 163–76. On Pombo and Longfellow, see Iván Jaksić, *The Hispanic World and American Intellectual Life, 1820–1880*, New York: Palgrave Macmillan, 2007, pp. 102–08.

[10] Domingo Faustino Sarmiento, *Travels in the United States in 1847*, translation and introductory essay by Michael Aaron Rockland, Princeton, NJ: Princeton University Press, 1970, pp. 216–17.

escaping the conflict, some again using the city as a base to try to overthrow Spanish rule. Inevitably, the largest rift in the Hispanic population over these years was between on the one hand the Cubans and Puerto Ricans seeking independence and on the other the Spaniards in support of monarchy and empire. The latter had their own benevolent society—widely known as La Nacional and still in existence—and their own newspapers such as *El Cronista* (1848–77) and the more liberal *Las Novedades*, founded in 1876 by José G. García, who ran it until 1914. Meanwhile, Cirilo Villaverde and his wife Emilia Casanova, whose father had bought the Whitlock mansion at Hunt's Point in the Bronx, stored arms and *matériel* in the house and shipped it out to Cuba from the East River. It was there that Villaverde wrote the classic Cuban novel of the nineteenth century, *Cecilia Valdés* (1882). Important Puerto Rican figures were also part of this generation—Ramón Emeterio Betances, Eugenio María de Hostos, and Francisco González Marín; and Mexicans arrived too after the French invasion of 1862, though most returned when the republic was restored in 1867. Among the meeting places for this generation was the house of Juan J. Peoli at 317 West 58th Street.[11] New York-born of a Venezuelan family, Peoli was an artist and collector whose home was first port of call for José Martí when he arrived in New York in 1880. Martí then galvanised the Hispanic community over the next 14 years, writing for many of the Spanish-language journals such as *La Revista Ilustrada de Nueva York* and *Las Tres Américas*, producing his own *Versos sencillos*, and in 1887 helping set up the Spanish-American Literary Society of New York, which met at 64 Madison Avenue (between 27th and 28th Streets). On the political front, Martí also founded the Partido Revolucionario Cubano (PRC) and its weekly newspaper *Patria*, produced at his office at 120–122 Front Street, close to the East River. The PRC had a Puerto Rican section, which involved figures such as Arturo Schomburg and Julio Henna, both of whom settled in the city.

After the Spanish defeat in the war of 1898, Cuban and Puerto Rican exiles flooded back to their islands and there was a notable hiatus in Hispanic literary and political, if not commercial, activities in New York. The third generation might be seen as beginning in 1905 when the Dominican writer and diplomat Fabio Fiallo arrived as his country's consul: he would host many writers over the next decade and would himself become a lightning rod for protests against the US occupation of his homeland. Whereas the first two generations had been dominated by the Cuban and Puerto Rican struggles for independence, the third was much more varied. The final years of Porfirio Díaz's autocratic rule in Mexico produced exiles such as the writer

---

[11] Manthorne, 'Painters, Politics, and Pastries', p. 146.

Rafael de Zayas Enríquez, along with his later more famous artist son Marius de Zayas, who reached New York in 1906; and then the turbulent years of the Revolution, beginning in 1910, would throw up successive waves, soon drawn back as the Mexican revolutionary tide turned and turned again. Salomón de la Selva belonged to this third generation, but he was different—possibly unique—in also spending his formative years in the city, allowing him to put down deeper roots and to become completely bilingual.

There are many different ways of being in a place. One quite typical Hispanic trajectory is that of Pachín (Francisco González) Marín (1863–97), the Puerto Rican poet and journalist who, between 1887 and 1897 spent time in Santo Domingo, Haiti, Curaçao, Venezuela, Jamaica, Martinique, New York, and Cuba.[12] In New York he worked on *La Gaceta del Pueblo*, was secretary of the Club Boriquén, and published two books of poetry, full of romantic and patriotic verses whose focus is determinedly outwards, back to the Caribbean, with no attention to the place in which he was writing. This exilic viewpoint was common and understandable. It no doubt helped provide psychological focus during years with little grounded domicile.

But the template for writing the Hispanic experience of New York was laid down by José Martí, who frequently wrote about the city he lived in for 14 years.[13] Martí would never fully embrace the city: he always felt himself in exile from his Cuban homeland and he was increasingly suspicious of US intentions towards it. But he walked the streets of New York and breathed its air; he came to understand the complexities within that tumultuous mingling; and he increasingly realised the importance of New York for the fate of the Caribbean. All of which means that he stands at the beginning of an autoptic tradition, very different from the Latin American stereotyping of the USA and New York associated with the Uruguayan essayist José Enrique Rodó (and examined in the next chapter) as simply in thrall to money-making.[14]

---

[12] See Laura Lomas, 'Migration and Decolonial Politics in Two Afro-Latin Poets: "Pachín" Marin and "Tato" Laviera', 'The Americas in New York: Writing and Arts in La Gran Manzana', *Review: Literature and Arts of the Americas*, 47, no. 2 (2014), 155–63.

[13] For the full range of Martí's journalism, see José Martí, *En los Estados Unidos: Periodismo de 1881 a 1892*, ed. Roberto Fernández Retamar and Pedro Pablo Rodrígues, Nanterre: ALLCA XX, Université Paris X, 2003.

[14] On Martí's notion of 'transpensar' (thinking through)—a predecessor to de la Selva, see Laura Lomas, 'Thinking-Across, Infiltration, and Transculturation: José Martí's Theory and Practice of Post-Colonial Translation in New York', *Translation Review*, 81, no. 1 (2011), 12–33.

As a Spanish speaker, Salomón de la Selva would have had no difficulty finding Hispanic writers in New York in 1914. The Hispanic habit of appointing intellectuals to diplomatic and consular posts directed a constant supply towards New York, and the development of the international telegraph system encouraged Hispanic newspapers to appoint correspondents in the city. There were established familial and other connections that kept some writers moving back and forth on a regular basis, particularly from Cuba and the Dominican Republic. Political upheavals in Mexico, Central America, and the Caribbean produced a steady stream of political exiles. And, once writers had a certain renown, New York was increasingly a magnet, recognised as a place where reputations could be enhanced: short term visits, often plural, ensued. Some, in all of these categories, having arrived, stayed. For nearly a century Spanish-language periodicals had been produced in New York, but by 1914 there was a weekly newspaper, *La Prensa*, which would become a daily paper under new ownership in 1919, and *Las Novedades*, the long-established, originally pro-Spanish magazine, now produced by *dominicanos*, which would become the home for outspoken criticism of US policy towards the Dominican Republic.

The year 1914 also saw the publication of what is often regarded as the first 'immigrant' Hispanic New York novel, *Lucas Guevara*, written in Spanish by the Colombian political exile Alirio Díaz Guerra, who had already published books in Colombia and Venezuela before he came to New York in 1895, where he practised as a physician and worked as an export manager for a firm of manufacturing chemists, as well as writing for the Spanish-language press. A novel in the picaresque tradition, written in ironic tones, *Lucas Guevara* is in the end equally scathing about life on the Lower East Side and about its Hispanic protagonist, who ends the book by throwing himself off the Brooklyn Bridge. Privately printed, its readership was probably minute. The book is dedicated to Díaz Guerra's friend Carlos A. Mendoza, the Panamanian politician of African descent who was briefly president of the new republic after its separation from Colombia. One of Díaz Guerra's few other appearances in the New York documentary record sees him giving a talk on the 'Panama Affair' at the University Club of Brooklyn in December 1903.[15]

---

[15] Alirio Díaz Guerra (1862–1940): see Nicolás Kanellos, *Hispanic Literature of the United States: A Comprehensive Reference*, Westport, CT: Greenwood Press, 2003, p. 95. Alirio Díaz Guerra, *Lucas Guevara*, New York: York Printing Company, 1914; Houston, TX: Arte Público, 2001; translated into English by Ethriam Cash Brammer, Houston,

A graphic snapshot of the kind of world that Díaz Guerra inhabited was offered in 1910 by that incomparable observer of the city in the opening years of the twentieth century, O. Henry:

> Where Broadway skirts the corner of the square presided over by George the Veracious is the Little Rialto. Here stand the actors of that quarter, and this is their shibboleth … Westward and southward from the Thespian glare are one or two streets where a Spanish-American colony has huddled for a little tropical warmth in the nipping North. The center of life in this precinct is 'El Refugio', a café and restaurant that caters to the volatile exiles from the South. Up from Chili, Bolivia, Colombia, the rolling republics of Central America and the ireful islands of the Western Indies flit the cloaked and sombreroed señores, who are scattered like burning lava by the political eruptions of their several countries. Hither they come to lay counterplots, to bide their time, to solicit funds, to enlist filibusterers, to smuggle out arms and ammunitions, to play the game at long taw. In El Refugio they find the atmosphere in which they thrive.[16]

Union Square, with its famous bronze statue of George Washington, was both the eastern boundary of the area identified as Little Spain, centred on West 14th Street, and the early theatre district or Rialto. O. Henry's 'El Refugio' was the restaurant at the Hotel America at 105 East 15th Street, which reserved its third floor for Hispanic guests. It had been recommended by José Martí to numerous Latin American visitors, and had been home in 1895 to Tomás Estrada Palma, Martí's successor as leader of the PRC and first president of the republic of Cuba in 1902.[17]

TX: Arte Público, 2003. Cf. Regina Galasso, 'Latin from Manhattan: Transatlantic and Interamerican Cultural Production in New York (1813–1963)', PhD thesis, Johns Hopkins University, 2008, pp. 87–102; and Jeffrey Browitt, 'Sexual Anxiety in Alirio Díaz Guerra's *Lucas Guevara*', *Hispania*, 88, no. 4 (December 2005), 677–86.

[16] O. Henry, 'The Gold That Glittered' [1910], in *More O. Henry: One Hundred More of the Master's Stories* [1933], London: Hodder & Stoughton, 1959, pp. 494–505, at p. 495.

[17] 'To Mr Robert Rudd Whiting, with whom he had been associated in the early days when he first began to contribute to the columns of *Ainslee's Magazine*, Sidney Porter once extended an invitation to a luncheon. It was to be a Spanish-American luncheon in the course of which O. Henry was to make his guest familiar with certain flavours and dishes that he himself had learned to like or at least to endure in the days of his exile in the lands of the Lotus Eaters. 'The two men at the time were crossing Union Square, "Come with me," said O. Henry, "I will show you the real place. Over

Another renowned Hispanic meeting place in the first quarter of the century was the splendidly named Joel's Bohemian Refreshery, owned and run by Joel Rinaldo. Located on West 41st Street, right behind the Ziegfeld Follies, Joel's was an important watering hole where local writers and Hispanic exiles met and drank and talked. It made a point of advertising itself in the Spanish-language magazine *El Gráfico*: 'This is the cabaret', it says in Spanish, 'preferred by all Hispanic-American visitors to New York. Here one breathes an atmosphere of familiarity and friendship found nowhere else. It is the main meeting-place for all New York bohemians, painters, musicians, caricaturists, actors …'. Its restaurant, the advert suggests, is the only place in New York offering authentic Mexican food. In addition, an invitation is offered to sit at 'the table of revolutions', 'where famous Hispanic-American revolutionaries used to sit'.[18]

On a completely different social plane was the Hispanic Society of America (HSA), a relatively new institution founded and presided over by Archer Milton Huntington, the dominant figure in Hispanic studies in early twentieth-century New York. Huntington was a multi-millionaire collector (Fig. 1), well-connected to New York high society but with a genuine love for and knowledge of Spanish art and literature. Though he could be abrupt in his manner, he was often generous with his fortune.

Huntington's family background was unusual, and is still rather murky. Aged 14, Archer had been adopted by Collis P. Huntington when the businessman married the boy's mother, his second wife, Arabella; but Archer may have been—as he himself maintained—Collis's natural son, the outcome of an affair which overlapped with the last years of a first marriage.[19]

---

at M's (mentioning a restaurant in a street to the south) you may see the Senors, the Capitans, the Majors, the Colonels. But if you would sit with the Generalissimos, the Imperators, the truly exalted of those countries of Central and South America, accept my guiding hand." And from the square they turned into Fifteenth Street and found, on the south side, some 75 yards east of Fourth Avenue the Hotel America, with its patronage of volatile Latins, who, if they were not actually planning revolution and the overthrow of some unstable government, at least had all the appearance of arch conspirators. It was the atmosphere which went to the making of "The Gold That Glitters"' (Arthur Bartlett Maurice, *The New York of the Novelists*, New York: Dodd, Mead and Company, 1916, pp. 207–08).

[18] The advert appeared frequently during *El Gráfico*'s lifetime (October 1916–June 1918). This example is taken from I, no. 2 (November 1916). The 'revolutionary table' was a reference to the artist Carlo de Fornaro's campaign against Porfirio Díaz, which landed him a 12-month prison sentence. A variety of Mexican political exiles ended up here: see Peter Hulme, 'Joel's Revolutionary Table: New York and Mexico City in Turbulent Times', *Comparative American Studies*, 15, nos 3–4 (2017), 117–45.

[19] The most thorough account of Huntington, which I draw on here, is Melvin

1 Archer Milton Huntington [1903]. Photogravure by E.W. Histed.
Courtesy of the Hispanic Society of America, New York.

Privately educated in New York, Archer was taken by his mother to the art galleries and museums of London and Paris during a European trip when he was 12: reading George Borrow was his introduction to Spain. Back in New York he began assiduously to learn Spanish. There was a family trip to Mexico in 1889, when Archer met the president, Porfirio Díaz, with whom his father was discussing railroad matters. In 1890, after some meagre efforts to accede to his father's wish that he learn the family business, Huntington gave himself over to Hispanic scholarship and collecting: the scheme to build a museum was an early idea although it would have a long gestation. Over the next few years, he visited Cuba and then Spain twice, learned Arabic, and worked on a translation of Spain's famous medieval epic, *Poema de mío Cid*. After marrying his cousin, Helen Gates, Huntington had a mansion built at 1083 Fifth Avenue, just north of East 89th Street. He began a series of facsimiles of rare books and published his work on the *Cid* in three volumes: a verbatim reproduction of the manuscript, his English translation, and notes and concordance.[20] It was scholarship of the highest calibre. Further book-collecting trips to Spain followed, but by now prospective sellers were coming to Huntington. Collis P. Huntington died in 1900, leaving a fortune calculated at the economic power equivalent in 2015 of over $65 billion, of which Archer received approximately a fifth, with more later inherited from his mother.[21] His museum began to take shape in 1904. The initial board of trustees included Porfirio Díaz, ex-president of Argentina, Bartolomé Mitre, whom Huntington had met on a visit to Buenos Aires, and John Hay, William McKinley's Secretary of State. He settled on Audubon Terrace, up in Washington Heights, as the site, and building began in 1905, the museum opening in January 1908 (Fig. 2). Huntington's private collection of 40,000 books formed the basis of the library, and his

---

Duane Davis, 'Collecting Hispania: Archer Huntington's Quest to Develop Hispanic Collections in the United States', PhD thesis, University of Alabama, 2005. See also Mitchell Codding, 'Archer Milton Huntington: Champion of Spain in the United States', in *Spain in America: The Origins of Hispanism in the United States*, ed. Richard Kagan, Urbana: University of Illinois Press, 2002, pp. 142–70 and Claudio Iván Remeseira, 'A Splendid Outsider: Archer Milton Huntington and the Hispanic Heritage in the United States', in Claudio Iván Remeseira, ed., *Hispanic New York: A Sourcebook*, New York: Columbia University Press, 2010, pp. 443–56.

[20] *Poem of the Cid*. Text reprinted from the unique manuscript at Madrid. With an English translation and notes by Archer M. Huntington, 3 vols., New York: G. P. Putnam's Sons, 1897–1903.

[21] Archer's mother Arabella later married his cousin (and her step-nephew), Henry Huntington, who had previously been married to the sister of Collis's first wife. The Huntingtons believed in keeping the money in the family.

2 Hispanic Society of America, 1906–07. 613 West 155th Street at Broadway. Courtesy of the Hispanic Society of America, New York.

mother donated paintings by Velásquez and Goya. Joaquín Sorolla was a particular beneficiary of Huntington's patronage, and an exhibition of 350 of his paintings in 1909 was the Hispanic Society of America's first popular success, garnering 160,000 visitors over two months. Salomón de la Selva would soon find his way to Huntington's door.

The Poetic Waters

All things considered, 1915 was not a bad year to launch a career as a poet in New York. Admittedly, Salomón de la Selva had no social standing and no financial backing, but he had talent and assurance, was well-read, and knew his way around the city. Neither would his youthful good looks hold him back. And now, more than ever before, there were institutions ready to welcome new writers and journals eager to publish new work. On the ground, at the time, it is not always easy to see exactly what is going on, but, with the benefit of hindsight, there was great deal of cultural ferment. The visual arts led the way, both in painting (John Sloan, Robert Henri, Edward Hopper) and in photography (Alfred Stieglitz, Paul Strand, Edward Steichen). The Armory Show in 1913 had brought attention to this work as well as introducing to New York a new wave of post-impressionist painting (Paul Cezanne, Vincent Van Gogh, Marcel Duchamp). The film industry was growing apace: indeed, was still largely located just across the Hudson River from Manhattan. 'Muckraking' journalism (Ida Tarbell, Lincoln Steffens, Ray Stannard Baker) was pioneering new ways of writing prose in its analyses of political and business corruption. Modern anthropology was being developed by Franz Boas at Columbia. Jazz was emerging as a new musical form, alongside many new ways of dancing. New meeting places such as the salons run by Mabel Dodge and Walter and Louise Arensburg, the relocated Liberal Club, and Petitpas' restaurant brought together writers, artists, journalists, and political figures, leading to collaborations such as the Paterson Strike Pageant in 1913. The Provincetown Theatre was taking its first steps. The outbreak of war in Europe had begun to bring European, especially French, artists and writers to New York (Marcel Duchamp, Francis Picabia). Advances in printing encouraged the founding of more journals, even if many of them didn't last very long.[22]

In terms of poetry, the three years between 1912 and 1914 saw books by Robinson Jeffers, Vachel Lindsay, Amy Lowell, Witter Bynner, Robert Frost, Conrad Aiken, Joyce Kilmer, James Oppenheim, and Gertrude Stein. The poetry journals were publishing Carl Sandburg, Wallace Stevens, and Ezra Pound. The newest poetic star in the New York firmament was Edna St Vincent Millay, whose poem 'Renascence', given a mere honourable mention in *The Lyric Year* (1912), had widely been regarded as the outstanding poem in the collection by reviewers of the book.[23] Jessie Rittenhouse had immediately asked her to give a poetry reading at a new and prestigious venue: the Poetry Society of America. She had quickly acquired a patron, made her New York debut in February 1913, and taken classes at Barnard so that she could go to Vassar in September 1914.

---

[22] The best overview is in Steven Watson, *Strange Bedfellows: The First American Avant-Garde*, New York: Abbeville Press, 1991.

[23] Ferdinand Earle, ed., *The Lyric Year: One Hundred Poems*, New York: Mitchell Kennerley, 1912, pp. 180–88; and see Daniel Mark Epstein, *What Lips My Lips Have Kissed: The Loves and Love Poems of Edna St. Vincent Millay*, New York: Henry Holt and Company, 2001, p. 67.

*

Writers have always met, usually in small groups, almost always informally. Early in the twentieth century, however, there was clearly an impetus, at least in the Anglo-American world, towards more formal structures: regular meetings, constitutions, membership fees, officers, prizes. To give the literary vocation respectable standing risked sacrificing all the advantages derived from the general perception of its essential *difference* from respectable kinds of work but, as Louis Menand notes: 'by the early twentieth century, the ideology of professionalism had established itself to the extent of making anything that smacked of amateurism look second-rate'.[24] Some writers inevitably felt such things to be inimical to the creative process and stayed away, or more often joined but then sniped from the sidelines. Nevertheless, networks formed, manifestos were produced, collaboration and competition became the norms.

An Authors Club had been set up in New York as early as 1882 at 103 East 15th Street by established figures such as Edmund C. Stedman, the journalist, poet, and critic, Charles deKay, art and literary critic for the *New York Times*, and Brander Matthews, writer and Professor of Dramatic Literature at Columbia University. It eventually received funding from Andrew Carnegie and moved into the Carnegie Building at Seventh Avenue and West 56th Street. All its members were gentlemen who had published books.[25] That more and more people were trying to make a living from writing and needing help in negotiations with publishers is suggested by the founding in Boston in April 1887 by the writer and editor William Henry Hills of *The Writer: A Monthly Magazine for Literary Workers*, which is still in existence.

New York saw a proliferation of new clubs and associations around the turn of the century. The National Arts Club was founded in 1898 and took up residence at 15 Gramercy Park South in 1906. The elite American Academy of Arts and Letters was created in 1904 on the model of the French Academy by the membership of the National Institute of Arts and Letters (itself established in 1898), electing William Dean Howells, Samuel

---

[24] Louis Menand, *Discovering Modernism: T. S. Eliot and His Context*, New York: Oxford University Press, 1987, p. 117. For the general background to professionalisation, see Magali Sarfatti Larson, *The Rise of Professionalism: A Sociological Analysis*, Berkeley: University of California Press, 1977.

[25] The Authors Club published an annual manual. Some surviving papers are in Authors Club (New York, NY), The New York Public Library, MSS Col 161; and Authors Club (New York, NY), [Collection of programs, lists, etc., of Authors Club activities], 1888–1937, New-York Historical Society Main Collection F128 HS2725.A9 Box 1.

L. Clemens, Edmund C. Stedman, John Hay, Augustus Saint-Gaudens, John La Farge, and Edward MacDowell. The number of academicians eventually grew to 50, while the membership of the Institute was limited to 200. Archer Huntington was a prominent member and gave the Institute and its Academy rooms on Audubon Terrace next to his Hispanic Society of America. Founded in 1894, the Pen and Brush Club for women writers and artists was incorporated in 1912 under the presidency of writer and suffragist Grace Seton. Ida M. Tarbell, Margaret Widdemer, and Jessie Tarbox Beals were among its members.

While the Authors Club had a slightly amateur feel to it, and was very much a club for men only, the Authors' League of America, started in April 1913, made it very clear that writers were central to New York professional life, and indeed to US society. Modelled on the British Society of Authors (founded in 1884 with Tennyson as its first president), the Authors' League started with the highly successful author Winston Churchill as president and Theodore Roosevelt as vice-president. Within a year it had 685 members. Its headquarters were at 33 West 42nd Street, right opposite the New York Public Library. It welcomed women authors: Helen S. Woodruff was on the council. It published a regular bulletin with articles such as 'Income Tax Statements: How Authors and Artists Should Prepare Them'. And in April 1914 its Legal Bureau reported on no fewer than 68 complaints received from members.[26] It later split into the various guilds which still protect the interest of authors, dramatists, and screen writers.

Poets were writers too, equally as concerned with contracts and copyright, but still attached to the notion that poetry was a special and distinct activity. Here, then, professionalisation took rather different forms. Anthologies of poetry (which suited anthologising better than other kinds of writing) began to have a significant influence in grouping new writers together and in beginning the process of canon-formation.[27] Dedicated journals came into being. Societies and associations brought writers together for discussion and readings. Boston was home from 1913 to an annual anthology of new poems compiled from magazines by William Stanley Braithwaite, literary

---

[26] See Isabel Howe, 'The Founding of the Authors' League of America', *Authors' League Bulletin*, Fall 2012/Winter 2013, 15–19; *Bulletin of the Authors' League of America*, V, nos 9–10 (December 1917–January 1918), 3–5; and *Year Book of the Authors' League of America*, 1 April 1914, pp. 16–35.

[27] See W. Scott Cheney, 'Anthologizing Modernism: New Verse Anthologies, 1913–1953', PhD thesis, Loyola University Chicago, 2014; and, more broadly, Alan Golding, 'The History of American Poetry Anthologies', in his *From Outlaw to Classic: Canons in American Poetry*, Madison: University of Wisconsin Press, 1995, pp. 3–40.

editor of the *Boston Evening Transcript*, Chicago from 1912 to the pioneering journal *Poetry* edited by Harriet Monroe. New York would have the Poetry Society of America.[28]

The origins of the Poetry Society of America (PSA) lay in a social gathering held by Mr and Mrs Isaac L. Rice at their apartments in the Ansonia, the fashionable residential hotel at 2109 Broadway between West 73rd and 74th Streets.[29] Successful businessman, musicologist, and president of the Manhattan Chess Club, Isaac Rice was also the founder and owner of *The Forum*, now in the possession of the thrusting young publisher Mitchell Kennerley.[30] George Sylvester Viereck was one of the moving forces behind the PSA, along with Edwin Markham, Hermann Scheffauer, Gertrude Atherton, Arthur Guitermann, and Leonard D. Abbott. After the poets started to take the idea too seriously for their tastes, the Rices stepped aside and the first official meeting—an 150-setting dinner—took place at the National Arts Club (NAC) on 27 May 1911, with Edward J. Wheeler appointed as chairman and Viereck as secretary.[31]

Monthly meetings ensued, hosted at the NAC premises, a splendid setting which tended to underline the respectability of the PSA. Here poets read from their work and there were lively discussions. So, for example, at the December 1913 meeting Rabindranath Tagore (who'd just been awarded the Nobel Prize in literature) was discussed; in March 1914, Mary Austin talked about 'aboriginal poetry'; and in December 1914, the topic was contemporary Belgian poetry, especially Emile Verhaeren.[32] PSA

---

[28] In London there had been The Poets' Club, started in 1908 by T. E. Hulme, under the influence of W. B. Yeats but then taking its distance from him. In 1909, Hulme seceded, as did the Poetry Recital Society, more wedded to Irish (that is, Yeatsian) recital, which was founded in February 1909 by William Galloway Kyle and became the Poetry Society in 1912: Margaret Sackville was president of both.

[29] 'Poets' Union and Less Noise', *The Sun*, 28 February 1910, p. 4.

[30] See Matthew Joseph Bruccoli, *The Fortunes of Mitchell Kennerley, Bookman*, San Diego, CA: Harcourt Brace Jovanovich, 1986.

[31] 'The Poets' Circle and Syndicate Open', *New York Times*, 2 June 1911, p. 7. On US poetry during this period, see Lisa Szefel, *The Gospel of Beauty in the Progressive Era: Reforming American Verse and Values*, New York: Palgrave Macmillan, 2011; and John Timberman Newcomb, *How Did Poetry Survive? The Making of Modern American Verse*, Urbana: University of Illinois Press, 2012.

[32] See the *Poetry Society of America Bulletin*, produced monthly during the early years, and then irregularly; Gustav Davidson, ed., *In Fealty to Apollo: Poetry Society of America, 1910–1950*, New York: The Five Editions Press, 1950; and *Poetry Society of America records ca. 1917–ca. 1948*, Manuscripts and Archives Division, The New York Public Library, MSS Col 2444. Anna Catherine Markham was on the PSA executive committee for many years, often serving as secretary after 1922, and so some PSA

membership was white and middle class. There were no membership fees, with richer members supplying funds and the NAC providing rooms free of charge. Non-poets could join. Salomón de la Selva, the young, voluble, and charming Nicaraguan, already steeped in the traditions of English poetry, must have made an immediate impression.

Although scarcely remembered today, the PSA members were significant names in US writing in 1915. Margaret Widdemer, born in Pennsylvania, though brought up in New Jersey, and who in 1919 would be awarded the Columbia University Prize (later known as the Pulitzer) for her poetry collection *The Old Road to Paradise*, had two of her early novels quickly adapted into films. She moved in 1915 to Greenwich Village, but with her family, which led to a more conventional social life than many of the other Villagers. Widdemer and Aline Kilmer (four years Margaret's junior) bonded at a PSA reading in 1915 as they giggled over a bad poem being recited by an earnest young brunette. Coincidentally, Widdemer soon ran into Aline's husband, Joyce Kilmer, in similar circumstances, and she quickly became a fast friend and regular visitor to the Kilmers' home in Mahwah, New Jersey. Widdemer describes Aline as disorganised—too disorganised to write short stories, the most marketable genre of the time; but gentler than her quick-tempered husband, with a 'slow, half-ironic, southern humor': she'd been born in Virginia.[33] Joyce had been born in New Jersey and was a Columbia graduate and staff writer for *New York Times Review of Books*. The couple were both Catholic converts. Joyce had become famous in 1913 for his short poem 'Trees', still much anthologised. William Rose Benét was the eldest of a trio of sibling Brooklynite writers: Laura and Stephen Vincent were the others. David H. Morton, born in Kentucky and a graduate of Vanderbilt, was working as a teacher in Morristown, New Jersey, from where he travelled assiduously to attend the PSA, eventually winning one of its prizes in the 1918–19 season. Shaemas O'Sheel, third-generation Irish-American, born in New York, was a committed Irish nationalist. Alan Seeger, young and intense, had grown up partly in Mexico City. Louis Untermeyer, New Yorker, had already published two books of poetry by 1914. Clement Wood, from Alabama, was an ardent socialist as well as a poet. Floyd Dell, born in Illinois, had arrived from Chicago in 1913 and was managing editor of *The Masses*, the journal of the moment in New York, where his poetry, as well as Wood's and Untermeyer's, was appearing.[34]

---

material is also to be found in the Edwin Markham Archive at Wagner College, Staten Island, Box 38.

[33] Widdemer, *Golden Friends*, pp. 155–56.
[34] On O'Sheel, see Wallace Winchell, 'Shaemas O'Sheel and his Unique Contribution

PSA president was Edward Jewitt Wheeler, a very minor poet himself, but certainly an important figure in the New York literary world. Wheeler was a long-time associate and protégé of the publisher Isaac K. Funk (both came from Ohio), one of the original trustees of the Westerleigh Collegiate Institute (which de la Selva attended), and editor of *Current Opinion*, an important journal of politics, literature, and culture. Wheeler had edited Funk's journals *The Voice* and *Literary Digest* and acted as a general literary advisor. He was clearly a cultured figure, though a relatively conservative one.

Jesse Rittenhouse soon took over as PSA secretary from Viereck. Another New Yorker, Rittenhouse was a published poet but also an important cultural broker as poetry reviewer for the *New York Times Review of Books* and editor of the *Little Book of Modern Verse* (1913), the first of a series of influential anthologies that would help determine the shape of modern US poetry: Millay's 'Renascence' made its second appearance here. In her rôle as anthologist, Rittenhouse would play an important part in de la Selva's eventual departure from New York in 1919.

And then there was Edwin Markham, in 1914 the best-known living US poet. Originally from Oregon, Markham and his wife Anna settled in 1902 on Staten Island, neighbours to Edward Wheeler. Their home became a meeting place for writers, but Markham was often found at literary and social events in Manhattan, staying overnight if need be at the Hotel di Rinaldo, above Joel's Bohemian Refreshery on West 41st Street. He was a PSA stalwart.

This was the New York literary world into which Salomón de la Selva stepped and these were his first fellow-poets and friends. It was obviously a new world for him, but he was not without preparation. He knew the streets of New York, he was fluent in English and already well-read in English poetry as well as Spanish. The PSA, like all such organisations, contained many strands. If the society's officers tended to be established figures such as Wheeler and Rittenhouse, who were in their forties and fifties, there was a younger generation of writers, such as the Kilmers, Widdemer, O'Sheel, Untermeyer, Dell, and the Benéts, who were in their late twenties and early thirties, not that much older than Salomón. Like its English counterpart,

---

to American Letters', *Markham Review*, no. 3 (October 1968), 12–15; on Seeger, Irving Werstein, *Sound No Trumpet: The Life and Death of Alan Seeger*, New York: Thomas Y. Crowell, 1967; on Dell, Douglas Clayton, *Floyd Dell: The Life and Times of an American Rebel*, Chicago: I. R. Dee, 1994. The prominence of women poets in the PSA is worthy of note. As Lisa Szefel writes: 'The reading culture surrounding poetry provided space for women to inscribe their lives outside the private sphere and expected norms' (*The Gospel of Beauty*, p. 7).

the PSA had members who were primarily interested in recitation and those who just knew that it was only poetry if it rhymed. But the writing of Markham, Widdemer, and O'Sheel had a strong social dimension and at least some of the members were open to what would soon become the new wave of imagists and futurists: Ezra Pound and Amy Lowell visited the PSA and Marinetti was discussed at the end-of-year dinner in December 1914. However, the PSA members little knew that visiting New York and even attending some of their meetings that winter was the most famous poet in the Spanish-speaking world, Rubén Darío. De la Selva would soon educate them about Hispanic poetry.

Modernity and Modernism

The conventional literary historical account sees the true literature of modernity—modernism—as incubating during these years, but not fully emerging until 1922, when *The Waste Land* and *Ulysses* appeared. New York, in any case, was not in this account at the forefront of modernist developments: Ezra Pound had gone to Italy, T. S. Eliot to London, and *Ulysses* had been prosecuted and banned in New York and so was published in Paris. Apart from the small magazines such as *Others*, signs of modernism in New York before 1920 were more apparent—the conventional story goes—in art than in literature, but often in the form of visitors from Europe, either on display in the Armory Show that so shocked New York in 1913, or later produced by the visitors themselves, Marcel Duchamp's scandalous 1917 'Fountain' being a prime example.

Salomón de la Selva's poetry—and that of most of the writers with whom he rubbed shoulders in New York—falls on the 'wrong' side of the watershed, which is why writers such as Edna Millay, Edwin Markham, and Jessie Rittenhouse tend to appear in literary histories, when they appear at all, under the sign of condescension. Literary history has usually been written by the winners, particularly when a generation of writers contains major critics and academics who can determine what gets published and taught; and Anglo-American modernism—'high modernism'—certainly won, in the sense that it became seen as the dominant and defining literary movement of the twentieth century. Already in the summer of 1919 Eliot would publish his essay 'Tradition and the Individual Talent', offering a first sketch of the new literary history and suggesting a brutal oblivion for writers not regarded as part of the main literary current as defined by Eliot himself.[35] In the fullness

---

[35] T. S. Eliot, 'Tradition and the Individual Talent', *The Egoist*, 6, no. 4 (September 1919), 54–55 and no. 5 (December 1919), 72–73.

of time, some judgements might be tempered or even reversed, and the occasional forgotten author resurrected, but the version of early twentieth-century literary history established by those high modernist protagonists is only very slowly being questioned a century later.

By the 1950s, as this story began to take hold in the academy, writers seen as not having contributed to high modernism began to disappear from anthologies and literary histories. In some cases established reputations suffered; in other cases strands of literary culture simply never made it onto the pages of literary history in the first place. Two writers who feature prominently here fall into that first category. Edwin Markham was the most famous US poet in 1915, but is hardly a footnote in any kind of recent literary history; while Edna St Vincent Millay's reputation was first established in these years, grew immeasurably in the 1920s, and was then largely eclipsed, though never as thoroughly as Markham's.[36] The second category includes writing in Spanish, unless that writing is situated in its appropriate chronological position, well after and therefore—so the story goes—probably influenced by its Anglo-American forerunners. The complicating factor here—relevant to *The Dinner at Gonfarone's* in ways I'll explain shortly—is that the Hispanic literary movement known as *modernismo* considerably pre-dates Anglo-American modernism, the first use of the term coming in an 1890 essay by the Nicaraguan poet Rubén Darío, in a Peruvian journal. Historians of modernism have tended to play down this fact—where they recognise it at all—on the grounds that *modernismo* is 'really' a Hispanic offshoot of French symbolism or Parnassianism, and therefore not properly modernist at all. So, although a standard early critical work such as Bradbury and McFarlane's *Modernism 1890–1930* starts its chronology as early as 1890—the very year in which Darío published his essay—the Nicaraguan features nowhere in the book's 684 pages. Chronologically, the first Hispanic writers to appear in the book are Miguel de Unamuno and José Echegaray, neither of whom would feature high on most critics' lists of Hispanic modernists of any ilk (although Unamuno's novel *Niebla* certainly deserves consideration). *Modernism 1890–1930* belongs to a series of guides to European Literature, but that doesn't prevent all the usual US suspects from appearing, just not any Latin American or Caribbean writers: no Rubén Darío or José Martí or César Vallejo. In the opening essay, the editors underline Eliot's metaphor: modernism is the *main stream*, leaving

---

[36] For more on Markham and Millay, see below, pp. 158–62 and 118–35. A recent sign of Millay's growing stature is the first critical edition of her work: Edna St Vincent Millay, *Selected Poems of Edna St. Vincent Millay: An Annotated Edition*, ed. Timothy F. Jackson, New Haven, CT: Yale University Press, 2016.

modernismo as—at best—a minor tributary or backwater.[37] Some critics have at least recognised that the presence of *modernismo* might represent something of a challenge to the scholarship on modernism and modernity, indeed a 'scandal', as Fredric Jameson puts it, although he doesn't tease out the nature of that scandal.[38] However, to be literal about it, just as modernity as a term began with Charles Baudelaire discussing Constantin Guys and *modernité* in Paris in 1863, so modernism as a term began with Rubén Darío discussing Ricardo Palma and *modernismo* in Lima in 1890. In that year Darío was at the beginning of his career as a poet. In 1915, he was at the end of that career, in New York, with his compatriot Salomón de la Selva.

In recent years, three developments have worked to complicate the hegemonic modernist story. A transnational and planetary version of modernism has taken shape, considerably broadening the horizons of the movement. *Modernismo* has itself been redefined in broader terms. And early twentieth-century US poetry has been given a different kind of attention, bringing some of the writers who feature here back into the literary–historical picture. Although its expansion is in geographical range rather than in definition, the *Oxford Handbook of Global Modernisms* does pay Rubén Darío and *modernismo* the compliment of a fine essay.[39] The scholarship on *modernismo* is substantial, but of particular importance is the argument—first advanced in 1966 by Iván Schulman (and here presented in shorthand)—that José Martí and journalism should be given equal billing with Rubén Darío and poetry.[40] Both Martí and Darío wrote far more journalism than poetry, and arguably the true engagement with modernity comes in the *crónicas* that both wrote for the Buenos Aires newspaper *La Nación*. Martí wrote many of his from and about New York in the 1880s and early 1890s; Darío wrote his very last *crónica* from and about New York, in 1915 (to be discussed in Chapter 3).[41]

---

[37] Malcolm Bradbury and James McFarlane, eds, *Modernism 1890–1930*, Harmondsworth: Penguin, 1976, p. 28.
[38] Fredric Jameson, *A Singular Modernity: Essay on the Ontology of the Present*, London: Verso, 2002, pp. 100–04; see also Matei Călinescu, *Five Faces of Modernity: Modernism, Avant-garde, Decadence, Kitsch, Postmodernism*, Durham, NC: Duke University Press, 1987, pp. 68–78.
[39] Gerard Aching, 'The Temporalities of Modernity in Spanish American *Modernismo* Darío's Bourgeois King', in *The Oxford Handbook of Global Modernisms*, ed. Mark Wollaeger, New York: Oxford University Press, 2012, pp. 109–28.
[40] Iván A. Schulman, *Génesis del modernismo: Martí, Nájera, Silva, Casal*, Mexico: Colegio de México, 1966. See also his *El modernismo hispanoamericano*, Buenos Aires: Centro Editor de América Latina, 1969.
[41] The broader view of *modernismo* is apparent in, for example, Cathy L. Jrade,

Schulman's argument develops out of the Spanish poet and critic Juan Ramón Jiménez's prolonged effort to have *modernismo* seen as an aspect of a broader modernism.[42] Although their perspectives and language may be very different, Jiménez's view chimes with Marshall Berman's definition of modernism: 'any attempt by modern men and women to become subjects as well as objects of modernization, to get a grip on the modern world and make themselves at home in it'.[43] If modernism is a reaction against dogma—as it surely is for Berman—then the religious element (stressed by Jiménez, who sees the genesis of modernism in the attempt to combine faith and scientific reason)[44] becomes more relevant. As Federico de Onís put it: 'el modernismo es la forma hispana de la crisis universal de las letras y del espíritu, que inicia hacia 1885 la disolución del siglo XIX' [modernism is the Hispanic form of the universal crisis that initiates around 1885 the dissolution of the nineteenth century].[45] What Jiménez, Onís, and Berman share is that their view of modernism was formed by and in New York.

Because periodisation always carries an element of the arbitrary, the thought-experiments of exact dating are difficult to resist, which is why Virginia Woolf's famous 'on or about' remark concerning 1910 is so

---

Modernismo, Modernity, and the Development of Spanish American Literature, Austin: University of Texas Press, 1998; the editors' introduction, 'Modernism and Its Margins: Rescripting Hispanic Modernism' to Anthony L. Geist and José B. Monleón, eds, *Modernism and Its Margins: Reinscribing Cultural Modernity from Spain and Latin America*, New York: Garland, 1999, pp. xvii–xxxv; David Craven, 'The Latin American Origins of "Alternative Modernism"', *Third Text*, 36 (1996), 29–44; Alejandro Mejías-López, *The Inverted Conquest: The Myth of Modernity and the Transatlantic Onset of Modernism*, Nashville, TN: Vanderbilt University Press, 2009; and Ericka Beckman, *Capital Fictions: The Literature of Latin America's Export Age*, Minneapolis: University of Minnesota Press, 2013. On journalism, see Aníbal González Pérez, *La crónica modernista hispanoamericana*, Madrid: Porrúa Turanzas, 1983; Susana Rotker, *La invención de la crónica*, Buenos Aires: Ediciones Letra Buena, 1992; and Andrew R. Reynolds, *The Spanish American Crónica Modernista, Temporality, and Material Culture: Modernismo's Unstoppable Presses*, Lewisburg, PA: Bucknell University Press, 2012.

[42] As discussed by Gayle Rogers, *Incomparable Empires: Modernism and the Translation of Spanish and American Literature*, New York: Columbia University Press, 2016, p. 110.

[43] Marshall Berman, *All That Is Solid Melts Into Air: The Experience of Modernity*, London: Verso, 1983, p. 5.

[44] Juan Ramón Jiménez, *El modernismo; notas de un curso (1953)*, Mexico: Aguilar, 1962, p. 68.

[45] Federico de Onís, 'Introducción', to *Antología de la poesía española e hispanoamericana* [1934], 2nd edn, New York: Las Américas, 1961, p. xv.

often invoked.[46] Onís's 'around 1885'—written just ten years after Woolf's pronouncement—perhaps contains a deliberate echo, as well perhaps as a hint of Hispanic or American correction. It is tempting to imagine the different versions of modernity to be constructed on the basis of a defining text published in 1885: *The Adventures of Huckleberry Finn*, Anténor Firmin's *De l'Égalité des Races Humaines*, or perhaps José Martí's essay 'Los indios en los Estados Unidos'?

The third development involves a more fundamental rethinking of the nature of literary history, and is associated with two key books: Cary Nelson's *Repression and Recovery: Modern American Poetry and the Politics of Cultural Memory, 1910–1945* (1989) and John Timberman Newcomb's *How Did Poetry Survive? The Making of Modern American Verse* (2012). Nelson points out how literary theory has neglected the whole process of literary historiography, which is in fact always ideological and usually carried out by self-anointed custodians of the literary tradition who pass off their decisions as self-evident and natural—that mere identification of the 'main current'. Those custodians are in fact, Nelson argues, operating a process of canon-formation, which he wants to separate out from literary history proper, which ought to be as inclusive and explanatory as possible—fully historicist, although he doesn't use that term.[47]

Newcomb's approach is similarly historicist. He points out that writers at the time referred to the 'new verse' or the 'new poetry', terms which suggested an engagement with modernity, but in registers which went much wider than the experiments in form characteristic of what only much later became known as modernism, referring to writing with a much more restricted range of formal experimentation.[48] The new verse was catalysed as much by a polemical expansion of subject matter as by innovations of style, he suggests, and it included a turn toward the city, which resulted in a poetics of metropolitan modernity—precisely the area occupied by many of the writers considered here. Newcomb places himself therefore within the larger definition of modernism adumbrated by Raymond Williams and Marshall Berman, both of whom emphasise the variety of forms that

---

[46] 'On or about December 1910, human character changed', in Virginia Woolf, *Mr Bennett and Mrs Brown*, The Hogarth Essays no. 1, London: L. & V. Woolf, 1924, p. 4.
[47] Cary Nelson, *Repression and Recovery: Modern American Poetry and the Politics of Cultural Memory, 1910–1945*, Madison: University of Wisconsin Press, 1989, pp. 3–11, 23.
[48] Newcomb, *How Did Poetry Survive?*, p. 2. See, for example, Alfred Kreymborg's 1929 *A History of American Poetry: Our Singing Strength*, New York: Tudor, 1934, which has several chapters on early twentieth-century poetry, including 'Singing New Things in Old Forms' (pp. 395–437), but nowhere even mentions the term 'modernism'.

Setting the Scene: New York in 1914

modernism has taken, if one views it as what has been written in response to the experience of modernity, especially in the city.[49]

These developments provide the framework for what follows here, even though reading Salomón de la Selva's poetry and project into the texture of the times hardly constitutes a *recovery* since they didn't register in the first place. But de la Selva came of poetic age with the new verse being written in New York and paying particular, though not exclusive, reference to that city. He also—uniquely for a poet writing in English—inherited the *modernista* tradition associated with Rubén Darío, and arrived on the poetic scene with the baggage of the citizen of a country under US occupation. When Eliot's main currents have been surveyed from London, or New York, or Paris, Salomón de la Selva has never been identified as even a ripple. It is perhaps time for him to make at least a small splash.

There are then many approaches to the history of modernism. If the appearance of the word itself is granted some significance, 8 November 1890 counts as a watershed on account of Rubén Darío's coinage of the term in an essay of that date to refer to a literary movement.[50] Certainly his own extensive work, including vast amounts of journalism, might easily be seen—given his extensive travels—as a continental response to the pressures of modernity. If Lima in 1890 initially seems an unlikely location, then the adverts in the issue of *El Perú Ilustrado* in which Darío's essay appeared give a lively sense of the modern framework: Palmer & Rey sewing machines from San Francisco, Harwood furniture from Boston, Liberty printing presses from New York. Lima in 1890 was fully part of the modern world—and a market for US manufacturing. Once the criterion for modernism becomes the literary *response* to modernity, then even Ricardo Palma, the subject of Darío's essay, becomes a contender. Though Darío does not name him among the modernists in that essay, Palma's *tradiciones*, produced between 1872 and 1910, can be read as subtle modernist responses, as formally innovative as more typographic or syntactic experimentalism.[51] For the latter, look no

---

[49] Raymond Williams, 'When Was Modernism?' and 'Metropolitan Perceptions and the Emergence of Modernism', in his *The Politics of Modernism: Against the New Conformists*, ed and introd. Tony Pinkney, London: Verso, 1989, pp. 31–35, 37–48; Berman, *All That Is Solid Melts Into Air*.

[50] Rubén Darío, 'Fotograbados: Ricardo Palma', *El Perú Ilustrado*, 8 November 1890, p. 1051. Cf. Allen W. Phillips, 'Rubén Darío y sus juicios sobre el modernismo', *Revista Iberoamericana*, XXIV, no. 47 (1959), 41–64; and Alfred A. Roggiano, 'Modernismo: origen de la palabra y evolución de un concepto', in *Nuevos asedios al modernismo*, ed. Ivan A. Schulman, Madrid: Taurus, 1987, pp. 39–50.

[51] See Elisa Sampson Vera Tudela, 'Hearing Voices: Ricardo Palma's Contextualisation

further than the Brazilian Sousândrade's *O inferno de Wall Street*, written after his residence in New York in the 1860s, published in 1874–77, and which would read like an imitation of Ezra Pound's *Cantos* were it not for the date of composition:

(Guesa writing *personals* in the Herald and consulting the Sibyls
of New York:)
—*Young—Lady* from Fifth Avenue,
Celestially flaunting her wares
In Grace Church one day ...
—Such prey
Just th'*almighty dollar* ensnares.
...
(*Freeloves* meditating on the *free-burglars* fine arts:)
—Rome, robbed right from the beginning;
Robbery's rampant in New York town,
Rio, *anthropophagous;*
Ophiophagous
Newark ... wholly turned upside down ...[52]

Add in Edgar Allan Poe's New York tales (1845), Herman Melville's *The Confidence-Man* (1857), Joaquim Maria Machado de Assis's *Posthumous Memoirs of Brás Cubas* (1881), and José Martí's journalism, and there is a respectable canvas of trans-American modernism running from the 1840s through to 1915. This is the lightest of sketches, intended merely to suggest that other histories of modernism are possible, ones in which America is not a latecomer, ones in which Hispanic writing (including Brazilian) has a prominent place. Even more pertinently, for current purposes, the writing of four of these authors shows the impress of New York: directly and dramatically in Poe, Sousândrade, and Martí, more subtly in Darío, but more relevantly here too because Darío was in New York in 1915, where—at least in Nicaraguan terms—he handed on the lyric torch to his young compatriot, Salomón de la Selva.

---

of Colonial Peru', in Christopher Prendergast, ed., *Debating World Literature*, London: Verso, 2004, pp. 214–32.

[52] [Joaquim de Sousa Andrade], 'The Wall Street Inferno (From "O Guesa")' (Sousândrade) (1832–1902)', trans. Robert E. Brown, *Latin American Literary Review*, 14, no. 27 (1986), 92–98, at 93–94. See Rachel Price, *The Object of the Atlantic: Concrete Aesthetics in Cuba, Brazil, and Spain, 1868–1968*, Evanston, IL: Northwestern University Press, 2014, pp. 85–89.

Chapter Two

American Geopolitics in the New Century (1898–1914)

It's only hatred you shall get
From all my folks and me.[1]

After 1492 there had first been four worlds—America having been added to Asia, Europe, and Africa—and then just two: the old world and the new. America was 'new' to the old world in part because that old world was determined to ignore what was old in the 'new' world; but the designations stuck and maps of the world were organised into two halves. Politically, the American continent began in the late eighteenth century to free itself from European control: first the USA gained its independence, then Haiti, then most of South and Central America. The new American creole nations had much in common, and the USA offered a secular, republican, and materialist model that the rest of the continent was eager to emulate. However, the relationship between the USA and at least its closest neighbours to the south soured considerably during the course of the nineteenth century as a result of the US–Mexico War of 1848 and of the recurrent attempted invasions of Cuba from the USA aimed at establishing an insular extension to the slave system. Alongside US military, political, and commercial initiatives, there developed an ideology of Pan-Americanism around a set of institutions dominated by the USA. The Spanish–American War of 1898, which resulted in Cuba, Puerto Rico, and the Philippines passing from Spanish hands into US control, concentrated minds and clarified dividing lines. Nearly a century after independence for most South and Central American countries, the cultural and linguistic ties to Spain—and through Spain to the rest of Europe—again began to tug; and the example of US materialism began to pall, at least for some. The period between 1898 and 1914 was dominated by

---

[1] From Salomón de la Selva, 'A Song for Wall Street', *Tropical Town and Other Poems*, New York: John Lane Company, 1918, p. 27.

Theodore Roosevelt and the implementation of his interventionist American policy, which enormously increased US influence in the countries to the south of the USA. In the face of US power, and against the official ideology of Pan-Americanism, Hispanic America produced a set of competing ideas about the continent and its identity which were still in ferment as the old world erupted into conflict in 1914.

The Famous States

The European discovery of America in 1492 had posed difficult questions for views of the world with foundations in classical and biblical traditions. One powerful argument, famously proposed by the French naturalist Buffon in the middle of the eighteenth century, stressed American difference: new world flora and fauna were simply poorer and weaker imitations of their old world originals, a view given philosophical substance in the lectures delivered by G. W. F. Hegel at Jena in 1805–06 and later published as his *Philosophy of History* (1833–35). Deeply Eurocentric in conception, Hegel's theory offered a picture of America as a young and immature continent: a 'new' world in the full sense, which was also different and inferior. Contestation of Hegel's views came both from his contemporary, Alexander von Humboldt, who had spent five years as a scientist–traveller in South America between 1799 and 1804 and who knew first-hand the richness and vitality of American nature, and from local creole writers who were forging new identities for themselves and for their nations. In this sense figures such as Thomas Jefferson, Andrés Bello, and Francisco Clavigero were united in their high valuation of the American continent, that new world or western hemisphere, as it was increasingly called.[2]

With the USA to the forefront, American cultural identity soon assumed political shape with John Quincy Adams's formulation in 1823 of what became known as the Monroe Doctrine: 'The occasion has been judged proper for asserting, as a principle in which the rights and interests of the United States are involved, that the American continents, by the free and independent condition which they have assumed and maintain, are

---

[2] See Antonello Gerbi, *The Dispute of the New World: The History of a Polemic, 1750–1900* [1955], trans. Jeremy Moyle, Pittsburgh, PA: University of Pittsburgh Press, 1973; Laura Dassow Walls, *The Passage to Cosmos: Alexander von Humboldt and the Shaping of America*, Chicago: University of Chicago Press, 2009; Arthur P. Whitaker, *The Western Hemisphere Idea: Its Rise and Decline*, Ithaca, NY: Cornell University Press, 1954; and John C. Chasteen, *Americanos: Latin America's Struggle for Independence*, Oxford: Oxford University Press, 2008.

henceforth not to be considered as subjects for future colonization by any European powers'.³ That formula notionally protected all the American republics, but Adams's view that Cuba would eventually become part of the USA gave Latin Americans pause for thought, as might that very early use of the plural 'continents', which inserted a blade into the map of America, presumably somewhere around the isthmus of Panama.⁴

The multiplication of continents came about during the nineteenth century, but it was by no means straightforward or easily agreed: even now there is no consensus as to whether there are five or six or seven continents, and five and six can be reached in different ways. Already by the second decade of the twentieth century, the idea of the seventh continent was in play, but at the same time some geography books were still teaching that there were only two continents, corresponding to those old and new worlds.⁵ Certainly, one of the pioneers of the study of Latin American history in the USA, Bernard Moses, suggested in 1898 that '[i]n order to see any portion of American history in its true light, we must stand where the whole continent lies within our horizon.'⁶ Indeed, the idea that North and South America might count as two continents is inherently strange: the adjectives 'north' and 'south' would logically imply an entity they have in

---

³ James Monroe, Seventh Annual Message (2 December 1823) <https://www.presidency.ucsb.edu/documents/seventh-annual-message-1> accessed December 2018.

⁴ John Quincy Adams to Hugh Nelson, 28 April 1823, in US Congress, House of Representatives, *Island of Cuba*, 32nd Congress, 1st. Session, Doc. no. 121 (Washington, DC, 1852), pp. 6–7.

⁵ See Helen S. Wright, *The Seventh Continent: A History of the Discovery and Explorations of Antarctica*, Boston: Richard G. Badger, 1918. William Hughes (*A Class-book of Modern Geography* [1859], 8th edn, London: George Philip & Son, 1873, p. 6) has six continents, including North America and South America, but also Eastern (Europe, Asia, Africa) and Western (America), a formulation similarly found in Thomas Cramer Hopkins, *Elements of Physical Geography*, Boston: Benjamin H. Sanborn & Co., 1908, p. 235. Walter J. Kenyon, *A Teacher's Handbook in Geography, Part 1: North and South America*, San Francisco, CA: C.A. Murdock & Co., 1905, has two sections: 'The Continent of South America' and 'The Continent of North America'. Richard Elwood Dodge, *Dodge's Advanced Geography*, Chicago: Rand McNally, 1904, has five continents (Europe, Asia, Africa, North America, South America), while the five in Ralph S. Tarr, *New Physical Geography*, New York: Macmillan, 1904, pp. 23–26 are Africa, Australia, Eurasia, North America, and South America.

⁶ Bernard Moses, 'The Neglected Half of American History', *University Chronicle*, 1 (April 1898), 122, quoted in James E. Watson, 'Bernard Moses: Pioneer in Latin American Scholarship', *Hispanic American Historical Review*, 42, no. 2 (1962), 212–16, at 213.

common. The tendency to think of them as separate continents was probably encouraged by cartographic convenience: a single plate for an entity the length of America will inevitably contain little detail, so from the middle of the eighteenth century cartographers would often include separate plates in their world atlases for North and South America, with North America including the Central American countries and the Caribbean islands. For a spell in the late nineteenth and early twentieth centuries it also became common to speak about the 'three Americas'—North, Central, and South, perhaps in recognition that the political dynamics of the latter two looked rather different, especially when viewed from the North. The Venezuelan writer, Nicanor Bolet Peraza, ran a journal in New York called *Las Tres Américas* (1896-99) and the concept appears intermittently in book titles until the 1930s.[7]

However you slice it, America is not easily divided into two or three on simple geographical lines—unless you use the equator as a dividing line, which fits with nobody's ideology. And ideology is the point: from the middle of the nineteenth century, North and South America are ideological categories corresponding fairly directly to Anglo America (or just the USA) and Hispanic America. This opposition between the 'Anglo' and 'Hispanic' parts of the continent had stiffened into warfare in 1846 following the annexation of Texas. The war with Mexico was a clear statement of US willingness to use force to extend its territory—what now became known as Manifest Destiny. Monterrey and Chapultepec were bitter defeats for Mexico and for Hispanic America; but the conflict also split US opinion, indicative of divisions which would soon lead to the Civil War. 'Go, blind worm, go, / Behold the famous States / Harrying Mexico / With rifle and with knife', as Ralph Waldo Emerson put it.[8] The Spanish possession of Cuba was also harried by the invasions of Narciso López launched from US territory, as was Nicaragua by the filibuster from Nashville, William Walker. López's actions were frowned upon by the US government, but the US President, Franklin Pierce, recognised Walker's rule in 1856 (Fig. 3). There's a strong argument—well pursued by Michel Gobat—that the shock waves from this act of recognition explain the almost immediate, and surprisingly long-lasting, resonance of the term 'Latin America'.[9] The act also served

---

[7] Bolet Peraza's 'third' America was probably Cuba and Puerto Rico, still Spanish colonies in 1896.

[8] 'Ode, Inscribed to W. H. Channing' [1846], in Ralph Waldo Emerson, *Collected Poems and Translations*, ed. Harold Bloom and Paul Kane, New York: The Library of America, 1994, pp. 61-64, at p. 62.

[9] Michel Gobat, 'The Invention of Latin America: A Transnational History of

3 William Walker's entrance into Granada. Copy of an engraving in Scrapbook, John P. Heiss Papers, Tennessee Historical Society Collections.

to put Nicaragua at the centre of the story of US imperialism, leading to particular pressure on its poets—Darío and de la Selva—to respond on behalf of 'the South'.

During the last quarter of the nineteenth century, the USA exported to the south of the continent its technical expertise and its ideas of individual freedom and enterprise. Many Latin American countries received considerable US investment and some consequent economic growth. Gratitude was by no means universal. There was selective incorporation of the comprador class that benefited most, but also substantial resistance from rural and indigenous communities as well as urban artisans and landowners whose interests were threatened. Resistance often adopted the symbols and rhetoric of nationalism.[10] But many Latin American intellectuals and politicians, the Argentine Domingo Sarmiento prominent among them, visited the USA and saw there progressive notions which they thought necessary to modernise

---

Anti-Imperialism, Democracy, and Race', *American Historical Review*, 118, no. 5 (2013), 1345–75.
[10] Thomas F. O'Brien, *The Revolutionary Mission: American Enterprise in Latin America, 1900–1945*, Cambridge: Cambridge University Press, 1996, pp. 1–6.

their own traditional, that is backward, societies.[11] So opposition between 'North' and 'South' America was never straightforward.

A growing issue, however, was the development and hardening of racial ideas, including the assertion that the Anglo-Saxon race, embodied in the USA, was in the process of demonstrating its superiority in a global context. One of the most popular books of the late nineteenth century was *Our Country* by Josiah Strong, originally published in 1885 but with multiple re-editions over the following 15 years. Strong's chapter on 'The Anglo-Saxon and the World's Future' ends with a startling prediction:

> It seems to me that God, with infinite wisdom and skill, is training the Anglo-Saxon race for an hour sure to come in the world's future. Heretofore there has always been in the history of the world a comparatively unoccupied land westward, into which the crowded countries of the East have poured their surplus populations. But the widening waves of migration, which millenniums ago rolled east and west from the valley of the Euphrates, meet to-day on our Pacific coast. There are no more new worlds. The unoccupied arable lands of the earth are limited, and will soon be taken. The time is coming when the pressure of population on the means of subsistence will be felt here as it is now felt in Europe and Asia. Then will the world enter upon a new stage of its history—*the final competition of races, for which the Anglo-Saxon is being schooled*. Long before the thousand millions are here, the mighty *centrifugal* tendency, inherent in this stock and strengthened in the United States, will assert itself. Then this race of unequaled energy, with all the majesty of numbers and the might of wealth behind it—the representative, let us hope, of the largest liberty, the purest Christianity, the highest civilization—having developed peculiarly aggressive traits calculated to impress its institutions upon mankind, will spread itself over the earth. If I read not amiss, this powerful race will move down upon Mexico, down upon Central and South America, out upon the islands of the sea, over upon Africa and beyond. And can anyone doubt that the result of this competition of races will be the 'survival of the fittest'?[12]

---

[11] Domingo Faustino Sarmiento, *Travels in the United States in 1847*, translation and introductory essay by Michael Aaron Rockland, Princeton, NJ: Princeton University Press, 1970; and see Julio Ramos, *Divergent Modernities: Culture and Politics in Nineteenth-Century Latin America*, trans. John D. Blanco, Durham, NC: Duke University Press, 2001, p. 154.

[12] Josiah Strong, *Our Country* [1885], ed. Jurgen Herbst, Cambridge, MA: Harvard University Press, 1963, pp. 213–14.

This kind of Anglo-Saxon mythology tended to be directed at a domestic readership, shoring up some version of national identity against a growing tide of immigration from the peripheries of Europe; not that the language thereby sounded less threatening to those in the south of the continent promised the 'impress' of Anglo-Saxon institutions. Southern American counter-currents stirred—and strengthened in response to Northern action and Northern rhetoric. At least three different strands can be identified. From the earliest years of the wars of independence, and embedded in the writing of Simón Bolívar in particular, was the idea of a united Spanish America.[13] Bolívar organised the Congress of Panama in 1826 to pursue this idea but the resulting Treaty of Union, League, and Perpetual Confederation was not generally ratified and the plan collapsed—though the dream has often been revisited. In its wake, after the annexation of Texas and the US invasion of Mexico, and in immediate response to Pierce's recognition of Walker's regime in Nicaragua, the discursive construct of *Latin* America began to appear in the 1850s in writings by the Chilean Francisco Bilbao and the Colombian José María Torres Caicedo, both part of a liberal émigré group based in Paris.[14] In a speech he delivered in Paris in June 1856, Bilbao renewed the Bolivarian call for collective action by 'la raza latinoamericana' [the Latin American race] in the face of 'the Saxon jaws of the magnetizing boa constrictor that is unrolling its tortuous coils' through Texas and the north of Mexico, a graphic image, despite the relative absence of boa constrictors in Saxon countries. Panama remains suspended, he writes: will it belong to the North or to the South?[15] Bilbao offers a compelling picture:

> The Disunited States of South America are beginning to discern the smoke from the US campfire. We are beginning to feel the footsteps of the colossus which, fearlessly, every year, with its diplomacy, with its cast of adventurers, with its growing influence and power that magnetises its neighbours, with the complications it causes in our countries with pre-treaties, mediations, and protectorates, with its industry, its navy, its businesses, watching out for our failures and fatigues, taking advantage of our divisions, every year more impetuous

---

[13] See Sara Castro-Klarén, 'Framing Pan-Americanism: Simón Bolívar's Findings', *CR: The New Centennial Review*, vol. 3, no. 1 (2003), 25–53.

[14] On Pierce's recognition of Walker's regime, see Robert E. May, *Manifest Destiny's Underworld: Filibustering in Antebellum America*, Chapel Hill: University of North Carolina Press, 2002, pp. 119–23.

[15] 'El Congreso Normal Americano', in Francisco Bilbao, *El pensamiento vivo de Francisco Bilbao*, 6th edn, Santiago: Editorial Nascimento, 1940, pp. 145–65, at p. 148.

and more daring, that young colossus that 'believes' in its empire just as Rome believed in its, infatuated with its successes, it advances like a flood tide waiting to unleash its waters in a cataract over the South.[16]

Bilbao develops an extraordinary classical analogy. The USA is Rome. Seventeen seventy-six was a glorious moment in its history. Wealth, power, and freedom grew; forests were torn down, deserts were populated. Scorning tradition, a new nation was forged. But then, turning inwards, it fell into the temptation of the Titans, believing itself arbiter of the world. Its personality hardened: the Yankee replaced the American, patriotism replaced philosophy, wealth replaced morality, righteousness replaced justice.[17] Without actually identifying Latin America as Greece, Bilbao identifies the divisions which destroyed Greece as the serpents that threatened Hercules. They must be destroyed, as Hercules destroyed the serpents, if Latin America is to fulfil its destiny. The pillars of Hercules are in Panama, which symbolises the future of the continent. If Latin America is united, Panama will be 'the sentinel of our future'. Disunited, then it will be the Gordian knot cut by the Yankee axe. William Walker is emblematic of the threat posed by the USA: 'Panamá es el punto de apoyo que busca el Arquímedes yanqui para levantar a la América del Sur y suspenderla en los abismos para devorarla a pedazos' [Panama is the fulcrum sought by the Yankee Archimedes in order to lift South America, suspend it over the abyss, and devour it bit by bit].[18]

Caicedo's poem of the same year—equally prompted by Walker's filibustering in Nicaragua—was called 'Las dos Américas' [The Two Americas]:

> La raza de la América latina,
> Al frente tiene la sajona raza,
> Enemiga mortal que ya amenaza
> Su libertad destruir y su pendón.[19]

> The race of Latin America
> Confronted by the Saxon race,
> The mortal enemy who now threatens
> To destroy its liberty and its banner.

---

[16] Bilbao, *El pensamiento*, p. 151.
[17] Bilbao, *El pensamiento*, pp. 150–51.
[18] Bilbao, *El pensamiento*, pp. 156–57.
[19] The full text is in Arturo Ardao, *Génesis de la idea y el nombre de América Latina*, Caracas: Centro de Estudios Latinoamericanos Rómulo Gallegos, 1980, pp. 175–85.

The obvious advantage to the new creole elite of that designation 'Latin America' was that it established a partial identification with European civilisation while keeping the old colonising power of Spain at a distance—not to mention the indigenous or African-descended elements of the population. 'In that shift, internal colonialism was born', writes Walter Mignolo.[20]

Unlike many of his European contemporaries, who tended to take a rather condescending view of the USA, the French Saint-Simonian economist Michel Chevalier, who travelled extensively through the USA, Mexico, and Cuba in the early 1830s, saw America as the continent of the future ('réservée à de hautes destinées' [destined for great things]), in part—and here he demonstrated a truly *global* vision—because of its situation between the two main blocks of civilisation, western and eastern, foreseeing that the United States would soon extend to the western coast of the American continent.[21] European thought had inherited from classical writers a broad distinction between Latin (Roman) and Teutonic (German) races, which Chevalier transferred across the Atlantic as 'the two Americas'.[22] Latins may have dominated in the time of Rome, or even of the Holy Roman Empire, but the Teutons now had the upper hand and the Hispano-Americans, as Chevalier called them, were 'an impotent race', in danger of being overrun.[23] It was the destiny of France, as the modern epitome of *latinité*, to protect and develop

---

[20] Walter D. Mignolo, *The Idea of Latin America*, Oxford: Blackwell, 2005, p. 65. See also John Leddy Phelan, 'Pan-Latinism, French Intervention in Mexico (1861–1867) and the Genesis of the Idea of Latin America', in *Conciencia y autenticidad históricas: Escritos en homenaje a Edmundo O'Gorman*, Mexico City: Universidad Nacional Autonóma de México, 1968, pp. 279–98; Ardao, *Genesis de la idea*; Monica Quijada, 'Sobre el origen y difusión del nombre 'América Latina' (o una variación heterodoxa en torno al tema de la construcción social de la verdad)', *Revista de Indias*, LVIII, no. 214 (1998), 595–616. Miguel Antonio Rojas Mix, '"América, no invoco tu nombre en vano": la idea de la América Latina de Neruda a la geopolítica contemporánea', *Revista de la Casa de las Américas*, no. 253 (2008), 4–19; Aims McGuinness, 'Searching for "Latin America": Race and Sovereignty in the Americas in the 1850s', in *Race and Nation in Modern Latin America*, ed. Nancy P. Appelbaum, Anne S. Macpherson, and Karin Alejandra Rosemblatt, Chapel Hill: University of North Carolina Press, 2003, pp. 87–107; Greg Grandin, 'Your Americanism and Mine: Americanism and Anti-Americanism in the Americas', *American Historical Review*, 11, no. 4 (2006), 1042–66; Gobat, 'The Invention of Latin America'; and Mauricio Tenorio-Trillo, *Latin America: The Allure and Power of an Idea*, Chicago: University of Chicago Press, 2017.
[21] Michel Chevalier, *Lettres sur l'Amérique du Nord*, 3rd edn, 2 vols., Paris: C. Gosselin et compagnie, 1837, vol. 1, p. vi.
[22] Chevalier, *Lettres sur l'Amérique du Nord*, vol. 1, p. ii. The Slav sometimes made a third part.
[23] Chevalier, *Lettres sur l'Amérique du Nord*, vol. 1, p. xi; vol. 2, p. 378.

Latin communities across the world: 'La France est dépositaire des destinées de toutes les nations du groupe latin dans les deux continents. Elle seule peut empêcher que cette famille entière de peuples ne soit engloutie dans le double débordement des Germains ou Saxons et des Slaves'.[24] [France is the guarantor of the destinies of all the Latin nations on the two continents. Only she can prevent the whole family of peoples from being swallowed up by the double influx of Germans and Slavs.]

That imagery of swallowing, shared by Chevalier and Bilbao, would feed into—as we shall see—the characterisation of the USA as a Cyclops or Caliban, a figure that would dominate the period between 1898 and 1914. Meanwhile, Chevalier's notion of 'Latinity' provided a second strand of response to Anglo-Saxon ideology, supporting the idea of a 'Latin America' which had inherited from mainland Europe the classical civilisation that both the Anglo-Saxon America to the north and the Indian and *mestizo* masses in the south were incapable of appreciating—but with France remaining firmly at the head of this particular family.

The supposed global struggle between the Anglo-Saxon and Latin races took an unusual turn, however, in 1862, when the army of the Latin patriarch, Napoleon III, invaded independent Mexico, deposing the president of the republic and installing a minor Hapsburg prince as Emperor Maximilian I, with none other than Michel Chevalier as his economic adviser. After Maximilian's ignominious defeat and execution, Chevalier justified the invasion on the grounds of the need to preserve Latin Catholic culture in the face of the spread of Anglo-Saxon Protestantism— not a rationale likely to go down well with most Mexicans.[25] The proposition that Latin America should find its identity as one part of the Latin family of nations never recovered from this misstep, despite the longevity of the adjective 'Latin' to name the southern part of the continent and despite persistent Latin American admiration for French culture. After this French intervention, some Hispanic Americans, such as Francisco Bilbao, became in response continental Americanists.[26] Bilbao was—as Mignolo pointedly puts it—'located at the receiving end not at the giving end of the equation', meaning that he was less interested in sweeping racial or cultural generalisations, and more likely to change his opinion in the face of changing political circumstances.[27]

---

[24] Chevalier, *Lettres sur l'Amérique du Nord*, vol. 1, p. xiii.
[25] Michel Chevalier, *Le Mexique, ancien et moderne*, Paris: L'Hachette et compagnie, 1863.
[26] See Rojas Mix, '"America, no invoco tu nombre en vano"', p. 10.
[27] Mignolo, *The Idea of Latin America*, p. 70.

The third strand of the counter-current, although it didn't appear until later in the piece, was *hispanismo*, which re-emphasised the centrality of Spanish culture to Spanish-speaking America, welcoming back into the fold—as it were—the children who had left home long enough ago to recognise their true identification with the values of the mother country.[28] But the Spanish proponents of the terms 'Hispanic America' or 'Iberoamerica' would fight a losing battle against the usage 'Latin America'.[29]

By the time the US Civil War was over, uniting the disunited States, the idea of two Americas, North and South, Anglo and Hispanic, divided by race, language, and culture, was firmly entrenched—however incoherent it might be, since Brazil was usually excluded and nobody knew what to do with the smaller Caribbean islands. The Argentine politician and writer Domingo Sarmiento founded a journal published in Spanish in New York, urging South America to follow US models and the US intelligentsia to recognise the intelligence of South America. He involved the US Hispanist elite, such as George Ticknor, and called it *Ambas Américas: Revista de educación, bibliografía y agricultura* (1867–68). The Venezuelan Ramón Páez, who lived in New York, wrote *Ambas Américas: Contrastes* (1872). In both cases it was taken for granted that there were now two Americas.[30]

In all these developments, the emphasis given in Spanish-speaking American countries to a supposed Latin vs. Anglo-Saxon contrast between 'North' and 'South' America tended to ignore the fact that the USA already had an increasingly large immigrant population from many parts of Europe which were far from Anglo-Saxon. By 1914, New York in particular was not an Anglo-Saxon city, so contrasts were bound to be complicated, at least if they took account of the actual lie of the land. Meanwhile, US foreign policy in the first two decades of the twentieth century tended further to sharpen the perceived division, even if lines were often also blurred, particularly—in ways that interest this book—by personal Hispanic experience of the USA, which, to many, meant experience of New York.

---

[28] See Fernando Ortiz, *La reconquista de América: Reflexiones sobre el panhispanismo*, Paris: Sociedad de Ediciones Literarias y Artísticas, 1911; and Fredrick B. Pike, *Hispanismo, 1898–1936: Spanish Conservatives and Liberals and their Relations with Spanish America*, Notre Dame, IN: University of Notre Dame Press, 1971.
[29] See Aureliano M. Espinosa, 'The Term *Latin America*', *Hispania*, 1, no. 3 (1918), 135–43.
[30] Tenorio-Trillo, *Latin America*, pp. 7–8.

Pan-Americanism

The soothing counter-melody to the strident interventionist tune of US foreign policy came to be known as Pan-Americanism: it saw its heyday in the period between 1898 and 1919. 'Pan-American' appears first as a term in the last quarter of the nineteenth century, probably on the model of pan-Slavic and pan-Hellenic, which were in wide use at the time. Earlier in the nineteenth century, inter-American congresses had been held exclusively for Latin American countries. The USA began to embrace a pan-American agenda only in 1881 when it proposed a conference which eventually took place in 1889–90 in Washington, DC as the First Conference of American States (also known as the International American Conference), which one newspaper referred to by the term 'Pan-American Conference'.[31]

To its admirers, Pan-Americanism stood for hemispheric brotherhood. US Secretary of State James G. Blaine promised as much when he inaugurated that first conference on a chilly October day in 1889. Addressing delegates from throughout the continent, Blaine promised a future of peace and accomplishments to dwarf those of the old world. 'No conference of nations has ever assembled to consider the welfare of territorial possessions so vast and to contemplate the possibilities of a future so great and so inspiring,' he proclaimed, invoking common heritage and common destiny. Latin Americans need not fear Yankee imperialism, he promised. Working together, Americans 'can show to the world an honorable, peaceful conference of eighteen independent American Powers, in which all shall meet together on terms of absolute equality.'[32] The outcome was not altogether auspicious. Most of the US delegates were businessmen, most of the Latin Americans diplomats and jurists; few spoke the others' language. The Latin Americans were taken on an exhausting six-week railroad trip to impress them with US achievements, which gave them plenty of time to get to know each other and to form a united front against US proposals. And, most damaging of all, the conference attracted the analytical skills of the Cuban patriot and revolutionary José Martí. Martí began by reporting in *La Nación* on US

---

[31] *New York Evening Post*, 5 March 1888; quoted in Joseph Byrne Lockey, *Essays in Pan-Americanism*, Berkeley: University of California Press, 1939, p. 1. The first citation in the *Oxford English Dictionary* is from 1879. See also John E. Fagg, *Pan Americanism*, Malabar, FL: R. E. Krieger Pub. Co., 1982.

[32] International American Conference (1st: 1889–90: Washington, DC), *Reports of Committees and Discussions Thereon* (Washington, DC, 1890), no. 1, 39–42, quoted in Benjamin Coates, 'The Pan-American Lobbyist: William Eleroy Curtis and U.S. Empire, 1884–1899', *Diplomatic History*, 38, no. 1 (2014), 22–48, at 22.

press reaction, which was decidedly mixed, along party lines; and on the intrigues attendant on the early unofficial meetings.[33] Further dispatches for *La Nación* were consistently downbeat, including a long piece, dated New York, 2 November 1889, and published on 19 and 20 December, in which Martí was sceptical of the motives of the USA, 'repletos de productos invendibles, y determinados a extender sus dominios en América' [full of products they can't sell and determined to extend their dominions].[34] Martí was even invited to address the Spanish-speaking delegates at a meeting of the Sociedad Literaria Hispanoamericana on the evening of 19 December 1889.[35] Later, in the preface to his book of poems *Versos sencillos*, he recalled the whole conference in sombre tones:

> It was during that anguished winter when, out of ignorance, blind faith, fear, or mere politeness, the peoples of Latin America gathered in Washington beneath the fearsome eagle. Who among us has forgotten that seal, on which the eagle of Monterrey and Chapultepec, López and Walker, clutched all the flags of America in its talons?[36]

However, despite Martí's somewhat melodramatic rhetoric, Blaine's proposals for various kinds of continental uniformity were defeated, and yet all concerned were positive enough about the outcome to commit to a Union of American Republics (UAR), which organised subsequent International American conferences in Mexico City (1902), Rio de Janeiro (1906), and Buenos Aires (1910) (all frequently referred to informally as Pan-American conferences) and to the formation of the Pan-American Union (PAU), which became the agent of the UAR and the permanent secretariat for the

---

[33] Letter to *La Nación* (dated 4 October 1889, published 14 November 1889), in José Martí, *Argentina y la primera conferencia panamericana*, ed. Dardo Cúneo, Buenos Aires: Transición, 1955, pp. 89–91.

[34] José Martí, 'Congreso Internacional de Washington: Su historia, sus elementos y sus tendencias', *Obras escogidas*, 3 vols., ed. Ela López Ugarte and Adiala González Naranjo, La Habana: Editorial de Ciencias Sociales, 1992, vol. 2, pp. 379–94; 'The Washington Pan-American Congress', in *Inside the Monster by José Martí: Writings on the United States and American Imperialism*, trans. Elinor Randall et al., ed. Philip S. Foner, New York: Monthly Review Press, 1975, pp. 339–67.

[35] José Martí, 'Madre América', *Obras escogidas*, vol. 2, pp. 420–27; 'Mother America', *José Martí Reader: Writings on the Americas*, ed. Deborah Shnookal and Mirta Muñiz, Melbourne: Ocean Press, 1999, pp. 101–10.

[36] José Martí, 'Versos sencillos', *Obras escogidas*, vol. 2, p. 519; 'Simple Verse/*Versos sencillos*', *Selected Writings*, trans. Esther Allen, Harmondsworth: Penguin, 2002, p. 270.

conferences, with the US Secretary of State always its president. By 1910, the PAU had a new headquarters in Washington, DC with the first two Pan-American Commercial Conferences taking place there in 1911 and in early June 1919. In the wake of the establishment of the PAU, various inter-American agencies mushroomed to deal with particular issues and a number of non-governmental and private organisations began to use the Pan-American designation.[37]

In 1914, the diplomat John Barrett announced 'the beginning of a great Pan-American era'.[38] During this period Barrett was the director general of the PAU and its most prominent spokesman. Officially, as he would often explain, the PAU consisted of the 21 American republics, all with equal voice. PAU headquarters was in Washington, DC merely because that was the one place on the continent where all 21 had diplomatic representation. However, that official rhetoric could not always hold: the language of the two Americas was never far away. Punctiliously, Barrett could suggest that the PAU brought together North and South America, with North America including all the republics as far south as Panama, an eleven to ten split purely geographical in nature, with no cultural or linguistic elements involved.[39] Intriguingly, it took architecture to show how ideology could trump geography. The handsome new PAU building in Washington, largely funded by Andrew Carnegie, was a not unattractive mishmash of architectural styles, several of them 'Hispanic', but the decorative sculpture easily lent itself to less 'geographical' depictions of the two Americas. So, on either side of the main entrance—as Barrett himself explained it—'are two sculptured groups depicting respectively North America and South America':

> The two groups are similar in motive. In each a draped female figure represents the genius of its division of the Western Hemisphere; each cherishes with maternal affection a nude boy approaching adolescence. These boys typify the youthful character of their respective portions of the World. In the North American group the boy, strikingly alert in feature and action, expresses the more energetic spirit of the fully

---

[37] For a clear account of these early years, see M. Margaret Bell, *The Problem of Inter-American Organization*, Stanford, CA: Stanford University Press, 1944. The Pan-American Union was turned into the Organisation of American States in 1948. Also Clifford B. Casey, 'The Creation and Development of the Pan American Union', *Hispanic American Historical Review*, 13, no. 4 (November 1933), 437–56.

[38] John Barrett, 'Pan-American Possibilities', *Journal of Race Development*, 5, no. 1 (July 1914), 19–29, at 19.

[39] John Barrett, *The Pan American Union: Peace, Friendship, Commerce*, Washington, DC: Pan American Union, 1911, p. 110.

awakened North .... The figure of 'South America,' while young and strong, has a softer and more sensuous quality, expressive of tropical ease and luxuriance. The boy has likewise an easy grace of carriage; his friendly, lovable expression, imaginative and dreamy, conveys a sense of great future possibilities of which he is not yet conscious. The woman holds an olive branch, the boy a winged sphere. Contemplating this, he seems to be vaguely stirred by the impulse of a high destiny.[40]

'Throughout the design the two grand divisions of North and South America are held in view', he continues. 'These are represented on the front elevation by the two marble pylons on either side of the triple entrances. Here this motive is given emphasis first by colossal groups, then by two historical subjects in low relief, and finally by the eagle and condor, the great birds of the North and the South'.[41] The Andean condor (*Vultur gryphus*) is the national symbol of six South American republics, so a not unreasonable 'representative', but the bald eagle (*Haliaeetus leucocephalus*) is the national animal of just one North American republic and indeed outside the USA is only found in northern Mexico: none of the Central American or Caribbean republics could possibly feel 'represented' by it. Similarly, two sculpted panels represent Washington and San Martín, both great liberators, but the former only of North America taken as the USA.[42] Thus do 21 republics separate into North and South America, with North America tending to resolve itself symbolically and therefore ideologically into the USA.

When it came to Pan-American organisations, the distinction between state and private was not always very clear. So, for example, the Pan American Society (PAS) of the United States was founded in February 1912 by John Barrett with the support of Elihu Root, who had been Theodore Roosevelt's first Secretary of War and second Secretary of State. Its main objectives were 'To promote acquaintance among representative men of the United States and those of other republics of America' and 'to show hospitality and attention to representative men of the other republics of America who visit the United States'. In other words, it was the private—and New York-based—equivalent of the PAU, of which John Barrett was the Director General in

---

[40] Barrett, *The Pan American Union*, pp. 109–10. See Robert Alexander González, *Designing Pan-America: U.S. Architectural Visions for the Western Hemisphere*, Austin: University of Texas Press, 2011, pp. 79–80.
[41] Barrett, *The Pan American Union*, p. 101.
[42] Barrett, *The Pan American Union*, pp. 110–11.

1912. The PAS's first president was Henry White, a career diplomat who had been US delegate to the Fourth Pan-American Conference in Buenos Aires in 1910. He was succeeded by John Bassett Moore, a leading international lawyer who had provided Roosevelt with a defence for his Panama Canal venture. The PAS's 25-year celebratory volume notes 525 luncheons and dinners, which is probably a good indication of the society's priorities.[43]

The PAU had an official bulletin, published monthly from 1893, and known from 1910 as the *Bulletin of the Pan American Union*. Around it clustered other publications, mostly supportive of the PAU's general orientation but with a wider remit, including matters of culture. Most prestigious was the *Pan American Magazine*, founded in 1900 by the inveterate traveller William W. Rasor and edited by him for many years. *The Pan American Review* was the magazine of the PAS, which began publication in New York in February 1919. Commercial in orientation, it eventually provided short sections on books and lectures, but only lasted until December 1921. Pan-American in orientation, yet not using the designation, and without institutional support, were the twin magazines, *El Norte Americano* and *The South American*, the former, distributed throughout Latin America, carrying essays from US magazines translated into Spanish; the latter, distributed in the USA, carrying essays from Latin American magazines translated into English.[44] The oldest surviving journal of this ilk was *América: Revista Mensual Ilustrada*, which for several years from 1910 was edited by the exiled Mexican writer Rafael de Zayas Enríquez, and which was notable for the illustrated chronicles of New York life produced by his son, Marius de Zayas. Marius also provided a series of Parisian chronicles which culminated in his essay introducing Pablo Picasso to a Hispanic readership.[45]

---

[43] The Pan American Society, *Twenty-fifth anniversary 1912, February fifteenth, 1937*, New York: The Pan American Society, 1937.

[44] The series ran from 1914 to 1921, produced by the South American Publishing Co. at 61 Broadway, whose president was Wing B. Allen.

[45] The first of Marius de Zayas's chronicles was 'La vida en Nueva York: la noche (crónica artística)', *América: Revista Mensual Ilustrada*, IV, no. 3 (March 1910), 173–76; his Picasso essay was 'Pablo Picasso', *América: Revista Mensual Ilustrada*, VI, no. 5 (May 1911), 363–65; translated in *Camera Work*, 34–35 (April–July 1911), 65–67. Rafael de Zayas Enríquez's positive take on pan-Americanism is seen in an unattributed editorial, 'Panamericanismo-panhispanismo', *América: Revista Mensual Ilustrada*, VI, no. 2 (February 1911), 124–25. See also his unpublished book manuscript, 'El problema vital del continente americano: panhispanismo y panamericanismo' [1919], MZP, Box 8. MZP is the Marius de Zayas Papers, 1914–1948 (MS 1407), Rare Book and Manuscript Library, Columbia University. Although it originally had considerable cultural content, *América* was always a business-oriented magazine directed at a Latin

So the term 'pan-American' and the ideas associated with that term, however nebulous, permeated New York by 1914 and would, if anything, become even more widely discussed as the American nations began to think about the consequences of the war in Europe. When Salomón de la Selva began to use the term to describe the project into which he was investing so much of his energy, it was already carrying considerable baggage.

Roosevelt's Vision

If the story proper behind the dinner at Gonfarone's starts in January 1915, as it will in the next chapter, then the prologue begins in 1898, the year when the geopolitical plates in the larger Caribbean region underwent a dramatic shift, changing forever the relationship between the USA and its Spanish-speaking neighbours and, indeed, arguably ushering in a whole new planetary order.[46] New York played a central rôle in that process from the moment one of its favourite sons, Theodore Roosevelt, as part of his successful campaign for the governorship of New York in late 1898, commissioned Frederic Remington to paint the colonel leading the charge of his Rough Riders up San Juan Hill, in Cuba, in July that year. The Rough Riders had walked or crawled up the hill, and it was Kettle Hill, not San Juan, but such inaccuracies were never likely to derail Roosevelt's bandwagon.

The forces driving increased US engagement with the lands to its south were many and various, but Roosevelt certainly embodied them and articulated them better than anybody and after assuming the presidency in September 1901 he was in pole position to press them forward. From his time as Assistant Secretary to the Navy, Roosevelt had headed an informal expansionist coterie in Washington who lunched and dined at the Metropolitan Club, close to the White House: 'men linked', in Edmund Morris's words, 'as much by Roosevelt's motley personality as by their common political belief, namely that Manifest Destiny called for the United States to free Cuba, annex Hawaii, and raise the American flag supreme over the Western Hemisphere'.[47] This group favoured what was sometimes referred to as the 'large policy', a continuation

---

American readership, a focus sharpened when it was taken over at the beginnning of 1913 and became *América y industrias americanas*: Rafael de Zayas Enríquez was demoted from editor to 'literary collaborator'.

[46] Julio Ramos, 'Hemispheric Domains: 1898 and the Origins of Latin Americanism', *Journal of Latin American Cultural Studies*, 10, no. 3 (2001), 237–51, at 238.

[47] Edmund Morris, *The Rise of Theodore Roosevelt* [1979], New York: Modern Library, 2001, p. 592. For more detail, see Peter Hulme, *Cuba's Wild East: A Literary Geography of Oriente*, Liverpool: Liverpool University Press, 2011, pp. 171–80.

of the ideas of US Manifest Destiny first articulated in the middle of the nineteenth century. Roosevelt provided the political driving force, the naval strategist, Captain Alfred Thayer Mahan, the strategic vision, and the Republican politician, Henry Cabot Lodge, the ideological underpinning based upon a sense of Anglo-Saxon primacy.[48]

Manifest Destiny had surfaced as a concept in 1839, guiding the USA through its western and southern expansions. Popular writers such as Josiah Strong had ensured its dissemination and development. The 'large policy' inherited the idea of Manifest Destiny and sought ways of putting it into practical effect on a continental, and indeed global, scale, building on the Monroe Doctrine. As an early twentieth-century US diplomat put it, even the original Monroe Doctrine was based on the assumption that the USA should have its cake and eat it too; in other words that it should reserve the right to interfere in the world outside America when it saw its interests involved, but forbid anyone else from interfering in the Western hemisphere.[49]

Under the auspices of Pan-Americanism, the Monroe Doctrine supposedly offered equal protection to all American countries, as Henry Cabot Lodge pointed out in his assessment of its relevance to the border dispute between Britain and Venezuela which erupted in the 1890s.[50] So, although no US national interests were involved, Grover Cleveland's administration invoked the Doctrine to suggest the need for arbitration via a memorandum to the British government delivered in July 1895 by Richard Olney, Cleveland's Secretary of State. Olney's words offer perhaps the best indication of US determination in the 1890s to change the global order:

> To-day the United States is practically sovereign on this continent, and its fiat is law upon the subjects to which it confines its interposition.

---

[48] See Julius W. Pratt, 'The 'Large Policy' of 1898', *Mississippi Valley Historical Review*, 19, no. 2 (1932), 219–42; Paul T. McCartney, *Power and Progress: American National Identity, the War of 1898, and the Rise of American Imperialism*, Baton Rouge: Louisiana State University Press, 2006, pp. 174–82; and Evan Thomas, *The War Lovers: Roosevelt, Lodge, Hearst, and the Rush to Empire, 1898*, New York: Little, Brown, and Company, 2010.

[49] See Walter LaFeber, 'The Evolution of the Monroe Doctrine from Monroe to Reagan', in *Redefining the Past: Essays in Diplomatic History in Honor of William Appleman Williams*, ed. Lloyd C. Gardner, Corvallis: Oregon State University Press, 1986, pp. 121–42, at p. 125. For relevant background, see Gretchen Murphy, *Hemispheric Imaginings: The Monroe Doctrine and the Narratives of U.S. Empire*, Durham, NC: Duke University Press, 2005.

[50] Henry Cabot Lodge, 'England, Venezuela, and the Monroe Doctrine', *North American Review*, 160 (1895), 651–58.

Why? It is not because of the pure friendship or good-will felt for it. It is not simply by reason of its high character as a civilized state, nor because wisdom and justice and equity are the invariable characteristics of the dealings of the United States. It is because, in addition to other grounds, its infinite resources, combined with its isolated position, render it master of the situation and practically invulnerable as against any or all other powers.[51]

In fact, the USA wasn't interested in Venezuela's territorial claims: the arbitration committee largely accepted the British case. Rather, it was interested in asserting its own right to control the American continent.

Indeed, Venezuela under the dictator Cipriano Castro proved a significant irritant to Roosevelt, repudiating arbitration awards and confiscating foreign property, therefore opening up the possibility of British and German intervention. This was something Latin American countries wanted no more than did the USA, and the Argentine diplomat Luis M. Drago proposed a policy initiative that would see all American nations combining to protect each other from such interventions merely to collect debts—in effect, as Arthur P. Whitaker points out, a pan-American corollary to the Monroe Doctrine. Thanks to the skills of Elihu Root, this truly—as opposed to cosmetic—pan-American initiative was sidelined while Roosevelt announced his own corollary to the Monroe Doctrine in his 1904 Annual Presidential Address: 'All that this country desires is that the other republics on this continent shall be happy and prosperous; and they cannot be happy and prosperous unless they maintain order within their boundaries and behave with a just regard for their obligations towards outsiders.'[52] The USA would take it upon itself to determine whether those other republics' regard was just or not. In a letter to John Hay on the subject, Roosevelt spelled it out in less diplomatic language: 'It will show those Dagos that they will have to behave decently.'[53]

---

[51] From the full version of Olney's message reprinted in the appendix to William Eleroy Curtis, *Venezuela: A Land Where It's Always Summer*, London: Osgood, McIlvaine & Co., 1896, pp. 261–309, at p. 284.

[52] Theodore Roosevelt, Annual message 6 December 1904 <http://en.wikisource.org/wiki/Theodore_Roosevelt%27s_Fifth_State_of_the_Union_Address> accessed December 2018. See Whitaker, *The Western Hemisphere Idea*, pp. 86–107; and Richard H. Collin, *Theodore Roosevelt's Caribbean: The Panama Canal, the Monroe Doctrine, and the Latin American Context*, Baton Rouge: Louisiana State University Press, 1990, pp. 80–96.

[53] Theodore Roosevelt, *The Letters of Theodore Roosevelt*, ed. Elting E. Morison, 8 vols, Cambridge, MA: Harvard University Press, 1951, vol. 4, p. 917 (2 September 1904). Cf. Edmund Morris, *Theodore Rex*, New York: Random House, 2001.

Roosevelt himself had a lively interest in naval history, which led him to seek the advice and friendship of the naval strategist Captain Alfred T. Mahan. In May 1897, Mahan published the latest in his series of analyses of sea-power, suggesting the centrality of the Caribbean for contemporary geopolitics: 'In the cluster of island fortresses of the Caribbean is one of the greatest of the nerve centers of the whole body of European civilization; and it is to be regretted that so serious a portion of them now is in hands which not only never have given, but to all appearances never can give, the development which is required by the general interest.'[54] In response, Roosevelt wrote a revealing and confidential letter to Mahan, studded with the prophetic phrase, 'if I had my way': Hawaii would be annexed, Spain would be turned out of the Caribbean, the Danish islands would be acquired.[55]

Guantánamo Bay had been on the US agenda for many years, so it was hardly a surprise when it was the first place US troops landed on Cuban soil after the declaration of war with Spain in May 1898. They never left. In a memorandum Mahan wrote on behalf of the Naval War Board in August 1898, he mentioned Guantánamo Bay, along with two other Cuban bays, saying, with a revealing turn of phrase, 'When Cuba becomes independent, the United States should acquire, as a naval measure, one of these ports, with a portion of adjacent territory.'[56] Roosevelt ensured that it did, giving the USA control of the huge harbour that dominates the Windward Passage, the main route for shipping en route to and from any isthmian canal—the construction of which was the next item on Roosevelt's agenda.

The national and commercial advantages of having an isthmian canal under US control were self-evident: the Pacific coast could be more efficiently populated, with consequent increases in business of all kinds. For Roosevelt and his allies, however, the military reasons were undoubtedly paramount: as Captain Mahan noted, without a canal it would take the national fleet four months to reach Pearl Harbor; with a canal, four weeks. In Mahan, Roosevelt had an able apologist who could articulate what even Roosevelt knew it would be unwise for him to say himself. Possession of the canal zone, Mahan pointed out, along with Guantánamo Bay, 'advanced the southern maritime frontier of this country'.[57]

---

[54] Alfred T. Mahan, *The Interest of America in Sea Power, Present and Future* [1897], Port Washington, NY: Kennikat Press, 1970, p. 261.
[55] Roosevelt, *The Letters of Theodore Roosevelt*, vol. 1, pp. 607–08 (3 May 1897).
[56] Alfred T. Mahan, *Letters and Papers of Alfred Thayer Mahan*, ed. Robert Seager II and Doris D. Seager, 3 vols, Anapolis, MD: Naval Institute Press, 1975, vol. 2, p. 588.
[57] Alfred T. Mahan, *Armaments and Arbitration, or The Place of Force in the International Relations of States*, New York: Harper and Brothers, 1912, p. 166.

Once Roosevelt became President it was clear that an isthmian canal would be built, though both Panama (still part of Colombia) and Nicaragua offered possible routes, and playing them off against each other was part of the strategy to ensure the best possible deal. In June 1902, Congress authorised Roosevelt to negotiate a concession with the moribund French Panama canal company, which was keen to extricate itself after its spectacular failures. The Colombian *chargé d'affaires* in Washington was persuaded to sign the Hay-Herrán Treaty in January 1903, which was quickly ratified by the US Senate in the face of opposition from a handful of senators who still preferred the Nicaraguan option. The Colombian government, however, viewed the treaty as an assault on its sovereignty and rejected it in August.[58]

Roosevelt, meanwhile, had found somebody he could do business with: Philippe Bunau-Varilla, a major shareholder in the French canal company, who was able to encourage a Panamanian uprising against Colombian rule while Roosevelt, it seems, ordered the US Navy to prevent Colombia from landing troops on the isthmus. The USA immediately recognised Panama's independence and concluded an agreement with Bunau-Varilla which was only ratified by Panama's new legislature when Roosevelt threatened to remove the US warships that were keeping Colombian troops at bay.[59] Even sympathetic biographers think that Roosevelt took some shortcuts here and, after he died, the USA quietly paid $25 million to Colombia in compensation. His own defence, provided by the lawyer John Bassett Moore, was to look to a higher authority: 'If ever a government could be said to have received a mandate from civilization ... the United States holds that position with regard to the interoceanic canal'.[60] To those who called Roosevelt's dealings with Colombia and Panama 'a chapter of national dishonor', Mahan responded that those who oppose what is best for human progress are 'worthless cumberers of the ground, and therefore rightly dispossessed'.[61] That view hardly bode well for the inhabitants of tropical America. In a letter to his friend Rudyard Kipling, Roosevelt reckoned these as his major

---

[58] See Dwight Carroll Miner, *The Fight for the Panama Route: The Story of the Spooner Act and the Hay-Herrán Treaty*, New York: Columbia University Press, 1940.
[59] John Lindsay-Poland, *Emperors in the Jungle: The Hidden History of the U.S. in Panama*, Durham, NC: Duke University Press, 2003, pp. 24–26.
[60] Theodore Roosevelt, Special Message to Congress, 4 January 1904 <https://www.presidency.ucsb.edu/documents/special-message-438> accessed December 2018. Roosevelt was heavily dependent on legal advice from John Bassett Moore, who also acted as a public apologist for Roosevelt's actions: see Bassett Moore's unpublished autobiography in John Bassett Moore Papers, Library of Congress, MSS 33332, Box 297.
[61] Mahan, *Armaments and Arbitration*, pp. 155, 249.

achievements: 'I would consider myself a hundred times over repaid if I had nothing more to my credit than Panama and the coaling stations in Cuba.'[62]

With the Panama Canal under construction and the Guantánamo Bay Naval Base being developed to provide protection, Roosevelt's main concern was now with the political stability of the rest of the region. Particularly problematic, for slightly different reasons, were the Dominican Republic and Nicaragua. In the middle of the nineteenth century, the Dominican Republic had been occupied by Haiti and also returned briefly to Spanish control. Never a rich country, it began in the 1860s to build up massive external debts after successive—often corrupt, certainly venal—presidents took out very large loans with successive—often corrupt, certainly unscrupulous—bankers, beginning with a German fraudster called Edward Herzberg, who changed his name to Hartmont and set up a bank in London, not known, then like now, for its close oversight of banking practices. The debt kept being bought and kept growing. Small investors in Europe were ripped off and the Dominican Republic saw little economic development, but foreign bankers and a few local politicians got very rich. Occasional periods of stability were punctuated by civil wars and assassinations.

As far as the USA was concerned, the chief danger was that some European power—probably Germany—would use debt default as an excuse to take over the country, thereby breaching the Monroe Doctrine. So the US government encouraged the formation of a US company, the San Domingo Improvement Company (SDIC)—basically three New York lawyers—to take over the debt: that way the US government could keep an eye on things and keep the Europeans out.[63] Matters started coming to a head early in the twentieth century and in January 1905, under the Roosevelt Corollary, the USA assumed administration of the Dominican Republic's customs houses, the country's main source of income, and quickly became its only foreign creditor. Another presidential assassination in the Dominican Republic in 1911 led to further civil war. At the end of 1914, Juan Isidro Jimenes was elected president but was under pressure from the USA to allow US control of the treasury and armed forces.

In Nicaragua, José Santos Zelaya seized power in 1893 for the Liberal Party, whose power base was in the coffee-growing areas around the

---

[62] *The Letters of Theodore Roosevelt*, vol. 4, p. 1008 (1 November 1904).
[63] For a study of the SDIC, see Cyrus Veeser, *A World Safe for Capitalism: Dollar Diplomacy and America's Rise to Global Power*, New York: Columbia University Press, 2002. For subsequent events, see Ellen D. Tillman, *Dollar Diplomacy By Force: Nation-building and Resistance in the Dominican Republic*, Chapel Hill: University of North Carolina Press, 2016.

city of León. His project was modernisation: commercialising agriculture, promoting domestic industries via foreign investment, and incorporating the semi-detached Atlantic coast into the national economic and political system. Conservatives had notionally been modernising agriculture but their traditional interests in cattle-raising and cacao production meant that their efforts had lacked vigour.[64] In theory, therefore, Zelaya should have been the kind of politician trusted by US interests, but in practice he ran into all sorts of problems. He instituted what was in effect a labour draft which threatened communal practices, particularly among indigenous villages. The availability of virgin land meant that labourers would often simply run away. He encouraged large-scale foreign investment but struggled to juggle the protection of its interests with the protection of local producers. Both blamed him for the resulting conflicts, but the US investors could call in support from their government: the US minister to Central America, William Lawrence Merry, had family connections to the United Fruit Company, whose control of the banana industry gave it significant political clout in the region. International coffee prices fell during the period of Zelaya's presidency and entrenched transportation problems meant that Nicaraguan coffee was rarely competitive with that of its neighbours. Zelaya also enriched his family and friends through the granting of domestic monopolies, alienating other elite families. Eventually, it was the local Bluefields governor on the Atlantic Coast, Juan José Estrada, who rebelled in October 1909, gaining immediate support from the Conservative leaders, from US corporations, and from the US government, which broke diplomatic relations with Zelaya after the execution of two US mercenaries, Leonard Groce and Lee Roy Cannon, on 29 November 1909. Seeing the writing on the wall, Zelaya resigned and went into exile in France, although he later moved to New York.[65]

US corporate interests had done much to destabilise Nicaraguan society—as they would continue to do, and as would the US government, which insisted that loans from US banks to the new administration should be secured by customs receipts: the introduction of 'dollar diplomacy', financial intervention often in practice to be followed by military intervention as the attempt to create an environment conducive to the expansion of corporate

---

[64] For background, see Justin Wolfe, *The Everyday Nation State: Community and Ethnicity in Nineteenth-Century Nicaragua*, Lincoln: University of Nebraska Press, 2007.

[65] For a revisionary view of Zelaya, see Charles A. Stansifer, 'Una nueva interpretación de José Santos Zelaya, dictador de Nicaragua, 1893-1909', *Anuario de Estudios Centramericanos*, I, no. 1 (1974), 47–59.

culture proved futile.[66] The Liberals were no less committed to encouraging US investment than the Conservatives, but the Conservatives were a minority party tied to old land-owning interests, whereas the Liberals could now bolster their widespread support among various sectors of the country with a nationalistic and anti-US ideology. In 1912, Luis Mena, a renegade Conservative, rebelled with Liberal support, endangering the interests of the Nicaraguan Pacific Railway, controlled by J. W. Seligman and Co. and Brown Brothers. The US government committed 3,000 troops and eight warships. Graft and corruption remained endemic, but between 1913 and 1924 an uneasy peace was maintained by a US Marine guard stationed in Managua. This US occupation, along with that of the Dominican Republic, form constant elements in the background to this book.

Roosevelt left office in 1909, but his successor, William Taft, and Taft's Secretary of State, Philander Knox, continued the lines of Rooseveltian Caribbean policy, if with less subtlety. As 1915 broke, the Democrat president Woodrow Wilson had been in office for two years. Nicaragua and the Dominican Republic, along with Haiti, were under effective US control, and the Panama Canal had just opened, introducing a seismic shift in global geopolitics. As the acute observer Morton Fullerton put it in 1913: once the Panama Canal opens 'the geographical centre of gravity will have shifted from the Mediterranean to the Caribbean', and the ships of all nations will pass 'between the fortifications of the United States'.[67]

The Shakespearean Allegory

From a Spanish perspective that year of 1898 marked the end of empire and a moment when Spanish intellectuals started to question their country's rôle in the modern world. For the Caribbean in particular, and for Spanish America more generally, 1898 marked the moment when the United States emerged as the dominant military and political power in the region, displacing both Spain and Britain. If there were a dominant Spanish-American view of the USA in the first two decades of the twentieth

---

[66] See O'Brien, *The Revolutionary Mission*, p. 67. On Zelaya and the aftermath of his removal, see John E. Findling, *Close Neighbors, Distant Friends: United States–Central American Relations*, New York: Greenwood Press, 1987, pp. 53–68; Noel Maurer, *The Empire Trap: The Rise and Fall of the U.S. Intervention to Protect American Property Overseas, 1893–2013*, Princeton, NJ: Princeton University Press, 2013, pp. 104–17; and Michel Gobat, *Confronting the American Dream: Nicaragua under U.S. Imperial Rule*, Durham, NC: Duke University Press, 2005.

[67] William Morton Fullerton, *Problems of Power: A Study of International Politics from Sadowa to Kirk-Kilissé*, London: Constable, 1913, p. 310.

century, then it would be what has come to be called *arielismo*, a name taken from the short book, *Ariel*, written by the Uruguayan essayist José Enrique Rodó in 1900, in the aftermath of the disaster of 1898, a book which invoked Shakespeare's ethereal character from *The Tempest* and became the standard reference point for the defence of latinity or *hispanidad* against supposed US aggression and materialism.[68] Despite this, Rodó's development of an Americanist allegory in *Ariel* is rather slight: his influences are commentaries and adaptations of *The Tempest* by late nineteenth-century French writers, such as Ernest Renan and Alfred Fouillée, for whom Caliban tended to play the part of 'the people' in an examination of changing political imperatives after the European revolutions of 1848. Rodó's *Ariel* is almost entirely concerned with the connotations of the title character's creativity and spirituality. If Caliban is Ariel's opposite, as at that moment he surely was, and if he was to be associated with the USA, then Rodo's readers were largely left to draw that conclusion themselves. As Carlos Jáuregui astutely notes, the fear of US territorial ambition was often phrased in terms of US voracity and thirst, making its eventual identification as the supposed cannibal, Caliban, seem logical.[69] However, the modalities of Rodó's prose operate well above the level of mundane geopolitics; rather, he sees dangers to spirituality in the debilitating effects of democracy, cosmopolitanism, and immigration.

Arielismo was a significant phenomenon in Latin America in the first quarter of the twentieth century, though it tended to simplify Rodó's ideas. As the editor of Rodó's complete works points out, even before *Ariel* was published Rodó had to correct a newspaper announcement describing his book as a study of the pernicious influence of the 'raza anglo-yankee' [anglo-yankee race] on Latin America.[70] That was the kind of book that was *expected* from leading Latin American intellectuals in 1900; just not the one that Rodó wrote. For him Ariel was the symbol of idealism, an aspiration presented to his students by the figure of Prospero, to be contrasted with the evils of a utilitarian and levelling society of the kind that Caliban symbolised for Ernest Renan, if hardly for Shakespeare.

---

[68] *Ariel* was a best-seller, with further editions in the Dominican Republic (1901), Cuba (1905), and Mexico (1908). There were nine editions in Rodó's lifetime, and an English translation as early as 1922.
[69] Carlos A. Jáuregui, *Canibalia: Canibalismo, calibanismo, antropofagía cultural y consumo en América Latina*, Madrid and Frankfurt: Iberoamericana/Vervuert, 2008, pp. 314–15.
[70] Emir Rodríguez Monegal, in his edition of Rodó's *Obras completas*, Madrid: Aguilar, 1957, p. 194.

In broad terms, the Spanish-American reading extended the materialism and sensuality associated with the plebeian figure of Caliban to the new colossus of the United States, while it suggested a Spanish-American identification with the character of Ariel. In this allegory Caliban could be related to earthly matters, while Ariel represented the spiritual and artistic realms in which Spanish America, now rediscovering its Hispanic roots, could count itself as superior. The seeds of this simplification were laid in Rodó's extended description of the USA as an example of the achievements and dangers of the elevation of utilitarianism to a national ideal. Those achievements are substantial, he began by suggesting. However, that they are first acknowledged by means of a rhetorical chivalresque salute is probably a reference to the solidity of the ironclad battleships against which the Spanish navy had so recently broken its wooden lances, and perhaps therefore an early sign of sympathetic identification with the losers in this conflict.[71] The modern concept of liberty is the first achievement acknowledged: the example offered to what would in time become the republics of the south of the continent. Second is 'the grandeur and power of work', whose accomplishment Rodó envisages, in a striking image, as 'un conjunto imaginario de ejemplares de Robinson' [an imaginary assemblage of Crusoes]—though he sensitively refrains from pointing out the extent to which that eighteenth-century Caliban, Friday, did much of the actual work as Robinson Crusoe's slave. Insatiable US curiosity is praised, as is the country's relentless focus on the importance of education, and its unparalleled ability to put science to work.[72] Rodó also admits to admiration for the strength of US willpower, though in a paragraph where that admiration has to struggle with descriptive terms such as 'titanic greatness' and 'enormous excesses', as well as a reference to 'the recent violence of their history'; as close as he gets to mentioning the events of 1898.[73] Dynamism, activity, originality, audacity, energy: those are evident US qualities praised by Rodó, even though the last carries a twist in the tail when he suggests that it is found even in the nation's divergent peculiarities. Edgar Allan Poe—the poet-martyr almost deified by Baudelaire and Rubén Darío—is of course the polar opposite of utilitarian: 'una individualidad anómala y rebelde' [one such

---

[71] José Enrique Rodó, *Ariel*, ed. Gordon Brotherston, Cambridge: Cambridge University Press, 1967, p. 73; Rodó, *Ariel*, translation, reader's reference, and annotated bibliography by Margaret Sayers Peden, Austin: University of Texas Press, 1988, p. 74. References continue in this form: to Spanish original [English translation].
[72] Rodó, *Ariel*, pp. 73–74 [p. 75].
[73] Rodó, *Ariel*, p. 76 [p. 77].

anomalous and rebellious individual].⁷⁴ Yet even Poe's heroes are marked by their superhuman willpower, a kind of crystallisation of the national characteristic where it might least have been expected.

Eventually the coin gets flipped. The key point is that this 'fervent pursuit of well-being' has no object 'beyond itself', which is why it ultimately creates 'a singular impression of insufficiency and emptiness'. There is no idealism, no spark: 'it is like a well-laid fire to which no one has set a match'. The resulting critique relates most evidently to the levelling tendencies of US civilisation—there is no good taste, no discrimination: 'a radical ineptitude for selectivity'.⁷⁵ The sense that higher ideals can be attained only by the few is deeply embedded for Rodó. There is no indication, he says, that the fine plans to disseminate basic education to the masses have been accompanied by any imperative towards selection 'to aid in allowing excellence to rise above general mediocrity'. The general level of education has been raised, but the higher level lowered. This allows Rodó to introduce a historical element into his argument: the early nineteenth century had seen the intellectual flourishing of cities like Boston and Philadelphia where the best of European thought had been transplanted, but this bequest has been squandered in the rush for material well-being with a resulting 'quiet winding-down [descomposición] of all the mainsprings of moral life'. That rush even has a geographical dimension: the cities of the east coast have been displaced by Chicago as indicative of the westward course of US expansion whose representative figure is 'the tamer of the only-yesterday-deserted Plains', the frontiersman, the westerner—or rough rider.⁷⁶

Theodore Roosevelt was not himself such a figure, but his willingness to embrace the values associated with this way of life, and to attempt to incorporate them into a national morality, mark his distance from Rodó. Rodó quotes here Michel Chevalier's prescient remark 'les derniers seront les premiers' [the last shall be first] made in the 1830s to predict that the US westerner, combining the characteristics of the easterner (Yankee) and southerner (Virginian), would come to dominate the expanding nation. Chevalier showed none of Rodó's distaste: he even seems to have thought it a good model, one that might profitably have been adopted in France after the Revolution rather than allowing the northerner to so dominate the southerner. This—admittedly simplistic—geographical thinking finds its echoes in *Ariel*. Rodó picks up in particular on one of Chevalier's dualisms— Sparta and Athens—to suggest that some kind of balance and mutual benefit

---

⁷⁴ Rodó, *Ariel*, p. 77 [p. 77].
⁷⁵ Rodó, *Ariel*, p. 78 [p. 79]; p. 79 [p. 79]; p. 80 [p. 81].
⁷⁶ Rodó, *Ariel*, pp. 81–82 [p. 82]; p. 83 [p. 83]; p. 86 [p. 85].

is permissible and indeed necessary between the utilitarian and the spiritual in the interests of a greater good: 'History clearly demonstrates a reciprocal relationship between the progress of utilitarianism and idealism.'[77] So some sort of higher harmony is notionally possible: indeed, US positivism might be seen in the long run as actually serving the interests of Ariel, however few signs it yet showed, as far as Rodó was concerned, of living up to that potential.

Earlier, the USA was a titan but, as *Ariel* proceeds, it takes on a more sinister rôle as 'that Cyclopean nation', the closest Rodó comes to associating the country with the supposed cannibalism of Caliban—whose name appears only three times in Rodó's text and without specific reference to the USA.[78] (Indeed the first of these notes that in *The Tempest* Caliban is a symbol 'de sensualidad y de torpeza' [brutal sensuality]—the very opposite of the characteristics of the USA according to Rodó.)[79] The danger to which Rodó wanted to alert his readers was the widely held view within Latin America that the southern half of the continent should be 'de-Latinized of its own will' and then regenerated in the image of the northern archetype: 'nordomania' as he calls this delusion.[80] This would be to 'denaturaliz[e]' the character of Latin America, home to 'a heritage of race, a great ethnic tradition, to maintain, a sacred place in the pages of history'.[81] This certainly suggests that the Hispanic component of Latin American culture is the source of its essence. Even the abstract duality between utilitarianism and idealism finds placial identity in Rodó's example of how the perfect axis of Greek culture was the centre of the dynamic poles of Athens and Sparta—and he hardly needed to spell out which would be which when it came to the American continent.[82] Havelock Ellis has a good summary:

> It is necessary, even for the sake of America as a whole, that Latin America should jealously guard the original character of its collective

---

[77] Rodó, *Ariel*, p. 89 [p. 88].
[78] Rodó, *Ariel*, p. 89 (pp. 22, 53, 101); [p. 88 (pp. 31, 58, 98)]. A whole repertoire of giants and monsters was deployed to describe the implacable growth of the USA, perhaps finding their origin in Bilbao's boa constrictor (see above, p. 39). Martí wrote in 1890 of the USA's 'gigantic appetites' (<www.josemarti.cu/publicacion/la-conferencia-de-washington-i/> accessed December 2018) and, famously, in one of his last letters as a 'monster' in whose belly he had dwelt (*Obras escogidas*, vol. 3, p. 604; *Selected Writings*, p. 347); and see Jáuregui, *Canibalia*, pp. 322–27.
[79] Rodó, *Ariel*, p. 22 [p. 31].
[80] Rodó, *Ariel*, pp. 69 and 70 ['USA-mania' p. 71].
[81] Rodó, *Ariel*, pp. 70 and 72 [pp. 72 and 73].
[82] Rodó, *Ariel*, p. 72 [p. 73].

personality, for nearly all luminous and fruitful epochs of history have been, as in Greece with the poles of Athens and Sparta, the result of two distinct correlated forces; the preservation of the original duality of America, while maintaining a genial and emulatory difference, at the same time favours concord and solidarity.[83]

As Gordon Brotherston puts it, given the timing of Rodó's essay it was bound to be interpreted as a manifesto: 'Rodó's least stricture on North American society, combined with his evasive but articulate admission of his own Latinity, encouraged the notion that his despicable Caliban was really the U.S.A., and led readers to consider Ariel as a symbolic justification of their own racial and spiritual superiority'[84]—an exaggeration and simplification by those readers, perhaps, but not a complete misreading of the text's implications.

This purely negative view of the USA was often repeated and elaborated in Latin America over these years, frequently by those who had never been there: it provided a comforting myth. But, on the positive side, a notion of Latin American cultural identity was created and 'idealism'—which could be interpreted in many different ways—began to displace the positivism that had previously dominated, nowhere more so than in Mexico where the Ateneo de la Juventud—in which Pedro Henríquez Ureña participated along with José Vasconcelos, Martín Luis Guzmán, and Alfonso Reyes—fomented an intellectual revolution which would spread across the continent. This was the kind of practical *arielismo* which ensured that the term maintained its positive connotations in Hispanic communities for much of the twentieth century.[85]

Ariel therefore helped entrench the idea that there were 'two Americas', North and South, Anglo-Saxon and Latin, however incoherent this dualism might actually be. As early as 1902, the Venezuelan Rufino Blanco Fombona was responding to W. T. Stead's *The Americanization of the World* by predicting that the new century would be dominated by wars of race and by weighing up the prospects of Hispanic or Latin American alliances.[86]

---

[83] Havelock Ellis, 'Rodó', in his *The Philosophy of Conflict and Other Essay in War-Time*, 2nd series, London: Constable and Company, 1919, pp. 235–45, at p. 237.
[84] Gordon Brotherston, 'Introduction' to José Enrique Rodó, *Ariel*, ed. Gordon Brotherston, Cambridge: Cambridge University Press, 1967, p. 12.
[85] Jean Franco, *The Modern Culture of Latin America: Society and the Artist*, Harmondsworth: Penguin, 1970, p. 66.
[86] Rufino Blanco Fombona, 'La americanización del mundo' [1902], in *Antología*, Barcelona: Red Ediciones, 2013, pp. 35–52. Cf. Cesia Ziona Hirshbein, *Rufino Blanco Fombona y su pensamiento americanista*, Caracas: Universidad Central de Venezuela, 1997.

The existence of such entities were 'proved', in entirely circular fashion, by writing about them. And with US foreign policy hardening as the opening of the Panama Canal approached, and with the State Department under Philander Knox lacking Elihu Root's interest in at least trying to understand Latin American attitudes, positions became more entrenched, as in these words from the Argentine Manuel Ugarte:

> We speak of the deep lines dividing the New World into two halves. Nobody can doubt that the Mexican frontier is a boundary between two civilisations. To the North shines forth the Anglo-Saxon spirit, to the South persists the Latin ethos. These are two antagonistic entities who synthesise a divorce of atavistic interests in a historical and geographical dilemma that nobody can resolve. The separating boundary is not some capriciously placed stone marking a diplomatic triumph, but rather an incompatibility which goes to the roots of the two sides.[87]

In 1913, the leading *dominicano* journalist and literary critic, Federico García Godoy, published a collection of book reviews which welcomed a whole string of what could be seen as *latinoamericanista* texts by Blanco Fombona, Ugarte, and Francisco García Calderón. He concluded that the division between the two Americas—Anglo-Saxon and Latin—was getting deeper: 'Yankee imperialism gets more aggressive by the day, hardly bothering to hide its true motives'. Events in Nicaragua clearly showed this: 'The vast majority of yankees now increasingly support an expansionist policy that flatters their pride and satisfies most of their appetites.'[88] He later wrote that, though a political alliance was unlikely, there could, in response, be an intellectual Hispanic-American federation.[89]

So by 1915 the dualism was firmly entrenched, an itch that both sides kept scratching. In his landmark literary history of Spanish America, Alfred Coester suggested that:

> Latin America and the United States resemble two neighbors who have long lived side by side, each too busy with private matters to take more

---

[87] Manuel Ugarte, *El porvenir de la América española: La raza, la integridad territorial y moral, la organización interior*, Valencia: F. Sempere y Compañía, 1911, p. iv.

[88] Federico García Godoy, *Páginas efímeras (Movimiento intelectual hispano-americano)*, Santo Domingo: Imp. 'La Cuna de América, 1913, pp. 91–92, 94.

[89] Federico García Godoy, *Americanismo literario*, Madrid: Editorial-América, 1917, p. 9.

than an indifferent if not hostile interest in the other. Recently we North Americans have been taking a broader interest in our neighbors. The building of the Panama Canal has directed our attention to the south. We have discovered that those vast unknown regions are inhabited by human beings worthy of being better known though their character differ widely from our own.[90]

The recourse to the domestic metaphor has always been the prime way US discourse has disavowed responsibility for its foreign policy. Even aside from the mismatch—a nation-state and the 20 or so republics to its south—the idea of neighbourliness is a considerable stretch: it might work for San Diego and Tijuana or El Paso and Ciudad Juárez, but Washington, DC and Caracas? let alone the more than 5,000 miles between Boston and Valparaíso? And, as often in disavowal, agency is shifted to some objective force: 'The building of the Panama Canal'—as if it built itself, 'has directed our attention'—as if we had just been woken from our slumbers by the noise of the canal-builders. In his review of Coester's book Waldo Frank picked up on the analogy of the neighbours, though he went on to suggest that the two parts of the continent were actually like brothers at the awkward age. Unusually, though, there was no hint of condescension. South America was 'less provincial than we', their literature 'certainly an older, a richer, and a hardier growth than ours':

> North and South America are like two suburban towns that cannot recognize each other's existence because neither one is fully aware of its own. Take the suburbs of New York or Boston or Chicago; they are all made up of people who have left the metropolis for much the same reasons and who find themselves face to face with much the same problems. And yet because they have no autonomous social life they are able to communicate with one another only through the medium of the metropolis itself. So it is with our two American continents. We throw no light on each other, although we are both largely in the same boat. While in the vital foreground of our lives we are confused by the same growing-pains and are seeking ends that are harmonious through means that are similarly conditioned, our understandings converge only in the European background of our common ancestral memories.[91]

---

[90] Alfred Coester, *The Literary History of Spanish America*, New York: Macmillan, 1916, p. vii.
[91] [Waldo Frank], 'The Literary History of Spanish America', *The Seven Arts*, I, no. 6 (April 1917), 667–68. The review is anonymous, but Frank was the editor with Spanish-American interests.

Meanwhile, Rodó himself continued to reinforce the idea that any attempt on the part of Hispanic America to emulate alien ways of life would be tantamount to what he called 'abdicación ilícita, mortal renunciamiento' [illicit abdication, deadly renunciation].[92] His essays were appreciative of those who shared his views. He did, however, hold out against the idea of *Latin America*, preferring 'Íbero-América', and redefining Spanish America as the 'magna patria', the nation-in-waiting, very much in the spirit of Bolívar.[93]

So the time was not exactly ripe for a Latin American writer to defend a pan-American position—certainly not a *Nicaraguan* writer—but Salomón de la Selva was never easily deterred.

*

The Spanish-American allegory was based on what had become during nineteenth-century Shakespearean criticism a quite traditional reading of the qualities of the characters of Ariel and Caliban in *The Tempest*. It was also, to a large extent, an allegory of consolation: US power—military, technological, commercial—was now ascendant. To identify the USA with Caliban was—on the basis of a traditional reading of the play's themes—to suggest the brutality of the aggressor and to indicate, perhaps subliminally, that the aggressor, like Caliban, might ultimately be defeated. After the appearance of *Ariel* it became difficult for Hispanic Americans to invoke *The Tempest* without alluding to Rodó, and *arielismo* became a significant intellectual movement in Spanish America. However, Rodó's *Ariel* had in fact been preceded by two much more uncompromising pieces of writing.

Within the Hispanic world, Rubén Darío was a cosmopolitan poet. He had left Nicaragua in 1883, aged 15, and only ever returned for very short visits, though he did occupy diplomatic posts for his country. Aged 20 he had gone to Valparaíso, in Chile, where his first book, *Azul*, was published and he then spent several years in Argentina before basing himself in Paris in 1900. His second book of poems, *Prosas profanas* (1896), had been a literary sensation and he was widely seen as having renovated the Spanish lyric tradition. Two further volumes of poetry and a collection of essays had consolidated his reputation, and he wrote ceaselessly for Hispanic newspapers, ensuring that his name was always before the eyes of Spanish-speaking readers across Europe and America. He was, as Roberto González Echevarría points out, the first poet of modern communications—one of

---

[92] José Enrique Rodó, *El mirador de Próspero*, Montevideo: José María Serrano, 1913, p. 38.
[93] Rodó, *El mirador de Próspero*, pp. 435–37, 290–91.

the ways in which *modernismo*, the literary movement with which he was associated, was indeed a fully modern phenomenon, carried across the Atlantic and through the American continent by steamship and underwater cable with a speed unthinkable even 20 years earlier.[94]

Like many Spanish-American writers and intellectuals, Darío was worried about the consequences of Spain's defeat in 1898. Aside from a general perception of the growing threat of US influence in Central America and the Caribbean, Darío himself had a deep commitment to the Spanish poetic tradition in which his genius had been nourished. Although he held diplomatic posts and was close—sometimes too close for comfort—to major politicians, Darío was never an overtly political figure nor a politically engaged writer in any narrow sense, but he did occasionally write political poems and sometimes comment on matters of politics in his newspaper columns.[95] The seriousness of this periodic engagement can be gauged by the essays he published in *La Nación*, such as 'La cuestión de los canales', 'Los Estados Unidos y la América Latina', and his long review of W. T. Stead's *Americanization of the World*, 'La fuerza yanqui'.[96]

Darío had travelled to New York in 1893 and hated his brief taste of the future. He wrote an essay about Edgar Allan Poe for the Buenos Aires journal *Revista Nacional*, published in January 1894, in which he referred to the French occultist Joséphin Peladan's use of the term 'féroces Calibans' to refer to the denizens of the USA.[97] 'Caliban rules on the island of Manhattan', Darío stated; indeed, throughout the country: 'Caliban saturates himself

---

[94] Roberto González Echevarría, 'The Master of Modernismo', *The Nation*, 13 February 2006 <https://www.thenation.com/article/master-modernismo/> accessed December 2018.

[95] See Alberto Acereda, 'La hispanidad amenazada: Rubén Darío y la guerra del 98', in *The Legacy of the Mexican and Spanish-American Wars: Legal, Literary, and Historical Perspectives*, ed. Gary D. Keller and Cordelia Candelaria, Tempe, AZ: Bilingual Review/Press, 2000, pp. 99–110.

[96] *La Nación*, 9 March 1902, 6 April 1902, and 18 May 1902, in Rubén Darío, *La caravana pasa: libros cuarto y quinto*, ed. Günther Schmigalle, Managua: Academia Nicaragüense de la Lengua; Berlin: Edition Tranvía, 2004, pp. 79–102, 145–65, and 61–77. Cf. Rubén Darío, *Escritos políticos*, ed. Jorge Eduardo Arellano and Pablo Kraudy Medina, Managua: Banco Central de Nicaragua, 2010.

[97] 'Psychiquement la société des Etats-Unis est un ramassis de Homais, de Prudhomme à base de bandits: dans ce milieu de féroces calibans subit son grand martyre, le Prospero: Edgar Allan Poe' (*Poésies complètes de Edgar Allan Poe: avec une introduction de Joséphin Peladan*, Paris: Camille Dalau, 1889, p. x). Quoted in Spanish as 'feroces Calibanes' in Rubén Darío, 'Edgar Allan Poe', *Revista Nacional*, 2nd series, XIX (January 1894), 28–37; reprinted in *Los raros*, *Obras Completas*, vol. 6 (Madrid: Editorial Mundo Latino, 1906), pp. 17–29.

with whisky, just as he does with wine in Shakespeare's play.' Free from the control of any Prospero, he multiplies himself: 'his name is Legion'.[98] But then, through God's will—*por voluntad de Dios*—which is presumably the only force strong enough to explain such a miracle, a being of superior nature, Edgar Allan Poe, is engendered by these monsters, someone who will stretch his wings towards what Darío calls 'the eternal Miranda of idealism', only to find himself persecuted in his own country.[99]

So when the USA declared war on Spain in May 1898, the identification with Caliban was at Darío's fingertips: his essay 'El triunfo de Calibán' [The Triumph of Caliban] was written in the heat of the moment, in that very month. For Darío, the Calibanic cultural context explains the plight of Edgar Allan Poe: 'that poor swan drunk on suffering and alcohol ... the martyr of his dreams in a country which will never understand him'.[100] Poe, by contrast, as Darío put it in the earlier essay, is like 'an Ariel made man'.[101] This seems an unlikely identification; and the very vigour of Darío's language begins to suggest an undercurrent of admiration for this demonic Calibanic force: after all, it was Poe who was saturated with whisky and whose works were legion. The more Darío describes him, the more Poe begins to seem a genuine son of Caliban, and Caliban begins to appear less purely brutal as a result.

In 'El triunfo de Calibán' the ratchet is tightened:

I have seen those Yankees in their oppressive cities of steel and stone, and the time I spent among them made me uneasy. I seemed to be living under a mountain. I felt I was breathing in a country of Cyclops, flesh-eaters, bestial blacksmiths living in the houses of mastodons. Ruddy, sluggish, and overweight, they push and shove each other up and down the streets like animals, in search of the dollar. The ideals of these Calibans are limited to the stock-exchange and the factory. They eat and eat, calculate, drink whisky, and make millions ... 'We have,' they say, 'all the biggest things in the world!'[102]

---

[98] Darío, 'Edgar Allan Poe', p. 20.
[99] Darío, 'Edgar Allan Poe', p. 20.
[100] Published in *El Tiempo* of Buenos Aires (20 May 1898) and then in *El Cojo Ilustrado* of Caracas (1 October 1898). Quoted here from Rubén Darío, 'El triunfo de Calibán' [1898], ed. and notes by Carlos Jáuregui, *Revista Iberoamericana*, 64, nos 184–85 (1998), 451–55, at 451. Cf. Gordon Brotherston, '*Arielismo* and Anthropophagy: *The Tempest* in Latin America', in '*The Tempest*' *and Its Travels*, ed. Peter Hulme and William H. Sherman, London: Reaktion Books, 2000, pp. 212–19.
[101] Darío, 'Edgar Allan Poe', p. 22.
[102] Darío, 'El triunfo de Calibán', pp. 451–52.

The poet in Darío seems almost to take delight in the accumulation of images of gigantism and consumption, from the silver-toothed buffalo of the first line ['no quiero estar de parte de esos búfalos de dientes de plata']—surely a reference to Theodore Roosevelt, the self-styled bullmoose with the flashing teeth—to the skyscrapers in the land of Brobdingnag and the closing biblical images of the Behemoth and the Great Beast; from the 'eaters of raw meat' to the open jaws of the serpent, to the sheer 'gluttony of the North'.[103] *Modernista* poetry is often described as effete, but this essay—more of a prose-poem—sometimes reads like Allen Ginsberg *avant la lettre*.

Darío announces his three heroes as Roque Sáenz Peña, José Tarnassi, and Paul Groussac, representative—for Darío's purposes—of Argentina, Italy, and France. The three of them had spoken at a meeting in the Teatro Victoria in Buenos Aires on 2 May 1898, the day after Admiral Dewey had annihilated the Spanish fleet in Manila, effectively ending a war that had only just been declared. Darío recalls Sáenz Peña standing up to James G. Blaine in the Pan-American Congress of 1890 in Washington. Groussac's French background and the Italian Tarnassi allow Darío to sketch a Latin alliance that he can set up against the Anglo-Saxon one formed by British rejoicing at US belligerence, a 'surge in the blood' that had to be countered by an alternative racial brotherhood.[104]

There is nothing particularly progressive about this Latin backlash. Argentina in 1898 hardly offered a model of modernity much different from the USA: it had similarly slaughtered its indigenous population, was in thrall to railway magnates, and was busy opening itself to international capital, much of it English, that is Anglo-Saxon. The Ariel–Caliban opposition—in Darío's hands as much as in Rodo's—was clearly Eurocentric, explicitly racial, and implicitly anti-democratic. It was also—despite some weasel words from Darío ('I who have been a supporter of a free Cuba')—obviously prepared to leave Cuba to stew in the bosom of mother Spain.[105] That Caliban was being oppressed by a white magician, that his land had been stolen, that he had at his disposal only the weapons of the weak: these aspects of the character left ajar the door that would eventually be smashed open in the second half of the twentieth century by George Lamming, Aimé Césaire,

---

[103] Darío, 'El triunfo de Calibán', pp. 451, 452, 455, 451, 453, 454.
[104] On the relationship between Groussac and Darío, see Florencia Bonfiglio, 'En zaga de tantos otros: Paul Groussac y la angustia de las influencias en el Río de la Plata', *Orbis Tertius*, 16, no. 17 (2011) <www.orbistertius.unlp.edu.ar/article/viewFile/OTv16n17a10/4927> accessed December 2018.
[105] Darío, 'El triunfo de Calibán', p. 455.

and Roberto Fernández Retamar.[106] The real opposition in Shakespeare's play is between Prospero and Caliban, not Caliban and Ariel.

But Darío's allegory is subtly different from the more familiar argument soon to be sketched by Rodó. The basic opposition between US materialism and Hispanic spirituality is the same, but for Darío Ariel represents Spain itself—a Spain of chivalry, idealism, and nobility, of Cervantes, Quevedo, and Góngora—while Spanish America (and, explicitly, Darío himself) is represented by Prospero's daughter, Miranda: 'Miranda will always prefer Ariel', Darío writes. 'Miranda is the soul of the spirit, and all the mountains of precious stones, of iron-ore, of gold, and of pork-barrels will never be enough to get my Latin soul to prostitute itself to Caliban.'[107] The gender implications of all this are intriguing. Spain is conventionally female, but there is no obvious mother figure in *The Tempest*: Prospero's wife is presumably dead, as is Sycorax, Caliban's mother, who would hardly be appropriate anyway. Ariel just about fits the bill as an androgynous character, unsullied by earthly concerns, although if Spanish America is Miranda, then you might have thought that Spain would be Prospero himself, teaching Miranda all she knows. In any case, it is Darío's own identification with Miranda, the young virgin, which is most unusual, and which remains so: Miranda doesn't tend to feature much in subsequent Spanish-American allegories of *The Tempest*. The implications are arguably problematic: there is no contest in the play between Ariel and Caliban over Miranda, because Ariel is asexual, and Miranda—obedient daughter and pawn in Prospero's political manoeuvrings—makes a strange identification for a postcolonial culture struggling to find its own identity, however much we might welcome Darío's unexpected willingness to break out of the masculinist stereotypes which often dominate the allegorical deployment of *Tempest* characters. In any case, Darío's essay sketches out a *hispanismo* whose influence would grow over the next two decades.

Despite the violent language of 'El triunfo de Calibán', Darío's line was never consistent, at least in part because of his sensitivity to changing contexts. So, for example, in 1901, after a visit to the US pavilion at the 1900 Paris Universal Exposition, he'd quickly been able to admit exceptions:

No, those strong men from the North are not without artistic gifts. They also have thoughts and dreams. We Hispanic Americans still

---

[106] See Peter Hulme, 'Reading from Elsewhere: George Lamming and the Paradox of Exile', in *'The Tempest' and Its Travels*, ed. Peter Hulme and William H. Sherman, London: Reaktion Books, 2000, pp. 220-35.
[107] Darío, 'El triunfo de Calibán', p. 455.

can't show the world an intellectual firmament filled with constellations where figures like Poe, Whitman, and Emerson shine bright. Up there, where the majority dedicates itself to the cult of the dollar, you can still find—in the face of the plutocratic empire—the development of a minority of undeniable excellence ... Among the millions of Calibans, the most marvellous Ariels are born.[108]

Then, in 1904, in Málaga, on a visit to his Colombian friend Isaac Arias in the aftermath of the Panama crisis, Darío wrote his most-cited political poem, 'A Roosevelt'. The statement made by the second stanza is often quoted:

> You are the United States,
> you are the future invader
> of America the innocent, with her indigenous blood,
> who still prays to Jesus Christ and still speaks Spanish;

as is the paean to 'our America, that has had poets / since the ancient times of Netzahualcoyotl,' which doubles as a warning to 'you men of Saxon eyes and barbarous soul'.[109] Indigenous America, Catholic America, Spanish America: these are all descriptions of the America that Darío sees as threatened by Roosevelt and his policies. Darío was never going to be a José Martí, but this poem did much to boost his status as a spokesman for Spanish America, someone willing to put his poetic gift to the service of his embattled culture. That enhanced status didn't last very long. Just three years after 'A Roosevelt', in Rio de Janeiro as a delegate to the third Pan-American conference, Darío wrote his 'Salutación al águila' [Salute to the Eagle], which seemed to many to offer a capitulation to northern forces:

> Welcome magical Eagle with your mighty and strong wings
> spreading over the South your great continental shadow,
> bringing in your claws, ringed with brilliant rubies

---

[108] Rubén Darío, 'Los anglosajones', in his *Peregrinaciones* [1901] Madrid: G. Hernández y Galo Sáez, 1922, pp. 57–58.
[109] 'A Roosevelt' was collected in *Cantos de vida y esperanza* [1905]: *Cantos de vida y esperanza. Los cisnes y otros poemas*, Barcelona: F. Granada y Cª, 1907, pp. 37–40. On the first appearance of the poem in the Madrid journal, *Helios*, see Andrew Reynolds, 'Transatlantic Sensationalism and the First Printing of Rubén Darío's "A Roosevelt"', *Decimonónica*, 12, no. 1 (2015), 53–65.

a palm of glory, the colour of immense hope,
and in your beak the olive of a great and productive peace.
...
Hail, Eagle! Limitless power to your immense flights,
queen of the blue sky—health, glory, victory and enchantment!
May Latin America receive your magic influence
May a new Olympus be reborn, full of gods and heroes![110]

The poem caused dismay and even outrage among the more hard-line *hispanistas* and *arielistas*, eager to assert racial solidarity against the northern menace. Darío's offence was the greater in that the poem was written during one of the Pan-American events widely seen in the south as providing the alibi behind which the USA pursued its ruthless imperial agenda. Darío even used as an epigraph for his poem the toadying words of the Brazilian politician and poet, Fontoura Xavier, spoken in English: 'May this grand Union have no end', borrowing the vocabulary of US nation-building at the end of the civil war to describe the putative union of the two 'halves' of the continent, although that kind of 'union' was not really what anybody had in mind. The circumstances of the poem's composition—while Darío was on a diplomatic mission, and delivery—at an event on the SS *Charleston* to honour the US Secretary of State, Elihu Root, have also, however, been used to excuse the poem on the grounds that it was an entirely *occasional* composition rather than an articulation of Darío's true beliefs. Although context is always important, and Darío may well have felt some obligation to one of the conference organisers, Joaquim Nabuco, who had probably arranged a meeting with the elderly figure of Machado de Assis, whom Dario revered, that argument ultimately doesn't wash.[111] To begin with, the earlier, supposedly hard-line 'A Roosevelt' is actually far more nuanced than much contemporary Spanish-American discourse about the USA. 'You are the proud and strong exemplar of your race; / you are cultured, you are skilful' are some of the words he also addresses to Roosevelt in that poem, a sentiment echoed in his 1904 essay 'El arte de ser presidente de la república: Roosevelt', an objective and rounded sketch, by no means hostile. Here Darío shows himself appreciative of Theodore Roosevelt's talents while still seeing a danger for 'conquerable America'. 'He is worthy of his people', Darío opines. 'He

---

[110] Rubén Darío, 'Salutación al águila', in *El canto errante* [1907], Madrid: Editorial Mundo-Latino, 1918, pp. 43–46, at p. 43.
[111] See Fred P. Ellison, 'Rubén Darío and Brazil', *Hispania*, 47, no. 1 (March 1964), 24–35.

is a representative yankee. He has great things in mind. We need to be careful.'[112]

Anyone can claim that one particular poem articulates Darío's real views, while another one doesn't, but there is no supporting evidence, and in any case Darío's views tended like most people's to change according to changing circumstances—and the political circumstances were changing vertiginously during the first decade of the twentieth century.[113] When *El canto errante* was published in 1907, its opening section, 'Dilucidaciones', contained further praise for Roosevelt as a President who recognised the value of poetry to the state.[114] Then, shortly after the Rio event, in the 'Epístola' dedicated to Mme Lugones, one of his finest late poems, Darío wrote what might count as a distancing comment on the occasion: 'Yo pan-americanicé / con un vago temor y con muy poca fe' [I pan-americanised / with a vague fear and with very little faith].[115] The superficially light mode of that poem shows Darío at his most skilful—and most difficult to read.[116] What exactly was he afraid of? 'With very little faith' seems to suggest that he was playing along with people's diplomatic expectations, perhaps trying not to rock the boat, and yet never really believing in the Pan-American rhetoric that his public persona was spouting. Perhaps so, or perhaps it was both convenient and satisfying to shift gears and modes in order to avoid pinning himself to a single position.

---

[112] Rubén Darío, 'A Roosevelt', p. 37; 'El arte de ser presidente de la república: Roosevelt', *La Nación*, 13 November 1904, p. 3, in *Escritos dispersos de Rubén Darío, recogidos de periódicos de Buenos Aires*, ed. Pedro Luis Barcia, La Plata: Universidad Nacional de La Plata, 1977, pp. 214–17, at pp. 216, 217.

[113] Ricardo Llopesa, *Rubén Darío en Nueva York*, Valencia: Instituto de Estudios Modernistas, 1997, tracks the changes in Darío's views; as does Rocío Oviedo Pérez de Tudela, 'Ruben Darío: panamericanismo y lenguaje', *Les Ateliers du SAL*, no. 4 (2014), 131–42. For a more subtle reading of the poem: Antonio Oliver Belmas, 'Rubén Darío y su "Salutación al águila"', in his *Ultima vez con Rubén Darío*, 2 vols., Madrid: Ediciones de Cultura Hispánica del Centro Iberoamericano de Cooperación, 1978, vol. 1, pp. 311–16.

[114] Rubén Darío, 'Dilucidaciones', in *El canto errante*, pp. 3–15, at p. 3.

[115] Rubén Darío, 'Epístola', in *El canto errante*, pp. 135–44, at pp. 135–36.

[116] See, for example, Susana Zanetti, 'Rubén Darío, cosmopolitismo y errancia: "Epístola a la señora de Leopoldo Lugones"', Actas del III Congreso Internacional CELEHIS de Literatura (Española, Latinoamericana y Argentina) (2008) <http://fh.mdp.edu.ar/revistas/index.php/celehis/article/viewFile/524/529> accessed December 2018; Maria A. Salgado, 'Félix Rubén García Sarmiento, Rubén Darío, y otros entes de ficción', *Revista Iberoamericana*, 55, nos 146–47 (2009), 339–62; and Gordon Brotherston, *Latin American Poetry: Origins and Presence*, Cambridge: Cambridge University Press, 1975, pp. 72–76.

Throughout Darío's writing, there is an urge—sometimes denied—toward some kind of synthesis of the two parts of the continent: in 1902, he noted that Caliban was looking for Ariel's wings.[117] As John Beverley and Marc Zimmerman suggest, Darío dreamed of a productive mating of the eagle and the swan in which the offspring would magically assume the best characteristics of both parents, while that dream was tempered by a realistic sense that any such mating would be accompanied by the bloodying of white plumage.[118] Yet Darío's pan-American dream—if not the commitment to the Pan-American institutions—remained intact and was strengthened by the outbreak of war in Europe, finding its final manifestation in the somewhat incoherent if intermittently powerful verses of his final poem, read by the poet in New York in January 1915, in the presence of his young compatriot, Salomón de la Selva.

*

In one of several essays written nearly four decades after his schooldays in New York, Salomón de la Selva makes a point of using *The Tempest* against Rodó. He claims to have arrived in New York—aged just 13—with a copy of *Ariel* under his arm: 'I'd decided not to let the Anglo-Saxon Caliban overcome the Latin spirituality of my national stock.'[119] To his surprise he found that *The Tempest* was being performed in Brooklyn.[120] Not only that: Johnston Forbes-Robertson, one of the finest English actors of his day, was alternating *Hamlet* and *Antony and Cleopatra* at a Times Square theatre, Julia Marlowe and John Barrymore were in productions of *Romeo and Juliet* and *Henry IV* at the Manhattan Opera House, Eva Le Gallienne had a repertoire that included *The Merchant of Venice* and *A Midsummer Night's Dream*, and Isadora Duncan was dancing *Oedipus Rex* at the Century Theatre. De la Selva is clearly collapsing a number of years here—Duncan didn't get to New York until 1914, Le Gallienne until 1915—in order to make the point that the New York he experienced as a young man was a centre of humanistic civilisation, by no means the desert

---

[117] Rubén Darío, *La caravana pasa* [1902], Madrid: Editorial Mundo Latino, 1917, p. 254.
[118] John Beverley and Marc Zimmerman, *Literature and Politics in the Central American Revolutions*, Austin: University of Texas Press, 1990, p. 58.
[119] 'Acróasis en defensa de la cultura humanista' [1957], in Salomón de la Selva, *Antología Mayor III: Ensayos*, p. 43.
[120] This is probably a reference to the outdoor production by the Ben Greet Players in June 1909 ('"The Tempest" Out of Doors: Ben Greet Players Give the Shakespeare Comedy in Brooklyn', *New York Times*, 16 June 1909, p. 7).

of barbarism that some Latin American writers had painted. His cultural interests were wide and there was plenty to detain him in these pre-war years: the ballet had Anna Pavlova and Lydia Lopokova, Diaghilev and Nijinsky, the designs of León Bakst and the music of Igor Stravinsky; the Armory Show brought the best of contemporary European painting. He just wanted to drown himself in culture, Salomón writes.[121] The famous *diseuse*, Yvette Guilbert, came to New York on tour. The Metropolitan Opera House staged the US premieres of Richard Strauss's *Der Rosenkavalier* and Enrique Granados's *Goyescas*. The Educational Alliance mounted modern Jewish plays, in Yiddish, throughout the Lower East Side. Classical music was heard at Carnegie Hall but also in open-air summer concerts in Central Park and in many a school auditorium. Then there were the seemingly endless riches of the Metropolitan Museum of Art and the newly opened New York Public Library.[122] De la Selva makes similar points in a 1950 essay about Edna St Vincent Millay, recalling Harriet Monroe's launching of *Poetry* and the raft of amazing skyscrapers that shot up during these years. Little of all this is known in Hispanic America, he laments, where the perspective of José Enrique Rodó still holds sway through the passionate lack of understanding demonstrated by writers such as Rufino Blanco Fombona and Manuel Ugarte. Other Hispanic American writers who have written about the USA have been 'too minor for so large a topic', he claims, with the result that the USA still remains largely unknown to its southern neighbours.[123] By 1957, de la Selva had travelled widely through the USA and so was in a position to affirm that the torch of culture that burned in New York illuminated wide swathes of the country, a situation he contrasts with the lands to its south where small pockets of culture are surrounded by huge areas dominated by poverty and illiteracy. No doubt he couldn't have put it quite as powerfully in 1915, and no doubt he exaggerates, but de la Selva here demonstrates the same kind of independent thinking that he was pioneering in his earlier days: anti-imperialist in politics, nationalist and regionalist in sympathy, Americanist in the larger sense, supportive of Spanish-American culture, and deeply humanist in its classical and European tastes. What undoubtedly made the difference—as it had done with José Martí (although their perspectives were different)—was his knowledge of New York on the ground. And that ground influenced de la Selva even more because he had encountered it at such a tender age.

---

[121] De la Selva, 'Acróasis', p. 45.
[122] De la Selva, 'Acróasis', pp. 45–49.
[123] Salomón de la Selva, 'Edna St. Vincent Millay', *América: Revista Antológica*, 62 (January 1950), 7–32, at 26.

In this later essay he reaffirmed his Americanism, again in terms more nuanced than his younger self could have articulated: 'I want to stress … that I've suffered personally, body and soul, from all the insults that the egoism of the strongest American nation has inflicted on our poor peoples.' But would we have behaved any differently, he asks? The idea of revenge is rejected, not least because of its impossibility. 'Since, however different we might seem, there is more that tends to unite us than tends to alienate us, I believe that the noble path, prudent and possible, is to make the effort to create a common culture.' Which does not mean, he emphasises, giving up *our* culture, but being loyal to it.[124]

---

[124] De la Selva, 'Acróasis', pp. 56–57.

Chapter Three

The Changing of the Poetic Guard (1915)

You could not tell the country where he came from;
He was so very vague and dazzling and so very young.[1]

'Shot through by the lightning bolt of sex' was one description of the film *A Fool There Was*, which premiered at the Strand Theatre in Times Square on 12 January 1915, getting the year off to a bracing start.[2] The film starred Theda Bara as 'the vampire', meaning a strong and independent woman to whom men were in helpless thrall: she would quickly become one of early cinema's most sensational stars. Film was the modern medium, now becoming very popular, but each performance of *A Fool There Was* began with an actor reading out Rudyard Kipling's poem on which the film, via a play, was based. Poetry still took precedence, just about. A different sign of modernity came on 10 April when the well-known sculptor Karl Bitter died after being struck by a car a couple of blocks south of the Strand, at Broadway and West 40th Street, perhaps the first artist to die in this way. Less dramatically, in the cultural field new journals began to proliferate: in March alone there appeared the *Ridgefield Gazook*, edited by Man Ray, *Rogue*, edited by Allen Norton, and *291*, edited by Marius de Zayas. None would survive for long, but all would eventually be seen as harbingers of new literary and artistic worlds in the process of creation.

The *Ridgefield Gazook* was the product of a group of young writers and artists who frequented the Grantwood colony at Ridgefield, a small collection of houses on the—still pastoral—Jersey Shore: Man Ray, William Carlos Williams, Alfred Kreymborg, Mina Loy, Wallace Stevens. A four-page

---

[1] From Salomón de la Selva, 'The Sword of Wonder', *Tropical Town and Other Poems*, New York: John Lane Company, 1918, p. 106.
[2] In the *New York Dramatic Mirror*, quoted in Eve Golden, *Vamp: The Rise and Fall of Theda Bara*, Vestal, NY: Emprise, 1996, p. 41.

newsletter, it had just the one issue. In town, many of that group attended the salon run by Walter and Louise Arensberg at their apartment at 33 West 67th Street: Marcel Duchamp joined it when he reached New York in June.[3] The Arensbergs' wealth also supported *Rogue*, a decadent but genuinely modernist magazine, now renowned for having published several of Wallace Stevens's early poems. Norton, Arensberg, and Stevens had all been to Harvard, but it was a Harvard, as one historian puts it, that had turned its back on Boston and opted for New York.[4] They called themselves the Patagonians, perhaps in ironic reference to a primitive Americanism.

Having established himself in New York with the help of the journalist friends he'd worked with in Mexico City, Benjamin de Casseres and Carlo de Fornaro, Marius de Zayas was invited to exhibit his caricatures by the photographer Alfred Stieglitz, founder and editor of *Camera Work*, at his gallery at 291 Fifth Avenue, beginning a fruitful collaboration between the two men. De Zayas was instrumental in bringing the new European painting to New York, and he provided an early Hispanic thread through the New York artistic avant-garde, later developed by Diego Rivera, Miguel Covarrubias, and Joaquín Torres García. That first issue of *291* included work by Apollinaire and Picasso, as well as by de Zayas himself, who was instrumental in organising Picasso's first New York exhibition at the end of the year, held at de Zayas's Modern Gallery at 500 Fifth Avenue.

Quite separate from this avant-garde activity, though equally committed to the art of poetry, two Nicaraguan writers were active in New York in the first months of 1915 but at very different stages of their careers. Salomón de la Selva was just beginning to write seriously and he would have his first poem published in July. Meanwhile, Rubén Darío, the greatest living poet in the Spanish language, was struggling to hold a pen in his hospital room on West 34th Street. Terminally ill, he left New York in April and died back in Nicaragua in February 1916. Already committed to translating poetry from English into Spanish, de la Selva made contact in August 1915 with the rising young star of US poetry, Edna St Vincent Millay, initiating a lengthy and passionate correspondence. Along with his friend the Dominican Pedro Henríquez Ureña, he also began the series of pan-American dinners that

---

[3] See Stephen Voyce, '"Make the World Your Salon": Poetry and Community at the Arensberg Apartment', *Modernism/modernity*, 15, no. 4 (November 2008), 627–46.

[4] Jay Bochner, 'The Marriage of *Rogue* and *The Soil*', in *Little Magazines and Modernism*, ed. Suzanne W. Churchill and Adam McKible, London: Ashgate, 2008, pp. 49–66, at p. 50.

form the backbone of this book, first honouring the poet many saw as Darío's successor, the Peruvian José Santos Chocano, whose visits to New York had already produced some short but haunting poems.

Growing Up in New York

The Delineator: A Journal of Fashion, Culture, and Fine Arts is not usually regarded as a vanguard publication: its stock in trade was sewing patterns. Nonetheless it was an extremely successful magazine, which could therefore afford to pay writers of quality such as Hamlin Garland, Arnold Bennett, and Jack London. Theodore Dreiser had even edited the magazine between 1907 and 1910. Aimed principally at women readers, it published features on 'women's issues', successful women, social campaigns, and women in sport and cultural life. With a circulation close to a million, *The Delineator* was published in English in the USA, Britain, and Canada as well as in French, German, and Spanish (as *El Espejo de la Moda*).[5] Its New York offices in the Butterick Building at Spring Street and MacDougal—the largest publishing plant in the city—housed teams of translators, and it was there in late 1914 that the aspiring Nicaraguan poet Salomón de la Selva found his first proper job (Fig. 4). Translating sewing patterns from English into Spanish was not the most glamorous or challenging of tasks, but the young man needed some kind of income while he tried to establish himself in the New York literary world, and in retrospect there could have been worse places to begin a career.

Salomón de la Selva had come to New York in 1906, aged 13 if the 1893 birthdate is correct, and had therefore had several years of education in English.[6] Hard facts about his early life in Nicaragua are difficult to come

---

[5] See Sidney R. Bland, 'Shaping the Life of the New Woman: The Crusading Years of *The Delineator*', *American Periodicals: A Journal of History & Criticism*, 19, no. 2 (2009), 165–88.

[6] Books and essays about de la Selva tend to recycle the same stories, some of them based on misleading biographical information supplied by the writer himself. Even his year of birth has been open to question since the published biographies give 1893 but all surviving official US documents—ship manifests, censuses, army registration, etc.—give, or imply from age, 1894, as does de la Selva himself in an undated (probably early 1918) letter to William Rose Benét, seemingly in response to a request for a biographical sketch: "Born León, Nicaragua, March 20, 1894" (Letter from Salomón de la Selva to William Rose Benét, WRBP). WRBP is the William Rose Benét Papers (YCAL MSS 1100, Box 39 Folder 1538), Beinecke Rare Book and Manuscript Library, Yale University. Perhaps de la Selva was correct and his biographers wrong; perhaps he was simply mistaken; perhaps, for reasons unknown, he decided at some point to take a year off his age.

4 The Butterick Building at Spring Street and MacDougal. Still standing. Provenance unknown.

by. He was born and brought up in León, a traditionally Liberal city in a country of traditional divisions between Liberals and Conservatives. His mother was Evangelina Escoto Baca. His father, Salomón Selva Glenton, was a lawyer, though less eminent a lawyer than *his* father, Buenaventura Selva, who had supposedly been driven from his home town of Granada by William Walker's incursion. This paternal grandfather had married Teresa Paula Glenton, daughter of Jonas Wilson Glenton, a young Liverpool businessman who had established himself on the Pacific coast of Central America after the end of the local wars of independence and married Teresa González Sol. Salomón de la Selva was always proud of this English strain in his lineage.

After a solid primary education, which reportedly included tuition in English from a black Jamaican named Charles Greenwood, Salomón received a government scholarship to study in the USA. He was sent to New York in the charge of one of Zelaya's ministers, Fernando Sánchez, who travelled with his family.[7] The SS *Panama*, sailing from Colón, reached New

---

[7] Sánchez had been educated in León and so probably knew the Selva family. Pío Bolaños, the Nicaraguan Consul in New York (based at 18 Broadway), was a protégé

5 Salomón de la Selva aged 16, probably on Staten Island. Photographer unknown. Colección Salomón de la Selva, Biblioteca Francisco Xavier Clavigero, Universidad Iberoamericana, Mexico City.

York in May 1906.[8] According to de la Selva's own accounts, he attended a military academy in Newton, Massachusetts, and then the Westerleigh Collegiate Institute on Staten Island (Fig. 5), a boarding school with a good academic record which had been established by the publisher Isaac K. Funk in a part of the city long associated with the temperance movement and, perhaps for both those reasons, favoured by families sending their children from abroad for a US education. A significant number of pupils at the school (19 out of around 50 in 1910) came from Spanish-speaking countries, including six from Nicaragua. By the time de la Selva attended, however, the original school building in Prohibition Park had burned down (in February 1903) and the school had relocated to a Greek-revival mansion on Richmond Terrace, facing across the bay to Manhattan.[9]

---

of Sánchez's and a second cousin of Zelaya's. See the letter of introduction from Zelaya to Bolaños, carried by de la Selva, in Pío Bolaños Álvarez, 'Memorias de Pío Bolaños', Archivo Histórico del Dr Andrés Vega Bolaños <http://sajurin.enriquebolanos.org/vega/docs/732.pdf>, pp. 65–66 accessed December 2018.

[8] See the List or Manifest of Alien Passengers for the U.S. Immigration Officer at the Port of Arrival. SS *Panama*, from Colon, 27 April 1906, arriving New York, 3 May 1906 (passenger ID 105525150068; frame 278; line number 6), where he is listed as Solomon Selva, aged 12. In the contributor's note to his first publication, de la Selva mentioned having travelled in Europe before coming to the USA (*The Forum*, LIV [July 1915], 761). This is not impossible, but no hard evidence has emerged, and he would have been too young for the experience to have made much of an impression. See also n. 14, below.

[9] See *Atlas of the Borough of Richmond, City of New York*, 2nd edn, New York: E. Robinson, 1907, Plate 1. The mansion had originally been built by John Haviland for John Q. Jones (President of the Chemical Bank). After Jones's death, the estate was acquired by the lawyer J. Evarts Tracy, who presumably rented the mansion to the Institute. The Institute's headmaster, Wilbur Strong, was indicted for fraud not long after de la Selva left (*New York Times*, 11 June 1916, p. 17).

De la Selva also then attended the engineering school at Cornell University, though very briefly—from September to November 1909. He later said that he went there because his father wanted him to build the Nicaraguan Canal, and indeed the Cornell Civil Engineering department taught its students by means of a 420 ft canal on Beebe Lake.[10] However, he seems an unlikely engineering student and later remembered taking much more interest in the library than in the canal.[11] He was following a brief non-degree course but even this was cut short because his scholarship from the Nicaraguan government was discontinued during the unrest in the country in the autumn of 1909.[12]

---

[10] See *Cornell University Register, 1909–1910*, Ithaca, NY: Cornell University, July 1910, pp. 419–20.

[11] Salomón de la Selva, *Ilustre familia: poema de los siete tratados = De praeclarae familiae historia: libri septem: novela de dioses y de héroes. Con tres acroasis informativas y apologéticas*, Mexico City, n.p., 1952, pp. x–xi.

[12] The few weeks at Cornell are sometimes inflated by de la Selva and others into having obtained a degree from, or even being appointed professor at the university. References to de la Selva (then Salomon Selva Jr) in Cornell official publications are meagre and not entirely consistent. He was on campus for the opening of the 1909 academic year: *Cornell University Register, 1909–1910*, p. 229. Fees were $150 p.a., with another $550 p.a. estimated for living expenses, but his scholarship from Nicaragua obviously stopped arriving sometime during the autumn of 1909 since the minutes of the Board of Trustees for 28 December 1909 notes that 'The Treasurer was authorized to cancel tuition and other fees for the current term of Salomon Selva, a student supported by the Nicaraguan Government, but whose allowance had been discontinued by the Government, and who was therefore compelled to withdraw from the University' (*Proceedings of the Board of Trustees of Cornell University, June 17, 1909–May 29, 1912*, Ithaca, NY: Cornell University, 1912, p. 788). De la Selva's entry in the 1922 alumni directory lists him in the class of 1913 (*Cornell Alumni Directory*, Cornell University Official Publication, 13, no. 12, Ithaca, NY: Cornell University, 15 May 1922, p. 289) despite there being no evidence on his transcript of attendance in that year, but the next edition has him simply as 09–09 (*Cornell Alumni Directory 1868–1931*, Ithaca, NY: Cornell University, 1931, p. 788), presumably correcting the earlier error. There are four other mentions of de la Selva in official Cornell publications. In the *Cornell Alumni News*, 19, no. 1 (5 October 1916), 10–11, his essay about the poetry of Thomas S. Jones, Jr is mentioned and quoted from—though in connection with Jones being an alumnus, not de la Selva. In the *Cornell Alumni News*, 30, no. 35 (7 June 1928), there is an entry: "13—Salomón de la Selva is a journeyman bookbinder and secretary of the Nicaraguan Federation of Labor'. He is listed in the section of those whose current addresses Cornell doesn't have, in *Cornell Alumni News*, 29, no. 35 (August 1937), supplement. His death is noted in *Cornell Alumni News*, 79, no. 8 (April 1977), 52, a mere 18 years after the fact. With thanks to Hilary Dorsch Wong, Reference Coordinator at the Division of Rare and Manuscript Collections, Cornell University, for help in clarifying these records.

The April 1910 New York census has de la Selva back at Westerleigh, but by then the young man's life had been further shaken by the death of his father in February. There were probably months of financial hardship: he later recalled shining shoes and selling newspapers.[13] The eldest son in a family of nine children, Salomón was doubtless expected to go home, which he did in September 1910, spending a year back in León, some of it studying law and founding and writing a student newspaper. He later told the New York journalist Prosper Buranelli that his adolescent fulminations provoked the new government to put him on the next steamer out of the country, which is how he ended up back in New York in September 1911, probably back in fact to Westerleigh, where he may have done some teaching; although he also told Buranelli that he was employed as a translator by a Brazilian con-artist who passed off Salomón's translations into Spanish and Portuguese of poems by Coleridge and Blake and Swinburne as his own work.[14]

During the key years of 1915 to 1919, de la Selva's base was the Upper West Side, but after leaving Cornell in 1909 he lived in Harlem (143th Street and Seventh Avenue) and later across the river in the Bronx (895 Cauldwell Avenue), probably always alongside his close Cuban friend Rufino González Mesa, whom he had probably met at school.[15] He says that it was through the Irish family he lodged with in Harlem that he got involved in local Tammany Hall politics, helping the mayoral campaign of William J. Gaynor (whom Salomón admired because he was always quoting Epictetus). Since Gaynor was elected at the beginning of November 1909, de la Selva must have moved directly from Ithaca to Harlem. It may have been in the period before he returned to Nicaragua that there developed what he calls the Order

---

[13] Salomón de la Selva, 'Al pueblo de Nicaragua' [1927], *Antología Mayor/III Ensayos*, pp. 577–92, at p. 580.

[14] Prosper Buranelli, 'Poet of Fantastic Fortunes', *World Magazine*, 29 August 1920, pp. 10, 13. That contributor's note to de la Selva's first publication also says 'In the winter of 1911–12 he landed at New York once more, after having visited, on his way from Nicaragua, Chile, the Argentine, Brazil, and Panama' (*The Forum*, LIV (July 1915), 761). He did arrive from Panama, but in September 1911. There is no evidence of, or further reference to, those visits to Chile, Argentina, and Brazil. It seems likely that he was trying to give the impression of extensive international experience: see also n. 8, above. Jorge Eduardo Arellano suggests that the DeBayle family helped finance his return to New York (*Aventura y genio*, p. 12).

[15] A letter to de la Selva from Archer Huntington was sent to this Bronx address on 5 March 1915, but by September he had moved into the more spacious premises at 115 West 97th Street (Letter from Salomón de la Selva to Archer M. Huntington, HSA (17 November 1915). HSA is the Hispanic Society of America.

of Ideal Friendship (OIF), a kind of neighbourhood educational initiative that he ran with Rufino González.[16] Salomón took Pedro Henríquez Ureña to the OIF in 1915 where his older Dominican friend was in his element.

At this time de la Selva also began to make the local contacts that would eventually enable his pan-American project to gain some traction in a crowded literary field. Possibly the first was Frank Crane, a syndicated newspaper columnist, writer of advertising copy, and author of best-selling homilies entitled 'Four-minute Essays'. Salomón would have had no interest in his facile writing, but Crane befriended the teenager and opened some doors for him. More important in the long term, though, were the contacts he made through the Poetry Society of America which, with a nice sense of timing, had just been getting into its stride as de la Selva came back to New York in the autumn of 1911.

Rubén Darío in Hospital

Rubén Darío had arrived in New York in November 1914. Not only was Darío also Nicaraguan, he had grown up in León, which he regarded as his home town, and had probably known Salomón's family. If news had not already reached him on the Hispanic grapevine, de la Selva would have been alerted to Darío's arrival by the nearly full-page piece in the *New York Times* with the headline 'Noted South American Poet Writes About New York', and the sub-head 'Ruben Dario of Nicaragua, Celebrated Throughout Spanish-Speaking World, Describes for The Times His Emotions on Arriving Here'. 'Little known in this country,' the introduction began, going on to explain something of Darío's reputation in France and listing some of the books he had written and some of the diplomatic posts he had held. The bulk of the piece consisted in what the *Times* reporter describes as 'a sketch of Senor Dario's impressions on first seeing New York, dashed off by the great Spanish-American poet especially for the New York Times after his arrival here a few days ago from Europe'. There was considerable journalistic sleight of hand here. What followed was indeed a translation of a piece by Darío describing his first impressions of New York, but it had been written 21 years previously, on the occasion of Darío's first visit to the city in 1893. In any case Darío never dashed anything off. In all likelihood, for an appropriate sum, the *Times* reporter had been given the rights to have this much earlier piece translated into English.[17]

---

[16] On this period of his life, see Salomón de la Selva, 'In Memoriam Pedro Henríquez Ureña', *Antología Mayor III: Ensayos*, pp. 99–165, at pp. 139–42.
[17] 'Noted South American Poet Writes About New York', *New York Times*,

For Darío, Paris was the literary capital of the world and Barcelona and Buenos Aires might be considered its avatars. New York—almost despite itself—had produced Whitman and Poe, but it was not in the same league. It was, however, where José Martí was living in 1893, which seems to have encouraged Darío to travel to Buenos Aires on an indirect route, via Panama, New York, and Paris. During this first visit to New York in 1893, the young Darío had been lionised by the vibrant Hispanic community. He had stayed in the Hotel America on Irving Place and East 15th Street, popular with Spanish-American visitors, and been given a banquet attended by a host of important literary and political figures: Nicanor Bolet Peraza, Benjamin Guerra, Néstor Ponce de León, Gonzalo de Quesada, José María Vargas Vila ... The only recorded exchange between Martí and Darío came when they met one evening in May 1893 before a speech Martí was to give at Hardman Hall on the corner of Fifth Avenue and East 19th Street. According to Darío, Martí approached and addressed to him just one word '¡Hijo!' [Son!].[18] Perhaps he was anointing Darío as his literary successor, which was how Darío probably understood the word; but perhaps he was asserting seniority, putting Darío—14 years his junior—into his place as a follower, a disciple. In any event, by 1914, Martí, Bolet Peraza, and Guerra were dead, Ponce de León was back in Cuba, Quesada was Cuban minister in Washington, and Vargas Vila—a constant traveller—was elsewhere.

On this first visit to New York in 1893, Darío had written a poem to a Cuban artist which distinguishes between three islands: of gold, silver, and iron, with no room for doubt that Manhattan is the third of these, the 'isla de Hierro' [island of iron] where the artist finds herself in exile, far away from 'el país del sol' [country of the sun] where the poet imagines her more fulfilled. So far, so conventional. Interestingly, though, this is a prose poem—perhaps indicative that Darío felt the need for a new form for a new place, rather as Baudelaire had in the 'new' Paris of the 1860s with his *petits poèmes en prose*.[19]

---

29 November 1914, p. XX6. During these years the *Times* did have a bilingual journalist, the Venezuelan-born Thomas Russell Ybarra, who may have written the piece and done the translation (though he would not have been responsible for the headline describing Darío as 'South American'). Darío's account of that first arrival in New York makes up the opening paragraphs of his essay 'Edgar Allan Poe' [1894], in *Los raros, Obras Completas*, vol. 6 (Madrid: Editorial Mundo Latino, 1906), pp. 17–29.

[18] Rubén Darío, *Autobiografía* [1912], Madrid: Editorial Mundo Latino, 1918, p. 109.

[19] Despite the title of the volume, this is the only prose poem in Darío's *Prosas profanas y otros poemas* [1896], Madrid: Editorial Mundo Latino, 1920, pp. 73–76.

Darío's intervening visits to the city in November 1907 and April 1908 had been very brief, basically just to change boats, but his stay in 1908 had produced two telling reminiscences. The first came in *El viaje a Nicaragua*:

> Pasé por la metrópoli yanqui cuando estaba en pleno hervor una crisis financiera. Sentí el huracán de la Bolsa. Vi la omnipotencia del multimillonario y admiré la locura mammónica de la vasta capital del cheque.
>
> Siempre que he pasado por esa tierra he tenido la misma impresión. La precipitación de la vida altera los nervios. Las construcciones comerciales producen el mismo efecto psíquico que las arquitecturas abrumadoras percibidas por Quincey en sus estados tebaicos. El ambiente delirio de las grandezas hace daño a la ponderación del espíritu. Siéntese algo allí de primitivo y de supertérreo, de cainitas o de marcianos. Los ascensores *express* no son para mi temperamento, ni las vastas oleadas de muchedumbres electorales tocando pitos, ni el manethecelphárico renglón que al despertarme en la sombra de la noche solía aparecer bajo el teléfono en mi cuarto del Astor: *You have mail in the office*.[20]

> [I passed through the Yankee metropolis when a financial crisis was at full boil. I felt the hurricane of the stock market. I witnessed the all-powerful multi-millionaires and I admired the Mammonic madness of the vast capital of the chequebook.
>
> Whenever I've gone there I've had the same impression. The headlong pace of life upsets the nerves. The business premises produce the same psychical effect as the overwhelming architectural images that De Quincey saw in his Theban hallucinations. Such magnitude in an atmosphere of delirium damages the balance of the spirit. One senses there something primitive and otherworldly, of Canaanites or Martians. The express elevators don't suit my temperament, nor the vast surges of electioneering crowds blowing whistles, nor the manethecelpharic line I see appear under the telephone in my room at the Astor when I wake up in the darkness of the night: *You have mail in the office*.]

Darío here again employs some of the conventional tropes about New York life, mostly based on its hectic pace: the hurricane of the Stock Exchange, the excessive speed of life embodied in the express elevators (a feature of the newly completed Woolworth Building where they travelled at 700 feet per

---

[20] Rubén Darío, *El viaje a Nicaragua; e Intermezzo tropical*, Madrid: Biblioteca 'Ateneo', 1909, pp. 10–11.

minute), the delirium induced by looking up at the skyscrapers. Vocabulary from Greek mythology and the Bible is called into play: the material avarice associated with the Mammons, the primitive passions of the Canaanites. Yet, as with his 'Edgar Allan Poe' essay, the sheer excess of US life seems to betray a grudging or perhaps unconscious admiration: these creatures seem to come from another planet (Martians);[21] the effect the buildings have on Darío identifies him with Thomas De Quincey, a much admired writer. And even the new technology that disturbs his beauty sleep in the Hotel Astor is the occasion for the spectacular neologism 'manethecelphárico'—the writing on the wall.[22]

The second reminiscence comes from a piece about the Dominican poet Fabio Fiallo, who was working as a consul in New York at the time:

> Allá en la imperial Nueva York ... de hierro, junto a los edificios babélicos y las oficinas de negocios, por Broadway o por Wall Street, adonde le llevaron sus funciones diplomáticas, Fabio y yo, entre el horror de la ciudad comercial, hablábamos de arte, de belleza, de poesía, viendo aún poesía, belleza y arte aún en el trabajo y tráfagos de aquellos cíclopes. Y luego en mi cuarto del Astor, o en nuestras sobremesas del Delmónico o en el Restaurante Martín, oía yo recitar a mi amigo, a mi buen amigo, sus versos de patria o de amor ... Y al oírle, yo pensaba no en nuestros maestros de simbolismo, en nuestros *mauvais maitres*, Verlaine y demás, harto perseguidos por los nuevos; sino en los Bécquer y los Heine de antaño, dolorosos y amargados, cisnes muertos de pena amorosa.[23]

> [There in the imperial iron city of New York, next to the towers of Babel and the business office, on Broadway or on Wall Street, where his diplomatic duties took him, Fabio and I—amidst the horror of the commercial city—would talk of art and beauty and poetry, even seeing poetry, beauty, and art in the hustle and bustle of those cyclops. And then in my room at the Astor, or after dinner at Delmonico's or Martin's, I'd listen to my friend, my good friend, recite his poems of patriotism or love ... And listening to him, I would think not of our

---

[21] Darío was a keen reader of science fiction. H. G. Wells's *The War of the Worlds*, featuring a Martian invasion, had been translated into French in 1900.
[22] 'And this is the writing that is written: MANE, THECEL, PHARES' (Daniel 5:25).
[23] Rubén Darío, 'Fabio Fiallo', in Fabio Fiallo, *Obras completas*, 4 vols., Santo Domingo: Editora de Santo Domingo, 1980, vol. 4, pp. 1–7, at p. 3. Originally published as 'Cantaba el ruiseñor', in *El Fígaro* [Havana] in 1911.

Symbolist teachers, our *mauvais maîtres*, Verlaine and the rest, chased by the new ones, but of the Bécquers and Heines of the old days, sorrowful and bitter, swans who died of the pangs of love.]

If in the first account Darío had presented himself as isolated and disoriented in the maelstrom of New York life, here the presence of Fiallo allows him to create a defiant enclave. The kinds of contrasts elaborated on the basis of Rodó's *Ariel* are starkly apparent, but given even greater weight because articulated from the belly of the beast itself. New York is still the 'isla de Hierro' he had seen in 1893, the city of business and commerce, Babylonian in scale and populated by cyclops, one of Darío's favourite words, presumably indicative of the monocular vision and cannibalistic intent of the denizens of Wall Street. Within this world move Darío and Fiallo, talking of higher things, of beauty and of poetry, even seeing beauty and poetry in the world of the cyclops, although the one-eyed monsters are incapable of returning the compliment. The poets' talk becomes more and more rarefied—from symbolism to Verlaine to Bécquer and Heine; those dying swans become further and further removed from the city of steel. And yet, in an irony Darío clearly doesn't appreciate, these poetic conversations take place at one of the smartest hotels in New York and two of its finest restaurants—a fact that the poet seems reluctant to interrogate. Surely these enclaves of 'luxe, calme et volupté' are imbricated with or even supported by the despised world of Babylon? Nonetheless, Darío seems almost as keen to underline the places in which his conversations with Fiallo took place as the topics of those conversations: the Hotel Astor on Times Square, opened in 1904, the height of modernity, with its 11 storeys housing 1,000 guest rooms; Delmonico's, right next to the Astor; and the Café Martin on West 26th Street and Fifth Avenue.[24] This poet is no ragpicker. His other close friend at the time in New York was the Nicaraguan consul Pío Bolaños—who had greeted the young Salomón Selva on his arrival in New York a couple of years earlier. Apparently, Bolaños and Fiallo had to bail Darío out after he had racked up a $300 bill at an upmarket brothel.[25]

---

[24] Juan Bautista Martín was a French restaurateur who had spent a number of years in Panama. The Café Martin attracted a large French and Spanish-American clientele. Martín eventually lost all his money on the Stock Exchange and returned to France.
[25] See Ricardo Llopesa, *Rubén Darío en Nueva York*, Valencia: Instituto de Estudios Modernistas, 1997, p. 31. Other relevant studies are Eliot G. Fay, 'Rubén Darío in New York', *Modern Language Notes*, 57, no. 8 (1942), 641–48, and José Agustín Balseiro, 'Ruben Darío y Estados Unidos', in his *Seis estudios sobre Rubén Darío*, Madrid: Gredos, 1967, pp. 117–43.

By 1914, Darío's situation was much more precarious. His fame in the Hispanic world had not diminished, but his health was deteriorating, his relationship with his companion, Francisca Sánchez, had broken down, and his financial position was increasingly parlous. This American tour, of which New York was supposed to be the first leg, was intended to boost his finances. The tour had been the brainchild of Darío's friend and fellow Nicaraguan Alejandro Bermúdez. Biographers differ as to whether Darío was unwisely seduced into the trip by Bermúdez or rescued by Bermúdez from an alcohol-induced captivity at the hands of Sánchez, once the love of his life, who stayed behind in Barcelona with their son. Bermúdez's proposed trip involved New York, Washington, Mexico City, various cities in Central America, and Argentina, although it seems to have been dependent on getting funding in New York from the Carnegie Endowment for International Peace: Nicholas Butler, president of Columbia University, was the head of its department for International Education and Communication. They left Barcelona on 25 October 1914 with Darío's new secretary, Juan Huertas. Friends who saw Darío in Cádiz described him as suffering from attacks of delirium tremens. Huertas disembarked in Havana and returned to Spain. The other two reached New York on 12 November 1914, just as winter was beginning to clasp the city in an icy grip. Bermúdez went back to Nicaragua in mid-February 1915, abandoning Darío at his lowest point.

The Hispanic community in New York could be relied upon to celebrate Darío and to offer him the occasional dinner, though some of the celebrants would also add their drinks to his not inconsiderable bar tab. Ricardo Llopesa's report of a 'triumphal reception' is almost certainly an overstatement.[26] Darío wrote occasional pieces for Francisco Peynado's magazine, *Las Novedades*, and the journal gave him a dinner shortly after his arrival.[27] For somebody always notoriously self-conscious about his provincial background and prickly about his social status, it must have been difficult for Darío to deal with the cascading impoverishment of his New York accommodation. During his first few weeks in the city he stayed at the respectable, but not luxurious, Hotel Earlington on West 27th Street before moving to an apartment opposite and then to a boarding house called Casa Méndez at 313 West 14th Street.[28] Darío wrote to the Nicaraguan

---

[26] Llopesa, *Rubén Darío en Nueva York*, p. 34.
[27] See the account from *Las Novedades* reprinted in Emilio Rodríguez Demorizi, *Papeles de Rubén Darío*, Santo Domingo: Editora del Caribe, 1969, pp. 138–40.
[28] See Alejandro Bermúdez's letter to his wife dated 12 January 1915, in Demorizi, *Papeles*, pp. 154–55; Letter from Rubén Darío to Archer M. Huntington, HSA (7 April 1915).

agent in Washington pointing out that he was owed a considerable amount of money for his previous services to the state—but to no avail.[29] He also wrote to Leo S. Rowe, an influential academic teaching at the University of Pennsylvania but with links to the State Department, whom Darío had probably met in Rio de Janeiro at the Pan-American Conference, but Rowe could do little. Darío was still in receipt of payment for newspaper articles for *La Nación* and Archer Huntington bestowed some of his largesse. After founding the Hispanic Society of America in 1904, Huntington had supported publications and events as well as sponsoring writers: he knew exactly how important a figure Darío was.[30] But none of this was enough to keep Darío in any kind of comfort and, in the depths of winter, increasingly weak and increasingly penurious, he ended up spending nearly a month in the French Hospital on West 34th Street with an attack of double pneumonia. Dr Aníbal Zelaya, nephew of the ex-Nicaraguan president, tended Darío when he was ill; Juan Arana Turrol, a Colombian poet and journalist working for *Las Novedades*, managed to gather together some funds; and eventually Manuel Estrada Cabrera, the Guatemalan dictator, sent money and arranged Darío's passage to Guatemala. Gustavo Alemán Bolaños writes bitterly of the 'friends' who flocked to Darío's side in the good times and who abandoned him when the money ran out.[31] This was a sad decline from cosy lunches at Delmonico's and warm nights in the Hotel Astor. One letter in January 1915 from Darío to his Mexican friend Amado Nervo was written on Hotel Astor notepaper, perhaps suggesting that he sometimes popped in there to remind himself of happier days (Fig. 6).[32]

Although it was only six years since Darío's previous visit, New York was a different city. Mabel Dodge's salon was in full swing at 23 Fifth

---

[29] Letter to Pedro Rafael Cuadra, probably January 1915, in Demorizi, *Papeles*, pp. 179–80. For background, see David E. Whisnant, 'A Prodigious Child of Nicaragua: Rubén Darío and the Ideological Uses of Cultural Capital', in his *Rascally Signs in Sacred Places: The Politics of Culture in Nicaragua*, Chapel Hill: University of North Carolina Press, 1995, pp. 313–43.

[30] In May 1916, Pedro Henriquez Ureña offered Alfonso Reyes a survey of the reception Darío had received on his last visit to New York, noting that Huntington did most: a big reception as well as paying for the reading at Columbia University: Letter from Pedro Henríquez Ureña to Alfonso Reyes (May 1916), *Epistolario íntimo, 1906–1946*, ed. Juan Jacobo de Lara, 3 vols., Santo Domingo: UNPHU, 1981–83, vol. 1, p. 244.

[31] Gustavo Alemán Bolaños, 'Lo que no se hizo y lo que se hace con Rubén Darío', *El Gráfico*, II, no. 1 (1917), 234.

[32] The authenticity of these letters to Nervo, written as to a lover, is disputed: see Alberto Acereda, '"Nuestro más profundo y sublime secreto": los amores transgresores entre Rubén Darío y Amado Nervo', *Bulletin of Spanish Studies*, 89, no. 6 (2012), 895–924.

6 Rubén Darío in New York in 1915. Photograph by Sarony dedicated to Huntington. Courtesy of the Hispanic Society of America, New York.

Avenue, down on Washington Square the Liberal Club was humming with discussions and lectures, and the excitement from the Armory Show of spring 1913 was still in the air.[33] Unfortunately, Darío had few opportunities to engage with any of this. De la Selva's project had not yet started—in fact, his experience with Darío may have acted as a catalyst: he took Darío to some Poetry Society of America meetings, but just as a member of the audience, and Darío was in any case socially awkward in English-speaking settings. Jessie Rittenhouse recalls that Darío was a frequent visitor to the PSA but that few people knew how important a figure he was outside the USA until the outburst of public mourning in Latin America that greeted his death the following year.[34] Then, de la Selva spoke for an hour and a half at the PSA, which published a note lamenting Darío's death: Joyce Kilmer had proposed the resolution.[35] De la Selva wrote an obituary for *Poetry*, and Pedro Henríquez Ureña also gave material to Edward Wheeler, some of which appeared in the June 1916 issue of *Current Opinion* as two short pieces, 'A Poet's Funeral' and 'Darío's Place in Spanish Poetry', noting that 'Señor Darío visited the United States a year or so ago but was not received with any degree of enthusiasm'.[36]

The best-known of the half dozen poems that Darío wrote on this final visit to New York is 'La gran cosmópolis (Meditaciones de la madrugada)' [The great cosmopolis: dawn meditations], which suggests an even deeper sense of alienation than on his previous visits. These are the opening stanzas:

> Casas de cincuenta pisos,
> servidumbre de color,
> millones de circuncisos,
> máquinas, diarios, avisos
> y ¡dolor, dolor, dolor!

---

[33] For the general ambience of 1915, see Adele Heller and Lois Rudnick, eds, *1915, The Cultural Moment: The New Politics, the New Woman, the New Psychology, the New Art & the New Theatre in America*, New Brunswick, NJ: Rutgers University Press, 1991. On the Liberal Club, see Peter Hulme, 'The Liberal Club and its Jamaican Secretary' (March 2017) < http://repository.essex.ac.uk/19768/1/Hulme%2C%20Liberal%20Club.pdf > accessed December 2018.

[34] Jessie B. Rittenhouse, *My House of Life: An Autobiography*, Boston: Houghton Mifflin Company, 1934, pp. 238–39.

[35] See Harriet Monroe, 'Editorial Comment', *Poetry*, VIII, no. 2 (May 1916), 88–89.

[36] Salomón de la Selva, 'Rubén Darío', *Poetry*, VIII, no. 4 (July 1916), 200–04; 'Carta de Pedro Henríquez Ureña a Alfonso Reyes sobre Rubén Darío (Nueva York, 9 de mayo de 1916)', in Ernesto Mejía Sánchez, ed., *Cuestiones rubendarianas*, Madrid: Revista de Occidente, 1970, pp. 53–59, at p. 59; *Current Opinion*, 60 (1916), 428.

> Estos son los hombre fuertes
> que vierten áureas corrientes
> y multiplican simientes
> por su ciclópeo fragor,
> y tras la Quinta Avenida
> la Miseria está vestida
> con ¡dolor, dolor, dolor … ![37]
>
> Homes in a fifty story high-rise,
> a serving class of color,
> millions of people circumcised,
> machines, billboards, newspapers,
> and grief, layer upon layer!
>
> So these must be the strong men
> who spread their golden needs
> and multiply their seeds
> with a Cyclopian fervor,
> while all along Fifth Avenue
> Misery is in full view
> And grief, layer upon layer![38]

The poem is highly conventional in its imagery and diction: the skyscrapers, the black servants, the industry, the contrast between wealth and poverty, the touch of anti-Semitism; all rounded off at the end of each stanza by that tolling bell of pain or grief: *dolor, dolor, dolor*. This is again the familiar discourse of *arielismo* in which New York, typical of the USA as a whole, is seen as the Calibanesque monster of materialism, in implicit contrast to the more spiritual values of the Latin American republics.

There were, however, signs that Spanish-American literature was beginning to be taken seriously in New York: in that sense Darío arrived just too early.[39] Alfred Coester had recently published an impressive bibliography of Spanish-

---

[37] Rubén Darío, 'La gran cosmópolis' [1914], in his *Poesía*, ed. Ernesto Mejía Sánchez, Caracas: Biblioteca Ayacucho, 1977, pp. 469–70.

[38] 'The Great Cosmopolis', in Rubén Darío, *Selected Writings*, ed. Ilan Stavans, New York: Penguin, 2005, p. 129.

[39] Hispanist scholarship already had a long and distinguished history in the USA, notably through the Smith Chair in Romance Languages and Literatures at Harvard, occupied by illustrious figures such as George Ticknor (from 1819 to 1835), Henry Wadsworth Longfellow (from 1836 to 1854), and James Russell Lowell (from 1854 to 1891).

American writing and was bringing to completion the first major study of the subject, which would be published in 1916.[40] Just the previous year Darío had himself engaged with an early US attempt to include Spanish-American poetry in the Spanish canon, E. C. Hills and S. G. Morley's anthology, *Modern Spanish Lyrics*. He commended their introduction as 'magisterial', quoting, with seeming admiration, Hills' judgements on Garcilaso, Quevedo, and others, approving of the sophisticated discussion of prosody, interjecting comments about his own verse forms, and noting, without comment, Hills' remark about Darío's use of assonance on alternate lines in his alexandrines as 'without precedent'.[41] Perhaps inevitably, Darío found fault with the Hispanic American selection, which he calls 'very limited'. Several countries were represented by just one poet, and even by just one poem. Eleven countries had no representation at all. But even here he found things to praise in the introduction, from which he quotes extensively, concluding that the book will be of great use for students and readers of Castilian poetry. One quotation he includes without comment is to the effect that the 'grandiloquent' José Santos Chocano is a 'disciple of Darío's'.[42] The one poem of Darío's that Hills and Morley include is, interestingly, 'A Roosevelt', about which Darío wrote to the editors: 'I do not think today as I did when I wrote those verses.'[43]

The Hispanic Society of America offered the one exception to the general lack of interest. On 8 January 1915, Huntington invited Darío to the HSA to receive the Hispanic Society's Silver Medal of Arts and Literature and he also visited Darío in his hotel, possibly taking de la Selva with him, possibly de la Selva's introduction to Darío. In addition, he co-sponsored (with Columbia University's relatively new outreach association, the Institute of Arts and Sciences) the event on the evening of Thursday, 4 February 1915 where Darío would read a long new poem about the need for peace. Perhaps tellingly, on the official invitation Darío's name came below that of Bermúdez:

---

[40] Alfred Coester, *A Bibliography of Spanish-American Literature*, New York: Columbia University Press, 1912; and *The Literary History of Spanish America*, New York: The Macmillan Company, 1916.
[41] Elijah Clarence Hills and S. Griswold Morley, eds, *Modern Spanish Lyrics*, New York: Henry Holt and Co., 1913; Rubén Darío, 'Un libro norteamericano', *La Nación*, 15 September 1913, p. 7; 16 September 1913, p. 9; 18 September 1913, p. 11, in *Escritos dispersos de Rubén Darío, recogidos de periódicos de Buenos Aires*, ed. Pedro Luis Barcia, La Plata: Universidad Nacional de La Plata, 1977, pp. 274–87, with quotations from pp. 274, 277, 277, and 278.
[42] Darío, 'Un libro norteamericano', pp. 278 and 285.
[43] Hills and Morley, *Modern Spanish Lyrics*, p. 314.

THE HORRORS OF WAR, THE NECESSITY OF PEACE
AND THE MEANS OF OBTAINING IT
SEÑOR ALEJANDRO BERMÚDEZ
Formerly Secretary Nicaragua Legation at Washington
and
SEÑOR RUBÉN DARÍO
Poet and Author.[44]

The event took place in room 309 of Havemeyer Hall, a steeply raked lecture theatre in the Department of Chemistry. The building had been funded by Theodore Havemeyer, whose money came from the family sugar business. Professor Adolphe Cohn, head of the Department of Romance Languages and Literatures since 1890, introduced the speakers. Bermúdez spoke first, then Darío said a few words about his poem, before reading 'Pax'. None of this sounds particularly controversial, but the event occasioned wildly divergent accounts.

Las Novedades reported that the capacity audience had listened 'ecstatically'.[45] According to Alejandro Bermúdez, in a letter to his wife, attenders included 'a multitude of ladies and gentlemen from Cuba, Colombia, Argentina, Chile, and Costa Rica, as well as prominent figures from the USA such as bankers, senators, journalists'.[46] 'I think I did a serious job', he reported, 'brilliant and with many highlights ... The reception was sensational'.[47] Darío was much applauded too, he notes. He estimated the number attending at 800 to 1,000. Bermúdez was writing soon after the event, but he certainly had an interest in it being considered a success and so may well have exaggerated: the hall's capacity is 330 and the local *Columbia Daily Spectator* reported an audience of about 150.[48]

Other accounts introduced negative notes. Pedro Henríquez Ureña, writing soon afterwards and presumably (since he hadn't attended) basing himself on reports from friends, wrote to Alfonso Reyes that the audience was 'numerous but not select'—because invitations had gone out to diplomats rather than writers.[49] Arturo Torres Rioseco, who did attend, called it a

---

[44] Reproduced in Theodore S. Beardsley, Jr, 'Rubén Darío and the Hispanic Society: The Holograph Manuscript of *¡Pax!*', *Hispanic Review*, 35, no. 1 (1967), 1–42, at 3.
[45] In Demorizi, *Papeles*, pp. 173–74, at p. 173.
[46] Alejandro Bermúdez to his wife, 9 February 1915. In Demorizi, *Papeles*, pp. 176–78, at p. 177.
[47] Bermúdez in Demorizi, *Papeles*, p. 177.
[48] *Columbia Daily Spectator*, 6 February 1915, p. 4.
[49] Letter from Pedro Henríquez Ureña to Alfonso Reyes (11 May 1915), *Epistolario íntimo*, vol. 2, p. 241.

failure because Darío, never renowned as a good reader of his own work, mumbled his way through his poem.[50]

Thirty-five years later, in a lecture for the Ateneo Americano in Washington, DC, Salomón de la Selva recalled every detail:

> Y bien, llegó la noche del acto en la Universidad. Oh Dolor. Para la presentación del exquisito poeta no se halló disponible más que una vieja sala de clases de química, lo mas destartalado imaginable, una especie de anfiteatro con graderías que convergían hacia un mostrador largo lleno de retortas, de grifos larguiruchos para el agua y de quemadores Bunsen, con un fondo formado por un gran pizarrón ya blanquecino de viejo. Y detrás de ese mostrador tuvo el poeta que presentarse y leer sus versos. Presidía la ceremonia el anciano Professor Cohn, Jefe entonces del Departamento de Idiomas Romances, maestro de francés, idioma al que estaba supeditado el español. Y de público no había arriba de catorce personas: Mr Huntington con su señora; no sé quién más de Norteamérica; el Dr Luis H. Debayle, de Nicaragua; el Dr Luis Felipe Corea, también nicaragüense; y un puñado de periodistas dominicanos.[51]

> [And so the night of the reading at the university arrived. What grief! For the performance by such an exquisite poet the best they could manage was an old chemistry classroom, as shabby as could be imagined, a sort of raked amphitheatre converging on a counter full of retorts, oversized water taps, and Bunsen burners, in front of an old blackboard whitened with age. It was behind this counter that the poet was introduced and had to read his poem. Chairing the event was the ancient Professor Cohn, then head of the Department of Romance Languages, a teacher of French, the language to which Spanish was subordinate. The audience was no more than fourteen strong: Mr Huntington and his wife; other North Americans I didn't know; Dr Luis H. Debayle, from Nicaragua; Dr Luis Felipe Corea, also Nicaraguan; and a handful of Dominican journalists.]

---

[50] Arturo Torres Rioseco, *Vida y poesía de Rubén Darío*, Buenos Aires: Emecé editores, 1944, p. 104.

[51] Salomón de la Selva, 'Discurso sobre Rubén Darío', *Antología Mayor III: Ensayos*, pp. 276–88, at pp. 281–82. The Ateneo Americano in Washington ran from 1949 to 1959. This lecture was attended by Juan Ramón Jiménez, who was living in Washington at the time while teaching at the University of Maryland.

Room 309 was not exactly an old classroom—it was less than 20 years old; but it was a chemistry teaching room, so probably full of equipment and perhaps more 'destartalado' than the salons at the National Arts Club that de la Selva was used to from PSA meetings. Amado Nervo had also read in that room and Ramón Pérez de Ayala would later lecture there; so there was no slight to Darío involved. The lecture theatre is now what the Columbia University website describes as the 'signature architectural feature' of Charles Follen McKim's original six-building campus, doubtless having been tarted up somewhat since 1915.[52] The event was hosted—de la Selva complains—by 'el anciano Professor Cohn', chair of the Department of Romance Languages and Literatures, a French specialist despite the event being entirely in Spanish. Cohn was 64 years old in 1915, but then de la Selva was only 21, so the professor did probably seem 'anciano'. Most startlingly, de la Selva remembers an audience of 14—against the *Daily Spectator*'s 150 and Bermúdez's 800 to 1,000. No doubt wishful thinking in Bermúdez's case, although it's intriguing—and perhaps more puzzling—that de la Selva should have wanted to exaggerate the inability of anyone in New York, Hispanic or Anglo, himself excluded, to give full due to the prince of poets. To sum up the occasion, de la Selva quite consciously chooses the word 'dolor' that resounds like a mournful toll through Darío's poem, 'El gran cosmópolis'.

*

For years, Darío's only steady income had come from the articles he wrote for the Buenos Aires newspaper *La Nación*—*crónicas*, in the tradition of those that José Martí had written from New York, many for the same newspaper. Poverty-stricken, Darío seems to have written intermittently, or at least taken notes, some via dictation to his son, during his hospital stay; and his final contribution to *La Nación*, 'Apuntaciones de hospital' [Notes from hospital], was published in August 1915, dated 'New York July 1915', though he had left the city in April.[53] From one perspective, this is a disjointed piece of writing, perhaps reflecting the circumstances of its composition. Only four pages long, the *crónica* is divided into eight sections of varying length, several of which recount incidents from his hospital stay. The pieces were written—or give the impression of having been written—on the evening of each reported incident, with their tone often shifting sharply.

---

[52] <http://ieor.columbia.edu/files/seasdepts/industrial-engineering-operations-research/pdf-files/Havemeyer_Map.pdf> accessed December 2018.
[53] Rubén Darío Contreras, Darío's first-born son, 22 years old, was living in New York at the time.

A reasonably coherent opening explains how he caught a chill on coming out of the restaurant where *Las Novedades* had been giving him a dinner. By the time he got back to his room, he was almost unconscious and with a high fever. Fortunately, his friend Dr Aníbal Zelaya was with him and could arrange for his admittance into the French Hospital. 'Mi Martín Reibel centroamericano', Darío calls him, with reference to his doctor in Buenos Aires. He immediately thinks of Lélian, the *maudit* Paul Verlaine, whose experience of hospital was extensive enough to provide material for a whole book (*Mes Hôpitaux* [1891]). The hospital itself he describes as 'mediocre and antiquated'. Despite its name, hardly anybody speaks French. Some of the nurses are nuns, which makes the hospital feel like a cross between a prison and a convent, even if some of the lay nurses are really pretty. Old habits clearly die hard.

A French doctor suddenly appears, takes some blood, and is gone again. A nurse comes in to give him medicine; he hears the other patients moaning and coughing; he hears the rapid footsteps of the night nurses. Then 'around two in the morning', he hears something that sounds like the howling of a wolf, the screams of an animal being tortured—a 'demonic, lycanthropic, and tragic ululation'. New York has rarely seemed so infernal.

> La soledad parece que se duplicase. El aislamiento, la casi destrucción de la personalidad, el sentirse solitario, abandonado, olvidado, ponen en el alma una inexpresable opresión de angustia y de desesperanza, sobre todo, en un pueblo de seres distintos, de idioma distinto, de espíritu y mentalidad distintos.
>
> [It seems as if loneliness is doubled. The isolation, the near-destruction of the personality, feeling alone, abandoned, forgotten, press on the soul with an inexpressible weight of anguish and despair, especially in a nation of different beings, different language, different spirit and mentality.]

That emphasis on *difference*, not just differences of language and mentality but 'different beings', really seems to underline the chasm between the two cultures, the 'two Americas'.

At times Darío echoes the sentiments and even the vocabulary of 'La gran cosmópolis':

> Nieva. Un mundo de recuerdos me llena el cerebro. Todos mis afectos están lejos de mí. Soy algo que apenas existe entre diez millones de hombres duros, prácticos, que hacen su labor de cíclopes y de gnomos,

de edificios monstruosos, de una estética infernal. Y si me fijo más en la montaña que hierve, llego a pensar que ya no soy ni algo; soy nadie; no soy. Aquí el amor, la caridad, el hogar, la amistad, la generosidad, todo tiene un fin utilitario. Se cambia de sentir con facilidad, y con tranquilidad. No hay el apasionamiento ni el relámpago latinos.[54]

[It's snowing. A world of memories fills my head. Everything I hold dear is far away. I'm something that hardly exists among ten million hard and practical men doing the work of cyclops and gnomes, of monstrous buildings, of an infernal aesthetic. And if I stare any longer at the swarming mass, I come to think that I'm no longer anything; that I'm nobody; that I am not. Here, love, charity, the home, friendship, generosity, everything has a utilitarian end. Feelings are easily and calmly changed. There is no Latin passion or fire.]

Here in New York all the human virtues of love, charity, and friendship have a utilitarian end—Rodó's point exactly. As the Uruguayan had put it: 'a well-laid fire to which no one has set a match'.[55] No passion, no fire.

According to other accounts—not necessarily accurate—Darío was visited in the hospital by José Ignacio Vargas Vila, brother of the writer, and by Juan Arana Torrol, but in 'Apuntaciones' Darío only reports four visitors, none of them Hispanic. Early on, the visit of an unnamed—and possibly to Darío unknown—woman ('robust and friendly matron'), carrying a large bunch of tulips, briefly raises his spirits. Her Spanish is limited to 'Buenos días', so they converse in his fractured English, with the doctor helping out. The piece ends—almost absurdly—with the arrival of Archer Huntington who, Darío writes, deserves a chapter of his own, which he never managed to write.[56] Earlier he reports the visit of Robert J. Shores and his wife Marie, among the best friends he has had in New York, Darío says. The Shores had held a dinner for Darío on 1 January 1915 at their house at 248 West 76th Street and the journalist Frances England had described Shores as Darío's 'friend

---

[54] 'Apuntaciones de hospital', in *La Nación*, 22 August 1915, p. 5. Reproduced in *Escritos dispersos de Rubén Darío, recogidos de periódicos de Buenos Aires*, ed. Pedro Luis Barcia, La Plata: Universidad Nacional de La Plata, 1977, pp. 305–09, at pp. 306–07. See also Susana Zanetti, 'Itinerario de las crónicas de Rubén Darío en *La Nación*', in *Rubén Darío en La Nación de Buenos Aires, 1892-1916*, Buenos Aires: Eudeba, 2004, pp. 9–59.
[55] See above, p. 59.
[56] The fact of Huntington's visit rather contradicts de la Selva's memory: 'Y recuerdo a su amigo el millonario / De Nueva York, hecho el desentendido' (*Antología Mayor/I Poesías*, p. 345).

and literary representative'.[57] Darío calls Shores 'the foremost essayist in the United States' and compares him with Dr Johnson and Jonathan Swift, comparisons which say more about Darío's gratitude for Shores's willingness to help Darío get his books published in English than they do about his critical acuity: Shores's essays are long forgotten.[58] However, he was a US writer with no particular axe to grind who had a genuine interest in Latin American poetry and who was clearly also concerned about Darío's physical well-being, so the poet's gratitude was well-earned.

The day following the dinner he had given for Darío, Robert Shores wrote to the semi-monthly Chicago literary magazine *The Dial* to gently berate the literary establishment, himself included, for moments when 'our own ignorance of foreign literature become[s] so obvious as to be embarrassing'. He continued:

> When Señor Ruben Dario arrived in New York not long ago, we went about asking one another, 'Who is this Dario, and what has he done? And this same Dario is the foremost poet in the Spanish tongue today, author of twenty-odd books of poetry and prose, and acknowledged a classic writer by all Spanish-speaking peoples.[59]

After Darío's death the following year, Shores wrote again to *The Dial*, striking a rather different note from his previous letter but offering a valuable pen-portrait of Darío in New York in 1915:

> Though I saw Ruben Dario a number of times and talked with him in rather intimate fashion regarding his plans and his work, he was something of an enigma to me. In personal appearance he was swarthy, stout, and gave the impression of being a larger man than he really was. He was not in fact very tall, but he seemed tall as well as broad.

---

[57] See 'Social Notes', *New York Times*, 2 January 1915, p. 9; and Frances England, 'Latin American Poet Suggests an International Thought Exchange to Help Spanish Women Free Themselves', *New York Times*, 8 February 1915, p. 5.

[58] Shores' publications are *Gay Gods and Merry Mortals: Some Excursions in Verse*, New York: Broadway, 1910 and *New Brooms*, Indianapolis: Bobbs-Merrill, 1913. In 1917, he was also publishing poetry books at 225 Fifth Avenue. The Huntington-financed English edition of Darío was originally announced as translated by Thomas Walsh, Salomón de la Selva, and Robert Shores, but de la Selva seems to have eliminated the translations by Shores as not up to his exacting standards (*Current Opinion*, 60 [1916], p. 428).

[59] Robert J. Shores, 'Entertaining Genius Unawares', *The Dial*, 58 (16 January 1915), 41.

The Changing of the Poetic Guard (1915) 99

He had a pleasant smile; but when his face was in repose, he had almost an oriental cast of countenance. His head was fine,—the sort a sculptor likes; the sort which looks well upon a medal or coin. Dario was not sociable. He did not like to meet people; seemed really to be averse to making new acquaintances, though he was affable enough when he did meet them. In many respects he was like a child; when he was pleased with anything, he showed his pleasure very plainly. He was vain but not conceited; he did not boast but accepted praise, and even flattery, with great equanimity. He liked to hear his poetry praised and on one occasion asked me to read three times a letter which he had received from a lady who admired his poems, and each time he exclaimed, 'That is good for me.' During his stay in New York, he complained very much of the cold, and did not like to go out unless the sun was hot. He was very remiss in keeping his engagements, and would often telephone at the last moment to say he could not attend a repast given in his honor.[60]

The Spanish journalist Julio Camba spent 1916 in the USA, mostly in New York, which he hated. He read Shores's letter and opined that Darío's exclamation was what the French—always blame the French—call 'hablar negro' [talking black]. The language and the thought, and indeed the poetry, Camba says: 'toda la obra de Rubén Darío es la obra de un negro de genio' [all Rubén Darío's work is the work of a black genius].[61]

The only other writer to feature in Darío's piece is again recalled for her kindness:

Pienso escribir largamente en La Nación sobre el desarrollo mental de la mujer en los Estados Unidos ... Me refiero, por ejemplo, a esa encantadora Mrs Woodruff cuyos exquisitos libros son para pocos, y la cual tuvo la gentileza de presentarme como guest en una recepción que presidía el ex embajador Mr Choate, a lo más brillante de la intelectualidad de la imperial ciudad.[62]

I'm thinking of writing a long piece for *La Nación* about the mental development of women in the United States ... I'm referring, for

---

[60] Shores' letter is quoted by Theodore Stanton in his column 'Literary Affairs in France', *The Dial*, 60 (8 June 1916), 528.
[61] Julio Camba, *Un año en el otro mundo*, Madrid: Biblioteca Nueva, 1917, p. 90.
[62] 'Apuntaciones de hospital', 308. Darío had long been interested in this issue, even writing 'La mujer americana' in 1892, before he had visited the USA.

example, to that enchanting Mrs Woodruff whose exquisite books are for the select few, and who was kind enough to introduce me as a special guest at a reception for the ex-ambassador Mr Choate to the intellectual elite of the imperial city.

On 10 February 1915, Mrs Woodruff had invited Darío to a reception for the Authors' League of America at her splendid house at 14 East 68th Street.[63] Joseph Hodges Choate was a distinguished lawyer who had spent six years as President McKinley's ambassador in the United Kingdom, but there is certainly an element of social snobbery on Darío's part here: he must have been desperate to indicate to his Latin American readership that *somebody* in New York beyond his immediate friends had recognised his significance. Again, Darío's critical judgement is awry when he notes that Mrs Woodruff's exquisite books are for the few. The books—written for what would now be described as the young adult market—were far from exquisite and they were read by many: very many indeed. Helen Smith Woodruff was an independently wealthy Southern lady and she gave her royalties to charity. *The Lady of the Lighthouse*, which is about a woman who helps blind children, raised $300,000 for the New York Association for the Blind—the equivalent of more than $7 million today.[64] Yet there is no resentment in Darío's words or tone for Mrs Woodruff's wealth, just an appreciation of her intellect and discernment.

'Apuntaciones de hospital' is quite atypical in that Darío's *crónicas* tend to recount the arrivals, impressions, and departures of a man almost constantly on the move, either from place to place or within a city like Paris. As Julio Ramos notes, the *crónica* is really a form of travel writing.[65] By contrast, there is here a sense of stasis—enforced of course in Darío's situation. The world comes to him in the hospital, but that feels like a metaphor for his life in New York where he has largely been dependent on

---

[63] 'Greets Authors' League', *New York Times*, 11 February 1915, p. 9. The Hispanic Society of America was probably key because of Archer Huntington's connections to other New York institutions like the Authors' League. See also the letter from Pedro Henríquez Ureña to Alfonso Reyes (11 May 1916), *Epistolario íntimo*, vol. 2, p. 241.

[64] See <www.encyclopediaofalabama.org/article/h-3012> accessed December 2018. Nine years later Mrs Woodruff committed suicide by jumping from a second-storey window of her house.

[65] Julio Ramos, *Divergent Modernities: Culture and Politics in Nineteenth-Century Latin America*, trans. John D. Blanco, Durham, NC: Duke University Press, 2001, pp. 126, 173. See also Graciela Montaldo, 'Guía Rubén Darío', in Rubén Darío, *Viajes de un cosmopolita extremo*, ed. Graciela Montaldo, Mexico: Fondo de Cultura Económica, 2013, pp. 11–51.

the kindness of strangers. The *crónica* has little coherence or consistency but, as so often, much depends on the context in which something is read. Read biographically, the piece is an index of Darío's declining health; read against his other *crónicas*, it just looks disjointed and incoherent. But read alongside Baudelaire's *petits poèmes en prose*, his classic take on Parisian modernity, which were also first published in newspapers, or alongside some of Juan Ramón Jiménez's prose pieces in the *Diario de un poeta recien casado*, or even alongside *The Waste Land*, and what might seem trivial and disjointed begins to look like an extended image of life in the modern city *in extremis*, fragmentary in form and offering a compelling metaphor of the challenges of modernity in its central collapsing consciousness trying with limited success to register what goes on around him. It's a haunting piece, particularly because it comes right at the end of Darío's career, one of the last things—if not the very last—he wrote. Darío's extraordinary career has never been integrated into the larger story of modernism, but 'Apuntaciones' does offer a means to do so, as—against the grain—Darío finally leaves behind the Parisian lodestar that had previously guided his writing, and produces a gripping version of life and death in Manhattan. When Darío sent that piece to *La Nación*, T. S. Eliot was still in Harvard and Ezra Pound was in London, and William Carlos Williams was delivering babies just across the Hudson.

As we saw in the previous chapter, Darío's views—inasmuch as 'views' can be inferred from poems—were hardly consistent over the years, but then neither were the circumstances in which he lived. If his mature years had been dominated by the multiple effects of the Spanish *desastre* of 1898, his final months were lived in the shadow of a war which seemed to herald the destruction of all the values of European civilisation that he had held dear. Little surprise, then, that his calls for peace should be coupled with a sense that the future of the world was now in the hands of the American continent. As he says in the final lines of 'Pax', the poem he read at Columbia University in February 1915:

> Ved el ejemplo amargo de la Europa deshecha;
> Ved las trincheras fúnebres, las tierras sanguinosas,
> Y la Piedad y el Duelo, sollozando los dos:
> No, no dejeis al Odio que dispare su flecha,
> Llevad a los altares de la Paz miel y rosas:
> ¡ Paz en la inmensa América! Paz en nombre de Dios.[66]

---

[66] Beardsley, 'Rubén Darío and the Hispanic Society', 29.

> Look at the bitter example of Europe undone;
> At the funereal trenches and the bloody earth,
> And Piety and Grief, sobbing together:
> No, don't let Hatred fire off its arrow,
> Take honey and roses to the altars of Peace:
> Peace in America the immense! Peace in the name of God!

José Agustín Balseiro sees this poem as 'his final and mature testament of continental transcendence'.[67] In the essay he wrote for the Chicago journal *Poetry*, after Darío's death, de la Selva had him coming to America 'to preach peace, and to work for a Pan-American Union based on a community of ideals and the intellectual fellowship of the two Americas'.[68] De la Selva may have been projecting his own ideals onto Darío, but there is at least an element of truth in his assessment. 'Pax' was a word copiously displayed in the new Pan American Union building in Washington, DC. The director general, John Barrett, described it as the PAU's 'shibboleth'.[69] So Darío's poem could perhaps accurately be described as 'Pan-American' in an almost official sense, particularly in the four lines he added to the poem after the reading:

> Y pues aquí está el foco de una cultura nueva,
> que sus principios lleva desde el Norte hasta el Sur,
> hagamos la Unión viva que el nuevo triunfo lleva;
> *The Star-Spangled Banner*, con el blanco y azur ...[70]

> And since here is the seat of a new culture,
> its principles carried from the North to the South,
> let us make live the Union won by this new triumph;
> *The Star-Spangled Banner*, with the blue and the white ...

In an interview with the *New York Times* conducted shortly before his Columbia reading (but published afterwards), Darío announced that he would 'go to Buenos Ayres and other Spanish speaking cities of South

---

[67] José Agustín Balseiro, 'Rubén Darío y Estados Unidos', in his *Seis estudios sobre Rubén Darío*, Madrid: Gredos, 1967, pp. 117–43, at p. 143.
[68] Salomón de la Selva, 'Rubén Darío', *Poetry*, VIII, no. 4 (July 1916), 200–04, at p. 203.
[69] John Barrett, *The Pan American Union: Peace, Friendship, Commerce*, Washington, DC: Pan American Union, 1911, p. 137.
[70] See Niall Binns, '"¡Pax!" de Rubén Darío: testamento poético y acto de clausura', *Anales de Literatura Española*, 28 (2016), 53–69, at 62–63.

America and start a nucleus of literary men, who will come to the United States to become acquainted with some of the writers of this country. We know very little of your present day poets, and you here know still less of the writers of South America.'[71] It is likely that his enthusiasm fired de la Selva, but not impossible that the influence was the other way around.

De la Selva's views about Darío were inevitably complicated. The elder poet was undoubtedly a father-figure and a writer of enormous stature, but therefore also in some sense a rival. In addition, de la Selva recognised—and largely shared—Darío's ambivalent feelings about Nicaragua. In a letter written in 1919, de la Selva recalls how news of Darío's embrace of Argentina had been received at home in León:

> Darío, her greatest poet, after gaining to universal reputation, was accorded—as a most unique honour—the citizenship of the Argentine Republic for an ode he sang in praise of that great country. I remember how ill-worded was the cable-news of that event that reached Nicaragua. We were given to understand that Darío had of his free will renounced Nicaragua for an honour from a prosperous nation.—That day, only the little children ate their dinner at my home. My heart broke, with shame, with pain, when, without a word, my father took all Darío's books and ordered a man-servant take horse to the sea-shore and cast them to the tide. When the whole family had gathered around my mother, late that evening, for the family devotions that always sealed our days and prepared us for a Christian night, my father's order was terrible to hearts that loved the poet with excess of pride in him. 'Henceforth,' my father said, 'let not the name of Rubén Darío be spoken in this house.'[72]

After Darío's death, de la Selva wrote a piece for the New York magazine *Revista Universal*, under a pseudonym, about Darío's funeral in León.[73] While describing the magnificent ceremony the poet was given, the essay

---

[71] England, 'Latin American Poet Suggests', p. 5. (The women of the article title seem something of an afterthought to Darío, although the journalist chose to emphasise the point.)

[72] Letter from Salomón de la Selva to Jessie B. Rittenhouse, JBRC (2 August 1919). JBRC is the Jessie B. Rittenhouse Collection at Rollins College, Winter Park, Florida.

[73] Hipólito Mattonel [Salomón de la Selva], 'Ecos de la muerte de Rubén Darío', *Revista Universal*, 3, no. 27 (1916), 27.

is marked by a real bitterness towards the backward Nicaraguan society that had made life so difficult for Darío, effectively driving him out of the country. Returning there to die was the first time in Darío's life that he had any patriotic feelings, de la Selva suggests. (The pseudonym may have been a form of self-protection.) But de la Selva emphasises that Darío was made in Nicaragua: he didn't leave in order to learn how to write, he left in order to find readers who would appreciate his writing. The essay appears under an infamously intrusive photograph of Darío on his deathbed.

De la Selva wrote another essay about Darío which was published in Mexico and Costa Rica in 1941, on the 25th anniversary of Darío's death.[74] Here Darío is seen as a large literary figure to be compared with Dante and Shakespeare and Shelley: he offers a 'true encyclopedia de our America'.[75] Finally, in 1957, as part of his 'Evocación de Píndaro', de la Selva dedicated several stanzas to Darío, one of which paints a startlingly black picture of the poet during these months in New York:

> Yo lo recuerdo, presa de terrores,
> sumido en el dolor y en la penuria,
> con el color terroso de panal destruído,
> con la mirada de águila, extraviada,
> con la sonrisa en boca adolorida,
> con no sé qué, animal o primitivo,
> que buscaba rincón donde morirse,
> escondido, de espaldas a la Muerte.
> El invierno era crudo, el cuarto frío.
> Como en un cuento de Edgar Poe, un negro
> magro y macabro le bailaba danzas
> grotescas, de esqueleto,
> descoyuntadas,
> le cantaba lamentos sincopados,
> con la bocaza abierta roja y blanca.
> Los rascacielos (¡nuevos!) levantaban brazos
> de imploración y de tortura antiguas.
> El río iba de luto, iba de llanto,
> iba de miedo a dar a la bahía,
> frustrado el darse al mar, ¡como Darío![76]

---

[74] Reprinted in Salomón de la Selva, 'Rubén Darío', *Antología Mayor/III: Ensayos*, pp. 266–75.
[75] De la Selva, 'Rubén Darío', p. 266.
[76] De la Selva, *Antología Mayor/I Poesías*, p. 344.

The Changing of the Poetic Guard (1915)   105

[I remember him, terror-stricken,
pain-ridden, sunk in poverty,
his skin the colour of bleached cotton,
his eagle's glance wild-eyed,
his smile a rictus round his mouth,
like—I hardly know—an animal or savage
looking for a corner to hide away
and expire, his back to Death.
The winter was cruel, his room cold.
Like in a story by Poe, a scrawny
and macabre negro danced for him
grotesque jigs, skeletal,
disjointed;
and sang him syncopated blues
with a mouth gaping red and white.
The skyscrapers (new ones!) raised their arms
imploringly, victims of ancestral torture.
The river grieved, the river cried,
as if fearful of reaching the bay,
yet eager to give itself to the sea—like Darío.]

The invocation of Poe brings Darío's New York sojourn full circle. The scrawny and macabre negro is no doubt an image of imminent death, but also perhaps a reminder—though who knows with what intent on de la Selva's part—of Darío's African ancestry, which clean-blooded Spaniards like Julio Camba were not beyond noticing in print. The river wants to give itself to the sea, like Darío: the way home, to Nicaragua or to death, which would now amount to the same thing.

The intricate geography of New York's waterways has always left its rivers bereft of a clear literary identity. The short passages between Manhattan and New Jersey across the Hudson, and Manhattan and Long Island across the East River make the waterways look truly riverine, yet the East River isn't actually a river at all, and both stretches of water give so quickly into Upper New York Bay and the Atlantic beyond that the world's vastness has always seemed so close—which is doubtless why the river is so fearful of reaching the bay, where it will quickly lose its identity. A poem referencing New York, death, Poe, and the river inevitably calls to mind 'The Mystery of Marie Roget', Poe's story based on the death of the beautiful young Mary Rogers, whose mutilated body was found floating in the Hudson in 1843, the story that began modernism's fascination with death.

Shortly after Darío left New York, the chances of the USA staying out of the European conflict sharply decreased with the sinking of the *Lusitania* off the Irish coast on 7 May. De la Selva's friend, Joyce Kilmer, made a public impression with his poem 'The White Ships and the Red', which was given prominence in the *New York Times*:

> When God's great voice assembles
> The fleet on Judgment Day,
> The ghosts of ruined ships will rise
> In sea and strait and bay.
> Though they have lain for ages
> Beneath the changeless flood,
> They shall be white as silver,
> But one—shall be like blood.[77]

Befriending Pedro, Loving Edna

An early snapshot of Salomón de la Selva in New York comes in a letter from Pedro Henríquez Ureña to his friend and constant correspondent, the Mexican writer and intellectual, Alfonso Reyes, written from New York on 3 July 1915. It seems that de la Selva and Henríquez Ureña had been introduced by Manuel Florentino Cestero, the Dominican journalist and writer: Henríquez Ureña mentions a dinner with the three of them plus Mariano Brull, the Cuban poet who had been mentored in Havana by Henríquez Ureña and then posted to New York to work in the Cuban consulate. Pedro reports that Frank Crane had referred to de la Selva as the best young poet in the country. An intellectual of Henríquez Ureña's calibre was never likely to take Crane's judgement seriously, but he sat up when he heard that the respected journal *The Forum* was about to publish one of de la Selva's poems: 'a consecration', he calls it in the letter.[78] A pen-portrait follows:

---

[77] Joyce Kilmer, 'The White Ships and the Red', *New York Times*, 16 May 1915, SM1.
[78] De la Selva's 'The Tale from Faerieland' appeared in *The Forum* in July 1915. Perhaps inspired by this example, Henríquez Ureña submitted an essay about Anatole France, which appeared in the journal in November. There were only two other poems in that July issue: one by Edna Millay, 'The Dream', with the issue dominated by essays discussing the war. In the same 1915 volume, as well as Henríquez Ureña's essay, is Carlo de Fornaro explaining the latest development in the saga of the Mexican Revolution while offering a vindication of the new president Venustiano Carranza, and an essay by Marius de Zayas on modern art.

> De la Selva is twenty-one years old; shorter than me, fair, with a flat face and round cheeks. A great enthusiast, if not exactly magnetic. Widely read, especially in English poetry. He's friends with half the literary world, and through him I've met some curious people, such as a blind poet called Doyle who composes conceptual sonnets along the lines of Milton, and a Polish beginner who is all Slavic soul (Gorki's *The Three*, not Dostoevsky) and a young yankee who seriously studies the literary art of advertising: the last two belong to a unique group called the Order of Ideal Friendship.

'De la Selva will be a magnificent poet', Henríquez Ureña declares, and he puts him alongside other young poets such as Joyce Kilmer and Shaemas O'Sheel.[79] It was de la Selva, the 21-year-old ingénu, who had just introduced the established writer Henríquez Ureña to the famous Joyce Kilmer: the young man really did know everybody.

Salomón quickly became Pedro's 'amigo predilecto' [best friend],[80] and Pedro became Salomón's mentor. Almost ten years older, and from a family which formed part of the Caribbean intellectual aristocracy, Pedro's influence on the young Nicaraguan was immense, as de la Selva always recognised. Pedro's mother, Salomé Ureña, had been one of the region's finest poets as well as an educator who had worked closely with the great Puerto Rican writer and intellectual, Eugenio María de Hostos, during the years he spent in the Dominican Republic. She had died in 1897, but Pedro's father, Francisco Henríquez y Carvajal, and his uncle, Federico, were both involved in Dominican politics: Federico had also been close to José Martí. Pedro had lived in New York with his father between 1901 and 1904, becoming fluent in English, then travelled widely, including a spell in Mexico City, before returning to New York in November 1914.[81] He also had published books to his name. The following year his father would be elected President of the Dominican Republic, a position that the US State Department would prevent him from occupying. Pedro's brother Max also became a literary

---

[79] Letter from Pedro Henríquez Ureña to Alfonso Reyes, *Epistolario íntimo, 1906–1946*, ed. Juan Jacobo de Lara, 3 vols., Santo Domingo: UNPHU, 1981–83, vol. 1, p. 61. Pedro also sent some of de la Selva's poems to his Mexican friend, the poet Julio Torri: Letter from Julio Torri to Pedro Henríquez Ureña (5 September 1915) in Julio Torri, *Epistolarios*, Mexico: Universidad Nacional Autónoma de México, Coordinación de Humanidades, 1995, p. 226.

[80] Arturo Torres Rioseco, *La hebra en la aguja*, Mexico City: Editorial Cultura, 1965, p. 31.

[81] See Victoria Núñez, 'Writing the Migration: Pedro Henríquez Ureña and Early Dominican Migrants to New York City', *MELUS*, 36, no. 3 (2011), 111–35.

critic and historian, and his sister Camila was an academic who taught at Vassar for many years and who is the focus, along with her mother, of Julia Álvarez's novel, *In the Name of Salomé.*

Despite his love of the classics, Pedro Henríquez Ureña was excited by novelty in the arts, writing in Spanish about experimental writers such as Paul Fort and H. D. Shortly after they became acquainted, Pedro and Salomón went together to Carnegie Hall to see a performance of Alexander Scriabin's *Prometheus: The Poem of Fire* with its colour organ which projected coloured light onto a screen in the concert hall rather than sound, the machine being specially built for the performance by Preston S. Miller, president of the Illuminating Engineering Society.

After Pedro died, in Argentina in 1946, de la Selva wrote a series of eight articles for the Mexican newspaper *El Universal*, which recall their life together in New York and offer perhaps the richest picture we have of the Hispanic life of the city in the years 1915 to 1919, while also giving us a sense of the friendships the two men forged.[82] De la Selva's own networks were already wide, obviously facilitated by his complete fluency in English. He recalls a spring day before the First World War, perhaps 1914, when Frank Crane took him to the Hotel Brevoort for lunch to meet the young Chicago journalist Edgar Mowrer, who had with him a highly refined young man called Ralph Roeder, who became one of de la Selva's best friends. Roeder had just come back from Mexico where, like John Reed, his fellow Harvard graduate, he had become a partisan of Pancho Villa—who was probably about as far removed from a Harvard graduate as it's possible to be. Whereas Nicaragua and the Dominican Republic—homelands of de la Selva and Henríquez Ureña—would struggle to make an impact on US consciousness, despite the presence there of US forces, Mexico, with its ever-developing revolution and constant stream of exiles, remained *the* Hispanic reference point in New York during these years.

For all his refined manners and love of the Renaissance, Roeder was a man of the left, as de la Selva became at this time, working on the Socialist journal *The Call*. Here de la Selva name-checks Charley Ervin, who took over as editor in 1916; the Rand School of Social Science, centre of Socialist activity; and Clement Wood, the poet and anarchist whom de la Selva met there.[83] Socialist

---

[82] The articles appeared between 12 July 1946 and 4 October 1946. They are quoted from the version contained in Salomón de la Selva, 'In Memoriam Pedro Henríquez Ureña', *Antología Mayor III/Ensayos*, pp. 99–165. When mentioning the names de la Selva recalls, I have made silent corrections to the spellings where either he has slightly misremembered or they have been mangled in publication.

[83] De la Selva, 'In Memoriam', p. 111. On *The Call*, see Charles W. Ervin, *Homegrown*

circles in New York were full of exiles, but rarely Hispanic ones: they tended to come from Bucharest and Petrograd, the Abruzzo and Sicily. In this milieu de la Selva read *Das Kapital* and rubbed shoulders with figures like Carlo Tresca, the Industrial Workers of the World organiser—later assassinated by the Mafia, Benjamin Feigenbaum, the Jewish editor of *Vorwärts*, and Joseph Gollomb, journalist and English teacher at the Rand School.

Through Clement Wood de la Selva also met the poets Floyd Dell and Louis Untermeyer: 'We formed a daring group, committed to renewing poetry through political economy and psychology, and to remaking the world through renewed poetry.'[84] Salomón was the baby of the group: in his early 20s while the others were in their late 20s and were already publishing books. It was through Floyd Dell that de la Selva started attending the Liberal Club, which had just relocated to Greenwich Village. Although he doesn't say, it was probably there that he met Walter Adolphe Roberts, who was the club secretary in the latter part of 1913.[85] The Liberal Club was almost an offshoot of the journal *The Masses*, and it incubated both the Provincetown Players, who performed two doors away, and the Washington Square Players (WSP), who became the Theatre Guild. Ralph Roeder acted with the WSP, and de la Selva also recalls Helen Westley, Phillip Moeller, and Edward Goodman.[86] Oddly he doesn't mention Theresa Helburn, to whom he later became very close.

Clearly Salomón had Hispanic friends and interests: he shared a house with Rufino González Mesa and he knew Manuel Cestero (Fig. 7), who was the link to Pedro; and with the Mexican jurist Rafael Mallén he organised protests in the streets of New York against the US occupation of Veracruz from April to November 1914;[87] but these circles in which he was now moving—Greenwich Village and the Lower East Side, the Rand School, the Liberal Club and the new theatres—were young and bohemian and socialist and literary and polyglot, but largely white and with little identifiable Hispanic presence.

As they became acquainted, Salomón told Pedro about Tresca and Feigelbaum and Irwin and Roeder, while Pedro told Salomón about Alfonso Reyes, Antonio Caso, and José Vasconcelos, three of the figures he'd known

---

Liberal: The Autobiography of Charles W. Ervin, ed. Jean Gould, New York: Dodd, Mead & Co., 1954, pp. 78–101.

[84] De la Selva, 'In Memoriam', p. 112.

[85] See Roberts' account in W. Adolphe Roberts, *These Many Years: An Autobiography*, ed. Peter Hulme, Kingston: University of the West Indies Press, 2015, pp. 131–34.

[86] De la Selva, 'In Memoriam', p. 114.

[87] As he recalled in the long 1954 essay, 'El agua y la rosa en la poesía mexicana', *Antología Mayor III/Ensayos*, pp. 172–247, at p. 215.

7 Manuel Florentino Cestero. *La Prensa*, 7 May 1919, p. 5.

in Mexico City. This was the beginning of pan-American cultural exchange in action. Mariano Brull shared an apartment on West 45th Street with Pedro before the Cuban's diplomatic duties took him elsewhere. At that point Pedro proposed that he and Salomón should take an apartment together and, along with Salomón's old friend, Rufino ('a Cuban who writes nice little humorous stories in bad English'),[88] they rented two floors of a fine old brownstone at 115 West 97th Street, not far from Central Park, with a large living room full of handsome mirrors. Pedro's Mexican friends came to stay and visit: Manuel Gamio, Luis Castillo Ledón, José Vasconcelos, Martín Luis Guzmán, Balbino Dávalos, and Javier Icaza: 'Our New York was filled with Mexican faces and voices and problems.'[89] The house was also always full of books, Salomón recalls—borrowed from the New York Public Library. Other

---

[88] Letter from Henríquez Ureña to Reyes (17 September 1915), *Epistolario íntimo*, vol. 2, 191.
[89] De la Selva, 'In Memoriam', p. 134.

The Changing of the Poetic Guard (1915) 111

Hispanic figures they associated with were the Dominican Cestero cousins, Manuel Florentino and Tulio Manuel, the Cuban José Antonio Fernández de Castro, whom de la Selva had taught at Westerleigh Collegiate Institute,[90] Alfonso Guillén Zelaya, who worked at the Honduran Consulate, and the Colombian Ricardo Arenales, later to rename himself Porfirio Barba Jacob. The meeting between de la Selva and Henríquez Ureña was crucial for the pan-American project in that in 1915 de la Selva's contacts were mostly with US writers, Henríquez Ureña's mostly with Hispanic writers: their address books were complementary and, once they shared the same house, they could begin to bring these groups together.

Henríquez Ureña died just three weeks after John Maynard Keynes so de la Selva uses the coincidence to recall the fleeting presence in their lives of Lady Keynes in her earlier incarnation as the dancer Lydia Lopokova. After her wild success with the Ballets Russes in Paris, Lopokova had been tempted by the money offered by a US dance entrepreneur but then disillusioned by the kinds of productions in which she was asked to appear, which were little better than vaudeville. She had retreated to the Catskills and retrained as an actress, eventually accepting a position with the Washington Square Players, who had moved north from Greenwich Village to the 40-seater Bandbox Theatre at East 57th Street and Third Avenue. After evening performances, actors, audience, and critics would all repair to a nearby bar, possibly P. J. Clarke's (915 Third Avenue, at East 55th Street) to drink beer and talk into the night. De la Selva remembers Lopokova as 'a golden dream-like creature, as if she's stepped out of a picture in a book of fairy tales'.[91] He recounts how she was courted by both Ralph Roeder and Heywood Broun, the theatre critic, while Pedro tried to quiz her on the influence of Isadora Duncan on Russian dance, Lydia wondered out loud about how somebody from a Caribbean island could know so much about ballet, and Salomón marvelled at how anybody could prefer to talk to Lydia instead of just adoring her.[92] It all, of course, ended unhappily. She briefly became Broun's girl, a relationship ended when he found her in the arms of Diaghilev's business manager, Randolfo Barocchi, to whom she was then briefly married (while also having an affair with Igor Stravinsky, *inter alios*). Swept back into the artistically more nourishing environment of the Ballets Russes, she toured England and was courted by Maynard Keynes, whom she met—according anyway to the story that Ezra Pound told de la Selva—at a supper party given

---

[90] De la Selva, 'El agua y la rosa', p. 215.
[91] De la Selva, 'In Memoriam', p. 131.
[92] De la Selva says that he would have adored her, 'si hubiese tenido libre el corazón' [if his heart had been free] ('In Memoriam', p. 132).

by Clive Bell in honour of Pablo Picasso.[93] After a brief disappearance in 1919—when she ran off with a Russian general—Lydia returned to London and accepted Keynes's proposal of marriage, somewhat to the surprise of Keynes's gay lover Duncan Grant.[94] Broun took to drink. Roeder consoled himself with a young painter called Jo Nevison, who would later marry Edward Hopper, before himself marrying another Russian, Fania Mindell, who had been imprisoned alongside Margaret Sanger for opening the first birth control clinic in the country, in Brownsville, Brooklyn, in 1919. But in the context of remembering Henríquez Ureña, de la Selva is more interested in recalling how the two of them went to performance after performance of Lopokova in *The Firebird*, forming a group with Troy and Margaret Kinney, the illustrators and students of dance, in whose apartment they would drink Turkish coffee and eat baklava.[95] Those were certainly the days.

Heywood Broun, de la Selva notes, was the son of a rich Wall Street dealer and was well-connected through his friends from Harvard—Ernest Gruening, Walter Lippmann, and José Camprubí, who was to become a key figure for Hispanic New York when he bought and expanded *La Prensa*, the city's leading Spanish-language newspaper.[96] Pedro and Salomón were together—typically—in a theatre watching a production of Euripides' *Trojan Women* when a newspaper vendor dramatically broke onto the stage displaying his 'extra': 'LUSITANIA SUNK'.[97] Writing his memoir not long after the US deployment of an atomic bomb, de la Selva is struck in 1946 by the disasters of war: Troy, the *Lusitania*, Hiroshima. But, looking back, he provides a detailed sense of the kinds of networks woven in New York during those golden years.

Slowly, however, as de la Selva notes, the balance of their social circle shifted. They began to drift away from Salomón's US friends. An important development here was the arrival of the Alfau family in New York. De la Selva recounts that Pedro knew the family beforehand because Señora Alfau came from Santo Domingo, though he doesn't mention the literary connection: Eugenia Galván Velázquez de Alfau was the daughter of Manuel Jesús de Galván, author of the novel *Enriquillo*, practically the national epic of the Dominican Republic. Antonio A. Alfau was a Spanish diplomat,

---

[93] De la Selva, 'In Memoriam', p. 135.
[94] De la Selva, 'In Memoriam', pp. 131–34; and see Judith Mackrell, *Bloomsbury Ballerina: Lydia Lopokova, Imperial Dancer and Mrs John Maynard Keynes*, London: Weidenfeld & Nicolson, 2008.
[95] De la Selva, 'In Memoriam', p. 133.
[96] De la Selva, 'In Memoriam', p. 136.
[97] De la Selva, 'In Memoriam', p. 162.

politician, and journalist who had lived in Puerto Rico and the Dominican Republic. He had founded an Ateneo in Santo Domingo. In New York he edited *Las Novedades* and wrote political articles under the name Doctor Kronos.[98] Salomón recalls five children: three brothers and two sisters— Alfonso, Felipe, Jesusa, Monna (María Montserrat), and another whose name he forgets (Rafael). Jesusa was beautiful but decorous and intelligent; the younger Monna had large dark eyes and 'looked as capable of as much mischief as Jesusa did of kindness'.[99] He recalls Jesusa's long commute from their house (he remembers 125th Street, but it was even further north, at 540 West 136th Street) down to Canal Street where she worked for *La Prensa*. The father died in 1919 and the family probably relied on Jesusa, the eldest child, for support.[100] She also worked with Pedro Henríquez Ureña on *Las Novedades*. Jesusa had already written and published a novel in Spain, *Los débiles* (1912). Felipe, although only a teenager, made an impression on Salomón as a lively boy—he would also later write novels in English.[101] Salomón's Puerto Rican friend, Luis Muñoz Marín, would recall his own visits to what amounted to a Hispanic *tertulia* or salon—'chaotic evenings', Salomón calls them, and Alfonso Alfau would be drawn into the literary projects that Salomón and Luis would concoct in 1918.[102]

What Muñoz Marín remembers are the enthusiastic discussions about events in Russia. In his *Memorias* he recalls the father Antonio ('noble and conservative patriarch'), his sons Felipe ('taciturn adolescent') and Alfonso, and two unnamed daughters. They were not themselves radicals, he says. However: 'A combination of intellectual curiosity and resentment about the Spanish American War, still quite recent, and the US occupation of Santo Domingo, made them look with sympathy on the Russian experiment'.[103] Presumably the resentment saw them particularly enjoying the disquiet that the Russian Revolution caused in the USA.

Throughout de la Selva's recollections of his friend Pedro runs a strain of surprise at his lack of interest in women, despite their often open admiration for his intellect and good looks. This, of course, at a time when Salomón

---

[98] See his obituary in *La Prensa*, 14 January 1919, p. 1.
[99] De la Selva, 'In Memoriam', p. 144–45. Monna Alfau later lived in Mexico, married (sequentially) to a Catalan poet (Rafael Sala) and then writer (Felipe Teixidor).
[100] There was an older brother, José, who didn't accompany the family to New York.
[101] These were rediscovered in the 1980s: *Locos: A Comedy of Gestures* [1936], Champaign, IL: Dalkey Archive Press, 1988; and *Chromos*, Champaign, IL: Dalkey Archive Press, 1990.
[102] De la Selva, 'In Memoriam', p. 145. See below, p. 237 n. 76.
[103] Luis Muñoz Marín, *Memorias. Autobiografía pública 1898–1940*, 2nd edn, San Juan, Puerto Rico: Fundación Luis Muñoz Marín, 2003, pp. 58–59.

8 Jesusa Alfau Galván.
La Prensa, 8 May 1919, p. 4.

himself was in love with at least half a dozen women at once. Jesusa Alfau (Fig. 8) obviously seemed to de la Selva an ideal mate for Pedro, but he was only interested in her conversation. Luis Muñoz Marín, barely 20, asked Jesusa to marry him, but she declined a proposal from such a stripling.[104] However, when the academic Antonio de Solalinde arrived from Spain, he found Jesusa very ready to fall in love: they married in 1924 and taught together at the University of Wisconsin in Madison. This may just have been a matter of personality, though one wonders whether Pedro was in any sense held back by a sense that his mixed race, apparent in his features and colouring, would lead to a rejection of his overtures at least in such *castizo* families as the Alfau Galváns (Fig. 9). Photographs are not always reliable evidence, but it does not seem as if Pedro could have passed as white at least in his younger years; and some Dominican scholars have recently made a point of underlining that his mother Salomé was a woman

---

[104] Muñoz Marín, *Memorias*, p. 58. He remembers her as ten years older than him; there was only three years' difference, but she was a very sophisticated young woman.

9 Pedro Henríquez Ureña in 1917. Provenance unknown.

of colour despite attempts to whiten her features in later portraits.[105] Henríquez Ureña hardly ever referred to his colour: there's just one passing reference in 1908 to antipathy on the streets of New York towards those who, 'like me, announce in their appearance that they belong to strange and "inferior" races'.[106] When he spoke about his family history, he tended to emphasise the paternal line which supposedly went back to the followers of Enriquillo who'd resisted the Spaniards in the sixteenth century.[107]

---

[105] See Dixa Ramírez, 'Salomé's Blurred Edges', *The Black Scholar: Journal of Black Studies and Research*, 45, no. 2 (2015), 45–56.
[106] Letter from Pedro Henríquez Ureña to Alfonso Reyes (13 March 1908), in Pedro Henríquez Ureña and Alfonso Reyes, *Epistolario íntimo, 1906-1946*, ed. Juan Jacobo de Lara, 3 vols., Santo Domingo: UNPHU, 1981–1983, vol. 1, pp. 74–75 [quienes, como yo, llevan en su tipo físico la declaración de pertenecer a pueblos y razas extraños].
[107] Although Enriquillo's group was mixed, including Africans and mestizos, so descent from it would in any case be no guarantee of indigenous purity: see Ida Altman, 'The Revolt of Enriquillo and the Historiography of Early Spanish America', *The Americas*, 63, no. 4 (2007), 587–614.

His historiographical work tended to exclude anything African from consideration, a move which, for such a scrupulous scholar, is bound to arouse suspicions of denial.[108]

Salomón reflects on how much he wished he'd been able to see the warm family man and father that Pedro eventually became in Argentina, though he did witness the *coup de foudre* that hit Pedro when he first laid eyes on the 17-year-old Isabel Lombardo Toledano in Mexico in 1920.[109] Pedro romanced her in his own special way by reciting from memory in Greek the catalogue of the heroes from the *Odyssey*. Isabel declared that she wanted to learn Greek and Pedro must teach her. And that was that. De la Selva notes that Isabel was 'of a dark Italian type'.[110] It was in 1915, in New York, that Madison Grant completed *The Passing of the Great Race*, which included a sideswipe at the Mexicans currently demonstrating their incapacity for self-government, a failure to be explained, he claimed, by the widespread racial mixture in the country.[111]

*

By September 1915, the two fast friends were already planning what Henríquez Ureña called a *salon* in that West 97th Street apartment. They would receive two or three times a month, he reported to Reyes: two separate groups, Hispanic-American and US, with the two hosts providing the common ground; rather less ambitious than de la Selva's eventual pan-American project. Henríquez Ureña claims in this letter not to frequent Hispanic-American circles but he mentions some figures he knows: Manuel Galván, Manuel Cestero, Rivas the Venezuelan historian, Romera Navarro ('a Spaniard who writes badly': Henríquez Ureña had trashed one of his books in a review), and Homero Serís, whom Henríquez Ureña calls Cuban, though he was a Spaniard. Of the US writers he knows, he mentions only Thomas Walsh, translator of Fray Luis de León and a poet himself, William Rose Benét, and the Kinneys, who wrote about dance and knew Spain like the backs of their hands.[112] But by January 1916, the *salon* had not made much

---

[108] See Arcadio Díaz Quiñones, 'Pedro Henríquez Ureña (1884–1946): la tradición y el exilio', in his *Sobre los principios: los intelectuales caribeños y la tradición*, Bernal, Argentina: Universidad Nacional de Quilmes Editorial, 2006, pp. 167–249.
[109] De la Selva, 'In Memoriam', p. 147.
[110] De la Selva, 'In Memoriam', p. 149. Her grandparents were Italian immigrants.
[111] Madison Grant, *The Passing of the Great Race, or The Racial Basis of European History* [1916], 4th edn, New York: C. Scribner's Sons, 1936, p. 17.
[112] Letter from Pedro Henríquez Ureña to Alfonso Reyes (17 September 1915), *Epistolario íntimo*, vol. 2, p. 191.

progress, which Henríquez Ureña put down to his workload and to de la Selva's laziness.[113] Instead they go together to the opera and to the Poetry Society of America. Indeed, they took with them to the PSA—at different times—Mariano Brull, José Santos Chocano, Martín Luis Guzmán, and Balbino Dávalos Balkin.[114]

We get here an early sense of the range of Hispanic writers in New York at this time. Manuel de Jesús Galván Velásquez was the son of the Dominican writer who had authored *Enriquillo* and sister to Sra Alfau.[115] Cestero, also *dominicano*, would become one of de la Selva's closest colleagues and will reappear in a number of different contexts throughout this book. Rivas was probably Ángel César Rivas, the Venezuelan political historian. Manuel Romera Navarro (with whom de la Selva worked on *The Delineator*) was writing a study of US hispanism which was published in 1917. Homero Serís de la Torre was a Spanish philologist and pupil of Ramón Menéndez Pidal. Balbino Dávalos Balkin was a young Mexican writer, as was Martín Luis Guzmán, who would reach New York in 1916.

Pedro Henríquez Ureña was himself a learned man and a rigorous critic, to whom all his poet friends gave their verses to read in trepidation, yet somebody who was always annoyed by poets: that's perhaps why he called de la Selva 'lazy'—almost anyone else was, by his draconian standards.[116] He distrusted improvidence and improvisation and was suspicious of the fluency of writers like Porfirio Barba Jacob and José Santos Chocano. He was, in de la Selva's contrast, Horace to the Nicaraguan's Catullus.

If Salomón de la Selva was precocious, he was also smart enough to recognise that Pedro Henríquez Ureña was a friend to be cherished, a man whose intellect and knowledge impressed everybody he met—including, eventually, Jorge Luis Borges—and who clearly acted as Salomón's adviser right through these New York years, although after autumn 1917 he didn't live in the city. Henríquez Ureña had contributed an essay to the *arielista* debate when he was only 20, but by then he had already added to the prodigious literary knowledge gained at the knees of his mother the experience of three years living in New York, which included training as

---

[113] Letter from Pedro Henríquez Ureña to Alfonso Reyes (16 January 1916), *Epistolario íntimo*, vol. 2, p. 219.
[114] De la Selva, 'Acróasis', p. 44.
[115] Eugenia Galván Velázquez de Alfau was Manuel de Jesús Galván Velásquez's sister, but then he married María Alfau Péréz, who was the daughter of Antonio Alfau Baralt by a previous marriage and therefore the Alfau Galván children's (step) brother-in-law as well as their uncle.
[116] De la Selva, 'In Memoriam', p. 100.

a typist and bookkeeper and working long hours to keep afloat financially after his father resigned from his position at the Dominican Ministry of Foreign Affairs; so he knew the USA on the ground. In that early essay Henríquez Ureña takes issue with some of Rodó's judgements about the USA, noting that they are more severe than those made by Martí and Hostos—both of course from the Caribbean and both with first-hand experience of the country.[117] Henríquez Ureña's own judgement was hardly mild, underlining the Anglo-Saxon pride which lay behind the country's imperialistic tendencies and racial prejudices.[118] But where he differed from Rodó was in allowing the USA a sustaining utopian ideal. And here—because he has lived among them—he can list the journalists and the painters and the writers and the scientists who embody this progressive principle of taking the gospel of moral and intellectual elevation to the masses. He would sustain this empirical and non-doctrinaire approach throughout a long and distinguished career.

Pedro's involvement in the pan-American project was curtailed when he decided on the need for an academic career to support himself. To that point he'd been employed as editor on the Spanish-language magazine *Las Novedades*, managed by the Dominican businessman and aspiring politician Francisco Peynado. De la Selva—doubtless drawing on Pedro's complaints over the dinner table—has him slaving away to correct the stupid articles that the magazine had agreed to publish.[119] In September 1917, Pedro moved to Minneapolis to take up a position in the Department of Spanish at the University of Minnesota, meaning that his time in New York was from now on limited to relatively brief visits.

*

In 1949, de la Selva wrote a long essay in the third person to introduce the publication of his translation of Edna Millay's 'Renascence' in the

---

[117] Pedro Henríquez Ureña, 'Ariel' [1904], in his *Obra crítica*, ed. Emma Susana Speratti Piñero, Mexico: Fondo de Cultura Económica, 1960, pp. 23–28, at p. 27.
[118] Henríquez Ureña, 'Ariel', p. 27.
[119] De la Selva, 'In Memoriam', p. 137. On *Las Novedades*, Francisco Peynado employed Manuel de Jesús Galván Velásquez as editor-in-chief and Manuel Florentino Cestero as editor, adding Pedro Henríquez Ureña in July 1915. In October 1916, Antonio Abad Alfau took control, being replaced on his death in November 1918 by Rafael Montafur. Manuel Florentino Cestero y Pedro Henríquez Ureña resigned when Peynado left, but Manuel de Jesús Galván Velásquez (Alfau's son-in-law) continued until the end of 1918. (Franklin Gutiérrez, 'Ensayistas dominicanos' <http://cvc.cervantes.es/lengua/anuario/anuario_08/pdf/literatura19.pdf> accessed December 2018.)

Mexican journal *América: Revista Antológica*.[120] He begins by recalling an occasion—a dinner organised by Pedro Henríquez Ureña at an Italian restaurant, doubtless in the Village, with a mountain of garlic spaghetti and a bottle of rough Sicilian wine on the table—when someone had asked him about Edna. Salomón immediately recited two stanzas in Spanish from 'Witch-Wife', which he had just translated that morning, taking time from his job as a translator for *The Delineator*.[121] At this stage he hadn't known Edna long but was madly in love with her: 'la veía con ojos de amor' [I looked at her with eyes of love].[122] She, cool and provocative, had sent him this poem with its opening lines: 'She is neither pink nor pale / And she never shall be all thine'. De la Selva discoursed at length about her colour; Mariano Brull chipped in with comparisons to the angels in the painting of Benozzo Gozzoli, though de la Selva thought that Agnolo Gaddi was a better reference point, while Henríquez Ureña posited Botticelli.

De la Selva gives a sympathetic biographical sketch of Millay, quoting generously from her poetry and recalling the help that Walter Adolphe Roberts ('alma latina' [a Latin soul]) gave her.[123] He discusses her renovation of the ballad form, the theme of suffering in her poetry, her poetic ancestors, her dogmatic pacifism during the First World War, her rooted opposition to fascism, her extraordinary recitals, as well as quoting his own poem about her: 'I loved a bit of New England once'.[124] He also discusses his translation of 'Renascence' with its four lines that are not in the original, a liberty which he both condemns and defends.[125] Finally, he recalls the world of 1920 when her poem 'My candle burns at both ends' seemed to speak for the attitude of a new generation, at least in New York.[126] He sees the poetry and the beliefs behind it as a female emancipation, with its South American equivalents in the figures of Delmira Agustini, Alfonsina Storni, and Juana de Ibarbourou.

To Salomón, Edna was special as both person and poet. Many of the New York poets he'd met were young, but still approaching 30, while Edna was 23, just a year older than he was, and within the world of poetry she was already famous for her poem 'Renascence'. A few more short poems had appeared in *The Forum*, including 'Witch-Wife', but it would be 1917

---

[120] Salomón de la Selva, 'Edna St. Vincent Millay', *América: Revista Antológica*, 62 (January 1950), 7–32.
[121] One or two names are confused: Edna's older sister Norma appears as Irma. He also dates the dinner as 1914 but he didn't meet Edna until the following year.
[122] De la Selva, 'Edna St. Vincent Millay', 12.
[123] De la Selva, 'Edna St. Vincent Millay', 10.
[124] De la Selva, 'Edna St. Vincent Millay', 14.
[125] De la Selva, 'Edna St. Vincent Millay', 28–29.
[126] De la Selva, 'Edna St. Vincent Millay', 19.

before she had written enough to publish her first slim volume, with *A Few Figs from Thistles* following in 1920.[127]

Although she wasn't close to her, Margaret Widdemer was nostalgic in 1964 about the glow that surrounded Edna Millay in those years:

> I wonder if anybody today can realize what she and her poems meant to our generation. It isn't enough to say that she had beauty, simplicity, and passion. She spoke for us: for the boys and girls caught in the wave of rebellion against narrowness and conventionality. Who ranged from the ones like me who only asked to be regarded as adult, to think and act for themselves, through the group which felt that freedom should be sexual as well as physical and mental, to the inevitable fringe which supposed that the proof of brilliance and greatness was licence. She spoke, in her lyrics and sonnets, those sonnets still wonderful to those of us who found them then, for us all.[128]

When he first wrote to Edna on 9 August 1915, de la Selva was already in the process of compiling an anthology of translations of modern US poems to be published in Argentina and writing an article on such poets for the journal *Cuba contemporánea*, a liberal magazine founded in Havana in 1913. As well as asking questions about her background and poetical credo, he confesses that the personality conveyed in her poems already binds him 'as with a spell', and that her poem 'Renascence' will not cease to trouble him until he has translated it into Spanish.[129] Even before he met her he was bewitched—and perhaps it always was the poetry that bewitched him. As a reference he mentions friends: William Rose Bénet, Joyce Kilmer, Joseph Edgar Chamberlin, and Frank Crane, demonstrating that he was continuing to add to his connections: between them these four wrote regularly for the *Literary Digest*, the *New York Times*, the *New York Evening Mail*, and the *New York Globe*.

In his next letter he's asking for a picture ('I'm curious to see it'), but this is to accompany an article his friend Pedro Henríquez Ureña is writing about

---

[127] Edna St Vincent Millay, *Renascence, and Other Poems*, New York: Mitchell Kennerley, 1917; *A Few Figs from Thistles: Poems and Four Sonnets*, New York City: F. Shay, 1920.

[128] Margaret Widdemer, *Golden Friends I Had: Unrevised Memories of Margaret Widdemer*, Garden City, NY: Doubleday & Company, 1964, p. 17.

[129] Letter from Salomón de la Selva to Edna St Vincent Millay, ESVMP (20 August 1915). ESVMP is the Edna St. Vincent Millay Papers (MSS 32920), Library of Congress, Washington, DC.

The Changing of the Poetic Guard (1915)   121

US poets for *El Fígaro*, another Cuban magazine.[130] By the end of August, having received two brief replies from Edna, as he already calls her, de la Selva is beginning to wax lyrical ('I am delighted with you', 'whole hearted admiration', 'such a queer child, withal most dear to me!'): she reminds him of his mother—rarely a good line to use in an attempt at seduction. He is also beginning to offer his uncompromising judgements ('what nice thing could I say of Percy MacKaye as a lyric poet'?).[131] Six days later, having received no reply, he is 'remorse-stricken' and 'bitter-sorry', convinced that he has offended her through over-familiarity: 'Perhaps because I secretly desired your friendship, I took your affected affability as inviting me out of ordinary formality'.[132] De la Selva was not the first man to be seduced by Edna's epistolary tone: artist and poet Ferdinand Earle had fallen under Millay's sway in the course of some erotically charged correspondence about the competition which eventually failed to award Millay's 'Renascence' a prize. Earle was a proponent of the so-called 'soulmate and affinity' movement; his multiple marriages and affairs were plastered all over the newspapers, so Millay knew exactly who she was dealing with, and on what terms. She was in no way offended by de la Selva's tone: she was a modern woman who enjoyed epistolary flirtatiousness almost as much as she did the real thing. In fact it was because she took the real thing so seriously that she was a tardy correspondent, at least by de la Selva's exacting standards.

When Edna's reply did arrive—it must have crossed with his abject apology—it clearly showed no signs of her having been upset because his immediate response leapt over all barriers, launching itself without even the formality of a salutation:

Should I tell you all?
But if I tell you that I love you, you will laugh at me, and hurt me, and ...
Edna!

He had been speaking about her with Joyce Kilmer, he reports. Kilmer had never laid eyes on her either but asserted that she was beautiful, so therefore, continues de la Selva: 'you must be beautiful—like a wilful princess loved of

---

[130] Letter from Salomón de la Selva to Edna St Vincent Millay, ESVMP (20 August 1915). One of the leading Cuban journals, *El Fígaro* ran from 1885 to 1929.
[131] Letter from Salomón de la Selva to Edna St Vincent Millay, ESVMP (31 August 1915).
[132] Letter from Salomón de la Selva to Edna St Vincent Millay, ESVMP (6 September 1915).

many, loving none, with a little dagger, in her hand, red with the blood of slaves'—a pretty good assessment.[133] But Edna was certainly intrigued. She wrote to her first and rather reluctant lover, Arthur Hooley: 'The Spanish boy who wrote the Tale from Faerieland in the July Forum has written me. Do you know him? If you have seen him, tell me, is he as good-looking as he ought to be?'[134]

Salomón describes himself as short and thin and often pale—probably not the dark South American type she might be expecting: 'my blood is a queer mixture—Indian, Spanish, English; my hair is light; green or blue my eyes; white my skin. But my cheek-bones are Indian, & my nose, and the way my eyes have of looking.' More animadversions on New York poets follow: Louis Untermeyer has the 'air of a tin-god on wheels', though 'he lives a few houses away from me & we are good friends'.

But the yearning note keeps returning:

> Why do you draw me to you and bind me so? I stretch out my arms to you, in the dark, and my lips seek yours, in the dark, and there is only dark and dark and dark, but I hear you, and you always call me, and I go on, and on, seeking, seeking, O Love! ...[135]

Later the same day he wrote again. He'd translated her poem 'Witch-Wife' into Spanish (with its equally telling final lines: 'But she was not made for any man, / And she never will be all mine'); he'd been thinking about her, dreaming about her; and now he tries to engage her in discussion of poetic technique ('I'd like to talk English metres over with you') before lapsing into a rather resentful account of how hard it had been to get a hearing for his work: 'And when, after three years, I managed to get a poem accepted, it was bitter to realize that no one cared.'[136]

---

[133] Letter from Salomón de la Selva to Edna St Vincent Millay, ESVMP (7 September 1915).

[134] Letter from Edna St Vincent Millay to Arthur Hooley, ESVMP (6 September 1915). On the relationship between Edna and Hooley, see Daniel Mark Epstein, *What Lips My Lips Have Kissed: The Loves and Love Poems of Edna St. Vincent Millay*, New York: Henry Holt and Company, 2001, pp. 76–80. Hooley, originally English, had been employed by his cousin, Mitchell Kennerley, to edit *The Forum*, and so, in accepting 'The Tale from Faerieland', was presumably the first person to publish a de la Selva poem.

[135] Letter from Salomón de la Selva to Edna St Vincent Millay, ESVMP (7 September 1915).

[136] Letter from Salomón de la Selva to Edna St Vincent Millay, ESVMP (7 September 1915).

About two-thirds of the way through September, they finally met—and de la Selva's worst fears were realised: she didn't find him attractive. His next letter suggests that he took this news badly. He opens with a poem, the first stanza of which reads:

> Your silence, Love, much sorrow tells.
> I hear the beat of flying wings,
> A far-away moaning of tolling bells,
> And faint goodbyes, & whisperings.

'I know you hate me. I don't blame you,' indicates the general tone. 'One can only love beautiful things ... you found me ugly. I will curse God and die'; though the letter swiftly moves on to a detailed discussion of the terrible power of her poem 'Interim' before returning to his dramatic performance of self-pity: 'I will die & no one shall care.'[137] For her part, Edna wrote to Arthur Hooley: 'It doesn't in the least matter about Salomón.'[138]

'I do not hope to hear from you again' was one of the sentences in de la Selva's letter, which didn't prevent his next one, eight pages long, from opening: 'Why have you not written to me, Edna?' Lovelorn hardly begins to cover it.

> You make me doubt you, against my will. I have wandered by many highways and my feet have wearied in many a strange path that led nowhere. Many a pilgrimage have I made to shrines untold, and I have hung many a wreath of false flowers on the altars of a host of untrue gods. But to you I have come, not by any road, but through a wood of mid-night and poppied fields of morning and daisied meadows of afternoon; and I have picked for you—a fair offering—a branch of laurel from the wood, and, from the fields, dreams, and, from the meadows, purities—laurel, poppies, daisies—true flowers for my goddess true. But you make me doubt you, against my will; and my heart is pregnant with a fear; and tonight I saw the moon and it seemed a sorrow growing round for me in heaven.

He calls himself unworthy of any woman: of her, of his mother ('white-haired now and sorrowing for her long-absent son'), or even of the 'offered

---

[137] Letter from Salomón de la Selva to Edna St Vincent Millay, ESVMP (24 September 1915).
[138] Letter from Edna St Vincent Millay to Arthur Hooley, ESVMP (17 September 1915).

loves I have refused'—'Edith, white of face and bosom; Vivian the witch; proud Helen of Ithaca; blue-eyed Anna; Gladys the frail and Marguerite of the wondrous hair'.[139] It's by no means clear that any of these 'loves' corresponded to flesh-and-blood women. The second half of the letter, written the following day, is markedly different in tone, offering a long discussion of what it means to be 'American'.

> I can be 'American' when I want to, that is to say: I can put myself in that frame of mind that is essential to believe that Conan Doyle, or Mark Twain, or Jack London are great novelists; that culture is a product of the universities & has no rôle in real life; that people are divided in two classes—our folks & other folks; that poets are queer things that do nothing but dream, have unhappy wives & starve in the end; that—Oh! Most surely, I can be 'American': I can, for a while, train myself to calling my sweet-heart 'kid,' to speak of a girl as a 'queen,' of my father as 'the old man,' of my mother as 'maw,' of my employer as the 'boss,' and my position as my 'job;' I can accustom myself to saying hell, tough, & 'lore' for law & 'sore' for saw, and 'ain't got' for have not. [...]
>
> And the first commandment of the Americanism I have adopted for myself is: 'Be yourself, & all else be damned.' Surely, you, also, are that sort of an American. No? And it isn't that I am 'American' or not 'American,' but that I am myself. There is no caste, tribe, race, or nationality that can say: he is molded after our patented model.
>
> You haven't sent me the copies of your poems that you promised. Suit your whim about it: I am not used to begging, it is a trade for which, decidedly, I am not fit. [...]
>
> Oh, well, if you feel that way about it ... I don't care. Get me?[140]

A note of resignation creeps in: 'Well, we will be friends.'[141] Then he sends another monster letter—18 pages, some of them double-sided—which again combines the literary and the personal. It begins with a discussion of his articles in Spanish about US writers. The one in *El Fígaro* has been published: he doesn't like the appearance of the magazine. But the article

---

[139] Letter from Salomón de la Selva to Edna St Vincent Millay, ESVMP (29 September 1915).

[140] Letter from Salomón de la Selva to Edna St Vincent Millay, ESVMP (30 September 1915).

[141] Letter from Salomón de la Selva to Edna St Vincent Millay, ESVMP (9 October 1915).

and translations for *Cuba contemporánea* have been delayed because the US poets are not really helping, though Percy MacKaye is an honourable exception. Edna herself has apparently been reluctant to send anything suitable to be translated. 'There is nothing worse than dealing with poets. They are many-worded, spineless, & can't be depended on. And they should all be boiled in hot oil—'.

Having got that out of his system, de la Selva returns to his old theme, scratching away at what Edna wants from him and whether he can be her friend: 'But you are only a poet, it seems; & poets have no friends'; before moving to a long discussion of classical music and then an account of an unhappy evening at a literary gathering he'd been invited to at Murray Hill Art Gallery.[142] The letter that he wrote at the end of October 1915 is the sixteenth he'd addressed to Edna: he has just received her fourth. The discrepancy may say much about what each meant to the other, although it may also indicate something about their respective social milieus. Some of this letter is about translation, de la Selva explaining the difficulties of translating her poems into Spanish—a language she has been learning. Intriguingly, he includes not just his Spanish translation of 'Afternoon on a Hill', but a literal back-translation into English.

De la Selva indicates his distaste for political poetry via a discussion of the music of Liszt. He notes some fine passages.

But there is in him too much of that trash that Vachel Lindsay writes now,—too much boomlay, boomlay boom! And clangaranga-clanga! ... Cowboys may like that, and old maids that don't know the abc of poetry, and brainless men who want to socialize and democratize and anarchicize poetry as if poetry had anything to do with social classes & forms of government & parties and all the other curses of mankind.[143]

De la Selva's letters are often playful in tone. Usually, even when sounding serious, he mocks himself and speedily shifts to other topics. His first letter in November initially seems written out of a real slough. Everyone around him is ill; he has been acting as nursemaid; and he gets a letter from Edna saying that she is also sick. Without salutation, he launches an opening salvo:

---

[142] Letter from Salomón de la Selva to Edna St Vincent Millay, ESVMP (21 October 1915).
[143] Letter from Salomón de la Selva to Edna St Vincent Millay, ESVMP (30 October 1915).

Why have you been ill? Do you like it? If you do, may I present you with a silken rope with which to tie a lovely noose about your kiss-memoried neck & hang your self? If you don't like being sick, then, why are you so? Aren't you a rational animal?

Having recalled some of his nursing experiences in Nicaragua, presumably when he was still a child, he recovers his composure enough to note that he could take care of Edna when she was ill: 'The difficult thing, I fancy, is to handle you when you are well.'

Edna could be every bit as playful—perhaps even more so—than de la Selva, though in this case her letters have to be imagined from his replies. He always wrote so admiringly of his good friend and mentor Pedro Henríquez Ureña that Edna obviously teased him about it. His response perhaps suggests that he didn't entirely appreciate the humour: 'What do you mean by saying that I may be married to Pedro? I beg you, most respectfully, to understand that though I can take care of babies, I am every bit a male of the species.' 'I may have described Pedro as Socrates', de la Selva writes, 'but the inference you seem to draw makes my bowels writhe with sheer disgust'.[144] Edna clearly touched a raw nerve, although Salomón was perfectly capable of drawing a line under that sentence and launching into a discussion of one of her poems, so perhaps there was also an element of deliberate archness in his outrage.

After what he apologises for as 'a long silence'—a week—he writes again to explain his 'one absorbing love-affair' which began 'years ago'. He describes its progress in terms of a developing symphony, impressionistic rather than rich in actual detail. After more than four pages of this, he concludes: 'If God wills, Helen and I will be married before long.' They had quarrelled five months ago, then met accidentally at a friend's house in New York and spent the previous weekend wandering about the city and talking about their future.[145] De la Selva wrote often to his women friends about his lovers, real or pretended. Sometimes perhaps to try to make them jealous, although there was often a large dose of fantasy and wishful thinking in his accounts, as we shall soon see in more detail.

---

[144] Letter from Salomón de la Selva to Edna St Vincent Millay, ESVMP (6 November 1915).
[145] Letter from Salomón de la Selva to Edna St Vincent Millay, ESVMP (13 November 1915).

10 José Santos Chocano drawn by Conrado Massaguer in 1917. From *Social*, 5. no. 9 (September 1920), p. 7.

The First Dinner

The origins of Salomón de la Selva's pan-American project were in the informal *tertulias* that he and Pedro Henríquez Ureña hosted in their apartment, but the first fully fledged dinner took place there in honour of José Santos Chocano on Saturday, 13 November 1915. Chocano had come to New York that autumn directly from Guatemala where he had several times visited the dying Rubén Darío, who had then gone home to Nicaragua in October. Darío and Chocano had long had what Günther Schmigalle calls 'a conflicted friendship'.[146] Their personalities were very different; Darío was the senior figure in poetic terms and Chocano was a demanding friend; but Chocano now knew that Darío had only a short time to live. Chocano would have to wait two more years to get full recognition in New York, but the dinner at de la Selva's was a useful staging post and Salomón's pan-American project was broadly in keeping with Chocano's own—by no means always coherent—views.

During the first third of the twentieth century, José Santos Chocano (Fig. 10) would become as well known as his Hispanic poetic contemporaries, the slightly older Rubén Darío and the slightly younger Juan Ramón Jiménez,

---

[146] Günther Schmigalle, 'Una amistad conflictiva: Rubén Darío y José Santos Chocano', *Anales de Literatura Hispanoamericana*, 41 (2012), 123–52.

although his reputation has fallen precipitously since his death. While Darío and Jiménez were reticent in character, Chocano was an imposing figure with a stentorian voice and a personality to match, who relished public life, dabbled in politics on a continental scale, enjoyed a chaotic love life, and was involved in a number of spectacular feuds, one of which ended with him murdering a fellow Peruvian writer in 1925. Nine years later he himself was stabbed to death on a tram in the Chilean capital, Santiago, by a deranged business associate.[147]

Chocano's poetic output was extensive but has always been difficult to categorise or to classify. He saw himself as a poet of America, somewhat along the lines of Walt Whitman and with some of same vatic tendencies. His most famous book of poems was called *Alma América*: 'Walt Whitman tiene el Norte, pero yo tengo el Sur' [Walt Whitman has the North, but I have the South], as he modestly put it.[148] Whereas, for Darío, Paris was always the literary capital to which he aspired, Chocano—who never knew French but had learned English at school—moved almost exclusively within an American ambit, frequently in Central America, then Madrid, then Mexico, moving back to Peru and Chile in the late 1920s, with occasional visits to New York and New Orleans. He wasn't beyond pointing out that Darío seemed to have forgotten that Baudelaire's literary hero was Edgar Allan Poe.[149]

Too much of an individualist to be associated with movements, Chocano's approach could nonetheless be bracketed with what the Chilean poet Francisco Contreras described in rather vague terms as *mundonovismo*: 'it's simply a question of creating the art of the New World, of the young land of the future.'[150] The novelty of Contreras's idea—and its relevance to Chocano—lies in its continental scope and in that sense it is a literary continuation of the affirmation, with its roots in Humboldt, Jefferson, and Andrés Bello, that the new world is a braver version of the old rather than a feebler cousin. Literature should not be local or regional or even national, argued Contreras: it should encompass the continent—with the 'mundo

---

[147] The standard biography is Luis Alberto Sánchez, *Aladino, o vida y obra de José Santos Chocano*, 2nd. edn, Lima: Editorial Universo, 1975.
[148] José Santos Chocano, 'Prólogo lírico' to *Oro de Indias* [1908], in his *Obras completas*, ed. Luis Alberto Sánchez, Mexico City: Aguilar, 1954, p. 731.
[149] See Sánchez, *Aladino*, p. 73.
[150] Ironically, Contreras's essay was originally written in French and published in 1917 in Paris, where he lived for many years. It appeared as 'El movimiento que triunfa hoy. Manifiesto sobre el mundonovismo' in his collection of essays *La varillita de virtud*, Santiago de Chile: Minerva, 1919, pp. 101-15. The predecessor here would be Andrés Bello's poem, *Silva a la agricultura de la zona tórrida* (1826).

nuevo' [new world] implying the *whole* continent, even if in practice the poetic vision in Spanish was often limited to south of the US border.

Like Darío, Chocano's attitude towards the USA was not always consistent, doubtless similarly swayed by the development of US foreign policy towards its southern neighbours over the first two decades of the century. And, rhetorically at least, Chocano could envisage some future union: in *Alma América* the North is Adam, the South is Eve, potentially a more productive coupling than Caliban and Ariel could ever be.[151] There are also signs—by no means unusual among Latin American intellectuals at the time—of an unstable mixture of admiration and resentment at the industrial and military power of the USA. For Chocano, whose tendency to admire strong figures saw him work for Pancho Villa and Manuel Estrada Cabrera before he flirted with fascism in the 1920s, the US exercise of power in, for example, spurring Panama into independence in order to force through the completion of the isthmian canal, demonstrated exactly what Latin America (called here just 'America') should be emulating:

> Los Estados Unidos, como argolla de bronce,
> Contra un clavo torturan de la América un pie,
> Y la América debe, ya que aspira a ser grande,
> Imitarles, primero e igualarles después.[152]
>
> Like a bronze ring against a nail,
> The United States tortures an American foot.
> And if it aspires to greatness, that America must
> First imitate them and then equal them.

Yet his involvement with the politics of Central America and Mexico, and especially his closeness to Pancho Villa, also led Chocano to a clearly anti-imperialist stance, which could look very like the defensive *hispanoamericanismo* which had its roots in Rodó's *Ariel*. This stance got stronger after US intervention in Mexico in 1914 when Chocano wrote about how he was working towards a Central American Union, a Caribbean Confederation, and a Federal Bolivarian Republic: he could never be accused of doing things by halves.[153] Twice during his life Chocano harboured political ambitions

---

[151] José Santos Chocano, 'El canto del porvenir', in his *Alma América: poemas indo-españoles*, Paris: Librería de la V^{da} de G. Bouret, 1906, pp. 24–26, at p. 26.
[152] José Santos Chocano, 'La epopeya del Pacífico', in his *Alma América*, pp. 17–20, at p. 17.
[153] Sánchez, *Aladino*, p. 295.

in which he appeared—at least to himself—as an intellectual reincarnation of Simón Bolívar, travelling through South America in order to bring about some kind of unification of the Latin republics. In Puerto Rico in late 1913 and early 1914 he gave a series of lectures which, while condemning Roosevelt's ruthlessness, still welcomed the imminent opening of the Panama Canal and spoke warmly of Woodrow Wilson as an idealistic president. The *New York Times* reported the lectures under the headline 'Famous Peruvian Author Urges Pan-American Unity'.[154]

Chocano was an inveterate traveller and New York inevitably exercised a pull. This 1915 visit was at least his fifth.[155] By the time Chocano arrived in Spain in 1905, as part of the Peruvian diplomatic mission concerned with the border dispute with Ecuador, he had a considerable reputation as a poet. He'd been employed on diplomatic missions to Central America by the Peruvian government, and had become close to Zelaya in Nicaragua and Estrada Cabrera in Guatemala, where he lived in some style and wrote much of *Alma América*, which was published in May 1906 in Madrid to great acclaim. Madrid had a thriving literary culture into which Chocano easily slipped: Spaniards such as Manuel Machado, Ramón Pérez de Ayala, and Juan Ramón Jiménez—the last two both later to make their own visits to New York—mixed with Americans such as Rubén Darío and the Mexican poet Amado Nervo.[156] Chocano had three happy and productive years in Madrid, ended by a financial scandal which led to him fleeing the country. He arrived in Havana in June 1908 penniless, which suggests that he didn't benefit from the underhand deals carried out by individuals in his circle.[157] He travelled eastwards through Cuba, spent six days in Santo Domingo, returned to Cuba, and then sailed for New Orleans and to New York by train to stay with the Dominican poet (and consul) Fabio Fiallo, in his apartment on West 61st Street. Fiallo therefore hosted both Darío

---

[154] 'Famous Peruvian Author Urges Pan-American Unity', *New York Times*, 18 January 1914, p. SM6. Chocano had had a finger in the Panamian pie too, and pointed out accurately that the main driving force here was Philippe Bunau-Varilla. See his 'Ante los Estados Unidos' [1913], in *Obras completas*, ed. Luis Alberto Sánchez, Mexico City: Aguilar, 1954, pp. 1010–26.

[155] Neither Sánchez nor Estuardo Núñez ('El poeta Chocano en Nueva York', *Cuadernos Americanos*, 75, no. 3 (1954), 292–98) gives accurate accounts of Chocano's visits to New York.

[156] See Schmigalle, 'Una amistad conflictiva', pp. 128–29.

[157] Schmigalle, 'Una amistad', has a thorough account of the incident (pp. 129–36).

The Changing of the Poetic Guard (1915) 131

and Chocano within six months.[158] During this short visit, of probably not more than two weeks, Chocano wrote some of the poems which were later called *Estampas Newyorkinas* [New York Scenes], completing the series on subsequent visits.

Chocano left New York in October 1908 by train to New Orleans and by November he was in Guatemala, where he translated his Brazilian friend Fontoura Xavier's book of poems, *Ópalos*, into Spanish, recalling in the prologue Darío's use of one of Xavier's lines as an epigraph to his 'Salutación al águila'.[159] He returned to New York in 1909, then again in December 1911 to complete a business deal of some kind, and again in 1912 to marry his second wife, Margarita Batres Arzu, whom he had been assiduously courting in Guatemala. The marriage took place in the Hotel Astor with Antonio and Manuel de Jesús Galván as witnesses.[160] The 1911 visit was probably short; the 1912 one lasted around two months. Although it is not clear when each of the *estampas* was written, they were probably all done by 1912, by which time Chocano had considerable experience of the streets of New York.

Chocano was now becoming deeply involved in the developing Mexican Revolution. He had been close to Francisco Madero, who had overthrown the dictator Porfirio Díaz only to be himself murdered in February 1913 on the orders of his general, Victoriano Huerta, who assumed control of the country and expelled Chocano. The poet then allied himself at different times with Pancho Villa and Venustiano Carranza, on whose orders he may have been in New York at the end of 1915, after falling out with Villa.[161]

What is most immediately striking about Chocano's poems written in New York is the difference in tone from the vatic—and to contemporary tastes overblown—language of his better-known work. Just one of the *Estampas*, 'La ciudad fuerte' [The strong city], is *arielista* in tone, comparing New York to Babylon and Nineveh, invoking the pride of a city which history will eventually bring down to earth like a collapsing house of cards. Against that background the poet can stand and describe the chaos around him—the grinding wheels which sound like ogres gnashing their teeth, the speeding cars, the steaming factories—and wonder where poetry and harmony might be found. Walt Whitman's trumpet will just be that of the angel sounding the last judgement. And yet, he concludes: 'Poesía: aquí

---

[158] Sánchez, *Aladino*, p. 238. See above, p. 85, for Rubén Darío's visit with Fiallo.
[159] Sánchez, *Aladino*, p. 252. See above, p. 70.
[160] Sánchez, *Aladino*, p. 265. Sons of the Manuel de J. Galván, author of *Enriquillo*, who had died in 1910.
[161] See Friedrich Katz, *The Life and Times of Pancho Villa*, Stanford, CA: Stanford University Press, 1998, pp. 284–85, 516–17.

mismo te encuentro' [Poetry: I find you right here], an almost Baudelairean recognition that the prose of the city can be alchemically transformed by the writer into eternal poetry.[162] But whereas Baudelaire is always actively engaged with his surroundings, the poet in Chocano's verse is an outsider, an observer—interested, amused, occasionally outraged, but never taking part in the scenes he describes, almost is if he were invisible; and Chocano in person was rarely invisible. Like Baudelaire, Chocano finds that the city throws up unexpected encounters with women, but when the poet in 'Pullman' watches a beautiful young woman on a train, alone, reading and then not reading, he identifies with her assumed loneliness ('La soledad se llama también melancolía' [Loneliness is also called melancholy]) but never exchanges a glance or gives any indication that she might also have seen him. They travel together 'en rápida huída / atropelladamente' [in rapid flight / helter-skelter] (853) on tracks that never meet. Chocano fell in love often and enthusiastically, but this encounter lacks the sexual spark of Baudelaire's 'A une passante' [To a passer-by], and if there is a tinge of voyeurism in his observation of ladies at tea ('Five O'Clock Tea' [855–56]) or smoking together ('Las damas fumadoras' [The smoking ladies] [858–59]), then it's the voyeurism of the excluded solitary rather than the sexual adventurer.

The prevailing tone of the *Estampas* is indeed melancholy. In 'El parque nevado' [The park under snow] (856–58) the poet wanders around a park—presumably Central Park—coming across the solitary figure of a woman who, her coat flecked with snow, looks like a marble statue, then a bunch of children playing, then a fine lady in a car who the poet fantasises as Snow White, then skaters on the frozen lake. Despite these signs of gaiety in the children and the skaters—just fantasies, he suggests—the park seems sad

---

[162] The *Estampas Newyorkinas* first appeared as a group in volume 3 (1941) of *Oro de Indias*, the four-volume collection (Santiago: Nascimiento, 1939–41) published after Chocano's death. Perhaps because they are difficult to square with the rest of Chocano's output, none of *Estampas Newyorkinas* is included in the 605 pages of the *Obras escogidas*, ed. Luis Alberto Sánchez (Lima: Occidental Petroleum Corporation of Peru, 1987), nor in *Los cien mejores poems de José Santos Chocano* (Mexico: Aguilar, 1971), nor in his *Antología poética*, ed. Alfonso Escudero (Buenos Aires: Espasa-Calpe, 1947). Just one, 'La ciudad fuerte', is included in *José Santos Chocano Poesía*, ed. Luis Fabio Xammar (Buenos Aires: Editions Jackson, 1945), even though the book includes a whole section called 'América' (pp. 181–254). The definitive edition is *Obras completas*, ed. Luis Alberto Sánchez, Mexico, Aguilar, 1954, from where the quotations that follow are taken (pp. 850–61), with page numbers henceforth included in the text. This quotation is from p. 851. Three of the *estampas* were published in 1909 in the *Pan American Magazine*.

and oppressed to the poet, with a strong indication that it's the poet who feels sad and oppressed.

The last poem of the sequence, 'El alma sola' [The lonely soul], places the poet at the very heart of the city, Times Square. Traffic—another Baudelairean motif—swirls around him: a carriage, a tram, a car, a bicycle, a painted young woman, and an athletic businessman; but in the middle of the tumult, surrounded by 20-storey skyscrapers which look to him like granite prisons for enchanted princesses, 'sentí toda la angustia de las desolaciones' [I felt all the anguish of their desolation]. Everything feels alien to him, yet there is no outrage or self-pity, or even philosophical reflection on the Calibanesque ways of northern life:

> ... Yo que en mi alma acrisolo
> todas las impresiones, ante aquella tal día
> permanecía inmóvil y helado ... y me sentía,
> entre esos miles de almas, completamente solo. (860)

> ... I, who in my soul refine
> all impressions, before the one that day
> stood frozen to the spot, immobile ... and felt,
> in the midst of those thousands of souls, completely alone.

The only companion in the poet's solitude, and the only hint of its possible implications, is the one he conjures:

> ... Sentí una angustia, viendo
> ese tropel de gente y escuchando ese estruendo,
> como hace medio siglo llegó a sentirla acaso
> Poe al cruzar las plazas con vacilante paso.

> ... I felt anguished, seeing
> that throng of people and listening to that uproar,
> just like half a century ago Poe perhaps felt it
> as his hesitant step crossed these squares.

'Los personajes de Edgardo' [Edgar's characters] were, the poet reflects, his old friends, but they are far away.

The last stanza of the poem, and therefore of the *Estampas*, emphasises the poet's solitude, and even a certain 'afán suicida' [suicidal impulse] but, at least in retrospect, the final emphasis has to be on the strengthening of the ego for which Chocano was so renowned. Although the *Estampas* are marked by a questioning and reflective lyricism, quite different from the rest of Chocano's poetry, they end with his assertion that

> ... me sentí, dentro de ese encrespado abismo
> cuanto más solo estuve, más dueño de mí mismo. (861)

> ... within that swirling chasm
> The more alone I was, the more I felt master of my self.

An assertion which—to the benefit of the poems—doesn't carry entire conviction.

His biographer, Luis Alberto Sánchez, sees Chocano as chastened by his experiences in Madrid, and it is indeed possible that the *estampas* written in 1909 bear the mark of that difficult time in the poet's life; but that would hardly explain the consistency of tone within the group as a whole when some were written as late as 1912.[163] Perhaps Chocano was slightly overawed by New York—almost all visitors were, at least initially. Perhaps he was never there quite long enough to overcome a sense of alienation. Yet what is interesting is that, like the true poet he was, Chocano felt the need to write out those sensations in his *estampas*: quiet and unassertive poems by his standards, but—with a century of hindsight—among his most impressive. Despite an early adherence to Darío and his project, Chocano was never a *modernista* poet in the narrow sense, nor even a modernist one in the broader sense; yet these poems, with their subtle rhythms and Baudelairean themes, come as close as he ever did to a modernist idiom. Call it the New York effect.

In many ways, then, nobody better than Chocano for Salomón de la Selva to honour with a pan-American dinner. In a letter to Archer Huntington a few days later de la Selva wrote:

> The evening, I hope, will be a memorable one; for, for the first time in the history of America, literary men of the Northern and Southern continents were gathered to exchange ideas and ideals, and to lay the basis for their better understanding. Poems were read by Sr. Chocano and by Mr Thomas Walsh, Mr Wm. Rose Benét, and others. I had the honor of translating, at sight, both the Spanish and the English poems for the benefit of all the company.[164]

---

[163] Sánchez, *Aladino*, pp. 245–49.
[164] Letter from Salomón de la Selva to Archer M. Huntington, HSA (17 November 1915); and see Huntington's replies of 26 and 30 November 1915. Huntington had been invited but he rarely attended social functions.

Instantaneous translation between the two languages, in both directions, was de la Selva's party piece.

On the same day as his letter to Huntington, de la Selva replied to a note from Edna written in Spanish. After congratulating her, in Spanish, he moved to English to describe the dinner for Chocano:

> Now, Love, last Saturday we gave a little feast to the great South American poet, Don José Santos Chocano, at my house. The American (U.S.) poets that attended read verses of their own, which I, in a tour de force that cost me a headache, translated at sight into Spanish. I wish you had been with us! The purpose of these receptions is to create friendly relations between the poets of North and South America. There is nothing selfish or commercial about these gatherings; and they are not literary meetings, but social evenings rather, where poets come to know poets, and where, already, several pleasant friendships have begun.
>
> So far I haven't dared to invite women. I know how to multiply myself, when I am among men, so as to seem to give myself entirely to each & every one of my guests. With women at my parties it would be, I have thought, all different ... But, joking aside, I am going to try women very soon. And, if you will allow me, my next reception will be in your honor, to introduce you to Latin American men & women of letters. And I shall invite American poets and their wives. Chaperones will abound: I shall name Jessie Rittenhouse chaperone-in-chief. (You ought to see Thomas Walsh describe her roundness. Fat Tom Walsh, beneath his pompous pretensions to respectability, is a comical old cuss.)[165]

He explained to Edna that he was hoping to arrange his reception in her honour for the evening of Saturday, 27 September 1915. It speaks volumes about Edna's elusiveness that this reception finally took place more than two years later, on the occasion of Chocano's *next* visit to New York.

---

[165] Letter from Salomón de la Selva to Edna St Vincent Millay, ESVMP (17 November 1915).

Chapter Four

New York through Spanish Eyes (1916)

Early December this year of grace
(*This year of sorrow*, the world's heart saith).[1]

New York had been a magnet for many years. During 1916, Marcus Garvey joined the ranks of black West Indians in the city: it wouldn't take him long to shake things up. The impending storm in Russia brought Nikolai Bukharin to Manhattan. Writers continued to arrive, Mina Loy perhaps the most renowned this year. Unable to tour Europe, the Ballets Russes arrived in January. Latin American elites were used to decamping to Europe in the summer. The war had put a stop to such tours but the Havana magazine *Social* helpfully produced a guide to New York, listing the best hotels and clubs over four issues, ensuring that rich Cuban tourists had something to spend their money on.[2] On 30 July, German agents blew up the munitions factory on Black Tom Island in New York harbour, proving that the war in Europe was not limited to Europe. On 16 October, Margaret Sanger opened the country's first birth control clinic, in Brooklyn, violating Section 1142 of the New York State Penal Code, which criminalised the distribution of materials about contraception due to their obscene nature. Sanger had been trying to provoke prosecution in order to push the previously obscure topic of birth control into public debate. The provocation worked: she was arrested.

The cultural revolution continued apace. Modern US drama can be dated from the November production of Eugene O'Neill's *Bound East for Cardiff* at the Provincetown Playhouse at 139 MacDougal Street in Greenwich

---

[1] From Salomón de la Selva, 'December 1916', *Tropical Town and Other Poems*, New York: John Lane Company, 1918, p. 73.

[2] 'New York', *Social*, 1, no. 6 (June 1916), 28; no. 7 (July 1916), 41; no. 8 (August 1916), 39; no. 9 (September 1916), 25.

Village, two doors up from the Liberal Club. The actors had had two informal summer seasons on Cape Cod, but that autumn they had organised themselves as 'The Provincetown Players', voting to produce a season in New York City. Mexican art made its first impression on New York when Marius de Zayas's Modern Gallery staged an exhibition of Diego Rivera's paintings in the autumn.

Salomón de la Selva doggedly pursued his pan-American project while benefiting from the job opportunities opening up in the teaching of romance languages. His path crossed that of the young Spanish poet Juan Ramón Jiménez, who came to New York in January to get married and wrote one of the longest and most intriguing of all early twentieth-century poems, partly about his experiences of what everyone was now thinking of as the city of the future. Meanwhile, Salomón painstakingly wrote his poems out in longhand and had his friend Rufino González design a simple cover. His growing list of correspondents now included the renowned Edwin Markham of Staten Island.

Courting Archer

Although Salomón de la Selva could later be quite rude about the reclusive Archer Huntington, the first surviving correspondence between them indicates that the poet had written to the philanthropist to tell him about his reduced circumstances, enclosing a poem for good measure: the latter had responded with a cheque for $100.[3] In another letter, de la Selva modestly summed up his experience as a translator: versions of Chaucer, Keats, Rossetti, and Stephen Phillips published in Mexico; of William Rose Benét, Joyce Kilmer, and Edna St Vincent Millay in the Havana *Fígaro*, and in *Las Novedades* translations of Thomas Walsh, more Millay, and now 'four versions of Mrs Huntington's very lovely songs', which he enclosed, asking for permission and any improvements the couple might offer, along with his ringing endorsement of the songs' 'delicate beauty'.[4] Despite his critical acumen, Salomón was—when his financial interests were at stake—capable of showing palpable insincerity. In fact, though, given that Helen Huntington was around this time beginning an affair with the English actor

---

[3] Letter from Salomón de la Selva to Archer Huntington, HSASS (5 March 1915). The HSASS is Salomón de la Selva, Member's File, Hispanic Society of America, New York.

[4] Letter from Salomón de la Selva to Archer Huntington, HSASS (18 January 1916).

Harley Granville Barker, which would lead to the Huntingtons' divorce in 1918, this may not have been the best way to Archer Huntington's wallet, though de la Selva was hardly in a position to know that.

Nonetheless, by 1916, de la Selva was closely involved in two important translation projects underwritten by Huntington. The first, an anthology of Spanish-language poetry covering nine centuries, was an ambitious undertaking which would offer originals and translations. In February, de la Selva was full of ideas for publicising the anthology, including having Huntington interviewed by Joyce Kilmer for the *New York Times*. De la Selva's seven-page prospectus gives a detailed outline—150 poems by 90 poets, all of which are listed with a note of existing translations or possible translators: de la Selva himself is slated to do more than 50 translations.[5] Eventually, an expanded version, called *Hispanic Anthology*, featuring around 175 poets, was published by the Hispanic Society of America (HSA) in 1920 with Thomas Walsh as sole editor.[6] The skeleton of de la Selva's original proposal is still visible in the published version but, though Walsh himself was responsible for a number of the translations, de la Selva's name appears nowhere. This project would be a source of ongoing friction between de la Selva and Walsh.

In March 1916, de la Selva wrote to Edna Millay: 'Rubén Darío died a month ago today and I haven't been able to sleep quietly since.'[7] But he had offered a set of ten of his translations of Darío's poems to the HSA, which Huntington accepted, paying him 25 cents per line, which amounted to $60. When *Eleven Poems of Rubén Darío* appeared later that year, de la Selva's ten translations had been supplemented by Thomas Walsh's translation of 'Portico', but his name appeared above de la Selva's on the title page.[8] In the *Hispanic Anthology*, the only translation of a poem by Darío that is reprinted from *Eleven Poems* is 'Portico'. The review in *The Sun*, while welcoming the translations of 'the greatest of Spanish poets', did regret that in most instances the name of the translator wasn't attached to each poem—and that, in the one where it was, 'Portico', Walsh's translation seemed to have fallen below his usual standards.[9] That must have brought a smile to the face of the Nicaraguan.

---

[5] Letter from Salomón de la Selva to Archer Huntington, HSASS (16 February 1916), with seven-page synopsis, 'An Anthology of Spanish Poetry'.

[6] Thomas Walsh, ed., *Hispanic Anthology: Poems Translated from the Spanish by English and North American Poets*, New York: G. P. Putnam's Sons, 1920.

[7] Letter from Salomón de la Selva to Edna St Vincent Millay, ESVMP (6 March 1916).

[8] Rubén Darío, *Eleven Poems*, translations by Thomas Walsh and Salomón de la Selva; introduction by Pedro Henríquez Ureña, New York: G. P. Putnam's Sons, 1916.

[9] 'Poems in All Keys', *The Sun* (17 February 1918), 4.

Relationships with Huntington and the HSA seem to have remained cordial. In May, Huntington accepted an invitation to hear de la Selva speak at Columbia; in July, de la Selva was elected a corresponding member of the HSA, and in May 1917, the HSA librarian, E. C. Hills, sent de la Selva two copies of his pamphlet on Latin American poets and Huntington sent books too, which de la Selva, now teaching at Williams College, distributed to his best students.[10]

*

The early twentieth century was the period when Latin America first became a subject of academic study in the USA and plenty of material was now being published. So, for example, William Robert Shepherd (1871–1934), who had a PhD in History from Columbia and who would later return there as Professor of History, was by 1908 considered an authority on Latin America and served that year as a delegate to the first Pan-American Scientific Congress at Santiago, Chile, and a year later as secretary of the US delegation to the fourth International Conference of American States in Buenos Aires. He participated in several later Pan-American conferences and lectured extensively abroad on Latin America. His *The Hispanic Nations of the New World* was published in 1919, offering a slightly bland account of the subject, with only the mildest of implied criticism of US foreign policy.[11]

The early development of US literary scholarship about Hispanic America owed most to J. D. M. Ford, appointed to the Harvard Smith professorship in 1907, aged just 34. Ford undertook an extensive tour of South American universities in 1913 and was the inspiration behind two path-breaking books, Alfred Coester's *The Literary History of Spanish America* (1916) and Isaac Goldberg's *Studies in Spanish American Literature* (1920). Coester's doctoral thesis under Ford had been on the *Poema de mio Cid* and he taught at a Brooklyn school for 15 years, but Ford encouraged his interest in Spanish-American literature, which would eventually lead Coester to a chair at Stanford. Coester was also one of the pioneers of the American Association of Teachers of Spanish, whose first chapter he helped establish on 21 October 1916 in New York. Published in August 1916, Coester's

---

[10] Letter from Salomón de la Selva to Archer Huntington, HSASS (11 May 1917); Letter from Salomón de la Selva to E.L. Stevenson, HSASS (26 September 1916); Letter from Salomón de la Selva to E. C. Hills, HSASS (7 May 1917).

[11] Shepherd was prominent enough to have a chair named after him, which is still extant at Columbia, though he was a publicist rather than a scholar.

The Literary History of Spanish America is a genuine milestone, the first book in any language to look at Spanish-American literature not as a sub-order of Spanish literature or as a mere imitation of French literature, but as something to be read on its own merits, having its own patterns, consistencies, and variations.[12] Even though Coester continued to give weight to the different national literatures involved and although inevitably it is dated in its opinions and prejudices, the book is well-informed and does a fine job of setting Spanish-American literature within its historical and political contexts. In his chapter on *modernismo*, Coester suggested two periods, symbolised by Darío's swan and condor. The first period focused on the creation of beauty; the second—shaken by political events around the turn of the century—looked outwards, although, after mentioning Darío's depiction of the USA as 'el futuro invasor de la América ingenua' [the future invader of ingenuous America], Coester laid more stress on Darío's 'Salutación al águila' and on Chocano's continental invocations.[13] Just as Coester's book appeared, Federico de Onís was asked to help organise Spanish studies at Columbia, on the recommendation to Nicholas Butler of Archer Huntington, who had sought the advice of Ramón Menéndez Pidal. In 1920, Onís founded the Instituto de las Españas, which later became the Casa Hispánica. Onís encouraged the study of Spanish-American literature, with the first PhD in the subject awarded at Columbia in 1923.[14]

---

[12] Coester, *Literary History of Spanish America*, viii–ix. Coester thanks Paul Groussac, both Henríquez Ureña brothers, and J. D. M. Ford at Harvard (xii), so he clearly had good advisors. See the essays in the Coester number of *Hispania*, 25, no. 3 (October 1942). Latin American literary history had previously tended to operate on a national basis: see Beatriz González Stephan, *Fundaciones: canon, historia y cultura nacional: la historiografía literaria del liberalismo hispanoamericano del siglo XIX*, Madrid: Iberoamericana; Frankfurt: Vervuert, 2002; and Naomi Lindstrom, 'Shifting Tendencies in Latin American Literary History', *Chasqui*, 29, no. 2 (2000), 96–107; though there had been Marcelino Menéndez Pelayo's *Historia de la poesía hispanoamericana* (1893): see Arcadio Díaz Quiñones, '1898: Hispanismo y Guerra', in *1898: su significado para Centroamérica y el Caribe: ¿Cesura, cambio, continuidad?*, ed. Walther L. Bernecker, Frankfurt: Vervuert; Madrid: Iberoamericana, 1998, pp. 17–35. More generally, see Helen Delpar, *Looking South: The Evolution of Latin Americanist Scholarship in the United States, 1850–1975*, Tuscaloosa: The University of Alabama Press, 2008. For the situation in these years, see James D. Fernández, 'Longfellow's Law: The Place of Latin America and Spain in U.S. Hispanism, circa 1915', in *Spain in America: The Origins of Hispanism in the United States*, ed. Richard L. Kagan, Urbana: University of Illinois Press, 2002, pp. 122–41.
[13] Coester, *Literary History of Spanish America*, pp. 464–65, 470–71.
[14] See the series of essays called 'Hispanismo en los Estados Unidos' (pp. 677–745), including 'Historia de los estudios hispánicos en la universidad de Columbia'

The Recently Married Poet

José Santos Chocano had not long left Manhattan towards the end of 1915 when the rising star of Spanish poetry arrived in the city: Juan Ramón Jiménez (Fig. 11). Born in 1881 in southern Spain, and so 15 years younger than Rubén Darío and six younger than Chocano, almost all of Jiménez's considerable poetic output was written after 1898. Although even less of a political poet than Darío—his recent work had included a collection of spiritual sonnets and a lyrical prose work about a donkey—Jiménez could easily be seen in 1916 as representing the intellectual and sensitive Hispanic soul, deeply tied to traditional values and opposed to the brutalising materialism associated with Spain's antagonist and conqueror.

The picture was, of course, more complicated than that. Jiménez was travelling to New York to marry Zenobia Camprubí, daughter of a very cosmopolitan family, whose brothers had been educated in the USA (on the wishes of their mother, whose own father was the scion of the Aymars, New York merchants), as a result of which Zenobia had spent several years in the country.[15] The Aymar trust benefited only direct descendants, not spouses, so Isabel, Zenobia's mother, had an independent income which included money in trust for her children. Zenobia's brother José would shortly become the owner of *La Prensa*, the leading Spanish-language newspaper in New York. Juan Ramón's bride was, therefore, already embroiled in US life, where she had much more social freedom than in Spain, a freedom she didn't much feel like renouncing. Zenobia and her mother had reached New York in December 1915 and stayed at the women-only Hotel Martha Washington (30 East 30th Street) until the wedding, which took place on 2 March 1916 at St Stephen's church at 151 East 29th Street, followed by a reception at the National Arts Club in Gramercy Park.

If, as at least one critic has suggested, the book that Jiménez wrote about his visit, *Diario de un poeta reciencasado* [Diary of a Newlywed Poet], tells of a personal and yet archetypal journey away from the nourishing mother

---

(pp. 725-34) in Federico de Onís, *España en América*, San Juan: Ediciones de la Universidad de Puerto Rico, 1955. And cf. Concha Meléndez, 'Federico de Onís y la América hispana', *Revista Hispánica Moderna*, 34, nos 1-2 (1968), 31-36; and Hugo Rodríguez-Alcalá, 'Sobre el americanismo de Federico de Onís', *Revista Hispánica Moderna*, 34, nos. 1-2 (1968), 71-84.

[15] Zenobia had first travelled to the USA aged nine, and had lived there for four years as a teenager (1905-09), becoming bilingual. She visited again in 1912. She always spoke English with her mother and brothers. See Angel Sody, *Biografía de Zenobia Camprubí: la musa de Juan Ramón Jiménez*, Bilbao: Ediciones Beta III Milenio, 2009.

11 Juan Ramón Jiménez painted by Joaquín de Sorolla y Bastida. Courtesy of The Hispanic Society of America, New York.

and towards the conjugal partner, a journey fraught with an anxiety which is eventually and triumphantly overcome, then the association of the wife with the USA suggests at the very least a mature reckoning with that land and with its principal city.[16] Jiménez was determined to confront his experiences head-on by writing a poetic diary and, although many of the constitutive pieces were presumably revised after composition, the resulting *Diario* goes out of its way to present itself as a collection of daily reflections and impressions, often carrying date and place as headings. The 143 poems are divided into six sections. The *Diario* is to a large extent a travel book, so the first and fifth sections are set in Spain, the second and fourth on the Atlantic, forth and back, and the third in the USA. The sixth—typical of a book which never quite conforms to any tidy description—consists of 'Recuerdos de América del Este Escritos en España' [Memories of Eastern United States Written in Spain], as if the urge to capture that US experience was not assuaged by the journey back home. Nevertheless, a superficial *arielista* sense of contrast can easily be drawn from the volume. Jiménez's impressions of New York tend to come in the prose fragments which cluster in sections III and VI—satirical and off-hand, with occasional notes of bafflement and outrage. Many of the entries are very short, like fragments of thoughts and ideas and impressions. Some are more set pieces, like the poem called in English 'New Sky' written as from the top of the Woolworth Building, then the tallest structure in the world; but even here the syntax is often broken, with dashes for punctuation.[17] The old poetic theme of the moon turns into: 'Broadway. La tarde. Anuncios mareantes de colorines sobre el cielo. Constelaciones nuevas.' Those new constellations are the vast advertising hoardings: the boar, the bottle, the scotsman, the fountain, the book, the ship, the moon: '—¡La luna!—¿A ver?—Ahí, mírala, entre esas dos casas

---

[16] The original Spanish is from Juan Ramón Jiménez, *Diario de un poeta recien casado (1916)*, ed. Michael P. Predmore, 6th edn, Madrid: Catedra, 2011; the English translation from *Diary of a Newlywed Poet: A Bilingual Edition of 'Diario de un poeta recien casado'*, with an introduction by Michael P. Predmore; translation by Hugh A. Harter, Selinsgrove, PA: Susquehanna University Press, 2004. See also the perceptive article by John P. Devlin, 'The Prose of Jiménez's *Diario de un poeta reciencasado*: A Revaluation', *Bulletin of Hispanic Studies*, 59, no. 4 (1982), 301–16. Predmore reads the poem as a coming-of-age narrative in which Spain is in effect the mother, with the USA as the wife: 'Moguer. Mother and siblings. / The clean and welcoming nest …' (*Diario*, XIII, p. 110/*Diary*, 13, p. 106), as Jiménez put it. The impulse is towards love and maturity, but the journey involves insecurity and danger before the final resolution.

[17] *Diario*, LXXIV, p. 160; *Diary*, 74, p. 240.

altas, sobre el río, sobre la octava, baja, roja, ¿no la ves …?—Deja, ¿a ver? No … ¿Es la luna, o es un anuncio de la luna?' [Broadway. Afternoon. Dizzying advertising signs of bright colors across the sky. New constellations ….—The moon!—Let's see?—There, just look at it between those two tall houses over the river, above Eighth Avenue, down low, and red, don't you see it?—Wait a minute, let's see? No …. Is it the moon or is it an advertisement of the moon?]^[18]

The New York poems are dominated by the themes of death and fire. 'La muerte' [Death] (LXXIII) is undated, but its placing in the *Diario* would suggest late March 1916: the weather had been unrelentingly cold since the wedding, the temperature rarely rising above zero. On the voyage across the Atlantic, Jiménez had learned of the death, on 8 February, of his friend Rubén Darío, perhaps hastened by the harsh New York winter he had experienced the previous year. Jiménez would be aware of following some of Darío's traces, particularly at the Hispanic Society of America.[19] Then, to Darío's death had been added that of the composer Enrique Granados, drowned along with his wife Amparo when the SS *Sussex* was torpedoed by a German U-boat in the English channel. Juan Ramón and Zenobia had met the Granados just before the composer and his wife left New York to return to Europe after the triumphant premiere of Granados's opera, *Goyescas*, at the Met, so the shock of their death would have been acute: his elegy to the couple, 'Humo y oro' [Smoke and gold], dated very precisely 'New York, at my window on Eleventh Street, March 27, morning, with a yellow moon …' must have been written within hours of receiving the news in that morning's copy of the *New York Times*: '—the solitary moon / is dying, shattered, oh Poe!, over Broadway—'.[20] Death was in the air, so it would have been easy for Juan Ramón to see the seven taxis in a line that open 'La muerte' as a funeral procession. They may even have been a funeral procession struggling through the traffic: nothing stops the New York traffic, even a funeral. Just 57 words (60 in the English translation):

Seven taxis in a line, in a hurry, but with a haste that would leave them between snow and mist. No buses stop, no taxis for the living, no streetcars. The sequence is rational, though sadly touching to the

---

[18] *Diario*, CXI, pp. 182–83; *Diary*, 111, p. 254.
[19] See Juan Ramón Jiménez, 'Rubén Darío (1940)', in his *Españoles de tres mundos*, Madrid: Alianza Editorial, 1987, p. 62.
[20] *Diario*, LXXXI, pp. 164–65; *Diary*, 81, p. 218. Granados's librettist, Fernando Periquet, had written a piece about *Goyescas* for *Las Novedades*, which de la Selva translated as 'How "Goyescas" Was Written', *New York Times*, 23 January 1916, p. X5.

heart at times: fire, the young woman, the young man, the boy, the old man, the old woman, death.[21]

In '¡Fuego!' [Fire!] the poet addresses the irony of a city dedicated to untrammelled freedom caging its buildings in elaborate and unsightly fire-escapes. Not far from Jiménez's hotel was the site of the Triangle shirtwaist factory where 147 people had died just five years earlier, some of them killed when an inadequate fire escape collapsed beneath them. The danger and fear of fire evokes images of the inferno, as if this were a city knowing that it is on the way to eternal damnation. That imagery, and that particular descent, are then underlined in the 22 words of the untitled XCVIII: 'What anguish! Always down below! It seems to me that I'm in a great broken down elevator that cannot—that will not be able!—to ascend to the sky'.[22] The city is going to hell and it is taking the poet with it.

Whereas Darío had shown a rather touching appreciation for the interest in him shown by US writers who were operating in a much lower league, and Salomón de la Selva was in the process of cultivating a wide range of published and aspiring poets around the city, Jiménez's literary contacts seemed to have remained relatively sparse. He did attend literary events at the Poetry Society of America and at the Authors' League—where on 2 May 1916, at a dinner to mark the anniversary of Shakespeare's death, he sat next to Salomón de la Selva[23]—but his attitude is summed up in the remark: 'I always thought that in New York there might not be any poets. What I didn't suspect was that there were so many bad poets.'[24] He was taken to the Authors Club by Thomas Walsh, who certainly fitted that particular bill. New York was not, then, for Jiménez, a place of literary refinement. When he goes out onto Long Island and asks to see Walt Whitman's house, he has his interlocutor (presumably his host, Arthur W. Page, the editor and publicist)[25] express surprise that he should want to see Whitman's house rather than Theodore Roosevelt's: 'Nobody has ever asked me such a thing!'[26] Poe and Whitman always provided the two examples that proved the rule

---

[21] *Diario*, LXXIII, p. 159; *Diary*, 73, p. 208.
[22] *Diario*, XCI, p. 171; *Diary*, 91, p. 230. *Diario*, XCVIII, p. 175; *Diary*, 98, p. 238.
[23] Letter from Salomón de la Selva to Edna St Vincent Millay, ESVMP (2 May 1916).
[24] *Diario*, CCXXX, pp. 286–87; *Diary*, 230, p. 464. This was a writer's comment about poor writers rather than a disparagement of US writers per se. Elsewhere he has appreciative discussions of Amy Lowell, Emily Dickinson, Edgar Allan Poe, and Edgar Lee Masters.
[25] Editor of *World's Work* (and presumably friend of the Camprubí family) and later a big noise in public relations.
[26] *Diario*, CCXXXII, p. 288; *Diary*, 232, p. 468.

of general US philistinism—geniuses despised and cast out by their own societies. So identification would tend therefore to be sought—in another Romantic trope—with outcasts, of whom the *Diario* has various avatars, such as a sleeping negro woman, an elderly man harassed by a suffragist, and a blind organ-grinder.[27] Juan Ramón joins their ranks when, delighted to find an early edition of Garcilaso in the library of the Hispanic Society of America, he declaims the poems in the street to the amusement of the passing policemen.

Within these generally cold, infernal, and philistine surroundings, the Hispanic poet searches out places and moments of tranquillity. Washington Square is a frequent reference point, just round the corner from the Hotel Van Rensselaer at 17–19 East 11th Street to which the honeymooning couple had moved on 19 March from the equally close but apparently less salubrious Hotel Marlton at 5 West 8th Street. A tree outside the imposing 1 Fifth Avenue, a step north of the Square, provides notable solace, a glimpse of nature, the true poet's ultimate refuge.

And yet, such an *arielista* reading of the *Diario*—stressing the negative and even philistine elements of New York—risks ignoring its ambiguities. To begin with, the *arielista* tendencies are often incomplete or thwarted or countered by other remarks. There is little obvious anger or even frustration in the poet's words: the prevailing tone is humorous, if occasionally exasperated. The policemen smile—they do not beat him up. The Whitman house turns out to be inhabited by a Pole who has no idea who Whitman is and doesn't want to let them in. Yet the man seems to Juan Ramón like a reincarnation of Whitman himself:

De pronto, un hombre alto, lento y barbudo, en camisa y con sombrero ancho, como el retrato juvenil de Whitman, viene—¿de donde?—y me dice, apoyado en su barra de hierro, que no sabe quién es Whitman, que él es polaco, que la casa es suya y que no tiene ganas de enseñarsela a nadie. Y, encogiéndose, se mete dentro, por la puertecita que parece de juguete.

[All of a sudden, a tall man, sluggish and bearded, wearing a short and a wide-brimmed hat like the one in the youthful picture of Whitman, comes out—from where?—leaning on his iron bar, declares that he doesn't know who Whitman is, that he is Polish, that the house is his and that he doesn't feel like showing it to anyone. Then, with a shrug

---

[27] *Diario*, LXXXIX, LXXXVI, and 9. This last is one of the extra 27 pieces first published in the 1970 edition of the *Diario*.

of his shoulders, he goes inside through a door small enough to be for a doll house.]²⁸

It is almost as if Jiménez had conjured Whitman up through the spirit of the place to provide the brush-off, to represent the no-nonsense new world in the face of old-world curiosity. The poet allows himself to stand corrected and perhaps a little in awe.

Similarly, the *Tempest* imagery that Darío and Rodó had both made familiar with reference to the USA did not seem to tempt Jiménez. The opportunity arose when he and Zenobia went to see Percy MacKaye's masque 'Caliban by the Yellow Sands', written to celebrate the 300th anniversary of Shakespeare's death, but the poem he wrote afterwards, 'A Miranda, en el Estadio' [To Miranda in the Stadium], mentions neither Caliban nor Ariel: in fact he seems more interested in the actress who played Miranda, Gladys Hanson.²⁹

As with Darío, although on a different scale, it is formal innovation which marks the *Diario*'s response to New York, particularly the unusual combination of verse and prose. Although Jiménez's social calendar was far removed from Darío's sickbed, the Spanish poet also seemed not entirely conscious of his own achievement—or at least disposed retrospectively to undermine it. His preliminary note to the book offers a classic case of disavowal: 'No el ansia de color exótico, ni el afán de "necesarias" novedades. La que viaja, siempre que viajo, es mi alma, entre almas. Ni más nuevo, al ir, ni más lejos; más hondo. Nunca más diferente, más alto siempre' [Neither the longing for exotic color nor the desire for something 'necessarily' new. What travels, whenever I travel, is my soul, among souls. Neither newer, on going, nor farther; deeper. Never more different, always higher].³⁰ That's six denials in the opening four lines. The note is obviously written after the fact: probably his way of trying to cope with the disorientation of the experience which his poetic diary has registered. Jiménez then excluded the

---

[28] *Diario*, CCXXXII, p. 289; *Diary*, 232, p. 468.

[29] *Diario*, CXLVII, pp. 214–15; *Diary*, 147, pp. 320–21. Percy MacKaye wanted his 'community masque', as he called it, to be performed in Central Park but had to settle for the recently opened Lewisohn Stadium, at City College, in East Harlem, where around 20,000 people a night watched the spectacle, with 20 professional actors in the speaking roles and 2,000 to 3,000 people performing in the related spectacles and pageants and interludes: Percy MacKaye, *Caliban by the Yellow Sands*, Garden City, NY: Doubleday, Page & Company, 1916. And see Coppélia Kahn, 'Caliban at the Stadium: Shakespeare and the Making of Americans,' *Massachusetts Review*, 41, no. 2 (2000), 256–84.

[30] *Diario*, p. 98; *Diary*, p. 84.

prose pieces—almost all dealing with New York—from the selection he made at this time for his *Poesías escojidas (1899-1917)* (1917), as well as suggesting in the *Diario*'s closing note that it is a 'provisional' work which he may well later correct.[31] He did indeed subsequently speak about publishing the verse and prose separately, but never did so, despite plenty of opportunities, as if sensing unconsciously that the book's achievement came out of the novelty of its organisation, while his conscious mind wanted to tidy up the mixing of poetry and prose. As with Rubén Darío and José Santos Chocano, one senses in Jiménez's *Diario* a modernist response almost against the grain of authorial intention.

Through his wife's friends and connections, Jiménez had an active social life in New York and beyond—probably more active than he felt comfortable with, given that one of his nicknames for his new bride was 'Miss Rápida'. Zenobia's own more conventional diary gives a taste of this activity.[32] They frequently met friends and family in the Vanderbilt Hotel at Park Avenue and East 34th Street and took side trips to Boston and Washington, DC. But Jiménez made new Hispanic connections too. Huntington was predictably assiduous in his attentions, and as a result is the dedicatee of various entries in the *Diario*. Jiménez also had dinner with the Underhills, John Garrett Underhill, translator of Jacinto Benavente, being a friend of the Camprubí family. In April and May he met frequently with Pedro Henríquez Ureña.

And, more than any other visitor, Jiménez went on literary pilgrimages. As well as seeking out Whitman's house on Long Island, he took the long trek up to Fordham to see Poe's cottage—one of many houses Poe lived in in New York:

'Poe's House'
—What about Poe's house? What about Poe's house? What about Poe's house?
—...!?
The young people shrug their shoulders. One pleasant old lady whispers to me:
—Yes. A little house, white. Yes, yes, I've heard about it. And she wants to tell me where it is, but her shattered memory can't take a straight path. There is no guide. So we go where we've been half told, but we never find it.[33]

---

[31] *Diario*, p. 300; *Diary*, p. 492.
[32] Zenobia Camprubí, *Vivir con Juan Ramón*, ed. Arturo del Villar, Madrid: Los Libros de Fausto, 1986.
[33] *Diario*, CCXLI, pp. 296-97; *Diary*, 241, p. 486.

It perhaps suited Jiménez's purpose that the cottage proved impossible to locate. In fact it had only been in 1913 that it had been moved across the street from its original location, and was now in the process of being designated as a literary monument.

*

This year of 1916 also saw the arrival in New York of Martín Luis Guzmán (Fig. 12), who was soon reporting his impressions of Salomón de la Selva to his friend back in Mexico City, Alfonso Reyes:

> Salomón de la Selva: young, pale, enthusiastic, amorous. He turned up at my house on the day of my arrival and we talked for ages. He seems pretty knowledgable about his craft, and prepared to sympathise with all the others. He has a violinist girlfriend, about whom he speaks passionately, without blinking. He is refined in temperament, with the nimbleness and sensibility of a real poet.[34]

The violinist may have been another salomonic fantasy figure: the unblinking are usually making it all up. But it is surely suggestive that de la Selva appeared on Guzmán's doorstep on the very day of his arrival, so keen was he to add another writer to the network. Guzmán goes on to list for Reyes no fewer than 20 Hispanic figures he's already encountered in New York, most of them Mexican. De la Selva would be increasingly busy.

Born in 1887, Guzmán had come of age with the Mexican Revolution, of which he was eventually one of the most important chroniclers. Having been a supporter of Francisco Madero and then, briefly, of Pancho Villa, he had known Pedro Henríquez Ureña in Mexico City, which would doubtless have provided his connection to de la Selva. Guzmán had previous experience of New York: a brief six-day visit just after Huerta's coup in 1913, which he describes in the opening pages of his autobiographical novel *El águila y la serpiente* [The Eagle and the Serpent]; a slightly longer stay in early 1914, which was probably to buy arms for Carranza and during which he met several other Mexican political exiles at the McAlpin Hotel on Broadway and West 34th Street; and a passing stay en route to Madrid in 1915.[35] After several months in Madrid, he returned to New York for a

---

[34] Letter from Martín Luis Guzmán to Alfonso Reyes (9 March 1916), in Martín Luis Guzmán and Alfonso Reyes, *Medias palabras: correspondencia (1913–1959)*, Mexico City: Universidad Nacional Autónoma de México, 1991, p. 86.

[35] See Susana Quintanilla, *A salto de mata: Martín Luis Guzmán en la revolución*

12 Martín Luis Guzmán.
Provenance unknown.

fourth time, probably because he thought it would be easier there to make ends meet.

Guzmán's stay in New York was typical of the sojourner—unable at least temporarily to return to his own country, without a fixed job and not interested in permanent immigration; although untypical in that he had a wife and three young children to support: they lived at 36 West 93rd Street, just a few blocks north of de la Selva and equally close to the park. He made a living as best he could, working for The New Continent Commercial Corporation, at 42 Broadway, selling aspirin to relieve Mexico's headaches, while trying—without much success—to construct a book-selling business for himself, and writing articles for *Revista Universal* and *El Gráfico*.[36]

---

mexicana, Mexico City: Tusquets Editores, 2009; and her 'A orillas de la Revolución: Martín Luis Guzmán in Madrid (1915)', *HMex*, 44, no. 1 (2014), 105–57.

[36] Two studies of Guzmán's New York years are Federico Patán, 'Martín Luis Guzmán se exilia en el Hudson', in his *El espejo y la nada*, Mexico City: Coordinación de Difusión Cultural, Dirección de Literatura, UNAM, 1998, pp. 77–86; and Rafael Lemus, 'The Emergence of a Writer: Martín Luis Guzmán on the Banks of the Hudson', trans. Ann De León and Chris Schafenacker, *Translation Review*, 81, no. 1 (2011), 48–59.

For five months he took over as editor of the ambitious and well-illustrated *El Gráfico*, with offices at 1400 Broadway, just south of the 42nd Street branch of the New York Public Library. The magazine had been founded in 1916 by the Spanish businessman Joseph Branyas (who died before the first issue appeared) and with Francisco Pendas as managing editor. It covered politics, culture, current affairs, fashion, and literature, but was distinctly Spanish in orientation, rather than Latin American or Latino. It ran a long series of articles on Cervantes and other pieces on current Spanish novelists. During the war the quality of its paper declined dramatically, and it went through a series of managing editors, Guzmán overseeing what turned out to be its final months from February to June 1918.

Guzmán collected his essays written in New York and published them in Mexico in 1920 as *A orillas del Hudson* [On the Banks of the Hudson]. Some are reflections on events in Mexico, but others continue the Hispanic tradition of the *crónica* written from the belly of the beast. Rafael Lemus suggests that it was this New York experience that turned Guzmán into a serious writer. The book begins with the snow, which always came as a shock to writers from the American Tropics: the winters of 1915–16 and 1916–17 were especially brutal. He then moves from the white of the snow to the white clothes of the tennis players against the background of the verdant meadows of Central Park in a piece about lawn tennis, also the subject of a poem by Guzmán's compatriot, José Juan Tablada. Tennis had once been the preserve of the aristocracy but was now being played by the many, without—for Guzmán—the game losing its enchantment. One senses here some of the unexpected attractions for the Hispanic visitor: the large family groups, the informality of relationships between the sexes, women's increasing freedom—physical as well as intellectual. Guzmán certainly showed an interest in his cultural surroundings too: he takes notice of and writes about Isadora Duncan, Troy Kinney, Diego Rivera, cubism, H. G. Wells … But for the most part the pieces are short and impressionistic: there is nothing with the heft of Martí or Darío's *crónicas*. His main focus remains Mexico and its political controversies, though his northern location justifies an even-handed essay about Mexico's relationship with the USA, noting with a degree of objectivity how the countries misunderstand each other.[37] One piece might be taken as indicative of his response to the city. In 'Entre el cielo y la tierra' [Between heaven and earth], Guzmán suggests that every city has a soul and that it is the sacred duty of the traveller to

---

[37] Martín Luis Guzmán, *A orillas del Hudson*, Mexico City: Librería Editorial Andrés Botas e Hijo, 1920, pp. 95–97.

seek it out. From the 29th storey of a downtown skyscraper, he looks out, impressed by the views, and wonders:

> From the elevated vantage point we can see one of the greatest and most beautiful spectacles of man-made achievement. Perhaps it's there that dwells, like the secret spirit animating this brutal accumulation of energy, the soul of the people of New York. Let our gaze follow the tall towers of the houses, darts that spurt from the ground until their points are lost in the mist. Let's turn towards the rippling waves of Cyclopean roofs, crowned with a thousand delicate curls of escaping steam. Let's look down at the wide ribbon of the river, tied by the iron rings of the bridges, its banks jagged by the innumerable wharves, its restless water agitated by the countless boats and barges: a stream of trams and carts and cars rolls day and night over every bridge; every lighter carries whole trains across the river. And this gigantic panorama, swathed in the thick and jumbled sounds that drift up here like the shadows of the setting sun, is repeated as far as the eye can see. Is this vitality—arrogant, brutal, offensive, beautiful, magnificent—the soul of New York?
>
> Dwarfed by their handiwork, like bees beside the hive, humans scuttle about down below, diminutive and silent. Seen from on high, their gait acquires an unusual lightness and their movements a new grace. Their progress is unimpeded, their pace regular. They pass without bumping into or even brushing against each other. They move with such precision between the cars, the trams, and the little carts that we feel like going down to follow them in their play. Because it must be play, that perfect sauntering that produces no sound and no fatigue. Only when we look carefully at one place (as if examining a small picture full of figures) do we come across sudden collisions and falls and trips; but these are fleeting and perfect fluency is soon restored. A fine contrast it is between this panorama of brute force ruling over its tracks and the sweet glide of bodies through the flat streets, free of obstacles! Happy these mortals who've known how to load machines with their weariness while they disport themselves carefree! Does this make up the happy soul of the city? Does the easy coming and going we watch from on high express the soul of New York?[38]

Seriously, at length, and with some real empathy, Guzmán takes the pulse of the metropolis, only ultimately, in the last section of his essay, to decide

---

[38] Guzmán, *A orillas del Hudson*, pp. 42–43.

that any civilised city needs boulevards in which those who want to move can do so, and those who would rather watch can find a place. He doesn't mention the obvious examples: Paris, Madrid, and Mexico City. But, as the last line of the piece drily states, 'en Nueva York no hay bulevares' [in New York there are no boulevards].[39] When he wrote that sentence, Guzmán was committing himself to return to live in Mexico as soon as the political circumstances allowed.

*

Mexican exiles in New York came in many different colours and were separated by ideological and personal differences. De la Selva seems to have moved smoothly between them, becoming close to Martín Luis Guzmán and José Vasconcelos, but also socialising with José Juan Tablada, Pedro Requena, and José Castellot. Requena—de la Selva's exact contemporary—offers an interesting contrast. Pedro Requena belonged to one of the richest families in Mexico under the *porfiriato*: his grandfather made a fortune dealing in sugar cane and precious woods, and his father, José Luis Requena, a successful lawyer, increased the fortune through his investments in the mining industry, the family home becoming a showcase of Mexican art nouveau design.[40] After the fall of Porfirio Díaz, the Requenas stayed in Mexico City, only to fall foul of Madero's successor, Victoriano Huerta, who reneged on an agreement to work with the politician Félix Díaz, exiled Díaz, and then started to round up and shoot leading *felicistas*—a group that included José Luis Requena, who fled to New York with his family at the end of 1914. Pedro would die in the influenza outbreak of 1919, so he spent the most productive years of his short life in Manhattan, earning a reputation for his translations into Spanish of poems by Alan Seeger and, especially, Rabindranath Tagore. Luis Muñoz Marín wrote that Requena had no equal as a translator from English.[41] He worked as a lawyer (with his father) and a translator out of an office in Nassau Street and lived in an apartment on West 120th Street, just north of Central Park. However, at an Italian restaurant on 8th Street

---

[39] Guzmán, *A orillas del Hudson*, p. 44.
[40] See <https://grandescasasdemexico.blogspot.co.uk/2014/03/la-casa-de-la-familia-requenalegarreta.html> accessed December 2018.
[41] Quoted in 'In Memoriam', in Pedro Requena Legarreta, *Poesías líricas: rústicas, rimas paganas y diversas*, Mexico City: Miguel E. Castilleja e hijos, 1930, pp. i–xxiv, at p. xiii. Muñoz Marín's essay had first appeared in *La Revista de Indias* in 1918 and was reprinted in the *New York Evening Post* in December 1923.

he would meet *en tertulia* with José Juan Tablada, Joaquín Méndez Rivas, Antonio Castro Leal (all three Mexican), Alfonso Guillén Zelaya, Manuel Cestero, and Salomón de la Selva. José Santos Chocano and Amado Nervo were said to have visited when in town.[42]

Unlike, say, Chocano or Tablada, who in different ways engaged with New York in their poetry, Requena's poetic world was elsewhere. The name of the city appears just once, in the title of a poem called 'Desde Lejos (En Nueva York)' [From Afar (in New York)], where it merely provides skies 'de espesa neblina' which hide the stars 'con torpe cortina' [of thick mist … with a heavy curtain], forcing the poet's memory to fly like a swallow back to his homeland.[43] Requena's New York years were the years of the First World War, and the one book he completed during his lifetime was an anthology of verse by poets who had died during that war.[44]

Of these Mexican exiles, José Juan Tablada would ultimately stay longest and write most about New York, though this writing mainly came after de la Selva left the city. Tablada was based in New York for 20 years after his exile from Mexico in 1915 following the fall of Huerta, but he published little in the early years, and all of it outside the country, in Colombia and Venezuela (where he had brief diplomatic appointments), and in Cuba and Paris. In New York he founded and ran a 'Latin' bookshop (selling books in Spanish, French, and Italian) and taught French—marrying one of his pupils, a much younger Cuban woman. Appointed to a position in Ecuador which he clearly didn't want to take up, Tablada wrote a letter to Carranza in November 1919, listing his writings in a rather desperate attempt to prove his loyalty to the Mexican state.[45] Among the few traces of New York in his writing at this time are the three poems in a section of his 1918 volume *Al sol y bajo la luna* called 'En Nueva York', all of which touch on the question of the unavailability of young US women. As the beginning of one has it:

---

[42] Pável Granados, 'Mala suerte de Pedro Requena', in 'Requena: esplendor y olvido,' 3 pp. <http://www.milenio.com/cdb/doc/impreso/8899292> accessed December 2018. Granados reports the restaurant's name as El Angelo, though L'Angelo or Angelo's would seem more likely.

[43] Pedro Requena Legarreta, 'Desde Lejos (En Nueva York)', in his *Poesías líricas*, pp. 193–96, at p. 195.

[44] Pedro Requena Legarreta, ed., *Antología de poetas muertos en la guerra, 1914–1918*, Mexico City: Cultura, 1919.

[45] In Nina Cabrera de Tablada, *José Juan Tablada en la intimidad*, Mexico City: Imprenta Universitaria, 1954, pp. 151–52. See also Rodolfo Mata, 'José Juan Tablada and Cuba', *Literatura Mexicana*, 22, no. 1 (May 2011) <http://www.scielo.org.mx/scielo.php?script=sci_arttext&pid=S0188-25462011000100010> accessed December 2018.

New York through Spanish Eyes (1916) 155

>Mujeres que pasáis por la Quinta Avenida
>tan cerca de mis ojos, tan lejos de mi vida ...
>
>[You women who walk down Fifth Avenue
>so close to my eyes, so far from my life ...]

The poem then ends:

>Mujeres 'fire proof', a la pasión inertes,
>llenas de fortaleza, como las cajas fuertes,
>
>es vuestro seno el antro de la ambición histérica,
>¡vuestro secreto es una combinación numérica![46]
>
>[Fire-proof women, inert to passion,
>Full of resolution, just like a strongbox,
>
>your breast is a cavern of hysterical ambition,
>your secret is a combination lock!]

Fire-proofing was a big issue in a city so susceptible to damaging fires, but Spanish then had no equivalent adjective (it would now be *ignífugo*), so the English word is used, as if it would be linguistically unthinkable for a Spanish woman to resist the call of passion. 'Inert' is an insulting enough word in this context, but the poet then adds the strongbox protected by a combination lock, a kind of metaphorical chastity belt, only, presumably, to be unlocked by the supernumerate businessmen of Wall Street. But Tablada was rarely a crude poet, so there may be an element of self-mockery in this failure to find the combination to unlock the hearts of Manhattan maidens. He was, after all, 47 years old when he published these poems.

Part of the problem was that these were not now the swaddled and prim ladies of 1914, but athletic young women who were showing more of their bodies than ever before, some of them in enhanced and magnified fashion on the proliferating movie screens. The French called this new figure 'la jeune fille américaine': sporting, free-spirited, independent. Jean Cocteau summed her up in 1919: 'les États-Unis évoquent une jeune fille chez qui le plaisir d'aller bien l'emporte sur le sentiment de sa beauté. Elle nage, boxe,

---

[46] José Juan Tablada, *Obras*, vol. 1, *Poesía*, Mexico: Universidad Nacional Autónoma de México, Centro de Estudios Literarios, 1971, p. 624. This was the original version, subsequently modified: see p. 327.

danse, saute sur des trains en marche, sans se savoir belle. C'est nous qui admirons sa figure au cinématographe, grande comme une figure de déesse' [The United States ... evokes a girl more interested in her health than in her beauty. She swims, boxes, dances, leaps onto moving trains—all without knowing she is beautiful. It is we who admire her face, on the screen, enormous, like the face of a goddess].[47] Cocteau put the figure in *Parade*, performed by the Ballets Russes in May 1917; but her true incarnation was the film star Mary Pickford.

The young woman's game of choice was lawn tennis: athletic enough but not exhausting, allowing graceful movement, and offering an opportunity for even looser, and fewer, clothes than normal. Having started in New York within cricket clubs, tennis was in these years spreading to the parks, particularly Central Park, where whole families could gather to play at weekends. Perhaps because it had been such an elite activity in Mexico, both Guzmán and Tablada seem to have been fascinated by the spectacle, and Tablada—in full experimental mode in these years—produced an image of the game's hypnotic movement in his poem entitled, in English, 'Lawn Tennis' (327–28), soon translated by Salomón de la Selva—apparently without Tablada's knowledge:[48]

> Clothed in such rippling
>   White robes as these,
> You seem to sport in
>   Peplos of Greece,
>
>   Feigning the glory,
>   Fleetness and grace
>   Of the wing'd Victory
>   Of Samothrace.
>
> Vain are your poses—
>   What is the use!
> For, far from being
>   Dryad or Muse,
>
>   You cannot even
>   Discern the lewd
>   Winds that would have you
>   Ungirdled, nude ...

---

[47] Jean Cocteau, *Carte blanche: Articles parus dans Paris-Midi du 31 mars au 11 août 1919*, Paris: Aux éditions de La Sirène, 1920, p. 108.

[48] José Juan Tablada, *Obras*, vol. 4, *Diario (1900–1944)*, ed. Guillermo Sheridan, Mexico City: Universidad Nacional Autónoma de México, 1992, p. 164.

>   Your feet on Yankee
>   Soil ever press:
>   High is the soaring
>   Of the Nikés!⁴⁹

*

Edna Millay didn't improve as a correspondent, so by 18 January 1916 Salomón was threatening to leave for Japan and Java: she would never see him again. As far as Edna was concerned, further intermittent declarations of Salomón's love ensued, usually immediately followed by statements of how foolish he was to have loved her.⁵⁰ He was also frequently rude about the Poetry Society: 'that poor hencoop that gets so stirred when a real rooster comes in'.⁵¹ No prizes for guessing who he saw as the rooster.

In September, de la Selva took up a teaching position in modern languages at Williams College in Williamstown, just across the state line in Massachusetts. He was soon conveying to Edna an invitation from his head of department Professor and Mrs Rice to visit them, so enchanted had they been by de la Selva's account of her. Having not heard back in a week, he was getting impatient, trying out various forms of blackmail: 'The Rices ask me: Have you heard from Ednecita?' In case she still worries about leading him on, he insists: 'Edna, I wish once & for all to dispel whatever fear you may have of my making love to you.—I made love to you once, & you did not care for it. I will not make love to you again.' In the same letter he also makes an unusually direct political comment in connection with a visit that Woodrow Wilson has made to Williams College: 'I was glad that he was reëlected. He has done more than any other American to do away with the hatred for the U.S. that generations of distrust had fostered in my peoples.'⁵² This was a view that would soon be severely tested.

After several more persistent inquiries, Salomón finally heard on 29 November that she would indeed accept the invitation. She visited on Saturday, 2 December, and on the Monday he wrote, still overflowing with

---

⁴⁹ In *Pan American Magazine*, 27, no. 6 (October 1918), 332. Tablada's original layout didn't make it into this version, perhaps because de la Selva wasn't there to oversee production, so I've restored it here. The original is in Tablada, *Obras*, vol. 1, *Poesía*, pp. 327–28.

⁵⁰ For example, Letter from Salomón de la Selva to Edna St Vincent Millay, ESVMP (6 April 1916).

⁵¹ Letter from Salomón de la Selva to Edna St Vincent Millay, ESVMP (2 May 1916).

⁵² Letter from Salomón de la Selva to Edna St Vincent Millay, ESVMP (11 November 1916).

excitement, as can be gauged from his closing remark: 'Ahora voy a un Faculty meeting, ¡qué fun!' He has been congratulated by various people: 'Ahora sí estamos comprometidos' he jokes: '¡Dios lo quiera!' [I'm just off to a Faculty meeting, what fun! Now we really are engaged. That's what God wants!][53] His next note asks for a lock of her hair; he signs himself 'Pierrot'. He declares his love, in Spanish: 'Mi amor para ti es mi religión', though some sense of realism has returned since the letter ends: 'El Faculty meeting fue muy estúpida' [My love for you is my religion. The Faculty meeting was very stupid].[54]

But the old problem quickly reappears: Edna can never write as quickly or as often as he would like her to. He wrote two letters on 6 December, one beginning 'You will never write?', the other 'Ednacita, escríbeme!' [write to me!]. The second of these letters talks of his conversations with the college president, H. A. Garfield. Harry Augustus Garfield, son of the assassinated 20th President of the USA, was a good friend of Woodrow Wilson and would later join his administration, so de la Selva's remark that 'Garfield le expondrá a Wilson my views ... sobre la política de los Estados Unidos con la América Latina' [Garfield will explain to Wilson my views about the politics of the USA with respect to Latin America] is perhaps not as far-fetched as it may initially sound. This, he declares, is evidence of his serious side, which Edna has perhaps not yet appreciated. Dig deep into me, he tells her: 'Now can you hear the thunder in my heart?'[55]

Edwin Markham on Staten Island

At some point, possibly in 1914, possibly through the Poetry Society of America, Salomón de la Selva became acquainted with Edwin Markham (Fig. 13). Judging from the first surviving letter, dated 29 September 1916, de la Selva had sent some of his early poems to Markham, who had eventually sent back comments.[56] De la Selva was now apologising for having troubled him with such callow efforts and assuring Markham of the esteem in which the renowned poet was held by Rubén Darío, who had

---

[53] Letter from Salomón de la Selva to Edna St Vincent Millay, ESVMP (4 December 1916).
[54] Letter from Salomón de la Selva to Edna St Vincent Millay, ESVMP (5 December 1916).
[55] Letter from Salomón de la Selva to Edna St Vincent Millay, ESVMP (6 December 1916).
[56] Letter from Salomón de la Selva to Edwin Markham, EMA (29 September 1916). EMA is the Edwin Markham Archive, Horrmann Library, Wagner College, Staten Island, New York.

13 Edwin Markham. Courtesy of the Edwin Markham Archive, Horrmann Library, Wagner College, Staten Island, New York.

died earlier in the year, apparently without writing the essay on Markham which he had wanted to add to his book, *Los raros*.[57] Salomón addressed Markham—old enough to be his grandfather—as 'dear Master', 'lyric king', 'master revered', 'King of Poets': the tone was light-hearted but the sentiments obviously heartfelt.

Markham's revered status was due almost entirely to the worldwide renown of a single poem, 'The Man with the Hoe'. So comprehensively

---

[57] At the back of Markham's *The Gates of Paradise* (New York: Doubleday, Page & Company, 1920) are no fewer than 55 quotations making up 'A Chorus of Critical Opinions' (pp. 139-49), probably a sign of anxiety that his poetry was no longer speaking for itself. Among them is 'Edwin Markham is both lamb and lion—humble yet tempestuous. I am eager to include him in my new volume, Los Raros—The Rare Ones'—Ruben Dario, the greatest poet of Latin-America' (p. 145). The sentiment was almost certainly conveyed to Markham by de la Selva, who may also have been responsible for that particular wording.

has Edwin Markham's reputation dissolved that it is not easy to convey how famous he was for the first quarter of the twentieth century: 'The Man with the Hoe' was, for many decades, the most famous US poem bar none. It had appeared in the *San Francisco Examiner* in January 1899 and within a week had, as one critic puts it, 'begun to run its wildfire course across the country', before being translated into some 40 languages.[58] It made Markham a national figure, the very embodiment of a poet with his flowing white beard. He continued to write popular poetry and was always available to read on public occasions, most notably perhaps at the dedication of the Lincoln Memorial in 1922 when he read his poem about Lincoln to an audience of several thousand.

'The Man with the Hoe' was based on Jean-François Millet's 1860 painting, 'L'homme à la houe', showing a downtrodden agricultural labourer. Markham had seen a woodcut as early as 1886 and written some notes towards a poem, which then lay dormant. However, having rediscovered the notes in 1898, he rushed to see the painting itself, brought to San Francisco in 1893 by the wife of William H. Crocker, heir to a railway baron who had made his fortune on the backs of Chinese labourers building the transcontinental railroad. She presumably saw no irony. In a burst of inspiration in December 1898, Markham then composed the final version of his cry of moral outrage.

> Bowed by the weight of centuries he leans
> Upon his hoe and gazes on the ground,
> The emptiness of ages in his face,
> And on his back, the burden of the world.
> Who made him dead to rapture and despair,
> A thing that grieves not and that never hopes,
> Stolid and stunned, a brother to the ox?
> Who loosened and let down this brutal jaw?
> Whose was the hand that slanted back this brow?
> Whose breath blew out the light within this brain? ...
>
> O masters, lords and rulers in all lands,
> How will the future reckon with this Man?
> How answer his brute question in that hour
> When whirlwinds of rebellion shake all shores?
> How will it be with kingdoms and with kings—

---

[58] Jesse Sidney Goldstein, 'Edwin Markham, Ambrose Bierce, and *The Man with the Hoe*', *Modern Language Notes*, 58, no. 3 (1943), 165–75, at 169.

With those who shaped him to the thing he is—
When this dumb Terror shall rise to judge the world,
After the silence of the centuries?[59]

Markham had grown up out west and encountered many debt-ridden farmers and downtrodden labourers, though one of the few recent critics to even mention the poem, Cary Nelson, suggests that he really had in mind the great US labour struggles of the second half of the nineteenth century: the coal strikes of the 1860s and 1870s, the rail strikes which had lasted into the 1890s, the Homestead strike of steel and iron workers in 1892, and the Haymarket massacre in 1886—the event which had radicalised so many, including José Martí and Emma Goldman.[60] Certainly, 'The Man with the Hoe' is in a broad sense a protest poem, casting exploitation as a violation of God's will, in a style both Christian socialist and progressive.

Nelson's reading of the poem is nuanced. He suggests that it is impossible to tell whether Millet's man with the hoe is too crushed to speak or has just stepped forward to tell his story, an interpretation which allows him to suggest that Markham is othering the peasant by declaring him unable to speak and therefore having to be spoken for. The fact that listeners and readers are not subjected to the voice or culture of the man with the hoe is then taken as the reason for the poem's widespread acceptability outside radical circles. It is not clear whether Nelson would have thought it preferable had Markham ventriloquised a voice not his own; and in any case 'just stepped forward to tell his story' is not an interpretation of the painting that has occurred to any of the eminent art historians who have discussed it. Nelson is right, however, to point out how the illustrations that framed the poem in the special Sunday supplement that the *Examiner* produced later in 1899 interpreted it as a symbolic confrontation between mythological forces, attempting to leech the poem of any possible contemporary resonance.[61]

In his younger days, Markham had been an ardent socialist, based on his reading of Shelley, Marx, Kropotkin, Hugo, and Ruskin. In an 1886 letter, he wrote:

---

[59] These are the first and last of the poem's five stanzas: Edwin Markham, *The Man with the Hoe*, New York: The Doubleday and McClure Co., 1900, pp. 9, 13.
[60] Cary Nelson, *Revolutionary Memory: Recovering the Poetry of the American Left*, New York: Routledge, 2001, p. 16. For a sketch of his overall career, see Lisa Szefel, *The Gospel of Beauty in the Progressive Era: Reforming American Verse and Values*, New York: Palgrave Macmillan, 2011, pp. 57–84.
[61] Nelson, *Revolutionary Memory*, pp. 17, 19–22.

Ours is certainly a sick world, and I can see no human help for it but in International Revolutionary Socialism. The present order is built up in the image of the Beast ... The Church is the consecration of Cant; the State, the consecration of Injustice. Let them perish. From their ruins may rise a new order.[62]

In August 1917, he wrote directly to Alexander Kerensky, saying that the hope was that 'a regenerated Russia would be the leader of the advancing Democracy of the world'.[63] He bracketed Kerensky's name with those of Washington and Mazzini and enclosed a copy of his poem 'Russia Arise!', written ten years earlier and read at the celebration of the events of February 1917 held in Madison Square Garden.

De la Selva wrote an essay introducing Edwin Markham to Hispanic readers, originally for the short-lived New York publication *Revista Universal: Magazine Hispano-Americano*, then reprinted in *Repertorio Americano*, Joaquín García Monge's new Costa Rican magazine.[64] He writes of Rubén Darío's regard for Markham, returned by the US poet at the PSA meeting commemorating Darío. He suggests Markham's deep interest in Latin America's literature and social problems. De la Selva's assessment of Markham's writing is warm but realistic: Markham provides one of the true pillars for socialism in the USA; his poetry is praised, while Max Nordau is taken to task for suggesting that it is superior to Whitman's, a verdict de la Selva does not allow to stand. While recognising that Markham has no relevance to the new poetic tendencies, de la Selva praises the encouragement and friendship that he has offered to young poets. The 1920 version includes Luis Muñoz Marín's translation of 'The Man with the Hoe' a copy of which the Puerto Rican would later hang on the wall of his living quarters at La Fortaleza in San Juan during his years as governor of the island.

The best insight into Edwin Markham's rather unlikely Staten Island salon comes in the form of an address given in July 1956 to the New York City Writers' Conference, held at Wagner College, on Staten Island, by Markham's

---

[62] Quoted in 'Markham and Gorky', *Markham Review*, no. 1 (February 1968), 1–2, at 1.

[63] Letter from Edwin Markham to A. F. Kerensky, 2 August 1917 [EMA].

[64] Salomón de la Selva, 'Edwin Markham', *Revista Universal: Magazine Hispano-Americano*, February 1917, p. 11; 'Edwin Markham', *Repertorio Americano*, II, no. 9 (15 December 1920), 124–25.

son, Virgil, himself a writer and a professor in English at Wagner.[65] The Markham family, Virgil recalls, arrived in 1901, seeking more trees than were noticeable in Brooklyn, their previous neighbourhood. Westerleigh—now fully suburban—was then still called Prohibition Park and was on the edge of woodlands. In 1909, they moved to a handsome new house at 92 Waters Avenue. 'Books were here,' Virgil remarks, 'the cornerstone and indeed the whole foundation of life';[66] and it is clear that at least a subsidiary attraction for visitors was the opportunity for borrowing some of them. Markham's library was probably one of the most extensive private collections in New York and he was apparently more than happy for his friends to take what they wanted—except from the Red Room, his study, from which no book could ever be removed.

Growing up on Staten Island, Virgil witnessed his parents working together in what he calls a 'literary collaboration'[67]—though everything appeared under his father's name. Anna Catherine Markham would rough out the materials for the prose works and essays; Edwin would polish the prose. Virgil even suggests that his mother had a significant hand in 'The Man with the Hoe' and 'Lincoln', though this claim was contested by Florence Hamilton, Markham's secretary and probably lover, who wrote but never published a semi-official (that is, probably largely written by Markham himself) biography.[68] Anna acted as secretary to the Poetry Society of America after Jessie Rittenhouse moved to Florida in 1924.

The Markhams' nearest literary neighbour, just across the street, was Edward Jewitt Wheeler, editor of *Current Literature*. Others that Virgil recalls include the Dutch poet and translator Leonard Van Noppen— serious but rather unproductive; and the novelist Florence Morse Kingsley, productive and wildly successful, if not of the highest quality. Born in 1899, Virgil's strongest memories of his parents' house were of the years from around 1908 to 1918, after which, as first a student and then a professor in California, he was less often at home. During those years, Russia was the great liberal cause. Ivan Narodny was the one exile who set up house on Staten Island, Virgil recalling that it was Van Noppen who introduced

---

[65] Published as Virgil Markham, 'Literary Tradition on Staten Island', (I) *The Staten Island Historian*, 17, no. 4 (October–December 1956), 33–36; (II) 18, no. 1 (January– March 1957), 1–5; (III) 18, no. 2 (April–June, 1957), 12–16.
[66] Virgil Markham, 'Literary Tradition', vol. 2, p. 3.
[67] Virgil Markham, 'Literary Tradition', vol. 2, p. 3.
[68] See Florence Hamilton's letter to the *New York Times* (27 June 1942, p. 12) in response to Virgil Markham's (21 June 1942, p. E8). Hamilton's manuscript biography is in the Library of Congress: Florence Hamilton collection relating to Edwin Markham, 1857–1959, MSS 31393, unfinished biography.

Narodny into the Markham coterie.[69] In fact, the most infamous New York Russian *cause célèbre* of the time touched Staten Island when Maxim Gorky and his companion—but not, strictly speaking, wife—Maria Andreyeva were thrown out of various New York hotels on grounds of immorality. They were offered hospitality by John Martin and Prestonia Mann Martin at their house on Staten Island. The Martins were serious Fabian intellectuals and probably the Markhams' closest friends at this time, and Edwin visited Gorky on several occasions at the Martins' home.

Much of Edwin Markham's time was taken up with the editing of the manuscripts of the visionary poet and utopian communist Thomas Lake Harris, who had died in 1906, a task in which he was assisted by the formidable Dr Laura Morgan, who Virgil describes as arriving one day at Waters Avenue to have a chat with Markham and staying for 19 years, until her death. Harris's manuscripts—dictated in a trance state and written in a crabbed hand—were voluminous and almost unreadable, in both senses of the word, so the task of editing them was, as Virgil puts it, 'unfinished—and … unfinishable'.[70] Markham's extensive lecture tours were undertaken in part to finance this labour, although one suspects that they were increasingly welcome as a way of escaping it.

But it was the gatherings of poets for which the Markham household was best known—four or five times a year, according to Virgil;[71] and that does not include all the individual visits. Some of the names Virgil recalls are Ridgely Torrence, Marion Mills Miller, Jessie Rittenhouse, Shaemas O'Sheel, Arthur Guiterman, Kahlil Gibran, Margaret Widdemer, Anna Hempstead Branch, Zona Gale, Anna Strunsky, Louis Untermeyer, Percy MacKaye, and John Hall Wheelock—most, if not all, members of the Poetry Society of America, once that institution was established, and many the friends and acquaintances of Salomón de la Selva.

Wilson's Crime in Santo Domingo

Through the at least intermittent residence there of Fabio Fiallo (Fig. 14), Manuel Cestero, Tulio Cestero, and Pedro Henríquez Ureña, the literary *dominicano* presence in New York was strong and Salomón de la Selva was inevitably drawn into their network of interests and activities. During 1916,

---

[69] Virgil Markham, 'Literary Tradition', vol. 2, p. 5. On Narodny, see W. Adolphe Roberts, *These Many Years: An Autobiography*, ed. Peter Hulme, Kingston: University of the West Indies Press, 2015, pp. 120–21.

[70] Virgil Markham, 'Literary Tradition', vol. 2, p. 2.

[71] Virgil Markham, 'Literary Tradition', vol. 3, p. 14.

14 Fabio Fiallo.
Provenance unknown.

the situation in the Dominican Republic began to reach crisis point and de la Selva's friendship with Pedro meant that the troubles would be brought even closer to home. The US president, Woodrow Wilson, had tried to impose a US financial advisor on the Dominican Republic, following the model for external control pioneered by the British in Egypt, but the Dominican Republic congress rejected the idea, leading to US Marine landings on the north coast of the island in May. At this point, the congress elected Pedro's father, Francisco Henríquez y Carvajal, as president but when he refused to meet US demands Wilson announced the imposition of a military government. After the US refused to allow him to take office, Henríquez y Carvajal spent the next few years wandering through the Caribbean and Latin America in search of support, and in Washington and New York trying to get the US State Department to hear his case. He became known as *el presidente errante*, the roving president.

Francisco Henríquez y Carvajal had lived in Cuba since 1904 while intermittently occupying Dominican governmental and diplomatic posts, most recently delegate to the International High Commission in Buenos Aires in April 1916. Returning from Buenos Aires, he passed through New York, where he wrote an analysis of the situation in his home country, which was published in *Las Novedades* in June and then, after his elevation to the presidency, in the Dominican press, where it became a programme for his government—although one he was prevented from carrying out. His analysis of the US occupation was dependent on acceptance of the Wilsonian ideal of the Pan American Union, a chain of sovereign and independent states of which the Dominican Republic was one link, 'aunque pequeña' [although small]:

> En los momentos mismos en que las fervorosas declaraciones del Presidente Wilson en pro del Pan-americanismo sirven de consagración definitiva a tal doctrina y la caracterizan, enfrente del gran desastre europeo, como una doctrina de interés mutuo, de amor nacional, colectivo, de acción internacional cooperativa para fines históricos de civilización, de libertad política internacional, entre los Estados de ambos continentes americanos, la subordinación, por la fuerza armada, de una cualquiera de las más pequeñas Repúblicas del mundo americano, a la más poderosa de ellas, dislocaría para siempre los eslabones de esa cadena, sembraría la más recóndita desconfianza en cada uno de los demás países y haría pensar a cada cual en la necesidad de buscarse en nuevas orientaciones los recursos adicionales al propósito de precaverse contra futuras posibles emergencias.[72]

> [At the very moment when President Wilson's fervent declarations in favour of Pan-Americanism serve as definitive consecration of that doctrine and characterise it, in stark contrast to the great European disaster, as a doctrine of mutual interest, of national and collective love, of co-operative international action among the States of both American continents, the subordination by armed force of any of the smallest republics of the American world by the most powerful of all of them, would dislodge in perpetuity the links of that chain, would sow the deepest distrust in all the other countries and would make each one ponder the need to seek in new directions the additional means to forestall possible future emergencies.]

Because of its ignorance of the true causes of the political conflicts on the island, US intervention, he argued, would not resolve any problems but would just make matters worse. He wasn't wrong.

That summer the Dominican journalist Manuel de Jesús Galván Velasquéz—fourth son of the novelist—wrote in bewilderment and exasperation of the US failure to live up to its expressed ideals: 'Nothing is

---

[72] Francisco Henríquez y Carvajal, 'El problema de la República Dominicana' [1916], in Max Henríquez Ureña, *Los Estados Unidos y La República Dominicana: La Verdad de los Hechos Comprobada por Datos y Documentos Oficiales*, Havana: Imprenta 'El Siglo XX', 1919, pp. 111–16, at p. 113.

more extraordinary than the conduct of the United States in its relations with Hispanic American countries.' He entitled his essay, 'Ubinam gentium sumus', one of Cicero's rhetorical questions in his Catiline orations: 'Where on earth are we? What is the government we have? In what city are we living?' In tone, and in choice of analogy, this is very different from the *arielista* contrast between civilised Hispanic Athenians and uncultured US Spartans. We are all Romans now, but we are not getting the government we deserve.[73]

The US minister in the Dominican Republic, William W. Russell, presented Henríquez y Carvajal with a series of demands. Negotiations followed but were cut short by the appearance of Captain Harry S. Knapp, who proclaimed US military control over the country on 29 November. A severe censorship was immediately imposed. A few days later, now powerless, Henríquez y Carvajal left the island and travelled via Puerto Rico to New York where again he published an analysis of recent events in *Las Novedades*, which appeared on 31 December. The US claim that its actions fell short of removing the Dominican Republic's sovereignty was given short shrift: 'It is ridiculous and puerile to affirm that despite the suspension of its treasury and its army, both now under foreign control, a State still possesses its sovereignty.'[74] Hispanic New York was firmly in sympathy. *La Prensa's* headline didn't mince words: 'Military dictatorship in Santo Domingo'.[75]

On the island itself there was no local support for the occupation. Thousands of peasants were soon dispossessed by a Land Registration Act, some of them then forming armed groups called *gavilleros* to fight the US Marines. The Marines behaved with considerable brutality—which didn't increase their popularity. The *gavilleros* also tended to fight against each other, and were almost entirely separate from the intellectual nationalists based in the city of Santo Domingo—but also in New York.

In Santo Domingo, the *cause célèbre* was the imprisonment of the poet Fabio Fiallo, a close friend and supporter of Henríquez y Carvajal—and who

---

[73] Manuel de Jesús Galván Velásquez, 'Ubinam gentius sumus', *Las Novedades*, 27 August 1916, reprinted in *Literatura dominicana en los Estados Unidos: Historia y trayectoria de la diáspora intelectual*, Santo Domingo: Fundación Global Democracia y Desarrollo, 2004, pp. 15–19.

[74] Francisco Henríquez y Carvajal, 'La cuestión dominicana' [1916], in Max Henríquez Ureña, *Los Estados Unidos y La República Dominicana: La Verdad de los Hechos Comprobada por Datos y Documentos Oficiales*, Havana: Imprenta 'El Siglo XX', 1919, pp. 193–206, at p. 196.

[75] 'Dictadura militar en S. Domingo', *La Prensa*, 6 January 1917, p. 1. On the occupation, see Bruce J. Calder, *The Impact of Intervention: The Dominican Republic during the U.S. Occupation of 1916–1924*, Austin: University of Texas Press, 1984.

we have already met as the host in New York of both Darío and Chocano. Fiallo wrote a newspaper article very critical of the US occupation. He was arrested and a court martial established with the power to impose the death penalty. He was eventually sentenced to five years' hard labour, commuted to one year's imprisonment only after widespread outrage across Latin America. Years later, Fiallo wrote an excoriating account of what he referred to as 'the monstrous hypocrisy of Wilson's double-faced policy in 1916–1920' under the unambiguous title *The Crime of Wilson in Santo Domingo*.[76]

In September, Pedro wrote a letter from New York to the *Minneapolis Journal* in response to a leader in that newspaper entitled, 'Mexico and Pan-Americanism', which had discussed the cases of Mexico, Nicaragua, and Haiti. Pedro wanted to add information about the Dominican Republic on the grounds that the US public was hearing very little about what was happening on account of the press censorship in the country. He pointed out that the preservation of peace was invoked as the pretext for intervention despite the evidence that interference by the USA has always tended to *foster* revolutionary disturbances rather than end them:

> In the present situation, the reasons given for the American intervention could not be vaguer nor its good results less evident. But for the people of Santo Domingo the reasons appear clear enough: they know that the United States is trying to obtain the absolute control of the Caribbean Sea, and that the Wilson Administration, in spite of its rhetorical utterance on the subject, thinks little of violating the territorial sovereignty of smaller countries.[77]

In April 1921, with the occupation still continuing and his father still roaming the continent, Pedro Henríquez Ureña would give a talk to the International Relations Club at the University of Minnesota. We only have his notes, in Spanish, for this talk. The keynote is in the first sentence: No nation has the right to try to civilise another. He poses a number of questions: Who decides which country is civilised and which isn't? Seemingly, he says, with the Dominican Republic in mind, only force decides, but in

---

[76] Fabio Fiallo, *The Crime of Wilson in Santo Domingo*, Havana: Arellano y Cia, 1940, p. 9. Originally published in Spanish in 1935.

[77] Pedro Henríquez Ureña, 'Letter to The Minneapolis Journal' (26 September 1916), in Alfredo A. Roggiano, *Pedro Henríquez Ureña en los Estados Unidos*, Mexico City: n.p. [State University of Iowa Studies in Spanish Language and Literature, 12], 1961, pp. lxxiii–lxxiv.

that case why complain about what Germany did? And then perhaps the most interesting sentence: If Haiti needs to be civilised, why not civilise the state of Georgia? Haiti of course was also under US occupation at the time. Haitians complained that US Marine brutality was particularly bad because the Marines came disproportionately from southern US states. Why might Georgia be in need of civilising? Henríquez Ureña doesn't say, but he almost certainly had in mind that there were more than 50 lynchings in the USA in both 1915 and 1916 and that in both years the state with the highest number of lynchings, more than a quarter of the total, was Georgia. So, when Henríquez Ureña came really to turn the screw into US hypocrisy, he did it—as a *dominicano*—by invoking his neighbour, by bringing the two countries on the island together, at least for a moment, and by implying that neither should be taking lessons in civilised behaviour from a country still permitting lynching to occur with such frequency.[78]

Henríquez Ureña spent the last 20 years of his life in Argentina, though he never attained a university chair—according to Borges precisely because of his colour. He received no official academic recognition until Harvard appointed him to the annual Charles Eliot Norton Professorship of Poetry in 1940. The roll call for that award, established in 1926, is highly esteemed: T. S. Eliot and Robert Frost were among the first; Henríquez Ureña came between Igor Stravinsky and Erwin Panofsky. The 2015 lecturer was Toni Morrison. Pedro Henríquez Ureña was therefore the first 'coloured' recipient, the first Caribbean recipient, the first Latin American, and the first Spanish speaker—Borges himself and Octavio Paz would follow. When Herbie Hancock was appointed in 2014, it was said that he was the first non-white recipient. Not so.

A Tale from Faerieland

What Salomón de la Selva wanted was to publish a book of his own poems. He laboriously copied out 32 of them and got his friend and flatmate, Rufino González, to design and make a cover.[79] 'A Tale from Faerieland and Other Poems' consists of 33 poems, of which one was published in *Ainslee's* in January 1916 and five survived into *Tropical Town and Other Poems*, de la

---

[78] Notes for a lecture delivered in English at the International Relations Club, University of Minnesota, 6 April 1921. In Pedro Henríquez Ureña, *Historia cultural, historiografía y crítica literaria*, ed. Odalís G. Pérez, Santo Domingo: Editora Búho [Archivo General de la Nación, vol. CXIV], 2010, p. 128.
[79] Salomón de la Selva, 'A Tale from Faerieland and Other Poems', New York, 1916, Brown University Library Manuscript Collections, 1901 S4686t.

Selva's first published collection, in 1918. The booklet opens with a short dedicatory poem to E. L. V. G., whom he calls his 'faerie-godmother'. It seems, the poem ends, 'so little pay / for all that you have given me'.[80] A footnote reads 'Vale. Xmas 1920', with de la Selva's initials, suggesting that he gave the book to Eugenia Geisenheimer when he left New York. If so, she disposed of it fairly rapidly because it was bought by Brown University Library in June 1925 for $1.00 from a New York bookseller called Barrett. It is not obvious that anyone then opened it until the present writer in October 2016.[81]

Young, slim, good-looking, Latin, silver-tongued, Salomón was clearly attractive to women, who fill his New York years. He seems to have been sexually attracted exclusively by those of the same age and younger—perhaps much younger; while a group of older women acted, depending on their own circumstances, as friends or patrons. Florence Schauffler, whom he would meet towards the end of this year, was probably the most important of the figures in this second category: he called her his 'mamita'; but Eugenia Geisenheimer perhaps earned the dedicatory poem by giving material support when it was most needed.

Eugenia Louise Victoria Geisenheimer had been born in Düsseldorf in 1870. She lived on the Upper West Side with her brother-in-law Theodore Geisenheimer, a dye-goods importer (with whom Salomón was also friends). Theodore was a widower with a young daughter, so Eugenia perhaps acted as stepmother, at least until the daughter's marriage in 1916. De la Selva first mentions Geisenheimer in his 1916 essay on Walter Pater, where he calls her a 'culta señorita alemana' [cultured German lady] and says that she is preparing a translation into Spanish of Walter Pater's novel, *The Child in the House*.[82] A longer description comes in an interesting letter to Joaquín

---

[80] De la Selva, 'Dedication', in 'A Tale from Faerieland', pp. 1–2. *Tropical Town* has no dedication, but the opening poem, 'Tropical Town', is inscribed 'For Miss Eugenia L. V. Geisenheimer'.

[81] There are two other unpublished collections of de la Selva's poems that may date from around this time: 24 poems in a collection in Princeton (Salomón de la Selva, ['Poems'], 2 typed and 22 handwritten. General Manuscripts Collection CO140, Princeton University Library), nine of which were collected in *Tropical Town*; and 11 also at Brown, evidently submitted for an anthology that Clement Wood was preparing but which was never published (*Poems by Many Singers* [ca. 1915–23]. Compiled by Clement Wood. MS Harris Codex 1344, Hay Library, Brown University). De la Selva presumably submitted his poems to Wood, but the provenance of the Princeton collection is unknown.

[82] Salomón de la Selva, 'Walter Pater', *Revista Universal* (November 1916), p. 28; it was reprinted in *Repertorio Americano*, II, no. 15 (15 March 1921), 206.

García Monge, published in *Repertorio Americano*, in 1921. De la Selva was writing from Geisenheimer's house at Shoreham, on Long Island, and he begins by thanking García Monge, on behalf of Geisenheimer, for his note in response to her Pater translation:

> Eugenia insists on pretending she isn't cultured; but Pedro Henríquez Ureña, her friend whom she admires, can tell you how unusual it is to find in these somewhat provincial United States women who, like her, are catholic in outlook, purely cosmopolitan in taste, and who have a refined knowledge of foreign literature and psychology. She is not a professional writer, and I think she's wary of being taken as such: her cultivation of literature is just an intellectual 'sport', a private satisfaction of personal tastes in no way intended for public consumption. But her cautious dabbling could easily have been turned into a professional career if she'd had to earn her daily bread or if in her modest and discreet spirit the tarantula eager for public acclaim had sunk its maddening teeth.[83]

De la Selva had a good critical eye, so it's no surprise that he kept just the best five poems from this youthful volume: he wrote with such facility that there were always going to be plenty more to choose from when he got a contract with a publisher. Some of discarded poems do, however, have possible biographical interest.

'Little Boy Dead' is about a mother's grief as the poet leaves home. The intriguing question is which departure it might refer to:

> All I remember is
> My mother's goodby kiss,
> And her crying
> Like the wail
> For one dead ...
>
> Blue sea, then, & rounded sky,
> And a port at the end of the sea:
> Foreign girls that passed me by
> Laughing very wistfully—

---

[83] Salomón de la Selva, 'Carta de Nueva York', *Repertorio Americano*, II, no. 28 (10 August 1921), 393–94, at 393.

> One was golden-haired & pale,
> Lily-lovely, fresh & frail,
> And the pallor of her skin
> Was like innocence to me,—
> Would to God it had not been.
>
> All I remember is
> My mother's kiss
> When goodby was said,
> And her crying
> Like the wail
> For one dead ...[84]

The original departure from Nicaragua was in 1906, aged 13, but it is difficult to imagine a mother thinking her child 'dead' when he goes off to school, even in New York. There is one other definite departure in 1911, when de la Selva went back to New York after a year in Nicaragua: that would fit better with the interest in the foreign girls. And there is the possibility of other visits home in the years 1912 to 1914, when little documentary evidence has been found. One theory—for which there is circumstantial support—is that de la Selva had an incestuous relationship with his younger sister María Isabel, who had been born in 1899.[85] An event of that kind might certainly explain why he became 'dead' to his mother, particularly if it is in fact the case that María Isabel gave birth to Mélida, who appears in the records as Salomón's youngest sister but—according to this theory—may in fact have been his daughter.

Two other poems from this unpublished collection could be read in the light of that hypothesis. Immediately following 'Little Boy Dead' comes 'Serpentina':

> She brought the flaming lure of Lucifer,
> The passion infinite of Sathanas,
> Silently creeping through the guileless grass
> To where I lay, desiring only her.

---

[84] De la Selva, 'Little Boy Dead', in 'A Tale from Faerieland', pp. 29–30.
[85] This circumstantial evidence is laid out in some detail in Steven F. White, *Rubén Darío y Salomón de la Selva: Ecos de la muerte y la guerra*, León: Promotora Cultural Leonesa, 2016.

She put to shame the roses red and white,
And wronged the lilies' dewy innocence.
The skies were wroth, at her so great offence
And not a star was lit in heaven that night.

And on the earth no fragrant love-wind sighed;
And the deep sea was loud with angry breath;
She made the wind's wings saturate with death
So that somewhere a maiden paled & died.

My Guardian Angel burned aloes & myrrh,
To God, that He might save me from her spell,
For when she whispers all earth's tongues are still,
And nevermore will pray, because of her.

But we had never need, for our delight
Of moon or wind, of flowers or of prayers:
She covered me with kisses & her hair
Shielded our troth from the offended Night.

And when dawn came, back to her hell she crept;
And tired of all, desiring only sleep,
I left my soul in a black dragon's keep,
And followed her & in her cavern slept.[86]

A powerful evocation of sinful love, with the man passive but desiring, the woman active, sinuous, seductive, irresistible; the heavens offended. Guilt diverted, unsuccessfully, by giving all agency—if the hypothesis has validity—to the 13- or 14-year-old sister. Against this might be set 'Lullaby For a Star':

Go out, you lonely star! I want to sing
But all the night you cry & make me weep;
Fling far away your grief, a useless thing,
    And go to sleep.

Are you not tired of seeking through the night
The resting places of the ravished moon?
Ah, seek no more, for you are mad outright
    And out of tune.

---

[86] De la Selva, 'Serpentina', in 'A Tale from Faerieland', pp. 31–32.

> O little sister hush! Your eyes are red
> With wasting in the darkness grief so wild;
> Fling far away your heart, & go to bed
>   Like a good child! ...[87]

Beyond these poems there are three further pieces of circumstantial evidence. One is a remarkable prose piece, called simply 'Confesión', which appeared in *Repertorio Americano* in May 1921, just after de la Selva had cut his last ties with New York. Strangely, however, the piece was sent to the journal in 1917 and there is no obvious explanation as to why it didn't appear for four years, and whose choice that delay was—presumably it must have been either the author's or the editor's. This is an extract:

> I once wanted to find out how sweet it was to kiss and be kissed, how good it was to cut roses, how to reach God riding the leopards of Dionysus; and when I awoke, I felt dirty and started to cry.
>
> Then I wanted to purify myself. I fasted and prayed, I stayed awake and denied myself all pleasures, I fixed my eyes on a skull; but again I felt disgusted and started to cry.
>
> Now look how infinitely beatific I appear, possessed by a calm intensity.
>
> I've sharpened and polished my feelings to such an extent that I don't need to open my eyes in order to see; my nose smells future roses in the mud; without moving, my lips are always smiling at life because of its beauty; my fingers caress the curve of the earth and the curve of the sky as the smooth round breasts of a lover are caressed ...
>
> I've clarified my feelings just as one cleans with great care the glass in the windows of a house occupied in spotless happiness.
>
> The world offers my feelings all its beauty because I keep them chaste and hidden, like prudent virgins, each one with its lamp.
>
> Because I married my body with my soul: 'This is your companion, enjoy yourself in her'. And to my soul: 'This is your companion: let him make you fruitful'.
>
> The children of this marriage will overcome death. They will populate space and inherit the earth.
>   (Sent by the author, New York, 1917).[88]

---

[87] De la Selva, 'Lullaby for a Star', in 'A Tale from Faerieland', pp. 49-50.
[88] Salomón de la Selva, 'Confesión', *Repertorio Americano*, II, no. 20 (20 May 1921), 277.

New York through Spanish Eyes (1916)

The second piece is equally remarkable, particularly if one considers it as a response. It is a poem written by Salomón's sister, María Isabel, under her pen-name of Aura Rostand, published in the same journal and with a dedication to her brother:

> El Dolor me ha elegido …
>   (Para Salomón de la Selva).
>
> El Dolor me ha elegido por su pálida novia
> y me ofrece sus crueles, lentas horas de angustia;
> soy como una azucena que su blancura agobia
> tomando el tinte lívido de la agonía mustia.
>
> Sus mejores caricias el Dolor me regala,
> sus ósculos más puros sobre mi frente imprime;
> Por eso digo que amo mi Dolor, y hago gala
> del murmullo que mi alma concierta cuando gime.
>
> Y digo que mi llanto es dulce y milagroso,
> que su sabor sagrado preserva y purifica,
> que es el agua bendita del escondido pozo
> donde lava mi alma su hermosa faz deífica! …
>
> Soy la pálida novia del Dolor ¡oh Dios mío!
> y el Dolor Tú lo hiciste … Me lo das, Te bendigo!
> Mi dolor de tu amor tiene el místico brillo,
> y en mi dolor Te siento tan mi padre y mi Amigo! …
>   Aura Rostand. León, Nicaragua, 1922.[89]

> [Grief has chosen me …
>   (For Salomón de la Selva)
>
> Grief has chosen me as his pale bride
> and offers me his slow cruel hours of anguish;
> I'm like a lily, whose whiteness he encumbers,
> Taking on the livid tint of withered agony.

---

[89] Aura Rostand, 'El dolor me ha elegido', *Repertorio Americano*, IV, no, 28–29 (25 September 1922), 399.

Grief presents me with its best caresses,
pressing its purest kisses on my brow;
for that I say I love my Grief, and glory
in the murmur my soul makes tuneful when it groans.

And I say that my weeping is a sweet miracle,
that its sacred taste can preserve and purify,
that it is the holy water from a hidden well
where my soul washes its beautiful and exalted face.

I am the pale bride of Grief, oh my Lord!
And a Grief that You created ... And gave to me, I bless You!
My grief in your love has the mystical radiance
and in my grief I feel You as my father and my Friend! ...
Aura Rostand. León, Nicaragua, 1922.]

In terms of the traditions of poetry in Spanish, one might place this poem within the mysticism of Santa Teresa or San Juan de la Cruz, in which the godhead painfully possesses the poet but the agony is welcomed as a blessing. All kinds of psychosexual analysis might be appropriate—but they are as nothing compared to what the dedication seems to suggest, where the elder brother becomes the father, the friend, and the lover—and, from a legal point of view, the incestuous rapist.[90]

The third piece of evidence is another poem. If the hypothesis holds water, and Mélida was in fact the daughter of the brother and sister, Salomón and María Isabel, she would have been born—as her documentation suggests—in 1914, when María Isabel was 14 years of age. One of the poems de la Selva published in *Poetry* in 1917 is 'The Tiny Maiden', which the poet passes off as a traditional Spanish folk song about a 19-year-old girl who is desperate because she hasn't yet had a baby. One stanza reads:

Girls of fourteen
Little babies bear;
I am almost twenty,
For this I despair.[91]

---

[90] Aura Rostand became a significant poet whose work has been the subject of recent reassessment: Aura Rostand, *Huerto cerrado*, ed. Helena Ramos, Managua: Banco Central de Nicaragua, 2013.

[91] 'The Tiny Maiden', *Poetry*, XI, no. 2 (1917), 79. When this poem appeared the following year in *Tropical Town* (as 'The Midget Maiden', firmly within the poems set

The following year, recalling his sister in the course of a rambling letter to Edna Millay about types of hair, clearly written when he was bored at work translating an advert for the hair treatment called Kurley-Kews, Salomón wrote: 'My sister María, she the poet, whose hair was long and straight—ever so straight—envied me my curls and loved me for them. Pobre Mariquita! Yo no sé si hubiese sido feliz o no. ¡Bien haya entre los ángeles de veras!' [Poor little Maria. I don't know whether she would have been happy or not. She is truly well off among the angels].[92] María Isabel didn't die until 1957.

---

in León), the line read 'Girls of seventeen' (p. 22). Existing documentation includes Mélida's marriage certificate (April 1937), which gives her age as 22, and a US border crossing identification card (dated 3 June 1949), which gives her date of birth as 2 August 1914.
[92] Letter from Salomón de la Selva to Edna St Vincent Millay, ESVMP (16 October 1917).

Chapter Five

Goading the Bull Moose (1917)

But now a cry like a red flamingo
Has winged its way to the Judgment gates.[1]

On the evening of Saturday, 13 January 1917 the steamer *Montserrat* entered New York harbour. The vast majority of the 364 passengers were Spanish, a mixture of immigrants and visitors. Four were Russian: Leon Trotsky, his companion Natalya Sedova, and their two young sons. They would only stay for just over two months, but Trotsky's presence would galvanise socialist New York, just at the moment that the Revolution triumphed in Russia.[2] One passenger was an Englishman, travelling as Avenarius F. Lloyd, though better known now as Arthur Cravan. Trotsky and Cravan chatted, but they would approach New York in very different ways. Trotsky's friends had arranged for the family to spend their first night in the Astor Hotel, where Rubén Darío had seen the writing on the wall. Cravan slept in Central Park before seeking out Robert J. Coady, who had already published some of Cravan's poems in his magazine, *The Soil*. He then moved into the apartment of a new Greenwich Village friend, the painter Arthur Frost, at 6 East 14th Street and after his friend Francis Picabia came back to New York in April he started frequenting the Arensburgs' salon.[3] Trotsky would soon spend his days working at the office of *Novyi Mir*, on St Mark's Place in the East Village, just on the edge of bohemian Greenwich Village, though representative of the very different world of the Lower East Side, where Russian and Yiddish predominated.

---

[1] From Salomón de la Selva, 'The Dreamer's Heart Knows Its Own Bitterness', *Tropical Town and Other Poems*, New York: John Lane Company, 1918, p. 42.

[2] See Richard B. Spence, 'Hidden Agendas: Spies, Lies and Intrigue Surrounding Trotsky's American Visit of January–April, 1917', *Revolutionary Russia*, 21, no. 1 (2008), 33–55; and Kenneth D. Ackerman, *Trotsky in New York 1917: A Radical on the Eve of Revolution*, Berkeley, CA: Counterpoint, 2016.

[3] Maria Lluïsa Borràs, *Arthur Cravan: una biografía*, Barcelona: Quaderns Crema, 1993, pp. 177–79.

Two weeks later saw the start of the trial of Margaret Sanger and Fania Mindell for opening a birth control clinic over in Brooklyn. Fania Mindell was a set designer who ran a shop called 'Little Russia' in the Village but as a radical feminist and gifted translator she became a valued assistant to Sanger. Mindell was found guilty on obscenity charges for selling the pamphlet, *What Every Girl Should Know*. A rich supporter paid the $50 fine, but the decision was reversed on appeal, a first victory in the birth control campaign. Having turned down the offer of a suspended sentence, Sanger herself was convicted and sentenced to 30 days' imprisonment at the Queens County Penitentiary.[4]

On the cultural front modern art was invented in April when the Society of Independent Artists at Grand Central Palace (Lexington and East 46th/47th) rejected Marcel Duchamp's 'Fountain'.

Salomón de la Selva's devotion to, and frustration with, Edna St Vincent Millay continued unabated as war raged in Europe and social unrest seethed in New York. José Santos Chocano eventually returned to New York at the end of 1917 and was fêted by the Poetry Society of America—before being whisked off by de la Selva to a pan-American dinner in honour, finally, of Edna Millay. Earlier that year, however, de la Selva had his greatest public triumph when he confronted Theodore Roosevelt in the grandest of all the pan-American literary occasions, held at the National Arts Club in Gramercy Park. This event took place, in all probability, because of Salomón's assiduity in making friends and connections on the New York literary scene. The year was soon overshadowed by the declaration of US intervention in the war in Europe—a war in which de la Selva was determined to fight. Another woman also entered Salomón de la Selva's life in the winter of 1916-17, but this time he wasn't falling head over heels in love.

Confronting Roosevelt

Just over a week after Trotsky and Cravan reached New York, on the evening of Tuesday, 23 January, poet Gertrude Drick, artists John Sloan and Marcel Duchamp, and Provincetown Playhouse actors Alan Russell Mann, Betty Turner, and Charles Ellis, possibly joined later by Allen Norton, slipped through an unlocked door on the west pier of the Washington Square Arch and climbed up the spiral staircase to the roof. They spread out blankets, sat

---

[4] See Ellen Chesler, *Woman of Valor: Margaret Sanger and the Birth Control Movement in America*, New York: Simon & Schuster, 1992, pp. 156-58.

on hot water bottles, hung Chinese lanterns, tied red balloons to the parapet, sipped tea and wine, shot off cap pistols, and conversed until dawn. At some point, Drick read out a proclamation of the 'Free and Independent Republic of Washington Square', largely consisting of the repeated word 'Whereas …'. Cravan hadn't yet got his bearings or else he might well have joined them; Trotsky would have scorned such child's play. Drick was Sloan's student, and he was politically radical, but this was somewhere between a prank and a proto-dada happening. Sloan's depiction of the event in a later etching called the group the Arch Conspirators, a multiple pun and something of a provocation at a time when 'conspiracy' was becoming a public issue: O. Henry had referred to the South Americans frequenting El Refugio as 'arch-conspirators'.[5] Several years later, interviewed by a *New York Tribune* reporter, Sloan described the conspirators as '[W]e of the small nation known as Greenwich Village'.[6] That month the German consul in San Francisco was convicted of conspiracy to blow up shipping in Seattle harbour and the Mexican consul general in New York was charged with conspiracy to ship arms across the border. The city had not yet been gripped by paranoia and there were no consequences for the Arch conspirators, but in one sense the timing of the event was meticulous. That morning the newspapers had reported Woodrow Wilson's speech to the US Senate in which he offered his latest outline for what the world ought to look like if only the old world nations would stop tearing each other to pieces. Before long, even Wilson's patience would run out and the USA would join the conflict, but for now he was keen to preach an equality of rights in which the guarantees exchanged 'must neither recognize not imply a difference between big nations and small'. His concluding recommendation was that the Monroe Doctrine should be adapted to the whole world, with every nation left to determine its own way of development, 'unhindered, unthreatened, unafraid, the little along with the great and powerful'.[7] Drick's plan had presumably been germinating for a while, so it was just a coincidence that the declaration of the Greenwich Village Republic, on the very day that Wilson's speech was

---

[5] See above, p. 15. The most thorough accounts of the incident are Michael Lobel, *John Sloan: Drawing on Illustration*, New Haven, CT: Yale University Press, 2014, pp. 164–72; and Paul B. Franklin, 'The State of Greenwich Village: Marcel Duchamp, John Sloan, and the 1917 Declaration of Independence', *Étant Donné Marcel Duchamp*, no. 4 (2002), 162–68. See also Peter Morse, *John Sloan's Prints: A Catalogue Raisonné of the Etchings, Lithographs, and Posters*, New Haven, CT: Yale University Press, 1969, p. 209.

[6] Margaret Christie, 'Arch Conspirators', *New York Tribune*, 30 December 1923, IX, p. 7.

[7] 'Text of President's Address to the Senate', *New York Times*, 23 January 1917, p. 1.

reported, should test through the means of dada statecraft the idea of just how small an autonomous nation might be. Nicaragua and the Dominican Republic would certainly want to know how seriously to take Wilson's vision; and, despite the President's honeyed words, the invocation of the Monroe Doctrine would probably have filled them only with apprehension.

*

On Thursday, 7 February 1917 a dinner and reception was given in honour of representative men and women of letters of South and Central America at the National Arts Club (Fig. 15). The hosts of the occasion were the members of the Joint Committee of the Literary Arts, an organisation made up of officers of seven New York literary societies and other men and women representing the art and literature of the United States: John G. Agar, president of the National Arts Club; Hamlin Garland, vice president of the Authors' League of America; Ernest Peixotto, president of the MacDowell Club of New York; Ida M. Tarbell, president of the Pen and Brush Club; Franklin H. Giddings, president of the Authors Club; Edward J. Wheeler, president of the the Poetry Society of America; Prof. William M. Sloane, chancellor of the American Academy of Arts and Letters; Augustus Thomas, president of the National Institute of Arts and Letters. This committee, with Garland as president and Wheeler as secretary, had been organised for the purpose of welcoming illustrious literary men from abroad.[8] Hamlin Garland was reported as stating the purpose of the dinner as 'a better understanding and a friendlier appreciation of the work which is being done by the poets and novelists of our sister Republics of the South. The great European war has already had the effect of sending many of the artists and authors of the South to the United States and without doubt many more will follow.'[9] Given that the evening included the reading of poems by Darío (read by Thomas Walsh) and Chocano (by John Pierrepont Rice), this may have been an elaborate attempt at restitution for the absence of official attention to their presence in the city two years earlier.[10]

---

[8] 'New Authors' Association', *New York Times*, 5 November 1916, p. 11.
[9] *The Bookman*, 44, no. 6 (February 1917), 666.
[10] John Pierrepont Rice was an Assistant Professor of Romance Languages at Williams College, fluent in French, Spanish, and Italian. He was older than de la Selva, but at 37 not *that* much older and, though what we would call Salomón's line manager, he became an enthusiast for the pan-American project of his young colleague. A copy of his notes for this pan-American occasion in February 1917 has been preserved in Florence Schauffler's papers (SFP, Box 23). SFP is the Schauffler Family Papers

15 The National Arts Club in Gramercy Park in 1975.
Courtesy of the National Park Service.

On this occasion the address of welcome was made by Agar, with Garland presiding. It was clearly a long evening. Sloane spoke on 'Literary Pan Americanism', Thomas on 'The Monroe Doctrine in Poetry', Peixotto on 'An Artist's Impressions of South America', Lilian Elliott on 'The Poets of Brazil,' and Alfred Coester on 'The Modernistic Movement in South America'.[11] In conformity with the theme of the evening, Coester ended by

---

(MS 1389), Manuscripts and Archives, Yale University Library. Rice's translations of Chocano appeared in prime position in *Poetry*, in February 1918.

[11] Later published as 'The Modernista Movement in South American Literature', *Bulletin of the Pan American Union*, 44 (1917), 173–77.

underlining the growing acquaintance between North America and Latin America, helped by the spread of the study of Spanish in US schools and colleges: after all, he concluded, 'the name America means, not a part of a continent, but a whole continent from Alaska to Cape Horn'.[12] There were brief addresses by various Latin American guests and a resolution was passed to the effect that a permanent Pan American Union of literary associations from across the continent should be formed for the purpose of securing a wider mutual appreciation.[13]

The February 1917 issue of the *Pan-American Magazine* also carried a report on the evening. It was anonymous, but almost certainly written by Lilian E. Elliott, the literary editor of the magazine. To the list of notable guests, she adds the names of Leopold Grahame, from Argentina, New York correspondent of *La Nación*; Dr Manuel Galván, son of the Dominican novelist; Federico de Onís, who had just taken up the chair in Spanish literature at Columbia; Dr Manuel Calero, late Minister from Mexico; José María Vargas Vila, Colombian writer; William Robert Shepherd, Columbia University historian; Peter Goldsmith of the Carnegie Endowment; and the ubiquitous Mr and Mrs Edwin Markham. She also notes that 'The Literary Editor of The Pan-American Magazine, L. E. Elliott, gave an address on "The Poets of Brazil," touching briefly upon the eloquence and oratorical gifts of Latin Americans, and speaking of the love of nature that has inspired in particular, so much of the beautiful and rich poetical output of Brazil.'[14] A two-page account of the address follows, with extensive quotations from her translations of Brazilian poetry, but with no further detail about the occasion as a whole.

A less formal account was produced by the evening's chairman, Hamlin Garland, in one of the books of his reminiscences which punctuated the first half of the century. Garland recalls that the evening was his idea: 'When I learned that a number of distinguished writers from South America were temporarily living in New York, I suggested to John Agar, the president of the National Arts Club, that a dinner in honor of these authors and artists would have a beneficial effect',[15] a formulation that leaves open

---

[12] Coester, 'The Modernista Movement', 177.
[13] *Bulletin of the Pan American Union*, 44, nos 281–85 (January–June 1917), 234–35. Nothing came of this admirable idea.
[14] 'Pan-American Literary Meeting in New York', *Pan-American Magazine*, XXIV, no. 4 (February 1917), 209–11, at 209–10. See also 'Una conferencia sobre literatura panamericana', *El Norte Americano*, 3, no. 3 (March 1917), 14.
[15] Hamlin Garland, *My Friendly Contemporaries: A Literary Log*, New York: The Macmillan Company, 1932, p. 141.

the question of just how he 'learned': possible routes would be from de la Selva to Markham to Wheeler to Garland, or from de la Selva to Lilian Elliott to Garland. That Salomón de la Selva should have had the last slot on the programme either suggests his hand in the organisation or the recognition by others of his pre-eminence in the pan-American literary field, no doubt bolstered by his mastery of English. Agar provided the premises of the National Arts Club, Archer Huntington helped finance the dinner, and Garland secured the services of Kermit Roosevelt, Theodore Roosevelt's second son, who had just returned from a visit to Brazil, and gave a talk entitled 'Conditions of Authorship in South America'. According to Garland, the dinner was just finishing and the room where the talks were being given was filling up, when Theodore Roosevelt suddenly arrived, filling the small room with his presence. He told Garland that he was here to listen to his son, and asked not to be called upon for a speech. In Garland's account everything went off swimmingly:

> It touched me to find in Roosevelt so much of the fond father. He sat upon one of our hard, narrow camp chairs for two hours, listening to all the speeches with alert interest. He stayed on till we put our resolutions of goodwill to vote, and congratulated me afterward on the success of the meeting.
> 'It is a good message to send to our sister republics in the South,' he said. 'The news of it will go to every capital.'[16]

Fortunately—for the sake of posterity and literary scholarship—one newspaper reporter sat through the evening, and his account, published the next day in the *New York Tribune*, made it sound like a much less staid occasion, at least in its final passage. In addition, several people wrote to Pedro Henríquez Ureña to inform him of what had happened, and he recorded their words in an essay he wrote for the Havana journal, *El Fígaro*.[17] The newspaper headline captured the important moment:

PATRIOT SILENCES T.R. AT ARTS CLUB
Nicaraguan, in Reciting Wrongs by U.S., Looks at Colonel
SPANISH-AMERICAN GATHERING THRILLED

---

[16] Garland, *My Friendly Contemporaries*, p. 141.
[17] Pedro Henríquez Ureña, 'Salomón de la Selva', *El Fígaro*, 36, no. 12 (6 April 1919), 288–89, quoted from Alfredo A. Roggiano, *Pedro Henríquez Ureña en los Estados Unidos*, State University of Iowa Studies in Spanish Language and Literature, 12, Mexico City: n.p., 1961, pp. 136–42.

Roosevelt, on Programme, Not Called On—'I Didn't Do Anything,' He Says.[18]

De la Selva had finally been called at 11 p.m., when everybody was beginning to get fidgety. 'A previous speaker referred to my country as "little Nicaragua,"' began Professor de la Selva (this is from the newspaper report) and it wasn't so much his words as his tone that caused a general straightening in chairs. The so-called professor undoubtedly was in earnest: 'Nicaragua may be small in size, but a land is as large as its hopes and aspirations,' he declaimed: 'A previous speaker said that governments derive their just powers from the consent of the governed. Through the United States my country is ruled by a government which its people have not chosen.' The speaker—the reporter noted—was making gestures and looking right in the direction of Colonel Roosevelt, who was leaning forward in his chair taking in every word. One US poet wrote to Pedro, he reported, that unconsciously de la Selva had given Theodore Roosevelt 'una mirada de fuego' [a fiery look].[19] Then (the newspaper again): 'I will now read a poem,' announced Professor de la Selva, without any warning whatsoever. According to the reporter, the *entente cordiale* seemed about to go up in smoke. One of Pedro's women correspondents said that Salomón's hair was standing on end throughout his talk: the young man's earnestness caught the audience's fancy, and his 'palabras inflamadas' [inflammatory words] were applauded furiously.[20] 'I see we can now come to an understanding,' de la Selva is reported as saying. 'It has been hard for me to talk of love for America while my own land was being tramped down by the United States. There can be no real Pan-America until wrongs have been righted.' Then, according to the newspaper account, rather than calling on Roosevelt as per the programme, which the chairman obviously thought would risk a firestorm, he quickly brought the evening to a close.[21] Journalists surrounded Roosevelt: 'Why, the young man didn't mean me,' Roosevelt explained. 'I never did anything to Nicaragua.' However, according to the letters Pedro received, Roosevelt became indignant at de la Selva's words and accused those who applauded him of being 'unpatriotic' and of not understanding what they doing; to which one woman replied, 'We were applauding the truth.'[22] The effectiveness of de la Selva's poetic harangue was all the greater

---

[18] 'Patriot Silences T.R. at Arts Club', *New York Tribune*, 8 February 1917, p. 9.
[19] Henríquez Ureña, 'Salomón de la Selva', 138.
[20] Henríquez Ureña, 'Salomón de la Selva', 139.
[21] It is unclear whether Roosevelt senior was scheduled to speak or not.
[22] Henríquez Ureña, 'Salomón de la Selva', 139.

in that it took place in Gramercy Park, just across Park Avenue from the house where Theodore Roosevelt had been born. He was being bearded in his own backyard.

The poem that de la Selva read—which he'd written specially for this evening—starts like a typical migrant's tale:

> From the South am I, from the tropic lands;
> I was born where the sunlight is molten gold:
> If you probe my heart, if you pierce my hands,
> You will know the blood that is never cold.
> ...
> To the North I came, with a dream, with a song,
> With a noise like the music of the rain in the Spring,
> For I held the Vision and it ruled my tongue,
> And North and South would hear me sing.[23]

It's a longish poem. The South he calls his mother while the North is his bride, and he obviously wishes to reconcile them. It is the mother who needs convincing, so he addresses her, though in language which echoes military destruction:

> And again I spoke in my Mother's face:
> 'This is your daughter, this foreign land;
> For my love of her I have dared disgrace:
> I have shattered the walls of creed and race,
> Love was so true that no walls could stand.'[24]

He denies the implied charge of falsity to his mother ('You have I cherished above all other'), but affirms a dual allegiance ('my flags are two') in the face of Roosevelt's recent insistence that Americanism should be 'unconditioned and unqualified'.[25]

---

[23] From Salomón de la Selva, 'The Dreamer's Heart Knows Its Own Bitterness', *Tropical Town and Other Poems*, New York: John Lane Company, 1918, pp. 38–43, at p. 38.
[24] De la Selva, 'The Dreamer's Heart', p. 39.
[25] Theodore Roosevelt, 'America for Americans' [Speech at St Louis, 31 May 1916], in *The Progressive Party: Its Record from January to July, 1916, Including Statements and Speeches of Theodore Roosevelt*, New York: n.p., 1916. 'Americanism' had been a consistent Rooseveltian theme from as early as 1894: 'True Americanism' [*The Forum*, April 1894], in Theodore Roosevelt, *American Ideals, and Other Essays, Social and Political*, New York: G. P. Putnam's Sons, 1897, pp. 14–32.

The allegory is never comfortable. The Past demands to be remembered, and acknowledgement is made of 'the heedless North' and 'the headlong South':

> But the Past was night, and I was the sun
> And the light of the morning was on my mouth.[26]

Still, the verses speak more often of war than of harmony. The Condor and the Eagle spring at each other—but are caught in the net of the dreamer's song. Then the waters are suddenly black with war-rigged ships sailing south, presumably in reference to the 1898 Spanish–American War, only again for the waters to be quieted by the poet's song.

Finally, though, US military and financial might seem to have outflanked the poet's idealism:

> But now a cry like a red flamingo
> Has winged its way to the Judgment gates:
> My Nicaragua and Santo Domingo
> Shorn in their leanness by the 'famous States'!
>
> Harried and thieved in their want, in their hunger,
> Their honour flaunted for a thing of laughter. …
> —You have done this because you are the stronger,
> Do you know what deeds may follow after?[27]

The 'famous States' was a pointed quotation from the protest poem by the revered US writer Ralph Waldo Emerson, written in 1846 in outrage at the US invasion of Mexico:

> But who is he that prates
> Of the culture of mankind,
> Of better arts and life?
> Go, blind worm, go,
> Behold the famous States
> Harrying Mexico
> With rifle and with knife.[28]

---

[26] De la Selva, 'The Dreamer's Heart', p. 40.
[27] De la Selva, 'The Dreamer's Heart', p. 42.
[28] 'Ode, Inscribed to W. H. Channing' [1846], in Ralph Waldo Emerson, *Collected Poems and Translations*, ed. Harold Bloom and Paul Kane, New York: The Library of America, 1994, pp. 61–64, at p. 62. See above, p. 36.

Appropriately enough, that very day—7 February 1917—had seen the formal end of General Pershing's Mexico expedition after he'd failed to locate Pancho Villa, who had been tweaking US tails across the border.

De la Selva therefore makes his critique part of a pan-American anti-imperialist tradition rather than simply a cry of anguish from the invaded countries. Even the unquoted echo of Emerson's carefully chosen verb demonstrates de la Selva's credentials as a poet in English fully aware of the US poetic tradition of which he himself is also now a part. 'Harry' is an old English verb, but Emerson may have picked it up from Thomas Carlyle's account of the French Revolution and its aftermath, where 'The Prussians were harrying and ravaging about Metz'.[29] And it was Prussian 'harrying' which was also now pertinent to the political situation of February 1917, as the last three stanzas of de la Selva's poem make clear. The auguries are dire. The poet fears that the birds he caught in his net will escape and that the sea will again 'blacken with warlike ships'. His Bride seems to be rejecting his wooing. And yet he insists that she listen once again to the 'song of hope on my lips'—another reference to the revered Darío and his *Cantos de vida y esperanza*.

Here things get complicated. De la Selva wrote the poem for this occasion, finishing it therefore in early February 1917, several weeks before the USA announced that it would enter the war in Europe, though just as, on 3 February, Woodrow Wilson had taken a large step in that direction by breaking off diplomatic relations with Germany. But de la Selva would have known that Roosevelt—its addressee on the night—was an outspoken advocate of US participation in the war. By the time de la Selva was preparing the poem for publication in *Tropical Town and Other Poems*, nearly a year later, US troops were getting ready to embark in large numbers. It seems likely that the published version underwent some amendment to take account of the new situation. In the absence of an original typescript it is impossible to know just what changes were made. In the final version, however, the contrast is probably stronger than it would have been on the occasion of the poem's recital. The words published in 1918: 'You have challenged the might of Belgium's wronger / Dreadful you stand like the winged Avenger' would not have described the case in February 1917.[30] The Prussians have done the harrying, but Nicaragua and Santo Domingo saw themselves as American Belgiums which, for de la Selva, left the USA in an invidious position:

---

[29] Thomas Carlyle, *The French Revolution* [*The Works of Thomas Carlyle*, vol. 4] (London: Chapman & Hall, 1903), III, p. 10.
[30] De la Selva, 'The Dreamer's Heart', p. 43.

> Will you let this thing be said of you,
> That you stood for Right who were clothed with Wrong?
> That to Latin America you proved untrue?
> That you clamoured for justice with a guilty tongue?[31]

The analogy had the US Marines playing the rôle of the brutal German army—not quite the image the US wanted to cultivate. So now, having stood for Right with respect to Belgium, there is an opportunity for the USA to redeem itself, which allows the pan-American dream to survive—by the skin of its teeth—in the poem's closing lines:

> So, blameless and righteous, your strength shall be
> The power of God made manifest,
> And I pledge the South shall never rest
> Till your task is accomplished and the world is free.[32]

This allows him to subtitle the poem: '(A Pan-American Poem on the Entrance of the United States into the War)'. Mother and wife were reconciled for the moment.

A letter from Salomón to Edna mentions his 'fight with and victory over Teddy Roosevelt'. Then, recalling the occasion over a year later, in a letter to Amy Lowell, de la Selva claimed that news of the affair had made a big splash across Latin America and had secured his loyalty from further attacks—though it is unclear whether there had been attacks or whether he had just been feeling the insecurity of his own position as self-appointed cultural go-between.[33]

Mamita Schauffler

Among Salomón de la Selva's pupils at Williams College were two brothers, named Bennet and Goodrich Schauffler—'Beanie' and 'Gigs' to their family and friends—who seem to have introduced Salomón to their parents in New York: Florence and Charles. In a letter home, Bennet called Sal (as they referred to him) 'perhaps the most thoroughly Quixotic, impulsive, and admirable little man I know.'[34] By the spring of 1917, he was visiting

---

[31] De la Selva, 'The Dreamer's Heart', p. 43.
[32] De la Selva, 'The Dreamer's Heart', p. 43.
[33] Letter from Salomón de la Selva to Edna St Vincent Millay, ESVMP (21 March 1917); Letter from Salomón de la Selva to Amy Lowell, ALP (9 April 1918). ALP is the Amy Lowell Papers (MS Lowell 19 [1095]), Houghton Library, Harvard University.
[34] Letter from Bennet Schauffler to his family, SFP, Box 1 (12 February 1917).

the family and writing to them, usually to the mother. He was obviously welcomed into their home almost like another son and was soon calling Florence 'mamita' and referring to her as his second mother.[35]

Florence Manvel had been born in 1867 into a railroad family: her father was manager of various companies, including the Atchison, Topeka and Santa Fe Railway. She and her younger sisters had been prominent young society women in St Paul, Minnesota, and then in Chicago. Judging from her surviving papers, Florence had a literary bent from an early age, hand-producing a book of poems, writing essays on a series of authors including Whitman, Browning, and Dante, and co-writing and copyrighting a musical comedy called *Complexity* with her friend George Colburn. Chicago had a thriving literary scene in the 1890s and Florence Manvel seems to have been at least on the fringes of it, though the five sons born in the seven years following her marriage in 1889 must have been something of a distraction. Her husband, Charles E. Schauffler, son of a theologian, worked as a salesman for cement and oil companies in Chicago, but after his health broke down in 1910, he moved to a less stressful job in the New York office of his friend Ralph Modjeski's bridge-building company.[36] By 1915, the family was installed in the Northhold, a new apartment block at 3647 Broadway, in Hamilton Heights, not far from the Hispanic Society of America. In the 1920 census Florence's occupation was listed as housewife and she was cooking and cleaning for husband and now six sons living at least intermittently at home, aged 24, 23, 21, 20, 18, and 12.

Florence Schauffler had tried hard to get her writing published, sending poems and essays to respectable journals such as *The Century*. Mostly she got polite rejections, although one poem eventually appeared in print under her name.[37] This was a period when New York was full of young, often well-educated, single women from the midwest and the south, making their way in the literary world—Aline Kilmer, Muna Lee, Theresa Helburn— many of whom Florence Schauffler would now meet at the Poetry Society of America. But at 48 she was old enough to be their mother, the age in

---

[35] The relationship can be reconstructed from de la Selva's letters to the Schauffler family, mostly to Florence, and from other material in the the Schauffler Family Papers. Many of the letters are undated, so some guesswork is involved in reconstructing the chronology.

[36] On the Schauffler family history, see Robert McEwen Schauffler, *Schauffler Chronicle: A Roster and Biographical Sketches of the Schauffler Family in America*, Kansas City: privately printed, 1951.

[37] Florence M. Schauffler, 'The Watch-Night', *The Century*, 83, no. 3 (January 1912), 338.

fact of the established matrons of the PSA such as Anna Markham and Jessie Rittenhouse.

One of Florence's unpublished poems, dated New York, September 1915, is particularly revealing:

> I do not understand
> All this stirring within me;
> I do not know what this new pulse
> And flush through me means;
> For am I not nearly old?
> The time of my blossoming is as far gone
> That it may not be fitly remembered.
> I have entered into fruition
> And accomplished its wills and joys.
> They would laugh and say 'She is only a seed husk,
> Shattered and parching!'
> The rime of winter is already dusted upon me.
>
> And I stand like a foolish girl-child
> At my window.
> And reach out my arms to you,
> Crying,
> 'Sweetheart!'[38]

If read biographically, the sexual yearning may refer to a seemingly unrequited crush on a family friend called John Kerfoot, who was for many years the literary editor of *Life* magazine and a close associate of Alfred Stieglitz.[39] But more telling is that sense of her self-image as a woman with whitening hair newly moved to a realm where the young have inherited the world. Poignantly, she entitled this verse 'Renascence', echoing the scintillating poem that had recently announced the arrival on the poetic scene of the 19-year-old Edna St Vincent Millay, who was not known for standing at windows waiting to be rescued.

---

[38] Florence M. Schauffler, 'Renascence' (New York, September 1915), SFP Box 15.
[39] John Barrett Kerfoot (1865–1927). Associate editor and contributor to *Camera Work* and himself a photographer; and the author in 1911 of a book about Broadway. He features in Marius de Zayas's 1912 painting, *The Picnic*, along with Alfred Stieglitz, Agnes Meyer, and others. Over these years Kerfoot seems to have been having an affair with his brother-in-law's wife, so he may have been reluctant to complicate his life any further (*New York Times*, 27 October 1920, p. 11).

The dissociation that followed was logical. Mrs Schauffler was the nurturing mother of six, renowned for her fine cooking. She used the pseudonym Ellen Harrington for 'Renascence' and other poems of that ilk. Only one was ever published, though it was in the groundbreaking women's issue of *Others*, guest-edited by Helen Hoyt:

Matrix

I stretch my hands out toward you;
And by all the ways that are surer than seeing
I see that they are filled with gifts of your giving;
A coronet tipped with leaves and star dust,
And little slippers of gold with wings upon them.
And a glowing girdle of crimson,
And coin of royal mintage.
I hold my hands up to you;
And by all the ways that one knows without knowing
I know that you know I have filled them with gifts for your taking;
A cloak of eider as softly warm as satisfied desire,
And a clasp of living emerald to hold it,
And tingling wine in a jeweled goblet,
And a rare red rose to grace it.

But the cruel resolvent of actuality
Is fallen upon them:
And I stand and gaze at my upturned hands;
And they are only full
Of wistfulness.[40]

Nobody has ever connected Florence Schauffler with Ellen Harrington. The 'cruel resolvent of actuality' kept the two well apart.

Reconstructing these years from her papers leaves the impression of a talented, driven, but frustrated woman. She wrote poems of erotic yearning and long essays about feminism; she sent her work to the prestigious *Atlantic Monthly*, who politely returned it; and she cooked for her family and her family's friends and for Salomón de la Selva, whose youthful enthusiasm drew her into his pan-American projects.

---

[40] *Others: A Magazine of the New Verse*, 3, no. 3 (September 1916), A Woman's Number, ed. Helen Hoyt, 63.

Her relationship with de la Selva was intense, though maternal. De la Selva's charm and silver tongue often helped him beguile older women who could help his career, but his feelings for Florence Schauffler were stronger than that. When his first published poem, 'A Tale of Faerieland', originally unassigned, appeared in his book, *Tropical Town and Other Poems*, it was dedicated to Mrs Charles E. Schauffler.

By the beginning of 1917, Salomón de la Selva had a secure foothold in the literary world of New York: Pedro Henríquez Ureña wrote to Alfonso Reyes that de la Selva was *the* success story of US poetry.[41] He and his brother Max had been with Salomón at the Poetry Society of America and then at a party given for Salomón by Mrs Schauffler—very literary but very yankee, with the latter destroying the former, Pedro sniffed.

In 1917, Florence Schauffler seems to have been living in Williamstown, or at least spending a great deal of time there. She may temporarily have left her husband; she may just have been looking after her two sons who were at Williams College. One letter from de la Selva to Charles Schauffler celebrates how Florence wiped the floor with a professor of English, George Dutton, after a lecture she had given at Williams—so she obviously had some academic standing.[42] From a passing reference in another letter, it seems as if she may have been lecturing on the 'new poetry', with Dutton defending a more traditional position.[43]

In April 1917, towards the end of de la Selva's teaching year at Williams, the USA entered the First World War. Salomón registered on 5 June 1917 and began some military training at the college. His poem 'Drill', dated Williams College, April 1917, expressed his sense of joy at the prospect of fighting:

> Battle fields are far away.
> All the world about me seems

---

[41] 'Es *el* éxito del día en la poesía yanqui'(Letter from Pedro Henríquez Ureña to Alfonso Reyes [10 January 1917], in Pedro Henríquez Ureña and Alfonso Reyes, *Epistolario íntimo, 1906–1946*, ed. Juan Jacobo de Lara, 3 vols., Santo Domingo: UNPHU, 1981–1983, vol. 3, p. 42).

[42] Letter from Salomón de la Selva to Charles E. Schauffler, SFP, Box 1 (undated [March 1917?]).

[43] 'Old sad bones Dutton, clever dog, is married: he'll acknowledge vers-libre soon enough. There's nothing like the fatal step to make a man open his eyes to free and wild things' (Letter from Salomón de la Selva to Florence Schauffler, SFP, Box 1 [9 August 1917]).

> The fulfillment of my dreams.
> God, how good it is to be
> Young and glad to-day!
> ...
> Now, as never before,
> From the vastness of the sky,
> Falls on me the sense of war.
> Now, as never before,
> Comes the feeling that to die
> Is no duty vain and sore.
> ...
> So it shall be
> In Flanders or in France. After a long
> Winter of heavy burthens and loud war
> I will forget, as I do now, all things
> Except the perfect beauty of the earth.[44]

'So it shall be / In Flanders or in France': a prediction or a promise, or perhaps both.

Meanwhile, de la Selva established The Williams Poetry Society, a branch of the PSA, through which he encouraged the writing efforts of his students, including the Schauffler boys (Bennet was President). This group was evidently the core of the Williams College Ambulance Unit, which set off for France in the summer of 1917. Salomón sent to their sergeant, Harold Van Doren, via Florence, a letter of introduction to Archer Huntington, who was then in Paris.[45]

De la Selva's determination to fight must have been strengthened by the patriotic example set by the family to which he was closest in New York, the Schaufflers. A Chicago newspaper picture (Fig. 16) showed the six Schauffler boys, who would all serve in Europe, along with their father, who worked for the Army in New York. Four of Charles's brothers and two nephews are also mentioned as being in uniform. Florence is on the right of the picture, her mother on the left. War was clearly beginning to dominate Salomón's life. His first great plan was for a pan-American regiment and he even went to Washington for discussions: 'Hope to be made 1st lieutenant to serve as interpreter with the first Pan-American contingent to go over

---

[44] Salomón de la Selva, 'Drill', *Tropical Town, and Other Poems*, New York: John Lane Company, 1918, pp. 74–77.

[45] Since the originals are in the Schauffler Family Papers, it may be that they never reached Van Doren.

A 100 PER CENT FIGHTING FAMILY
Captain, His Five Sons, Four Brothers, and Two Nephews Are All in U. S. Uniform.

(Top row)- Goodrich, Henry, Bennett, Leslie and Charlie Schauffler (oval) Allan Schauffler -(bottom row)- Mrs. Manville, Captain and Mrs. Charles E. Schauffler

16 'A 100 Per Cent Fighting Family', *Chicago Daily Tribune*, 25 April 1918, p. 3. Clipping courtesy of the Schauffler Family Papers (MS 1389), Manuscripts and Archives, Yale University.

to France'.[46] When that plan fell through, 'It's Russia where they promise to send me with my 150 Pan-American immortals,' he wrote to Edna. 'But the government is disheartening, being so slow to act, so uncertain in its promises. What if the War should end before I get a manly scar on my breast, over my heart, a souvenir for you?'[47]

Mrs Charles E. Schauffler sat proudly alongside her uniformed husband and sons as the *Chicago Tribune* photographer took their picture. Back home, Florence Manvel Schauffler wrote the searing poem, 'The Woman Speaks':

---

[46] Letter from Salomón de la Selva to Clement Wood, CWP (undated [March 1917?]). CWP is the Clement Wood Papers (Box 31), Hay Library, Brown University.
[47] Letter from Salomón de la Selva to Edna St Vincent Millay, ESVMP (22 August 1917).

> I,
> Who am the chalice of very life itself,
> The fragile glass whence men have drunk their joy,
> The cup of homely peace that sits beside
> The strength and sustenance of their daily bread,
> Require of you an answer to this thing,
> This widespread field of tortured hideous death,
> These maggot-gnawed repulsions that were once
> My sons and lovers, beautiful and glad
> Against the whiteness of my nurturing breasts.[48]

There's no evidence that she showed it to anyone. Her men would probably not have understood.

*

Throughout his year at Williams College de la Selva's letters to Edna continued unabated. He was often apologising for his own thoughtlessness and then quickly berating her for not writing more often. In July 1917, he acknowledged a letter from her, 'al fin' [at last]. 'No creas que de ti tengo recuerdos amargos. Tú sabes que te quiero todavía' [Don't think that I have bitter memories of you. You know that I still love you]. And, in August: 'In all the world there are not any two quite so wonderful as we are, and it would be a pity if we were not to be fast and everlasting immortal friends', and yet, on the same day: 'It is true, I have never known you! I have loved you, worshiped you, sung your praises, built all manner of unstable and even perishable dreams about you, but "even as we are deceived in the stars", so I have been deceived in you.' But by the end of the month there was a further lurch in tone. She hasn't written ('You must rouse yourself') and he no longer wishes to love her but wants them to be friends. Her attitude to correspondence remained a barrier: 'Dear, time is so quick with me, and he busies me so, that the long two or three weeks you take to answer, ever so briefly, my letters of no end of pages, seem centuries interminable.'[49]

A 12-page letter in August picks yet again at the scab of his feelings for Edna, before turning into a self-flagellation about his struggles with the temptations of the flesh:

---

[48] Florence M. Schauffler, 'The Woman Speaks', SFP Box 23.
[49] Letters from Salomón de la Selva to Edna St Vincent Millay, ESVMP (9 July 1917, 22 August 1917, 26 August 1917).

I want you to know the faun in me, only don't get too near him, don't awake him! He is not young any more; he is no longer clean and bristling with laughter. He has been shut-up so many centuries that he is deformed and smells of cellar air that has not been wind and has not lifted flames for years and years. Only last spring, when the bark of the birches grew rose and skin-like and the lovely round trees seemed imminently turning into flesh, the ancient vigour quickened in my old faun and he leaped on light feet and pricked his ears and sniffed the air and ran himself ever so weary chasing—after you! Oh, Edna, you were in the air that spring day! Always in the distance, for only afar can we see air, and the air was you, I saw you. The wind kept caressing your ankles, and now and then I could see your legs, so marvellously pink—Oh, only white birches in April! When it was sunset, you spread your hair over all the hills, and in the keeping of the night you went to sleep, so far from me.

It was only <u>one</u> day of spring, Edna. Now Summer is all too fattened, and the old faun feels like vomiting when he enters the subway. The old faun is vile again. I don't know what to do with him. To starve him, I used to fast long days; I used to spend nights kneeling down telling my rosary, fighting sleep and him; for he would sometimes come to me in my sleep, and shame me when I woke. But that only left me haggard and old and made my mouth bitter.—Well, I will not give in. Although I know that the faun will not die until I die, I will not give in. I'd rather see my flesh rot with leprosy than be filthy with the spume and froth of him. Edna, it is pure I want to be all my days! Pray for me.[50]

On other occasions Salomón took Edna into his confidence about his romantic liaisons—or fantasies. So, in an undated letter which may have been written in the summer of 1917, he reports on three women. 'The little lady is in Southampton, although she may be in Billtown again, for all I know. May God be good to her always.' Billtown is Williamstown, which may suggest that the 'little lady' is a friend or lover from the College. 'The tiny Elizabeth Barrett Browning has written to me four or five times, and once I have been to see her.' This is probably Marya Zaturenska, who certainly had a teenage crush on de la Selva, which would eventually lead to trouble. And then, 'The wife—poor soul! You know, I really get thinking that she loves me. I wish she did not. I cannot love her. I cannot love anyone that way. It is the tragedy

---

[50] Letter from Salomón de la Selva to Edna St Vincent Millay, ESVMP (22 August 1917).

of my life, that I am a being of fine, but unsustained impulses.'[51] 'The wife' was a fantasy Salomón constructed for himself which acts as a counterpoint to his accounts of his relationships with real women. I'll come back later to this oddity, which is probably a key to his complex psychology. Yet, in another letter from the same period, he wrote: 'We have decided to separate, divorce would be too noisy and too rash, only less rash than our marriage. I thought it would break my heart, but I don't feel anything. She and I will go on being friends; and if love really enters our life, all shall be well.' He calls the wife 'Margaret'. Edna, who was more interested in romancing Bennet Schauffler than Salomón, wrote to the—possibly jealous—student to explain her relationship with the poet: 'As for Sal, oh well, he gets as much fun out of it as I do. We're really just good friends, and when we seem to be more, why we're just playing—that's the truth.'[52]

Another older woman makes an appearance in his letters around this time: 'And I haven't told you about Mrs Griswold,' he wrote to Edna in August 1917. 'She's a marvelous beautiful virtuous wife and mother and friend. I am desperately, but in a very pure way, in love with her. I have been young Socrates and she my Diotima of Mantinea. That is the most beautiful friendship of all my life: an intense, unselfish, chaste devotion; and it has meant the salvation in me of all the goodness & loveliness my Mother gave me for a heritage.'[53] In the *Symposium* Diotima gives Socrates the idea of Platonic love. Elizabeth H. Griswold was 36 at the time, wife of Chester Griswold and mother of three young children.

Chicago

In the autumn of 1917, de la Selva suddenly went to Chicago after, he wrote to Florence Schauffler, 'three things offered themselves'. One was the opportunity to address the Latin Americans in Chicago 'and so strengthen my position as the leader of my peoples in this country'. No false modesty there. When he wrote this letter to Florence, he had already made two speeches and was due to address a mass meeting 'of about five hundred' on the coming Friday. The second thing drawing him to Chicago was the

---

[51] Letter from Salomón de la Selva to Florence Schauffler, SFP Box 1 (undated [July 1917?]).

[52] Letter from Edna St Vincent Millay to Bennet Schauffler, SFP Box 1 (undated [June 1917?]).

[53] Letter from Salomón de la Selva to Edna St Vincent Millay, ESVMP (2 August 1917). Mrs Griswold is the dedicatee to 'Ode to the Woolworth Building' (*Tropical Town*, p. 82).

possibility of obtaining a position as a French instructor to soldiers going to France from the city. The authorities seem to want foreign officers, he reported, so he has sent to Nicaragua for documents attesting to his commission as captain in the Revolutionary Army of the Liberal Party. He seems to enjoy his own cheek in making the request of the Nicaraguan Congress while knowing that nothing will come of it. And, thirdly, *The American Exporter* in Chicago is in need of a Spanish translator.[54] This may well have been the clinching reason for the sudden move: a breakfast egg to be added to his usual diet of rice and beans, as he puts it.[55] Even the drudgery of translating business letters inspires him:

> It is so wonderful to know that even in this mean way I am a factor in bringing North and South America together ... I laugh to think what courteous and much obliging gentlemen I make these Swedes and Yankees, and what concise precise little businessmen I am turning many a wordy Latin American into.[56]

Through Harriet Monroe—editor of *Poetry* magazine—he has met the Chicago poets, he reports. He and Carl Sandburg have become fast friends and take long walks together. He had argued with the 'vampirish Mary MacLane' about Gertrude Stein. MacLane had confessed she was half in love with him, but at the same time she said she was 'half Lesbian', which caused Salomón some confusion: 'Oh freaks! And yet I like her: she is half cracked, and perfectly without reticence'.[57]

> This City you love so much is beginning to be dear to me. I have been so happy here! I told you Harriet Monroe gave Muna Lee and myself a dinner. Carl Sandburg wrote it up in his paper, the Daily News.[58]

---

[54] *The American Exporter* was one of a number of trade periodicals published by the Johnston Export Publishing Company. It appeared in English, Spanish, French, and Portuguese.
[55] Letter from Salomón de la Selva to Florence Schauffler, SFP Box 1 (10 September 1917).
[56] Letter from Salomón de la Selva to Florence Schauffler, SFP Box 1 (undated [September 1917?]).
[57] Letter from Salomón de la Selva to Florence Schauffler, SFP Box 1 (undated [October 1917?]). Mary MacLane, who was originally Canadian, had written a scandalous memoir published as *The Story of Mary MacLane* (1902). It was republished under its original title: *I Await the Devil's Coming*, New York: Melville House, 2013.
[58] Letter from Salomón de la Selva to Florence Schauffler, SFP Box 1 (undated [October 1917?]).

De la Selva had, he writes, given a speech defending literary conventions, which had provoked a lively discussion. Helen Hoyt, Muna Lee, and Mary MacLane had called him too logical; Harriet Monroe had defended him.

The first of the three letters from Chicago to Florence announces an important decision:

> Saturday night, at exactly 35 minutes after one o'clock, I made up my mind to get rid of that pink marble and quite useless ornament the Law calls my wife, and get as a real companion for my moods and fortunes in the shape (some shape!) of Sofia Barsay. There's a girl can be mother and mistress and sweetheart and pal and God to me![59]

But, just to complicate matters:

> Muna Lee has fallen very pathetically in love with me and I with her. She has written me the most wonderful sonnets in the world. Truly she is a great poet ... I have cried and cried thinking if she had come before I turned fool how happy we would have been.[60]

They have sworn eternal love, he reports, while both knowing—according to Sal—how meaningless that idea is. He knows—he says—that she is thinking of 'that lad in Oklahoma who has her heart', and he knows that she knows—he says—that he is longing for his true love, Sophia Barsay (though he seems unsure just how to spell her first name).[61] At the same time he asks:

> And what did Cousin Phil Rogers say? Did you tell him I loved Florence? He knew me only by hearsay, I am afraid; and I tremble to think of the wild stories he may have told that precious little girl. Isn't it funny, I love Florence. But as I love Sophia, no; but still I have no other name for it except love. May be it isn't love with any of them.[62]

---

[59] Letter from Salomón de la Selva to Florence Schauffler, SFP Box 1 (10 September 1917).

[60] Letter from Salomón de la Selva to Florence Schauffler, SFP Box 1 (undated [October 1917?]).

[61] The 'lad from Oklahoma' was John Peebles McClure, a not insignificant poet himself: see Jonathan Cohen, ed., *A Pan-American Life: Selected Poetry and Prose of Muna Lee*, Madison: University of Wisconsin Press, 2004, p. 7 and p. 70 n. 8.

[62] Letter from Salomón de la Selva to Florence Schauffler, SFP Box 1 (undated [October 1917?]). Florence Shepard Rogers was Phil Rogers's sister, children of the well-connected New York couple Noah Cornwell Rogers and Anna Shepard Rogers.

Goading the Bull Moose (1917)

His love life was getting seriously complicated, which seems to have been how he liked it. De la Selva sent Edna Millay 'Four Poems for Florence'; one of them, the lovely 'Guitar Song with Variations', retains its dedication to her in *Tropical Town*.[63] The covering letter explains who Florence is:

> She must be now about twenty-two or -three; when she was but one year old, she suffered from infantile paralysis, since when she has been a cripple. She is a graduate of Barnard, and has travelled a lot, in Italy and France. She is very beautiful: worlds of dark hair, and a splendid forehead, and passionate lips in the control of a most prim and rectitudinous nose. What I love best of her is an expression of suffering that her eyes have, not *old*, but immortal; eyes like those of a Mater Dolorosa, full of pain and sweetness! She and I are very excellent friends. I have found her as malleable as gold.[64]

No mention of course in any of this of his 'wife'.[65]

From Chicago de la Selva also reported to Florence Schauffler that John Lane Company had backed out of the agreement to publish his book—presumably referring to *Tropical Town*, which they did indeed publish the following year. 'They will', he wrote, 'inform you of that as soon as they get up enough courage to do so.' It is unclear why John Lane backed out, or why they backed in again later, but that they would inform *Florence* confirms the force of a letter of attorney that de la Selva wrote later that year, empowering her to make decisions about the publication of his poems, with royalties from any book published going to Edna. Less conventionally, '[r]equest to her is hereby solemnly made that she discredit any story told, retold or heard about as that does not give me a serious, upright, decent character. She is especially warned against fantasies regarding affairs of my heart and the vicissitudes thereof.'[66] 'I know that in your precious generous heart my interests are safe,' he wrote to Florence. 'Only don't love me too much. It is a curse I bear, that of making all who love me suffer.'[67]

---

[63] De la Selva, *Tropical Town*, p. 20.
[64] Salomón de la Selva to Edna St Vincent Millay, ESVMP (2 August 1917).
[65] Salomón de la Selva to Florence Schauffler, SFP Box 1 (undated [September 1917?]). There was a Sophia Barsay of about the right age living in Manhattan at the time, the daughter of Russian parents. She married in 1918.
[66] Salomón de la Selva conferring power of attorney on Florence Schauffler, SFP Box 1 (undated [May 1917?]). In a later, also undated, letter to Florence Schauffler [August 1917?] de la Selva refers to having to add another section to *Tropical Town*, so perhaps John Lane thought the original too slim.
[67] Salomón de la Selva to Florence Schauffler, SFP Box 1 (undated [September 1917?]).

Salomón had introduced Edna to Florence and to her son Bennet. 'I see a great deal of the Schaufflers,' Edna wrote to her mother and sister in late October 1917. She was much taken with Beanie: 'a great big, handsome dark-eyed thing of twenty-four—too cute for words in his sailor-suit & stunning in evening-things'.[68] According to a letter he wrote to his fiancée, Bennet resisted Edna's advances: if so, he would have been one of very few. In any case, the friendship seems to have lasted: he and Florence sat next to Edna at the January 1919 PSA dinner.[69]

Introducing Edna

There is a gap in the correspondence with Edna between March and July 1917, although—perhaps surprisingly—it is Edna who reignited it, leading to a slew of letters from Salomón in the summer and autumn of 1917, often again complaining that she doesn't write often enough or at sufficient length. In August, he begins his long story of trying to get to war. 'They demand impossibles of me. That I take papers of citizenship out, that I grow four pounds heavier, that—. As I stand, I am enrolled in the "Wild 12th" N.Y. Ntl. Guard. I have not yet been sworn into Federal Service, and I am meeting my difficulties fighting them inch by inch …'.[70] Right from the beginning of US involvement in the war, he is determined to fight, although the reasons he gives tend to vary. He writes to Edna that he will be fighting for no country:

> I will fight for the same reasons—rather for analogous reasons for which a young woman uses delicate perfume & fine array: to appear best. Having fought in the great War will bring out my best qualities to advantage & will cover up a multitude of defects. But believe me that I act instinctively; that I am conscious of the instinct merely shows that I am not altogether a fool.[71]

---

[68] Edna St Vincent Millay, *Letters*, ed. Allan Ross Macdougall, New York: Harper, 1952, pp. 79, 81.
[69] Letter from Bennet Schauffler to Marjorie Page, SFP Box 1 (undated [late 1917]); Program for Poetry Society of American Dinner, 30 January 1919, at the National Arts Club, EMA. EMA is the Edwin Markham Archive, Horrmann Library, Wagner College, Staten Island, New York.
[70] Letter from Salomón de la Selva to Edna St Vincent Millay, ESVMP (2 August 1917).
[71] Letter from Salomón de la Selva to Edna St Vincent Millay, ESVMP (March 1917).

Goading the Bull Moose (1917)

By November 1917, Salomón was back in New York from Chicago, writing of making plans for an immediate return to Nicaragua, perhaps in December. His mother calls him home and he has informed the military authorities, he writes to Edna. He will then be done with Nicaragua and will bring his brothers and single sisters to New York. Mrs Schauffler will be his literary representative; royalties from *Tropical Town* are to go to Edna; royalties from his second book, *The Lonely Exile*, expected out in February, to Edna's sister Norma—with whom he is now in love. Despite what he says about his brothers and sisters, this makes it sound as if he thinks he will never return. He feels guilty about not fighting and what people will say about him:

> I have to be dismissed first, from service. To think of the shame makes me sweat. How those who know me will sneer at me. They will say it was all a pose. They will say—Oh my God!
>
> I was so willing to go and die, without asking why or caring. It was such a generous gesture for all the world to see and say: 'He is magnificent!'—Poor Sali!—If only the war lasts long enough![72]

Edna was also seeing a lot of Salomón in these months: 'how we raise the devil', she wrote to her family.[73] It seems likely that it was around this time that they spent the night on the Staten Island ferry—at five cents a ticket for as many trips as you wanted, a popular form of cheap entertainment—an occasion commemorated in one of Millay's best-loved poems, 'Recuerdo', whose Spanish title would have meant the world to Salomón:

> We were very tired, we were very merry—
> We had gone back and forth all night on the ferry.
> It was bare and bright, and smelled like a stable—
> But we looked into a fire, we leaned across a table,
> We lay on a hill-top underneath the moon;
> And the whistles kept blowing, and the dawn came soon.[74]

As John Timberman Newcomb notes, this is one of the most resonant city verses of the period, offering 'a compressed portrayal of the varied spaces

---

[72] Letter from Salomón de la Selva to Edna St Vincent Millay, ESVMP (15 November 1917).
[73] Millay, *Letters*, p. 80.
[74] Edna St Vincent Millay, 'Recuerdo', *Poetry*, XIV, no. 2 (May 1919), 68. The poem had probably been written in late 1918: see Millay's March 1919 letter to Harriet Monroe: Millay, *Letters*, p. 88.

and modes of experiencing the modern city'.[75] He makes no connection to de la Selva (and doesn't interrogate the significance of the Hispanic title), but takes from the poem itself an ambiguity in the relationship between the couple in the poem: emotional intimacy which might or might not have a sexual dimension, with the absence of gendered pronouns lending the verse a utopian feel.

Another intriguing friend that de la Selva made around this time was the Italian Emanuel Carnevali. Born in Florence, Carnevali had emigrated to New York in 1914 where he worked at menial jobs while very quickly learning English and beginning to write his own poetry as well as translating from the Italian. De la Selva makes references to employing 'that Italian boy' as secretary: this was probably Carnevali, who is mentioned by name—as a mutual friend—in a letter to Edna Millay.[76] After winning a prize in a competition run by *Poetry*, and meeting Harriet Monroe on one of her visits to New York, Carnevali moved to Chicago in the summer of 1919 and was invited in November to become associate editor of *Poetry*, though he soon fell ill with a debilitating disease. Even more than Salomón, he was a shooting star, appearing for a scant two years in the pages of *Poetry*, *The Little Review*, and *Others*.

His remarkable deployment of a truly vernacular American idiom, particularly in his translations of contemporary Italian poets such as Salvatore di Giacomo, Corrado Govoni, and Piero Jahier, makes him another of the unsung poets of New York modernism.

Then, as 1917 drew to a close, Salomón finally managed to inveigle Edna Millay into attending an event in her honour. It must have been some evening. José Santos Chocano was back in town. After his earlier visit, he'd been fêted in Puerto Rico and then been able to return to Mexico once Victoriano Huerta had been removed in July 1914. During 1916 and 1917,

---

[75] John Timberman Newcomb, *How Did Poetry Survive? The Making of Modern American Verse*, Urbana: University of Illinois Press, 2012, p. 245.

[76] Letter from Salomón de la Selva to Edna St Vincent Millay, ESVMP (13 November 1917). On the friendship between de la Selva and Carnevali, see Francesca Congiu, 'Una parabola letteraria: il caso di Emanuel Carnevali. Alcune traiettorie interpretative fra Italia e Stati Uniti', PhD thesis, University of Cagliari, 2008, p. 18. For an account of his life: Emanuel Carnevali, *The Autobiography of Emanuel Carnevali*, compiled and prefaced by Kay Boyle, New York: Horizon Press, 1967.

on the payroll of the Guatemalan dictator Estrada Cabrera, he'd lived in Cuba and Honduras, with frequent trips back to Guatemala to see his wife.

Now a better-known figure, and with New York literary antennae more attuned to the presence of Latin American poets—due in no small part to de la Selva's efforts—Chocano was asked to read at a PSA event at the National Arts Club. He read four of his short poems, with Peter Goldsmith reading John Pierrepont Rice's translations before Rice rounded off the segment with a brief conclusion. Chocano then read 'Fragmento preliminar de una epopeya cíclica' [Preliminary fragment of a cyclical epic]—a very Chocano-esque title—which is partly about the USA, with de la Selva translating. To mark the occasion, Chocano's portrait, painted in oils, was presented to the National Arts Club.[77]

Directly from the PSA event, de la Selva took Chocano to a dinner at the Felix-Portland Hotel—132-134 West 47th Street and Broadway—to introduce Edna Millay to a group of Hispanic writers. They made an impressive collection. Pedro Henríquez Ureña, Martín Luis Guzmán, and Mariano Brull we've met already. Aged 30, the Honduran Alfonso Guillén Zelaya was a promising young poet. The Chilean Alberto Ried Silva, also 30, was working as a correspondent for *La Nación* in New York and had already published a book of poems. Ricardo Arenales was the current pseudonym of the poet born in Colombia in 1893 as Miguel Ángel Osorio Benítez. Already widely travelled and published, he would soon become known as Porfirio Barba Jacob.

Two copies of the programme to the dinner have survived. The one in Edna Millay's papers is more or less pristine, but Florence Schauffler scribbled some notes on hers (Fig. 17), which help us fill out the details of the evening. Under Edna's name, she wrote, 'who didn't know it was given in her honor until she arrived, 45 minutes late, and had to leave early to attend a rehearsal of the Provincetown Players, in which she was performing.' Pure Edna. Then, at the bottom of the page, next to the phrase 'Also ran', Florence gives a list of other names:

Florence M. Schauffler, of Chicago, Ill.
Helen Powell of Saginaw, Mich.

---

[77] Luis Alberto Sánchez has Chocano reading 'Oda cíclica' at the Hispanic Society of America on 27 December 1914 (*Aladino, o vida y obra de José Santos Chocano*, 2nd. edn, Lima: Editorial Universo, 1975, p. 318), but the HSA didn't do readings. Eduardo Núñez also has 27 December 1914 for the NAC event ('El poeta Chocano en Nueva York', *Cuadernos Americanos*, 75, no. 3 [1954], 292–98, at 296). Both are mistaken.

PAN-AMERICAN DINNER

IN HONOUR OF

Edna St. Vincent Millay

of the United States

UNDER THE AUSPICES OF

"PAN AMERICAN POETRY"

GIVEN BY

JOSÉ SANTOS CHOCANO, of Perú

ALFONSO GUILLÉN ZELAYA, of Honduras

PEDRO HENRÍQUEZ UREÑA, of Santo Domingo

LUIS MARTÍN GUZMÁN, of Mexico

MARIANO BRULL, of Cuba

ALBERTO RIED, of Chile

RICARDO ARENALES, of Colombia

and SALOMÓN DE LA SELVA, of Nicaragua

Representing Intellectual Latin America

THURSDAY DECEMBER 27TH, 1917

AT THE FELIX-PORTLAND HOTEL

IN NEW YORK CITY

17 Programme for the pan-American dinner in honour of Edna St Vincent Millay, Felix-Portland Hotel, 27 December 1917. Courtesy of the Schauffler Family Papers (MS 1389), Manuscripts and Archives, Yale University.

Norma Millay of Camden, Maine
Jessie Rittenhouse of New York City, N.Y.
Archie Coates of Manhattan and military
Calum Hohe of New York and Columbia University
Miss Elliot of Wales (British Isles) and Pan America
    Representing our intellectual United States.[78]

That 'Also ran' sounds like a barb: the programme invitation does rather suggest that Edna is being shown off to his Hispanic friends by Salomón, with the others making up the numbers and providing some additional female company. However, as we've already seen, Jessie Rittenhouse and Lilian Elliott were in fact substantial figures in their own right; Helen Powell was one of Florence's sisters-in-law, and Norma was one of Edna's sisters. The other two were Columbia students and budding playwrights. But they were all in one room at the same time. Salomón de la Selva's pan-American dream was still alive.

---

[78] 'Pan-American Dinner in Honour of Edna St Vincent Millay', SFP Box 23.

Chapter Six

The Pan-American Dream (1918)

> I am the man who dreamed the new day dawned
> And so arose at midnight with a cry.[1]

By the beginning of 1918, the mind of President Woodrow Wilson—ever the visionary—was turning to the post-war settlement. It was clear that his voice would be dominant, so particular attention was paid to his pronouncements. By the summer it was clear that the war was going the way of the Allies: the Battle of Amiens in August would prove decisive. By November, the fighting was over and on 4 December Wilson set off for the peace conference in Paris which would, he believed, finally bring a Woodrovian order to the unruly world. Imposing order at home would prove equally challenging. To date, New York had kept open its doors, which was one reason why it was such an exciting place to live. But a country at war is always likely to see enemies within. In May, the so-called 'Sedition Act'—actually a set of amendments to the 1917 Espionage Act—severely limited freedom of expression. The radical magazine *The Masses* was charged with publishing 'treasonable material' and brought to trial twice, in April and September, both trials ending with deadlocked juries.

The war limited travel, though two notable arrivals in the city in June were the Caribbean writer Eric Walrond and the painter Georgia O'Keeffe. In retrospect, the literary event of the year was the first instalment of James Joyce's *Ulysses* in Margaret Anderson's *The Little Review*. Meanwhile, however, Hispanic culture was becoming a real presence in New York. Following the success of Enrique Granados's opera, Jacinto Benavente's plays appeared in English translation in New York in 1917, with the one-act 'His Widow's Husband' performed by the Washington Square Players in late October. Nineteen eighteen would see no fewer than 24 printings of

---

[1] From Salomón de la Selva, 'To Those Who Have Been Indifferent to the Pan American Movement', *Tropical Town and Other Poems*, New York: John Lane Company, 1918, p. 119.

Vicente Blasco Ibañez's novel, *The Four Horsemen of the Apocalypse*, which would become the best-selling novel of 1919.[2] And now came the Spanish music and dance of *La Tierra de la Alegría*, a show which had played to acclaim in Madrid, Paris, London, Buenos Aires, and Havana. An operetta by Joaquín Valverde based on a book by two young writers, José F. Elizondo and Eulogio Velasco, and translated by Ruth Boyd Ober, *The Land of Joy* was a big success in New York, breaking box office records at the Park Theatre on Columbus Circle from the end of October 1917 to the end of January 1918, and then touring the country. An article in *Current Opinion* assessed this Hispanic phenomenon, the miracle—as it called it—in which Spanish dancing took New York by storm, largely thanks to the Spaniards and Latin Americans in the audience who, as one critic noted, 'unlocked the lips and loosened the hands of us cold Americans', shouting 'Olé!' and throwing hats onto the stage. Carl Van Vechten was no less enthusiastic:

> The revue ... is calculated ... to hold you in a dangerous state of nervous excitement during the entire evening, to keep you awake for the rest of the night, and to entice you to the theatre the next night and the next. It is as intoxicating as vodka, as insidious as cocaine, and it is likely to become a habit, like these stimulants ...[3]

It was certainly the talk of the town. Both Martín Luis Guzmán and Tom Walsh recommended it to Salomón, who asked Edna Millay if she would like to go. The new year had got off to a colourful start.[4]

Early 1918 was a particularly busy time for Salomón de la Selva. As well as trying to get his new poetry magazine up and running, which must have seemed like a full-time job, he was finalising his own collection of poems, to be published that spring by John Lane, while increasingly determined to join the fighting in Europe, though that proved easier said than done. Much easier was falling in love with beautiful women—and two more now

---

[2] Jacinto Benavente, *Four Plays*, trans. John Garrett Underhill, New York: C. Scribner's Sons, 1917; Vicente Blasco Ibañez, *The Four Horsemen of the Apocalypse*, trans. Charlotte Brewster Jordan, New York: E. P. Dutton & Co., 1918.
[3] 'Spanish Dancers Who Have Made New York Sit Up and Take Notice!', *Current Opinion*, 64, no. 1 (January 1918), 27–28; Carl Van Vechten, 'The Land of Joy' [3 November 1917], in his *The Music of Spain*, New York: A. A. Knopf, 1918, pp. 91–101, at pp. 98–101.
[4] Letter of Salomón de la Selva to Edna St Vincent Millay, ESVMP (January 1918).

entered his life. Having eventually got to England in August 1918, he kept up his correspondence with his friends in New York, his letters providing insights both into life in the British Army and what was going on in his head. The Armistice in November left him free to spend time in London and Paris over the winter.

Is America Honest?

Woodrow Wilson's initial determination to keep the USA out of the European war had burnished his credentials as an 'Americanist' president who would focus his attention on the western side of the Atlantic. To that end he enthusiastically adopted the rhetoric of Pan-Americanism, assiduously speaking at Pan-American conferences of various kinds and using the term as a central plank in his re-election campaign in 1916: one section of the official campaign book, entitled 'Wilson's Policy Welds the Americas Together', reprinted sections of his speeches and favourable quotations from Latin American newspapers. Phrases such as 'international co-operation' and 'interchange of values' were prominent. Pan-Americanism was going to be turned from theory into actuality.[5] The actuality didn't quite pan out as many hoped. Haiti, the Dominican Republic, and Nicaragua remained under US occupation. Incursions into Mexico didn't look much like the heralded respecting of each other's territorial integrity. US entry into the European war in the spring of 1917 divided opinion south of the US border as much as it did at home, but there were certainly those—like Salomón de la Selva—who initially thought that a concern for the fate of small countries such as Belgium must bode well for the future fate of those such as Nicaragua, which would surely benefit from the provisions of the kind of international agreement that Wilson had in mind. That inkling hardened into a certainty when Wilson started to use the word 'self-determination'.

With a century of hindsight it is easier to see how Wilson felt pressured into the adoption of that term. The idea behind it had initially been outlined by Lenin in October 1916 and articulated by the new provisional government in Moscow—under the influence of the Bolshevik-controlled Petrograd soviet—in April 1917.[6] Trotsky had then prominently denounced

---

[5] 'Wilson's Policy Welds the Americas Together', in *The Democratic Text Book 1916*, Washington, DC: The Democratic Congressional Committee and Democratic National Committee, 1916, pp. 183–91.

[6] V. I. Lenin, 'The Socialist Revolution and the Right of Nations to Self-Determination' (1916) <https://www.marxists.org/archive/lenin/works/1916/jan/x01.htm> accessed December 2018; Erez Manela, *The Wilsonian Moment: Self-Determination and the*

the hypocrisy of Western countries—including the USA—in claiming to fight for the rights of small nations in Europe while oppressing other national groups within their empires.[7] On the back foot, the Allies started to adopt the same terminology. In January 1918, David Lloyd George spoke about the need for the post-war settlement to respect 'the right of self-determination or the consent of the governed'.[8] Woodrow Wilson's 'Fourteen Points' speech merely called for the 'interests' of colonial people to be taken into account, leaving open who would decide what those interests were; but his address to Congress on 11 February 1918 (the 'Four Points' speech) was crystal clear: 'In the coming settlement', he said, 'national aspirations must be respected; people may be dominated and governed only by their own consent ... "Self-determination" is not a mere phrase. It is an imperative principle of actions which statesmen will henceforth ignore at their peril.'[9]

In June 1918, Wilson made a less famous speech to Mexican journalists in which he suggested that all American countries should sign a declaration guaranteeing each other's political independence:

> Some time ago, as you probably all know, I proposed a sort of Pan-American agreement. I had perceived that one of the difficulties of our relationship with Latin America was this: The famous Monroe Doctrine was adopted without your consent, without the consent of any of the Central or South American States.
>
> If I may express it in the terms that we so often use in this country, we said, 'We are going to be your big brother, whether you want us to be or not.' We did not ask whether it was agreeable to you that we should be your big brother. We said we were going to be. Now, that was all very well as far as protecting you from aggression from the other side of the water was concerned, but there was nothing in it that protected you from aggression from us, and I have repeatedly seen the uneasy feeling on the part of representatives of the states of Central and South America that our self-appointed protection might be for our own benefit and our own interests and not for the interest of our neighbors

---

International Origins of Anticolonial Nationalism, New York: Oxford University Press, 2007, p. 37.

[7] Manela, *The Wilsonian Moment*, p. 38.

[8] Manela, *The Wilsonian Moment*, p. 39.

[9] As 'Only One Peace Possible', in *Americanism: Woodrow Wilson's Speeches on the War—Why He Made Them—And — What They Have Done*, ed. Oliver Marble Gale, Chicago: Baldwin Syndicate, 1918, pp. 103–09, at p. 106. Cf. Mark T. Gilderhus, *Pan American Visions: Woodrow Wilson in the Western Hemisphere 1913–1921*, Tucson: University of Arizona Press, 1986.

... So let's have a common guarantee signed by everyone. And that's the kind of guarantee that we will need throughout the world.[10]

These were not words that Theodore Roosevelt could ever have uttered, and they gave rise to considerable Hispanic American optimism that the tectonic plates of US foreign policy might be shifting as Wilson saw the need to align that policy with his dreams for a League of Nations that would re-order the whole world. So, in October 1918, the journal *Inter-America* seized on an editorial piece that had appeared in *La Nación* (Buenos Aires) praising Wilson to the skies for his idealistic and disinterested participation in the war in Europe, which he, Wilson, had in this interview with Mexican journalists, associated with his larger Pan-American policy.[11] The editorial suggested that Latin America need no longer fear that by Pan-Americanism the USA might mean political hegemony, military expansion, and economic domination. Wilson was now articulating a spiritual and civilisational ideal which *La Nación* associated with an idealistic movement towards 'the ethnic unity of humanity: the supreme ideal'.[12] That the newspaper immediately suggested that the obstacles to this ideal would include 'the inconsequence of the African populations' indicated that the ideological framework still needed some tweaking—as subsequent history would rapidly confirm.[13]

Wilson's record had always been far removed from his rhetoric. De la Selva had himself protested in New York against the US occupation of Veracruz in 1914. The US justification—doubtless penned by Wilson, though signed by his Secretary of State, William Jennings Bryan—revealed one of the problems that would plague the idea of self-determination. 'The purpose of the United States,' it read, 'is solely and singly to secure peace and order in Central America by seeing to it that the processes of self-government there are not interrupted or set aside'.[14] Setting aside the relocation of Mexico into Central America, this statement justified the intervention of an outside power (the USA) to determine which group within another country best represented the processes of self-government. In other words, it promoted

---

[10] Woodrow Wilson, 'An Address to a Party of Mexican Editors' (7 June 1918), in *Wilson and Revolutions 1913–1921*, ed. Lloyd C. Gardner, Washington, DC: University Press of America, 1982, pp. 66–69, at p. 68.
[11] 'President Wilson and Pan American Ideals', *Inter-America*, 2 (October 1918–August 1919), 3–6.
[12] 'President Wilson and Pan American Ideals', 5.
[13] 'President Wilson and Pan American Ideals', 5.
[14] Telegram from The Secretary of State to Chargé O'Shaughnessy, Department of State, Washington, 24 November 1913 <https://history.state.gov/historicaldocuments/frus1914/d651> accessed December 2018.

the idea of self-government in the same words with which it undermined the notion. Typical, his critics would say, of Wilson's slippery way with words. What exactly was the 'self' which was going to do the determining? Nation, ethnicity, community? As if those were easy to define in any particular circumstance.

The Dominican Republic and Nicaragua had continued to get in the way, despite the best efforts of Roosevelt and Taft to keep them under the US thumb. Wilson's difficulties were to a large extent of his own making. In trying to think through a just settlement for Europe's problems, he'd borrowed the idea of self-determination from Lenin, but two difficulties had then ensued. First, American countries saw no reason why self-determination should apply in Europe but not in America; and, second, Lenin underlined the discrepancy in Wilson's version by indicating that the concept of self-determination was key to his policy of anti-colonialism—thereby boosting the attraction of Bolshevism to the inhabitants of countries under what they saw as colonial or neo-colonial rule.

An early but fierce examination of the inconsistencies in Wilson's position put the Dominican Republic in the spotlight when the March 1918 issue of *Metropolitan* magazine published an original and biting satire called 'Is America Honest?' by the freelance journalist William Hard—who had been editor of *The Delineator* when Salomón de la Selva worked there.[15] 'Is America Honest?' was announced as 'An Imaginary Conversation' with four interlocutors: Woodrow Wilson, Kaiser Wilhelm, the Greek Prime Minister Eleutherios Venizelos, and Vincentino Evangelista, 'a Bandit of Santo Domingo'. Evangelista had been a real thorn in the side of the Marines in the Dominican Republic, responsible for the brutal execution of two US civilian engineers but also in some ways operating as a traditional *caudillo* with a power base in the east of the country, using a mixture of family ties, persuasion, and force: 'bare-bones state-making', Alan McPherson calls it.[16] In July 1917, he was eventually lured into a trap and shot 'while trying to escape'. He was immediately enshrined in Dominican mythology as a martyred patriot.[17]

---

[15] William Hard (1878–1962). Hard belonged to the 'muck-raking' school of journalism. Later in his career he worked for NBC and then *Reader's Digest* as well as writing biographies of Theodore Roosevelt and Herbert Hoover.
[16] Alan McPherson, *The Invaded: How Latin Americans and Their Allies Fought and Ended U.S. Occupations*, New York: Oxford University Press, 2014, pp. 48–49.
[17] See Bruce J. Calder, 'Caudillos and Gavilleros versus the United States Marines:

In Hard's piece the Kaiser begins by taking Wilson to task, in a friendly way, for acting against the principles announced in his second inaugural address by encouraging revolution in Germany. Wilson explains that he wasn't thinking universally when he announced those principles: 'I was speaking of the Americas ... In the Americas we have had too many revolutions. They are a nuisance. They keep me busy with messages and Marines. Too much. I am obliged to set my face unflinchingly against revolutions—in the Western Hemisphere.'[18] To which the Kaiser mildly responds that Wilson should think about issuing his speeches with geographical footnotes. Announcing himself as 'the ghost at this table', Evangelista then leaps up to quote Wilson's 'Jackson Day' speech from 8 January 1915 in which he had welcomed the Mexican Revolution and proclaimed 'It is none of my business and it is none of yours how they go about the business. The country is theirs. The government is theirs.'[19] And then, says Evangelista, you contradicted yourself by coming down to Santo Domingo with your Marines and taking the bread out of the mouths of honest men who were living by revolutions. But in another speech in January 1916 I'd pronounced *against* revolutions, claims Wilson. The Kaiser quietly states that this was exactly his point all along: principles are a matter of time and place and can easily be changed to suit changing circumstances. Venizelos then makes his first contribution, suggesting that if there is a distinction between the hemispheres, then Wilson should at least make it clear. He himself started off, he points out, as a revolutionary, fighting for Crete against Turkish claims to territorial integrity that were backed by the great European powers. Eventually, Crete's revolutionary aims were recognised as justified—as once had been those of the USA. At this point Wilson resorts to the international argument—the outline of what would become his proposal for a League of Nations. Sheer hypocrisy, claims the Kaiser, pointing out that the USA has no international credentials at all: when it was on the point of invading Haiti it refused the invitation to confer with other nations: 'In your words you are indeed the world's greatest internationalists. In your actions you are the world's greatest monopolists. You monopolize a whole hemisphere.'[20] Which brings them inevitably to the Monroe Doctrine. Venizelos offers a history lesson about

---

Guerrilla Insurgency during the Dominican Intervention, 1916-1924', *Hispanic American Historical Review*, 58, no. 4 (1978), 649-75.

[18] William Hard, 'Is America Honest?', *Metropolitan*, 47, no. 4 (March 1918), 15-16 and 66-69, at 15.
[19] Hard, 'Is America Honest?', p. 16.
[20] Hard, 'Is America Honest?', p. 16.

how Monroe's final revision of his message removed an acknowledgement of Greek independence so as to maintain a strict division of spheres of influence. That, Venizelos says, is when the USA abandoned internationalism in favour of the Monroe Doctrine. The Kaiser chips in with a quick rundown on the USA's 'vassal states' to its south: Cuba, Haiti, Santo Domingo, Porto Rico, Nicaragua, Panama ... and a mention of US disregard for the Central American Court of Justice. Here's an idea, says the Kaiser: 'Why not put Haiti and Santo Domingo into the Peace Conference? What? All conquests, by anybody, during the war, into the Peace Conference!'[21] Unapologetic, Wilson claims that he had embraced internationalism by convincing the American people in his address to the Senate on 22 January 1917 that internationalism was just the Monroe Doctrine writ large, at which Evangelista, finally getting flustered, makes him read more sentences from that speech: 'that every people should be left free to determine its own polity, its own way of development, unhindered, unthreatened, unafraid, the little along with the great and the powerful.'[22] Evangelista gives a rundown on the US intervention in the Dominican Republic, reserving his greatest scorn for Wilson's underhand dealing in not mentioning what he was doing in the Caribbean to his own people. Evangelista even refers to Wilson's 1916 Campaign Text Book with its chapter called 'Wilson's Policy Welds the Americas Together' which foregoes any mention of intervention in Haiti and the Dominican Republic in favour of detailing the new parcel post treaty with Brazil and the imposition of a two-cent postage on letters from the USA to the Leeward Islands. Evangelista is allowed the last word, addressed to Wilson: 'Say what you mean.'[23]

Hard's article created quite a storm. Venizelos was a respected international statesman, and the Kaiser—though an enemy—was a head of state. But, in early 1917, Evangelista had been portrayed as a murderous brute, yet here he was sitting at the same table as the president of the United States. The article was also remarkably even-handed—Wilson was allowed to refute the charges laid against him and the other three played strong hands too; but being even-handed in times of war could easily be seen as unpatriotic, even treasonable. The Kaiser is presented with a degree of sympathy, even humour; and Evangelista is allowed a disquisition of which a seasoned diplomat would be proud. Apparently in response to public complaints, the Postmaster General, Albert S. Burleson, stated that the issue would

---

[21] Hard, 'Is America Honest?', p. 67.
[22] Hard, 'Is America Honest?', p. 69.
[23] Hard, 'Is America Honest?', p. 69. It was officially called *The Democratic Text Book*, but Hard wasn't making anything up: see above, p. 210.

have been banned if Hard's piece had been known about in advance. As it had already been distributed there was no action to be taken, but the New York Postmaster was instructed to keep a close eye on the magazine and it was reported that the article had been sent to the Attorney General.[24] A complicating factor was that Theodore Roosevelt was a contributing editor to *Metropolitan*, which had been the main outlet for his writing since 1915, originally for a long series of articles in which he excoriated Wilson's interpretation of 'neutrality'.[25] Once Wilson had taken the USA into the world war, Roosevelt had had to moderate his tone, although he'd felt free to criticise Wilson's *conduct* of the war.[26]

Roosevelt weighed in against Burleson, a conservative Texan Democrat, accusing him of using the Espionage Act to discriminate against newspapers critical of Wilson; though Roosevelt didn't offer any specific defence of Hard's piece: satire was not his genre of choice.[27] Burleson responded to Roosevelt's charges, denying that the *Metropolitan* had been punished for criticising the administration's conduct of the war, and affirming that Roosevelt was the only 'patriotic' reader who had expressed approval of Hard's piece, referring to correspondence from around the country calling it not only unpatriotic but actually treasonable, and claiming to be 'reliably informed' that German propagandists had already had it translated into Spanish and distributed in Mexico and South America.[28] There was certainly

---

[24] 'Magazine Wasn't Barred From Mails', *New York Times*, 10 March 1918, p. 4; 'Slap at America Sent to Gregory', *New York Times*, 3 March 1918, p. 8.

[25] See Edmund Morris, *Colonel Roosevelt*, New York: Random House, 2011, pp. 196-97. These articles were collected in his *America and the World War*, New York: C. Scribner's Sons, 1915 and *Fear God and Take Your Own Part*, New York: George H. Doran Company, 1916.

[26] Despite its lavish illustrations, *Metropolitan* had generally pursued a fairly radical line: Israel Zangwill, George Bellows, and John Reed all wrote for it; but—in accordance with Roosevelt's views—it had been in favour of 'preparedness' and was fully behind the US entry into the First World War.

[27] 'Roosevelt Gives the Facts Called for by Burleson', *New York Times*, 11 May 1918, 1, 13. Burleson was responsible for introducing racial segregation into the Federal Post Office. He was notorious for pursuing supposedly subversive writing with all the resources given to him through the Espionage Act. His first target had been *The Masses*.

[28] 'Burleson Denies Colonel's Charge', *New York Times*, 20 May 1918, p. 8. See also 'Roosevelt Again Assails Burleson', *New York Times*, 26 May 1918, p. 19. 'Is America Honest?' did appear in Spanish in the Mexico City newspaper *El Demócrata*, which also republished articles by Roosevelt critical of the administration: see James R. Mock and Cedric Larson, *Words That Won The War: The Story of the Committee on Public Information 1917-1919*, Princeton, NJ: Princeton University Press, 1939, p. 325.

an element of party politics involved here. Hard was a strong Republican and there were rumours that Roosevelt was again going to be the Republican candidate in the next presidential election.

Translating Poetry

The European war gave a boost to various forms of pan- or inter-American communication in New York. On the political front, La Asociación Ibero-Americana de los Estados Unidos was formed on 30 July 1918 in order to present a united Latin American position. The officers and committee, representing all the republics, mostly had diplomatic or political or business backgrounds. The stated aims of the association were to facilitate acquaintance between Latin Americans residing in the USA and those on temporary sojourns; and to develop closer relations with 'the national Anglo-Saxon element' so as to establish harmony and understanding 'between the two branches in which the great American family is divided'.[29] That family metaphor can play out in many ways: two branches suggests division, but equality.

Literature may not have seemed the most obvious focus for these efforts, but it certainly played a rôle, in official circles as well as in de la Selva's more personal crusade. So, for example, on 31 May 1918, the National Arts Club hosted a meeting to promote interest in Spanish and Portuguese literature under the auspices of the Committee on Cooperation in Latin America (CCLA), an organisation founded in 1913 to introduce protestant religion into a part of the world in thrall to the Roman church. The Pan American Union was present in the person of its Director General, John Barrett. One of the CCLA representatives, Samuel G. Inman, would later write extensively about pan-American initiatives. The CCLA's interest seems to have been in the propagation of 'wholesome' literature, which any writers present might well have considered a contradiction in terms. The report of the meeting published in the *Pan-American Magazine*, and therefore probably written by Lilian Elliott, gave most space to the contribution to the discussion of a Miss L. E. Elliott, representing magazine editors. She made three excellent points. She noted the need for a good file of Latin American newspapers and magazines at a central New York location; she remarked that no true pan-Americanism could exist which did not include Canada and the Caribbean; and she stressed that one of the great stumbling blocks to the forging of social links was South America's condemnation of the treatment

---

[29] 'Editorial Comment: The Ibero-American Association', *Pan-American Magazine*, XXVII, no. 5 (September 1918), 224.

of 'coloured' people in the United States. 'South America,' she concluded, 'cannot understand this treatment as compatible with democracy.'[30] She fails to mention how this observation was received. One imagines like a lead balloon.

Just four days after this meeting, the Spanish-language newspaper *La Prensa* became a daily, a long step forward for the representation of Hispanic interests in New York. Founded by a Spanish entrepreneur called Rafael Viera, in 1913, *La Prensa* had undergone various changes of ownership and editorial team before José Camprubí bought it in 1918, probably seeing the newspaper as a natural accompaniment to the Unión Benéfica Española, of which he had been president since January 1917. Alfredo Collao, the Chilean editor, was the one element of continuity, undoubtedly necessary because Camprubí himself had no journalistic expertise.[31] He moved the offices to Canal Street, employed his old Harvard friend Ernest Gruening as a business manager, expanded the number of journalists, and improved the quality of the print. The move to daily publication helped consolidate the newspaper's position and its circulation began to rise sharply.[32]

Alongside the Spanish-language newspapers and the established journals that would accept poems and other forms of writing from Hispanic authors, a new cultural journal had appeared in October 1917 with the not inconsiderable financial muscle of the Carnegie Endowment behind it, specifically its Interamerican Division. It described itself like this: 'The purpose of *Inter-America* in to contribute to the establishment of a community of ideas between *all the peoples of America* by aiding to overcome the barrier of language, which hitherto has kept them apart.'[33] *Inter-America/ Inter-América* was published in alternate months in English and Spanish, the English-language version offering translations of essays, stories, and articles from Spanish and Portuguese journals, the Spanish-language version

---

[30] 'Literature for Latin America', *Pan-American Magazine*, XXVII, no. 3 (July 1918), 144–46, at 145.

[31] A piece by Manuel Cestero praising Collao's efficiency as a journalist noted that he was not yet 30 and lived a quiet family life: 'En broma y en serio', *La Prensa*, 28 October 1918, p. 4.

[32] See Amparo de Juan Bolufer, 'Recepción de la literatura española en *La Prensa* de Nueva York (con un apéndice sobre la visita de Blasco Ibáñez)', in *Literatura hispánica y prensa periódica*, ed. Claudio Rodríguez Fer et al., Santiago de Compostela: Universidad de Santiago de Compostela, 2009, pp. 533–64; and Regina Galasso, 'The Mission of *La Prensa*: Informing a Layout of the Literature of Hispanic America', *Hispania*, 95, no. 2 (2012), 189–200. On Gruening's rôle, see Ernest Gruening, *Many Battles: The Autobiography of Ernest Gruening*, New York: Liveright, 1973, pp. 82–86.

[33] Statement on the back cover of all issues of the journal (my italics).

doing the same from US journals. The topics ranged widely, from education to commerce, literature to politics. The journals involved were certainly reputable ones, such as *Plus Ultra* (Buenos Aires), *Revista Americana* (Rio de Janeiro), *Cuba Contemporánea* (Havana), *Variedades* (Lima), or from the USA, *The North American Review*, *Atlantic Monthly*, *Scribner's Magazine*, *The Yale Review*. The writers chosen for translation were of similar repute, although from the US side they tended to be rather conservative figures such as John D. Rockefeller Jr, George Washington Goethals, and Nicholas M. Butler—or, as they appeared in the pages of *Inter-América*, Róckefeller, Wáshington, and Bútler, the editor paying scrupulous attention to Spanish-American sensitivity about accents to mark pronunciation. No translators are mentioned, but Peter H. Goldsmith, Director of the Interamerican Division of the American Association for International Conciliation, edited the journal, initially alongside James C. Bardin. It is perhaps indicative that the translation process was entirely invisible, as if the essays were just introduced into a machine in one language and emerged in the other, with no sense of the texture and difficulties of process. Since the idea behind the journal was to introduce two worlds to each other, that world in-between, of Hispanic New York, where the translations were made, had no real part to play. Of de la Selva's friends and contemporaries in New York, only Pedro Henríquez Ureña and Rufino Blanco Fombona make appearances in the journal during these years (1917–20).

In terms of translating poetry from the Spanish, there was only one other game in town apart from de la Selva, but it went under the very distinguished name of William Carlos Williams. As a working doctor in Rutherford, New Jersey, Williams could only participate on an occasional basis in the literary life of the city but he was increasingly committed to his poetic avocation: his first major book, *Al Que Quiere!* appeared in November 1917. The Spanish title was no accident. Williams's mother, Raquel Elena Hoheb Williams, was Puerto Rican, and his father, William George Williams, English by birth, grew up in the Caribbean and was fluent in Spanish. Williams even had a link back to an earlier revolutionary generation: his first medical mentor had been José Julio Henna, a friend of Williams's father who had worked with Martí in the Puerto Rican wing of the Partido Revolucionario Cubano in New York in the mid-1890s and then settled in the city.[34]

---

[34] On Williams's Hispanic background, see Julio Marzán, *The Spanish American Roots of William Carlos Williams*, Austin: University of Texas Press, 1994; and Lisa Sánchez González, 'Modernism and Boricua Literature: A Reconsideration of Arturo Schomburg and William Carlos Williams', *American Literary History*, 13,

Williams's literary connections were very much to experimental modernism. He was an old friend of Ezra Pound's, spent time at Alfred Kreymborg's Ridgefield cottage—easy driving distance from Rutherford—with Man Ray and Adon Lacroix, and was an occasional visitor at the Arensbergs' salon on West 67th Street: he remembered an uneasy exchange there with Marcel Duchamp. Yet Williams's modernism was determinedly American, and part of that Americanism was its understanding of the Hispanic soil out of which the United States had grown.

The new magazine *Others*, which ran from 1915 to 1919, had been Kreymborg's idea, with Walter Arensberg providing some initial funding. Kreymborg remained notionally in charge but roped in a number of guest editors, such as Mina Loy, Helen Hoyt, and Williams.[35] The August 1916 issue—described on the cover as 'Spanish-American Number'—doesn't formally have a guest editor, though Williams's fingerprints are all over it given that the translations were done by his father (probably in association with the son).[36] The issue's opening 'Manifesto'—unsigned but almost certainly written by William Carlos Williams—highlights the contribution made by the young Honduran poet Alfonso Guillén Zelaya, who had '[n]ot long ago ... materialized in New York'.[37] In fact, Guillén Zelaya had been appointed in April 1915 to a position in the Honduran consulate in New York after spending the previous two years in Guatemala. Given the prominent showing in the issue of the Guatemalan writer Rafael Arévalo Martínez, who has six out of the 12 poems featured, it seems reasonable to assume that Guillén Zelaya brought a recent enthusiasm—probably based on personal encounter—with him to New York. He may also have brought a copy of Arévalo Martínez's as yet unpublished story, 'El hombre que se

---

no. 2 (2001), 243–64. As the ungrammatical title *Al Que Quiere!* suggests, Williams' grasp of Spanish was not entirely secure: see the centennial edition, edited and with an introduction by Jonathan Cohen, New York: New Directions, 2017. On Henna, see Gervasio Luis García, 'José Julio Henna Pérez: tema del traidor y el héroe (o los bordes dentados del fin de siglo)', *OP.CIT. Revista del Centro de Investigaciones Históricas*, no. 11 (1999), 73–108.

[35] See Suzanne W. Churchill, *The Little Magazine* Others *and the Renovation of Modern American Poetry*, London: Ashgate, 2006.

[36] See Jonathan Cohen, 'Introduction', in William Carlos Williams, *By Word of Mouth: Poems from the Spanish, 1916–1959*, ed. Jonathan Cohen, New York: New Directions, 2011, pp. xxi–xliii, at pp. xxviii–xxx. Cohen offers the best study of Williams's translations from the Spanish; see also Gabriele Serena Hayden, 'Routes and Roots of the New World Baroque: U.S. Modernist Poets Translate from Spanish', PhD thesis, Yale University, 2016.

[37] 'Manifesto', *Others*, 3, no. 2 (August 1916).

18 Alfonso Guillén Zelaya. Provenance unknown.

parecía a un caballo', which Williams son (with father's help) translated and published in *The Little Review* in 1918.[38] The six other poets featured in the *Others* issue, with one poem each, were—with the exception of the long-dead Colombian *modernista* José Asunción Silva—part of what in Spanish was called the 'post-modernist' generation, José Santos Chocano the most prominent, Guillén Zelaya himself the youngest (Fig. 18).[39]

The 'Manifesto' also noted Guillén Zelaya's enthusiasm for the idea of translating writers from *Others* into Spanish, and even having a Spanish edition under the title *Otros!*, though this never happened. The *Others* poets were not exactly de la Selva's cup of tea, with the notable exception of Wallace Stevens, but Guillén Zelaya's ideas and enthusiasm were certainly up his street and the Honduran would quickly be brought on board the

---

[38] Rafael Arévalo Martínez, 'The Man Who Resembled a Horse', trans. William Carlos Williams, *The Little Review*, 5, no. 8 (December 1918), 42–53. The story had been read to Arévalo Martínez's friends and privately published in Quetzaltenango, Guatemala in May 1915: see Dante Liano, 'Nota filológica preliminar', in Rafael Arévalo Martínez, *El hombre que se parecía a un caballo y otros cuentos*, Nanterre: ALLCA XX; Paris: Ediciones UNESCO, 1997, pp. xxxi–xlii, at pp. xxxii–xxv. See also Raúl Arturo Pagoaga, *Alfonso Guillén Zelaya*, [Tegucigalpa?]: n.p., [198?].

[39] The other three were two Argentines, Juan Julián Lastra (1881–1948) and Leopoldo Díaz (1862–1947) and a Colombian, Luis Carlos López (1879–1950).

pan-American project. De la Selva greatly admired his poetry, writing, 'There is nothing of Europe in him, he is all tropical, of this continent.'[40]

So it was into these fairly crowded waters that Salomón de la Selva launched *Pan-American Poetry*.[41] Although he was often rude about it, the Poetry Society of America had been a useful meeting place and the source of many of de la Selva's US contacts, so it was logical that he should approach its secretary and his good friend Jessie Rittenhouse about his new venture, asking her for the Society's mailing list. She had obviously wanted a note about *Pan-American Poetry* that she could include in the monthly bulletin that the PSA sent to its members, and he obliged:

> Under the leadership of Salomón de la Selva, there has been founded at the Felix Portland Hotel, a literary society called Pan American Poetry, whose purpose is to bring together the poets of all the continent. Pan American Poetry will publish a monthly magazine in Spanish and English containing the representative work of the best poets of North and South America, and it shall welcome in its pages Northern and Southern discussion of what it will print. And besides this venture, Mr de la Selva and his associates intend to undertake the work of editing books of Northern poets in Spanish and of Southern poets in English ... And in order to bring the poets from the different countries personally together, Pan American Poetry will give, from time to time, intimate dinners and receptions. The first of these, given on Dec 27th by seven Latin American poets each of a different nationality, was in honour of Miss Millay. A group of about twenty men and women of letters from Latin America and the United States were present.[42]

---

[40] Salomón de la Selva, 'Of Latin American Poetry', *Pan-American Magazine*, XXVI, no. 3 (January 1918), 145–47, at 146–47.

[41] Salomón later said both that *Pan-American Poetry* was started with his savings from his job at Williams College (Letter from Salomón de la Selva to Amy Lowell, ALP [12 March 1918]) and that it was partly financed by money his mother had sent him, raised from the sale of a family farm, so that he might return to Nicaragua and not go off to war (De la Selva, 'El agua y la rosa en la poesía mexicana', in *Antología Mayor/III Ensayos*, p. 217).

[42] Letter from Salomón de la Selva to Jessie B. Rittenhouse, JBRC (January 1918). JRBC is the Jessie B. Rittenhouse Collection, Rollins College, Winter Park, Florida. A version of this information appeared in the *Poetry Society of America Bulletin*, January 1918, pp. 7–8.

So not just a new journal, but a literary society which will also have a book series and intermittent receptions, formalising the ones that had been running since late 1915. This announcement was the height of de la Selva's ambition.

In the covering letter he then gave Jessie a valuable and more personal outline of what he had in mind:

> I hope that you may give Pan American Poetry a kind word among your friends. I am on fire about it, and perhaps it is God's wisdom and knowledge of what I am best fit for that has impeded my going to war. To sentimentalize is bad, especially now that I have so much work to do that requires every inch of my strength, but I can't help feeling that this I have started is a worthy thing, to be proud of, and in which to succeed. I cannot think of any one dull or hard enough to refuse aiding me, and I trust all the poets will come with willing hands to help spread far and wide the seeds of their own singing. I will depend greatly on you to put us Latin Americans in touch with the poets of your country. My idea is to prove in glowing print: to the Latin Americans, that the land where grew the gardens of Poe and the woodlands of Whitman is fruitful still, with what rich orchards and forests of song; to the North Americans, that Latin America is not merely a restless hive of barren bees, busy with ineffectual revolutions (as your countrymen are unjustly said to be bent on dollar making only), but a honeycomb heavy with what nutritious sweets, the labour of daily toil under the sun in gardens of home. We do not intend to preach fraternity; we will merely, in each number of Pan American Poetry give the best each country has to offer in song, and that gesture shall be sermon aplenty.

The poetic idealism is simon-pure, but de la Selva's own letters have already shown how little response he had tended to receive from the hands of other poets. And there were sharks in the water:

> The only people I fear are the editors of those spurious magazines, slovenly gotten up and written so badly, that claim to be interpreting Latin American song and thought. To be frank, I mean especially Dr Goldsmith's pretentious bundle of hopeless mediocrity. I hate so much to feel this way about it, but, my dear, have you seen what trash his Inter-American has been publishing? The truth must out of me! That man, like every worthless friend, is more dangerous than an enemy. Americans of intelligence reading that stuff cannot be blamed for believing that we in the South are a bunch of idiots swollen with nonsense.

This must count as rampant paranoia on the part of de la Selva, who probably felt that he was in danger of losing his self-appointed leadership rôle in the pan-American cultural movement. *Inter-America* was not really a rival, since it didn't publish poetry, but he clearly saw it as some kind of threat—hence the language of war and betrayal, which perhaps seeped into his prose from the spirit of the city in these days. The opening three issues of *Inter-America*—which came out before de la Selva wrote this letter—were probably too political in a broad sense for his taste, but they did include essays by Paul Groussac, Ramiro de Maeztu, and Leopoldo Lugones, and essays about Rubén Darío and the recently deceased José Enrique Rodó. They were by no means trash.

De la Selva took his new editorial duties seriously. It seems as if he had two standard letters, one to US poets and one to Hispanic poets, which he sent out with personalised variations. He wanted poets both to send original poems to be translated and to offer their own translations from the other language. That was always going to be a challenge: some of the Hispanic poets—long resident in New York—had good enough English to offer translations, but very few US poets had enough Spanish. Edna Millay got a letter of this kind, with translations of her work for her to revise for publication—presumably just in Edna's case because she knew some Spanish. The letter ends on an optimistic note: 'Soon we will be in a position to pay royally for work accepted for publication in our magazine, and we hope you will send us original poems, or translations from living Latin American poets'.[43] As so often, he would be disappointed in the response.

Salomón's second port of call was Amy Lowell. As a wealthy woman, she was a potential patron, but de la Selva also admired her poetry. Perhaps bruised by some of her encounters with US contemporaries, who could be less than flattering about her figure as well as her poetry, she may have welcomed the interest that a young Hispanic writer showed in her work—and his epistolary tone was always extremely respectful towards her. Kenneth W. Porter tracked down de la Selva's correspondence with Amy Lowell in the 1970s, noting perceptively that 'Salomón seems to have assumed the rôle of Miss Lowell's brilliant, rather boyish nephew and cast her in consequence in that of the indulgent spinster aunt'.[44] Lowell would be a loyal supporter

---

[43] Letter from Salomón de la Selva to Edna St Vincent Millay, ESVMP (2 January 1918). The letter is dated 2 January 1917 and filed accordingly in the Millay papers, but it was clearly written at the beginning of 1918, de la Selva making the common January error of writing the previous year.

[44] Letter from Kenneth W. Porter to Theodore S. Beardsley, Jr, KWPP (10 March 1977). KWPP is the Kenneth Wiggins Porter Papers (Sc MG 222, b. 73 f. 6: Notes for

and de la Selva wrote her some long, appreciative, and heart-felt letters, perhaps because she—unlike some of his other friends—had no doubts about the propriety of fighting in the war in Europe. De la Selva had first visited Lowell at her home in Brookline, Massachusetts in late 1916 and spoken to her about translating her work. He wrote in early January 1918 to get her permission to publish these translations: one by Guillén Zelaya, one by Martín Luis Guzmán, and a 'notable translation' of 'Patterns' by Hipólito Mattonel—who was Salomón himself.[45] She was never less than encouraging about his pan-American projects, to which she gave financial and moral support, and even tried to organise for the *Boston Transcript* to take some of his essays.[46] In turn, de la Selva wrote an essay about Lowell which appeared in New York in June 1918 and in Caracas in July under the title 'Una gran poetisa americana', and which offers a description of her work and a carefully worded assessment of the merits of free verse and imagism.[47]

Pan-American Poetry appeared in February 1918. It was bilingual, representing equal numbers of US and Latin American poets, with metrical translations on opposite pages and full biographical and critical notes. De la Selva had no difficulty recruiting prestigious names for his editorial board—although, as always, this did not necessarily mean that they would take any significant share of the workload. Impressive headed notepaper was ordered, listing de la Selva as editor-in-chief, Alfonso Guillén Zelaya as managing editor, and Pedro Henríquez Ureña, Martín Luis Guzmán, and John P. Rice (de la Selva's departmental chair from Williams College) as contributing editors. By the time the first issue appeared, Thomas Walsh's name had been added to the list. The first issue of the journal was similarly impressive. The main point, obviously, was the balance: seven US poets and seven Hispanic poets. But the quality was sterling. Edna St Vincent Millay had not yet published much, but was widely regarded as the coming figure of US poetry; Robert Frost and Amy Lowell had strong and burgeoning reputations; Vachel Lindsay and Carl Sandburg represented the socially conscious strain of US writing; Shaemas O'Sheel the political edge; and Muna Lee would be a new face. José Santos Chocano, Rubén Darío, and the Argentine Leopoldo

---

Manuscript Salomon de la Selva), Schomburg Center for Research in Black Culture, The New York Public Library. Porter (1905–81) was a distinguished historian and poet who developed an interest in de la Selva, did some serious research into his life and work, but died before he could publish anything.

[45] Letter from Salomón de la Selva to Amy Lowell, ALP (5 January 1918).

[46] See, for example, Letter from Amy Lowell to Salomón de la Selva, ALP (4 April 1918).

[47] Salomón de la Selva, 'Una gran poetisa americana', *El Gráfico*, II, no. 8 (June 1918), 596, 610, and *El Universal*, 4 July 1918, p. 5.

Lugones were probably the three biggest names in poetry from Latin America in 1918, Darío only recently dead. Mexican Enrique González Martínez and Colombian Rufino Blanco Fombona represented the new generation that had broken with *modernismo*. As a Brazilian, Olavo Bilac broadened the range even further. And, although not well-known in the USA, Froylán Turcios was an important Central American figure, the key Honduran writer and intellectual of his day.[48]

The purpose of the journal, the editorial note in the first issue announced, was to become 'a spiritual bond between the United States and the Latin republics of the continent':

> By means of an unselfish exchange of thought and feeling, as expressed in song, it hopes to let flow in the soul of both Americas an inexhaustible current of sympathy which, washing away all prejudices, may reveal to each other their real values and make it possible for them to have reciprocal understanding and respect.[49]

Assembling poems by 14, mostly living, writers was difficult enough. None of these poets had submitted poems to the new journal; all had to be communicated with and asked permission for their poems to be translated … and then the translations had to be made. All were translated as poems, with appropriate line-form and rhyme. The names of nine translators appear. Of the contributing editors, Guillén Zelaya undertook two translations, of poems by Millay and Frost, while Guzmán translated Amy Lowell's long poem, 'The Breaking out of the Flags'. Lilian Elliott translated the Bilac poem from the Portuguese, and Jorge Molina (who was probably the Chilean diplomat Jorge Molina Wood) Sandburg's 'They Will Say'. The other nine translations—in both directions—were all done by de la Selva himself, three under his own name, the others posing as Hipólito Mattonel, Laurence Greenough, J. Glenton, and Nicolás Escoto.[50] It obviously wouldn't do for the magazine to look like a one-man band, even if that is basically what it was.

The poems themselves were varied in theme and approach, but offered a fair cross-section of US and Latin American poetry in 1918. As would be expected, the war in progress left its trace: in Santos Chocano's paean to

---

[48] Froylán Turcios (1875–1942): see Carlos Manuel Arita Palomo, *Vida y obra de 'Froylán Turcios'*, Tegucigalpa: Editorial Universitaria, 1983. Enrique González Martínez (1871–1952); Olavo Bilac (1865–1918).
[49] 'Our Purpose', *Pan-American Poetry*, no. 1 (February 1918), 1.
[50] Glenton was de la Selva's paternal grandmother's maiden name; Escoto his mother's maiden name (and therefore his second surname, although he never used it).

King Albert of Belgium, who had stood up to the Kaiser ('Solemnly sad, he saw his sceptre bloom a sword') and in Amy Lowell's patriotic 'The Breaking out of the Flags' ('The flags ripple and jar / To the tramp of marching men').

De la Selva clearly did what he could to promote the journal. The previous month he published a piece called 'Of Latin American Poetry' in the *Pan-American Magazine* by way of drumming up interest in some of the names that would appear in his new journal, such as Alfonso Guillén Zelaya, and he called on many friends: so, for example, Jeanne Robert Foster adopted de la Selva's words in announcing the new journal in the *Review of Reviews*.[51] De la Selva is referred to as asserting that the realisation of the pan-American ideal is the task of poets, not diplomats or businessmen. Only poets can create 'a lasting and effectual bond between the two Americas that have been antagonistic through heedless underestimation on the part of the North, and a wounded pride on the part of the South'.[52] In the *Pan-American Magazine*, Lilian Elliott wrote a short welcoming article: 'With *Pan-American Poetry* preaching ceases and practise begins'.[53]

When he sent a copy of the first issue to Amy Lowell in March, de la Selva's tone was initially upbeat. He referred to the 'specially satisfactory article' in *Review of Reviews* (which he had probably, to all intents and purposes, written himself) and quoted (in translation) from a piece that Enrique González Martínez had supposedly written in the Mexico City newspaper, *El Imparcial* (which he edited):

We have had American bullets and they inclined us to hate the Yankee; we have had American diplomacy and it has tickled us into laughing at the Yankee; we have seen American adventurers and they have taught us to despise the Yankee; but now comes *Pan American Poetry*: there is at least one poem in it with sufficient convincing power as Poetry and as *rational expression* to make for respect, if not for outright sympathy, towards the Yankee, here and in all lands.

And, Salomón adds, here he quoted your poem.[54] Knowing that Amy Lowell

---

[51] Salomón de la Selva, 'Of Latin American Poetry', *Pan-American Magazine*, XXVI, no. 3 (January 1918), 145–47; [Jeanne Robert Foster], 'The Mission of Poetry in Pan-American Relations', *Review of Reviews*, 57, no. 3 (March 1918), 319–20.
[52] [Foster], 'Mission of Poetry', p. 319.
[53] 'Pan-American Poetry', *Pan-American Magazine*, XXVI, no. 3 (January 1918), 156.
[54] Letter from Salomón de la Selva to Amy Lowell, ALP (12 March 1918). Most accounts have *El Imparcial* as ceasing publication in 1914, so this may have been a piece of invented salomonic flattery.

shared his views on the war, de la Selva opened up about his hope that the USA would realise the need to project southwards the music of its soul, through its poets, which he compares to a kind of advertising. Germany has been doing this to great effect in Mexico, he says, whipping up anti-American feeling, and the USA has not responded adequately to such claims. So it is now up to the USA to demonstrate that musicality—which the songs of *Pan-American Poetry* could supply. Except that, despite the laurels it had received, the newly launched enterprise was already badly holed: there had only been seven subscriptions, his savings are gone, he is in debt, 'and the magazine will surely die unless someone comes to the rescue'. It was drowning and she was being asked to act as life guard. At the end of a ten-page letter, he gives it his best shot:

> I hope I have made my case clear to you, and I am sure you will not fail me. The demands of War are so heavy that what I am asking for is indeed a sacrifice. But this is War Service too, and of an important kind, considering that it cannot be made popular. My time, my energy and all I had I have given up that this ideal I have come to champion may flourish and gain permanence. The royalties of my book of English poems (to be issued this month; John Lane Co. publishers) have been pawned to support *Pan American Poetry*; and if I had more, it is more I would give. Two hundred dollars are needed for the continuance of the magazine. This amount will tide us over until subscriptions (owing to us) are paid. If the magazine gets to pay its expenses and to yield a little over, this excess will be utilized in paying off contributions.[55]

All to no avail. In April 1918, a new section began in *Pan-American Magazine* called 'Pan-American Poetry', indicative that the material which was to have been published in the new journal was having to find a new home—hardly an ideal one, in the magazine widely regarded as almost a house journal of the Pan American Union, the instrument of US corporations seeking profitable markets in the rest of the continent. But beggars cannot be choosers, and de la Selva obviously wanted to get into print the material he had commissioned or produced himself. De la Selva's brief foreword to this section notes that much of the promised financial support for his poetry journal had failed to materialise. Ever optimistic, he announced the setting up of a Pan American Poetry Fund to collect the money to enable a relaunch of the journal. Needless to say, this never happened. Meanwhile, he thanked *Pan-American Magazine* for its courtesy—doubtless due to Lilian Elliott—in

---

[55] Letter from Salomón de la Selva to Amy Lowell, ALP (12 March 1918).

The Pan-American Dream (1918)

opening its pages to continue the work he had begun, offering a reminder of the political importance of such work. During the ongoing war, the US attitude to Latin America may seem generous, he writes:

> But the United States forgets, or overlooks, the fact that the majority of Latin Americans believes the United States to be without 'music in its soul,' and that all it may do is but 'dark stratagem.' Plausible counsellors pointing this out, the Latin Americans do not lack. New presses are at work throughout the Latin American countries groaning under the memories of the sorry Panama affair, of the irretrievable loss of Mexican territory at one period of the country's history, of the treatment dealt out to Nicaragua, to Santo Domingo … Pan-American Poetry is therefore a War necessity. For if the United States desires to win the confidence of the Latin Americans, it must first pour out to them the music of its heart.[56]

The poets featured in this first segment were Carlos Pezoa Veliz (Chilean), Amy Lowell, Joyce Kilmer, Guillermo Valencia (Colombian), and Amado Nervo (Mexican). New translators to feature were James Crowhurst-Rand and Ernest F. Lucas—further avatars of the tireless de la Selva.[57] The May issue featured three poems by Enrique González Martínez, along with others by William Dean Howells, Edna St Vincent Millay, Mariano Brull, José Santos Chocano, Jessie B. Rittenhouse, Amy Lowell, James Weldon Johnson, Alberto de Oliveira (Brazilian), and William Rose Benét. New names among the translators were John Pierrepont Rice, Oswald Tenney, Jane McDonald, María Isabel de la Selva, M.L.S., and Cristina Salvatierra. Apart from Rice, these were all versions of the man himself, including the name of one of his sisters.[58]

In his own name de la Selva translated another of Amy Lowell's ringingly patriotic war poems, 'Before War is Declared'; and, as Hipólito Mattonel, Joyce Kilmer's 'In Memory of Rupert Brooke': Kilmer himself would be killed in France two months later. The May 1918 issue even contained a short prose poem *by* Hipólito Mattonel with that name as the *author* in both English and Spanish versions: in other words with no translator.[59]

---

[56] Salomón de la Selva, 'Pan-American Poetry', *Pan-American Magazine*, XXVI, no. 6 (April 1918), 330, 338.
[57] *Pan-American Magazine*, XXVI, no. 6 (April 1918), 326–37.
[58] On María Isabel de la Selva Escoto, see above, pp. 172–77.
[59] 'The Good Shade'/'La buena sombra', *Pan-American Magazine*, XXVII, no. 1 (May 1918), 42, 43.

De la Selva may have been showing off, or just having a small joke. He came clean in a letter to Amy Lowell:

> I could do much better work had I leisure for that. At present I am filling the shoes of a dozen men. It is fun, but like all fun it exhausts. ... You see, no one hardly cares to translate; it is hard, wearisome inglorious business; so I have to do it nearly all myself. ... My sole motive has been, in the first place, not to let it be known that Pan Americanism almost has in me its beginning, middle and end. People would get discouraged. From perusal of Pan American Poetry it does appear as if there were indeed quite a number of men and women interested in translating. That is ever so much more practical than to have my name paraded up and down at the bottom of nearly every translation, a thing that I would hate for it might even seem as if I were greedily showing off.[60]

May 1918 also brought an editorial from de la Selva on 'Spain and Pan Americanism', which demonstrated his derision towards the idea that Latin America might owe Spain a debt of idealism and spirituality—a notion that Spanish writers had been keen to propagate and that was fundamental to the ideology of Hispanism. It is Latin American writers who have given the Spanish language a new lease of life, de la Selva claims, but that lease has had to consist of 'a violent infusion, so to speak, of foreign blood into Spanish linguistic arteries', an infusion for which Rubén Darío wielded the syringe. De la Selva quotes (translated into English) the claim by the Spanish novelist and critic Clarín (Leopoldo Alas), in an article about Rodó, that 'the United States of the North are trying to attract the Latin Americans, the entire South, with the shibboleth of Pan-Americanism' in order to make those Southerners forget their Hispanic heritage.[61] There are some Southerners willing to do just that, Clarín had suggested: to embrace Anglo-American utilitarianism. De la Selva rejects the charge with a fine colloquialism: 'Clarín is talking through his hat'. But—like Martí before him—de la Selva does not

---

[60] Letter from Salomón de la Selva to Amy Lowell, ALP (18 June 1918).
[61] 'Ya se sabe que hoy los Estados Unidos del Norte procuran atraer a los americanos latinos, a todo el Sur, con el señuelo del panamericanismo; se pretende que olviden lo que tienen de latinos, de españoles, mejor, para englobarlos en la civilización yanqui; se les quiere inocular el utilitarismo angloamericano. Y como los triunfos exteriores, brillantes, positivos, del americanismo del Norte son tantos, en la América española no falta quien se deje sugestionar por esa tendencia' (Clarín [Leopoldo Alas], review of *Ariel, Los Lunes de El Imparcial* [Madrid], 23 April 1900, p. 4).

reject the comparison between North and South simply in order to affirm Southern superiority. Rather, he says that Latin Americans are no more spiritual than North Americans; it is just that they are to date less successful in achieving the material satisfactions which they desire as avidly as their Northern counterparts. If there is a leaven of spirituality in the South, then that leaven exists equally in the North: 'And it is exactly this struggling germ of spirituality that is the only thing of worth that the two Americas have in common. It is upon it that their relationship should be founded, their friendship built.' This relationship is 'of geographical imperativeness'. For that reason they should work together, rising side by side, and—here de la Selva deploys one of the most resonant of Caribbean metaphors—'each a wing of the one and indivisible soul of America'.[62]

The failure of *Pan-American Poetry* prompted a deal of soul-searching and self-justification. A 23-page letter to Amy Lowell offers a sweeping assessment of the challenges facing Latin America. As always, de la Selva is sustained by vast optimism that an intellectually united Latin America will be able to flourish in a post-war world in which the most powerful nations will be those 'that are the richest in intellectual and in spiritual accomplishment'; not those with the largest armies, but those 'with the best thinkers and poets that will mold the destinies of the world'. That, he says, is his prophecy and his desire. But at the same time he recognises that there are others ('traffickers in politics') who see things differently, who see the USA as imperialistic, who remember its land grabs from Mexico, who point to the occupations of Nicaragua and Santo Domingo. These things, the others say, 'are of yesterday and of today; they will be of tomorrow unless Latin America unites as an antagonistic power to check and balance North American rapacity'. 'You will admit,' Salomón writes, 'that they are not wholly without justification.' The proponents of this argument, he complains, have attacked him, branding him as a traitor and a matricide. (This may have happened, though no published examples have ever come to light.) His fracas with Theodore Roosevelt had, in any case, put an end to such attacks.[63]

June's poetic offering in the *Pan-American Magazine* included Robert Frost's 'Mending Wall' (translated by Miguel del Carmen Urcas), short lyrics by Sara Teasdale (Cristina Salvatierra), the Mexican, Luis G. Urbina (Laurence Greenough), and the Argentinian, Juan Julián Lastra (de la Selva), two poems by Alberto de Oliveira (the Black writer and educator, Leslie Pinckney Hill), and long poems by Robert Haven Schauffler (Nicolás Escoto)

---

[62] Salomón de la Selva, 'Spain and Pan Americanism', *Pan-American Magazine*, XXVI, no. 1 (June 1918), 50–52.
[63] Letter from Salomón de la Selva to Amy Lowell, ALP (9 April 1918).

and Rufino Blanco Fombona (James Crowhurst-Rand). Hill is the only one of these translators who is *not* de la Selva. Then, to round off a remarkable issue, there is one of the finest poems published in recent years, Wallace Stevens's 'Peter Quince at the Clavier' (1915). No prizes for guessing who translated that one, in his own name.[64]

July 1918 has Bilac, González Martínez, Muna Lee, William Rose Benét, Kilmer, Millay, and Schauffler, but some new voices too: a prose poem by the Mexican, Alfonso Reyes, two young Nicaraguans, Félix María Baca and Pedro Maldonado, the Brazilian, Bruno Henriques de Almeida Seabra, Justo A. Facio, Panamanian-born but living in Costa Rica, and the innovative US poet, Adelaide Crapsey. More translators appear, but Adela Ugarte, Julián Vargas, and Galán Puchaca y Moya are just further disguises for the editor. In a concluding note, de la Selva reports two of the contributors, William Rose Benét and Robert Haven Schauffler, as having recently become soldiers, as he himself would do, just as this issue appeared. His tone is one of discouragement: support has not been forthcoming: 'With our September issue ... we will have finished over half a year's unencouraged and unencouraging work; we will have earned a rest, assuredly'.[65] Well, at least a change.

The size of the last two issues dwindles. August has poems by Guillén Zelaya (the very fine 'Dios te haya perdonado', about the death of his brother), Santos Chocano, Guillermo Valencia, Joseph Warren Beach, and the Colombian, Julio Flores. Two new translators appear: Alice Stone Blackwell and the Mexican poet and academic, Balbino Dávalos, who was teaching at the University of Minnesota. The other new name, Effie Marguerite Shores, is a further de la Selva *nom de plume*. But a footnote indicates that with de la Selva's departure for the war the section 'is bereft of its moving spirit'. It calls on others to help, though de la Selva had also left some translations behind.[66] Elsewhere in that issue it is noted—presumably in Lilian Elliott's words—that Salomón de la Selva has joined the British Army and left New York on 22 July, shortly after the publication of his book of poems, *Tropical Town*. 'The literary circles of New York will miss this slim, boyish figure, always like a bright-eyed, ardent child.'[67]

September has Rubén Darío, the Mexicans Rafael Cabrera Camacho and Salvador Díaz Mirón, and Raymond Weeks, with Alice Stone Blackwell doing

---

[64] *Pan-American Magazine*, XXVII, no. 2 (June 1918), 97–112.
[65] Salomón de la Selva, 'Pan American Poetry', *Pan-American Magazine*, XXVII, no. 3 (July 1918), 164.
[66] *Pan-American Magazine*, XXVII, no. 4 (August 1918), 207–13.
[67] 'Editorial Comment: Salomón de la Selva in the British Army', *Pan-American Magazine*, XXVII, no. 4 (August 1918), 172.

the translating from the Spanish (apart from one poem by Balbino Dávalos) and Weeks presumably translating himself: he was chair of the Department of Romance Languages at Columbia. October only has a fine Edgar Lee Masters' poem, 'Silence', and 'Lawn Tennis' by José Juan Tablada (both translated pseudonymously by de la Selva); and January 1919 has poems by Amy Lowell, Chocano, Nervo, Bilac, the Chilean Ricardo Fernández Montalvo, and the Scottish war poet Joseph Lee, the last translated by Guillén Zelaya. And that was that. An impressive roster overall, but very much dependent on de la Selva's efforts, and so tailing off once he had left for Europe.

Alongside that 1916 Spanish-American issue of *Others*, *Pan-American Poetry* (with its afterlife in the *Pan-American Magazine*) stands as the origin of contemporary translation of poetry from Spanish America into English. The two ventures offer different models, both of which have found followers. Both aimed for accuracy. Later, Williams *hijo*, whose Spanish was patchy but who was a great poet, would often choose the creative option in his translations when he didn't have his father to chide and correct him. Here, however, in the *Others* translations it seems as if there is a serendipitous match between the father's desire for literalness and the son's preference for a plain vernacular style of poetry. It is as if the father had produced the most straightforward prose translation possible, and the son had turned the prose into poetry merely by reproducing the line lengths of the original Spanish. By contrast, de la Selva's project was to translate poems into their poetic equivalents in the other language. So, to give a simple example, these are lines from José Santos Chocano's poem, 'La canción del camino' [A Song of the Road]:

> Súbito, allá, a lo lejos,
> por entre aquella mole doliente y pensativa
> de la selva, …

The Williamses' translation is:

> Suddenly, there, in the distance
> within that sad and pensive mass
> of the wood, …

If it were not that the single word 'within' translates the Spanish phrase 'por entre', this would be an exact word for word, comma for comma, translation.

John Pierrepont Rice's translation is:

> But suddenly, afar, beyond the wood,
> Beyond the dark pall of my brooding thought, ...

The changes are noticeable: three lines into two; the more 'poetic' term 'afar' instead of the quotidian 'there'; the introduction of the repetition of 'beyond'; the significant shift from the image of the sad and pensive wood to *my* brooding thought, probably brought about by the rhyme scheme, so 'thought' can rhyme with 'caught' two lines later.[68]

There could be arguments in favour of the 'accuracy' of both versions. Word for word, the Williamses' version scores, but it doesn't reproduce the poet's rhyme, as Rice does, which is arguably essential to the poem's incantatory quality, heavily influenced by Poe. Arguably, Williams turned Chocano into a modernist poet, which might improve the poem but significantly *changed* its mode, whereas de la Selva wanted the translation to stand as a poem in its own right, a poem within the host language's poetic tradition, and he didn't recognise the Williamses' version as poetry.[69] Few people yet did, though they soon would. But de la Selva sensed what these young US poets were doing and what they had to offer the Spanish language: in one of his letters to Amy Lowell he complains about how hard it has been to translate Robert Frost's 'Mending Wall'. 'Hill Wife' was slightly easier and he looks forward to it being a 'heart of controversy', along with Masters' poems and some of Lowell's: 'You see, we have been so rhetorical that all our literary shiftings have been but a change of rhetoric. The "unliterary" downright sheer poetry of you Americans will shock our readers. So much the better.'[70]

*

In June 1918, with one magazine holed and sinking fast, what better move than to lash oneself to the mast of another under-financed craft. De la Selva

---

[68] José Santos Chocano's 'Nocturno no. 18 (La canción del camino)' [1908], from *Chocano: poesía*, ed. Luis Alberto Sánchez, Lima: Universidad Nacional Mayor de San Marcos, Patronato del Libro Universitario, 1959, pp. 135–36; 'The Song of the Road', trans. William G. Williams, *Others*, 3, no. 2 (August 1916), 43; 'The Song of the Road', trans. John Pierrepont Rice, *Poetry*, XI, no. 5 (February 1918), 234.

[69] He wrote that Guillén Zelaya had been 'poorly and insufficiently translated' in *Others* (Salomón de la Selva, 'Of Latin American Poetry', *Pan-American Magazine*, XXVI, no. 3 (January 1918), 145–47, at 146.

[70] Letter from Salomón de la Selva to Amy Lowell, ALP (29 April 1918).

heard news of a venture after his own heart being launched by the Puerto Rican poet Luis Muñoz Marín, and immediately went to offer his services to *La Revista de Indias* where he was welcomed with open arms and appointed editor of the English section of this bilingual project. Salomón wrote to Amy Lowell on paper with the new letterhead asking for an unpublished poem for the second number. The long letter gives a clear assessment of his priorities and plans, and of the larger pan-American project to which he was still committed:

> This is another effort to push ahead with my hope of establishing a worthy Pan American organ. Pan American Magazine is very fine in its way; but it is almost a trade journal. Pan American Poetry is giving it a higher character, but the thing is not mine to do with it as I could wish altogether: I have to be consulting editors who consult advertisers and all that sort of thing … Just now I wish Pan American Magazine to devote itself merely to translations of things already printed. Revista de Indias will push a step further and offer first hand goods. It will have two main sections, one in Spanish, the other in English. The make up is ambitious: 80 pages; there are also illustrations and we have quite a number of advertisements …[71]

Lowell admitted that her business sense would caution against a new venture so soon after the failure of the previous one, but she also recognised that de la Selva was not the kind of individual 'to hold himself in leash'.[72]

The first issue of *La Revista de Indias* came out in August 1918, shortly after de la Selva left for Europe, the second and third in September and October, and then it folded. No copy seems to have survived but a short account of the first issue appeared in the *Hispanic American Historical Review*:

> The first number of La Revista de Indias, a 'monthly Spanish-American Magazine of Arts, Letters, and Sciences' was issued in New York under date of August [1918]. This new periodical is published by the Indias Publishing Company at 1416 Broadway under the editorship of Sr. Luis Muñoz Marin. The managing editor is Sr. Antonio Alfau and the editor of the English section, Sr Salmon [sic] de la Selva. As implied above, there are both Spanish and English sections, but these are different throughout. The subscription price is $5.00 per annum;

---

[71] Letter from Salomón de la Selva to Amy Lowell, ALP (18 June 1918).
[72] Letter from Amy Lowell to Salomón de la Selva, ALP (22 June 1918).

$3.00 for six months; and $1.50 for three months. The literary element predominates, but the periodical will have an interest to students of Hispanic American history.

It went on to list some of the contents, including the essay 'Mexico and the United States', by Martín Luis Guzmán, and concluded by hoping that the review 'will have a long and useful career'.[73]

It didn't; but in Luis Muñoz Marín de la Selva had found a fellow spirit: bilingual, passionate, a keen poet and translator. Muñoz Marín would eventually pursue a political career, becoming three-times governor of Puerto Rico. Visitors to the island now land at the Luis Muñoz Marín International Airport in San Juan. There was little hint in 1918 of what was to come, but his subsequent importance for Puerto Rican history ensures that Muñoz Marín's biography has been subjected to close analysis and relevant documents have been retained in the archive that forms the heart of the Fundación Luis Muñoz Marín in San Juan. Gaps, however, still remain in the picture of his years in New York.

Muñoz Marín's father, Luis Muñoz Rivera, was himself a prominent Puerto Rican politician in the early years of the twentieth century, years that coincided with the establishment of US authority on the island after the defeat of Spain in the war of 1898. Muñoz Marín spent much of his youth in the USA, growing up bilingual in Spanish and English. As a teenager, his interests and enthusiasms seem to have switched every couple of years from the bright lights and dynamism of Washington or New York to, and from, his island roots and culture.[74]

At the end of 1916, after his father's death, Luis Muñoz Marín lived with his mother up in Harlem, on Broadway and 141st Street, where he tried his hand at writing stories, published as *Borrones*.[75] In the summer of 1917 he

---

[73] *Hispanic American Historical Review*, 1, no. 3 (1918), 377. No. 1416 Broadway was between West 39th and West 40th Streets and therefore close to where *El Gráfico* was published at 1400 Broadway.

[74] On Muñoz Marín's New York years, see his own *Memorias: Autobiografía pública 1898-1940* [1982], 2nd edn, San Juan, Puerto Rico: Fundación Luis Muñoz Marín, 2003; and the studies by Carmelo Rosario Nadal, *La juventud de Luis Muñoz Marín (Vida y pensamiento 1989-1932)*, San Juan: n.p., 1976; A. W. Maldonado, *Luis Muñoz Marín: Puerto Rico's Democratic Revolution*, San Juan: La Editorial, Universidad de Puerto Rico, 2006; and Giannina Delgado Caro, *Luis Muñoz Marín y la palabra trashumante*, San Juan, Puerto Rico: Editorial Isla Negra, 2009.

[75] Collected, along with all his other literary work, in *La obra literaria de Luis Muñoz Marín (Poesía y prosa: 1915-1968)*, ed. Marcelino J. Canino Salgado, San Juan, Puerto Rico: Fundación Luis Muñoz Marín, 1999.

was back in Puerto Rico; in the autumn, in Washington, working briefly as secretary to the Puerto Rican Resident Commissioner to Congress; and then again back in Puerto Rico trying to get subscriptions for the bilingual magazine he wanted to start.[76] This seems like an idyllic interlude, at least as he recalls it in his *Memorias*: *tertulias* in the Café París in Guayama, presided over by the rising poetic figure on the island, Luis Palés Matos. But, at the same time, almost in a parallel universe, he was hearing speeches about agricultural strikes in Ponce and seeing the local doctor called away to treat workers shot and beaten up by police. After a spell back in Puerto Rico, Muñoz Marín settled down in Manhattan in the spring of 1918. Like Salomón de la Selva, he got an editing and translating job for *The American Exporter*, which provided enough money to launch his journal.

*

Some time in the first half of 1918, de la Selva wrote a short handwritten note to Florence Schauffler:

> Well, mamita, you are the only mamita I have on earth now.—I had to tell someone, or go mad, so I told it to you. — Please don't tell Edna. She has no right in the world to my sorrow. And please don't write to me, or call me up, or anything—I beg to be let alone—alone—alone.— Please! Sal.[77]

There seems no ambiguity about the news being conveyed. However, Salomón's mother, Evangelina Escoto Bata, didn't die until January 1932.

Tropical Town

After the publication of 'The Tale from Faerieland' in July 1915, de la Selva had continued writing poems in English. He wrote more than 150 over the next three years, a handful published in journals: in November 1917, three had appeared in *Poetry*; James Joyce and Ezra Pound both had contributions in that same issue.[78] Other poems had appeared in *Century*

---

[76] Luis Muñoz Marín attributes the name of *La Revista de Indias* to Alfonso Alfau (1892–1963), Jesusa's brother. Partly archaic, recalling the Columbian expeditions, the name also fitted the journal's 'interamerican character' (*Memorias*, p. 58).

[77] Letter from Salomón de la Selva to Florence Schauffler, SFP Box 1 (undated [May 1918?]).

[78] De la Selva's poems were 'My Nicaragua', 'The Tiny Maiden', and 'The Merchant':

Magazine ('Hatred'), *Ainslee's* ('The Cup of Life', 'Winged Words', 'After the Tryst', 'St Francis' Tale to the Birds', 'Sorrow', 'I am not perfect …'), *Harper's Monthly Magazine* ('Measure'), *Contemporary Verse* ('The Singer Exults', 'The Singer Despairs'), *Washington Times* ('The Beehive'), and a pro-Allies publication, *Defenders of Democracy* ('Tropical Interlude' and 'Drill').[79] Then 80 poems were collected into his first book, *Tropical Town and Other Poems*, which appeared on 15 May 1918, published in New York by John Lane Company.[80] Poets with a Hispanic background such as Rafael Pombo and Miguel Teurbe Tolón had earlier written and published the odd poem in English, but *Tropical Town* was the first book of poems by such a writer—not of course that anyone in 1918 had any awareness of its historical significance.

John Lane Company was a prestigious house for a young poet writing in his second language. It published major figures such as Theodore Dreiser and H. L. Mencken. Its contemporary poetry list was perhaps less than cutting edge from a modernist perspective, but then modernism didn't really yet have a cutting edge. Vita Sackville-West, Richard Le Gallienne, and Rupert Brooke were substantial names on its books, and it had recently published Ezra Pound's memoir about Henri Gaudier-Brzeska. And by now—thanks to his contributions to magazines—de la Selva had a small but growing reputation within the poetry world. In September 1917, de la Selva reported to Edna Millay that he had been to see Jefferson Jones at John Lane Company, who had told him that he was the only poet whose work they had ever solicited; though he also later wrote to her that John Lane had taken him

---

Poetry, XI, no. 2 (1917), 77–80. The editor's note on contributors said that 'Mr de la Selva has published a number of books abroad'—which was untrue; and that he was the godson of Rubén Darío, which was equally untrue. It also quoted his words about the last two lyrics: 'The two folk-songs are genuine, the first one especially—centuries old; and there is hardly a country where Spanish is spoken but possesses its versions of these songs' (113)—which was equally untrue: they were his own compositions.

[79] Oddly enough, although earlier publications are acknowledged in the preface to *Tropical Town*, *The Forum* is not, despite having originally published 'A Tale from Faerieland', the longest poem in *Tropical Town*.

[80] Salomón de la Selva, *Tropical Town and Other Poems*, New York: John Lane Company, 1918; reprinted: edited, with an introduction, by Silvio Sirias, Houston, TX: Arte Público Press, 1999. The poems in English from these years not in *Tropical Town* appear in Salomón de la Selva, 'A Tale from Faerieland and Other Poems', New York, 1916, Brown University Library Manuscript Collections, 1901 S4686t, and in *An Unknown Songster Sings: Salomón de la Selva's Collected Poems: 1915–1958*, ed. Luis M. Bolaños-Salvatierra, Managua: Academia Nicaragüense de la Lengua, 2015, pp. 49–245.

'because a silly rich woman says I am a genius'.[81] That may have been Eugenia Geisenheimer exerting some financial muscle on his behalf.

On the whole, the reviewers were appreciative of *Tropical Town*: deeply impressed by the poet's command of verse-writing in English, complimentary about at least some parts of the book, even if with reservations about others. An anonymous review of 'Soldier Poets' in *The American Review of Reviews* said that *Tropical Town* showed 'a remarkable mastery of a foreign tongue as a medium for poetic expression'.[82] In *The Nation*, O. W. Firkins found the versatility 'astounding' and noted particularly the New England idylls 'for which Whittier would have been thankful'.[83] Another anonymous reviewer, in the *New York Times Book Review*, wrote that de la Selva 'gets a value from words and a freshness of meaning that come only with a command of English and a culture seldom found in the case of so young a poet, and especially in one so wildly temperamental'.[84] Out in California, 'ABS' noted in the poems 'an apparent simplicity and a genuine depth'.[85] Even the most critical of the reviewers tended to find something positive to say. An anonymous reviewer in *The Dial* criticised the 'lack of finished artistry' to be expected in a writer 'to whom English is not native', but still praised the power, realism, and sincerity of some of the poems.[86] Orrick Johns admitted that de la Selva was beyond him: 'I suspect him of being that extinct bird, an ego unashamed'. The book contains, he wrote, 'some charming conceits and … some ambitious fol-de-rol.' His summation is 'a promising mountebank, not beyond admiring for his versatility and enjoying for his candor.'[87] Firkins expressed strong admiration, then some doubt, and then a doubt about his doubt. The source of doubt was that he found de la Selva 'a rather dispersed personality; I have a feeling he should be reassembled'. But, '[p]ossibly in all this I am thankless and captious; as

---

[81] Letters of Salomón de la Selva to Edna St Vincent Millay, ESVMP (6 September 1917 and 27 September 1917).

[82] 'Soldier Poets', *The American Review of Reviews*, 58 (July–December 1918), 555. Jeanne Robert Foster was the literary editor of the *Review*, so she may have written this piece.

[83] O. W. Firkins, 'Assorted Poets', *The Nation*, 26 October 1918, pp. 488–89, at p. 489.

[84] Anonymous review of *Tropical Town*, *New York Times Book Review*, 16 June 1918, p. 284 [in KWPP].

[85] ABS, 'Salomon de La Selva, Young Poet of Pan-Americanism, Sings Fiery and Wistful Songs Born of Love for Nicaragua and of the United States', *Oakland Tribune*, 16 June 1918, p. 23.

[86] Anonymous review, *The Dial*, 65 (15 August 1918), 123.

[87] Orrick Johns, 'The Verse, Free and Otherwise, of Contemporary Poets' [originally in *Reedy's Mirror*], *New York Tribune*, 22 September 1918, p. 8.

I have said, the poet is finally strong enough to make me distrustful of my doubt.'[88] Most of the critics, however, were disturbed by the eroticism of the sonnet-sequence, 'The Box of Sandalwood': 'offerings to Eros in which Priapus dips a sodden finger', as Firkins put it, a little too graphically; poems, according to the *New York Times Book Review* 'in which Mr de la Selva's tropical nature seems to have gotten the better of his sense of fitness'.[89]

Probably the reviews de la Selva most appreciated were the private ones he received from Edwin Markham and Amy Lowell. Markham's generous response to the book brought de la Selva to tears, he reported, and he was equally appreciative of Amy Lowell's kind words. 'I cannot tell you how delightful I think it is,' she wrote. 'It all has personality and feeling and is thoroughly poetical … You have humour and sincerity, and an excellent pictorial sense, and how you write the way you do in an acquired tongue is a matter of wonder and admiration to me … It is a first volume to be exceedingly proud of.'[90] But the warmest and most perceptive published review was written by none other than the poet and translator Thomas Walsh, de la Selva's old friend and enemy (Fig. 19). Walsh took the lines from 'The Sword of Wonder' to be a self-description: 'You could not tell the country where he came from / He was so very vague and dazzling and so very young':

> It is a vagueness, however, characteristic not only of his youth and the modernist style in which he sings, but it is in a way typical of all Latin-American poetry—a hardly realized product, when one comes to analyze the thought and music of it. Rubén Darío seems to have sensed this, and escaped his native penalty by adopting a French clarity and logical quality in his work, which nevertheless possesses much of the vague splendor, the starry-splash, that is shown in many of the poems of 'Tropical Town'.

He saw the greatest achievements as 'The Tale from Faerieland' and 'The Box of Sandalwood'. Overall, 'his work still reveals a soul troubled and unsettled between his native and his adopted literature'.[91] Walsh's knowledge of poetry in Spanish stood him in good stead and he obviously wasn't fazed by the

---

[88] Firkins, 'Assorted Poets', p. 489.
[89] Firkins, 'Assorted Poets', p. 489; Anon., *New York Times Book Review*, p. 284.
[90] Letters from Salomón de la Selva to Edwin Markham, EMA (15 June 1918 and 18 June 1918); Letter from Amy Lowell to Salomón de la Selva, ALP (25 May 1918).
[91] Thomas Walsh, 'Prose and Poetry from the Pens of South Americans', *Chicago Daily Tribune*, 1 February 1919, p. 12.

19 Thomas Walsh. 26 April 1924. Edward Loughborough Keyes, Jr, papers, GTM010101, Georgetown University Library Booth Family Center for Special Collections, Washington, DC.

open sensuality of 'The Box of Sandalwood'—surely, we can now see, one of the finest twentieth-century sonnet sequences in English. Interesting too is that he saw de la Selva singing in 'the modernist style'—an early use of the term in English with a literary application, perhaps influenced by Walsh's knowledge of *modernista* poetry in Spanish. Above all, though, Walsh saw through the lyric fluency to the unsettled soul.

To round off the book's reception, the title poem, 'Tropical Town', was immediately included in the massive (4,110-page) *The Home Book of Verse*, the first—and for many years almost the only—domestication of de la Selva's poetry in English.[92] He had in a sense arrived; but he wouldn't be staying long.

Just where to place *Tropical Town* with respect to poetic movements is a question that would merit a book of its own. In the meantime, it gets a couple of paragraphs. The book has never had much attention, so there aren't many verdicts to disagree with. Latin American critics have never known what to do with a book by a Nicaraguan written in English,[93] and US critics have been reluctant, to say the least, to give the book any status within early twentieth-century US poetry; and indeed de la Selva himself, as we'll see in the next chapter, refused the opportunity for that kind of placement. It was only once the idea that Hispanic writers—by initial language or cultural background—might write and publish in English had become comprehensible in the 1990s, that *Tropical Town* could be 'recovered' and republished in Silvio Sirias's new edition, which 'placed' the book as one of the fountainheads of the US Hispanic literary heritage. That is certainly one of the places where the book now belongs; but how might it be seen in its historical context? Superficially, it might seem like one of the many volumes published in this period (1915 to 1919) that were quickly left behind in the backwaters of poetic history as the main current of literary modernism gathered force. After all, de la Selva's poetic heroes were Francis Thompson and John Keats, his critical muses Alice Meynell and Walter Pater. He loved writing sonnets; most of his poems use metre and rhyme.

---

[92] Burton Egbert Stevenson, ed., *The Home Book of Verse American and English 1580–1918*, 3rd edn., New York: Henry Holt & Co., 1918, pp. 3374–75. The same poem appeared in Edwin Markham's equally vast (3,243-page) *The Book of Poetry: Collected from the Whole Field of British and American Poetry*, New York: W. H. Wise, 1927, p. 785.

[93] There was a brief notice, more biographical than critical, by the Peruvian, François G. de Cisneros, 'El gesto de Salomón de la Selva,' *El Fígaro*, 35, no. 31 (1918), 937.

Silvio Sirias suggests—following de la Selva's own lead—that his poems of these years were written in dialogue with Edna Millay, which makes perfect sense, although Sirias tends to read them too literally as a chronicle of their relationship.[94] Salomón was clearly obsessed with Edna, translating her poetry assiduously, discussing poetry and poetics with her, and sending her poems he had written, some of which remained uncollected in her papers until 2015. Like Millay, de la Selva favoured sonnets, short lyrics, and a loose-limbed form modelled on traditional ballads. So that parallel at least helps to place his poems with respect to one significant contemporary. The great difference between them is that whereas Millay was self-evidently part of a poetic tradition, one which at this stage still saw itself as simply English—her own models were Tennyson and Housman—de la Selva's Nicaraguan origins and his intimate knowledge of Spanish poetry put him into a rather different place; indeed, so different as to be without precedent.

The first chapter of this book summarised some recent critical developments that have moved away from the more restrictive sense of high modernism to include other forms of new writing and to take better account of antecedent Spanish-American poetry. If, as a result, modernism becomes a broad enough church to include Rubén Darío, then de la Selva must have a claim to a pew since, alongside Edna Millay, Darío is the clearest influence on the poems of *Tropical Town*.[95] If we are now newly alert to varieties of novelty which go beyond formal experimentation, then the eroticism of the ten sonnets of 'The Box of Sandalwood' would certainly take their place within modernist explorations of sexuality but, perhaps even more important, the introduction of imperialism as a theme in those deceptively simple lyrics dealing with Nicaragua would add a wholly new strand to US poetry of this period.

Having lived so long in New York and become so familiar with its contours, de la Selva didn't feel the need to write about the city in the way that short-term Hispanic visitors did. There are only three direct references to New York in the book. 'Ode to the Woolworth Building' opens in seemingly perverse fashion by addressing the recently completed skyscraper, then the tallest building in the world and therefore iconic of American modernity, in language more suited to fourteenth-century subject matter:

---

[94] Silvio Sirias, 'Introduction' to Salomón de la Selva, *Tropical Town and Other Poems*, Houston, TX: Arte Público Press, 1999, pp. 1–50, at pp. 18–30.
[95] See Silvio Sirias, 'La presencia de Rubén Darío en la literatura estadounidense: el caso de Salomón de la Selva y *Tropical Town and Other Poems*', *Hispanófila*, no. 147 (May 2006), 9–23.

O lyric-ardent, lily-white, arrayed
Like some knight-worshipped medieval maid
The evening of her nuptials, in a gown
Whose long chaste folds fall rigorously down
And hide your earth-shooned feet; a thinnest veil
Of woven mist about you, and a frail
Tiara of gold blossoms in your hair,—
Why do you tarry all the seasons there?[96]

This may seem a long way from the language current in 1918, but then the Woolworth Building, though technologically innovative, had also been inspired by the great medieval buildings of Flanders and eastern France, decorated as it was by Gothic tracery, tourelles, gables, and finials: a promotional booklet had deliberately called it *The Cathedral of Commerce*.[97] In addition, many of the impeccably modernist photographs of New York skyscrapers—such as Alfred Stieglitz's of the Flatiron—clearly sought the visual equivalent of de la Selva's imagery, choosing weather conditions, time of day, and developing technique in order to settle veils of woven mist around the buildings, emphasising architectural continuity with their soaring medieval equivalents in the old world, such as the cathedral of Rheims ('Your elder sister, gray and glorious grown', as de la Selva has it), pictures of whose destruction had caused outrage across the world in the autumn of 1914. That's why the poem is included in the section called 'In War Time'. The poem also perhaps contains a glimpse of the poet's earlier, difficult years when, just after its construction, the building

> ... gladdened many a bitter nightmare night
> When homeless, hungry, with no dawn in sight,
>
> I walked the cruel streets, longing to be,
> In that sheer midnight of my misery,
>
> A corpse upon the waters mourning clad
> That round the City flow forever sad.[98]

---

[96] De la Selva, *Tropical Town*, p. 78.
[97] Edwin A. Cochran, *The Cathedral of Commerce: The Highest Building in the World*, New York: Broadway Park Place Co., 1916. Cf. Gail Fenske, *The Skyscraper and the City: The Woolworth Building and the Making of Modern New York*, Chicago: University of Chicago Press, 2008.
[98] De la Selva, *Tropical Town*, p. 81. For other poetic responses, see Newcomb, *How Did Poetry Survive?*, 182–97.

The Pan-American Dream (1918)

Another New York reference comes in 'A Song for Wall Street', where in Blakean fashion the simplicity of the verse-form and the vocabulary conceal a sharp kick in the groin. The poem begins in seeming pathos as the poet stresses his country's simplicity:

> In Nicaragua, my Nicaragua,
>   What can you buy for a penny there?—
> A basketful of apricots,
>   A water jug of earthenware,
> A rosary of coral beads
>   And a priest's prayer.

A little more is available for two pennies. And for a 'bright white nickel' the poet seems to offer a good investment opportunity:

>   It's lots of land a man can buy,
> A golden mine that's long and deep,
>   A forest growing high,
> And a little house with a red roof
>   And a river passing by.

But just as the US investor reaches into his pocket for his wallet, the tone changes abruptly:

> But for your dollar, your dirty dollar,
>   Your greenish leprosy,
> It's only hatred you shall get
>   From all my folks and me;
> So keep your dollar where it belongs
>   And let us be![99]

One of the most striking features of *Tropical Town* is that no fewer than nine poems have the word 'tropical' in the title, all within the section 'My Nicaragua'. They themselves are not in any obvious way political poems, although they do lead towards the more political poems at the end of that section. Tropicality had been an issue inseparable from the debate about

---

[99] De la Selva, *Tropical Town*, p. 27. By this time 'Wall Street' had become a synecdoche for the banking system which was gaining a stranglehold on the region: see Peter James Hudson, *Bankers and Empire: How Wall Street Colonized the Caribbean*, Chicago: University of Chicago Press, 2017.

the relationship between the USA and its southern neighbours which had intensified since 1898. By an accident of geography—at least in the first instance—the southern border of the US mainland, even after its southern dive in 1848, lay just north of the Tropic of Cancer. But the USA had recently been accumulating tropical possessions: Hawaii, Puerto Rico, the Philippines; had growing interests in other tropical countries such as Cuba and Panama; and was occupying still others such as the Dominican Republic, Haiti, and Nicaragua. Throughout the colonial period, the tropics had been regarded as dangerous for settlers from temperate climes, and the recent death rate from yellow fever during the construction of the Panama Canal had underlined that peril. Yet, with US commercial, not to mention political, interests now at stake, a different image was being cultivated in official and semi-official media, helped by advances in understanding the transmission of tropical diseases. As Colonel William C. Gorgas, the chief sanitary officer on the Panama Canal project, had put it in a speech to the American Medical Association in Atlanta on 9 June 1909: 'Our work in Cuba and Panama will be looked upon as the earliest demonstration that the white man could flourish in the tropics and as the starting point of the effective settlement of these regions by the Caucasian.'[100] So the tropics could still be home to steamy sensuality with its attendant dangers in, say, the stories of *Tropical Tales* by the prolific writer Dolf Wyllarde, which went through three editions in 1909–10 published by John Lane Company.[101] But at the same time the New York entrepreneur G. M. L. Brown could launch in 1908 a journal called *Tropical and Subtropical America* aimed particularly at US businessmen and tourists. The journal opened with a survey by the well-known travel writer Frederick Albion Ober, whose latest book, *A Guide to the West Indies and Bermudas*, was published that year, followed by a piece by John Barrett, director of the International Bureau of American Republics (soon to be renamed Pan American Union).[102] Behind all this lurked the influential warning issued by Benjamin Kidd in 1898:

---

[100] William C. Gorgas, 'The Conquest of the Tropics for the White Race,' *Journal of the American Medical Association*, 52, no. 25 (1909), 1967–69, at 1969.

[101] Dolf Wyllarde was the pseudonym of Dorothy Margarette Selby Lowndes (1871–1950).

[102] Frederick A. Ober, 'America's Mediterranean', *Tropical and Subtropical America*, 1, no. 1 (1908), 1–7; John Barrett, 'The Opportunity in Latin America', 13–17. Among Ober's many other books is *Our West Indian Neighbors: The Islands of the Caribbean Sea, 'America's Mediterranean'* (1904). On the development of tropical tourism, see Catherine Cocks, *Tropical Whites: The Rise of the Tourist South in the Americas*, Philadelphia: University of Pennsylvania Press, 2013.

The first step to the solution of the problem before us is simply to acquire the principle that in dealing with the natural inhabitants of the tropics we are dealing with peoples who represent the same stage in the history of the development of the race that the child does in the history of the development of the individual. The tropics will not, therefore, be developed by the natives themselves.[103]

Against this background, and with these connotations attaching themselves to the word 'tropical' in US public discourse, de la Selva seems deliberately to be guiding his readers towards some different implications. 'My Nicaragua' introduces US readers to the country, almost as if he were a travel guide, making use therefore of his native knowledge of his homeland and his acquired knowledge of New Yorkers' new-found enthusiasm for tropical excursions during the colder months:

> When the Winter comes, I will take you to Nicaragua,—
> You will love it there!
> You will love my home, my house in Nicaragua,
> So large and queenly looking, with a haughty air
> That seems to tell the mountains, the mountains of Nicaragua,
> — 'You may roar and you may tremble, for all I care!'[104]

At first sight the verse seems innocent, almost naïve. What we find in Nicaragua, at least initially, seem to be the kinds of things that feature in tourist brochures: 'Blue, pink and yellow houses', 'a rumbling ox-cart', 'Indian girls from the river with flowers in their hair', 'walls of honeysuckle and orchids all around', a 'street that's bounded by ancient houses'.[105] Even the tropical thunder gives way to 'rainbows overhead' and the 'turmoil of mysteries' that darkens 'Tropical Childhood' is reassuringly like childhoods everywhere else; but the innocence soon turns out to have a real edge to it:

> But if you hire a guide, no guide will ever
> Think of directing you to see this mere
> Unhonoured dailiness of people's lives
> That is the soil the roots of beauty know.
> ...

---

[103] Benjamin Kidd, *The Control of the Tropics*, New York: The Macmillan Co., 1898, p. 51.
[104] De la Selva, 'Tropical House', in *Tropical Town*, p. 12.
[105] De la Selva, *Tropical Town*, pp. 12, 11, 11, 15, 12, 29.

> The parlours of the ruling class adorned
> With much the same bad taste as in New York,—
> That never was my country! But the rows
> Of earthen little houses where men dwell,
> And women, all too busy living life
> To think of faking it, that is my country,
> My Nicaragua, mother of great poets![106]

'All too busy living life to think of faking it'. So there's some claim to integrity and authenticity here, undermining the clichés of tropical tourism that had been slowly developing after 1898. But it's not till the tenth poem in this section that the tone shifts decisively:

> Shattered walls
> The rain has eaten,
> The earthquakes shaken,
> The swift storms beaten,—
>
> No one owns them,
> No one would care
> To mend them and roof them
> And live there.
>
> They say that house
> Was burned down
> By the Yankee filibusters
> When they sacked the town.[107]

US 'visitors' to the tropics therefore turn out to include people like William Walker, the filibuster active in the 1860s who had recently (in 1906) been hailed by Theodore Roosevelt's favourite journalist, Richard Harding Davis, as a forgotten military genius.[108] It was Walker's exploits, it will be remembered, that had first galvanised Latin American sentiment.[109] León is haunted, even traumatised, by this memory, even if the poet's bold response to the fact that no one wants to mend the walls and live in the house is: 'I

---

[106] De la Selva, 'My Nicaragua', in *Tropical Town*, p. 36.
[107] De la Selva, 'The Haunted House of León', in *Tropical Town*, p. 25.
[108] Richard Harding Davis, 'William Walker', in his *Real Soldiers of Fortune*, New York: C. Scribner's sons, 1906, pp. 145–90.
[109] See above, pp. 36–37.

will marry a Yankee girl / And we will dare!'[110] It is obviously no accident that this poem precedes the warning of 'A Song for Wall Street', aimed at a modern version of filibustering, nor that the final poem in the section, 'The Dreamer's Heart Knows Its Own Bitterness', starts by underlining the poet's origins in 'the tropic lands'.[111]

There may even have been a more recent and more personal motive behind 'The Haunted House'. US soldiers of fortune were, after all, still operating in Nicaragua. The two most notorious in Salomón's youth were Leonard Groce and Lee Roy Cannon, mining engineers who had joined Juan José Estrada in his revolt against President Zelaya in 1909, using their expertise to try—unsuccessfully—to blow up troop ships. Both had been militarily active in Central America for several years—Groce as a police chief in El Salvador, Cannon involved in political unrest in Honduras—so they knew the risks they were running.[112] They had been captured and executed on 15 November 1909, the case against them put by Zelaya's attorney general, Salomón Selva Glenton, father of the poet.[113] Philander Knox, Taft's Secretary of State, used the executions as a reason for supporting the revolt against Zelaya, who was forced out of office—one consequence being the ending of Salomón's scholarship. There were widespread reports in the US newspapers that 'prompt action' would be taken against Selva Glenton for his rôle in the 'miscarriage of justice' which had led to the shooting of Groce and Cannon.[114] He was indeed accused by the new Nicaraguan regime of violating legal procedure, but acquitted on 28 January 1910 on the grounds that he had received written instructions from Zelaya. The atmosphere in Managua was fervid. Undoubtedly affected by the controversy, Selva Glenton died of a heart attack

---

[110] De la Selva, *Tropical Town*, p. 26.

[111] See above, pp. 186–89, for a discussion of 'The Dreamer's Heart'. While these poems are clearly addressed to an anglophone readership, de la Selva was at the same time writing a much more personal tribute to his home town in the poem 'Oda a León de Nicaragua' (*Diario de El Salvador*, San Salvador, 29 December 1919), in *Antología Mayor/I Poesías*, pp. 473–75.

[112] See Lester D. Langley and Thomas Schoonover, *The Banana Men: American Mercenaries and Entrepreneurs in Central America, 1880–1930*, Lexington: University Press of Kentucky, 1995, pp. 86–88; John E. Findling, *Close Neighbors, Distant Friends: United States–Central American Relations*, New York: Greenwood Press, 1987, p. 60.

[113] That case, powerfully made, is reproduced in Zelaya's collection of documents compiled in exile: José Santos Zelaya, *La revolución de Nicaragua y los Estados Unidos*, Madrid: Impr. de B. Rodríguez, 1910, pp. 138–64. See also Jorge Eduardo Arellano, 'La ejecución de Cannon y Groce en 1909', *El Nuevo Diario*, 28 November 1909 <https://www.elnuevodiario.com.ni/especiales/265183-ejecucion-cannon-groce-1909/> accessed December 2018.

[114] *Elyria Evening Telegraph*, 18 January 1910, p. 4.

on 2 February, aged just 50.[115] Two weeks later, the soldier in charge of the firing squad was shot dead in the street.[116] Late in life, de la Selva was still chewing over these events. He recalled them in a letter to his brother Rogerio, dated 23 June 1958, noting that the concessions of the House of Fletcher in Pittsburgh had suffered when Zelaya had realised that the USA had—as he saw it—been misleading him about their intentions to build a Nicaraguan canal.[117] When Taft had appointed as his Secretary of State Philander Knox, the Fletcher brothers' lawyer, who was socially close to the family, Zelaya's fate was sealed. Knox was a principal shareholder in the Fletcher brothers' La Luz and Los Angeles Mining Company, of which Groce had been an employee. Going into considerable detail, de la Selva fingers the US consul, Thomas P. Moffat, as the instigator of the revolution against Zelaya, in accordance with evidence from US Senate hearings from the 1920s.[118] He quotes, with page number, from *United States Statutes at Large* to the effect that US citizens expatriate themselves if they take the citizenship of another country, in order to underline that, having taken Honduran citizenship, Cannon and Groce were no longer US citizens, although Knox's ultimatum to Zelaya was based on the premise that they were.[119] In this case the dreamer's heart certainly remembered the reasons for its own bitterness.

*

As was happening elsewhere in New York, Salomón de la Selva's friendships were tested and sometimes sundered by US involvement in the European

---

[115] The *Diario del Salvador* noted the death of Salomón Selva Glenton, 'víctima de diabetes, agravada por la ejecución de los americanos' [victim of diabetes, aggravated by the execution of the Americans] (15 February 1910, p. 1). His death was also reported in the *Washington Post*, 15 February 1910, p. 1.

[116] 'Madriz Bombards Town Held By Foes', *New York Times*, 15 February 1910, p. 3.

[117] 'Dos textos de Salomón de la Selva', in William Krehm and Salomón de la Selva, *Nicaragua en la primera mitad del siglo XX*, Managua: Ediciones Populares, 1976, pp. 33–35.

[118] Moffat does a good job of incriminating himself in his 1927 Senate testimony: see *Foreign Loans. Hearings before the Subcommittee of the Committee on Foreign Relations*, United States Senate, Sixty-Ninth Congress, Second Session, Pursuant to S. Con. Res. 15, January and February 1927, Washington, DC: US Government Printing Office, 1927, pp. 31–44; and for relevant government documents: *Papers Relating to the Foreign Relations of the United States with the Annual Message of the President Transmitted to Congress December 7, 1909*, Washington, DC: Government Printing Office, 1911, pp. 446–59.

[119] See Benjamin Harrison, 'The United States and the 1909 Nicaragua Revolution', *Caribbean Quarterly*, 41, nos. 3/4 (1995), 45–63.

war. His engagement with radical New York had never been that deep, but he had maintained at least some of the friendships forged in earlier years—and indeed some of the friends were less radical than they once had been, though not Clement Wood. Wood had visited Williams College at Salomón's invitation and correspondence between them in 1917 was relaxed, Salomón writing to him as 'my dearest lad' and 'Sir Clement'.[120] However, at the beginning of the new year, de la Selva was asked by Harriet Monroe to review Wood's first book of poems, *Glad of Earth*, for *Poetry*, alongside Joyce Kilmer's *Main Street and Other Poems*. He had next to nothing to say about any of the poems themselves, but offered a general opinion that 'the problems and aspirations that are Mr Wood's themes' are approached 'with insufficient or unconvincing mastery', just as Kilmer's 'seem pale by the light of what have become common hopes and fears'. As these words suggests, '[t]he pity of these books is chiefly that they were born beyond their time', made irrelevant by the war, thought of which was certainly coming to dominate de la Selva's imagination.[121] Kilmer was already fighting in France, would be killed in July, and probably never saw the review. Wood was obviously hurt by it and wrote a long and dignified letter to de la Selva rebutting his criticisms—one of the relatively few surviving letters *to* de la Selva since Wood kept a carbon copy in his files. Wood lists some of his poems' weighty themes—death, psychology, love—but also understands that for de la Selva *all* other themes are rendered insignificant by war:

> Even your viewpoint underlying the criticism—that the conflicts of peace, the labor upheaval etc., are pale beside war's problems—is wholly at variance with the world's belief and practice; why are all the papers full of Bolsheviki and German and Austrian revolution, American labor matters, etc? The war is a surface matter, compared to the oppressed's struggle for the better things of life. If you do not know this, if the glamor of shiny buttons and braying bugles has fired your volatile fancy to the point where you cannot see the superficiality of it all as compared with the bigger class and individual problems, you are not a worthy critic of anything written today.

That somebody whom he thought of as a friend should criticise his work like this in public obviously also rankled. He throws out a piece of casual racism—'Perhaps the fault is mine, in choosing as friend a member of the

---

[120] Letter from Salomón de la Selva to Clement Wood, CWP (undated [March 1917?]). CWP is the Clement Wood Papers (Box 31), Hay Library, Brown University.
[121] Salomón de la Selva, 'Strains of Yesterday', *Poetry*, XI, no. 5 (February 1918), 281–82.

volatile Spanish-American race; you cannot be other than you are'—before getting close to the bone: 'do you think that literary stabbing of your intimates will earn you the respect of anyone, or even of yourself? Yours cannot be a happy life, if you live it so.'[122]

Falling in Love Again

Salomón may not always have been lucky in love, but he did have good taste. If Edna Millay was widely regarded as one of the most desirable women in New York, Jeanne Robert Foster was one of the most beautiful—her face and figure prominently displayed on the covers of fashion magazines (Fig. 20). She was also one of the cleverest, working as literary editor on the prestigious and influential *American Review of Reviews* and herself a published poet. Born Julia Elizabeth Oliver in Johnsburg, New York, in 1879, Jeanne had an impoverished Adirondack upbringing which she escaped through marriage to Matlack Foster when she was 18.[123] He was 46, older than her father. Living in Rochester, she had helped in her husband's business while taking diplomas and beginning to experiment with writing. Matlack's health problems encouraged him to semi-retire and spend time in New York City, where Jeanne took the opportunity to spread her wings, acting for the American Stock Company, working as a fashion model for *Vanity Fair* and the *Ladies Home Journal*, often sketched by Harrison Fisher, one of the pre-eminent illustrators of the early twentieth century, and taking a position as assistant fashion editor on William Randolph Hearst's New York newspapers. Caring for her typhoid-stricken sister in Boston then gave her the opportunity to take some courses at Harvard. Her husband was supportive, but by now Jeanne was clearly living an independent life. She stayed in Boston between 1905 and 1910, contributing to newspapers there and in New York, and still doing some modelling. Then, at a party in New York in late 1909, she met Albert Shaw, editor of the *American Review of Reviews*, who got her to move to the city to work on an oral history project collecting poetry and songs from Civil War veterans. She was soon contributing regularly to his journal—finally adopting the name Jeanne Robert Foster—and being sent by him to do research into housing reform in France, Scotland, and Ireland. Shaw's marriage was as unfulfilling as Jeanne's, and a liaison ensued. With Shaw's encouragement Jeanne developed the literary section of the *American*

---

[122] Letter from Clement Wood to Salomón de la Selva, CWP (6 February 1918).
[123] Biographical details are drawn from Richard Londraville and Janis Londraville, *Dear Yeats, Dear Pound, Dear Ford: Jeanne Robert Foster and Her Circle of Friends*, Syracuse, NY: Syracuse University Press, 2001.

20 Jeanne Robert Foster. Provenance unknown.

Review of Reviews, often writing the pieces herself. Her affair with Shaw petered out, though they remained friends.

Jeanne Foster had long had an interest in theosophy and the occult. The latter turned up in person in New York in the form of Aleister Crowley, who captivated Jeanne for a while, including during a trip she took through California with her husband late in the autumn of 1915. 'Deliver me from the snares of the flesh', she wrote in her diary. 'Deliver me from its sharp delights. Deliver me from its lures and its tender secrets.'[124] Crowley was determined to sire on Hilarion (his name for Jeanne) the son prophesied by his guardian angel. She soon tried to distance herself from Crowley, but he seems to have pestered her until early in 1917. Although Jeanne Foster and the lawyer and collector John Quinn had known of each other and even corresponded, they didn't meet until the end of December 1918—while de la Selva was still in England. By the time he returned, Foster had committed herself to John Quinn and would be by his side until his death in 1924.

An important element of Jeanne Foster's life in New York was Petitpas' restaurant, at 317 West 29th Street, where John Butler Yeats, the artist father of W. B. Yeats, held court every evening. She started taking her dinners there early in 1911, meeting over the years some of the city's most prominent artists and writers, including John Sloan, Van Wyck Brooks, and W. Adolphe

---

[124] Quoted in Londraville and Londraville, *Dear Yeats*, p. 95. See also Tobias Churton, *Aleister Crowley: The Biography. Spiritual Revolutionary, Romantic Explorer, Occult Master—and Spy*, London: Watkins Publishing, 2011; and Richard B. Spence, *Secret Agent 666: Aleister Crowley, British Intelligence, and the Occult*, Port Townsend, WA: Feral House, 2008.

Roberts. She may have met Salomón de la Selva there—he certainly attended on occasion; although the Poetry Society of America was another meeting place they had in common.

Jeanne herself never had children, but while volunteering as a social worker in Manhattan in 1912 she befriended an ill-nourished 11-year-old Russian immigrant earning a few cents as a seamstress. She eventually got the girl, Marya Zaturenska, a job at Brentano's bookshop and enrolled her for night-school classes. Zaturenska called Jeanne her fairy-godmother. In 1918, Zaturenska began to submit her poems to magazines, beginning a career which would culminate in a Pulitzer Prize in 1938.

Jeanne Foster's own first two books of poetry, *Wild Apples* and *Neighbors of Yesterday*, were both published in 1916. Although in 1918 de la Selva thought highly of Jeanne's recent poems, he was critical of both her published books. *Wild Apples* consists of conventional and often mawkish poems, of little interest, many written when she was very young, but *Neighbors of Yesterday*—as John Butler Yeats recognised—is a startlingly original set of Adirondack stories told in free-flowing verse.[125] The book was ignored in its day but has more recently had at least some local recognition.[126] It is an as yet unacknowledged modernist masterpiece.[127]

De la Selva didn't get to know Jeanne Foster and her young protegée Marya Zaturenska until the spring of 1918, when she was between her two major extramarital relationships. His first mention of her comes in a letter to Amy Lowell in which he asks her whether she knows anything about the work of Jeanne Robert Foster (she didn't): 'the matter is this: I have seen Mrs Foster, and lost my heart to her, quite completely and irretrievably. As she is married (or is she a widow?) I am perfectly unhappy. The Spring is my worst enemy, and this time it has struck me a mortal blow.'[128]

Of the two largest sets of de la Selva's love letters that survive, the ones to Edna Millay are by turns passionate, playful, despairing, lyrical, and angry, while the ones to Jeanne Robert Foster begin conventionally but quickly disappear into the realms of fantasy.[129] Although both poets, and women of

---

[125] Londraville and Londraville, *Dear Yeats*, pp. 74–77.
[126] Jeanne Robert Foster, *Neighbors of Yesterday*, 2nd edn, West Cornwall, CT: Locust Hill Press, 2002.
[127] See Cathy Fagan, 'The Excitement of an Afternoon Call: A Move Toward the Modern Voice in the Poetry of Jeanne Robert Foster', in Janis Londraville, ed., *Prodigal Father Revisited: Artists and Writers in the World of John Butler Yeats*, West Cornwall, CT: Locust Hill Press, 2003, pp. 237–54.
[128] Letter of Salomón de la Selva to Amy Lowell, ALP (undated [April 1918?]).
[129] Some of Salomón's letters to Jeanne are undated: Londraville and Londraville's suggested datings are unreliable.

The Pan-American Dream (1918)

luminous beauty, Edna and Jeanne were very different. For a start, Edna was more or less the same age as Salomón, just six months older, while Jeanne was 14 years his senior. By 1918, she had a powerful position within the New York cultural establishment. Her marital situation was unconventional, if not that unusual for this period: she and her husband led largely separate lives. Mr Foster lived in the marital home in Rochester, while Jeanne often overnighted at the National Arts Club, where many writers and artists had rooms. The first surviving letter from Salomón to Jeanne Robert Foster, written in June 1918, reads as if written in the immediate aftermath of a night of passion and is addressed to Jeanne-Julie—a combination of her original and assumed first names: 'We will teach the world how love of man and woman can be a form of mysticism ... Anointed with your kisses, my lips are sacrosanct; their holiness shall fashion all my utterance.'[130] He does not, he wrote, want to telephone her house too often in case his voice becomes familiar. But soon, and suddenly, the opportunity to join the British army appeared and he was up and away. From England he would send her a sonnet, 'With reference to the Box of Sandalwood', which suggests that what he really wanted was to leave the country with the love of a woman in his heart, and to leave behind an heir in her body:

> I could not go unloved, I could not give
> Death my sweet body whole-unsatisfied,
> Leaving, to tell how poorly I had died,
> Love-willing songs that I had meant to live;
> But now that all is true which I have sung,
> Now that in pain of virgin offering
> You have been Autumn to my perfect Spring
> Full-ripening what Death had found too young
>
> And hoarding in your body's granary
> That much of me not Death but Life should reap,
> Gladly I run to meet whatever doom
> The gods ordain, & if some mourn for me
> Be it not you for whom I did not weep
> But left my life in keeping of whose womb.[131]

---

[130] Letter of Salomón de la Selva to Jeanne Robert Foster, FMC (16 June 1918). FMC is the Foster-Murphy Collection, Manuscripts and Archives Division. The New York Public Library. Astor, Lenox, and Tilden Foundations.
[131] Poem (July 1918) sent by Salomón de la Selva to Jeanne Robert Foster, FMC (August 1918?]).

When he enlisted, de la Selva hastily left a sheath of poems with the Hispanic Society of America. This sonnet is one of them; underneath it (but not sent to Jeanne) is another called 'The Answer'. Scrawled in the margin in pencil is 'Mrs de la Selva': he has answered his own poem with one in the persona of his fictitious wife, who suggests that if she is indeed pregnant and if he, the poet, should die, then he should 'Usurp that dwelling place and softly lie / Secure beneath my heart, in the pulsing gloom', and await the moment 'when your lips shall suck from my full breast'.[132]

'I could not go unloved' is a masterful leaving-for-war poem, but in matters of the heart de la Selva liked to keep his options open. Jeanne Foster was stunningly beautiful but perhaps a little too old (autumn to his spring as he puts it, rather ungallantly) and perhaps a little out of his league. It's not clear just when or where Salomón met Theresa Helburn—'Thery', as he insisted on writing her name—but she was also writing poetry and attending the PSA, so that is a likely venue (Fig. 21). He first mentions her in a letter to Adolphe Roberts, editor of *Ainslee's*, probably written in June 1918 and enclosing for his consideration some of her poems, 'of which and of whom I think the world'.[133] She isn't mentioned in any of his other correspondence until he is in England, but by July the relationship had been strong enough for Theresa to be the last friend he saw before he left New York: they had breakfast together on Monday, 22 July before he gathered at Grand Central with other recruits to travel to Windsor, Nova Scotia, for training. Thery would join the list of his correspondents: his letters to her were less frequent than to Jeanne Robert Foster, but they do include the letter which gives decisive evidence about his disappointment at not being sent to the trenches to fight.

Part of that glittering generation of women writers and intellectuals who flocked to New York in these years, Theresa Helburn would eventually make her considerable name in theatre administration: from 1919, she worked as a producer for the Theatre Guild and was therefore largely responsible for bringing serious theatre back onto Broadway. In 1918, she was still a young bohemian woman, from a more privileged background than many—Bryn Mawr, Radcliffe, the Sorbonne—but still trying to make ends meet in

---

[132] 'The Answer' (July 1918), from Salomón de la Selva, Members File, Hispanic Society of America, New York.

[133] Salomón de la Selva to W. Adolphe Roberts, WARA (undated [June 1918?]). WARA is the Walter Adolphe Roberts Archive (MS 353), National Library of Jamaica. Roberts was evidently not impressed since none of them appeared in *Ainslee's*.

21 Theresa Helburn. *New York Herald*, 21 May 1922, p. 2.

Greenwich Village and writing some poetry and stories and theatre criticism. Born in 1887, she was a few years younger than Jeanne and a few older than Edna. Her work was published in the *The Century*, *Harper's*, and *The Bellman*, but she also—no doubt through her connection with de la Selva— had a feminist story published in *La Revista de Indias*, one of the very few surviving pieces from the three issues of that journal.[134]

Fighting for England

De la Selva had registered for the draft while teaching at Williams College and trained enthusiastically, as his poem 'Drill' suggested, but when the USA declared war, the US army would only accept US citizens—and de la Selva would not renounce his Nicaraguan citizenship. His attempts to join the French Foreign Legion and the Red Cross were similarly thwarted before the British Army, running short of soldiers and identifying British West Indians living in east coast US cities as a potential pool, set up a recruiting

---

[134] Theresa Helburn, 'The Homecoming' (THP) [August 1918?]. THP is the Theresa Helburn Papers (MSS864), Beinecke Library, Yale University.

office in New York. De la Selva seized his opportunity and was soon a member of the 3rd Battalion of the Loyal North Lancashire Regiment, a reserve unit based at Felixstowe as part of the Harwich Defences, guarding the east coast of England against the expected German invasion. The Loyal North Lancs wasn't de la Selva's choice, but it was appropriate enough given that he was already one-eighth Lancastrian through his paternal great grandfather.

The enthusiasm for the war Salomón de la Selva displayed in his writing made it difficult to imagine him not enlisting, and even more difficult to imagine him not fighting. Apart from the six poems collected in *Tropical Town* under the heading 'In War Time', he wrote another 20 or so poems about the war between 1914 and 1918, mostly published in newspapers and magazines either before his enlistment or while he was serving. Many of these poems strike the same note as 'Drill':

> So, with the rush of summer rain
> I shall have swept across the earth,
> And if it chance myself be slain
> My self shall have a richer birth.[135]
>
> I, too, will go and sing and do my part![136]
>
> I go to the wars faithful to you.[137]
> War is song too, and this shall have my heart.[138]
>
> Her heel has stepped too heavy on my heart;
> I were no man to let this outrage be![139]
>
> Therefore, I sing, though it may come to pass
> That we lie dead—for France!—before the night![140]

Salomón de la Selva explained his reasons—after a fashion—for wanting to fight in the First World War in personal terms, although the number of different accounts he gives does suggest that he was never altogether clear

---

[135] From 'The Knight in Gray', *Tropical Town*, p. 84.
[136] From 'Enrolled', *An Unknown Songster Sings*, p. 251.
[137] From 'To My Aztec Ancestors', *An Unknown Songster Sings*, p. 253.
[138] From 'These Emotional Rhetorics', *An Unknown Songster Sings*, p. 255.
[139] From 'On Germany', *An Unknown Songster Sings*, p. 259.
[140] From 'For France', *An Unknown Songster Sings*, p. 279.

about his motivation. The one possible reason that he firmly denies is that he was fighting as a Nicaraguan, for any nationalist reason. Perhaps so; but just as de la Selva was waiting impatiently in Felixstowe for the chance to enter the trenches of Flanders his friend and fellow Central American Alfonso Guillén Zelaya wrote a passionate piece for the *Pan-American Magazine* called, 'Why the Central American Republics Should Take Part in the War'. Guillén Zelaya was responding to the declarations of war on Germany made by Guatemala, Nicaragua, Costa Rica, and Honduras between April and July 1918. To declare war and then stay comfortably at home is rather comic, he wrote, a bit like fighting a duel by mail. So those declarations of war were 'mere expressions of complimentary sympathy thrown into that trench of the ideal which the Allies are defending with blood, brain and heart'.[141] Given the sparse populations and negligible armies of these Central American countries, what is needed to enable effective participation, he argued, is what has just been proposed by the Honduran President, Dr Francisco Bertrand: a Union of Central America which could, if El Salvador were to join in, sustain and equip an army of 250,000 men. Now Bertrand's proposal, like the declaration of war itself, had far more to do with internal Central American politics than it did with joining the fight against Germany, and of course within a month any such arguments would become nugatory; but Guillén Zelaya's heated advocacy of such a step perhaps suggests the powerful psychological motivations that might lead a Central American to want to fight. Central America, Guillén Zelaya argued, has never done anything for the benefit of great human ideals:

> we have never written a page of heroism, created anything or made a sacrifice worthy of taking a place among the broad interests of the world. We ought, therefore, to go actively into war ... to save ourselves from the calamity of being regarded as mere groups of human beings without culture and without ideals, without any national sentiment, with nothing to defend, with nothing to die for, even with nothing to destroy ... Taking part in the war is an imperious necessity for us. And we must go to do what we have never done or had; we must go to make history.[142]

Perhaps, on an individual level, such thoughts also animated Salomón de la Selva.

---

[141] Alfonso Guillén Zelaya, 'Why the Central American Republics Should Take Part in the War', *Pan-American Magazine*, XXVII, no. 6 (October 1918), 341–42, at 341.
[142] Guillén Zelaya, 'Why the Central American Republics', 342.

He later gave many reasons. He claimed in 1946 to have felt the tragedy aesthetically 'with complete disinterest'.[143] He fought under the flag of George V, he said, as much as for any other reason for Alice Meynell—as a representative of the best of English culture.[144] At the time he certainly rejected Edwin Markham's praise for the 'sense of duty' he had shown by enlisting:

> Alas, and how you are mistaken! I owed allegiance to none of the flags that wave so bravely over the battlefields of Europe; and there is no warring country that could have had any claim of service to put forward upon me. Neither did I conceive it as an obligation of any sort to enlist in any army or for any cause. My own flag remains furled; my own country has not called me and does not need me; and as for the ideals of the war, allow me to remain a sceptic. I have seen in this war, for myself ... only an opportunity, not otherwise to be had, of making a glorious sacrifice ... And for this I wish no praise, inasmuch as praise testifies to understanding of the praised in the praiser, and, though it is nothing to be ashamed of, I much rather prefer to be the only one to understand my motives. Not, of course, that I do.[145]

But perhaps his most telling comment was made in a letter to Edna: 'I will, however, go and be finally a man, even in man's beastliness'.[146] He seems to have in front of him the example of those six Schauffler boys, two of whom he'd taught. If they were all fighting in Europe, he just had to be there too, embracing human beastliness, if he was ever to really think of himself as a 'man'.

When he first tried to sign up to fight in late 1917 and early 1918, de la Selva's commitment to the USA took a battering. He tells the story in two long and rambling letters to Amy Lowell written in late July and early August from Windsor, Nova Scotia, where he was undergoing training prior to being shipped across to Europe. His overt commitment at first seems intact: he asks for some window in the USA to show a service flag for him,

---

[143] De la Selva, 'In Memoriam', p. 115.
[144] De la Selva, 'In Memoriam', p. 124.
[145] Letter from Salomón de la Selva to Edwin Markham, EMA (20 October 1918).
[146] Letter from Salomón de la Selva to Edna St Vincent Millay, ESVMP (2 August 1917).

adopting him as a serviceman even though he is fighting for the British. But, as the story unfolds, his sense of hurt becomes apparent. 'I had wished to follow the American colours!' he writes, '& under them to fight for Pan America'.[147] Pan-America was not at war, but a Nicaraguan fighting in US colours might offer a small but potent symbol of continental unity, and he had earlier offered to raise a Pan-American regiment. But fighting in any shape or form proved problematic:

> Again and again I tried to volunteer, in any sort of Army service, including Red Cross, Y.M.C.A., & what not. My second choice was the French Foreign Legion, but I had to get to France to join that, and ... my Local Board (Mass, No 1., at North Adams) stubbornly refused to grant me passport-permit. Why? God knows. I could not get those damn fools to say a word of explanation, & you cannot imagine how unpleasant it was to be treated so, especially after I had had to explain to the Intelligence Department that the anonymous accusations they had received about my being anti-American were pure bunk.[148]

These accusations had come after de la Selva had been consulted by the US Committee on Public Information for advice about checking German propaganda in Latin America, even suggesting, he writes, that he take up a salaried position in charge of a department of poetry—a suggestion that soon fell through. He wanted to think that German tricks were behind his treatment since he 'felt so crushed, so miserably deceived, betrayed, rejected when called upon, as an enemy, to clear myself of false charges'.[149]

He pieces together the story for Lowell. Sometime around 14 June he was still asleep near midday having worked until after dawn translating, when a plain clothes man called on him.

> He simply asked me whether I had recently published a book, whether I had been a professor of French and whether I knew English well. Then he wrote on a slip of paper an address and said that the War Department wanted me there that very day ... I went to the address given, fondly believing that I would receive an appointment as interpreter, for which I had on several occasions applied ... Imagine my astonishment when I was led to a private room, saw the door

---

[147] Letter from Salomón de la Selva to Amy Lowell, ALP (29 July 1918).
[148] Letter from Salomón de la Selva to Amy Lowell, ALP (29 July 1918).
[149] Letter from Salomón de la Selva to Amy Lowell, ALP (5 August 1918).

locked and guarded, and was made to face a sort of tribunal. The questioning officer, Lieut. Veley, informed me that I was before the Intelligence Department, charged with being a violent pro-German and a spy. He blandished [sic] a pile of letters, accusations from 'many reliable sources.'

Most of them were 'sheer falsehoods', de la Selva writes, 'the rest travesties of things I had really said.' They wouldn't tell him the names of his accusers. The interrogation 'was a sort of third degree', led by a group of Army officers who 'informed me that from the room into which I had been led in secrecy, I could be taken out and be shot and not a word of it known, "for this," he [Veley] said, "is war".'[150] Having failed to establish any truth in the accusations, the last question they put to de la Selva was, 'Is there any reason why you should feel inimical to the United States?' And Salomón clearly felt some satisfaction in having conjured up the courage to reply: 'Yes, that there are moments when I am made to feel not in the United States but in Germany.'

De la Selva's whole project was based on the possibility of dual allegiance, but official US policy—and the popular mood—was in favour of 100 per cent Americanism. He didn't look or sound like an 'alien', but any resident not willing to become a citizen fell under suspicion. To cap it all, that very week had been declared Loyalty Week in New York.[151] It is likely that de la Selva had fallen foul of Archibald Stevenson, the lawyer who was chairman of the Committee on Aliens, working for the New York Mayor's Committee of National Defense. A true zealot, Stevenson had volunteered earlier that year to assist the Department of Justice in its investigation of German propaganda and had supervised the construction of a card-index of people suspected of pro-German leanings. On this project he worked under Captain Trevor of the Military Information Division, with offices at 302 Broadway, which may be where de la Selva's interrogation took place.[152]

Although warned to keep quiet about the interrogation, de la Selva was telling Lowell, he wrote, because, should he die, he wanted somebody to be able to counter the official lies that would be told. 'Even my enlistment in the British Army may be taken as proof of my dislike for the United States'; such an untruth, he insists, that he carried a small US flag in his cap:

---

[150] Letter from Salomón de la Selva to Amy Lowell, ALP (5 August 1918).
[151] Ross J. Wilson, *New York and the First World War: Shaping an American City*, London: Routledge, 2016, p. 199.
[152] See *The Truth About the Lusk Committee: A Report Prepared by The Legislative*

[I]f, as it may be, they question with a sneer why I should so love a country not my own, where, for a time, I starved, where my services as a teacher were underpaid, and whose officials were teutonic in dealing with me, say that it was because I loved my country and my race, loved them wisely as well as passionately, with the sure knowledge that only through the brotherhood of the Americas could continental peace and solidarity and true progress be accomplished.[153]

He was certainly not going to compromise on his ideals.

*

There'd been a long debate within the British Army about the rôle that colonial troops should play. 'Not in combat roles, and certainly not in Europe' had been the mantra. The Army was initially opposed to having black soldiers at all, but by early 1918 it was desperately short of men. West Indies Regiments were recruited and involved in combat, though not in Europe. Finally, the Army decided to recruit among the large number of British citizens—most of them black West Indians—who were living on the east coast of the USA. Recruiting offices were set up, and the campaign was underlined in March 1918 by sending across the Atlantic one of the newfangled tanks, which rolled up Fifth Avenue. One of its celebrity passengers was the wife of Edward M. House, who the following month would become special presidential liaison with the Allied nations.[154]

The initial idea behind the British–American Recruiting Mission was to give British and Canadian citizens the opportunity to volunteer ahead of a possible draft.[155] As the need for troops increased, the pace of recruitment stepped up. By the early summer of 1918, the language was becoming much stronger. A new recruiting drive was reported as being underway, aiming to reach the '300,000 who have failed to volunteer': 'It is planned to force the attention of British subjects in New York on the plans for recruiting under the treaty arranged between the United States and Great Britain.'[156] British male subjects between the ages of 18 and 45 resident in the USA would have

---

Committee of the People's Freedom Union, New York: The Nation Press, 1920, p. 4.
[153] Letter from Salomón de la Selva to Amy Lowell, ALP (5 August 1918).
[154] *New York Times*, 3 March 1918, p. 8. On the cultural history of tanks during the war, see Trudi Tate, *Modernism, History and the First World War*, Manchester: Manchester University Press, 1998, pp. 120–46.
[155] *New York Times*, 28 November 1917, p. 24.
[156] *New York Times*, 29 July 1918, p. 7.

60 days to enlist in the British Army. If they didn't do so, they would be drafted into the US army. Meanwhile, the British Army was quite happy to sign up stray foreigners such as Nicaraguan poets.[157]

De la Selva's enlistment at the British and Canadian Recruitment Mission at 220 West 42nd Street (the Candler Building, a fine skyscraper completed in 1914) was unusual enough to merit a photograph in the *New York Herald* (Fig. 22): he looked so very young. Never one to miss an opportunity, Salomón composed a martial sonnet on the spot, invoking his appropriate 'Aztec ancestry': 'Sustain my knee and strengthen heart and hand'.[158] The potted autobiography he provided for the newspaper reporter continued the elaborations of his CV and his reputation. He was now, it seemed, 'regarded as the foremost poet of his generation in Latin-America'. He was accompanied, the article notes, by the writer and sculptor William Ordway Partridge, foreigners needing a sponsor.[159]

A letter to Edna announced his enlistment in the British Army: he would leave on Monday (which would be 22 July).[160] The same story is told to a number of correspondents in the summer and autumn of 1918: the refusal of his local military board to grant him a passport permit to France; the rejection by the Red Cross (for not being disabled), by the YMCA (for not being over 40), and by the Rehabilitation of Devastated France (for not being American); and then finally the successful visit to the British Recruitment Mission.

His sudden departure necessitated some arrangement of affairs. Huntington was asked to fly Salomón's service flag over the Hispanic Society of America, on the grounds that he was going to war 'for all the society stands for in fellowship among civilized people'. He had left the material for his next book, *The Lonely Exile*, with Jeanne Robert Foster, he reported to Huntington: he later asked for this material to be sent to his Manhattan address prior to his

---

[157] For documentation, see National Archives WO 32/4765, and *Who's Who in the British War Mission in the United States of America 1918*, New York: Edward J. Clode, 1918. For general background, see David Killingray, 'All the King's Men? Blacks in the British Army in the First World War, 1914–1918', in *Under the Imperial Carpet: Essays in Black History 1780–1950*, ed. Rainer Lotz and Ian Pegg, Crawley: Rabbit Press, 1986, pp. 164–81; Richard Smith, *Jamaican Volunteers in the First World War: Race, Masculinity and the Development of National Consciousness*, Manchester: Manchester University Press, 2004; and Ray Costello, *Black Tommies: British Soldiers of African Descent in the First World War*, Liverpool: Liverpool University Press, 2015.
[158] 'Nicaragua Poet Enlists; Writes Lines to Ancestors for Herald', *New York Herald*, 19 July 1918, p. 3.
[159] De la Selva blamed Partridge for the inaccuracies: Letter from Salomón de la Selva to Archer M. Huntington, HSASS (23 July 1918).
[160] Letter from Salomón de la Selva to Edna St Vincent Millay, ESVMP (18 July 1918).

22 Salomón de la Selva enlists in the British Army. 'Nicaragua Poet Enlists; Writes Lines to Ancestors for Herald', *New York Herald*, 19 July 1918, p. 3.

return from England, and then decided not to go ahead with the publication. He also speaks of a marriage 'duly performed before the wondering court of Heaven'. A postscript asks Huntington to pay a $30 debt to his landlady.[161]

Between July and November 1918 de la Selva must have written scores of letters judging from the 30 that survive in the archives of Jeanne Robert Foster, Archer Huntington, Amy Lowell, Edna Millay, Edwin Markham, Theresa Helburn, and W. Adolphe Roberts. He writes in detail about the hard training in Nova Scotia. The recruits piling up in Windsor he describes, with at least a touch of self-mockery, as 'Jews, negroes, human derelicts and other volunteers like myself'. He mentions Cubans,

---

[161] Letter from Salomón de la Selva to Archer M. Huntington, HSASS (23 July 1918). This letter comes after a gap of more than a year in the correspondence with Huntington, but presumably the contact had continued because this one is signed 'Affectionate wishes, Salomón'.

Mexicans, Argentinians, Russians, Italians, Hindus, and Australians, and is appreciative of the spirit of fellowship that prevails—except for 'the Yanks', or at least one stuck-up Yale student who rubs him up the wrong way.[162] He writes of how he was denied entry to the Grenadier Guards by reason of being a foreigner and assigned to the 3rd battalion of the Loyal North Lancashire Regiment; of avoiding the hordes of prostitutes around Trafalgar Square; of being fed and wined by Edward Wheeler at the Ritz: 'he was so proud of me, so affectionate, that I was really moved ... I reminded him of his son, he said, I talked like him'.[163] His Lancashire comrades are 'very innocent, very kind, very stupid, very brave, very honest'. They tend not to wash and their language and habits are unspeakably filthy. Salomón learns to adapt: 'I have grown to love these lads very much, and they like me well, too.'[164] He's keen to get the front: 'If any of the Schauffler boys have fallen, I here swear that when my innings came, I will take no German prisoners. It isn't vain boasting, Thery. The bayonet is my favourite weapon, and I have become incredibly proficient in it. It is the most expressive method of warfare, and as such it takes my fancy.'[165] His love of the bayonet—at least in training—becomes a troublingly obsessive trope in his letters.

He also involves Theresa with the story of his marriage: 'I love my woman more and more; you always thought her an idle wife play-acting with me; well, you didn't know her name even, and I swear to you that she is as good, as brave, as true a woman as she is beautiful and has been unfortunate ... And for her I will keep my flesh untainted as it is, untouched, clean'.[166] At first blush that 'marriage' seems to refer to his relationship with Jeanne Robert Foster, though in truth it has no factual basis. At the beginning of August he wrote to Jeanne (calling her 'My woman'): 'Write me that you love me, that you love me really, that you can hardly live without me.' Army life isn't easy, but he wants to be worthy of her: 'To have done something to make my woman proud of her man!' After several pages of detail about camp life—ill-fitting boots, kitchen duties, and the like—the letter ends,

---

[162] Letter from Salomón de la Selva to Archer M. Huntington, HSASS (30 July 1918).
[163] Letter from Salomón de la Selva to Theresa Helburn, THP (6 October 1918). Edward Wheeler was part of a delegation of US newspaper editors visiting London to investigate war work ('American Editors Feted in London', *The Sun*, 12 October 1918, p. 3). Wheeler had published his son's letters to him from Europe: Curtis Wheeler, *Letters from an American Soldier to his Father*, Indianapolis: Bobbs-Merrill, 1918.
[164] Letter from Salomón de la Selva to Theresa Helburn, THP (6 October 1918).
[165] Letter from Salomón de la Selva to Theresa Helburn, THP (6 October 1918).
[166] Letter from Salomón de la Selva to Theresa Helburn, THP (6 October 1918).

'Can you give me news of our son?'—an inquiry unlikely to have amused Jeanne after her experiences with Aleister Crowley.[167]

His next letter to Jeanne was written while crossing the Atlantic. He hopes to glimpse Ireland, he writes, 'for old Yeats's sake'—John Butler, the genial host at Petitpas'. He muses about his companions, whom he admires, not least for their grasp of the importance of the war. 'If I were before God, I could not sum up and make a brief of my reasons for becoming a soldier. I have tried to put those reasons on paper, and the result has been mere literature, Verlaine's abomination.' There are more protestations of love—'You are my woman, and I am yours as wholly and selfishly as I want you to be mine'; anxieties concerning 'my boy'; and a strange postscript in which he suggests that she ask Mrs Foster to forward some letters that he is enclosing to various people in New York.[168]

Having reached England and his base in Felixstowe, de la Selva was obviously granted almost immediate leave, which he spent in London. His next letter (sent to Jeanne but addressed to 'Mrs Salomón de la Selva') was written on the notepaper of the King George and Queen Mary Victoria League Club for Men of the Overseas Forces, on Charing Cross Road. He'd planned to write poetry, but hadn't; had visited the Bodley Head to get some money from John Lane, where he met 'that famous Mr C. Dawson,' whose war-wound he envies:

> The more I see of this war-mushroom-writers [sic], the less I wish to write about war-experiences. So you may as well inform Mr Jones that there is not going to be any war-poetry first section in my next book. And if he doesn't like it, the bargain is off.[169]

There is some literary gossip and some talk of girls he has met, though 'I have been faithful dear. And if you wish to know what I talk to the girls about, it's about you, and the tram-ways' strike, and slang, and food'. And again the son:

---

[167] Letter from Salomón de la Selva to Jeanne Robert Foster, FMC (4 August 1918).
[168] Letter from Salomón de la Selva to Jeanne Robert Foster, FMC (23 August 1918).
[169] Letter from Salomón de la Selva to Jeanne Robert Foster, FMC (10 September 1918). Despite this statement, some lists of de la Selva's writing—including at least one he himself produced—include *A Soldier Sings*, London: The Bodley Head, 1919. There is no evidence—and little likelihood—that such a book was ever published. Though British-born, Coningsby Dawson (1883–1959) served in the Canadian Army from 1916. After being wounded, he came to the USA on two lecture tours and was the author of *Khaki Courage: Letters in War Time*, which John Lane had published in 1917.

23 Salomón de la Selva in the uniform of the British Army.
Courtesy of the Schauffler Family Papers (MS 1389), Manuscripts and Archives, Yale University.

And my boy? Ah, my dear! This is my testament: that for him, I will not try to evade a soldier's death. My legacy shall be heroism. You shall tell him that the words of men, or the so called ideals of the war, moved not his father; but that somewhere in the world men were freely facing death, bravely bearing sacrifice, renewing so the chivalry of days when poets were warriors as well as lovers, and that a spirit in my blood, that he shall inherit, led me on. I will endeavour at the cost of all my life to distinguish my self in action; that pride in his father may also be his heritage. You shall tell him that in the midst of the roughest living, I never forgot I was a gentleman.[170]

Something of the English manner was clearly rubbing off.

A letter of 22 September 1918 didn't reach its destination, or at least hasn't survived, because one dated the following day—and opened in New York by the censor—refers to his 'silly letter of yesterday' when he let the blues get the better of him. He is now fully recovered and determinedly upbeat, he says, though increasingly worried 'that peace may come before I see the real show.' However, the complaints begin to multiply: 'England is a slow, sad, irritating place … It rains so damn often.' And it isn't just the weather: 'Why are the English so unclean? No wonder there's not a mouth in all the realm with a good set of teeth.' Individual soldiers begin to come in for criticism for their blank expression or their habit of spitting. As well as the West Indians, he mentions an Irishman, a Russian, a Chinese, a Swiss, and an East African. As the letter proceeds, his mood improves, so soon 'England is lovely', with its red roofs and trim little gardens.[171]

On 4 October, still entrenched in Felixstowe, and with the weather doubtless getting wetter and colder, he welcomes the arrival of Jeanne's poem, 'The Song of a Shulamite', which he describes as 'so beautiful!' When his friend Michael (the Cuban Miguel Ramos) saw Salomón's photograph of her, he asked if Salomón would will her to him if he were to be killed. He goes back to the poem, then discusses Joyce Kilmer as a poet, then his lover's ancestry, before ending with another description of how much he wants to use his bayonet on some real flesh.[172]

Jeanne Robert Foster clearly knew what de la Selva was up to. Having kept his letters and other writings for nearly 50 years, she returned them to

---

[170] Letter from Salomón de la Selva to Jeanne Robert Foster, FMC (10 September 1918).
[171] Letter from Salomón de la Selva to Jeanne Robert Foster, FMC (23 September 1918).
[172] Letter from Salomón de la Selva to Jeanne Robert Foster, FMC (4 October 1918).

his family in 1964: 'The letters are to myself and to two women—sent in my care. Despite the address "Mrs Salomon de la Selva", he was not married.' He was, she writes, 'one of the greatest poets of our time'. She is 'shocked beyond measure' at hearing of his death: 'It seemed to me that Salomon de la Selva had eternal and immortal youth.'[173]

To what extent Jeanne was a real object of Salomón's affections is difficult to say with certainty. The early letters seem full of passion for her and Adolphe Roberts certainly recalls Jeanne as being the most important woman in his friend's life around this time.[174] Jeanne herself said that he was her contribution to the war effort—a formulation which could be read in several different ways.[175] The most likely hypothesis is that—as with other women: many other women—de la Selva fell for Jeanne, possibly slept with her, but that the coalescence of fantasy object and real woman was brief: he continued to address the fantasy *through* the real woman but separate from her. The address on the envelopes: 'Mrs Salomón de la Selva c/o Mrs Jeanne Robert Foster' sums it up all too accurately.

*

By September, Salomón had settled into the routine of army life in his battalion. The North Lancashire regiments had initially been recruited, as one might expect, in North Lancashire: regimental headquarters were in Preston, and all the early recruits were white. By the summer of 1918, now based in Felixstowe, the 3rd Battalion of the Loyal North Lancs looked rather different (Fig. 24). The photograph on this postcard was probably taken in late 1918. There are hundreds of thousands of these First World War RPPCs (Real Photographic Postcards) in existence. The images were usually printed by hand directly from a negative onto photographic card with a 'postcard' back; and their popularity kept small photographic studios in business during the war. In most cases the print run would be half a dozen, made for an individual to send to his family. This one would have been good business for the Pier Studio in Felixstowe if each of the 36 soldiers pictured took a few copies, although only this one copy seems, by chance, to have survived. Fifteen of the 36 soldiers in this photograph are black,

---

[173] Letter from Jeanne Robert Foster to Family of S. de la Selva, FMC (18 March 1964). Apart from the play she mentions called 'The Blindness of Homer', copies of the returned material remain in the FMC.
[174] W. Adolphe Roberts, *These Many Years: An Autobiography*, ed. Peter Hulme, Kingston: University of the West Indies Press, 2015, p. 212.
[175] Londraville and Londraville, *Dear Yeats*, p. 114.

The Pan-American Dream (1918)

24 Salomón de la Selva and his platoon in Felixstowe, 1918. Postcard sent by de la Selva to W. Adolphe Roberts, 10 December 1918. Walter Adolphe Roberts Archive (MS 353), National Library of Jamaica. Courtesy of the National Library of Jamaica.

probably all of them West Indians who had been living in the USA and had been recruited in that same West 42nd Street office in Manhattan, or similar ones in Washington and Philadelphia. Salomón de la Selva is third from the right in the back row. In the message on the postcard, referring to the mixed nationalities in his squad, de la Selva wrote to Adolphe Roberts: 'They call us the foreign legion.'[176] In their way, these are also unknown soldiers: no history of the First World War—not even the regimental histories of the North Lancs—mentions West Indians in this rôle, let alone the other nationalities. These particular black soldiers are probably among the British West Indians listed on the manifest of the *Mauretania* that took them back to New York next year: James Moore, 39, porter; Alex Pinnock, 27, printer; Arnold Petrie, 27, shipyard worker; William Harris, 22, cooper; Perceval Jenkins, 29, baker; Clement Hewitt, 21, pipe maker; Claremont Thornhill, 23, porter; Allan Keppel, 36, telephonist ... Among which sits Salomón de la Selva, 24, professor.[177]

---

[176] Postcard from Salomón de la Selva to W. Adolphe Roberts, WARA (10 December 1918).
[177] List of Manifest of Alien Passengers for the United States, SS *Mauretania*, from

By October, de la Selva had retreated to the warmer YMCA hut to write, with the clink of billiard balls and a concert in the background. After a paean to Bach, Salomón offered his opinion of the war poets: Alan Seeger out in front, followed by Ledwidge and Brooke. The others, including Kilmer and McIntosh, are trash, though he admits it's hard to speak that way of those who have given their lives.[178] He also recalls his difficult years in New York, living in the Bowery to avoid compromising himself. He mentions that Huntington wanted to be his patron—which is not exactly the story that emerges from their correspondence; and that he damned Dr Frank Crane to hell for trying to help him out of the 'three months of pauperdom' he suffered when he was 15 and stranded in New York.[179]

De la Selva's last surviving letter before the Armistice was written to Edwin Markham on 20 October 1918. Its ten pages range widely, beginning with an explanation of why his religious nature rejects church attendance as enforced by military discipline. He suggests that though army life provides excellent material for real poetry, none of it would be printable, despite his having clearly come to terms with some of the things that most offended him in earlier months: 'farting is one of our chief delights; and more than a delight: it is also the basis of dear friendship, of true comradeship'. He claims, indeed, to have become an animal, with dog- or horse-like traits of obedience and innocence. 'Our hearts', he claims, 'are clean', with women unoffended, indeed put into their place: 'Once in a while we would like warm, tender, intimate company; but once in a while we would like apple-pie also, with equal force; and we are none the less pure or frugal for abstaining from both from no virtue but because neither are to be had.' He notes that his literary tastes have changed, with old favourites such as Thackeray, Tolstoy, and Austen now found unreadable; and he continues his running paean to the joys of the bayonet: 'when I charge with the bayonet, though it is only against painted sacks filled tight with straw, my own soul leaves me and a savage spirit, haply that of my blood-thirsty forefathers, enters into my flesh.'[180]

And then, after the months of waiting and hoping, came the sickening

---

Southampton on 31 March 1919, to New York on 7 April 1919 (passenger ID: 610083050445, Frame 299, Line Number 27). He appears as Salamon De-la-Selva.

[178] On Seeger and Kilmer, see above, p. 24. Francis Ledwidge (1887–1917), Irish poet, killed at Passchendaele; Rupert Brooke (1887–1915), English poet, died of sepsis en route for Gallipoli; E. Alan Mackintosh (1893–1917), Scottish poet, killed at second Cambrai.

[179] Letter from Salomón de la Selva to Jeanne Robert Foster, FMC (7 October 1918).

[180] Letter from Salomón de la Selva to Edwin Markham, EMA (20 October 1918).

disappointment of the announcement of peace. He wrote to Theresa Helburn:

> Ah Thery, I came too late! And it has disheartened me to the extent that I am planning never to return to the States or to Nicaragua and never to appear again before the world as a poet. As soon as I can get away I'll flit over to Belgium or France or Roumania and work there as a labourer in the reconstruction of any of those countries. This past month has been a devilishly nervous one for me. It was every day I expected to be among the lucky ones to be drafted for France but my turn never came; and I am a well-trained, nicely-fattened, perfectly eager would-be fighter left in the lurch. All dressed up and nowhere to go to, sums up my case. But we shall see who is stronger, luck or I. I shall be the poet of the Reconstruction, only I shan't write any verse, or if I do, I won't publish it, and if I ever do write for publication, it won't be in English any more. As for Spanish, I gave up writing seriously in it one time I was as let down about Nicaragua as I am about this war.—I would like to be a mason or a carpenter at Audenarde or Ramillies—here Nicaraguans, lads who have always looked up to me to do the glorious things, fell there and, falling, attained to more than I ever could with my words: Damn words![181]

'All dressed up and nowhere to go'. As so often, always the writer, he finds the perfect phrase to describe the situation. As might be expected, rash things are said in the first blaze of disappointment: Salomón was an unlikely mason or carpenter. But 11 November 1918 does represent a real turning point in his life. He would go back to New York and live in the States for several more months, but one senses that the decision to leave the country—or at least the desire to leave it—dates from this moment: the leaving of New York, but also the leaving of English as his lived language.[182] Tantalisingly, there is also here in this letter a glimpse of a future path. Not only did the Schauffler boys fight, there were—de la Selva suggests—even Nicaraguans who fought and died in Flanders and in France, at Audenarde and Ramillies, the two place names that would feature in de la Selva's next book of poems, *El soldado desconocido* (1922), as if he were trying to insert himself into a Nicaraguan war experience that had, to his lasting chagrin, been denied him:

---

[181] Letter from Salomón de la Selva to Theresa Helburn, THP (14 November 1918).
[182] He would continue to write poems in English, but all subsequent book publications were in Spanish.

Álamos destrozados de Oudenarde,
hayas truncas de Ramillies,
¡ya echaréis nuevas ramas
cuando vuelva abril![183]

Poplars destroyed in Oudenarde.
beeches cut down in Ramillies,
you'll throw out new branches
when April comes round!

Perhaps predictably, even more women now begin to feature in Salomón's letters. The first surviving letter after the one written to Theresa Helburn about his disappointment at not fighting is addressed to Catherine ('Mrs de la Selva'), but begins by stating: 'Should inquiries concerning my amorous affairs continue to reach Mrs Foster, you may tell her that she's at liberty to say that I have given my promise of marriage to Miss Gwendolen Wardman, an English young lady who is quite the loveliest thing I have seen in my life.'[184] *Continue to reach* suggests some earlier communication. And 'Catherine' can hardly be 'Mrs de la Selva' if Gwendolen Wardman has been promised that title. Vera Gwendolen Roma Wardman was born in 1899 in Ipswich, just up the road from Felixstowe. She worked as a nurse in 1918 and so may have looked after de la Selva when he was ill with flu. If any promise of marriage had been given, it was probably in jest or delirium. Perhaps understandably, his plans seem confused: 'My demobilisation has been ordered and I will soon return home. I want to arrange my muddled affairs in America, then return to England and probably settle at Oxford. I also must go to Nicaragua & attend to matters there. I don't know yet whether I'll be going to Nicaragua before going to the States, or the reverse.' Salomón had never seen Oxford, but it no doubt stood in his mind for the kind of refined Englishness that may briefly have seemed a refuge from the complications of his American life. The letter also offers a slightly bitter farewell to Catherine (Jeanne): 'Do have a good, exciting time, Catherine, but be careful with young fellows' hearts'.[185]

The next letter to Theresa, written from The Salvation Army Soldiers' Hostel in Whitechapel, London, unsurprisingly doesn't mention his

---

[183] Salomón de la Selva, 'Cantar', in *El soldado desconocido* [1922], Managua: Editorial Nueva Nicaragua, 1982, p. 141.
[184] Letter from Salomón de la Selva to Jeanne Robert Foster, FMC (22 December 1918).
[185] Letter from Salomón de la Selva to Jeanne Robert Foster, FMC (30 July 1919).

impending nuptials with Miss Wardman since it announces that has decided to fall in love with Theresa herself:

> It won't be hard. Just think of the fun we will have! I leave it to you to maintain a standard of sanity throughout it all. If you fail in this, well, I shall be defeated in the beautiful resolutions I am making. Because a good woman, in you, to love (mind you, I do not say 'to love me'), will, instead of taking strength from me, herself strengthen my heart and reassure me in my high purposes. I have had fits of passion sufficient to last me an ample life-time. I want the better love now, the calm, the sweet, the warm and enduring sort. Perhaps what I mean is what other people call friendship.

Considering his disappointment at not having been called upon to fight, the letter is surprisingly upbeat, full of plans to continue his project: 'I can do good work pan-Americanizing. The idea is bound to succeed, and I think it is I who has most nobly expressed it. It is great work for a great man, and with God's help I will be that great man'. She has sent him money, some of which he's spent on a couple of 'swell dinners' with a new Australian friend. He even asks about her recent play. But the news that most excites him is his visit to the Meynells, who clearly took to him. There is something of Darío's warmth towards Helen Woodruff in the way de la Selva writes about Alice Meynell: 'Mrs Meynell is very frail. She smokes, but very little,—three or four cigarettes a day. Mr Meynell is very beautiful. And how kind they are! So austere she is, but not severe ... No wonder Francis Thompson worshipped her! What a woman!' And Mrs Meynell's appreciation of him has increased his own sense of self-worth: 'Alice, my dear, likes me so much! I am so proud of that! I believe in myself now more than ever. At last I know, on Alice Meynell's authority, that I possess an "extraordinary felicity in the command of English."—They call me Sal! Think of it!'[186]

Ever the networker, de la Selva obviously found the Meynells' circle rather self-enclosed, so he wrote directly to the prime mover and shaker of the time, Ezra Pound, introducing himself as a friend of Amy Lowell and Harriet Monroe, and a writer of 'verse in Spanish'—even though most of his verse to date had been in English. He praises Pound's translations from the Spanish and floats the idea that Pound might contribute to a Spanish

---

[186] Letter from Salomón de la Selva to Theresa Helburn, THP (undated [early December 1918?]). He probably visited the Meynells at their London home: 47 Palace Court, Bayswater. They also had a house in Greatham, West Sussex. The 'beautiful' Mr Meynell was Alice's son Francis, just a couple of years older than Salomón.

Review (published in English) that he is going to edit in New York for the Hispanic Society of America. He expresses his wish to meet 'the literary people of London':

> So far, I know only the Meynells, who were extremely courteous to me; but like the stabler planets, they seem to move in a fixed plane, & but very seldom brush a comet or a shooting star. Will you not be my optic & reveal to me the frantic luminaries of London? You are their Saturn, I am told, & they take the madness from you.[187]

How could Pound resist? Back in New York de la Selva reported to Amy Lowell on his meeting:

> He's a funny fellow, merely funny. Had he really more life in him than he pretends to have, he'd be mad, which is a state of mind and heart to be lauded, whereas his pose, and I use the word advisedly, for though posing may be natural in him it is posing nonetheless, has a touch of the foolish that forces a derogation of his quality. It hurt me to find him so.[188]

What Ezra thought of Salomón remains unrecorded.

---

[187] Letter from Salomón de la Selva to Ezra Pound, EPP (22 February 1919). EPP is the Ezra Pound Papers (YCAL MSS 43), Beinecke Library, Yale University. This letter was written from the Eagle Hut, YMCA, in the Aldwych, set up to accommodate visiting US servicemen.

[188] Letter from Salomón de la Selva to Amy Lowell, ALP (11 April 1919).

Chapter Seven

The Last Dinner (1919)

> And a madness fell upon the king
> Watching the white and red grape drip.[1]

The death in January 1919 of Salomón de la Selva's old antagonist, Theodore Roosevelt, cast a long shadow across New York, suggesting the end of an era. Other titans of New York life died this year: Woolworth, Carnegie, Frick.[2] Although the fighting in Europe was over, the USA itself seemed in more turmoil than ever. Wall Street boomed while the cost of living soared and there were many strikes for higher pay. In February, 14 Spanish anarchists were arrested in New York on suspicion of plotting to assassinate Woodrow Wilson. In June, bombs exploded in eight US cities. The Attorney-General, A. Mitchell Palmer, created the General Intelligence Division of the Bureau of Investigation, headed by J. Edgar Hoover, which immediately moved to deport foreign radicals: 249 left for Russia in November, including Emma Goldman. The Red Scare permeated the city. In May, almost unnoticed, an earlier US bogeyman, José Santos Zelaya, died in Washington Heights.

There was action in many other fields. In March, the First Feminist Congress opened in New York; in June, the US Senate adopted a joint resolution submitting to the States the Women's Suffrage Amendment. That same month the Irish leader, Éamon de Valera, was smuggled off a ship in New York harbour, soon to make a dramatic public appearance—and to forge an important friendship with the Puerto Rican *independentista*, Pedro

---

[1] From Salomón de la Selva, 'Delgadina', *Tropical Town and Other Poems*, New York: John Lane Company, 1918, p. 131.

[2] Frank W. Woolworth (1852–8 April 1919), entrepreneur and store-owner; Andrew Carnegie (1835–11 August 1919), Scottish-born industrialist and philanthropist who made his fortune in steel; Henry Clay Frick (1849–2 December 1919), Pennsylvania-born industrialist who made his fortune in coal and then worked with Carnegie on the development of railroads.

Albizu Campos. Marcus Garvey's Black Star Line steamship, the SS *Frederick Douglass*, launched in September, the same month in which the founding of the African Blood Brotherhood was announced in *The Crusader*, edited by the Crucian, Cyril Briggs, one of Garvey's main critics.

The largest international context in the first half of 1919 was the Paris peace conference: Woodrow Wilson's articulation of the importance of self-determination to his view of a lasting post-war settlement had attracted much interest and support in Hispanic America, particularly since that articulation tended to draw on examples from the American continent. It therefore proved a major disappointment when Wilson refused to contemplate American issues at the conference.[3] In June, the Treaty of Versailles was signed, but the US Senate refused to ratify it, ending Wilson's dream of shaping the new world order. He was reminded of problems closer to home by a meeting of protest against the continuing US occupation of the Dominican Republic held in the Hotel Waldorf-Astoria in August. The Second Congress of the Pan-American Federation of Labor met in July at the less luxurious Hotel Continental, at West 41st and Broadway.[4]

In the cultural field, John Reed's *Ten Days That Shook the World* was published in March, reminding everyone of events in Russia—as if they needed reminding. Margaret Anderson's *The Little Review* continued serialising *Ulysses*. The Washington Square Players reorganised as the Theatre Guild, with its first production being *The Bonds of Interest*, a translation of Jacinto Benavente's *Los intereses creados*, in April, with Edna Millay in the rôle of Columbine. The appearance in November of Waldo Frank's *Our America*, in seeming ignorance of José Martí's 1890 essay of that title, demonstrated that US knowledge of its neighbours to the south still had some way to go, even though Frank offered a critique of US culture not very different from that of the *arielistas*. In the spring of 1919, at a party at Lola Ridge's apartment on East 14st Street, Emanuel Carnevali gave a dramatic speech attacking the city's poets: William Carlos Williams's response was in July the last act of *Others*.[5]

---

[3] Margaret MacMillan, *Peacemakers: The Paris Conference of 1919 and Its Attempt to End War*, London: John Murray, 2003, p. 17.

[4] See William K. Klingaman, *1919: The Year Our World Began*, New York: St Martin's Press, 1987; and William D. Miller, *Pretty Bubbles in the Air: America in 1919*, Urbana: University of Illinois Press, 1991.

[5] Carnevali's denunciation was published in his *A Hurried Man*, Paris: Three Mountains Press, 1925, pp. 247–68; Williams's not unsympathetic response was 'Belly Music', *Others*, 5, no. 6 (July 1919), 25–32.

Salomón de la Selva was out of the country for nearly a year and much had changed in his absence. Peace soon made travel easier and a new generation of Hispanic travellers made their way to New York. The Hispanic community in the city was more confident of its place, though concerns about US foreign policy remained. De la Selva reached New York in April to find his old friends Adolphe Roberts and Edna Millay had become lovers. Roberts had a book of poems in the pipeline and so Salomón took the opportunity to organise another—and what would be the final—pan-American dinner. It was a grand occasion, but a last hurrah—not least because the drinking of alcohol was about to become illegal.

Nueva York

Pan-Americanism was a contested idea during these years, but there was little doubt that in terms of street-level experience New York was the pan-American city *por excelencia*. In March 1919, three months before the dinner at Gonfarone's, the city's Spanish-language newspaper, *La Prensa*, made this point. It noted the various pan-American initiatives in operation: the Pan American Union in Washington, DC, the various inter-American congresses and conferences, the academic and political visitors between what it saw as the two continents, the growing number of Spanish-American students in the USA, and the international press. But *La Prensa* itself, the writer (probably the editor, Alfredo Collao) claimed, offered 'a daily course in Pan Americanism':

> Nowhere better to do this work of interamerican contact than the city of New York because this is the crucible where the Latin-American spirit is forged. There is no other city in the world where there are more Latin Americans from all countries. Here an Argentinian, a Chilean, or a Mexican can find out more about their brother countries than in their homelands. New York is precisely called the centre of true pan-Americanism.[6]

In other words, there is important pan-American work to be done and nowhere better to do it than New York. But, at the same time—and this is a perspective entirely *nuevayorkino*—America is not just two continents, it is 20 or so different countries, and even the ones speaking Spanish benefit from a neutral ground in which to get to know each other.

---

[6] 'Lazo de unión entre las dos Américas', *La Prensa*, 7 March 1919, p. 4.

A similar note was struck, but even more loudly and at greater length, in an essay by the Venezuelan writer Jesús Semprúm, which had originally appeared in *Actualidades* (Caracas) in December 1918 and was eagerly seized on by Peter Goldsmith for the June 1919 number of *Inter-America* on account of its argument that South American perception of the North had been 'profoundly and perceptibly altered' by selfless US participation in the recently concluded war.[7] Perhaps most striking, though, is Semprúm's blithe obliviousness in his essay to the fact that he himself had once enthusiastically embraced *arielismo* in Venezuela. Aged 19, he had founded a literary group called Ariel, whose members announced their *modernista* credentials by wearing their clothes black and their hair long. Their journal was called *Ariel*, and Semprúm wrote an essay called … 'Ariel'. His first longer work, *El canal de Panamá* (1912) was a denunciation of US imperialism. So this 1918 essay was very much a volte-face, implicitly critical of his earlier, naïve self. He recalls how South Americans, 'envenomed by a multitude of purely rhetorical phrases and falsehoods', had sarcastically communicated the victory of the lusty Calibanic barbarian of the North over the delicate and exquisite spirituality of the South.[8] He namechecks the most popular writers at whose door this misrepresentation might be laid: José Enrique Rodó, José María Vargas Vila, Rubén Darío, Rufino Blanco Fombona, and Manuel Ugarte. Almost magically, he reports, Caliban has vanished and in his stead stands Ariel. Admittedly, if the USA had an Ariel figure, it would probably be Woodrow Wilson, whose moment this was, but nonetheless, as a characterisation of US culture as a whole, this is quite some transformation. To the extent that the transformation is a real one based in changes in US politics, as opposed to a mere correction in Latin American perception, then Theodore Roosevelt is figured as the Caliban whose attitudes no longer hold sway. But Semprúm offers much more: a self-excoriating, if simplistic, analysis of the differences between North and South American cultures based on their very different histories; and a rather perceptive critique of the gap visible in the *modernista* generation between intellectuals and the masses.

To a large extent, this embrace of woodrovian idealism was a will-o'-the-wisp which would quickly dissipate during the Paris Peace Congress. Coincidentally or not, a few weeks after the English translation of his essay appeared in New York, Semprúm arrived in the city himself, yet another

---

[7] Jesús Semprúm, 'The North and the South: The United States and Latin America—Observations upon a Timely Subject', *Inter-America*, 2 (October 1918–August 1919), 327–39, at 327.

[8] Semprúm, 'The North and the South', 327.

self-exile from the unfriendly regime of Juan Vicente Gómez. He would stay until 1926, following his beloved Poe into alcoholism and eventually dying in abject poverty back in Venezuela in 1931.[9]

The *Juegos Florales* organised by *La Prensa* in May 1919 were the clearest sign yet of a newly confident Hispanic community in New York—as well as of the new financial health of the newspaper itself. The poetic contest of floral games dated back to the troubadour tradition in Toulouse in the fourteenth century, but had been revived in Barcelona in the late nineteenth. Perhaps more pertinently, a Chilean version had been held in 1914 in Santiago, launching the career of Lucila Godoy, who had entered under the name of Gabriela Mistral. These New York games—the first to be held in the city— were constantly advertised in *La Prensa* during the early months of the year, with the festivities taking place at the beginning of May in Carnegie Hall. An imposing advert in the paper emphasised the significance of the occasion: 'North Americans,' it noted, 'generally say that everything coming from the Hispanic community is a failure.'[10] But—the message was—we will prove them wrong. There were cash prizes in three categories—poetry, fiction, essay—with the winner of the poetry competition also getting to choose the Queen of the event. Prize money totalled $950. The essay title set was 'The spiritual and material unity of Hispanic and Anglo-saxon America. Why hasn't it been achieved? How can it be brought about quickly and effectively?' The jury was a distinguished one: Federico de Onís, José Castellot, Thomas Walsh, Orestes Ferrara, and Pedro Henríquez Ureña (although only the first three were present in Carnegie Hall for the awards). Submitted were 200 lyric poems, 50 essays, and 135 stories. The Spanish Embassy, the HSA, and PAU all sponsored the prizes. There were speeches and music as well as the prize presentations. Everybody was dressed elegantly, and everything was warmly applauded. This was a community demonstrating—*La Prensa* underlined—that it was well-organised, well-behaved, and highly cultured.

On the Monday after the prize-giving (5 May), the report on the games filled the front page of *La Prensa*. José Castellot *hijo*—the son of the Mexican banker and translator—had been MC for the day. The Mexican poet, Joaquín Méndez Rivas, had been awarded first prize in the poetry competition for his poem 'La sementera'. He had immediately crowned as

---

[9] He wrote a series of letters from New York back to Venezuelan newspapers: in Jesús Semprúm, *Crítica, visiones y diálogos*, Caracas: Fundación Biblioteca Ayacucho, 2006, pp. 445–78.
[10] *La Prensa*, 3 May 1919, p. 5.

Queen, Luz Requena Legarreta, sister of Méndez Rivas's recently deceased countryman, Pedro Requena Legarreta. The essay prize was awarded to none other than Manuel F. Cestero, the newspaper's own columnist, with the story prize going to Jesusa Alfau for 'Mentira'. Luz Requena had been glowingly profiled by Cestero a couple of months earlier.[11] Everything was being kept in the family. On the following days, *La Prensa* printed tributes to Luz from five admirers, including Manuel Cestero, Alfonso Guillén Zelaya, and José Juan Tablada; an appreciation of Cestero by Rene Borgia, followed by Cestero's essay; Alfau's story and profile came the next day; then one of the runners-up in the poetry contest, 'Yo soy tu flauta', by Luis Muñoz Marín.[12]

With uncanny timing, on Sunday, 4 May 1919, *The Sun* had a full-page feature entitled 'New York's Latin Colonies Form Picturesque Sections of City Life', which offers a useful snapshot of Hispanic life in the city just as de la Selva returned. The journalist, Eileen O'Connor, noted the vigorous growth of the Hispanic community. She estimated the number at around 1,500 in 1898, falling to 400 early in the century, before beginning the spurt which saw it grow to around 250,000 in 1919, about 4 per cent of the population of Manhattan. It's now difficult to miss them:

> They appear in smiling, dark complexioned groups, casting nuts to the squirrels in Central Park. We meet them in the furthest downtown districts and along the wharves. They congregate in and about the Hispanic Museum and the contiguous green squares on fete days. They give hearty handed and soft voiced applause at the theatre and operas.[13]

She notes four particular clusters on the island. One is in and around the apartment hotels that the better-off of the long-term residents and sojourners favour—the Ansonia, the Majestic, and the Walton, roughly Broadway and the lower 70s on the West Side. The Asociación Ibero-Americana de los Estados Unidos had its meeting place at Broadway and West 72nd.[14] Another cluster is further up Broadway, near the Hispanic Society complex, between 155th and 160th—still, or again, in 2019 a solidly Hispanic

---

[11] Manuel F. Cestero, 'En broma y en serio', *La Prensa*, 20 February 1919, p. 4.

[12] *La Prensa*, 6 May 1919, p. 4; 7 May 1919, pp. 4, 6; 8 May 1919, pp. 2, 4; 14 May 1919, p. 4.

[13] Eileen O'Connor, 'New York's Latin Colonies Form Picturesque Sections of City Life', *The Sun*, 4 May 1919, Magazine section, p. 3.

[14] Almost all of the individual Hispanic countries had their own clubs too. The President of the AIA was F. A. Pezet, a Peruvian government official, who was also president of the Peruvian Club.

neighbourhood.[15] (Another Hispanic club, La Luz, was further south at 200 Lenox Avenue [120th Street].)[16] A third area is the older Spanish section around West 14th Street, including the Spanish church at 229 on that street and, a little further east, the Hotel America at Irving Place. And the fourth area is down by the East River docks: South, Cherry, Maiden, Pearl, Wall streets—another traditional Hispanic area, but poorer: home to two of the city's best-known Spanish restaurants, Angelo's and Don Americano's.

In some ways—although *The Sun* article doesn't mention it—a sign of the growing importance of the transient Hispanic element in the city was the extent to which the larger hotels went out of their way to attract the custom. The Felix-Portland advertised in the Spanish-language press; the McAlpin ran a Latin American supper dance every Tuesday evening through the summer of 1919 on its rooftop garden and its ninth was 'the Spanish-American floor' where all employees were Spanish-speakers.

The article in *The Sun* mentions a long list of notable Hispanic figures resident in or spending significant time in New York: Orestes Ferrara, originally Italian but a *mambí* general in the Cuban war of independence and an influential politician and journalist in Cuba; Manuel Calero, prominent Liberal politician in Mexico, exiled by Huerta; Enrique Gil, the Argentine lawyer. There is also a whole raft of Hispanic businessmen in Wall Street—perhaps more in 1919 than in 2019. These particular figures don't feature in the story here, but they would only be a couple of degrees of separation away from de la Selva and his friends, partly because many of them, like Ferrara, were also journalists, partly because through the Henríquez Ureñas there was a direct connection to state-level politics.

Earlier in 1919, *The Sun* had inaugurated a South American section every Monday, called the 'Latin American Colony in New York', usually two pages of news, mostly but not exclusively commercial: it advertised itself as 'A valuable ally for manufacturers and business houses anxious to obtain a firmer footing in the rich South American markets.'[17] As well as news of trade missions and advertisements by banks and corporations seeking to invest in South America, the pages contained specially commissioned articles by

---

[15] Interestingly, of the half dozen reasons O'Connor gives for the rise in the Hispanic population of the city in the early twentieth century—trade, the education system, etc.—one of them is simply Archer Huntington.

[16] There were plenty of other Hispanic clubs too: Mexican Union and American Friendship, Chile-America Association, Centro Hispano Americano, Ibero-American Knights, the Spanish American Benevolent Society. The Club Aspiraciones was founded specifically to study Latin American literature and had as early members Dmitri Ivanovitch and Rene Borgia (*The Sun*, 20 October 1919, p. 10).

[17] *The Sun*, 14 April 1919, p. 12.

Hispanic journalists, notes from the various consulates, and the occasional poem or book review. With *La Prensa* now being published daily, there was a growing sense of a consolidated Hispanic community in New York. In April, *The Sun* announced the return to New York of Salomón de la Selva.[18]

A Soldier Returns

The troop ship SS *Mauretania* docked at Pier 54 at the foot of West 13th Street at 7 p.m. on the evening of Monday, 7 April 1919, carrying 1,080 US troops and 2,700 who had served with the British Army, including de la Selva. Salomón's old friend, Pedro Henríquez Ureña, was there to greet him, having arrived in the city that same week to act as one of the judges for the *Juegos Florales*.

Between the middle of July 1918 and the middle of November, just after the Armistice, de la Selva wrote 25 letters that have been located: many more, in all probability. From the middle of November 1918 until the end of 1919 (excluding dinner invitations), only 16, many of them undated. We are now used to the idea of post-traumatic stress disorder, or what at the time was called shell shock. De la Selva's letters from this period suggest that he had psychological difficulty in coming to terms with the fact that he had *not* been in combat, after having spent many months preparing himself to fight in the trenches.

One senses an initial feeling of inadequacy: heroism in combat, preferably with a (not-too-serious) wound as visible evidence, would prove his manhood—as much to himself as to anyone else. The dreamer in him even fantasised a heroic death. The instruction to Jeanne Robert Foster to tell his son that 'I never forgot I was a gentleman' is ridiculous on several levels, if chiefly for the fact that he had no son. One might speculate about some deep sense of failure, compounded when he didn't get to wield his bayonet in anger; or about the sense of guilt if, instead of a son left behind in New York, he actually had a daughter growing up in shameful circumstances in León. In the end, we don't know his motivation, so can only trace the strange lineaments of the profile his mind leaves on the pages of these letters.

Back in New York his chief correspondents remained Jeanne Robert Foster and Theresa Helburn, but the letters are sparser, both women having acquired lovers in de la Selva's absence.[19] There are two letters to Florence Schauffler, but then they seem to have quarrelled, probably on account of Jeanne's young

---

[18] *The Sun*, 21 April 1919, p. 11.
[19] In her autobiography, Helburn says that she fell in love with her future husband on 8 April 1919, perhaps coincidentally Salomón's first day back on US soil. De la

protégée, Marya Zaturenska. The first letter to Florence was probably written in late April or early May since it refers to a visit to Archer Huntington which had also involved meeting Thomas Walsh—a meeting Huntington refers to in his diary as taking place on 12 April, just five days after de la Selva's return to New York. This letter touches on some of Salomón's usual themes, but there is a bitter edge to the tone, and he adopts the characteristic technique of the unhinged in referring to himself in the third person: 'Nothing threatens Sal that he knows of.' At the beginning of the letter he's making arrangements to open a little school of his own; by the end he's planning on setting up in business as an interior decorator in partnership with Phil Culkin (a young neighbour on West 98th Street). Huntington has disappointed his hopes of getting a job as editor of one of the Hispanic Society of America magazines—and is rewarded with the epithet 'jelly fish'; while Tom Walsh, whom Huntington has forced him to shake hands with, is called 'the fat louse'.[20] 'Military training has made a new man of Salomon de la Selva,' Huntington notes.[21] It certainly seems to have expanded his vocabulary.

The second letter to Florence suggests even more psychological disturbance. There has been a disagreement or misunderstanding with Charles Schauffler ('the Fraternal Pa'), which has occasioned letters and telegrams from the Schaufflers, but Salomón is taking the blame on himself:

Not the Fraternal Pa, but *I* was foolish & unreasonable. Nothing he would do should hurt me; for my better self—what is in me the Poet—knows him for a true friend and filled with nothing but the most unquestioning love for little Sal.—But the devil in me has the upper hand; it had been too long under control, gathering power it seems, & the trifling occurrence at your house was merely a basis for his sophistries.

The self is divided:

That *I* that is good felt no offence and harbours no ill feeling, no regret, no sense of wounded pride. But the bad self is all hot and unappeasable; it is bound to unmake all my friendships: I have quarrelled with everybody, & from those I love most I keep myself the farthest away.—

Selva makes no appearance in her memoirs, although she kept his letters (Theresa Helburn, *A Wayward Quest*, Boston: Little, Brown and Co., 1960, p. 62).

[20] Letter from Salomón de la Selva to Florence Schauffler, SFP (undated [late April 1919?]).

[21] Archer M. Huntington, 'Dairies', Hispanic Society of America (12 April 1919).

Too long a stretch of mental & sentimental strain; army bother, poems, deep concerns over my Mother & my two little sisters' fate when her guidance is gone;—these things have unmade me. Apparently, & that is the tragedy of it, I am neither sick nor insane. But I should be sent to a hospital, or to a prison.—I feel all this, I know it as well as God Himself, and am powerless. It is a most strange case of soul-disorder. You cannot imagine what vile things I have done, those very things that are most repugnant to me, most unlike my ways & taste. And I can't help it!—All the badness in me must waste itself away before I can be again the only *I* you know, for whom you have cared so devotedly. Please wait!

Just one girlfriend gets a mention: 'The Little Lady G. is in town; she 'phoned me, but I don't answer any calls; I have told my landlady to say I am out. What her address is, I don't know; this is her 'phone number: Mad. Sq. 8619.—Please tell her I died in some accident.'[22] The Little Lady G. is Grace, the daughter of Elizabeth H. (Mrs Chester) Griswold. Salomón had written about his strong but chaste feelings for Elizabeth back in 1917. Grace—now aged 12—seems to have had a childish crush on Salomón, which was perhaps beginning to annoy him.

There are a few letters to Jeanne Foster, but without the passion of the previous year. In July 1919, Salomón was working for Potter Brothers, and staying in the city for Amanda's birthday: Amanda Culkin (Philip's sister) would turn 17 that summer. Salomón had bought her a wristwatch. She seems—if he can be trusted—to be another teenage girl infatuated with him, because he writes to Jeanne: 'If you do not love me truly, & if you do not intend to love me forever, you are doing Amanda a great wrong keeping me from her. Poor Amanda! either way she cannot have me.'[23] Three weeks later, a final letter to Jeanne (but calling her Catherine) suggests that he's working hard, both at the office and at his own writing: 'Amanda goes to the country Saturday. Work is pouring on me at the office. But I can manage it all without getting tired. I still love you and ever will; but if you were here, and called me, I would not go to you. I must write something very great, very worthy of you, before I feel that I deserve you again'.[24]

---

[22] Letter from Salomón de la Selva to Florence Schauffler, SFP (undated [May 1919?]).
[23] Letter from Salomón de la Selva to Jeanne Robert Foster, FMC (11 July 1919). Potter Brothers—originally from Liverpool—was a New York banking firm with extensive coffee plantations around Matagalpa in northern Nicaragua.
[24] Letter from Salomón de la Selva to Jeanne Robert Foster, FMC (30 July 1919).

25 Marya Zaturenska. Provenance unknown.

The most troublesome youngster to now join the epistolary harem was Marya Zaturenska (Fig. 25), who in later life would marry Horace Gregory and become a pillar of the New York literary establishment, but who was now in 1919, under Jeanne Robert Foster's tutelage, just beginning to submit her poems to magazines. The correspondence between Jeanne and Salomón had begun in June 1918, in that frantic month before he joined the British Army, though they may have known each other from the PSA for some time before that. Marya must have met him through Jeanne and was clearly in thrall, if a little shocked. Jeanne reports one of Marya's anecdotes, which probably dates from autumn 1918:

> Mr Kreymborg introduced me to Muna Lee, a Russian Jewish poetess ... who said that Salomón was engaged to her for three blissful months but failed to turn up at the time appointed for the wedding. I think he left her waiting on the steps of City Hall! She was quite unreserved about her disappointment! Did you ever hear of another such lady-killer

---

Amanda Culkin and her family lived opposite Salomón on the Upper West Side at 131 West 98th Street (he was now at 128). The father was a New York policeman. Philip Culkin, now 21, seems to have been a protégé of Salomón's: he studied art at Columbia Extension and at night played piano in Greenwich Village. He would attend the dinner at Gonfarone's.

26 Muna Lee in 1930.
Courtesy Jonathan Cohen.

as our Sal! I have lost all my respect for him, though my affection for him is as strong as ever. Besides he was always good, and sweet, and a brother to *me*. So I am going to stick by him if everybody else in the world leaves him.[25]

Alfred Kreymborg was an important editor and poet, but there was nothing Russian or Jewish about Muna Lee (Fig. 26), from Mississippi via Oklahoma. She, however, had clearly taken the previous year's flirtation in Chicago a good deal more seriously than Salomón, although by now she had met Luis Muñoz Marín: they would marry in July.

De la Selva had written to Marya from England, she tells Jeanne, announcing his arrival.[26] Marya is obviously concerned that he be kept apart from a Mr Levy, though whether she sees them as rivals for her

---

[25] Londraville and Londraville, *Dear Yeats*, pp. 107–08. Unreferenced, so presumably taken either from Foster's unpublished diary or from a letter now in a private collection.
[26] Letter from Marya Zaturenska to Jeanne Robert Foster, FMC (undated [March 1919?]).

affection or something else altogether is unclear. In March 1919, Marya was sixteen and a half. In his first 1919 letter to Florence Schauffler, de la Selva wrote: 'I went to see Marya, & was very mean to her, but it's because she has queer ideas about reforming me, just as if I had come out of a penitentiary instead of having been a soldier in a glorious cause.'[27] A few months later, on holiday in upper New York State, Marya wrote to Jeanne to enquire about Florence Schauffler, asks if Jeanne sees Sal, and announces that she is going to be bridesmaid at the wedding of Luis Muñoz Marín and Muna Lee.[28]

Exactly what happened between Marya and Salomón is unclear. He denied any romantic involvement with her, but he was certainly not above a bit of flirting—and this with a girl who was still in her teens and whose head was almost bound to be turned by the attention. The following year he received a letter from her that he replied to on 27 March 1920, shortly after returning to New York from a trip home to Nicaragua. Since he didn't have her address, he sent the letter to Jeanne Robert Foster, asking her to forward it. She probably did so, but she typed out a copy to keep. He recalls the last time they met:

> I saw you—I had looked forward very much to seeing you!—and I was very glad that you winged me a kiss at sight of me across the crowded hall. I love intimate messages that come tripping over fools' heads and that reach me out of breath; but I love even better the things that fly to me, and your kiss flew! Had it had no wings, had it had to run, it would have reached me breathing hard and open-mouthed, and I would not have liked it a bit. I thought now that I have never kissed you; and was a little sorry, a little happy, thinking also that should either of us die, there would be that one dear thing that never was to remember of the dead: a memory somehow like a lovely cup—empty! For when I was a soldier you wrote me promising a kiss, and I dreamed much of it, so wrought a bright pure chalice of desire. I still have that cup of longing.

One can understand Jeanne's anxiety: this was epistolary grooming.

De la Selva also recalls their first meeting, introducing an extraordinary image in which he appears as her mother:

---

[27] Letter from Salomón de la Selva to Florence Schauffler, SFP (undated [late April 1919?]).
[28] Letter from Marya Zaturenska to Jeanne Robert Foster, FMC (undated [June 1919?]).

> I remember the hungry-mouthed heart I met at a concert in a shabby hall in the poor district of New York; and I remember how very motherly my soul, that is always wet-nursing, gave that starving heart his fullest breasts to nourish it,—Marya whatever you may do, milk of my soil is blood in your heart's conduits; you are my child; I cannot choose but love you! ... I shall not kiss you yet, but hold you warm and close to my breast and feed you so, and do you gurgle when you have had your fill, and do you go to sleep and to your dreams: I will watch over you.

The letter is long enough to contain advice about her writing ('You must learn to punctuate') and details of his plans ('I am marrying a Central American girl'); but a central paragraph recalls an obscure incident for which Marya has contritely apologised in the letter to which de la Selva is replying:

> By that dreadful accusation you brought against me, although I tried not to be hurt, you hurt me very much. I had liked the Schaufflers very dearly, but they believed your stories and [for] a time—telling me not—they smiled and chatted while I play-acted harmlessly for the sake of a release from the grief of living, and in their minds, hiddenly and openly when my back was turned, they said to themselves of me 'The hypocrite'. They were glad they 'had my number' and I 'could not fool them'. Now I find it painful to be in their company. They are sure now that I did you never any wrong; they have tried to reassure me that I am well in their opinion; but I have once given my friendship to them, I have once felt for them that all I might do I would for their sake; that all the world might say of them, I would stand by them; but for me, when the least they might have done, considering that I called them 'Mother, Father, Brother' was to doubt, they had no such charity but in their conscience damned me. They may take me to their topmost heaven: I have been in their hell and there is no balm in any Gilead for those infernal burns.[29]

It is difficult to see beyond the idea that she had accused him of some sexual impropriety. The accusation had soured at least some of his friendships and may perhaps have been one of the reasons he left New York in 1919.

Having observed his teacher and friend at close quarters Bennet Schauffler was under no illusions. From Europe he wrote to his fiancée: 'Of course you would enjoy Sal. His attitude toward women I find, as you suggest,

---

[29] Letter from Salomón de la Selva to Marya Zaturenska, FMC (27 March 1920).

thoroughly selfish and generally damnable, with all that he is the most generous, open hearted and kindly soul in so many ways.'[30] Given this, his later defence of de la Selva must be considered as solid:

> I don't know what to do about Marya. I have undeniable written evidence that she has deliberately lied and put forward the most shameful implications in order to discredit Sal with his friends. Curiously enough, she herself gave me the letter which is conclusive proof of his innocence of any wrong toward her, and she gave it to me as proof of his guilt. I do not understand that … I am glad, very glad, that Sal was not guilty of those things, and that there was proof of that, because I can not ever be quite sure when he is telling the truth.[31]

Just the following day, Bennet reported with much glee on a 'poetical party' he'd attended the previous evening: 'You would have died to see Sal confronted at the same time by three very different girls to each of whom he had evidently made more or less violent love upon one occasion or another. (Marya was not there.) It was a sight worth watching.'[32] Edna and Theresa Helburn were both there, probably equally amused.

The Dinner at Gonfarone's

Walter Adolphe Roberts (Fig. 27) appeared in the last chapter as a new friend of de la Selva's: a recipient of correspondence and somebody to be asked after during Salomón's sojourn in the British Army. They'd been moving in the same circles since 1914: Salomón went to the Liberal Club in Greenwich Village while Roberts was secretary there, so they may have become acquainted; but Roberts had then spent two years in Paris, only returning to New York in 1916, so equally they may not have met until early 1918. Born in Jamaica to a genteelly impoverished white family, Adolphe Roberts had been a keen writer from childhood and as a teenager was already working as a journalist on local Kingston newspapers.[33] He moved to the USA in 1904, aged 17, and after a few years of travel settled down in New York, initially eking out a precarious existence. As a child, Roberts had had a romantic attachment to the Cuban war of

---

[30] Letter from Bennet Schauffler to Marjorie Page, SFP Box 1 (undated [late 1917]).
[31] Letter from Bennet Schauffler to Marjorie Page, SFP Box 1 (4 May 1919).
[32] Letter from Bennet Schauffler to Marjorie Page, SFP Box 1 (5 May 1919).
[33] See W. Adolphe Roberts, *These Many Years: An Autobiography*, ed. Peter Hulme, Kingston: University of the West Indies Press, 2015.

27 W. Adolphe Roberts in 1917. Walter Adolphe Roberts Archive (MS 353), National Library of Jamaica. Courtesy of the National Library of Jamaica.

independence, fought just 150 miles to the north of Kingston. In the USA, travelling across the country and trying to make a living as a journalist, he was tempted by a job with a railroad construction firm just across the border in Sonora where he got to witness first-hand the Mexican attempt to exterminate the Yaqui Indians. Once in San Francisco, he wrote 'The Tragedy of the Yaqui' for *The Overland Monthly*, one of the first accounts in English of the genocide that would soon be denounced in New York by John Kenneth Turner in an essay for the *American Magazine*.[34] He also wrote other stories with a Mexican theme such as 'A Beat on El Correo' and 'La Sonorense', so he was probably disposed to respond warmly to the denizens of Hispanic New York.[35] Travelling to Paris, Roberts managed to get a job on the *Brooklyn Daily Eagle* and, when the First World War broke

---

[34] As Walter Adolf Roberts, 'Tragedy of the Yaqui', *The Overland Monthly*, 53, no. 2 (August 1908), 119–21; John Kenneth Turner, 'The Tragic Story of the Yaquis', *American Magazine*, 69 (November 1909), 44.

[35] 'A Beat on El Correo', *The Overland Monthly*, 54, no. 1 (July 1909), 85–89 and 'La Sonorense', *The Smart Set*, 33, no. 1 (January 1911), 75–79, both as Walter Adolf Roberts.

out, he worked as a war correspondent, visiting the trenches, interviewing Georges Clemenceau, and interpreting the intricacies of European politics for his New York readers.

Back in New York around November 1917 Roberts was asked by the editor of *Ainslee's Magazine*, Robert Rudd Whiting, to take temporary charge while Whiting took up a position with the Bureau for Public Information in Washington. *Ainslee's* was a middle-brow monthly owned by Street & Smith and famous for having published the first O. Henry story. When Whiting died in the influenza outbreak in October 1918, Roberts's position became permanent. *Ainslee's* had been an important outlet for Salomón de la Selva, publishing five of his poems from November 1915 onwards under Whiting's editorship, so the Nicaraguan soon visited Roberts at the Street & Smith offices in Chelsea (the 6th floor of 79 Seventh Avenue, between West 15th and 16th Streets) to ensure that the sequence would continue.[36] The tastes of the two men proved entirely compatible and they became good friends. *Ainslee's* published another 12 de la Selva poems under Roberts's editorship. They knew each other well enough for Salomón to write warmly to Roberts from England in the summer of 1918 and for him to organise the party to celebrate the publication of Roberts's first book in June 1919—the dinner at Gonfarone's. Roberts's Hispanic interests may also have been a factor in Salomón's determination that the publication of his friend's book was suitable for a *pan-American* event.

De la Selva's friendships were distinctly gendered. Most of his close male friends were Hispanic: his mentor, Pedro Henríquez Ureña, his long-term room-mate, Rufino González Mesa, the Cuban he spent his army months alongside, Miguel Ramos; while most of his US friends were female: too numerous to mention. There may be good reasons for this: *most* Hispanic writers in New York were men—but by no means all, as we'll shortly see. And, as always, researchers are at the mercy of what has survived in the archives. However, as far as is known, Clement Wood and Adolphe Roberts are the only male contemporaries to whom de la Selva wrote with any consistency. (Edwin Markham was a generation older.) In his autobiography, Roberts wrote a deft pen-portrait, noting that Salomón was 'full of Catholic sentiment rather than mysticism, and … liked to portray himself as a sinner fallen under the spell of the old pagan gods'. He produced sonnets with the utmost fluency, Roberts writes: 'At dinner one night I heard him reel off, on a challenge, an unrhymed sonnet in iambic pentameters that somehow rang with the traditional sound effects'.[37]

---

[36] Roberts, *These Many Years: An Autobiography*, pp. 210–12.
[37] Roberts, *These Many Years: An Autobiography*, pp. 211–12.

De la Selva had mentioned Edna Millay to Roberts as one of the three most important young poets in the country: Stephen Vincent Benét was the third. But Roberts, like all poetry aficionados, already knew of Millay from the 'Renascence' scandal, so once he had his feet under the desk at *Ainslee's* he invited her to his office, offered to publish her poems on a regular basis and concocted the scheme of getting her to write short stories under the pseudonym Nancy Boyd, which—since *Ainslee's* paid by the word—made her much more money than her poems. Within weeks they were lovers.[38]

Roberts's own love-life was fairly tangled at this time. At the end of 1917, he had married Katharine Hickey, whom he'd meet at Petitpas' before the war. In his autobiography he is at a loss to explain just why they got married, and they didn't stay together very long. In all probability he married her on the rebound from his passionate relationship with Margaret Sanger. This may have begun in 1913 (he certainly knew her then) and been interrupted by his Parisian interlude (during which time he lived with a woman called Madeleine Lebourg), but it was at its height during 1916 and the first part of 1917, when he was working with her on *The Birth Control Review*. Edna would be his chief focus for most of 1919, but she always had more than one string to her bow. Roberts may also have been dating the writer Vennette Herron (Fig. 28) during these months: he was certainly publishing plenty of her stories in *Ainslee's*.

Adolphe Roberts had been writing poems for many years and getting the odd one published in newspapers and magazines, but the inspiration for collecting his poems into a book had probably come from the success of his adaptation of a 1915 French poem, 'Pierrot Blessé', by Pierre Alberty, which he must have come across in Paris. Roberts's translation, 'Pierrot Wounded', had appeared in the *New York Times* in February 1917, and then had been picked up by the Chicago-based The Brothers of the Book, who included it in an anthology on the Pierrot theme as well as having it printed in a brochure, the proceeds from which were devoted to the American Fund for French Wounded. It was also set to music and performed at Columbia University, in July 1917.[39] These are the opening lines:

> Pierrot has wakened, stricken in the night—
> Wounded and stricken in the pale moonlight!

---

[38] Roberts, *These Many Years: An Autobiography*, pp. 215–26.
[39] W. Adolphe Roberts, 'Pierrot Wounded', *New York Times*, 21 February 1917, p. 9; *Mon ami Pierrot: Songs and Fantasies*, ed. Kendall Banning, Chicago: Brothers of the Book, 1917; *Pierrot Wounded with Music for the Pianoforte by Rossetter G. Cole*, op. 33, Boston: Arthur P. Schmidt Co., 1917.

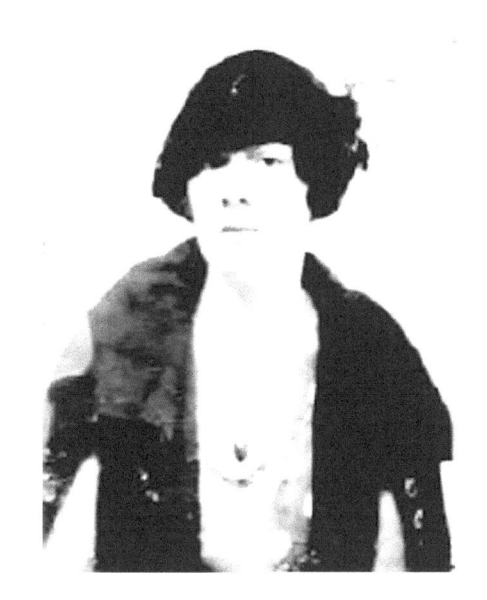

28 Vennette Herron.
Passport photograph 1921.
Provenance unknown.

>See, with the mud,
>The crimson flood
>That, drop by drop, is fed by his young blood!
>A thicket shields his bed upon the ground.
>He will not listen to the cruel sound
>Of shells on high,
>That shrieking fly
>And rend the somber velvet of the sky.[40]

The *commedia dell'arte* figures of Pierrot, Columbine, and Harlequin had seen a surge of popularity in the early years of the century. Influenced by Jules Laforgue, T. S. Eliot's early poems were using them, and they appeared in many of Picasso's paintings at this time, as well as in the performances of the Ballets Russes.[41] After appearing as Columbine in *The Bonds of Interest*, Edna Millay herself used the Pierrot and Columbine figures in what is regarded as her anti-war play, *Aria da Capo*. Pierrot was, then, already

---

[40] W. Adolphe Roberts, 'Pierrot Wounded', in *Pierrot Wounded and Other Poems*, New York: Britton Publishing Co., 1919, p. 3.
[41] For background, see Robert F. Storey, *Pierrot: A Critical History of a Mask*, Princeton, NJ: Princeton University Press, 1978; and Martin Green, *The Triumph of Pierrot: The Commedia dell'arte and the Modern Imagination*, University Park: Pennsylvania State University Press, 1993.

familiar as a war figure: in his downcast mode he could personify Belgium or France, as in the popular story *Pierrot, Dog of Belgium*.[42] Roberts's book *Pierrot Wounded and Other Poems* was dedicated to his wife Katharine, but each of the four sections carries its own dedication: 'Songs from France' to Salomón de la Selva; 'Villanelles' to Edna St Vincent Millay; 'Dialogue at Sunset' to Harold Hersey (another friend with whom Roberts had worked on *The Birth Control Review*); 'Juvenilia' to his mother, Josephine Fannie Roberts.[43]

*

The temper of the New York times in which this last dinner took place can be indicated by several other events from the spring and early summer of 1919. At the beginning of June 1919, the Second Pan American Commercial Conference took place in Washington, DC. The disposition of the conference can be gauged by the remarks of Manuel de J. Camacho, Consul General of the Dominican Republic in New York—the Dominican Republic currently occupied by US troops and controlled by a US colonel:

> It is not to be denied that the work of the Pan American Union has been more than efficient, and therefore worthy of praise, because that institution has carried to the remotest corners of the American Continent the ego of the sentiment of the trade of the United States and has made the North American public familiar with the Latin American standpoint.
>
> It is my opinion, like that of many others, that if American commerce continues to be carried on in the manner that it has been conducted lately. there will be no other market in the whole world for Latin American products than the United States.[44]

Total abjection was the order of the day. Pan American commerce had nothing to do with trade between the countries of the continent: it was focused entirely on trade between the USA and all the other countries. To

---

[42] Walter A. Dyer, *Pierrot, Dog of Belgium*, Garden City, NY: Doubleday, Page & Company, 1915.

[43] 'Ce livre est affectueusement dédié à Katharine Amelia Roberts, une amie de la France'.

[44] *Report of the Second Pan American Commercial Conference. Prepared by John Barrett, Director General of the Pan American Union*, Washington, DC: Pan American Union, 1919, p. 153.

underline the situation of the Dominican Republic, Camacho's remarks on trade were followed by remarks on the commerce and industry of the island made by Colonel G. C. Thorpe of the US Marine Corps. As the conference finished, the Director-General, John Barrett, hailed the benefits of a continental vision based on improved communications— better passenger, freight, and mail steamship services, improvement in the administration of consular offices, the construction of highways and railroads, the improvement of news and cable services.[45] In other words, lots more opportunities for US commercial interests to expand. This was the Pan-Americanism that made the rest of the continent nervous and that made de la Selva's task harder and harder.

Apart from Roberts and Millay, top of de la Selva's guest list would have been Edwin Markham. No serious literary occasion could pass without him—which probably explains the decline in his poetic output: he rarely turned down invitations. Markham had already had a busy year. On 30 January, he attended and spoke at the Annual Dinner of the Poetry Society of America, held at the National Arts Club, with around 270 guests. On 23 February, he was at the Hotel Biltmore (335 Madison Avenue) for a dinner given for John Galsworthy by the Society of Arts and Science. Then a birthday dinner was given in *his* honour on 23 April by the Joint Committee of Literary Arts at the Commodore Hotel on Park Avenue and East 42nd Street, 'in recognition of his genius as a poet and his worth as a man'.[46] The theme of the evening was 'Arts and Letters as Welding Forces in International Relationships'. Galsworthy was present to return the compliment, and there was official French and Italian presence too as well as the great and the good of literary New York: John G. Agar, Edward J. Wheeler, Hamlin Garland, Ernest Poole, Augustus Thomas, and so on. But the most telling of Markham's dinner engagements that spring suggests how thinly he was spreading himself, as well as giving a nice indication of the forms of left-liberalism at the time. A few years earlier a Russian immigrant called Misha Appelbaum, who had made a fortune in the metals business, founded an organisation called The Humanitarian Cult. It campaigned for social causes such as the fights against capital punishment, poverty, and the war, and in favour of women's suffrage. Instead of dues or membership fees, aspiring members were directed to pay grocers' and butchers' bills for impoverished families. Meetings at Carnegie Hall were sold out. Membership was over 100,000 and a journal called *The Humanitarian*

---

[45] 'New Era Between North and South America Seen As Conference Ends', *The Bisbee Daily Review*, 7 June 1919, p. 1.
[46] 'Dinner in Honor of Edwin Markham, 23 April 1919', EMA.

was established. An advisory council was appointed, along with committees on areas such as criminal law, legislation, child labour, women's welfare, and capital punishment. Markham had been asked by Appelbaum in September 1916 to address one of the Carnegie Hall meetings—and of course to write a poem for the cause.[47] The 1919 occasion was a nine-course dinner in March given by members of the Cult in honour of their founder and leader. It was held at the Hotel Commodore, where Markham's birthday dinner would take place the following month. Markham was one of 14 speakers, many of the others being justices and magistrates. Mme Eugenie Zanco de Primo played the Steinway. The programme—a copy of which survives in Markham's papers—contains two poems, one specially written for the occasion by Dorothy F. Cummins, the other, Markham's 'The Day and the Work', 'inscribed to Misha Appelbaum'.[48]

It seems to have been a last hurrah for the Humanitarian Cult. Appelbaum's world had already given signs of unravelling. He and his wife Irma had lived in one of the finest West End Avenue mansions (no. 266), where committee meetings of the Cult had taken place. But in 1917 Irma sued Misha for divorce on grounds of cruelty: she claimed he had ridiculed and humiliated her in public. He had sunk a large amount of money into the Cult while making a point of not having fees or collections, and his fortune was nearly exhausted. The journal's last issue was in May 1919 and the West End Avenue mansion was sold. The following year, Appelbaum married a 23-year-old singer named Helen Yorke after a 13-day courtship. Six months after the wedding, the couple were rushed to hospital after taking bichloride of mercury in an apparent suicide attempt. Appelbaum nearly died. Once he recovered, now nearly bankrupt, he auditioned for a vaudeville spot in an attempt to pay off his debts before disappearing from the historical record. It is perhaps a sign of things to come that the programme for the March 1919 dinner contains six misprints in Markham's poem, including spelling 'work' as 'mork'.

Markham was out of town at the end of May, otherwise he would doubtless have attended the celebration of the 100th anniversary of Walt Whitman's birth at the Hotel Breevort. Several incidents enlivened the evening. First a telegram from Emma Goldman was read out. Goldman was in prison, and would soon be deported to Russia, but she had lectured about Whitman, whom she saw as embodying the best qualities of the USA, and so wanted her voice to be heard. 'With you we celebrate Walt Whitman,' she wrote,

---

[47] Letter from Misha Appelbaum to Edwin Markham, EMA (13 September 1916).
[48] 'Dinner Given by the Members of the Humanitarian Cult in Honor of Misha Appelbaum, Founder and Leader, 7 March 1919', EMA.

'the dauntless rebel against all sham, the singer of the free city.' And then, in a neat political barb: 'Let the clarion voice of Walt call a halt to the Prussianization of America.'[49] At this point some members of the audience walked out.

Whitman's capaciousness meant that he could be claimed by just about everybody. The Unitarian minister, Dr John Haynes Holmes, argued that Whitman was deeply conservative; indeed, 'the most conservative person in the world'. This was hardly special pleading since Holmes, one of the founders of the NAACP, had six days earlier been one of the speakers at Madison Square Garden demanding that the US government stop support for the enemies of the Bolshevik regime in Russia.[50] But, by contrast, Whitman's old friend Charles B. Harned declared that the poet was 'a radical of the radicals'.[51]

Next up was George Viereck, not on the programme but called to speak by the compère, George Jay Smith. Viereck was already a controversial figure. His father was reputedly the illegitimate son of Kaiser Wilhelm I. The family had emigrated to New York in the late 1890s (Viereck's mother, Laura, had been born in the USA). Something of a poetic prodigy, Viereck had become nationally famous with his 1907 collection, *Nineveh and Other Poems*. In some ways he was the German equivalent to Salomón de la Selva, lecturing in Berlin on US poetry while trying to support German culture in the USA. A friend of Theodore Roosevelt and an editor on *Current Literature*, Viereck was a figure of some influence. But with war raging in Europe, he edited the German-sponsored magazine, *The Fatherland*, which made him unpopular in some quarters; and, after 1917, he increasingly found himself a literary and social outcast, expelled from the Authors' League and eventually even from the Poetry Society of America, which he had helped found, despite being defended by Edwin Markham and Shaemas O'Sheel.[52]

Called to speak about Whitman, Viereck launched into an attack on Woodrow Wilson: Whitman would not, he declared, have supported Wilson's vendetta against Germany, recently concluded in Versailles. This

---

[49] 'Viereck Stirs Poets to Fight', *The Sun*, 1 June 1919, pp. 1 and 13; 'Viereck Breaks Up Whitman Tribute', *New York Times*, 1 June 1919, p. 17; and cf. Timothy Robbins, 'Emma Goldman Reading Walt Whitman: Aesthetics, Agitation, and the Anarchist Ideal', *Texas Studies in Literature and Language*, 57, no. 1 (2015), 80–105.
[50] 'Bolshevists Win Cheers In Garden', *The Sun*, 26 May 1919, p. 20.
[51] 'Walt Whitman's Virtues Glorified', *The Sun*, 1 June 1919, p. 13.
[52] See Phyllis Keller, *States of Belonging: German-American Intellectuals and the First World War*, Cambridge, MA: Harvard University Press, 1979, pp. 121–88; and Lisa Szefel, *The Gospel of Beauty in the Progressive Era: Reforming American Verse and Values*, New York: Palgrave Macmillan, 2011, pp. 86–103, 210–16.

was too much for some patriots. The prominent lawyer George Dana Mumford walked out with his wife and some friends, Mumford shouting out 'The rotten German swine'. Shaemas O'Sheel told Mumford to shut up: 'What sort of American are you anyway?' To which, 'Mr Mumford made some reference to the Mayflower.' The two men squared up but Mrs Mumford intervened.[53]

The final reported provocation came from James Waldo Fawcett, editor of *The Modernist*, whose first—and only—issue had just appeared. Fawcett used his five minutes to lay into the Poetry Society of America who, he claimed, were now hypocritically praising the safely dead Whitman when 30 years ago they would have torn him to pieces: 'How dare people of this sort speak of celebrating Whitman?' The Poetry Society of America was 'only another mutual appreciation society' and its President 'neither a poet nor a friend of poets'—a barb directed against Edward J. Wheeler.[54] Poetry can rarely have seemed to matter so much.

The Whitman celebration took place three weeks before the dinner at Gonfarone's. But on the very day of the dinner, a few hours before the guests gathered just north of Washington Square, a very different kind of 'gathering' occurred, one which helps us understand the political context of these summer months of 1919. Just 800 yards north of Washington Square, the Rand School of Social Science was a place with very different priorities, but with some overlap in personnel. The Rand School had been formed in 1906 by adherents of the Socialist Party of America (SPA). Run by the American Socialist Society, with the aim of providing a broad education to working people, it offered evening classes, as well as housing a research bureau and a publishing arm. Several of the leading members of the SPA had offices there. On the streets of Manhattan, the first half of 1919 had, to put it mildly, been a fraught time. With the war now in some sense over, New York was—at least for the moment—a very inward-looking city. Things had started to come to a boil on May Day which saw vigilante attacks on socialist and radical targets in New York, led by returning soldiers, the press whipping up anti-foreigner hysteria. The Rand School was one of the targets, the fourth time it had been attacked since the Armistice. F. Scott Fitzgerald used the events of that night for his early short story, 'May Day'.[55]

---

[53] 'Viereck Stirs Poets', p. 1.
[54] 'Viereck Stirs Poets', p. 13.
[55] F. Scott Fitzgerald, 'May Day', *The Smart Set*, 62, no. 3 (July 1920), 3–32. See 'Rand School and Other Nests of Anarchy Are Wrecked by Mobs', *The Sun*, 2 May 1919, p. 1.

After the Armistice, private vigilante bodies such as the American Protective League, originally set up to counter German espionage in New York, started to look for new targets; and those new targets were the anarchists, labour agitators, and radical socialists, usually referred to in the round as Reds or Bolsheviki. The war was only *in some sense* over, because in 1919 the USA was still formally in a state of war with Germany (as it in fact remained until the summer of 1921), which meant that wartime legislation was still in force throughout 1919. It was also the case that many official and unofficial agents of the US state saw the Bolsheviki as German-inspired revolutionists, so that for them the campaigns of 1919 could be seen as a continuation of the war.

That was certainly the case with Archibald Stevenson, the lawyer who during the war had been the Director of the Military Information Division's Bureau of Propaganda, and who may have been behind de la Selva's interrogation the previous year. Stevenson had wanted to continue his work at federal level but the US Senate gave him the brush-off, so he held his own investigation of radicalism in New York City under the auspices of the private Union League Club. The Union League Club then petitioned the State of New York, which set up a Joint Legislative Committee Investigating Seditious Activities in the State of New York, chaired by junior State Senator Clayton R. Lusk. Stevenson offered himself as unpaid special counsel; so he was basically an unelected zealot who was prepared to do the hard work and was therefore allowed to drive the agenda.

Just knowing that the Rand School was a centre of sedition, Stevenson organised a raid on its premises for the afternoon of Saturday, 21 June, arriving with three furniture removal vans in which to take away confiscated documents—basically all the documents in the building. Just a week later, Stevenson was ready to make public what he called the 'worst' of the evidence, which he did at a public hearing. This 'worst' turned out to be a 'startling plan for the organization of the negroes into radical units' written by a black Jamaican named Wilfred A. Domingo.[56] Coincidentally, 17 years later, Adolphe Roberts and Wilfred Domingo would meet in Harlem and found the Jamaica Progressive League to press for self-determination for the island of their birth; but for the moment they were operating on parallel tracks.

---

[56] 'Moves to Close Rand School', *New York Times*, 28 June 1919, p. 1, 3. Domingo's essay, 'Socialism Imperilled, or the Negro—a Potential Menace to American Radicalism', was published in the Lusk Committee report: *Revolutionary Radicalism: Its History, Purpose and Tactics, with an Exposition and Discussion of the Steps being Taken and Required to Curb it*, 4 vols., Albany: J. B. Lyon Company, 1920, pp. 1489–510.

Salomón de la Selva had certainly frequented the Rand School a few years previously, though his contacts with Charley Ervin and Joseph Gollomb had probably cooled. The Rand School was still, however, the natural habitat for Edwin Markham. Adolphe Roberts had once been an ardent socialist, but was less so in 1919. The one dinner guest with a definite, yet murky, relationship with the institution was the writer Vennette Herron, whose father, George Herron, had been instrumental in setting up the Rand School: it had been financed by a bequest in his mother-in-law's will. Vennette, however, was Herron's daughter with his first wife, whom he had abandoned for Carrie Rand, his then mistress—leading to his defrocking as a Congregationalist minister. Rand and his second wife had to decamp to Italy to escape the scandal, and he was decreasingly content with the Rand School's political line, thinking it too sympathetic to the Bolsheviki, all the while the Rand School was considered by the real Bolsheviki—such as the Washington Square radical, John Reed—to be much too right-wing. The SPA was indeed in the process of tearing itself apart.

Another division within the SPA was over its relationship with the Third International, which had been established in Moscow in March 1919. That year a left-wing faction within the SPA had looked like winning seats on the National Executive Committee, leading the current executive to declare the election invalid and suspend various of its federations. At exactly the time of the dinner at Gonfarone's—precisely that evening of 21 June 1919—this left-wing faction of the SPA was meeting in New York City to decide how to react. It soon pulled away to form the Communist Party of America. June 1919 was a moment of maximum political tension, and the pace of political change was frantic.

This was also the summer of the some of worst mob attacks in US history as black soldiers returned home from defending their country only to face discrimination and street violence from white racists. Just a couple of weeks after the Gonfarone dinner, the most powerful literary response to those attacks—perhaps the most powerful anti-racist poem ever written—appeared in the pages of *The Liberator*, written by the Jamaican poet, Claude McKay:

> If we must die—let it not be like hogs
> Hunted and penned in an inglorious spot,
> While round us bark the mad and hungry dogs,
> Making their mock at our accursed lot.[57]

---

[57] Claude McKay, 'If We Must Die', *The Liberator*, 17 (July 1919), 21.

Another way in which poetry was at the very centre of New York political life in 1919.

*

Organisation for the dinner at Gonfarone's was a touch chaotic, in part because, as de la Selva's enthusiasm grew, so did the size of the guest list, necessitating two changes of venue, with every guest having to be updated by letter of the new arrangements. De la Selva's letter to the guest of honour, Adolphe Roberts, just eight days before the planned event, is the first piece of surviving evidence. Along with a personal note, de la Selva enclosed the general invitation he was sending out, which began:

Dear Fellow:
You are hereby summoned to attend an informal Pan American dinner at the home of Mrs C. E. Schauffler (The Northold, South-West corner of Broadway & 151st Street) on Saturday June 21st, this year, at 7.15 sharp in the evening.[58]

The dinner would celebrate the publication of Roberts's first book of poems, and de la Selva underlined that it will be 'a Pan American literary affair': 'You are to be the guest of Latin Americans'. (Presumably the Hispanic guests received a differently worded version.) A guest list was also enclosed, divided by country: eight from the USA (Roberts, Edna Millay, Jeanne Robert Foster, Muna Lee, Edwin Markham, Edward Wheeler, Jessie Rittenhouse, Florence Schauffler), two from Chile (Graciela Mandujano, Ernesto Montenegro), two from Spain (Jesusa Alfau, Alfredo Collao [who was actually Chilean]), and one each from Mexico (José Castellot), Colombia (Dmitri Ivanovitch), Venezuela (Tiberio Faria), the Dominican Republic (Manuel F. Cestero), Peru (Carmen Torres Calderón de Pinillos), Puerto Rico (Luis Muñoz Marín), Cuba (Laura Guiteras Gener Keller), and, of course, Nicaragua. Five writers have been asked to read, de la Selva reports: Roberts, Millay, Wheeler, Ivanovitch, and Montenegro; and translations would be rendered from English to Spanish by de la Selva and Luis Muñoz Marín, and from Spanish to English by de la Selva and Muna Lee.

An unexpected complication was introduced just four days before the dinner when *La Prensa* published a short piece about the forthcoming

---

[58] Letter from Salomón de la Selva to W. Adolphe Roberts, WARA (13 June 1919). Edwin Markham got a similar letter the next day: Letter from Salomón de la Selva to Edwin Markham, EMA (14 June 1919).

event under the heading 'Se Renanudan Las Reuniones Iberoamericanas' [The Iberoamerican Reunions Start Up Again].[59] Since Collao was the editor of *La Prensa*, he was probably the initiator if not the author: that may have been Manuel Cestero, who wrote a report on the dinner the following week. The piece noted that the event was a renewal of the series of pan-American *causeries*, as it called them, initiated by de la Selva and Pedro Henríquez Ureña. Strangely, though, it also suggested that anyone wanting to attend could send a donation to de la Selva, whose address it usefully provided, of not less than $2 and not more than $5. Collao must have imagined that Mrs Schauffler's dining room was almost infinitely expandable. The understanding, it went on to say, was that those attending would be 'si es hombre, poeta, escritor o artista, y si es mujer, hermosa y digna de la sociedad de los poetas' [if male, then a poet, writer, or artist, and, if female, beautiful and worthy of the company of poets], prompting a sharp letter from de la Selva noting that attendance was by invitation only, while taking the opportunity to announce that the venue had been changed to the Gonfarone. It was not until the day of the dinner that the newspaper printed de la Selva's note of clarification.[60] He refrained from pointing out that not all the men attending would be good-looking and that most of the women would themselves be writers. According to the *La Prensa* piece, the confirmed attendees would include (in addition to those already mentioned) Alfredo Ortiz Vargas, Arturo Torres Rioseco, Rene Borgia, José Frexas, 'y otros muchos escritores y poetas' [and many other writers and poets]. Millay would speak in Spanish and Ivanovitch in English.

With the list of invitees growing apace, de la Selva had to find a bigger venue. A postcard to Adolphe Roberts on the Wednesday (18 June) announced that they were now holding the dinner at the apartment of Mme Rosa Culmell Nin—mother of the then teenager, Anaïs—at 158 West 75th Street—with news of an additional guest, the young Spanish piano prodigy, Paquita Madriguera.[61] But that venue didn't hold for long, and the Gonfarone's private dining room was booked on the Thursday or Friday. De la Selva must have spent ages sending postcards to keep his puzzled guests up to date with the latest arrangements.

Roberts's complicated love-life gave his host additional dilemmas. De la Selva was keen to insist that Roberts should have the final say on those invited and on the seating plan, even though he had already sent out a whole slew of invitations. Roberts would, of course, sit between his host and Edna

---

[59] *La Prensa*, 17 June 1919, p. 4.
[60] Letter from Salomón de la Selva, *La Prensa*, 21 June 1919, p. 4.
[61] Postcard from Salomón de la Selva to W. Adolphe Roberts, WARA (18 June 1919).

Millay, his current lover. But would Edna object to Vennette Herron being invited, de la Selva inquired—a clear indication that she was a previous flame, perhaps not entirely extinguished. Certainly, Roberts should not be placed between them. Then, almost as an afterthought, but surely as a way of teasing his friend, de la Selva solemnly inquired as to whether 'Mme Roberts' was in town: if she was, 'she should come, that goes without saying'—no doubt to watch across the table as her husband tried to juggle his two lovers. 'But perhaps she is not in the city at present.'[62]

On the Thursday (19 June), de la Selva wrote to Edna, enclosing a longer guest list than he had sent to Roberts, one which now also included all three Millay sisters, Vennette Herron's sister (Miriam), Marjorie Page (Bennet Schauffler's girlfriend), Constance Murray Greene, and Enric Madriguera (Paquita's brother, also a musician). The following day he wrote to Jeanne Robert Foster to tell her of the second change of venue, although she had already indicated that she was probably not going to be able to attend. Edwin Markham got a similar letter, noting that Mrs Markham was also expected.[63] The plan was final. It was going to be dinner at Gonfarone's.

*

By 1919, Greenwich Village was already thought of as a multinational bohemian community, but it was still a basically migrant Italian neighbourhood with bohemian trimmings.[64] Gonfarone's was one of its popular *table d'hôte* Italian restaurants, started up in the early years of the century by a widow called Caterina Gonfarone, but now run by her business partner Anacleto Sermolino, both from the north of Italy. What had started out as a small restaurant patronised exclusively by northern Italians had by 1919 become a much larger proposition.

A lively sense of the atmosphere at Gonfarone's is conveyed in the memoirs of Sermolino's daughter, Maria, who had been brought up on the premises. The restaurant had originally been in the basement of the house on the corner of MacDougal and West 8th Street, seating 50 or 60. With Sermolino's encouragement, first as a chef, then as a partner, Madama

---

[62] Letter from Salomón de la Selva to W. Adolphe Roberts, WARA (13 June 1919).
[63] Letter from Salomón de la Selva to Jeanne Robert Foster, FMC (20 June 1919); Letter from Salomón de la Selva to Edwin Markham, EMA (20 June 1919).
[64] Donald Tricarico, *The Italians of Greenwich Village: The Social Structure and Transformation of an Ethnic Community*, New York: Centre for Migration Studies of New York, Inc., 1984, p. xvi.

Gonfarone—as she was known—took over four adjoining houses to create the large establishment. It could then serve 4,000 to 5,000 dinners a week. The private dining room, where this party was held, was on the 8th Street side. Maria Sermolino offers a typical Gonfarone menu, which is probably the closest we can get to knowing what the diners ate on the evening of 21 June 1919:

> Assorted Antipasto (celery hearts, black olives, salami, sardines, anchovies, sliced tomatoes with basil, tuna, pimento)
> Minestrone
> Spaghetti with meat sauce
> Half a boiled lobster with mayonnaise
> Boiled salmon with caper sauce
> Sweetbread with mushroom patty
> Prime rib of beef with brussel sprouts, spinach, and mashed potatoes
> Green salad
> Biscuit tortoni
> Fresh fruit
> Assorted cheeses
> Demi-tasse.[65]

This would cost 65 cents a head, with a pint of 'red ink' (Californian wine) each thrown in free. Anything drinkable would have to be paid for. The summer of 1919 was, however, something of a last hurrah for Gonfarone's, as for many such establishments. These restaurants made their profits from selling alcohol and Prohibition would kill many of them off, including Gonfarone's. Sermolino sold the business the following year and it closed soon after. In 1930 the buildings were torn down.

There are only two accounts of the night itself. A brief report in *The Sun* took a jocular tone.[66] The dinner was for 'thirty-two North and South American poets of assorted sizes'. Since Mr de la Selva had been unfortunate enough to misdirect his guests (perhaps not all had been informed of the change of venue), it seemed as if he would lose many of them, but only Harry Kemp was irretrievably mislaid. The Markhams arrived late having made a detour of 180 blocks—presumably having gone to Mrs Schauffler's apartment in Washington Heights, the original venue. Markham still gave 'a resounding address'—his speciality; and others who read poems are mentioned: Roberts

---

[65] Maria Sermolino, *Papa's Table d'Hôte*, Philadelphia: J. B. Lippincott Co., 1952, pp. 125–27.
[66] *The Sun*, 29 June 1919, p. 2.

himself, José Castellot, David Morton, and Aline Kilmer, the last two PSA stalwarts. Aline had always written poetry, much of it about her children, and while husband Joyce was in Europe she put together a collection called *Candles That Burn* (1919)—the candles in question being on one of their five children's birthday cakes. It is tempting to set these candles against the one in Edna Millay's famous 'First Fig', published the previous year, which she burns at both ends.[67] The two women sat at the same dinner at Gonfarone's in that summer of 1919, but their ways of life, like the poetic imagery, could hardly have been more different. *The Sun* also mentioned Vennette Herron, who 'recited an original vampire poem in costume'. The reporter concluded that 'Every one agreed that it showed a great deal of native talent': whether poem or costume was no doubt left deliberately ambiguous.

La Prensa struck a more serious note, recalling that the point of these pan-American occasions was through agreeable reunions for writers of the two parts of the hemisphere to get to know each other's writing. Three of these reunions had taken place, the piece says, in the house Pedro Henríquez Ureña shared with de la Selva.[68] On this occasion at Gonfarone's, most of those present had read from their work and there were toasts to Roberts, to the absent Pedro Henríquez Ureña, and to literary pan-Americanism, seen as more effective than its diplomatic variant. The gathering closed around 2 a.m. A long list of those present follows—though since it includes Jeanne Robert Foster, who certainly did *not* attend, and Harry Kemp who, according to *The Sun*, got lost en route, it may have been based, at least in part, on an *invitation* list. Previously unmentioned names are J. M. Bada, Ramón Pérez de Ayala, Bennet Schauffler, Julia Rivas, Elena de Seves, and Margarita de Seves. *The Sun*'s 'thirty-two' is the only indication of the final size of the gathering. In the burst of invitations and preparations, and news reports, 43 names had been mentioned and we only know of two of that number who almost certainly did not make it. Twenty-one of those 43 are Hispanic names. Twenty-two of the 43 are women. Salomón de la Selva was clearly an equal opportunities party organiser.

The Hispanic pack had been shuffled during de la Selva's absence in England, but he probably had more names to choose from than ever before as he began to put together his guest-list, which provides a final snapshot of the Hispanic cultural presence in New York in the summer of 1919. Some old friends were still around, notably Manuel Cestero and Jesusa Alfau, but there were quite a few recent arrivals. Records are inevitably

---

[67] 'My candle burns at both ends; / It will not last the night; / But ah, my foes, and oh, my friends—/ It gives a lovely light!' (*Poetry*, XII, no. 3 [June 1918], 130).
[68] Manuel Cestero, 'Notas de sociedad', *La Prensa*, 23 June 1919, p. 5.

patchy. Tiberio Faria seems to have left no trace. There was a Julia Rivas, Venezuelan, aged 22, living on 7th Avenue in 1920. Each of the de Seves' sisters had a poem written about her by one of the male guests, suggesting that they were both love interests, but nothing further emerges.[69] The Argentine José Frexas had been brought in as an editor on *La Prensa*: he was a career journalist, although he also translated books from the French (Alphonse Daudet, Alfred de Vigny) after he returned to Buenos Aires.[70] The Venezuelan journalist Napoleón Acevedo, who wrote under the name Rene Borgia, was a new arrival.[71] He leapt into debates in *La Prensa*, responding to a writer who had pointed out that Nicaragua, the size of Massachusetts, had failed to produce a William Taft, that Massachusetts had failed to produce a Rubén Darío; though his title, 'Ellos y Nosotros', was indicative of the kind of antagonistic thinking that de la Selva was constantly opposing.[72]

Paquita and Enric Madriguera belonged to a gilded generation of Catalan musicians and artists. Enric was only 15 in 1919, so probably didn't attend the dinner. He was in New York with his sister, Paquita—Francesca de Asís Madriguera y Rodón—who was herself only 18, although already a vastly experienced international pianist who had studied with Enrique Granados. She had given her first concert aged five, and had performed at the Royal Albert Hall aged 13. While playing a series of concerts in New York that summer, she was living with her mother (Francesca Rodón Canudas) in the house of Rosa Culmell Nin, with the young Anaïs, in her own words, dazzled by the teenage pianist's beauty, assurance, and flirtatiousness.[73] Rosa Culmell had taught in the Granados Academy when Paquita was studying there and it was probably her part-Cuban background that gave her connections in New York, where she had moved with her children in 1914 after leaving her abusive husband. It is tempting to imagine that Paquita played on the house piano at Gonfarone's.

---

[69] 'Dulce Elena de Seves' begins Dmitri Ivanovitch's poem, 'Ave María', in his *La ventana y otros poemas*, San José de Costa Rica: Ediciones Sarmiento, 1921, p. 11; Arturo Torres Rioseco, 'Margarita de Seves', *En el encantamiento*, San José de Costa Rica: Ediciones Sarmiento, 1921, pp. 80–81.

[70] Manuel Cestero noted that Frexas was small in stature, solitary by temperament, a fluent French speaker, and a lover of theatre: 'En broma y en serio', *La Prensa*, 2 November 1918, p. 4.

[71] Borgia (Venezuela, 1892–1961) was later a scriptwriter investigated for un-American activities.

[72] Rene Borgia, 'Ellos y nosotros', *La Prensa*, 17 March 1919, p. 3.

[73] *The Diary of Anaïs Nin*, vol. 6, *1955–1966*, ed. Gunther Stuhlmann, New York: Harcourt Brace Jovanovich, 1976, p. 136.

The most recent Hispanic arrival in New York to get an invitation to Gonfarone's was the Spanish novelist Ramón Pérez de Ayala, who had landed on 12 June. Pérez de Ayala had come to the USA in 1913 to marry his Pennsylvanian fiancée, Mabel Rick. They had spent time at her parents' home in Allentown, with Pérez de Ayala making occasional forays to New York. This time he was the beneficiary of a US overseas fellowship. He already had an established reputation on the basis of several novels, although his best work would be produced in the 1920s. Having parked his wife and two children in Allentown, Pérez de Ayala was soon back in New York where he visited Archer Huntington at the HSA on Friday 20 June.[74] This shuttling would become the pattern. As he wrote to a friend: 'Sometimes I escape to New York; but for one thing I'm on my own, and for another it's very expensive here, I get bored and then I have to go back straight away.'[75] His fellowship ran until November, but he negotiated an extension until February 1920 despite a growing disillusion with the country he had liked so much in 1913. His opinion was that the country had changed, not him; and he was right. He hoped, however, that the change was temporary: 'The USA finds itself in a state of maximum stubbornness and maximum stupidity. What most concerns me and irritates me above all is the unanimous sense of uncouth and brutal reaction.'[76]

José Castellot and Dmitri Ivanovitch form a nice contrast, both confirming O. Henry's thesis about the effects of volcanic political eruptions, while themselves occupying very different parts of the political spectrum. José Castellot Batalla (Fig. 29), aged 63 in 1919, so very much the senior Hispanic figure at the dinner, was a Mexican landowner, lawyer, banker, and politician, born in Campeche, who had benefited from the patronage of Joaquín Casasús and Porfirio Díaz.[77] Carleton Beals called

---

[74] Archer M. Huntington, 'Diaries', Hispanic Society of America (20 June 1919). On the writer's long relationship with the HSA, see Amparo de Juan Bolufer, 'Ramón Pérez de Ayala y la Hispanic Society: nueva documentación y un poema inédito', *Moenia*, 18 (2002), 175–99.

[75] Ramón Pérez de Ayala, *Cincuenta años de cartas íntimas (1904–1956) a su amigo Miguel Rodríguez-Acosta*, ed. Andrés Amorós, Madrid: Editorial Castalia, 1980, p. 200. For general background, see Agustín Coletes Blanco, *Gran Bretana y los Estados Unidos en la vida de Ramón Pérez de Ayala*, Oviedo: Instituto de Estudios Asturianos, 1984.

[76] Pérez de Ayala, *Cincuentas años*, p. 200. His newspaper articles were more measured, although he was clearly baffled by Prohibition: see Ramón Pérez de Ayala, *El país del futuro: Mis viajes a los Estados Unidos (1913–1914–1919–1920)*, Madrid: Biblioteca Almagro, 1959.

[77] See Raquel Padilla Ramos, 'Los Partes Fragmentados: Narrativas de la Guerra y la Deportación Yaquis', doctoral thesis, University of Hamburg, 2009, pp. 181–98.

29 José Castellot Batalla, ca. 1900. Instituto Nacional de Antropología e Historia, Mexico.

him 'a voracious, unscrupulous business man, with a mattress beard'.[78] He was also Grand Commander of the Supreme Council of the Scottish Rite Masons in Mexico. After the fall of Díaz, he lay low and concentrated on business before becoming President Huerta's representative in New York and then a conduit between Huerta's successor Carvajal and the US government. When that mission failed, and unable to return to Mexico, he moved into exile in New York, where he was cut off from his sources of wealth. His friend José Juan Tablada followed him to New York and seems to have helped him financially. 'Businessman and socialite, politician and diplomat, intellectual and *littérateur*', Tablada called him: small in stature, but cordial and loquacious, with a noble head and profuse red beard—as virile as those belonging to King Darius's lancers in the palace at Persepolis.[79] Castellot's translation into Spanish of Edward Fitzgerald's

---

[78] Carleton Beals, *Porfirio Díaz, Dictator of Mexico*, Philadelphia: J. B. Lippincott, 1932, p. 379. Beals details Castellot's financial shenanigans.
[79] José Juan Tablada, 'Prólogo' to *Rubaiyat de Omar Khayyam*, trans. José Castellot, New York: n.p. 1918, pp. 9–23, at pp. 21–22.

translation of the *Rubáiyát of Omar Khayyám*, with a prologue by Tablada, was advertised regularly in *La Prensa* throughout 1919 at the cost of one dollar.[80]

Dmitri Ivanovitch was the pen-name of the Colombian José Luis Betancourt Román, born in Cartagena in 1888.[81] He seems to have come to New York around 1912: in 1920, he was living on West 109th Street with his wife and two daughters. According to the pen-portrait written by his friend Manuel Cestero as an introduction to a collection of his poems, Ivanovitch was a gentle and retiring soul, a committed socialist, and a dedicated writer of love poems.[82] Like other Spanish-American poets (Cestero recalls his fellow *dominicano*, Fabio Fiallo), Ivanovitch insisted on separating his political views—Bolshevik, anti-imperialist—from his writing: poetry should, he thought, be entirely dedicated to praising the beauty of women. New York is never mentioned in his poems, though in the delicately beautiful 'La ventana', one senses the streets of Manhattan as well as the speaker's memory of the tropical warmth of Cartagena.

> Vióla abrirse en la sombra de la calle
> como una bienvenida. En torno suyo
> estaba todo negro. Sin estrellas,
> el cielo daba la impresión de un techo
> próximo a desplomarse. El vagabundo
> sentía la tristeza de su noche
> sin hogar y sin pan, y ambulaba
> con el aire extraviado de un sonámbulo
> por las calles hostiles ... De las casas
> ningún rumor surgía, las aceras
> ahuecaban sus pasos ¡entre el sueño
> de todos los humanos, sólo él iba,
> con su hambre cruel y su dolor, despierto!

He saw it open in the shadow of the street
like a welcome. Round about him
everything was black. Starless,
the sky looked like a roof

---

[80] In 1922, judgment was filed against Castellot for a debt of $1581.37 (*New York Tribune*, 24 August 1922, p. 18).
[81] Taken from the protagonist of Tolstoy's novel, *Resurrection* (1899).
[82] Manuel F. Cestero, 'Dmitri Ivanovitch', in Dmitri Ivanovitch, *La ventana y otros poemas*, pp. vii–xv.

> about to collapse. The vagrant
> felt the sadness of his night
> without home or bread, and he wandered
> with the distraught look of a sleepwalker
> through the hostile streets ... No sound
> came from the houses and his footsteps
> rang hollow on the pavements: among the mass
> of sleeping humanity, he alone,
> with his cruel hunger and his grief, was awake!

The starless night, the homeless and hungry wanderer, the quiet houses. Too much in the minor key to be Darío, though Edgar Allan Poe shines through, as so often, with the speaker seemingly condemned to walk the streets, as in Poe's 'The Man of the Crowd'. There is a window opening, as if in welcome. There is no welcome, but at least a sense of fellowship: somebody else is awake in the middle of the night. It might be a miser poring over his books or an obscure disciple reading Bakunin. No matter: he feels less lonely, though he is also taken back—in that contrast that often animates Hispanic depictions of New York—to the the star-filled sky of 'esa villa de los trópicos' [that tropical villa] where, as a young man, he had stood outside such a nocturnal window talking of love.[83]

Two of Dmitri Ivanovitch's poems are dedicated to fellow *gonfaronistas*, the Colombian Alfredo Ortiz Vargas and the Chilean Arturo Torres Rioseco.[84] Both were even younger than de la Selva—22 and 21 respectively—and of course much newer to the city. Both would settle in the USA and become published writers as well as teachers—but with very different outcomes. Ortiz Vargas was quickly involved with the campaign of protest against the US occupation of the Dominican Republic, and he may already have begun writing the epic poem eventually published as *Las torres de Manhattan* in 1939.[85] However, whereas Torres Rioseco went on to win glittering academic

---

[83] Ivanovitch, 'La ventana', *La ventana y otros poemas*, San José de Costa Rica: J. García Monge, 1921, pp. 3-4, at p. 3. The poem was first published in early 1920 and so may have been written in 1919: *Cuba Contémporanea*, 22 (January–April 1920), 401–02.

[84] Ivanovitch, 'Magdalena' and 'La Ventana', *La ventana y otros poemas*, pp. 74-77 and 3-4.

[85] He was part of the support group for the Comité de Damas pro Santo Domingo, formed in New York on 26 November 1919: see Alejandro Paulino Ramos, 'Libertad de prensa en República Dominicana' (2 March 2008) <http://historiadominicana.blogspot.co.uk/2008/03/libertad-de-prensa-en-rep-dominicana.html> accessed December 2018. Alfredo Ortiz Vargas, *Las torres de Manhattan*, Boston: Chapman & Grimes, 1939;

prizes, Ortiz Vargas was murdered in 1951 in Kansas City by a deranged ex-student.[86]

Although Torres Rioseco (Fig. 30) is now best remembered as the long-time professor of Spanish at Berkeley and author of several of the foundational works on Spanish American literature, he wrote some of the sharpest accounts of life in Hispanic New York in the years just after the war: they deserve some attention. Torres Rioseco had arrived in New York in the spring of 1918, having been appointed as a translator for the Committee for Public Information, a rôle that ended with the Armistice in November 1918. He'd been quickly introduced to de la Selva, possibly via Ernesto Montenegro, the Chilean journalist, and Salomón had in turn introduced Arturo to Pedro Henríquez Ureña, who would eventually do much to further Torres Rioseco's academic career.

A short prose piece—*poema en prosa*—written while Torres Rioseco was teaching at Williams College nicely encapsulates the complicated feelings of an educated young Latin American experiencing bohemian New York, as well as hinting at the ways in which the two languages might be used together.[87] 'Rosas de nuestra América' celebrates the ways in which the beauty of Spanish-American women lights up the streets of New York—'niñas de Cuba, ardientes de corazón y boca ... dominicanas de piel morena, rosas de Puerto Rico, colombianas reidoras que llevan en los ojos la melancolía agreste de los bambucos, chilenas serias y pensativas' [Cuban girls, with burning hearts and lips, dark-skinned *dominicanas*, roses from Puerto Rico, laughing Colombians whose eyes betray the rural melancholy of the *bambuco* (genre of folk music), thoughtful and serious Chileans]. Plenty of them, it seems, and presumably less tightly chaperoned than in their home countries since they will, he says, talk freely to you about their lives, 'because nothing encourages spontaneous frankness quite so much as the incomprehension between a race of businessmen and a load of pompous believers in impossible dreams'. He hails the US suitors with a show of good grace: 'Good health, baby lampiño, hijo robusto de la gran *culture* del Norte. Salud, caballero moderno de dollar y del sombrero Panamá, del corazón reseco,

---

The Towers of Manhattan: A Spanish-American Poet Looks at New York, done into English verse by Quincy Guy Burris, Albuquerque: The University of New Mexico Press, 1944.
[86] *Lawrence Daily Journal-World*, 30 August 1951, p. 9.
[87] Arturo Torres Rioseco, 'Rosas de nuestra América', *Repertorio Americano*, II, no. 20 (20 May 1921), 277.

30 Arturo Torres Rioseco. Provenance unknown.

del talento rutinario. Salud, filósofo del aviso, psicólogo del cerdo, poeta de Chicago, cantor del humo y del acero' [Good health, you smooth-cheeked baby, robust son of the great culture of the North. Good health, modern knight of the dollar and the Panama hat, of the shrivelled heart, of ordinary abilities. Good health, philosopher of the advertisement, pork psychologist, Chicago poet, singer of smoke and steel]. And yet he wants the yankees to know 'that the beauty who drinks your cocktail still suffers from her infinite desires because her heart is poisoned by the wandering moons of our skies'. Perhaps so, though one senses the understandable resentment of the impoverished outsider unable to distract the dark-eyed tropical beauties away from the glamour of wealthy young US businessmen. The piece ends, not entirely convincingly, with seeming recognition of the inevitability of what he is witnessing:

> Andando por los bulevares neoyorkinos, por cabarets y music halls no es raro encontrar una rosa de la ardiente América Central del brazo de un caballero yanqui, lampiño, enjoyado, con el rostro sonriente de clavel.
> América del dollar y la usina, entre el harmonioso conjunto de continentes yo te proclamo:
> *The greatest in the world.*

> Wandering along the avenues of New York, through cabarets and music halls, it's not unusual to find a rose from burning Central America on the arm of a yankee man, clean-shaven, bejewelled, with a carnation smile across his face.

America of the dollar and the factory, across the harmonious conjunction of continents, I proclaim you:
The greatest in the world.

In later life Torres Rioseco produced a series of semi-autobiographical stories, the last of which, 'Antonio de Silva', offers a reflection on these New York years, partly in terms of where he lived.[88] The eponymous Antonio is a Chilean student who arrives in New York on a government mission to study typography with a monthly salary of $300. He had previously been a law student and journalist in Santiago until his brother got this soft posting for him. The narrator, Ernesto Ríos, and his friend, Pedro Aguilar, are obviously both envious, even though they themselves are reasonably well off as teachers at a college in Massachusetts. Silva is living at the top-end Hotel Astor, Aguilar and the narrator at the very smart Hotel King's Arms near Columbia University—by which he must mean the King's Crown at 420 West 116th Street, now a residence for Columbia law students. After a few months, the two friends move to a room on West 96th Street, their savings having much diminished. They are reluctant to return to rural— and cheaper—Massachusetts because they still regard New York as a kind of paradise: 'Even without much money New York offered us its museums, its subways, the Hudson, Broadway, the self-service restaurants, the blonde girls, Columbia University and our Chilean friends. For us New York was the enchanted city of our dreams.'[89]

Silva's bursary has been stopped by the government when it became aware that he wasn't doing any studying, so the three of them decide to draw lots as to which of them should take a job as a waiter in order to support them all. Silva draws the short straw but only lasts one night. His next brainwave, to give Spanish lessons, works out better in the short term, while Ernesto and Aguilar have to retreat to teach in Massachusetts, returning to New York at Christmas to spend their savings. To their surprise, they find that Silva is living in a luxurious apartment on Riverside Drive, opposite Grant's Tomb—so around West 122nd Street—courtesy of an arrangement to teach Spanish to two beautiful sisters who live next door, daughters of a rich mine owner and Utah senator. Christmas goes swimmingly only for Senator Kruger to terminate the deal after

---

[88] Arturo Torres Rioseco, 'Antonio de Silva', in his *Relatos chilenos*, New York: Harper & Brothers, 1956, pp. 121–36. Alfredo A. Roggiano called the book 'confessional' ('Homenaje a Arturo Torres-Rioseco', *Revista Iberoamericana*, 68, no. 200 [2002], 663–73, at 663).

[89] Torres Rioseco, 'Antonio de Silva', p. 124.

realising that Silva and his daughter Sarah are in love. She is removed to Washington, where even more unfortunately she falls in love with her father's secretary—who was presumably judged by the family to be a more appropriate match.

Over the years Ríos loses touch with Silva, except for reading a couple of his stories in journals. Then a chance meeting with a Spanish writer leads to the news that Silva had married a Spanish woman, older than him, not pretty or cultured, but a good housekeeper and fine cook. The story ends with Ríos wondering about the fate of Sarah, living in the mid-west, her husband the president of some Chamber of Commerce, and thinking about Silva still dreaming about New York as his wife prepares a delicious paella.

'Antonio de Silva' has the ring of a lightly veiled reminiscence, with a tang of cultural division, a lingering sense that the Hispanic figure, the Chilean writer, was denied his perfect love, the Barnard graduate Sarah, by the anglophone snobbery of her rich father. By 1956, when the story was published, Torres Rioseco was happily married to a Californian woman.

Salomón de la Selva and Muna Lee clearly helped Luis Muñoz Marín expand his personal contacts among US writers. During 1919, he wrote a series of 'Retratos contemporáneos' [Contemporary portraits] for his Puerto Rican newspaper *La Democracia*, based on interviews with Upton Sinclair, H. L. Mencken, and Edwin Markham. The one with Markham suggests why the eminent poet was so attractive a figure to young Hispanic writers.[90] Part of the attraction was Staten Island itself, a rural retreat from the bustle of the Manhattan, where—Muñoz writes—the sunsets are more golden, the leaves fresher, the sky a deeper blue, and the smiles of the passers-by more affable. Markham's house itself is unpretentious but hospitable, Muñoz reports. It emanates—he says—'the placidity of houses that have never shut their doors to the sons of the road and in whose kitchens always shine the generous copper pot, red and glowing like a warm heart'.[91] Part of Muñoz's evident pleasure comes from the informality of the occasion. A note on the front door directs visitors to the kitchen, where Mrs Markham is resplendent

---

[90] According to de la Selva Markham wrote an article (now lost) for the first issue of *La Revista de Indias* calling Latin American poets to militant democracy.

[91] Luis Muñoz Marín, 'Retratos contemporáneos: Edwin Markham' [orig. *La Democracia*, 15 August 1919], reprinted in *La obra literaria de Luis Muñoz Marín: poesía y prosa, 1915-1968*, recopilación, estudio y notas de Marcelino J. Canino Salgado, San Juan de Puerto Rico: Fundación Luis Muñoz Marín, 1999, pp. 547-50.

in a full-length apron, her face angelic. She doesn't immediately recognise Muñoz because of his khaki outfit, what he calls his *traje de explorador* [explorer's outfit]: 'I dedicate my time', he explains, 'to exploring the villages and countryside of the USA in search of what is truly American, something not to be found in any abundance in the cities.'[92] It is a light-hearted comment, possibly even self-mocking, since Staten Island is not exactly the wilds of Montana; but it does suggest both a willingness on Muñoz's part to look behind the high-speed elevators and monstrous skyscrapers for the 'real' inhabitants of the USA, and an ultimately Romantic conviction that that reality will be found in the countryside. In fact, of course, Muñoz actually finds 'reality' in Markham's poetry, not necessarily in the man with the hoe, but in the man who understands and can speak on behalf of the man with the hoe. He probably pins down Markham's viewpoint when he writes in his *Memorias* of 'su compasión angélico-social' [social-angelic compassion], assuming that the 'kings' of 'The Man with the Hoe' were the leaders of the great monopolies and corporations.[93] A short description of Markham follows, based on the inevitable comparison with Whitman. Markham's beard is tidier, without it ceasing to be 'democratic'. The house is full of books, with even the staircase used as bookshelves. Muñoz notices the complete works of Swedenborg, well-thumbed; Markham talks of the book of philosophy he is trying to finish writing (and which he never did). Muñoz picks up a typed page at random and reads Markham's description of heaven as a divine fraternity, strictly ordered, in which everybody serves without thought of reward: Divine Socialism. This, Muñoz concludes, is the key to Markham's personality. He got Markham's permission to translate 'The Man with the Hoe' into Spanish.

During the early months of his marriage, in autumn 1919, living on Staten Island with his new wife in a wooden house rented from a Puerto Rican carpenter, only about half a mile from Markham's, Muñoz Marín was certainly productive: he wrote his essay on 'the poets of democracy', as well as poems of his own and his translation of 'The Man with the Hoe': 'El hombre de la azada' appeared in Nemesio R. Canales' journal *Cuasimodo*, published in Panama City, and in *La Democracia* in San Juan.[94] In addition—and as part of his same effort to describe US culture as he found it on the ground—Muñoz wrote a piece about Beatrice Fairfax, the first Miss Lonelyhearts, whose invention by Marie Manning in 1898 had

---

[92] Muñoz Marín, 'Retratos contemporáneos: Edwin Markham', p. 548.
[93] Muñoz Marín, *Memorias*, p. 35.
[94] Edwin Markham, 'El hombre de la azada', trans. Luis Muñoz Marín, *Cuasimodo*, 2, no. 6 (December 1919), 102; *La Democracia*, 13 February 1920, p. 4.

been an unexpected success, drawing up to 1,400 letters a day from the lovelorn. This, Muñoz suggested, tongue perhaps not entirely in cheek, was enough to indicate that Latin Americans were wrong to use the figure of Caliban to refer to the USA. If they wanted a Shakespearean character, then Romeo would be more appropriate. As he went on to point out, rather as de la Selva would later do, for every Wall Street in the USA there were a hundred parks, for every Rockefeller ten or more Beatrice Fairfaxes—as indeed by 1919 there were.[95]

Near their house on Staten Island was the Port Richmond branch of the New York Public Library where Muñoz immersed himself in the writings of Marx, Lenin, Kropotkin, Trotsky, Liebknecht, and Luxemburg—the last two very recently murdered in Berlin, as well as Bertrand Russell and the Webbs. In a general sense, Muñoz Marín's literary interests had led him in this direction: Shaw, Tolstoy, Ibsen, Zola, Whitman, Wilde. Muñoz cast a sympathetic eye on developments in Russia, motivated by 'a vague general discontent with the society around me'.[96] He must have expressed himself forcibly because he remembers that Muna Lee, a State Department employee until the time of their marriage, and so aware of official crackdowns, warned him to curb his remarks if he wanted to stay out of prison. He was also impressed by Eugene Debs, read the socialist paper, the *New York Call*, and went to some lectures at the Rand School.[97] Later he found Marxist ideas too mechanical. His sense of rebellion against injustice was deeper and more human, he writes.[98] He just rejected the brutalities of US capitalism, the barbarities of the Red Scare organised by Attorney General, A. Mitchell Palmer, and the inhumanity of sweatshop labour. His ideas—he now saw, writing his memoirs in later years—were too deterministic in comparison with the more mature views, formed by British Fabianism, of his friend and mentor, Nemesio Canales. Rosario Nadal sees Muñoz's outlook as being close to that of Kropotkin—anarcho-communism (not dissimilar perhaps to Markham's watered-down version), or to Wilde's 'The Soul of Man Under Socialism'.[99] But, from Muñoz Marín's rebellious heart, poetry flowed. In Puerto Rico he threw in his lot with Santiago Iglesias and the Partido Socialista—to the distress of his father's old colleagues. From New York he took with him a cheque from Dr Julio Henna to help with Iglesias's

---

[95] Luis Muñoz Marín, 'Beatriz Fairfax', *La Democracia*, 16 August 1919, p. 4, reprinted in *La obra literaria de Luis Muñoz Marín*, pp. 551–53.
[96] Muñoz Marín, *Memorias*, p. 34.
[97] Rosario Nadal, *La juventud*, pp. 94–95.
[98] Muñoz Marín, *Memorias*, p. 36.
[99] Nadal, *La juventud*, pp. 97–99.

newspaper, *Justicia*—the same Dr Henna who acted as mentor to William Carlos Williams.

Now that the war was over, different national priorities began to come to the fore. Higher education quickly expanded and, with Spain rehabilitated and Germany in the doghouse, and pan-American activities of all kinds flourishing, there was an increasing number of openings for academics, for translators, and for visiting students and writers. Just to give one example: one of the country's most prominent educationalists (with a modern language background, in German), Samuel P. Capen, then working at the Bureau of Education, had been asked in 1917 to serve as executive secretary of the recently formed Committee on Education established under the Council of National Defense. The Committee had been formed at the onset of the war to co-ordinate the higher educational interests of the country with a view to furthering various war-related projects. The work of co-ordination then continued with the establishment in 1918 of the American Council on Education, with Capen as its first Director. In 1915, Capen had compiled an impressive 222-page overview of higher education in the USA aimed at explaining the system to potential students from overseas. In 1919, the book was translated into Spanish for widespread distribution in Spain and Spanish America by a Peruvian woman named Carmen Torres Calderón de Pinillos, working under the direction of the Interamerican Division of the American Association for International Conciliation, a Carnegie Endowment-supported body.[100]

Carmen Torres Calderón (Fig. 31) was a writer, editor, and translator. Convent-educated and married to a well-to-do man, she had left her girlhood home at Trujillo in Peru and moved to Lima. When her husband lost his fortune, she became a fashion editor of a bimonthly magazine, the *Ilustración Peruana*, and then editor of a magazine for children. The small magazine met with unprecedented success, and Carmen eventually tried writing original articles, and translating French and Italian novels for the daily papers, but without ever using her own name: 'It would have hurt the papers and magazines,' she explained, 'to have it known that

---

[100] Samuel Paul Capen, *Opportunities for Foreign Students at Colleges and Universities in the United States*, Bulletin (United States Bureau of Education), 1915, no. 27, Washington, DC: GPO, 1915; *Facilidades ofrecidas a los estudiantes extranjeros en los colegios y universidades de los Estados Unidos de la América del norte*, trans. Carmen Torres Calderón de Pinillos, Bulletin (United States Office of Education), 1918, no. 16, Washington, DC: Imprenta del gobierno, 1919.

31 Carmen Torres Calderón de Pinillos. Public domain.

the articles—except the fashion articles— were written by a woman, and besides, it was never done.' When the editor of *Ilustración* died, Torres Calderón took his place, editing the magazine for a year, but still secretly. After the magazine was discontinued, and seeing no literary future for herself in her own country, she came to the United States— 'where women could work'—bringing with her a young daughter. Like de la Selva, her work in New York City began with the Butterick Publishing Company, on the Spanish edition of *The Delineator*, where the two may have met. She went on to do translations of newspaper articles and pamphlets published by the Carnegie Endowment for International Peace, as well as Capen's book, and then edited *Revista del Mundo*, the Spanish edition of *The World's Work*, before she became editor of *Inter-América*, succeeding Peter Goldsmith. She continued translating contemporary fiction into Spanish (Washington Irving, Hawthorne, Poe) as well as the five volumes of Frank Simonds's *History of the World War* (*Historia de la guerra del mundo*). She represented the American Association for International Conciliation at the Pan American Union and also attended the Pan-American Conference of Women in association with the National League of Women Voters in Baltimore in April 1922 (along with her friend Graciela Mandujano, a student at Barnard).[101] She and Graciela were both invited by Salomón to the dinner at Gonfarone's.

---

[101] See Dorothy N. Hubert, 'Peru Answers "Present"', *The Woman Citizen*, 6, no. 2 (11 March 1922), 7, 17, from where the quotations by Torres Calderón are taken.

Professional Hispanic women in New York were supported by local women's organisations. Sorosis had been the first professional women's club in the USA, organised in New York City with 12 members in March 1868, by Jane Cunningham Croly. During the First World War, Sorosis formed an Inter-American Committee 'to extend social and club courtesies to ladies of the Latin-American countries who are living or visiting in New York and vicinity', as well as more broadly to draw up a plan of affiliation which would bring Latin American women's movements into the worldwide International Council of Women.[102] A short piece appeared in the *Pan-American Magazine*, written by a member of the group, aimed at attracting the attention of such Latin American women. It must have worked, because a number were identified and invited to the luncheon on 18 March 1918 at the Waldorf-Astoria Hotel to celebrate the 50th anniversary of Sorosis. The flags of the Latin American countries hung alongside the Stars and Stripes, and the 15 visitors were placed at a special table. Lilian Elliott, although English, was allowed to represent Brazil on account of her long acquaintance with the country. The report of the luncheon singles out the two classical pianists, Rosita Renard (Chile) and Luisa Morales Macedo (Peru), the latter shortly to marry her piano teacher, the Polish composer Zygmunt Stojowski. Three other names of significance, because of their subsequent presence at the dinner at Gonfarone's, were Laura Guiteras, aka Mrs Herman Keller (Cuba), Graciela Mandujano (Chile), and Mrs Joachim Nin (Rosa Culmell), present with her daughter, Anaïs (for some reason representing Venezuela).[103]

The following month (April 1918) there was a meeting at the Long Island house of the chair of the Inter-American Committee, Mrs J. L. Childs. Salomón de la Selva's poem, 'Drill', was read by Mrs Childs, and Alfonso Guillén Zelaya read a poem of his own. Luisa Morales Macedo played Schubert and Liszt. Many of the women who had been at the luncheon attended this meeting, but also present was Carmen Torres Calderón. By mid-1919, the Inter-American Committee of Sorosis had been addressed by, among others, Genoveva Guardiola Estrada Palma, widow of the first President of Cuba and herself Honduran, and the writers José Santos Chocano, Martín Luis Guzmán, and Salomón de la Selva himself.[104] These sorts of

---

[102] 'The Sorosis Inter-American Committee', *Pan-American Magazine*, XXVI, no. 5 (March 1918), 246–47, at 246.
[103] 'Latin Americans at Sorosis', *Pan-American Magazine*, XXVII, no. 1 (May 1918), 31–32.
[104] 'The Inter-American Committee of the Sorosis Club', *Pan-American Magazine*, XXIX, no. 4 (August 1919), 217–18.

32 Graciela Mandujano.
Public domain.

meetings may not have had much lasting impact, but they were indicative of a desire on the part of the artistic and literary Hispanic community in New York to make connections across the cultural and linguistic divide.

Laura Guiteras Giner belonged to the Cuban revolutionary aristocracy. Three Guiteras Font brothers had married three Gener Solis-Puñales sisters, so the Guiteras Gener clan was vast—and a nightmare for researchers. They were wealthy, intellectual, liberal, and nationalist. Many of them lived at least part of their lives in the USA. Antonio Guiteras Font, Laura's father, was a well-known educationalist in Cuba who had once visited Longfellow in Boston.[105] Her uncles were both intermittently imprisoned for their work for independence, and Laura's eldest brother, José Ramón, was executed in 1870, aged 18, after twice being caught attempting to run guns into Cuba; which was why her family then moved to the USA. Her great nephew, Antonio Guiteras Holmes, later returned to Cuba where he fought against Machado, founded Joven Cuba, and was killed by the Cuban army in 1935. Laura wrote a short biography of one of her uncles, and translated into English *Cuba y sus jueces* by Raimundo Cabrera.[106]

Graciela Mandujano (Fig. 32) had come to the USA in 1915 to attend the Second Pan-American Scientific Congress in Washington. In Chile she had

---

[105] Iván Jaksić, *The Hispanic World and American Intellectual Life, 1820–1880*, New York: Palgrave Macmillan, 2007, p. 103.
[106] See Arnaldo Jiménez de la Cal, *La familia Guiteras: síntesis de cubanía*, Matanzas: Ediciones Matanzas, 2004.

graduated from the University of Santiago and had already helped translate James Fitzmaurice-Kelly's biography of Cervantes. During the four years she spent in New York, she studied at Barnard, worked on the *Pan-American Magazine*, and became involved with US suffragist movements, an interest she took back to Chile where she was part of a group that founded the Partido Cívico Femenino, edited its journal, and in 1935 co-founded the Movimiento por la Emancipación de la Mujer Chilena. She frequently returned to the USA: Eleanor Roosevelt wrote about meeting her in October 1941 when she came to New York to attend the ILO's International Labour Conference held in the city at Columbia University.[107] The women and men at Gonfarone's were intellectual equals.

The Gulf of Misunderstanding

The fighting in Europe might have been over, but the US occupation of the Dominican Republic continued to exercise the Hispanic American community in New York. Max Henríquez Ureña gathered together many of the documents he had collected while acting as his father's secretary between August and September 1916 and published them in Havana, along with a substantial historical background.[108] The volume was addressed to the Congress and people of the USA, but by this time it had probably become obvious to the whole family that Henríquez Carvajal was very unlikely to be allowed to take up his presidency, so the publication was mainly a statement for posterity about Wilson's hypocrisy, beginning as it does with juxtaposed epigraphs from Harry S. Knapp's declaration of US military control and Woodrow Wilson's infamous 1918 Pan-American speech to Mexican journalists in which he suggested that all American countries should sign a declaration guaranteeing each other's political independence.[109] At best, it was a last and despairing attempt to make a case for the cessation of the US military occupation on the grounds that such occupations threaten the very fabric of the Pan American Union. Not, it turned out, a consideration that would trouble either Wilson or his successors.

---

[107] For general background, see Francesca Miller, 'Feminism and Social Justice', in her *Latin American Women and the Search for Social Justice*, Hanover: University Press of New England, 1991, pp. 68–109.

[108] Max Henríquez Ureña, *Los Estados Unidos y La República Dominicana: La Verdad de los Hechos Comprobada por Datos y Documentos Oficiales*, Havana: Imprenta 'El Siglo XX', 1919. Manuel F. Cestero made a similar compilation: *The Dominican Republic and the Military Occupation*, New York: n.p., 1920.

[109] See above, pp. 111–12.

On the whole, the end of the First World War seems to have induced considerable confusion into the ranks of Latin American intellectuals. Pan-Americanism had never been a straightforward ideology. It was certainly possible to argue that Bolívar was its progenitor along with Jefferson; that the two of them had asserted the originality and sovereignty of republican America as against a largely monarchical Europe. In another article written in the warm post-Armistice glow, the Nicaraguan politician Rafael Urtecho embraced the term and pushed the claims of the Central American, José Cecilio del Valle as its true germinator.[110] But Urtecho obviously had difficulties in convincing even himself. If Pan-Americanism means guarantees of independence and territorial integrity, he suggested, then fine; but actions have sometimes run counter to words. Pan-Hispanism is not a real alternative, he wrote; but there's no reason why the two ideas cannot coexist. The war has awoken in Latin America admiration for the USA; but the USA needs to behave in a certain way—which Urtecho was happy to outline—in order fully to gain Latin American trust: it must know our language and history better, it must show more tolerance towards our customs and social environment. It must have occurred even to Urtecho himself that the USA was not likely to be listening to his words. Others, however, proved more than willing to believe in US goodwill.

The Chilean Tancredo Pinochet Le-Brun (1879–1957)—no relation to Augusto—offers an interesting pan-American life and career, which doubles and crosses Salomón de la Selva's. He spent some of his 20s in London, teaching at Kilburn Grammar School, and so became fluent in English. Back in Chile he was an ardent nationalist and a campaigning journalist. *La Conquista de Chile en el Siglo XX* (1906) criticises the sale of natural resources to foreign companies from a strongly nationalistic perspective but with the USA seen as the country to emulate.[111] Having left Chile because he feared for his life, he worked in Buenos Aires before being appointed Chilean representative to the International Congress of Chambers of Commerce in

---

[110] Rafael Urtecho, 'Pan Americanism from a Central American Standpoint', *Inter-America*, 3 (October 1919–August 1920), 347–49. The essay first appeared in *El Comercio* (Managua).
[111] See for background Patrick Barr-Melej, *Reforming Chile: Cultural Politics, Nationalism, and the Rise of the Middle Class*, Chapel Hill: University of North Carolina Press, 2001; and Fredrick B. Pike, *Chile and the United States, 1880–1962: The Emergence of Chile's Social Crisis and the Challenge to United States Diplomacy*, Notre Dame, IN: University of Notre Dame Press, 1963.

Boston in 1913 and stayed in the USA, working in Chicago in 1917, first in a biscuit factory, then in one making war materials, then as a high school teacher, all the while writing a book called *El diálogo de las dos Américas*.[112] His first wife, Chilean, having died young, Pinochet married Constance Alexander in New York in 1921. Alongside Tancredo Jr, from his first marriage, they had two further children.

While in Chicago, Pinochet had obviously acquired a reputation as a writer on South American affairs because was asked to contribute lead articles to the first four issues of the journal *El Estudiante Latino-Americano*, set up by the Federación de Estudiantes Latino-Americanos in 1918, originally in Ann Arbor, then from 1920 in New York. The journal was published by El Comité de Relaciones Amistosas entre los Estudiantes Extranjeros y los Estados Unidos (347 Madison Avenue). The aims of the organisation were listed as getting to know each other, encouraging good behaviour, getting 'our countries' known in the USA, and acting as a knowledge exchange hub.[113] The second of Pinochet's articles was directed at the supposed Latin American disease of 'scepticism': Latin Americans need to learn US self-belief and conviction was the message.[114] The fourth was a tribute to Theodore Roosevelt, uncritically praising his virtues.[115]

It was presumably this sterling contribution to the higher education element of the semi-official pan-American project that meant that when the publisher Wing B. Allan asked Peter Goldsmith and Samuel Inman to recommend a South American resident in the USA who might revive his magazine, *El Norte Americano*, which chose and translated into Spanish articles from US magazines, both mentioned Pinochet, whom Allan then successfully recruited. Pinochet published *El Diálogo* serially in *El Norte Americano*, attracting the attention of the *New York Times*, which translated excerpts under the title 'A Looking Glass for Two Americas'.[116] A full translation eventually appeared in 1920 as *The Gulf of Misunderstanding; or*

---

[112] For details on Pinochet's life, see his two entertaining memoirs: Tancredo Pinochet Le-Brun, *La biografía de mi smoking*, Santiago de Chile: Biblioteca de Alta Cultura, 1945; and *Mi smoking sale de viaje*, Santiago de Chile: Biblioteca de Alta Cultura, 1945.

[113] *El Estudiante Latino-Americano*, 1, no. 1 (August 1918), 28–30.

[114] *El Estudiante Latino-Americano*, 1, no. 2 (September 1918), 77–78.

[115] 'Al pie de una tumba en Oyster Bay', *El Estudiante Latino-Americano*, 1, no. 4 (January 1919), 135–36.

[116] 'A Looking Glass for Two Americas', *New York Times*, 13 April 1919, p. 28. When the book was published in English, the *Times* produced a long and thoughtful review: 'The Great American Gulf of Misunderstanding', *New York Times*, 9 January 1921, p. 46. The first Spanish edition was *El diálogo de las dos Américas*, Havana: Todamérica, 1918.

North and South America as Seen by Each Other, published by the leading modern publisher, Boni and Liveright, and therefore sitting alongside Ezra Pound and Eugene O'Neill, who both featured in the imprint that year.[117]

The literature of the 'two Americas' tended over the years, and particularly after 1898, to fall into predictable camps, with US writers defending the USA, often in ignorance of anything south of the Rio Grande, and Latin American writers promoting their own sub-continent against the northern behemoth, sometimes in ignorance, sometimes after experiencing life in the belly of the monster. *The Gulf of Misunderstanding* bucks that trend with some panache. The book's narrative premise is strikingly original. A Chilean businessman, travelling through the USA, mainly in the South and Mid-West, writes letters home to his wife in Chile criticising aspects of the USA. Since there is a war on, the letters are opened by a female censor in the New York post office, called Mabel Jones, who decides to add her own notes to the Chilean wife, contesting the husband's assertions and defending the good name of her nation. She signs herself 'Your Friend of the Other Continent'. The strength of the book comes in how well the two cases are put, on issues such as imperialism, religion, prohibition, and women's suffrage. The narrator's presence is minimal, with no opinion offered, so the two views are simply left in juxtaposition. The contest is never an equal one—and certainly never a 'dialogue', as the original Spanish title has it—since the censor is responding to the businessman's case and always therefore having the last word. Although educated, the Chilean relies strongly on newspaper reports for his evidence, while the censor has studied Latin American history and is in the process of writing a book about it. She always also has the moral high ground inasmuch as he is militantly anti-US in all his pronouncements while she is well-disposed towards Latin America and sees 'all America' as eventually becoming a 'moral entity' of note.[118] For a US readership, the Chilean is unlikely to prove sympathetic, belonging, as he does, to a small privileged class that looks to Paris for its sense of refinement and being quick to pour scorn on ragtime music, baseball, and skyscrapers. His is largely a conservative attack on modern democratic trends, such as unionism of the labour force, women's suffrage, and the ease of divorce. Workers intoxicated with democratic ideas will inevitably bring about Bolshevism, he suggests; the American suffragist is 'a completely new sex', neither woman nor man. His case is also undermined by his repeated use of Germany as a model

---

[117] Tancredo Pinochet Le-Brun, *The Gulf of Misunderstanding; or North and South America as Seen by Each Other*, trans. Cecilia M. Brennan, William Sachs, and Charles Evers, New York: Boni and Liveright, 1920.
[118] Pinochet Le-Brun, *The Gulf of Misunderstanding*, p. 5.

to be followed. His attack on prohibition as 'an attack on the liberty of the individual' would undoubtedly have garnered some support from the book's readership, though even here Miss Jones musters a strong case for the defence, largely on medical grounds.[119] That the businessman is a wine producer inevitably taints his argument with perceived self-interest. To his point that in a railroad car a US man seldom gets up to give his seat to a lady, Miss Jones is given the rather extravagant response that as a survivor from the *Titanic* she witnessed many cases of US men giving up their life-jackets to ladies. In her letters to the businessman's wife in Santiago, the censor underlines US philanthropy, its idealism, especially in the context of the current war, and its development of democracy.

Three of the subjects discussed are of particular relevance. One is the US exploitation of Latin American natural resources. In protesting against such exploitation the Chilean is on weak ground, as he himself admits, since the reason for his journey to the USA is to sell his copper deposits. However, he does make out the case for Latin American countries to retain ownership of, and to exploit, their own natural resources, an argument strongly put forward by Pinochet himself in *La Conquista de Chile*. Miss Jones responds that there is no place for seclusion in 'this epoch of internationalism' and that Latin American governments should become partners or stockholders in foreign enterprises.[120]

When it comes to US imperialism, the Chilean certainly lands some blows. He refers to the recent scandal—discussed above in Chapter 6—in which a US journalist, William Hard, had written a stinging critique in the *Metropolitan* of US behaviour towards the Dominican Republic. He has some fun with Roosevelt's fondness for domestic analogy: noisy neighbours requiring quietening down through use of a big stick. He waxes indignant about US appropriation of the name 'America'. He quotes at length the embarrassing defence of US imperialism offered by the Stanford historian H. H. Powers.[121] And he draws parallels between Germany's rape of Belgium and the USA's rape of Panama. Her response yields some ground—another indication of the ultimate superiority of her position since at this stage the Chilean is completely inflexible. So the annexation of Mexico is regretted—explained by the triumph of slave interests—and Powers is admitted as an inadequate commentator. Her defence, however, is straight down the line: African lives have been improved by transportation to the USA, and Indians live a better life now than before European colonisation. The development

---

[119] Pinochet Le-Brun, *The Gulf of Misunderstanding*, pp. 50, 119, 181.
[120] Pinochet Le-Brun, *The Gulf of Misunderstanding*, p. 88.
[121] Pinochet Le-Brun, *The Gulf of Misunderstanding*, pp. 57, 59, 63–67.

of these two groups is 'the most significant educational experiment in the world'.[122] And Roosevelt acted impeccably over the Panama revolution, as he did in Cuba and the Philippines.

Even Miss Jones, though, has some trouble in defending lynching. The Chilean creole distaste for Africans rather undermines the businessman's condemnation ('Thank God, we have no negroes in Chile'), but he does nevertheless pinpoint lynching as a manifestation of internal imperialism, just as imperialism is, in a startling phrase, 'lynching in distant seas'. For Miss Jones, lynching 'has no possible justification', but she nonetheless surrounds it with various pieces of mystification, such as the argument that its motive power comes from genuine indignation towards a delinquent who has offended society.[123]

Pan-Americanism is, for the Chilean, 'vain chatter'. 'We are two opposed worlds accidentally bearing the same name'. 'Latin Americans will never mix with Anglo-Saxon Americans': 'We have nothing in common: neither interests nor ideals.' Commercial union would just be a way of allowing US tyranny over Latin America: 'Our natural bond of union is with Europe.'[124] The civilisations of North and South America will always be antagonistic. Pan-Americanism is therefore just a con. The interested parties in the USA make believe that it means better understanding and mutual help, 'whereas it really stands for nothing else than the commercial conquest of Latin America by the United States'. Pan-Americanism should be opposed by Ibero-Americanism. In response, she admits that 'The Americas do not know each other', but wants to break down the 'mutual ignorance'.[125] Pan-Americanism is a step in that direction, just as the League of Nations will bring all countries and continents together. Although pan-Americanism has a commercial dimension, it is also moral and intellectual—aspects embodied in the Hispanic Society of America.

The narrative offers to gain complexity when the censor's notes are sent to the businessman by his wife, and the wife herself even gets to offer an opinion—that she would love to get to know the USA.[126] By now, the war over, his opinion has in any case modified as he begins to get insights into domestic and family life through his US acquaintances. Miss Jones's letters push at an opening door. The last chapter, entitled 'The Light of Truth', has a religious intensity. The Chilean businessman reverses all his views

---

[122] Pinochet Le-Brun, *The Gulf of Misunderstanding*, pp. 79, 100.
[123] Pinochet Le-Brun, *The Gulf of Misunderstanding*, pp. 99, 97, 98, 108, 109.
[124] Pinochet Le-Brun, *The Gulf of Misunderstanding*, pp. 60, 68. 70, 230, 231, 215.
[125] Pinochet Le-Brun, *The Gulf of Misunderstanding*, pp. 238, 235, 237, 72.
[126] Pinochet Le-Brun, *The Gulf of Misunderstanding*, p. 261.

one by one. He can't quite bring himself to advocate universal prohibition, although he attains 'a modicum of sympathy' for the movement, but he does realise that lynchers were 'athirst for justice', their only failing being a momentary lack of control. The book then ends with a toe-curling account of a meeting between businessman and censor in New York in which the Chilean pronounces himself a complete convert to the US way of life and thought. They have dinner together at the Waldorf-Astoria. He claims total transformation: 'I have a different soul in the same body.' As the narrator sententiously concludes: 'It was more than the awakening of a man; it was the awakening of a continent.' For this reason he agrees to the publication of the letters, 'so that they may serve as a torch to others who have fallen into the same errors'.[127]

There is however no *union*. They remain two souls, 'symbolical of two different races', 'an American of the North and an American of the South'. These kinds of encounters are often formal romances, but propriety demands that the businessman return to his wife, while Miss Jones is no doubt wedded to her writing. Nevertheless, in the final lines, as their dinner concludes and they turn from the lights of Fifth Avenue, '[t]heir eyes met; not the eyes of a man and woman lit up by passion, but those of one America and the other America that understood each other, two continents of a new world that had been divorced from each other and that wished to be re-united.'[128] If this is what pan-Americanism now looked like, then perhaps Salomón de la Selva's project had finally failed.

Nicaragua Has Me

In autumn 1919, de la Selva went back to Central America probably for the first time since 1911, sailing for El Salvador at the beginning of November. An extract from a letter he wrote to a friend was published in the *Pan-American Magazine* under the title 'Central Americanism'. The friend could have been Lilian Elliott herself, and Salomón probably wrote in English. On a personal level, the piece is a reaffirmation of his identity, though, interestingly, as a Central American rather than as a Nicaraguan: indeed, the word 'Nicaragua' nowhere appears. Partly this is a matter of *patria chica*, of feeling a special connection to the places and people of one's earliest years, in this case León, although de la Selva expresses the sentiment with characteristic forcefulness: to make a Central American into a citizen of another country would need

---

[127] Pinochet Le-Brun, *The Gulf of Misunderstanding*, pp. 263, 259, 271, 6.
[128] Pinochet Le-Brun, *The Gulf of Misunderstanding*, pp. 274, 275. The scene is similar to that at the conclusion of Israel Zangwill's play, *The Melting Pot* (1908).

the most thorough overhauling and refashioning: 'his heart must be plucked out and a different heart placed in his side, his blood drained and other blood poured into the red conduits of his flesh'.[129] But there is a political point too. Although Central America needs development, education, and democracy, those things must be 'of Central American growth, not a foreign varnish or an alien imposition'.[130] Aid should be aid, and nothing further. One can catch the hint of desperation in the tone, as if he knew this was a plea that would fall on deaf ears.

The most important letter de la Selva wrote in 1919 was to the PSA stalwart, Jessie Rittenhouse (Fig. 33). She had certainly been a friend for some years, but probably never an intimate one. That summer, however, Jeanne Robert Foster passed on to Salomón a letter from Jessie inviting him to be part of an anthology of US poetry she was compiling. Rittenhouse was a major figure in the New York poetry world: secretary of the PSA, poetry reviewer for the *New York Review of Books*, and editor of *The Little Book of Modern Verse* (1913). This new anthology, to be published later in 1919 as *The Second Book of Modern Verse: A Selection from the Work of Contemporaneous American Poets*, and including only poems published since 1913, would produce the first canon of modern US poetry: as de la Selva writes, 'a place there is somewhat of a consecration'.[131] Many of Salomón's old friends would feature: Edna Millay, Aline Kilmer, Joyce Kilmer, David Morton, Amy Lowell, Louis Untermeyer, Carl Sandburg, Muna Lee, Clement Wood, Thomas S. Jones, Jr, William Rose Benét, Margaret Widdemer, Thomas Walsh, Shaemas O'Sheel; as well as other writers with growing reputations: Vachel Lindsay, Robert Frost, Edward Arlington Robinson, Sara Teasdale, Adelaide Crapsey, H. D., Edgar Lee Masters. It was dazzling company and Salomón recognised the honour of being asked to join it for the poems that had been published in *Tropical Town*. Two years ago, he says, 'your request to establish my poem in your book would have exalted me in my own mind beyond all bounds'. If he refuses now, 'it must be because I have powerful reasons directing me'. The reason is, in a word, nationalism. The importance of the letter means that it needs quoting at length:

---

[129] Salomón de la Selva, 'Central Americanism', *Pan-American Magazine*, XXX, no. 4 (February 1920), 213–14, at 214.
[130] De la Selva, 'Central Americanism', 214.
[131] Louis Untermeyer's *Modern American Poetry* also appeared in 1919 but went back to Emily Dickinson and so didn't include just contemporary poetry.

33 Jessie Rittenhouse. Courtesy of the Department of College Archives and Special Collections Olin Library, Rollins College, Winter Park, Florida.

Jessie, mine is a little country; it is very poor—at the present time and for many years past and years to come, I fear me, there are, there have been, there will be, people starving there—; we have little. Ah, can you understand? Do you know what a child, already conscious of sorrow, feels when he has an invalid, suffering mother? Have you guessed what poignant grief is the lover's whose maid of maidens goes in rags? Such a mother have I in my country, and such a Love. I know, I know—but let that pass—that to most people I seem—though there are only superficial reasons for such an opinion of me—devoid of any great, simple, back-bone-like purpose, desire, ideal. You know me better. Judge me: Am I not wholly devoted to my country? Is not this honourable in me?—Because of my devotion to my country, I must not under any circumstances appear as anything but a Nicaraguan poet any-where. Eager for a glorious death, which would redound in glory for my country, I would have proudly gone forth among the first that bore your flag to the battlefields of France. I did not hesitate to enlist under the colours of England when my only opportunity to serve bravely lay in that. But to win to my proper place among the singers of today, to attain distinction that from all sides except this is denied me,—I'd rather remain unknown forever than to be careless in the least thing of my nationality. Nicaragua has me. In many things a starveling, penurious, let her have her fill of me.

Jessie, your book is of American poets, is of poets of the United States. Even now, among my people, there are [those] who accuse me of infidelity for that I write so much in English, forgetting to cultivate my mother tongue. What would be said of me if I allowed my work to appear as that of a North American? Apart from sentimental reasons, there are the practical ones. I have no future here. Bitter indeed is the bread I eat, and steep the stairs I climb; for I am an alien, and to be an alien is being regarded more and more as an offence, as a stigma, by your people. Again and again, and properly no doubt, my being an alien has proved to me an obstacle in the way of my earning a livelihood. I may dig your subway, I the alien; I may clean your sewers, I may do your hard labour or underpaid work, in which there is no honour; all else is barred to me. Yet I bear you no ill will. Your fine ideals of universal brotherhood are yet too much on your tongue; bye and bye they will reach your heart. Your candid embrace of me among your national poets is a proof sufficient that a time will come when, though loyal first to the flag God willed, when He gave me birth, I should be loyal to, will constitute no demerit of me. I have said it in one of my poems (*The Dreamer's Heart Knows* ...); the United States shall feel a special pride in me when my name is praised. But my future is in my country. A fruit must ripen ere it falls, unless calamitous winds or greedy hands shake it or pluck. When I have ripened, I will go back to my country. The United States is my sun; I will grow nutritive, wholesome, sweet, informed by its light, matured by its warmth. But my land shall draw me when the meat of me is ready. I abide my season.

Please believe me your lover and the lover of your country in the best sense, but consecrate to Nicaragua. I would there were but one flag for these two lands so dear to me![132]

There is undoubtedly a good deal of fantasy and deception—much of it perhaps self-deception—in de la Selva's writing, but it would be difficult

---

[132] Letter from Salomón de la Selva to Jessie B. Rittenhouse, JBRC (2 August 1919). JBRC is the Jessie B. Rittenhouse Collection, Rollins College, Winter Park, Florida.

to deny the sincerity of his feelings for his country, even if the return he envisaged proved elusive. Some of the dreams are simply impossible: logically there cannot be one flag for two nations. But it is telling, that when it comes to anthologising—canonising—his poetry, he feels that he has to choose: he either has to be a US poet or a Nicaraguan poet. Dual belonging, even in the aesthetic realm, is an impossibility. Roosevelt may have died at the beginning of the year, but his doctrine of 100 per cent Americanism still held sway, if anything even more powerfully in the fervent Red Scare months of the summer of 1919, with the enemy now within the city itself and therefore—so the argument went—even more of a threat than during the 18 months of the war. 'Alien' was the word of the moment, and Salomón, despite having lived in New York for half his life, felt interpellated by it. The fruit ripening on the tree was one of the infamous metaphors of US expansionism, so his deployment of it here is probably not accidental. He is himself the fruit on the tree, and he wants to feed the country of his birth rather than that of his adoption. The meat of him was, as it turned out, just about ready. Yet the USA remains his sun.

A postscript which is as long as the main part of the letter then takes off in different directions. He urges the inclusion of Jeanne Robert Foster in Rittenhouse's anthology (one of her poems was included). He discusses other poets, such as Edward Arlington Robinson and Adelaide Crapsey, which brings him to Muna Lee and hence back to the women in his life:

I am told that Muna Lee and Luis Muñoz Marín (of Porto Rico) are married. Muna is a good poet (if she may only grow!) and a fine girl. She was to have been my wife; I think we were engaged, but she forgot me while I was away. On the other hand, Marya Alexandrovna Zaturenskaia (of The Four Horse-men fame) published reports of a love affair that I had with her—all false. I have loved Muna, and I have loved a thousand others, but not Marya. I have taken no one; given myself to noone. Edna, I think, is the one I have loved most. María Teresa, the Cuban beauty (do you remember her?) has gone with her family to her native land ... My sweetheart now is an honest-to-God princess—niece of a King. What do you think of that? A princess has my heart; but if a beggar maid asked me for a kiss, how could I refuse? So, you see, I am not yet truly in love. However, I am writing sonnets to my wife and to my children! I have imagined a very wonderful wife for myself, and the loveliest boy!—I wooed enough in *Tropical Town*, I think; and the critics called me lewd. In my next book I'll show them that I am a very respectable husband and father!!!—oh, it's a merry world. My wife is a XVII century English lady—no; she is a XIV century Florentine Madonna. My boy is of all ages ... Do not forget, when you write to me, to send your love to my wife and boy. They send you theirs.[133]

'I think we were engaged' is a telling formulation, but the forgetting is much more likely to have been on Salomón's side, as Marya Zaturenska's report of him leaving Muna at the altar rather suggests.[134] After their brief but passionate attachment in Chicago in autumn 1917, de la Selva certainly pursued other love interests in New York, and their paths don't seem to have crossed that frequently even after she came to New York in June 1918. Luis and Muna attended the Gonfarone dinner together only ten days before their marriage. Marya's false report of a love affair still rankles: he clearly fails to understand the extent to which he led her on. The Cuban María Teresa is unidentified, but the princess, niece to a king, moves us firmly back into the realm of fantasy.

---

[133] Letter from Salomón de la Selva to Jessie B. Rittenhouse, JBRC (2 August 1919).
[134] See above, p. 287.

Aftermath

> So all our yesterdays, dissolved at length
> Into the soil of everlasting time,
> Make rich the present.[1]

The long letter to Jessie Rittenhouse in August 1919 reads like Salomón de la Selva's final reckoning with his New York years and his pan-American project, although the break was never clean. He left the city for El Salvador in the last week of October and was in Central America long enough to fall in love with yet another teenager, a gifted young poet called Margarita del Carmen Brannon Vega, whose Irish-descended father was a Blavatskian theosophist.[2] After a few months in El Salvador, Nicaragua, and Honduras, he returned to New York via Guatemala and New Orleans in late February 1920, moving quickly on to Washington, DC and Virginia where he spent the summer and autumn of 1920.[3] By the autumn of 1921 he was living in Mexico City. In the process of moving south de la Selva cut his personal ties with New York: he frequently returned to the city but rarely sought out his old friends, in person or by letter. At the same time, though, he never dug up the roots he'd put down there: they remained part of his identity. He was always proud of his pan-American efforts.

Leaving New York

There are two indirect accounts of this period, both fed via writer acquaintances. The first, written by Prosper Buranelli—friend and ghostwriter

---

[1] Salomón de la Selva, 'Of Time and Song', *Tropical Town and Other Poems*, New York: John Lane Company, 1918, p. 132.
[2] The news of his departure was reported in the 'Latin American Colony Notes' of *The Sun*, 3 November 1919, p. 12.
[3] He wrote to Marya Zaturenska in March 1920, saying that he was just back from a trip to Nicaragua: Letter from Salomón de la Selva to Marya Zaturenska, FMP (27 March 1920).

of the broadcaster and impresario Lowell Thomas—appeared in *The World Magazine* in August 1920.[4] With considerable journalistic licence, it reports de la Selva's arrival in the city as a newsworthy event: 'Recently there has come to New York a young man of curious mien', overlooking the fact that he had actually been living there for well over a decade. It rehearses his exotic background—half Spanish, quarter Indian, quarter English (though in fact he was one-eighth English). It tells of how his father sent him travelling alone to London, Paris, and New York (whereas he travelled to New York on a government scholarship under the protection of a family friend). Of how after overcoming all kinds of difficulties he managed to publish two volumes of verse (in fact just the one). But the overarching narrative is of how an unnamed woman—the *monna innominata*—has replaced Margarita DeBayle in de la Selva's affections. Margarita DeBayle Sacasa was a member of one of the most prominent Leonese families, her father a famous doctor; and when she was six years old, Rubén Darío had written for her the lovely poem, 'Margarita, está linda la mar' [Margarita, the sea is lovely].[5] Salomón and Margarita were children in León together, though she was six years younger than him; and he would have seen her again in 1910, though since she only had her tenth birthday that summer, his pronouncement, reported by Buranelli, that he would make her his would have to have been framed with some judicious use of the future tense.[6] All this, however, appears in the context of Buranelli's article the better to dramatise the *coup de foudre* that saw de la Selva—supposedly employed by a leading New York finance house to report on conditions in Central America—abandon the now 20 year-old Margarita, who had supposedly welcomed him back with open arms, in favour of the (unnamed) Carmen.[7] But alas!—and this is very much the tone of the piece—the father, himself a poet and therefore

---

[4] Prosper Buranelli, 'Poet of Fantastic Fortunes', *The World Magazine*, 29 August 1920, pp. 10, 13.

[5] 'A Margarita DeBayle', in Rubén Darío, *Poema del otoño y otros poemas* [1910], Madrid: Editorial Mundo Latino, 1918, pp. 69–80.

[6] When he had planned to return to Nicaragua in late 1917, Salomón had written to Edna: 'I will see Margarita Debayle, and I wish to look very handsome to her. Maybe I shall marry her. That would be the desire of the families' (Letter from Salomón de la Selva to Edna St Vincent Millay, ESVMP [15 November 1917]). Margarita could hardly, though, have been the 'maid of maidens', languishing in rags, referred to in his letter to Jessie Rittenhouse (see above, p. 331). That may have been his sister.

[7] In New York, in 1919, 'serví de secretario a uno de los jefes de una importante casa bancaria en Nueva York' [I worked as secretary to one of the heads of an important New York bank] (Salomón de la Selva, 'Al pueblo de Nicaragua' [1927], *Antología Mayor/III: Ensayos*, pp. 577–92, at p. 585).

distrustful of poets, forbad the new romance, leaving the lovelorn Salomón to send his *enamorata* to a convent while he himself retired to a Carthusian monastery. All this to be taken with a barrel of salt, as the jocular accent of the article suggests. At this stage, it seems as if de la Selva was still undecided about what route to take. He had not cut links with New York literary life, publishing a well-informed and rather modest essay in the *New York Evening Post* in the summer of 1920 called 'The Poets of Nicaragua' in which his own achievements occupied only a small place.[8]

The second indirect account—not substantially different but more soberly expressed—is found in a letter written by the Honduran writer and diplomat Rafael Heliodoro Valle to Joaquín García Monge to be published in the latter's *Repertorio Americano*, where it accompanied de la Selva's essay on Walter Pater and his poem 'Pajaritos de barro'.[9] Heliodoro Valle obviously got his information from the horse's mouth and in this instance the horse seems to have told the story fairly straight, although with some equivocation when it came to his war record: 'Es que el poeta estuvo, como nunca antes, más cerca del dolor diario, en diálogos con la Muerte' [The thing is that the poet was, as never before, closer to daily grief, in dialogue with Death] is a formulation which suggests experience in the trenches even if it doesn't specifically describe it; likewise, 'me leyó sus nuevos poemas escritos en medio de la catástrofe' [he read me his new poems written in the midst of the catastrophe]. The *monna innominata* appears again, a love that has sown new constellations in the poet's mental firmament.

Two months later, de la Selva himself wrote to García Monge to introduce his new protégée as 'una mágica poetisa de nuestra patria grande' [a magical poetess from our great homeland]—and finally to name her. He describes how they had met on a train in El Salvador towards the end of 1919: he, in soldier's uniform, was heading to Nicaragua to visit his family, she to Honduras to stay with friends over Christmas. They talked—of Giorgione, of Shakespeare, of Romain Rolland, of the Central American Union— and Salomón promised to visit her in Tegucigalpa, which he did, though well-chaperoned one would imagine.[10] Back in the USA—according now to the account that Carmen Brannon herself gave to de la Selva's Nicaraguan biographer, Jorge Eduardo Arellano—he took her under his epistolary wing,

---

[8] Salomón de la Selva, 'The Poets of Nicaragua', *New York Evening Post*, 3 July 1920, p. 7.
[9] Rafael Heliodoro Valle, 'Salomón de la Selva', *Repertorio Americano*, II, no. 15 (15 March 1921), 206–07.
[10] Salomón de la Selva, 'Una mágica poetisa de nuestra patria grande', *Repertorio Americano*, II, no. 21 (30 May 1921), 293–94.

introducing her to his favourite English poets and coaching her in English metrics.[11] After a year, he judged her ready to make her poetic début on an international stage and sent two of her poems along with his letter to García Monge, placing her in the exalted company of Edna St Vincent Millay, Alfonsina Storni, Juana de Ibarbourou, and Gabriela Mistral, all a few years older than Carmen. A couple of months later, Salomón published a series of six sonnets dedicated to C.B., and they continued to write to each other but, by the time they next met, in 1929, Carmen was married.[12] Carmen Brannon's talent was real enough: under the pseudonym Claudia Lars she later became a very fine poet. She always remembered de la Selva fondly and certainly regarded him as her poetic mentor; but it seems as if the *amour fou* he hinted at was mostly, if not entirely, in his imagination.[13]

De la Selva's conversations with Buranelli and Heliodoro Valle both offered the opportunity for him to embroider earlier parts of his biography, continuing the process of auto-mystification which—if nothing else— has made life difficult for biographers. In 1933, for example, the highly authoritative *Enciclopedia Universal Ilustrada Europeo Americana* published an entry on de la Selva which could only have been drawn from information he himself provided. It noted, among other things, that he was appointed at Williams College as 'catedrático de lenguas romances' [Chair of Romance Languages] (in fact, his title was 'Instructor'); that in an article in *Harper's Monthly Magazine* William Dean Howells had recognised him as 'uno de los escritores más ilustrados de la América Central' [one of the most famous writers in Central America] (though Howells had been complimentary about the single poem, 'Tropical Town', he'd made no such sweeping judgement); and that among his publications was the book of poems, *A Soldier*, published in London in 1919 (no such book ever appeared).[14] In 1935, a high-school principal from Silver Creek, Chautauqua, in New York State, went on a trip to the Panama Canal Zone and wrote an account for his local newspaper in which he recalled meeting a slim, blue-eyed Nicaraguan, wearing a drooping moustache, who was the secretary of the Centro de Estudios Pedagógicos.

---

[11] Jorge Eduardo Arellano, *Aventura y genio de Salomón de la Selva*, León: Alcaldía Municipal, 2003, pp. 98–100. Arellano interviewed her in San Salvador in February 1969.

[12] The sonnets were published in *Darío: Revista Quincenal Ilustrada* [León], II, no. 32 (June 1921), 8–9: see Arellano, *Aventura y genio*, pp. 100–02.

[13] See Claudia Lars, 'Recordando a Salomón de la Selva', *Cultura*, 36 (1965), 43–46.

[14] 'De la Selva, Salomón', in *Enciclopedia Universal Ilustrada Europeo Americana*, Madrid: Espasa Calpe, 1933, vol. 9, pp. 1225–26 (Apendice). See *Catalogue of Williams College, 1916–1917*, Williamstown: Williams College, 1916, p. 13; William Dean Howells, 'Editor's Easy Chair', *Harper's Monthly Magazine*, 134 (April 1917), 746–47.

To the principal's surprise, this Nicaraguan turned out to have a PhD 'from one of the greatest American Universities', had been a professor at Columbia and Williams, had served for two years as a British soldier on the front line, and had fought with Sandino against US Marines in Nicaragua. There was also another wife, a German woman.[15] None of this was true.

Prosper Buranelli's piece in *The World* had at least one eager reader. In August, Edwin Markham, Salomón's erstwhile master, wrote to inquire after his disciple: 'You know, my dear poet,' he began, 'that I have watched your kaleidoscopic fortunes with a fond fatherly interest.' He wondered, with evident dismay, why de la Selva hadn't visited or written. 'Send me news, then let your face shine in upon me. This is not so much an appeal as it is a command.'[16] Markham was still in 1920 the most famous living US poet, so this was not a relationship easily scorned. It seems that Markham's letter followed Salomón around until it reached him in Staunton, Virginia, where he was teaching at the military academy. Salomón replied in November. Aside from recommending to Markham a young poet from South Carolina whom he'd met at Staunton, de la Selva adopted the accustomed tone of his letters to his *cher maître*: 'Your anxious letter of ever so long ago … has reminded me that I am an ungrateful cur to have kept myself away from my lyric king so many months. I will make up for this as handsomely as I may, writing you a very long letter as soon as I get established in my new position in Washington, as editor for the Pan American Union, for which I leave today.'[17] 'Editor' was a rather grand term for de la Selva's employment at the PAU; and the very long letter never got written. Deliberately or not, he was starting to cut his ties with his friends in New York. This is the PAU, incidentally, which he had described two years earlier, in a letter to Amy Lowell, as 'a putrefact, stagnating, salary-drawing, selfish mass of half of the time-drunken mediocrity'.[18] He later suggested that he forced himself to work there in order to get to know 'so-called official Pan-Americanism'.[19]

---

[15] Ray C. Witter, 'Odds and Ends in Central America', *Silver Creek News and Times*, 22 August 1935, pp. 1–2. On the story behind the mythical German wife, see Steven F. White, *Rubén Darío y Salomón de la Selva: Ecos de la muerte y la guerra*, León: Promotora Cultural Leonesa, 2016, pp. 75–77.
[16] Letter from Edwin Markham to Salomón de la Selva, EMA (20 August 1920).
[17] Letter from Salomón de la Selva to Edwin Markham, EMA (7 November 1920).
[18] Letter from Salomón de la Selva to Amy Lowell, ALP (9 April 1918).
[19] Salomón de la Selva, 'Al pueblo de Nicaragua' [1927], *Antología Mayor III/Ensayos*, pp. 577–92, at p. 586.

One other letter survives from this period. Like Markham, Salomón's Jamaican friend, W. Adolphe Roberts, had written a concerned letter and got a fairly light-hearted reply from Washington:

> I was going to be a monk, then I decided to be military once more & got to be a Captain; the Union of Central America stirred me very deeply and I came here ostensibly to be an editor, in my heart of hearts to do all I could for Pan America; after two months of the job I had a fight, resigned, others resigned too, I went to teach, the fight went on, I won it, and here I am again. Have been here nine days now. That's the barest outline of it all. The details are as rich as a Florentine tapestry. There has been no marriage, but in the past year, past twelvemonth I mean, there have been: Marie, Margarita, Herminia, Julia, Leonorcita, Carmen, another Margarita, Fidelina, María, Elisita, Rosaura, Helen, otra Marie, Marguerite, Stella and the most recent one is Elizabeth. I have loved them all, and some I grew to hate and some to pity and Carmen and Stella I still love with a kind of worship the first one, with a kind of complete trust the star yclept. Carmen is too wonderful for words, the most beautiful creature in God's world and a poet that beats even Edna …
> What has become of Edna?—You know, I have always loved her with every atom of my being. And beautiful, gracious, queen-hearted J. R. F.? Her too I have loved.[20]

So monk and soldier during those four months, and then two spells of employment in the PAU in Washington, DC, broken by some time as a teacher. And over the last 12 months an inventory of 14 lovers, real or imagined. He compares his life to a Florentine tapestry, though his list sounds distinctly operatic: 'Madamina, il catalogo è questo.' He tells Roberts ('old man') that he thinks of his New York friends but doesn't write to them because he's always losing their addresses—not the most convincing of excuses. This was the last time he wrote to Roberts, and he had clearly already lost touch with Edna and Jeanne.[21] In early 1921, he was invited by José Vasconcelos, on the recommendation of Pedro Henríquez Ureña, to

---

[20] Letter from Salomón de la Selva to W. Adolphe Roberts, WARA (17 November 1920).

[21] Several years later Roberts wrote a short piece for the journal he had founded and edited, *The American Parade*, in which he quoted admiringly from *Tropical Town* and wondered what had become of Salomón de la Selva ('Poets of Nicaragua', *The American Parade*, 1, no. 3 [1926], 189–91).

take up a position as editor of the journal *El Maestro* in Mexico City, an offer he accepted with alacrity. He may have been in Mexico in spring 1921, though by June he was back in the USA. But by September he had definitely relocated because he attended the First International Congress of Students in Mexico City along with the Spanish writer Ramón del Valle-Inclán and Pedro Henríquez Ureña.[22]

The move to Mexico was not entirely surprising. Already in a letter to Amy Lowell in April 1918 describing his intellectual milieu, de la Selva's centre of gravity seems to have become mexicanised, even if several of the Mexicans were still at this stage in exile in New York. Included in the group were Martín Luis Guzmán, José Vasconcelos, Julio Torri, Enrique González Martínez, Balbino Dávalos, and Alfonso Reyes. Mexico was, he admitted, 'the capital of our literary republic'.[23] Once Vasconcelos had become rector of UNAM, and had tempted Pedro Henríquez Ureña to return, the move south must have seemed logical to de la Selva.

The only New York contacts de la Selva appears to have maintained beyond 1920—and these only briefly—were with Eugenia Geisenheimer and Theresa Helburn. He stayed with Geisenheimer at her house in Shoreham, on Long Island, in June 1921, and when he returned to New York in December 1921 to accompany Ramón del Valle-Inclán, he evidently met Theresa, as he recalls in a letter written just before his departure: 'you are the only girl I kissed this time'.[24] But that seems to have been his last letter to Thery; and, although the evidence is not conclusive, he may already have been involved in Mexico City with Katherine Anne Porter.

It is perhaps not accidental that de la Selva's final piece of writing from New York—the letter to Joaquín García Monge published in *Repertorio Americano* in August 1921—has some marked similarities to the equivalent Parthian essay written by Rubén Darío six years previously. Both offer extravagant praise of cultured and rich women whose recognition and support have given the writers some social cachet in the cut-throat world of Anglo-Saxon New York. But whereas Darío, at the end of his career and his life, had to write in desperation from his hospital bed, de la Selva writes from his patron's *quinta* on a perfect June day where the sea breeze smells of honeysuckle and his readers are asked to feel grateful that he dragged himself away from walking on the beach to tap out his letter.

---

[22] 'Se abrió el congreso de estudiantes', *Excelsior* [Mexico City], 21 September 1921, p. 1.
[23] Letter from Salomón de la Selva to Amy Lowell, ALP (9 April 1918).
[24] Letter from Salomón de la Selva to Theresa Helburn, THP (undated [December 1921]).

This is clearly a man who has arrived. He may be about to leave, but the impression he wants to give is of somebody leaving on his own terms, at the top of his game.[25]

In Mexico

De la Selva's years in Mexico fall outside the scope of the current volume, but they need mentioning because the early months there, in particular his ill-starred relationship with Katherine Anne Porter, cast some light, or perhaps some shadow, on the fully grown man—now in his late twenties—who had returned to live in a Hispanic country for the first time since he was 13.

Porter had gone to Mexico City in October 1920, having got to know Mexican artists, notably Adolfo Best Maugard, in New York. The details of her relationship with de la Selva, three years her junior, are hazy.[26] They probably met in the autumn of 1921, and she probably aborted their foetus sometime in 1922. They did not part amicably. Porter scholars are clear that de la Selva features—unsympathetically portrayed—in several of her stories, notably 'Virgin Violetta', which was published in *The Century* in December 1924, 'The Martyr', and 'The Lovely Legend'. In her unpublished notes, Porter says that de la Selva seduced the younger sister of Palma de Guillén, one of Diego Rivera's models. She also notes him as 'totally evil and without scruple', a judgement on which she elaborated in a conversation with Enrique Hank Lopez in Mexico City in 1964: '"He was one of the most evil men I've ever known," she said. "An absolute scoundrel, who thought nothing of seducing the teenage daughter of his best friend and then bragging about it. Yet there was something strangely compelling about Salomón de la Selva, a certain sinister magnetism that made him hard to resist"'.[27]

Whatever his motivations, de la Selva had been committed to fighting in the war. When it came to writing poetry about the war he was much more

---

[25] Salomón de la Selva, 'Carta de Nueva York', *Repertorio Americano*, II, no. 28 (10 August 1921), 393–94, at 393.

[26] The most reliable account is in Thomas F. Walsh, *Katherine Anne Porter and Mexico: The Illusion of Eden*, Austin: University of Texas Press, 1992.

[27] Walsh, *Katherine Anne Porter*, p. 65; the conversation is in Darlene Harbour Unrue, ed., *Katherine Anne Porter Remembered*, Tuscaloosa: University of Alabama Press, 2010, p. 202, reprinted from Enrique Hank Lopez, *Conversations with Katherine Anne Porter: Refugee from Indian Creek*, Boston: Little, Brown, 1981, pp. xiii–xviii.

ambivalent. As we saw earlier, there are poems full of bravado about the *prospect* of fighting, but he was scathing about the quality of other writers' war poems—while admitting that it seemed in bad taste to criticise poems written by those who had been killed. His ambivalence finds perfect expression in the phantom volume *A Soldier Sings*—often claimed, even by de la Selva himself, to have been published in London in 1919, even though he had written angrily to Jeanne Robert Foster that she should inform Mr Jefferson Jones, of John Lane Company, 'that there is not going to be any war-poetry first section in my next book'.[28] In fact, his next book consisted entirely of war poetry.

It is not clear just when de la Selva wrote the poems that make up *El soldado desconocido* [The Unknown Soldier], published in Mexico City in 1922, or whether some or all of them were first written in English and then translated into Spanish. It does, however, seem likely that the impetus for the title and prologue (dated New York, 1921) came from the movement initiated in 1920 when the Reverend David Railton, who had served on the Western Front, wrote to the Dean of Westminster proposing that an unidentified British soldier from the battlefields in France be buried with due ceremony in Westminster Abbey to represent the many hundreds of thousands of Empire dead. The Tomb of the Unknown Warrior was dedicated there on 11 November 1920, followed by The Tomb of the Unknown Soldier in Arlington Cemetery in Virginia on 11 November 1921. In October 1921, the body of an unidentified US soldier had been exhumed from each of four US cemeteries in Europe. The bodies were placed in identical caskets and taken to Châlons-sur-Marne where one was selected at random to become *the* unknown soldier. The reporting of this ceremony seems to have prompted de la Selva's prologue, which describes four typical Americans: one has gone back to his old life but failed to find work. A second is in hospital, not being cured of his injuries. Another came back in a coffin, and his girlfriend has just married someone else. The fourth just carried on as before as if the war had never happened. Since clearly none of these men can be heroes, de la Selva writes, the hero becomes the Unknown Soldier. They dug him up and sealed him in a coffin; then put the coffin in a splendid sarcophagus. He doesn't have a name or a family, just a country; so he satisfies everybody. And, most important of all, he makes no demands and there's no need to give him a pension. The bitterness of the returning soldier saturates de la Selva's prose. There certainly is no recognition of Nicaraguan unknown soldiers, which

---

[28] Letter from Salomón de la Selva to Jeanne Robert Foster, FMC (10 September 1918).

is where *El soldado desconocido* can make a contribution. A dozen years later John Dos Passos would write a devastating attack on the unknown soldier process at the end of his novel *Nineteen Nineteen*:

> In the tarpaper morgue at Chalons-sur-Marne in the reek of chloride of lime and the dead, they picked out the pine box that held all that was left of
> enie menie minie moe plenty other pine boxes stacked up there containing what they'd scraped up of Richard Roe
> and other person or persons unknown. Only one can go. How did they pick John Doe?
> Make sure he ain't a dinge, boys,
> make sure he ain't a guinea or a kike,
> how can you tell a guy's a hundredpercent
> when all you've got's a gunnysack full of bones, bronze buttons stamped with the screaming eagle and a pair of roll puttees?[29]

It is almost as if de la Selva were prospectively adding to Dos Passos's acerbic comment: 'And make damn sure he's not a spic', because the one thing everybody knew about the Unknown Soldier was that he was 'hundred-percent' *white American*.

Given the importance of his war experience for de la Selva, and given the vast extent of his writings, published and unpublished, over the 40 years he lived after 1918, it is remarkable that he never stated unequivocally whether or not he saw action in the trenches. *El soldado desconocido* seemed to almost all its readers to offer such a graphic account of a personal experience of war that its testimonial nature has never been publicly questioned. It was a young member of the next generation of Nicaraguan poets, Ernesto Cardenal, who came closest to doing so in a 1948 article, although even here the challenge was indirect, indeed doubly indirect inasmuch as the note of doubt that Cardenal appeared to introduce ('Aunque el poeta afirma en el prólogo haber estado realmente en la guerra ... las fechas de los poemas de su libro anterior difícilmente dan lugar a que se lo crea' [Although the poet affirms in the prologue that he really was in the war ... the dates of the poems in his previous book make that difficult to believe]) was itself based on some shaky reading: the prologue stated that the author

---

[29] John Dos Passos, *Nineteen Nineteen*, in *U.S.A.* [1938], Harmondsworth: Penguin, 1966, p. 722.

had served under the flag of King George, not that he had fought in the trenches, and the 1918 dates attached to some of the poems in *Tropical Town* restricted the time frame but by no means excluded the possibility of participation. Cardenal's conclusion, however, was acute: the book 'produce cierta impresión de autobiografía ficticia' [produces a certain impression of fictitious autobiography].[30] The official 'unknown soldier' is by definition dead, and so de la Selva does not offer himself as an example, but Cardenal insisted on using the term to describe him, with the implication that he is 'unknown' on account of the lack of information he has provided about his military experiences.

But Cardenal went further, also alighting upon the pervasive sense of shame ('vergüenza') in *El soldado desconocido*, as a theme but also as a mood or sentiment, suggesting that this may be an explanation for the poet's reclusiveness in the years following 1922. Either Cardenal intuited that the sense of shame related to de la Selva not having fought on the front line, or his poetic antennae allowed him to read between the lines of the poetry more acutely than others. As Jorge Eduardo Arellano explains, Ernesto Mejía Sánchez took a copy of Cardenal's essay to de la Selva, who was furious at its implication; not, however, at the implication that he hadn't actually fought in the war, but at the implication—supposedly conveyed in a remark about de la Selva's poem about Alexander Hamilton—that Salomón's mother had been a prostitute. This was an implication that only de la Selva could read into Cardenal's words, and he was not to be dissuaded, despite the best efforts of various Mexican friends and a letter from Cardenal himself.[31] It is impossible not to conclude that de la Selva was, consciously or unconsciously, refusing to see the real implication in Cardenal's essay and was diverting attention away from it by taking furious offence elsewhere—a diversionary tactic which worked rather effectively for 70 years.

Later Life

The briefest of sketches will have to suffice.[32] In August 1922, de la Selva was dismissed from his positions in the Mexican Ministry of Education after falling out with Vasconcelos. He worked for a while with CROM,

---

[30] Ernesto Cardenal, 'Salomón de la Selva: El soldado desconocido', *Rueca*, 5, no. 18 (1948), 12–19, at 15–16.
[31] Arellano, *Aventura y genio*, pp. 144–45.
[32] See, in general, Arellano, *Aventura y genio*; and Eddy Kühl, 'Salomón de la Selva, datos de su vida', *Revista de Temas Nicaragüenses*, no. 85 (May 2015), 340–49.

the federation of Mexican labour unions, and then from 1924, back in Nicaragua, with the equivalent national organisation, the Frente Obrero Nicaragüense.[33] In January 1926, he married Carmela Castrillo Gamez, with whom he had two children, a son, also Salomón, and a daughter, Carmen, who was killed in the 1931 earthquake in Managua. After persistent criticism of the presidency of José María Moncada, whose electoral victory had been engineered by the occupying US forces, de la Selva was expelled in October 1929: he had already expressed his strong support for Augusto Sandino's military revolt against the US occupation of Nicaragua.[34] After a short stay in New York, he lived in Costa Rica, working as a journalist and language teacher, but had to leave after a disagreement with the Minister of Education, which ended in a duel. Three years in Panama followed, including a spell editing the *Digesto Latinoamericano/Latin American Digest*, a bilingual supplement of *Panama American*, founded and edited by Nelson Rounsevell. *Digesto Latinomericano* demonstrated strong anti-imperialist and pro-Sandino credentials—which soon had to include an obituary for Sandino after his murder. During 1934, the leftist US journalist Carleton Beals was de la Selva's co-editor.[35]

De la Selva never fell into antagonistic thinking. Even at his moment of maximum opposition to US foreign policy with respect to Nicaragua, he was capable of quoting Theodore Roosevelt with respect on the nature of patriotism and saying that this is exactly how Nicaraguans should view their relationship with the USA. The problem, he insisted in 1927, is that there are individuals in the USA who do not respect this position. The problem is with these individuals, not with the culture as a whole.[36] Indeed, there will be other US individuals, 'hombres de buena voluntad' [men of good will], who will oppose the aggressors. His outlook was determinedly—perhaps naïvely—optimistic. The USA was founded on the principles of liberty and will always return to that path, he claims, even if its leaders have taken it down other ones.[37]

These, however, were the years when it became most difficult to defend

---

[33] On this period, see Jorge Eduardo Arellano, 'Salomón de la Selva: campaña sindical y antiintervencionista', *Revista de Temas Nicaragüenses*, no. 85 (May 2015), 201–04.

[34] Salomón de la Selva, 'Sandino', *The Nation*, 28 January 1928, pp. 63–64.

[35] On this period, see Jorge Eduardo Arellano, 'Salomón de la Selva: periodista y educador en Costa Rica y Panamá' <https://web.archive.org/web/20131014185919/http://www.revistaixchel.org> vol. 2 (2010), 58–73 accessed December 2018.

[36] De la Selva, 'Al pueblo de Nicaragua' p. 581.

[37] De la Selva, 'Al pueblo de Nicaragua', p. 582.

any form of pan-Americanism. Latin American attitudes were hardening, to the extent that in 1934 José Vasconcelos could simply define 'the politics of Pan-Americanism' as the method by which the 'nordic empire' would achieve its aim of incorporating the 20 Hispanic nations of the American continent.[38] By this time, admittedly, Vasconcelos's eccentrically racist views were hardening into fascism. But even de la Selva himself was finding it difficult to keep the faith. His moment of greatest despair arrived in 1930, expressed—characteristically—in an essay purportedly about Thucydides, when he wrote that there was no doubt that the USA could do to Nicaragua what Athens did to Melios: slaughter all its inhabitants because they refused to declare allegiance.

> There is no doubt that the North American imperialists find it necessary to 'round out their empire'. To dominate the whole Caribbean and not to permit any of us to have a free voice. There is no doubt that, in their twisted judgement, to deal with these nations as equals would seem like a 'dangerous weakness'.[39]

Four years later, Sandino was dead, but his example provided signs of hope, as expressed in de la Selva's obituary for the fallen hero:

> The continent owes Sandino, because of his defeat of the Marines that were infinitely better armed, better supplied, better equipped in every way than he, and that outnumbered him some times twenty to one,— the continent owes Sandino a change of psychology making for better friendship. The Latin American complex of physical inferiority Sandino did largely destroy, and whoever has studied inter-American relations knows that inferiority complexes as well as superiority complexes must be destroyed before there can be real feeling of continental solidarity in the peoples of this hemisphere.[40]

As a Nicaraguan, de la Selva was perhaps bound to feel strongly about the hunting and murder of Sandino, just as he had about the filibustering incursions of William Walker that had driven his grandfather from

---

[38] José Vasconcelos, *Bolivarismo y monroísmo: temas iberoamericanos* [1934], Santiago de Chile: Editorial Ercilla, 1937, p. 11.
[39] Salomón de la Selva, 'Discurso sobre los Melios y la Historia de Tucídides', *Repertorio Americano*, XXI, no. 22 (6 December 1930), 348–51, at 350–51.
[40] Salomón de la Selva, 'Sandino', *Digesto Latinoamericano*, 26 February 1934, pp. 1, 16, at p. 16 (English in original).

Granada, and of Groce and Cannon that had led directly to his father's death. But the Walker and Sandino incidents had continental resonance too.

In October 1935, de la Selva returned to Mexico, working as a journalist and for the government, with the Department of Press and Propaganda. In 1939, he applied unsuccessfully to the Rockefeller Foundation for a grant to write a 21-volume history of the USA. His brother, Rogerio, was private secretary to President Alemán (1946–52), and Salomón seems to have acted as a speech-writer: he was certainly involved in the organisation of Alemán's visit to the USA in 1947. This government involvement led to travel opportunities: in December 1941 he was in New York, where he met Edna Millay again; in 1948 he was in Spain, France, and Italy; and in 1950 he was Mexican cultural attaché in Washington, DC.

In Nicaragua, Salomón had known the Somoza family: the sister of his childhood friend Margarita DeBayle had married Anastasio Somoza García, the chief beneficiary of the US occupation of Nicaragua and effective dictator of the country between 1937 and 1956. Since it was Somoza who had ordered Sandino's assassination in 1934, de la Selva refused any official Nicaraguan recognition until after Somoza's own assassination—by the poet Rigoberto López Pérez, from León—in 1956.[41] From Somoza's younger brother Luis, de la Selva accepted the diplomatic post of European ambassador at large, which he was occupying at the time of his death from a heart attack in a Paris hotel on 5 February 1959. His remains were buried in the cathedral in his birthplace, León.

Throughout his life, de la Selva continued to write poems and essays as well as journalism. The three-volume anthology of his work probably only scratches the surface, and there is also an archive of unpublished writings.[42] Generally speaking, his later poetry leaves behind the two great experiments of his youth—writing in English (in *Tropical Town*) and writing in modernist style in Spanish (in *El soldado desconocido*).

---

[41] See Iván Molina Jiménez, 'Entre Sandino y Somoza: La trayectoria de Salomón de la Selva', *Secuencia*, 53 (2002), 139–61.

[42] See above, p. 170 n. 81. On the published work, see Jorge Eduardo Arellano, 'Bibliografía de Salomón de la Selva', *Boletín Nicaraguense de Bibliografía y Documentación*, no. 12 (1976), 102–09; on the unpublished work, Jorge Eduardo Arellano, 'Viaje a los papeles de Salomón de la Selva', *Boletín Nicaraguense de Bibliografía y Documentación*, no. 12 (1976), 95–101.

Taking Account

The wheel continued to turn. Franklin Roosevelt's 'good neighbor' policy offered some signs of continental understanding, soon bolstered—as Wilson's policy had been 20 years earlier—by a European war. With the war over, and now entering his sixth decade, Salomón de la Selva began to reflect on his New York years, writing about perhaps the three figures most important to him from that time: Pedro Henríquez Ureña, Edna Millay, and Rubén Darío. It was time to remember and to take account.

Pedro's sudden death in Argentina in May 1946 occasioned de la Selva's first flood of memories, which has already been drawn from in painting a picture of their friendship and activities.[43] His startling recall paints a vivid picture—without the exaggeration that a quarter of a century often lends; which is perhaps surprising given the constant embroidery of his own life-events in various previous tellings. His own verdict came slightly later, perhaps prompted by his appointment as Mexican cultural attaché in Washington, DC, probably a reward for his work for President Alemán. First came the long essay about Edna Millay, not just recalling their friendship but giving a sympathetic account of her whole career, particularly her work for the anti-fascist movement. Eventually he goes back to her dramatic appearance on the poetic scene in 1912, the year also, he notes, unexpectedly, which sees the beginning in one sense of the 'good neighbour' policy—an excellent policy if carried out intelligently, which it hadn't been. In Baltimore, in 1912, Salomón recalls, FDR, campaigning with Woodrow Wilson, gained the nomination that led to his appointment as Subsecretary to the Navy, the beginning of the career that would take him to the White House. Just before Wilson's inauguration, the 'bad neighbour' policy struck its cruellest blow when the US Embassy in Mexico City collaborated in the plot to assassinate Francisco Madero, who had just been deposed in a coup. Intellectuals fled Mexico, some to the USA, including Pedro Henríquez Ureña and José Vasconcelos, who influenced de la Selva's reintegration into 'Hispanoamérica'.[44] This may in a general sense be true, though it certainly didn't happen immediately after the murder of Madero, but rather when de la Selva went to Mexico in 1921. In any case, 'in a certain sense, this was a pity', he says; and he recalls his work from these years as 'interpreter of each culture to the other and the link between the two', translating poets from Spanish into English and vice

---

[43] See above, pp. 108–16.
[44] Salomón de la Selva, 'Edna St. Vincent Millay', *América: Revista Antológica*, 62 (January 1950), 7–32, at 27–28.

versa—the best that has been done in this field, he reasonably claims.[45] De la Selva was still clearly sore about paths taken, and critical of some of his own choices. The Department of State missed opportunities during the Second World War through its poor decisions, he writes, resulting in books of minimum value.[46] Clearly no one was up to the job Salomón had left incomplete.

Nonetheless, and making use of the third person to deflect charges of vainglory, his final verdict is positive: 'When all is said and done, the work undertaken—disinterestedly and solely for the satisfaction of doing it— during the years of his literary life in New York, is the best that has been done in this field, as would be recognised if it could be collected'.[47] For better and for worse, and looking at the results of such a collection, that seems a fair enough verdict on Salomón de la Selva's pan-American project.

In the same essay he briefly recalls his service in the British Army and his departure from New York for Mexico in 1921. He had last seen Millay in 1919, and only met her again in 1941, the day before the attack on Pearl Harbour, a meeting marked by affection and tears. Of their conversation, what de la Selva chooses to recall—presumably closer to his concerns than to hers—is the debate about Chamizal, that contested smidgeon of land by the Rio Grande on which he wanted, true to his old ideals, to build 'a great New World university'.[48] It was not to be. The essay ends by de la Selva recalling the heroic figure of Inez Millholland, whose widower, Eugen Bossevain, Edna had married and with whom she lived a largely contented and secluded life. By the time he finished writing the essay in September 1949, Bossevain had just died, so recently that the news hadn't reached Mexico; and the essay was published, in January 1950, just nine months before Edna's own death.

In Washington, DC, as Mexican cultural attaché, de la Selva accepted an invitation to speak at a relatively new forum (inaugurated on 12 October 1949) called the Ateneo, established under the auspices of the Pan American Union (Ermilo Abreu Gómez, the Mexican writer, was chief of the cultural division of the PAU at the time)—where de la Selva had briefly worked in 1920—and presided over by the eminent figure of Juan Ramón Jiménez, whom de la Selva had sat beside at a New York dinner

---

[45] De la Selva, 'Edna St. Vincent Millay', 28.
[46] He presumably refers to Luis Alberto Sánchez's *Un sudamericano en Norteamérica; ellos y nosotros*, Santiago de Chile: Ediciones Ercilla, 1942.
[47] De la Selva, 'Edna St. Vincent Millay', 28.
[48] De la Selva, 'Edna St. Vincent Millay', 31. The Chamizal dispute was not settled until 1963.

30 years earlier. The Ateneo seems sometimes to have met at Georgetown and sometimes at the Library of Congress, but de la Selva spoke in the Pan American Union building itself. Muna Lee, present at the dinner at Gonfarone's and now working in Washington, had been the only woman among the 22 founding members, and she was presumably also present at de la Selva's lecture.[49]

Beginning by noting that no great poet works entirely alone, Salomón took the opportunity to pay tribute to Juan Ramón, in whose presence, he says, he will speak about Rubén Darío. De la Selva was primarily concerned to defend the relevance of Darío's American vision—and perhaps his own—in the light of the recently concluded world war. He recalled the debt that the USA owed Darío for its less than warm welcome to him in 1915; he recalled the reading of 'Pax' at Columbia University; he recalled receiving the manuscript of the poem from Darío, which he had passed on to 'mi querido [my dear] Archer M. Huntington'. He noted how appropriate it was that he should be speaking in Washington, in the shadow of the Capitol, where wars are declared and peaces ratified, and where Spanish-Americans meet under diplomatic protocol with US ambassadors. His tone was optimistic: 'Here is where the most tenacious work is undertaken towards the peace of the world, and where most rapidly the shadow of Cain is vanishing, though cainite indeed was the US imperialism only yesterday we were fighting against.'[50]

The story of Cain and Abel had been at the heart of Darío's last great poem, 'Pax', the one he had read at Columbia University on 4 February 1915. In that poem the metaphor had universal application for a fratricide that Darío feared might destroy the world. On this occasion, de la Selva wanted to use it to address his perennial theme of the relationship between North America and Hispanic America. He asserted that despite appearances there was no contradiction between Darío's poems 'A Roosevelt' and 'Salutación al Águila'. Both are poems about brothers, he says: brothers fight, brothers make up, brothers join in union; in many ways a more reassuring metaphor than the one with the bride and the mother that had dominated de la Selva's own 1917 poem, 'The Dreamer's Heart Knows Its Own Bitterness'. US imperialism had indeed once been 'cainite', and needed to be resisted, but that did not mean that the USA would always act in the same way—as Darío knew. And now, in 1950, de la Selva said, the USA, via President

---

[49] Emilia Romero del Valle, 'Vida y muerte del Ateneo de Washington' <https://sajurin.enriquebolanos.org/docs/650.pdf> accessed December 2018.
[50] Salomón de la Selva, 'Discurso sobre Rubén Darío' [1950], in *Antología Mayor/III Ensayos*, pp. 276–88, at pp. 281 and 287.

Truman's Point Four Programme, had formally renounced imperialism in favour of the doctrine of fraternal responsibility. 'Let us hope there will be no betrayal,' he added.[51]

In the short term, Salomón de la Selva's pan-American project was a failure. It left no obvious mark on the cultural life of New York and, for the most part, when others later made similar attempts, they made no reference to de la Selva, usually describing themselves as pioneers in the field, what Harris Feinsod describes as 'an amnesiac sequence of false "firsts"': the 'First Inter-American Writers Congress' in Puerto Rico in 1941 or the 'First Encounter of American Writers' in Concepción in Chile in 1960 or the 'First Gathering of American Poets' in Mexico City in 1964.[52] We can be sure that none of the writers at these gatherings was recalling that evening at the Felix-Portland Hotel in December 1917 when Salomón de la Selva brought Edna Millay and José Santos Chocano together. And yet, unacknowledged, out of sight, there are threads that connect de la Selva's project to these later efforts. Whereas de la Selva never managed to create more than provisional and short-lived institutions, Muna Lee—*gonfaronista*, wife of Luis Muñoz Marín—made a career for herself as translator and administrator within the US State Department, where she could practise a pan-Americanism surely bolstered, if not learned from, her Nicaraguan friend. At the Sixth Inter-American Conference in Havana—notable for the strong feminist intervention—Muna Lee spoke forcefully of the 'spiritual country of Pan America'.[53] She tried to give matter to that spirit: as well as organising that 1941 conference in Puerto Rico, she was a moving force behind Dudley Fitts's landmark 1942 *Anthology of Contemporary Latin-American Poetry*, for which she provided a substantial number of the translations.[54] She, perhaps more

---

[51] De la Selva, 'Discurso sobre Rubén Darío', p. 288.
[52] Harris Feinsod, *The Poetry of the Americas: From Good Neighbors to Countercultures*, Oxford: Oxford University Press, 2017, pp. 4–5. De la Selva's primacy is briefly acknowledged by Feinsod, but described as an 'early moment of false promise' (p. 8).
[53] K. Lynn Stoner, 'In Four Languages but with One Voice: Division and Solidarity within Pan American Feminism, 1923–1933', in David Sheinin, ed., *Beyond the Ideal: Pan Americanism in Inter-American Affairs*, Westport, CT: Praeger, 2000, pp. 79–94, at p. 87.
[54] Dudley Fitts, ed., *Anthology of Contemporary Latin-American Poetry*, Norfolk, CT: New Directions, 1942. The volume was covertly funded by Nelson Rockefeller's Office of the Coordinator of Inter-American Affairs. It also includes a translation by Donald Walsh of de la Selva's 'Elegía' from *El soldado desconocido*. Another *gonfaronista*, Arturo Torres Rioseco, is also thanked in the acknowledgements.

than any other individual, can be considered as a carrier of de la Selva's ideas, if not his name, into the next generation.

And when Sergio Mondragón and Margaret Randall began the bilingual magazine *El Corno Emplumado/The Plumed Horn* in Mexico in 1962, it was de la Selva's old antagonist, Ernesto Cardenal, who wrote in a letter of support: 'Si los poetas no realizan el Panamericanismo nadie más lo hará' [If the poets don't achieve Panamericanism, then nobody else will], echoing the declaration on which de la Selva had built his project 44 years earlier.[55]

Everyone's life has its seasons. As summer ends, the grass is cut, and life moves on. But the cut stalks still grow, and that aftermath—though less spectacular than the first growth—can provide nourishment for the future, both for the individual life and for those who follow. Perhaps Salomón de la Selva's time in New York, forgotten for so long, can still make rich the years to come; or perhaps the true republic of the American poets will for ever remain a mirage.

---

[55] Ernesto Cardenal, 'Carta', *El Corno Emplumado*, 5 (January 1963), 146–47, at 146.

Biographies

Alfau Galván de Solalinde, Jesusa (1890–1943) Granddaughter of the author of *Enriquillo*, Manuel de Jesús Galván. Born in Spain, she moved to New York in 1916, writing for *Las Novedades*, a magazine edited by her father. She married the Spanish academic, Antonio García Solalinde, and became a teacher at the University of Wisconsin. Invited to the dinner at Gonfarone's.

Barba Jacob, Porfirio (1883–1942) Born in Colombia as Miguel Ángel Osorio Benítez, he wrote under a variety of pseudonyms, including Ricardo Arenales, before settling on Barba Jacob in 1922. A poet and journalist, he travelled widely throughout the continent, usually behaving scandalously.

Barrett, John (1866–1938) Born in Vermont, he worked as a journalist before becoming a diplomat. In 1907, he was appointed at the first Director General of the Bureau of American Republics, renamed the Pan American Union in 1910, and served for 14 years. He was therefore the public voice of official Pan-Americanism.

Benét, William Rose (1886–1950) Born in Brooklyn, he was the older brother of Stephen Vincent and Laura Benét. Poet, writer, and editor.

Broun, Heywood (1888–1939) Born in Brooklyn, he was a sportswriter, drama critic, campaigning journalist, and a member of the Algonquin Round Table alongside Dorothy Parker and Robert Benchley.

Brull Caballero, Mariano (1891–1956) Born in Camagüey, in eastern Cuba. A Symbolist poet, he was also known for a type of poetry called *jitanjáfora* in which sound is all-important. A diplomat by profession, he was posted to New York in 1916. Author of *La casa del silencio* (1916) and *Poemas en menguante* (1928).

Camprubí de Jiménez, Zenobia (1887–1956) Writer, poet, and translator, she married Juan Ramón Jiménez in New York in 1916.

Camprubí, José Aymar (1880–1942) Born in Puerto Rico, educated in Barcelona and Connecticut, and then at Harvard, he worked as an engineer before buying *La Prensa* in 1918 and turning it into a daily newspaper for the Hispanic population of New York. Sister of Zenobia Camprubí.

Carnevali, Emanuel (1897–1942) Born in Florence, Italy, he immigrated to New York where he worked at menial jobs while quickly learning English and beginning to write poetry. After winning a poetry competition, he was invited in 1919 to become associate editor of *Poetry*, but fell seriously ill with encephalitis lethargica and returned to Italy. Author of *A Hurried Man* (1925), *The Autobiography of Emanuel Carnevali* (1967), and *Furnished Rooms* (2006).

Castellot Batalla, José (1856–1938) Born in Campeche, Mexico, he was a landowner, banker, politician, and prominent Freemason, who benefited from the patronage of Porfirio Díaz. Exiled in New York during the early years of the Mexican Revolution and cut off from the sources of his wealth, he operated as a socialite and *littérateur*, translating Edward Fitzgerald and Thomas Gray into Spanish. Invited to the dinner at Gonfarone's.

Cestero, Manuel Florentino (1878–1926) Born in the Dominican Republic, he spent several years in New Year working as a journalist for *La Prensa* and becoming heavily involved in the campaign supporting Francisco Henríquez y Carvajal's presidency. He wrote a scathing account of life in the USA: *Estados Unidos por dentro* (1918). Invited to the dinner at Gonfarone's, about which he wrote an account.

Chocano, José Santos (1875–1934) Born in Lima, Peru. During his lifetime he became one of the best-known poets writing in Spanish, espousing American themes sometimes on an epic scale. Politically engaged, especially with the Mexican Revolution, he was a frequent visitor to New York. Briefly imprisoned in Peru for murder in 1925, he was himself murdered in Chile.

Crane, Frank (1861–1928) Born in Urbana, Illinois, he was an ex-church minister who became a popular journalist dispensing Christian common sense; best-known as the author of 'four-minute essays' or 'sermons' that were widely circulated and distributed. In his day he was one of the most widely read writers in the world, and seen as a serious intellectual figure. He befriended the young Salomón.

Culkin, Philip Harley (1898–1977) A young neighbour of de la Selva on the Upper West Side (along with his sister, Amanda), Culkin studied art at Columbia Extension and at night played piano in Greenwich Village. His musical comedy *Marjorie* ran for three months on Broadway and he published 'Four Woodcuts of Delia' (*Story*, vol. 12 (March 1938), 45–56). His daughter is the actor Bonnie Bedelia. Invited to the dinner at Gonfarone's.

Darío, Rubén (1867–1916) Born in Nicaragua, he became the leading Hispanic poet of his generation, associated with the literary movement known as *modernismo*. He travelled extensively, writing for newspapers, and visited New York on several occasions.

Dávalos Balkin, Balbino (1866–1951) Mexican diplomat and academic who taught at the universities of Minnesota and Columbia between 1917 and 1919.

Dell, Floyd (1887–1969) Born in Illinois after working as an influential book-reviewer in Chicago, he relocated to New York City in 1913 to become managing editor of the influential magazine *The Masses* and a regular at many Greenwich Village venues. Originally a playwright, he later wrote novels and memoirs.

Elliott, Lilian Elwyn (1874–1963) Born in London, she went to the USA in 1909, where she worked for the *Pan-American Magazine*, which she later edited. She travelled extensively in America, publishing *Brazil Today and Tomorrow* (1917) and the novel, *Black Gold* (1920). Later in life she married Thomas Joyce and undertook anthropological work with him in Central America.

Ervin, Charles (1865–1953) A socialist and journalist, he was editor for several years of the *New York Call*.

Fawcett, James Waldo (1893–1968) Born in Pittsburgh, Pennsylvania, he was briefly a writer and journalist in New York before moving to Washington, DC. In New York he founded and edited *The Modernist* in 1919 and worked with Margaret Sanger. During a much more conventional later life his main interests became genealogy and philately.

Feigenbaum, Benjamin (1859–1932) A socialist who was editor for many years of the radical Jewish newspaper *Forverts (The Jewish Daily Forward)*.

Fiallo Cabral, Fabio Federico (1866–1942) A Dominican writer and politician, he spent several years in the consular service in New York and was active in the opposition to the US occupation of his country.

Foster, Jeanne Robert (1879–1970) Born Julia Elizabeth Oliver in Johnsburg, New York. After a career as a fashion model, she became literary editor of the *American Review of Reviews* and later worked for the collector John Quinn, becoming close friends with Ford Madox Ford, Ezra Pound, and William Butler Yeats. She published several books of poetry. Invited to the dinner at Gonfarone's, but couldn't attend.

Galván Velásquez, Manuel de Jesús (1869–?) The fourth son of Manuel de Jesús Galván, who worked as a journalist on *Las Novedades* in New York.

Galván, Manuel de Jesús (1834–1910) Born and lived in Santo Domingo, Dominican Republic. Conservative in his political views, he wrote the historical novel *Enriquillo* (1880), widely seen as the country's national epic.

Geisenheimer, Eugenia Louise Victoria (1870–1946) Born in Düsseldorf, a rich spinster who produced translations into Spanish, she lived on the Upper West Side but had a house at Shoreham on Long Island, where de la Selva stayed on at least one occasion.

Gollomb, Joseph (1881–1950) Born in Petrograd, he reached New York with his family in 1891 and became a member of both the Socialist Party of America and the Industrial Workers of the World. He worked as a journalist and investigative reporter, but eventually became a popular and successful novelist.

González Mesa, Rufino (ca. 1890–1938) A childhood Cuban friend of Salomón de la Selva, who shared apartments with him during the period covered by this book. At the time of his death he was working as a sub-editor on the *New York Herald Tribune*.

Goodman, Edward (1888–1962) Born in New York, he was a director, producer, and writer associated with the Washington Square Players and the Theatre Guild.

Greene, Constance Murray (1891–?) The sister of Aline Murray Kilmer, she wrote book reviews. Invited to the dinner at Gonfarone's.

Guillén Zelaya, Alfonso (1887–1947) Born in Olancho, Honduras, he worked in the Honduran consulate in New York, as well as writing poetry and journalism. He attended the Versailles peace conference along with Rafael Heliodoro Valle and left New York in 1921. He died in Mexico.

Guiteras Gener Keller, Laura (1865–1940) Born in Cuba into a wealthy, intellectual, liberal, and nationalist family with strong connections to Philadelphia. Her eldest brother, José Ramón, was executed in 1870, aged 18, after twice being caught attempting to run guns into Cuba. Invited to the dinner at Gonfarone's.

Guzmán, Martín Luis (1887–1976) Born in Chihuahua, Mexico. After studying law, he joined the Mexican Revolution and served as a colonel with Pancho Villa. His novelised memoirs, *El águila y la serpiente* [*The Eagle and the Serpent*] (1928), is widely regarded as one of the finest books about the Revolution. He wrote several other novels and back in Mexico became a pillar of the Revolutionary establishment.

Helburn, Theresa (1887-1959) Born in New York. After studying at Bryn Mawr and Radcliffe, she lived the bohemian life in Greenwich Village, writing poetry, stories, and plays before becoming involved with the Theatre Guild from its inception in 1919, first as literary manager, then as co-producer with Lawrence Langner. She was a key Broadway figure for four decades.

Henríquez Ureña, Pedro (1884-1946) Born in Santo Domingo, the son of Francisco Henríquez y Carvajal, who would be elected president of the Dominican Republic in 1916, and the eminent poet and feminist, Salomé Ureña. He lived in New York as a teenager, then in Cuba and Mexico, before returning to the USA in 1915, working as a journalist. He taught at the University of Minnesota, then in Mexico and Argentina. He was the pre-eminent twentieth-century literary historian in the Spanish language.

Herron, Margaret Vennette (1895-1973) Born in Ohio, the daugher of the congregationalist minister and preacher of the social gospel George Herron. She attended Iowa College before becoming a writer based in New York, publishing in magazines such as *Ainslee's* and *The Smart Set*. Her collection *Perfume and Poison* appeared in 1917. She later travelled in Java and Europe and published two further collections of short stories. Invited to the dinner at Gonfarone's.

Huntington, Archer M. (1870-1955) Born in New York City, he was the stepson—and possibly natural son—of railroad magnate and industrialist Collis P. Huntington, from whom he inherited a large fortune. A Hispanist scholar, he founded and ran the Hispanic Society of America and was a major benefactor of Hispanic writers.

Ivanovitch, Dmitri (1886-1974) Pen name of José Luis Betancourt Román. Born in Cartagena, Colombia, he was a poet, translator, and political activist who worked as one of the editors of *La Prensa*. Author of *La ventana y otros poemas* (1921); *La sonrisa unánime* (1926); and *Tristezas en el mar* (1928). He returned to Colombia in 1946. Invited to the dinner at Gonfarone's.

Jiménez, Juan Ramón (1881-1958) A Spanish poet, born in Andalucía, he came to New York in 1916 to marry Zenobia Camprubí. From his visit came the book of poems *Diario de un poeta reciencasado* (1916). He later taught at the universities of Maryland and Puerto Rico, and in 1956 was awarded the Nobel Prize for Literature.

Kemp, Harry Hibbard (1883-1960) A well-known bohemian figure in Greenwich Village and Provincetown, known as 'the vagabond poet' and 'the poet of the dunes'. Invited to the dinner at Gonfarone's, but got lost en route.

Kilmer, Alfred Joyce (1886–1918) Born in New Brunswick, New Jersey, he joined the *New York Times Review of Books* and *New York Times Sunday Magazine* in 1913 and published several volumes of poetry, attaining worldwide fame for his poem 'Trees'. Having volunteered for the US army in 1917, he died during an attack on the hills above the Ourcq in France.

Kilmer, Aline Murray (1888–1941) Born in Norfolk, Virginia, she was a poet and writer of children's books, and the wife (married 1908) and widow of poet and journalist Joyce Kilmer. Her books include *Candles That Burn* (1919). Invited to the dinner at Gonfarone's.

Kinney, Troy (1871–1938) Born in Kansas City, he was an artist, writer, and expert on dance, who wrote books and essays with his wife, Margaret West Kinney (1872–1952), as The Kinneys.

Kreymborg, Alfred Francis (1883–1966) Born in New York City, he was a poet, novelist, playwright, and literary editor. Involved in various modernist magazines, including *Others*, he was also a world-class chess player and later President of the Poetry Society of America.

Lee, Muna (1895–1965) Born in Mississippi. A poet, feminist, and translator, she married the Puerto Rican writer and politician Luis Muñoz Marin in 1919 (legally separated in 1938). In later life she worked in cultural affairs for the US State Department. Invited to the dinner at Gonfarone's.

MacKaye, Percy (1875–1956) Dramatist and poet, born in New York City, he was best known for the concept of Civic Theatre and for his huge community productions such as *Caliban by the Yellow Sands* (1916).

Madriguera Rodon, Francesca 'Paquita' (1900–65) Spanish piano prodigy who in later life married the guitarist and composer Andrés Segovia. Invited to the dinner at Gonfarone's.

Mandujano, Graciela (1902–1984) Born in Chile, she was a feminist and political writer who lived in the USA between 1916 and 1920, participating in Pan-American conferences, and writing for the *Pan-American Magazine*. In 1935, she co-founded the Movimiento por la Emancipación de la Mujer Chilena. Invited to the dinner at Gonfarone's.

Markham, Edwin (1852–1940) During the years covered by this book, Markham was the best-known living poet in the US, having shot to fame with his poem 'The Man with the Hoe' in 1899. He became a friend and supporter of both Salomón de la Selva and Luis Muñoz Marín. Invited to the dinner at Gonfarone's.

Millay, Edna St Vincent (1892–1950) One of three sisters, all born in Maine and all of whom lived in New York for some of the years 1915 to 1919. Edna was a student at Vassar and already a published poet when she met de la Selva. Her early books made her famous, and she became one of the century's best-known writers, renowned for her readings of her work, which attracted large audiences. Her commitment to traditional forms led to her reputation falling away after her death but a recent critical edition of her poems has revived interest. Invited to the dinner at Gonfarone's.

Millay, Kathleen (1896–1943) Youngest of the three sisters, she was a moderately successful writer of novels, verse, and fairy tales whose career was limited by alcoholism and depression. Invited to the dinner at Gonfarone's.

Millay Ellis, Norma (1893–1986) Actress and singer. The first keeper of Edna's flame, she inherited Steepletop, Millay's house near Austerlitz, New York, and founded there the Millay Colony for the Arts. Invited to the dinner at Gonfarone's.

Montenegro, Ernesto (1885–1967) Born in Chile. A journalist and short-story writer, he was the representative of *El Mercurio* (Chile) in New York where he wrote on a variety of topics, literary and political, for the US press, including *The Sun*, and for Latin American journals. He translated many books from English into Spanish, including W. H. Hudson's *Green Mansions*. Invited to the dinner at Gonfarone's.

Morton, David H. (1886–1957) Born in Kentucky, he was a journalist and then teacher and critic, but always a poet. Invited to the dinner at Gonfarone's.

Muñoz Marín, Luis (1898–1980) Puerto Rican poet and journalist, later politician and statesman. Growing up, he spent several years in New York and was bilingual. He married Muna Lee in 1919 (legally separated in 1938). In 1948, he became the first democratically elected Governor of Puerto Rico. Invited to the dinner at Gonfarone's.

O'Sheel, Shaemas (1886–1954) Born James Shields in New York, he met Edwin Markham when the poet spoke at his school in 1900 and became part of his circle, publishing several books of poetry. He often worked closely with Louis Adamic. A committed Irish nationalist, he was also a heterodox communist and opponent of US entry into both world wars.

Onís, Federico de (1885–1966) Born in Salamanca. A brilliant protégé of Miguel de Unamano and José Ortega y Gasset, he was invited in 1916 to become Professor of Spanish Literature at Columbia University in New York, from where he made a large contribution to the establishment of Hispanic studies, including the study of Latin American literature, in the USA. He later taught in Puerto Rico.

Ortiz Vargas, Alfredo (1898–1951) Born in Bogotá, Colombia, he travelled extensively as a young man, including some time in New York in 1919. He later spent two years in the USA in the Colombian consular service before taking up teaching positions and writing the long poem *Las torres de Manhattan* (1939). He was murdered in Kansas City by a former student. Invited to the dinner at Gonfarone's.

Page, Marjorie (1897–1983) Part of the extended Schauffler family group in these years, she married Bennet Schauffler in 1920. She was later Director of the School Affiliation Service of the American Friends Service Committee in Philadelphia. Invited to the dinner at Gonfarone's.

Pérez de Ayala, Ramón (1880–1962) Born in Spain, he was a prolific novelist and Spanish ambassador to England in the early 1930s. After marriage to his US wife in 1913, he spent a considerable amount of time in New York. Invited to the dinner at Gonfarone's.

Peynado, Francisco (1867–1933) Born in the Dominican Republic, he trained as a lawyer and was a member of the Dominican Republic–Haiti boundary dispute commission which visited New York and Washington in 1911, and minister plenipotentiary to the USA in 1912–14. In November 1914, he took over *Las Novedades*. An opponent of the US military occupation of the DR, he supported Francisco Henríquez y Carvajal's presidency.

Pinochet Le-Brun, Tancredo (1880–1957) Born in Chile, he was a journalist and writer who spent a number of years living in the USA and whose second wife was American. Editor of the New York periodical *El Norte Americano*, he was the author of *The Gulf of Misunderstanding*.

Rice, John Pierrepont (1879–1941) Born in New York City, he studied French and German and took his PhD at Yale before teaching modern languages at Williams College between 1910 and 1924. He contributed translations to Thomas Walsh's *Hispanic Anthology* (1920) and spent the last part of his career at the University of Buffalo.

Ried Silva, Alberto (1886–1965) Chilean sculptor, poet, and short-story writer, he was a member of the literary group known as 'Los Diez' [The Ten]. He worked as a correspondent for *La Nación* in New York.

Rittenhouse, Jessie Belle (1869–1948) Poet, editor, and literary critic. Between 1905 and 1915, she lived in New York City, where she was poetry reviewer for the *New York Times Review of Books* and helped found the Poetry Society of America, of which she was secretary for ten years. She later taught at Rollins College in Florida and was awarded the first Robert Frost medal for lifetime achievement in poetry in 1930. Invited to the dinner at Gonfarone's.

Roberts, Walter Adolphe (1886–1962) Born in Jamaica, he was a journalist, novelist, editor, poet, travel writer, and historian, based in New York between 1909 and 1949. It was the publication of his book of poems *Pierrot Wounded* that was being celebrated at the dinner at Gonfarone's.

Roeder, Ralph (1890–1969) Born in New York and educated at Harvard and Columbia universities, he was a journalist, actor, leftist, and scholar, with a long-standing interest in Mexico. He married the theatre designer and feminist Fania Mindell of New York, and they moved to Mexico in the late 1940s.

Romera Navarro, Miguel (1888–1954) Born in Almería, Spain, he came to New York in 1912 where he worked on *The Delineator* while preparing his book *El hispanismo en Norte-América* (1917). He subsequently taught at the universities of Pennsylvania and Texas.

Sanger, Margaret (1879–1966) Born in Corning, New York, she pioneered the birth control movement in the USA, opening the first clinic in Brooklyn in 1916. She was also active in radical politics during the years covered by this book.

Schauffler, Bennet Fellows (1893–1979) Born in Chicago, son of Charles and Florence Schauffler, he was a student poet and close to de la Selva at Williams College. Invited to the dinner at Gonfarone's.

Schauffler, Florence Manvel (1867–1942) Born in St Paul, Minnesota, she was an aspiring poet and writer who eventually published little. The family moved to New York in 1910, where for a while she provided a home away from home for de la Selva. Invited to the dinner at Gonfarone's.

Schauffler, Robert Haven (1879–1964) Born in Brno, now in the Czech Republic, he moved to Ohio aged two. He was the younger brother of Charles Edward Schauffler (Florence's husband) and lived with the family for some time in New York. A poet, musician, and popular writer, he was briefly married to Margaret Widdemer from 1919.

Seeger, Alan (1888–1916) Born in New York, he spent some childhood years in Mexico City and was killed in France fighting for the Foreign Legion. His posthumously published poems and letters were extremely popular.

Shores, Robert James (1881–1950) Born in Butte, Montana, he was a journalist, editor, and writer, who befriended Rubén Darío in 1914–15.

Ordained in 1927, he spent the last years of his life in the Protestant Episcopal Diocese of Washington, DC.

Torres Calderón de Pinillos, Carmen (1881–?) Born in Trujillo, Peru, she was an editor and translator before moving to New York, where she worked on *The Delineator* before becoming editor of *Inter-América*. She married Herbert S. Houston in 1937. Invited to the dinner at Gonfarone's.

Torres Rioseco, Arturo (1897–1971) Born in Tasca, Chile, he was appointed in 1918 as a translator for the Committee for Public Information in New York. He was a poet and journalist during these years before teaching at Williams College and then at the University of Minnesota where he obtained his PhD, subsequently spending 33 years as Professor of Spanish American literature at Berkeley. Invited to the dinner at Gonfarone's.

Tresca, Carlo (1879–1943) Italian-born newspaper editor and labour organiser, he was prominent in the Industrial Workers of the World. During the 1930s, he opposed Mussolini and Stalin. He was murdered, probably by the Mafia.

Untermeyer, Louis (1885–1977) Born in New York City, he was a poet, but also an increasingly influential anthologist and critic. During these years he was a socialist who wrote for *The Masses*. In later life he was blacklisted from television on account of his earlier left-wing views.

Vasconcelos, José (1882–1959) Born in Oaxaca, he grew up in Texas and became bilingual. A vastly influential Mexican intellectual, he was named rector of the National Autonomous University of Mexico in 1920, in which capacity he drew many Latin American figures, such as Pedro Henríquez Ureña and Salomón de la Selva, to Mexico City. His best-known work is *La raza cósmica* [*The Cosmic Race*] (1925). Drawn to fascism in the 1930s, he ended as a Catholic political conservative.

Viereck, George Sylvester (1884–1962) Born in Bavaria, he emigrated with his parents to New York in 1897. He won early fame for his poetry but soon became a controversial figure because of his support for Germany during the First World War, leading to his expulsion from the Poetry Society of America, which he had helped found. His later support for National Socialism led to his imprisonment between 1942 and 1947.

Walsh, Thomas (1875–1928) Born in Brooklyn and educated at Georgetown. A poet and translator from the Spanish, he worked in postal censorship during the war, which is where he met Muna Lee, whom he introduced to Luis Muñoz Marín. He worked with de la Selva on the *Hispanic Anthology* project, which he took over and completed.

Weeks, Raymond (1863-1954) Born in Iowa, he took his PhD at Harvard and was Professor of Romance Languages at Columbia University from 1909 to 1929. He was good friends with Pedro Henríquez Urena, Ralph Roeder, and Salomón de la Selva.

Wheeler, Edward Jewitt (1859-1922) Born in Cleveland, Ohio, he was managing editor of *The Voice, Literary Digest*, and then *Current Opinion*; a leading member of the Prohibition movement; and first President of the Poetry Society of America (1909-1921). After the war he was decorated by the French government in recognition of his editorial services for the Allies. Invited to the dinner at Gonfarone's.

Widdemer, Margaret (1884-1978) Born in Pennsylvania but brought up in Asbury Park, New Jersey. A poet and novelist, she was briefly married in 1919 to Robert Haven Schauffler.

Williams, William Carlos (1883-1963) Born in New Jersey, he was brought up in a household where Spanish was spoken, and he translated poems and stories from the Spanish with his father. His first significant book of poems *Al Que Quiere!* was published in 1917. He went on to become one of the most highly regarded US poets of the twentieth century.

Wood, Clement (1888-1950) Born in Tuscaloosa, Alabama. A socialist, poet, and New York bohemian, he became a prolific writer of little distinction.

Woodruff, Helen Smith (1888-1924) Born in Alabama, she moved to New York on her marriage in 1906 and became a highly successful author of books for young adults. As a member of the executive council of the Authors' League of America she hosted a reception for Rubén Darío during his visit to New York in 1915. She died as the result of a fall from a second-storey window in her New York home, a probable suicide.

Yeats, John Butler (1839-1922) Artist and father of W. B. Yeats. Born in Ireland, he moved to New York in 1908 and presided over nightly *soirées* at Petitpas' restaurant attended by many artists and writers. He was especially close to Jeanne Robert Foster. See William M. Murphy, *Prodigal Father: The Life of John Butler Yeats (1839-1922)*, Ithaca, NY: Cornell University Press, 1978.

Zaturenska, Marya (1902-1982) Born in Kiev, she emigrated with her family to New York when she was eight. Encouraged to write as a teenager by Jeanne Robert Foster, she started publishing poems. She later graduated in library science from the University of Wisconsin-Madison, where she met her husband, the poet Horace Gregory. She received the Pulitzer Prize for Poetry in 1938.

Zayas Enriquez y Calmet, Marius de (1880–1961) Born in Veracruz, Mexico. His father, Rafael de Zayas Enríquez (1848–1932), was a noted writer and lawyer, originally supporter and then opponent of Porfirio Díaz. In 1906, Marius worked as a caricaturist on *El Diario*, but the family left Mexico under political pressure. In New York he worked on the *Evening World*, was exhibited by Alfred Stieglitz at his gallery, '291', and was soon acting as a liaison between Stieglitz and the Cubist and Surrealist artists in France. Back in New York he edited the *291* magazine and opened his own gallery.

Acknowledgements

My greatest debts are to Jonathan Cohen and Steven White, both of whom provided constant guidance, encouragement, information, and support, and were kind enough to read the whole manuscript and to offer invaluable suggestions. I'd also like to thank in particular Luis Bolaños-Salvatierra, Carmen Boullosa, Herbie Butterfield, Esthela Calderón, James Canton, Liz DeLoughrey, Jim Fernández, Lowell Fiet, Maria Cristina Fumagalli, Gordon Gebert, Susan Gillman, Orlando J. Hernández, Winsome Hudson, Laura Lomas, Jak Peake, Holly Peppe, Lisa Paravisini, María Cristina Rodríguez, Ana Rodríguez Navas, and Tim Youngs. Thanks too to Carlos Aguasaco, Sarah Aponte, Gloria Arjona, Ali Behdad, William Booth, Barry Carr, Andrea Castro, Deborah Cohn, Cecilia Cordero, Frederick Courtright, Cathy Fagan, Paul Firbas, Humberto García Muñiz, Janet Higbie, Nina Gerassi Navarro, Richard Gray, Rafael Hernández Rodríguez, Carlos Jáuregui, Janis Londraville, Richard Londraville, Shelley McConnell, Shawn McDaniel, Felipe Martínez Pinzón, Enid Mastrianni, Marysa Navarro, Mark Oberski, John O'Neill, Cristina Pérez Jiménez, James Proctor, Pedro Ángel Palau, Julio E. Quirós Alcalá, Gayle Rogers, Sharon Ruston, Verónica Salles Reese, Richard Smith, Silvio Torres-Saillant, Fionnghuala Sweeney, Javier Uriarte, Fabienne Viala, Stella Villagrán, and Mike Wallace. Thanks are also due to Liverpool University Press, and especially to Chloe Johnson; and to Carnegie Book Production.

Some of the research for the book was undertaken on a Leverhulme Emeritus Fellowship, for which I warmly thank the Leverhulme Trust. I'd also like to acknowledge institutional support from the Department of Literature, Film, and Theatre Studies at the University of Essex, the Department of Languages and Literatures at the University of Gothenburg, and the Department of Hispanic Languages and Literature at SUNY Stony Brook.

Work in progress was presented to the following, with thanks to those who invited me and to those who participated in the helpful discussions that followed: Department of Hispanic Studies, Vassar (2012); 'Cultural Encounters in the Luso-Hispanic World', conference at the University of Warwick (2013);

Society for Caribbean Studies, University of Warwick (2013); Department of Spanish and Portuguese, Indiana University (2013); 'Migration', British Comparative Literature Association conference, University of Essex (2013); Society for Caribbean Studies, University of Glasgow (2014); Instituto de Estudios del Caribe, University of Puerto Rico (2014); University of Gothenburg (2014); Department of English and Creative Writing, Lancaster University (2014); Department of English and Comparative Literature, UCLA (2015); West Indian Literature conference, Río Piedras, Puerto Rico (2015); Department of Modern Languages, St Lawrence University (2015); Department of Hispanic Languages and Literature, SUNY Stony Brook (2015); Department of Iberian and Latin American Studies, Columbia University (2015); Department of Romance Languages, Tufts University (2015); Society for Caribbean Studies, Newcastle University (2016); 'American Networks: Radicals Under the Radar' conference, London (2016); School of Arts and Humanities, Nottingham Trent University (2016); Department of English, Literature, Language, and Linguistics, Newcastle University (2016); Department of Spanish, Brown University (2016); Department of Spanish, Georgetown University (2016); Department of Spanish, NYU (2016); 'Transatlantic New York' conference, CUNY (2017); and the Society of Caribbean Studies conference, University of Essex (2017).

Most of the research for this book was carried out in the New York Public Library on West 42nd Street: I warmly thank the librarians there for their invaluable assistance. Other libraries and archives consulted—with similar thanks to their librarians and archivists—were: the Library of Congress and the Columbus Memorial Library, both in Washington, DC; the Hispanic Society of America, the Schomburg Center for Research in Black Culture, and the Greenwich Village Preservation Society, all in Manhattan; Wagner College Library on Staten Island; SUNY Stony Brook University Library; the Lilly Library, Indiana University; the National Library of Jamaica, Kingston; the Fundación Luis Muñoz Marín, San Juan, Puerto Rico; The Houghton Library, Harvard University; the Charles E. Young Research Library, UCLA; the Sterling and Beinecke Libraries, Yale University; the Cornell University Library; the Butler Library, Columbia University; the Hay Library, Brown University; the Firestone Memorial Library, Princeton; the British Library; and the libraries at the University of Essex and the University of Lancaster.

Quotations from *Letters of Edna St. Vincent Millay*, edited by Allan Ross Macdougall, copyright 1952 by Norma Millay Ellis, and excerpts of letters in the Edna St. Vincent Millay Papers, Library of Congress: all reprinted with the permission of The Permissions Company, Inc., on behalf of Holly Peppe, Literary Executor, The Edna St Vincent Millay Society <www.millay.org>.

Material from the Edwin Markham Archive is reproduced with the kind permission of the Horrmann Library, Wagner College, Staten Island, New York.

Material from the Schauffler Family Papers (MS 1389), Manuscripts and Archives, Yale University Library, is reproduced with the kind permission of the heirs of the donors.

Attempts to locate other copyright holders have been unsuccessful.

Select Bibliography

The bibliography has three sections. The first lists all the manuscripts referred to in the notes, along with abbreviations where they are used. The second lists many but probably not all of Salomón de la Selva's writings between 1915 and 1919, in date order as far as can be determined, along with a selection of his later writings. Collections are placed according to the latest date of the contents. The third section lists background sources for the study of New York in this period, particularly its culture.

1 Manuscripts

Amy Lowell Papers (MS Lowell 19 [1095]), Houghton Library, Harvard University = ALP.
Archer M. Huntington, 'Diaries', Hispanic Society of America, New York.
Authors Club (New York, NY), [Collection of programs, lists, etc., of Authors Club activities], 1888–1937, New-York Historical Society Main Collection F128 HS2725.A9 Box 1.
Authors Club (New York, NY), The New York Public Library, MSS Col 161.
Clement Wood Papers (Box 31), Hay Library, Brown University = CWP.
Colección Salomón de la Selva, Biblioteca Francisco Xavier Clavigero, Universidad Ibero-Americana, Mexico City.
Edna St. Vincent Millay Papers (MSS 32920), Library of Congress, Washington, DC = ESVMP.
Edwin Markham Archive, Horrmann Library, Wagner College, Staten Island, New York = EMA.
Ezra Pound Papers (YCAL MSS 43), Beinecke Library, Yale University = EPP.
Florence Hamilton collection relating to Edwin Markham, 1857–1959, MSS 31393, unfinished biography, Library of Congress, Washington, DC.
Foster-Murphy Collection, Manuscripts and Archives Division (MSS Col 1051), The New York Public Library = FMC.
Fundación Luis Muñoz Marín, San Juan, Puerto Rico = FLMM.
Jessie B. Rittenhouse Collection, Rollins College, Winter Park, Florida = JBRC.
John Bassett Moore Papers (MSS 33332), Library of Congress, Washington, DC.
Kenneth Wiggins Porter Papers (Sc MG 222, b. 73 f. 6: Notes for Manuscript Salomon de la Selva), Schomburg Center for Research in Black Culture, The New York Public Library = KWPP.

Marius de Zayas Papers, 1914–48 (MS 1407), Rare Book & Manuscript Library, Columbia University = MZP.

Poems by Many Singers (ca. 1915–23). Compiled by Clement Wood. Ms. Harris Codex 1344, Hay Library, Brown University.

Poetry: A Magazine of Verse. Records. University of Chicago Library.

Poetry Society of America records ca. 1917–ca. 1948 (MSS Col 2444), Manuscripts and Archives Division, The New York Public Library.

Salomón de la Selva, ['Poems'], 2 typed and 22 handwritten. General Manuscripts Collection CO140, Princeton University Library.

Salomón de la Selva, 'A Tale from Faerieland and Other Poems', New York, 1916, Brown University Library Manuscript Collections, 1901 S4686t. Accessed 22 June 1925.

Salomón de la Selva, Members File, Hispanic Society of America, New York = HSASS.

Schauffler Family Papers (MS 1389), Manuscripts and Archives, Yale University = SFP.

Theresa Helburn Papers (MSS 864), Beinecke Library, Yale University = THP.

Walter Adolphe Roberts Archive (MS 353), National Library of Jamaica = WARA.

2 Salomón de la Selva

[*] = a republication. I use 'publication' in the broadest possible sense.
[TT] = published in *Tropical Town* (1918)
[USS] = published in *An Unknown Songster Sings* (2015)

'The Tale from Faerieland', *The Forum*, LIV (July 1915), 96. [TT]
'La carta de mi madre', *Las Novedades*, 5 (August 1915), 9.
'The Lover' (8 September 1915). Edna St. Vincent Millay Papers (MSS 32920), Library of Congress, Washington, DC, ESVMP. [USS]
'There Were Black Roses There' (9 September 1915), ESVMP. [USS]
'A String of Colored Beads' (15 September 1915), ESVMP. [USS]
'Not All the Songs Are Sung!' (15 September 1915), ESVMP. [USS]
'Your Silence, Love, Much Sorrow Tells' (24 September 1915), ESVMP. [USS]
'Night', ESVMP. [USS]
'Hunger Chaunt', ESVMP. [USS]
'De Profundis', ESVMP. [USS]
'To Love Purifical', ESVMP. [USS]
'The Cup of Life', *Ainslee's*, 36, no. 4 (November 1915), 69. [USS]
'The Pilgrim's Tale' (sent to Archer M. Huntington 7 November 1915), Salomón de la Selva, Members File, Hispanic Society of America, New York = HSASS. [USS]
'Hatred', *Century Magazine*, XCI, no. 3 (January 1916), 446. [TT]
'Winged Words', *Ainslee's*, 36, no. 6 (January 1916), 150. [USS]
'How "Goyescas" Was Written', by Fernando Periquet, translated by Salomón de la Selva, *New York Times*, 23 January 1916, p. X5.
'After the Tryst', *Ainslee's*, 37, no. 1 (February 1916), 158. [USS]
'His Last Adventure', *Las Novedades*, 23 April 1916, p. 8. [USS]

Select Bibliography

'St Francis' Tale to the Birds', *Ainslee's*, 37, no. 4 (May 1916), 107. [USS]
'Rubén Darío', *Poetry*, VIII, no. 4 (July 1916), 200–204.
'The Singer Exults', *Contemporary Verse*, 2, no. 5 (November 1916), 65. [USS]
'The Singer Despairs', *Contemporary Verse*, 2, no. 5 (November 1916), 65. [USS]
'Candle Light', *Contemporary Verse*, 2, no. 5 (November 1916), 66. [TT]
'Tropical Town', *Contemporary Verse*, 2, no. 5 (November 1916), 66. [TT]
'To a Young Poet' (September 1916), in Mariano Brull, *La casa del silencio*, Madrid: M. García y G. Sáez, 1916. [USS]
Rubén Darío, *Eleven poems*, translations by Thomas Walsh and Salomón de la Selva; introduction by Pedro Henríquez Ureña, New York: G. P. Putnam's Sons, 1916. [ten of the translations are by Salomón de la Selva]

'Primaveral'. Translation of 'Primaveral', 3, 5.
'Autumnal'. Translation of 'Autumnal', 7, 9, 11.
'The Three Wise Kings'. Translation of 'Los tres reyes magos', 23.
'Song of Hope'. Translation of 'Canto de esperanza', 25, 27.
'Poets! Towers of God'. Translation of '¡Torres de Dios! Poetas', 29.
'A Sonnet on Cervantes'. Translation of 'Soneto a Cervantes', 31.
'On the Death of a Poet'. Translation of 'En la muerte de un poeta', 33.
'Antonio Machado'. Translation of 'Oración por Antonio Machado', 35.
'Bagpipes of Spain'. Translation of 'Gaita Galaica', 37.
'Song of Autumn in the Springtime'. Translation of 'Canción de otoño en primavera', 39, 41, 43.

[as Hipólito Mattonel] 'Ecos de la muerte de Rubén Darío', *Revista Universal: Magazine Hispano-Americano*, November 1916, p. 27.
'Walter Pater', *Revista Universal: Magazine Hispano-Americano*, November 1916, p. 28.
'A Tale from Faerieland and Other Poems', New York, 1916, Brown University Library Manuscript Collections, 1901 S4686t.

'Dedication'
'A Tale from Faerieland' [*] [TT]
'Youth'
'Song'
'The Rosebush'
'Alexandrines'
'Colloque Sentimental'
'Vox et Praeterea Nihil'
'Death'
'On an Oaten Reed'
'To His Beloved in Time of Despair'
'Notre Vie est du Vent Tissu'
'Winged Words' [*] [TT]
'The Beggar'
'Tropical Town' [*] [TT]
'Little Boy Dead'
'Serpentina'
'Carnaval Grotesque'
'Sal'
'Kiss Me Again'
'Hatred' [*] [TT]
'Dreams'
'Autumn Mood'
'Tryst' [TT]
'Impressions'
'Cave'
'Song'
'Even So'
'Ah, Brother!'
'The Muse'
'Lullaby for a Star'
'Song of Joy'
'Sunset' [TT]

'Poems', General Manuscripts Collection CO140, Princeton University Library [undated].

'To Bessie' [USS]
'At Noon in Nicaragua' [USS]
'The Singer Exults' [*] [USS]
'Measure' [TT]
'Winged' [USS]
'Chinese Motif' [USS]
'Le Chant Du Berger' [USS]
'Tryst' [*] [TT]
'Desire' [USS]
'Candle Light' [*] [TT]
'To a Young Man' [TT]
'Portrait' [TT]
'Deliverance' [TT]
'Poplars in Winter' [USS]
'Quintessence' [USS]
'Both Rhyme & Reason' [USS]
'More Reason' [USS]
'Homesick' [USS]
'Pastoral' [USS]
'After Seeing a Certain Picture of the Madonna' [USS]
'Song' [USS]
'Tropical' [later retitled 'Tropical House'] [TT]
'In León: The Haunted House' [later retitled 'The Haunted House of León'] [TT]
'Fleur D'Or' [TT]

Poems by Many Singers (ca. 1915–23). Compiled by Clement Wood. Ms. Harris Codex 1344, Hay Library, Brown University [undated].

'Canticling' [USS]
'You Shall Be Mine' [USS]
'Ghosts' [USS]
'The Bridal Couch' [USS]
'My Ways' [USS]
'A Kiss' [USS]
'My Beloved' [USS]
'My Sweetheart' [USS]
'The Poet to the Musician' [USS]
'The White Man Muses' [USS]
'Prostitutes' [USS]

'The Well-Tempered Clavicord', ESVMP. [USS]
'Edwin Markham', *Revista Universal: Magazine Hispano-Americano*, February 1917, p. 11.
'Sorrow', *Ainslee's Magazine*, 39, no. 1 (February 1917), 114. [USS]
'Silent' [15 February 1917], *Poetry: A Magazine of Verse*. Records. Box 32, folder 32. University of Chicago Library. [USS]
'The Beehive', *The Washington Times*, 18 August 1917, p. 8. [USS]
'My Nicaragua', *Poetry*, XI, no. 2 (November 1917), 77–79. [TT]
'The Tiny Maiden', *Poetry*, XI, no. 2 (November 1917), 79. [TT]
'The Merchant', *Poetry*, XI, no. 2 (November 1917), 80. [USS]
'Body and Soul', *The Pan-American Magazine*, XXVI, no. 1 (November 1917), 79.
'I Am Not Perfect', *Ainslee's Magazine*, 40, no. 6 (January 1918), 143. [USS]
'Of Latin American Poetry', *The Pan-American Magazine*, XXVI, no. 3 (January 1918), 145–47.
'Sonnets of Enlistment'
  'Rejected' [USS]
  'Enrolled', *Ainslee's Magazine*, 41, no. 1 (February 1918), 43. [USS]

'Our Purpose', *Pan-American Poetry*, I, no. 1 (February 1918), 1.
[as Hipólito Mattonel] 'From "Ode on the Andes"'. Translation of Leopoldo Lugones's 'De "odas seculares"', *Pan-American Poetry*, I, no. 1 (February 1918), 2.

[as Laurence Greenough] 'His Majesty Albert I of Belgium'. Translation of José Santos Chocano's 'Su majestad Alberto I de Bélgica', *Pan-American Poetry*, I, no. 1 (February 1918), 4.
[as Hipólito Mattonel] 'Las ventanas de las fábricas …' Translation of Vachel Lindsay's 'Factory Windows Are Always Broken', *Pan-American Poetry*, I, no. 1 (February 1918), 6.
'Throttle the Swan'. Translation of Enrique González Martínez's "Tuércele el cuello al cisne', *Pan-American Poetry*, I, no. 1 (February 1918), 6.
[as Laurence Greenough] 'What I Would Ask'. Translation of Rufino Blanco Fombona's 'Lo que yo pediría', *Pan-American Poetry*, I, no. 1 (February 1918), 8.
'Country Girl'. Translation of Froylan Turcios's 'Muchacha campesina', *Pan-American Poetry*, I, no. 1 (February 1918), 12.
'La queja de los nidos'. Translation of Muna Lee's 'The Moaning of the Doves', *Pan-American Poetry*, I, no. 1 (February 1918), 15.
[as J. Glenton] 'Salutation to His Native City'. Translation of Rubén Darío's 'Salutación a la tierra natal', *Pan-American Poetry*, I, no. 1 (February 1918), 16.
[as Nicolás Escoto] 'Los que lucharon siempre y sufrieron derrota'. Translation of Shaemas O'Sheel's 'They Went Forth To Battle But They Always Fell', *Pan American-Poetry*, I, no. 1 (February 1918), 17.
'Strains of Yesterday', *Poetry*, XI, no. 5 (February 1918), 281–82.
'One Day in Bethlehem', *Ainslee's Magazine*, 41, no. 3 (April 1918), 59–61. [USS]
'Pan-American Poetry', *The Pan-American Magazine*, XXVI, no. 6 (April 1918), 330, 338.
[as James Crowhurst-Rand] 'Fecundity'. Translation of Carlos Pezoa Veliz's 'Fecundidad', *The Pan-American Magazine*, XXVI, no. 6 (April 1918), 326.
'Antes de declararse la guerra'. Translation of Amy Lowell's 'Before War Is Declared', *The Pan-American Magazine*, XXVI, no. 6 (April 1918), 327, 329, 331.
'In Memoriam Rupert Brooke'. Translation of Joyce Kilmer's 'In Memory of Rupert Brooke', *The Pan-American Magazine*, XXVI, no. 6 (April 1918), 331.
[as Ernest F. Lucas] 'Translucency'. Translation of Amado Nervo's 'Diafanidad', *The Pan-American Magazine*, XXVI, no. 6 (April 1918), 334, 336.
'On a blank page of "Wild Apples"', Foster-Murphy Collection, Manuscripts and Archives Division (MSS Col 1051). The New York Public Library = FMC. [USS]
'The Siren's Song'. Translation of Enrique González Martínez's 'La canción de la sirenas', *The Pan-American Magazine*, XXVII, no. 1 (May 1918), 36, 38.
[as Hipólito Mattonel] 'The Weeping Water'. Translation of Enrique González Martínez's 'En el lloro del agua', *The Pan-American Magazine*, XXVII, no. 1 (May 1918), 38.
[as Nicolás Escoto] 'Amigos y enemigos'. Translation of William Dean Howell's 'Friends and Foes', *The Pan-American Magazine*, XXVII, no. 1 (May 1918), 39.
[as Oswald Tenney] 'My Heart'. Translation of Mariano Brull's 'Mi corazón', *The Pan-American Magazine*, XXVII, no. 1 (May 1918), 40.
[as J. Glenton] 'Soneto'. Translation of Edna St Vincent Millay's 'Sonnet' ['Not in this chamber …'], *The Pan-American Magazine*, XXVII, no. 1 (May 1918), 41.

[as Jane McDonald] 'Ploughers of the Sea'. Translation of José Santos Chocano's 'Aremos en el mar', *The Pan-American Magazine*, XXVII, no. 1 (May 1918), 42.

[as Hipólito Mattonel] 'La buena sombra', *The Pan-American Magazine*, XXVII, no. 1 (May 1918), 42.

[as Hipólito Mattonel] 'The Good Shade', *The Pan-American Magazine*, XXVII, no. 1 (May 1918), 43.

[as María Isabel de la Selva] 'Júbilo'. Translation of Jessie Rittenhouse's 'Joy', *The Pan-American Magazine*, XXVII, no. 1 (May 1918), 43.

'Spain and Pan Americanism', *The Pan-American Magazine*, XXVII, no. 2 (June 1918), 50–52.

[as Miguel del Carmen Urcas] 'Remendando la cerca'. Translation of Robert Frost's 'Mending Wall', *The Pan-American Magazine*, XXVII, no. 2 (June 1918), 97.

[as Cristina Salvatierra] 'Campo arado'. Translation of Sara Teasdale's 'The Broken Field', *The Pan-American Magazine*, XXVII, no. 2 (June 1918), 99.

[as Nicolás Escoto] 'Basura del mundo'. Translation of Robert Haven Schauffler's 'Scum of the Earth', *The Pan-American Magazine*, XXVII, no. 2 (June 1918), 101, 103, 104.

[as Laurence Greenough] 'Pobre Galleguito'. Translation of Luis G. Urbino's 'Pobre galleguito', *The Pan-American Magazine*, XXVII, no. 2 (June 1918), 105.

'The Thief of Songs'. Translation of Juan Julián Lastra's 'Después de algunos años', *The Pan-American Magazine*, XXVII, no. 2 (June 1918), 105.

[as James Crowhurst-Rand] 'From the Songbook of Unhappy Love'. Translation of Rufino Blanco Fombona's 'Del cancionero del amor infeliz', *The Pan-American Magazine*, XXVII, no. 2 (June 1918), 106, 108, 110.

'Peter Quince en el clavicordio'. Translation of Wallace Stevens's 'Peter Quince at the Clavier', *The Pan-American Magazine*, XXVII, no. 2 (June 1918), 109, 111.

'Measure', *Harper's Monthly Magazine*, CXXXVII (June 1918), 105.

'Una gran poetisa americana', *El Gráfico*, II, no. 8 (June 1918), 596, 610, and *El Universal* [Caracas], 4 July 1918, p. 5.

'Pan American Poetry', *The Pan-American Magazine*, XXVII, no. 3 (July 1918), 164.

'Cuando en el cementerio'. Translation of Muna Lee's 'When We Shall Be Dust', *The Pan-American Magazine*, XXVII, no. 3 (July 1918), 155.

'Yo que tan ciegamente'. Translation of Muna Lee's 'I Who Had Sought God', *The Pan-American Magazine*, XXVII, no. 3 (July 1918), 155.

[as J. Glenton] 'The Vulgar Idyll'. Translation of Félix María Baca's 'El idilio vulgar', *The Pan-American Magazine*, XXVII, no. 3 (July 1918), 154.

[as Oswald Tenney] 'Simon the Cyrenean'. Translation of Pedro Maldonado's 'Simón el cirineo', *The Pan-American Magazine*, XXVII, no. 3 (July 1918), 156.

[as Adela Ugarte] 'Voto'. Translation of Adelaide Crapsey's 'The Pledge', *The Pan-American Magazine*, XXVII, no. 3 (July 1918), 157.

[as Cristina Salvatierra] 'El sudario'. Translation of Edna St Vincent Millay's 'The Shroud', *The Pan-American Magazine*, XXVII, no. 3 (July 1918), 159.

[as James Crowhurst-Rand] 'La Hora'. Translation of Enrique González Martínez's 'La hora', *The Pan-American Magazine*, XXVII, no. 3 (July 1918), 158.

[as Julián Vargas] 'Domingo de resurrección'. Translation of Joyce Kilmer's 'Easter Sunday', *The Pan-American Magazine*, XXVII, no. 3 (July 1918), 161.

'Hatred'. Translation of Justo A. Facio's 'Odio', *The Pan-American Magazine*, XXVII, no. 3 (July 1918), 162.
[as Galán Pachuca y Moya] 'El soldado'. Translation of Sophie Jewett's 'The Soldier', *The Pan-American Magazine*, XXVII, no. 3 (July 1918), 163.
[as Nicolás Escoto] 'Al partir'. Translation of William Rose Bénet's 'Going', *The Pan-American Magazine*, XXVII, no. 3 (July 1918), 163.
'To My Aztec Ancestors', *New York Herald*, 19 July 1918, p. 3. [USS]
'With Reference to the Box of Sandalwood', FMC. [USS]
'Poems' (22 July 1918), HSASS.

'Rejected' (May 1917) [*] [USS]
'Heed Me, My Mother' [USS]
'This Summer Night' [USS]
'On Pacifists' [USS]
'On Germany' [USS]
'Enrolled' (July 1918) [*] Amended from the previous 'Enrolled'.
'When After the Last Kiss'. [USS]
'Sonnet (I would not go unloved)' (19 July 1918). [*] [Same as 'With Reference to the Box of Sandalwood'] [USS]
'The answer' [written as by 'Mrs de la Selva'] [USS]

'Sonnet (Souls of my fathers)' [*] [Same as 'To My Aztec Ancestors'] [USS]
'Sonnet (These emotional rhetorics)' [USS]
'On France' [USS]
'Sonnet (I said I would not let)' [USS]
'Sonnet (Below, the world)' [USS]
'Sonnet (But when night came again)' [USS]
'Pax animae'. Translation of 'Pax animae' by Mariano Brull.

[as Eppie Marguerite Shores] 'God Have You in His Care'. Translation of Alfonso Guillén Zelaya's 'Dios te haya perdonado', *The Pan-American Magazine*, XXVII, no. 4 (August 1918), 206, 208.
'Not Easily Could Me Say', ESVMP (31 August 1918). [USS]
'Two Sonnets: In the Country'   'The Wind' [USS]

'Summons Recalled', *Ainslee's Magazine*, 42, no. 2 (September 1918), 146. [USS]
[as Hipólito Mattonel] 'El silencio'. Translation of Edgar Lee Masters' 'Silence', *The Pan-American Magazine*, XXVII, no. 6 (October 1918), 331, 333.
'Lawn Tennis'. Translation of José Juan Tablada's 'Lawn Tennis', *The Pan-American Magazine*, XXVII, no. 6 (October 1918), 334, 336.
'Tropical Morning', *Defenders of Democracy*, ed. The Gift Book Committee of the Militia of Mercy, New York: John Lane Company, 1918, p. 141. [TT]
'Tropical Rain', *Defenders of Democracy*, ed. The Gift Book Committee of the Militia of Mercy, New York: John Lane Company, 1918, pp. 141–42. [TT]
'Tropical Park', *Defenders of Democracy*, ed. The Gift Book Committee of the Militia of Mercy, New York: John Lane Company, 1918, pp. 142–43. [TT]
'Tropical Town', *Defenders of Democracy*, ed. The Gift Book Committee of the Militia of Mercy, New York: John Lane Company, 1918, p. 143. [*] [TT]
'Tropical House', *Defenders of Democracy*, ed. The Gift Book Committee of the Militia of Mercy, New York: John Lane Company, 1918, pp. 143–44. [TT]
Tropical Town, and Other Poems, New York: John Lane Company, 1918.

'Tropical Town' [*]   'Tropical House' [*]

'Tropical Park' [*]
'Tropical Morning' [*]
'Guitar Song with Variations'
'Tropical Dance'
'The Midget Maiden' [*] [variant of 'The Tiny Maiden]
'The Girl That Was Wise'
'Tropical Rain' [*]
'The Haunted House of León' [*]
'A Song for Wall Street'
'Tropical Afternoon'
'Tropical Life'
'All Soul's Day'
'Tropical Childhood'
'Birds of Clay'
'Body and Soul' [*]
'My Nicaragua' [*]
'The Dreamer's Heart Knows Its Own Bitterness'
'Deliverance' [*]
'Portrait' [*]
'The Secret'
'Confidences'
'Finally'
'Measure' [*]
'Inmate'
'Song of the Magdalen'
'Cellini at the Metropolitan Museum'
'Make-Believe'
'Pennies'
'Moonrise'
'Sonnet (Are You Awake, Belovèd?)'
'Courtship'
'Tryst' [*]
'Worn Toy'
'The Birch Tree'
'A Prayer for the United States'
'Hatred' [*]

'December'
'Drill'
'Ode to the Woolworth Building'
'The Knight in Gray'
'Pastorale'
'The Tale from Faerieland' [*]
'To A Young Man' [*]
'The Box of Sandalwood (Ten Sonnets)' [Numbered I–X]
'Candle Light' [*]
'Fleur D'Or' [*]
'Song of the Poppy'
'Song of the Poppy's Lover'
'Aria in G'
'The Sword of Wonder'
'First Love Revived (Seven Sonnets)'
  'Spring Song in Winter'
  'The Claim'
  'On Her Photograph When She Was Nine'
  'The Difference'
  'Love's Selfishness'
  'Beginning of the End'
  'The End'
'The Little Foxes'
'The Sorry Madrigal'
'I Would Be Telling You'
'Her Wish Was That Myself Should Be'
'To Those Who Have Been Indifferent to the Pan American Movement'
'Oh Glorious Spendthrift Joy!'
'The Modern Eve'
'Joy'
'Hunger in the City'
'The Maker of Red Clay Jars'
'Delgadina'
'Of Time and Song'

'The Pulse of Love', *Ainslee's Magazine*, 42, no. 3 (October 1918), 85. [USS]
'For France', *Ainslee's Magazine*, 42, no. 4 (November 1918), 132. [*] [USS]
'The Wharves of God', *Ainslee's Magazine*, 42, no. 5 (December 1918), 42. [USS]
'On Being Issued a Pair of Worn Shoes', FMC. [USS]
'I Am No Flesh', *New York Tribune*, 15 December 1918, II, p. 1. [USS]
'I Am No Flesh', *Ainslee's Magazine*, 42, no. 6 (January 1919), 88. [*] [USS]

'So Love Has Taught Me', *Ainslee's Magazine*, 43, no. 1 (February 1919), 130. [Same as 'When After the Last Kiss'] [*] [USS]
'In Defense of Helen', *Ainslee's Magazine*, 43, no. 2 (March 1919), 103. [USS]
'The Calendar of a Great Love. A book of poems', FMC.

'Inspiration' [USS]
'Jeanne' [USS]
'To Jeanne' [USS]
'Moon of My Delight' (26 April 1918) [USS]
'Reincarnation' (29 April 1918) [USS]
'To a Modern Witch' (29 April 1918) [USS]
'Juliet' (30 April 1918) [USS]
'Melisanda' (30 April 1918) [USS]
'Spring Song' (3 May 1918) [USS]
'To An Apple Tree' (12 May 1918) [USS]
'To A Spider' (19 May 1918) [USS]
'To the Lady of the Spider' (19 May 1918) [USS]
'Who Knows?' (19 May 1918) [USS]
'Flower Bearer' (23 May 1918) [USS]
'Magic Tones' (23 May 1918) [USS]

'O Why "In Vain"?' (25 May 1918) [USS]
'To A Lovely Pessimist' (25 May 1918) [USS]
'Ambrosia' [USS]
'Happiness Deferred' (29 May 1918) [USS]
'Beloved' (2 June 1918) [USS]
'O May The Lily's Fragrance!' (2 June 1918) [USS]
'Rainbow of the Moon' (23 June 1918) [USS]
'Kiss of Rapture' (2 July 1918) [USS]
'Follies' (2 July 1918) [USS]
'Through Depths Profound' (10 July 1918) [USS]
'What Need?' (18 May 1919] [USS]
'Youthful Fancies' (30 May 1919) [USS]

'Judge Me The Thing I Am', *New York Sun*, 15 June 1919, VI: Books and the Book World, 2. [USS]
'To Atthis', *New York Sun*, 22 June 1919, VI: Books and the Book World, 6. [USS]
'That I Desire', FMC. [USS]
'Unredeemed', *Ainslee's Magazine*, 44, no. 1 (August 1919), 136. [USS]
'Birches', *Ainslee's Magazine*, 44, no. 2 (September 1919), 134. [USS]
'The Song About Death', *New York Sun*, 26 October 1919, VI: Books and the Book World, 6. [USS]
'Oda a León de Nicaragua', *Diario de El Salvador*, San Salvador, 29 December 1919.
'Two Humorous Poems' ['A Gentleman Amuses a Lady' and 'On a Dead Cat'] (1919), Colección Salomón de la Selva, Biblioteca Francisco Xavier Clavigero, Universidad Ibero-Americana, Mexico City. [USS]

'Central Americanism', *The Pan-American Magazine*, XXX, no. 4 (February 1920), 213–14.
'The Poets of Nicaragua', *New York Evening Post*, 3 July 1920, p. 7.
'Edwin Markham', *Repertorio Americano*, II, no. 9 (15 December 1920), 124–25.
'Confesión', *Repertorio Americano*, II, no. 20 (20 May 1921), 277.
'Una mágica poetisa de nuestra patria grande', *Repertorio Americano*, II, no. 21 (30 May 1921), 293–94.
'Carta de Nueva York', *Repertorio Americano*, II, no. 28 (10 August 1921), 393–94.

El soldado desconocido, Mexico City: Cultura, 1922.
'Sandino', *The Nation*, 28 January 1928, pp. 63–64.
'Discurso sobre los Melios y la Historia de Tucídides', *Repertorio Americano*, XXI, no. 22 (6 December 1930), 348–51.
'Sandino', *Digesto Latinoamericano*, 26 February 1934, pp. 1, 16.
'Edna St. Vincent Millay', *América: Revista Antológica*, 62 (January 1950), 7–32.
Ilustre familia: poema de los siete tratados = De praeclarae familiae historia: libri septem: novela de dioses y de héroes. Con tres acroasis informativas y apologéticas, Mexico City, n.p., 1952.
'Dos textos' ['La caída de Zelaya y sus consecuencias' and 'Las elecciones de 1924, la guerra civil de 1926, Moncada, Sandino, Sacasa ...'], in William Krehm and Salomón de la Selva, *Nicaragua en mitad del siglo XX*, Managua: Ediciones Populares, 1976.
El soldado desconocido [1922], Managua: Editorial Nueva Nicaragua, 1982.
Sandino: Free Country or Death, compiled by Jorge Eduardo Arellano, Managua: Biblioteca Nacional de Nicaragua, 1984.
La guerra de Sandino o el pueblo desnudo, Managua: Editorial Nueva Nicaragua, 1985.
Tropical Town and Other Poems [1918], edited and with an introduction by Silvio Sirias, Houston: Arte Público Press, 1999.
Antología Mayor/I Poesías, ed. Julio Valle-Castillo, Managua: Fundación UNO, 2007.
Antología Mayor/II Narrativa, ed. Julio Valle-Castillo, Managua: Fundación UNO, 2007.
Antología Mayor/III Ensayos, ed. Julio Valle-Castillo, Managua: Fundación UNO, 2009.
An Unknown Songster Sings: Salomon de la Selva's Collected Poems, 1915–1958 = Un bardo desconocido canta: poemas recolectados de Salomón de la Selva, 1915–1958, compilation, prologue, and annotation by Luis M. Bolaños-Salvatierra; translation by Luis M. Bolaños-Salvatierra, Guillermo Fernández-Ampieé, and Moisés Elías Fuentes, Managua: Academia Nicaraguense de la Lengua, 2015.

3 New York

Ackerman, Kenneth D., *Trotsky in New York 1917: A Radical on the Eve of Revolution*, Berkeley, CA: Counterpoint, 2016.
Allen, Esther, 'What Does Nueva York Mean in English?', *Translation Review*, 81, no. 1 (2011), 1–11.
'The Americas in New York: Writing and Arts in La Gran Manzana', *Review: Literature and Arts of the Americas*, 47, no. 2 (2014).
Antliff, Allan, *Anarchist Modernism: Art, Politics, and the First American Avant-Garde*, Chicago: University of Chicago Press, 2001.
Bell, M. Margaret, *The Problem of Inter-American Organization*, Stanford, CA: Stanford University Press, 1944.
Berkovici, Konrad, *Around the World in New York*, New York: The Century Co., 1924.

Bochner, Jay, *An American Lens: Scenes from Alfred Stieglitz's New York Secession*, Cambridge, MA: MIT Press, 2005.
Brooker, Peter and Andrew Thacker, eds, *The Oxford Critical and Cultural History of Modernist Magazines*, vol. 2, *North America, 1894–1960*, Oxford: Oxford University Press, 2012.
Brooks, Van Wyck, *Scenes and Portraits: Memories of Childhood and Youth*, New York: E. P. Dutton and Co., 1954.
—— *The Confident Years: 1885–1915*, New York: E. P. Dutton and Co., 1955.
Carr, Helen, *The Verse Revolutionaries: Ezra Pound, H.D. and the Imagists*, London: Jonathan Cape, 2009.
Churchwell, Sarah, *Careless People: Murder, Mayhem and the Invention of the Great Gatsby*, London: Virago, 2013.
Coates, Benjamin Allen, *Legalist Empire: International Law and American Foreign Relations in the Early Twentieth Century*, New York: Oxford University Press, 2016.
Collin, Richard H., *Theodore Roosevelt's Caribbean: The Panama Canal, the Monroe Doctrine, and the Latin American Context*, Baton Rouge: Louisiana State University Press, 1990.
Conrad, Peter, *The Art of the City: Views and Versions of New York*, New York: Oxford University Press, 1984.
Crundern, Robert M., *Ministers of Reform: The Progressives' Achievement in American Civilization, 1889–1920*, New York: Basic Books, 1982.
—— *American Salons: Encounters with European Modernism, 1885–1917*, New York: Oxford University Press, 1993.
Davidson, Gustav, ed., *In Fealty to Apollo: Poetry Society of America, 1910–1950*, New York: The Five Editions Press, 1950.
DeCasseres, Benjamin, *Mirrors of New York*, New York: Joseph Lawren, 1925.
Feinsod, Harris, *The Poetry of the Americas: From Good Neighbors to Countercultures*, Oxford: Oxford University Press, 2017
Fernández-Armesto, Felipe, *Our America: A Hispanic History of the United States*, New York: W. W. Norton, 2014.
Findling, John E., *Close Neighbors, Distant Friends: United States–Central American Relations*, New York: Greenwood Press, 1987.
Gilderhus, Mark T., *Pan American Visions: Woodrow Wilson in the Western Hemisphere 1913–1921*, Tucson: University of Arizona Press, 1986.
Greusz, Kirsten Silva, *Ambassadors of Culture: The Transamerican Origins of Latino Writing*, Princeton, NJ: Princeton University Press, 2002.
Heller, Adele and Lois Rudnick, eds, *1915, The Cultural Moment: The New Politics, the New Woman, the New Psychology, the New Art and the New Theatre in America*, New Brunswick, NJ: Rutgers University Press, 1991.
Hudson, Peter James, *Bankers and Empire: How Wall Street Colonized the Caribbean*, Chicago: University of Chicago Press, 2017.
Kanellos, Nicolás, *Hispanic Literature of the United States: A Comprehensive Reference*, Westport, CT: Greenwood Press, 2003.
Klingaman, William K., *1919: The Year Our World Began*, New York: St Martin's Press, 1987.

Krugler, David F., *1919, The Year of Racial Violence. How African Americans Fought Back*, New York: Cambridge University Press, 2015.

Lindner, Christoph, *Imagining New York City: Literature, Urbanism, and the Visual Arts, 1890-1940*, New York: Oxford University Press, 2015.

McPherson, Alan, *The Invaded: How Latin Americans and Their Allies Fought and Ended U.S. Occupations*, New York: Oxford University Press, 2014.

Maurer, Noel, *The Empire Trap: The Rise and Fall of the U.S. Intervention to Protect American Property Overseas, 1893-2013*, Princeton, NJ: Princeton University Press, 2013.

Maurice, Arthur Bartlett, *The New York of the Novelists*, New York: Dodd, Mead and Co., 1916.

May, Henry F., *The End of American Innocence: A Study of the First Years of Our Own Time, 1912-1917*, New York: Alfred A. Knopf, 1959.

Miller, William D., *Pretty Bubbles in the Air: America in 1919*, Urbana: University of Illinois Press, 1991.

Morán González, John and Laura Lomas, eds, *The Cambridge Companion to Latino/a Literature*, New York: Cambridge University Press, 2016.

Morris, Edmund, *The Rise of Theodore Roosevelt* [1979], New York: Modern Library, 2001.

—— *Theodore Rex*, New York: Random House, 2001.

—— *Colonel Roosevelt*, New York: Random House, 2011.

Nelson Cary, *Repression and Recovery: Modern American Poetry and the Politics of Cultural Memory, 1910-1945*, Madison: University of Wisconsin Press, 1989.

Newcomb, John Timberman, *How Did Poetry Survive? The Making of Modern American Verse*, Urbana: University of Illinois Press, 2012.

O'Brien, Thomas F., *The Revolutionary Mission: American Enterprise in Latin America, 1900-1945*, Cambridge: Cambridge University Press, 1996.

Onís, Federico de, *España en América*, San Juan: Ediciones de la Universidad de Puerto Rico, 1955.

Remeseira, Claudio Iván, ed., *Hispanic New York: A Sourcebook*, New York: Columbia University Press, 2010.

The Routledge Companion to Latino/a Literature, ed. Suzanne Bost and Frances Aparicio, Abingdon: Routledge, 2013.

Scott, William B. and Peter M. Rutkoff, *New York Modern*, Baltimore, MD: Johns Hopkins University Press, 1999.

Stansell, Christine, *American Moderns: Bohemian New York and the Creation of a New Century*, New York: Henry Holt and Company, 2000.

Sullivan, Edward J., ed., *Nueva York, 1613-1945*, New York: The New-York Historical Society in association with Scala Publishers, 2010.

Sullivan, Mark, *Our Times: The United States, 1900-1925*, 6 vols., New York: C. Scribner's Sons, 1926.

Szefel, Lisa, *The Gospel of Beauty in the Progressive Era: Reforming American Verse and Values*, New York: Palgrave Macmillan, 2011.

Veeser, Cyrus, *A World Safe for Capitalism: Dollar Diplomacy and America's Rise to Global Power*, New York: Columbia University Press, 2002.

Wallace, Mike, *Greater Gotham: A History of New York City from 1898 to 1919*, New York: Oxford University Press, 2017.

Watson, Steven, *Strange Bedfellows: The First American Avant-Garde*, New York: Abbeville Press, 1991.

Wertheim, Arthur Frank, *The New York Little Renaissance: Iconoclasm, Modernism, and Nationalism in American Culture, 1908–1917*, New York: New York University Press, 1976.

Whalan, Mark, *American Culture in the 1910s*, Edinburgh: Edinburgh University Press, 2010.

Index

A Fool There Was 75
Abreu Gómez, Ermilo 350
Acevedo, Napoleón *see* Borgia, Rene
Adams, John Quincy 34–35
Agar, John G. 181, 182, 183, 184, 297
Ainslee's Magazine 169, 256, 293
Alas, Leopoldo *see* Clarín
Albizu Campos, Pedro 278
Alemán Valdés, Miguel 348, 349
Alfau, Antonio A. 112, 118n119
Alfau Galván, Alfonso 113, 235
Alfau Galván, Felipe 113
Alfau Galván, Jesusa 113, 114, 282, 303, 307, 354
Allan, Wing B. 325
Almeida Seabra, Bruno Henriques de 232
Álvarez, Julia 8, 108
America (continent) 11, 33, 34–36
   'the two Americas'
      ideological division 35–43
      in Ruben Darío's writing 96, 102
      in Salomón de la Selva's project 226, 227, 231
      see also Ariel; Pan American Union building; Pinochet Le-Brun, Tancredo, *The Gulf of Misunderstanding*
American Academy of Arts and Letters 21, 181
American Association for International Conciliation 219, 319, 320
American Association of Teachers of Spanish 139

American Exporter, The 199, 237
American Tropics 4–5, 151
Anderson, Margaret 208, 278
Anglo-Saxon ideology 38–39, 42–43, 62, 67
Appelbaum, Misha 297–98
Arana Turrol, Juan 88, 97
Arellano, Jorge Eduardo 337, 345
Arenales, Ricardo *see* Barba Jacob, Porfirio
Arensberg, Louise 76, 220
Arensberg, Walter 76, 220
Arévalo Martínez, Rafael 220–21
Argentina 67, 103
   Buenos Aires 67, 83
   Pan-American conferences in 45, 48, 139
Ariel 57–61, 64, 66–69, 129, 147, 280
   see also The Tempest
Ariel see Rodó, José Enrique
arielismo 57, 61, 64
   in José Santos Chocano 131
   in Rubén Darío 91
   debated by Pedro Henríquez Ureña 117–18
   in Juan Ramón Jiménez 143, 146
   in, and rejected by, Jesús Semprúm 280
Armory Show 20, 26, 73, 90
Asociación Ibero-Americana de los Estados Unidos 217, 282
Ateneo de la Juventud 61
Athens 59, 60, 61, 347
Authors Club 21, 22, 145
Authors' League of America 22, 100, 145, 181, 299

Baca, Félix María 232
Bada, J. M. 307
Ballets Russes 111, 136, 156, 295
Bara, Theda 75
Barba Jacob, Porfirio 111
    at pan-American dinner (1917) 205
Barrett, John 217, 246, 297, 354
    on Pan American Union building
        in Washington DC 46–47, 102
Barsay, Sophia 200–01
Baudelaire, Charles
    comparison with José Santos
        Chocano 132–33
    and modernity 28
    deifies Edgar Allan Poe 58, 128
    prose poems 83, 101
Beach, Joseph Warren 232
Beals, Carleton 309, 346
Belgium 188–89, 210, 227, 296, 327
Bello, Andrés 34, 128
Benavente, Jacinto 148, 208, 278
Benét, Laura 24, 25
Benét, Stephen Vincent 24, 25, 295
Benét, William Rose 24, 25, 116, 330, 354
    friend of Salomón de la Selva 120
    and pan-American project 134
    poems translated into Spanish 137, 229, 232
Berman, Marshall 29, 30
Bermúdez, Alejandro 87, 92–93, 95
Best Maugard, Adolfo 342
Betances, Ramón Emeterio 12
Betancourt Román, José Luis *see*
    Ivanovitch, Iván
Bilac, Olavo 226, 232, 233
Bilbao, Francisco 39–40, 42
Blackwell, Alice Stone 232
Blaine, James G. 44, 45, 67
Blanco Fombona, Rufino
    and 'the two Americas' 62, 73
    reviewing *The Americanization of
        the World* (W. T. Stead) 61
    in *Inter-América* 219
    poem translated into English 280
    as *posmodernista* poet 226

Blasco Ibáñez, Vicente, *The Four
    Horsemen of the Apocalypse* 209
Boissevain, Eugen 350
Bolaños Álvarez, Pío 78n7, 86
Bolet Peraza, Nicanor 36, 83
Bolívar, Simón 39, 64, 324
Bolsheviki 251, 301, 302
Bolshevism 210, 213, 299, 311, 326
Borges, Jorge Luis 117, 169
Borgia, Rene 282, 308
Brannon Vega, Margarita del Carmen
    335, 337–38
Branyas, Joseph 151
Brazil 43, 81n14, 182, 184, 321
British American Recruiting Mission
    257–58, 263
British Army 263–64
    see also De la Selva, Salomón,
        First World War, experience in
        British Army
Brooke, Rupert 229, 238, 272
Broun, Heywood 111, 112, 354
Brull Caballero, Mariano 354
    friend of Pedro Henríquez Ureña
        106, 110, 119
    and pan-American project 205, 229
    at the Poetry Society of America
        117
Bryant, William Cullen 10, 11
Bulletin of the Pan American Union 48
Bunau-Varilla, Philippe 53
Buranelli, Prosper 81, 335, 336, 338
Burleson, Albert S. 215, 216
Butler, Nicholas 87, 140, 219
Butterick Building 77, 78

Cabrera Camacho, Rafael 232
Café Martin 86
Calero, Manuel 83, 283
Caliban
    USA as 42, 57–58, 60–61, 64,
        65–72, 129, 280, 318
    see also The Tempest
Camacho, Manuel J. 296–97
Camba, Julio 99, 105
Camprubí, José 112, 218, 355

Camprubí de Jiménez, Zenobia 141, 144, 147, 148, 354
Canada 77, 217
Canales, Nemesio R. 317, 318
cannibalism 60, 86
Cannon, Lee Roy 55, 249–50, 348
Capen, Samuel P. 319, 320
Cardenal, Ernesto 344–45, 353
Caribbean, the
  part of North America 36, 47, 217
  political upheavals in 14–15
  US policy towards 13, 49, 52–56, 168, 215, 347
Carnegie, Andrew 21, 46, 277
Carnegie Endowment for International Peace 87, 183, 218, 319, 320
Carnevali, Emanuel 204, 278, 355
Carranza, Venustiano 106n78, 131, 149, 154
Casanova, Emilia 12
Casseres, Benjamin de 76
Castellot Batalla, José 153, 281, 303, 307, 309, 310–11, 355
Castellot Paullada, José 281
Castillo Ledón, Luis 110
Castrillo Gamez de la Selva, Carmela 346
Castro Leal, Antonio 154
Cecilio del Valle, José 324
Central America
  Central American Court of Justice 215
  Central American Union 337, 340
  Central Americanism 329–330
  part of North America 36, 47, 212
  political upheavals in 14–15
  US filibustering in 249
    see also William Walker
  US policy towards 65
  and First World War 259
Cestero, Manuel Florentino 110, 355
  at dinner at Gonfarone's 303, 304
  friend of Pedro Henríquez Ureña 116
  friend of Dmitri Ivanovitch 311
  friend of Salomón de la Selva 106, 109, 111, 117, 154, 307
  works for *Las Novedades* 118n119
  works for *La Prensa* 282
Cestero, Tulio Manuel 111, 164
Chamberlin, Joseph Edgar 120
Chevalier, Michel 41–42, 59
Chile 81n14
  Pan-American conferences in 139, 322–23
  see also Pinochet Le-Brun, Tancredo
Chocano, José Santos 355
  Alma América 128–30
  and Rubén Darío 92, 127
  Estampas Newyorkinas 131–34
  'La canción del camino' 233–34
  and pan-American project 127, 135, 204–07, 352
  at the Poetry Society of America 117, 179, 181, 205
  translated into English 225, 226, 229, 232, 233–34
Clarín 230
classical analogies 40–42
Clavigero, Francisco 34
Cleveland, Grover 50
Cocteau, Jean 155–56
Coester, Alfred 62–63, 91, 139–40, 182–83
  The Literary History of Spanish America 62–63, 139–40
Cohn, Adolphe 93, 94, 95
Collao, Alfredo 218, 279, 303, 304
Colombia 14, 53, 93
Columbia University
  Spanish studies at 140
  see also Darío, Rubén, reading at Columbia University; De la Selva, Salomón, reading at Columbia University; Roberts, W. Adolphe, 'Pierrot Wounded' performed at Columbia University
Comité de Relaciones Amistosas entre los Estudiantes Extranjeros y los Estados Unidos 325

Committee on Cooperation in Latin America 217
Conferences of American States *see* Pan-American Conferences
continents, theory of 33–36
Contreras, Francisco 128
Costa Rica 93, 104, 162, 232, 259, 346
Covarrubias, Miguel 76
Crane, Frank 82, 106, 108, 120, 272, 355
Crapsey, Adelaide 232, 330, 333
Cravan, Arthur 178, 179, 180
Crowhurst-Rand, James *pseudonym* of De la Selva, Salomón
Crowley, Aleister 253, 266
Cuba
　Cubans in New York 10–12
　under US control 2, 35, 52, 54, 246
Culkin, Amanda 286, 355
Culkin, Philip 286, 355
Culmell Nin, Rosa 304, 308, 321
Cyclops
　USA as Cyclops 42, 60, 66, 85, 86, 91, 97

Darío, Rubén 64–72, 82–105, 356
　'A Roosevelt' 69–70
　'Apuntaciones de hospital' 95–101
　in Buenos Aires 67
　'Epístola a Madame Lugones' 71
　'La gran cosmópolis' 90–91
　and Archer M. Huntington 88, 92–93
　'Margarita, está linda la mar' 336
　and José Martí 83
　and *modernismo* 27–28, 31
　in New York 65–66, 83–103
　and pan Americanism 72, 102–03
　'Pax' 101–02, 351
　at the Poetry Society of America 90
　reading at Columbia University 92–95, 101–02, 351
　'Salutación al águila' 70–71
　translated into English 138, 232
　'El triunfo de Calibán' 66–68
　El viaje a Nicaragua 84–85
　see also Chocano, José Santos, and Rubén Darío; De la Selva, Salomón, views on Rubén Darío; Jiménez, Juan Ramón, and Rubén Darío; Markham, Edwin, praises Rubén Darío; Shores, Robert J., and Rubén Darío; Woodruff, Helen S., and Rubén Darío
Dávalos Balkin, Balbino 110, 117, 232, 233, 341, 356
Davis, Richard Harding 248
Dawson, Coningsby 267
De la Selva Castrillo, Salomón 346
De la Selva Castrillo, Carmen Evangelina 346
De la Selva, María Isabel *pseudonym* of De la Selva, Salomón
De la Selva [Escoto], Salomón
　adolescence in New York 81–82, 108–09
　automystification 79n8, 81, 264, 338–39
　and Margarita del Carmen Brannon Vega 335–38
　'Cantar' 273–74
　and Emanuel Carnevale 204
　visit to Chicago 198
　'Confesión' 174–75
　cultural life in New York 109, 111–12
　views on Rubén Darío 103–05
　with Rubén Darío in New York 90, 92, 94–95
　and Margarita DeBayle Sacasa 336
　dinner at Gonfarone's 303–07
　dinners at West 97th Street 116–17, 127, 134–35
　'The Dreamer's Heart Knows Its Own Bitterness', 186–89
　'Drill' 193–94
　early life in Nicaragua 77–78
　education 77–80
　employment 77, 198, 339–40
　First World War, determination to fight in 194, 202, 257–63

First World War, experience in
British Army 264–75, 344–45
First World War, return from
284–86
and Jeanne Robert Foster 252–56,
264, 267–70, 274, 286
and Alfonso Guillén Zelaya 111,
154
'The Haunted House of León'
248–49
and Theresa Helburn 256, 272–75,
341
and Pedro Henríquez Ureña 76, 82,
106–20, 126, 127, 184–85, 193,
225, 284, 307
Hispanic friends 109–11, 112–13,
117, 153–54, 303–05
and Archer M. Huntington 134,
137–39, 264–65, 272, 285
imagined lovers 124, 126, 268–70,
333–34
and Juan Ramón Jiménez 145, 350
and John Lane Company 201,
238–39
and Joyce Kilmer 107, 120, 121, 251,
269, 272
later life 342–49
and Muna Lee 199–200, 287–88,
333–34, 351
'Little Boy Dead' 171–72
The Lonely Exile 203, 264
and Amy Lowell 224–25, 227–28,
235, 240
'Lullaby for a Star' 173–74
and Edwin Markham 158–59, 162,
240, 339
marriage and children 346
and Alice Meynell 275
and Edna St Vincent Millay 118–27,
157–58, 196–98, 202–07
and modernism 26, 243
and *modernismo* 28, 31
and Luis Muñoz Marín 235–36
arrival in New York recalled 72–73
leaves New York 335–42
'My Nicaragua' 247

Nicaraguan identity 329–34
'Ode to the Woolworth Building'
243–44
pan-American dinner (1917)
205–07
pan-American project 8, 222–23,
226, 249–53
his parents 78, 237, 249
and the Poetry Society of America
24–26, 82
and Katherine Anne Porter 342
and Ezra Pound 111, 275–76
pseudonyms 104, 226, 229–30,
232–33
reading at Columbia University 139
reputation as poet 5–7
and Jessie Rittenhouse 329–34
and W. Adolphe Roberts 291–96,
340
confronting Theodore Roosevelt
179–89
and Florence Schauffler 189, 192–93
'Serpentina' 172–73
his sisters 172–77
El soldado desconocido 343–44
A Soldier [Sings] 267n166, 338
'A Song for Wall Street' 245
'A Tale from Faerieland and Other
Poems' 169–74
teaching at Williams College 139,
157, 189, 193–94
'The Tiny Maiden' 176
translation projects 138, 156,
222–34
'Tropical House' 247
Tropical Town and Other Poems,
203, 237–50
views of others about 106–07, 149,
175–76, 239–41, 290–91, 293
'With Reference to the Box of
Sandalwood' 255–56
and Clement Wood 251–52
and Marya Zaturenska 254, 287–91
De Valera, Éamon 277
DeBayle Sacasa, Margarita 336, 348
Delineator, The 77, 117, 119, 213, 320

Dell, Floyd 24, 25, 109, 356
Delmonico's 85, 86, 88
Díaz, Porfirio 18, 131
Díaz Guerra, Alirio 14
   Lucas Guevara 14
Díaz Mirón, Salvador 232
Digesto Latinoamericano/Latin American Digest 346
Domingo, Wilfred A. 301
Dominican Republic 14, 54
   US occupation of 3, 164–69, 296–97
   see also Henríquez y Carvajal, Francisco; Hard, William, 'Is America Honest?'
Dos Passos, John 344
Drago, Luis M. 51
Dreiser, Theodore 77, 238
Drick, Gertrude 179–80
Duchamp, Marcel 20, 26, 76, 179, 220
Duncan, Isadora 72, 111, 151
Dutton, George 193

Earle, Ferdinand 121
El Salvador 249, 259, 329, 335, 337
Eliot, T. S. 26, 101, 169, 295
   The Waste Land 26, 101
   'Tradition and the Individual Talent' 26, 31
Elliott, Lilian E. 217, 356
   as literary editor of *Pan-American Magazine* 227, 228, 232, 329
   at pan-American dinner (1917) 207
   'The Poets of Brazil' 182, 183
   at Sorosis luncheon 321
   as translator 226
Emerson, Ralph Waldo 36, 69, 187, 188
Ervin, Charles 108, 302, 356
Escoto Baca, Evangelina 78
Escoto, Nicolás *pseudonym of* De la Selva, Salomón
Estrada Cabrera, Manuel 88, 129, 130, 205
Estudiante Latino-Americano, El 325
Evangelista, Vincentino 213–15

Facio, Justo A. 232
Faria, Tiberio 303, 308
Fawcett, James Waldo 300, 356
Feigenbaum, Benjamin 109, 356
Felix-Portland Hotel v, 205, 206, 283, 352
Fernández de Castro, José Antonio 111
Fernández Montalvo, Ricardo 233
Ferrara, Orestes 281, 283
Fiallo, Fabio 356
   arrival in New York 12
   with José Santos Chocano in New York 130–31
   with Rubén Darío in New York 85–86
   imprisoned in Santo Domingo 167–68
Firkins, O. W. 239, 240
First World War 119, 154, 193
   poetry of 5, 272
   see also De la Selva, Salomón, First World War
Fitts, Dudley, *Anthology of Contemporary Latin-American Poetry* 352
Fitzgerald, F. Scott, 'May Day' 320
Flores, Julio 232
Fontoura, Xavier 70, 131
Ford, J. D. M. 139
Fornaro, Carlo de 16n18, 76, 106n78
Foster, Jeanne Robert 253, 356
   invited to dinner at Gonfarone's 303, 305, 307
   as poet 254, 333
   'The Mission of Poetry in Pan-American Relations' 227
   see also De la Selva, Salomón, and Jeanne Robert Foster
France
   as Latin nation 41–42, 67
   Paris
      and modernism 28, 31, 101
      Latin Americans in 39, 48, 64, 83, 128, 154, 210, 320, 348
Frank, Waldo 63, 278

French Hospital 88, 96
Frick, Henry Clay 277
Frost, Robert 9, 20, 169, 225, 330
    translated into Spanish 226, 231, 234
Funk, Isaac K. 25, 79

Galsworthy, John 297
Galván, Manuel Jesús de 112, 357
Galván Velásquez, Antonio de Jesús 131
Galván Velásquez, Manuel de Jesús 116, 117, 118n119, 131, 183, 357
    'Ubinam gentius sumus' 166-67
Galván Velásquez de Alfau, Eugenia 112, 117
Gamio, Manuel 110
García Godoy, Federico 62
García Lorca, Federico 5
García Monge, Joaquín 162, 171, 337, 338, 341
Garfield, Harry Augustus 158
Garland, Hamlin 77, 181, 182, 183, 184, 297
Garvey, Marcus 136, 278
Geisenheimer, Eugenia L. V. 170, 171, 239, 341, 357
Geisenheimer, Theodore 170
Gil, Enrique 283
Glenton, J. *pseudonym of* De la Selva, Salomón
Glenton, Jonas Wilson 78
Glenton, Teresa Paula 78
Goldberg, Isaac, *Studies in Spanish American Literature* 139
Goldman, Emma 161, 277, 298
Goldsmith, Peter H. 219, 223, 280, 320, 325
    and pan-American project 183, 205
Gollomb, Joseph 109, 302, 357
Gonfarone, Caterina 305
Gonfarone's *see* Hotel Gonfarone
González Marín, Francisco 12, 13
González Martínez, Enrique 226, 227, 229, 232, 341

González Mesa, Rufino 81, 82, 109, 293, 357
    draws cover for 'A Tale from Fairieland' 137, 169
González Sol, Teresa 78
Gorgas, William C. 246
Gorky, Maxim 164
Gráfico, El 16, 150, 151
Grahame, Leopold 183
Granados, Amparo 144
Granados, Enrique 73, 144, 208, 308
Grant, Madison 116
Greene, Constance Murray 305, 357
Greenough, Laurence *pseudonym of* De la Selva, Salomón
Greenwood, Charles 78
Griswold, Chester 198
Griswold, Elizabeth H. 198, 286
Griswold, Grace 286
Groce, Leonard 55, 249-50, 348
Groussac, Paul 67, 140n12, 224
Gruening, Ernest 112, 218
Guantánamo Bay 2, 52, 54
Guardiola Estrada Palma, Genoveva 321
Guerra, Benjamín 83
Guillén Zelaya, Alfonso 282, 321, 357
    at pan-American dinner (1917) 205
    as translator 225, 226, 227, 233
    and *Others* 220-21
    translated into English 232
    'Why the Central American Republics Should Take Part in the War' 259
    see also De la Selva, Salomón, and Alfonso Guillén Zelaya
Guiteras Font, Antonio 322
Guiteras Gener Keller, Laura 303, 321, 322, 357
Guiteras Holmes, Antonio 322
Guiterman, Arthur 23, 164
Guzmán, Martín Luis 61, 110, 117, 149-53, 357
    A Orillas del Hudson 151-53

H. D. (Hilda Doolittle) 108, 330
Haiti
  under US control 56, 168–69, 210, 246
Hard, William, 'Is America Honest?' 213–17
Harrington, Ellen *pseudonym of* Schauffler, Florence Manvel
Harris, Thomas Lake 164
Havemeyer, Theodore 93
Hawaii 49, 52, 246
Hay, John 18, 22, 51
Hegel, G. W. F. 34
Helburn, Theresa 190, 256–57, 291, 358
  see also De la Selva, Salomón, and Theresa Helburn
Heliodoro Valle, Rafael 337, 338
Henna, J. Julio 12, 219, 318–19
Henríquez Ureña, Camila 108
Henríquez Ureña, Max 107, 323
Henríquez Ureña, Pedro 358
  in Argentina 169
  as critic 6, 108, 117
  on Rubén Darío in New York 88n30, 90, 93
  and Juan Ramón Jiménez 148
  in Mexico 61, 149, 341
  his mixed race 114–16, 169
  at pan-American dinner (1917) 205
  on US occupation of the Dominican Republic 168–69
  see also De la Selva, Salomón, and Pedro Henríquez Ureña
Henríquez y Carvajal, Federico 107
Henríquez y Carvajal, Francisco 107, 165–67, 323
Henry, O. 15, 180, 293, 309
Heredia, José María 10
Herron, George 302
Herron, Miriam 305
Herron, Vennette 294–95, 302, 305, 307, 358
Hickey, Katharine 294, 296, 305
Hill, Leslie Pinckney 231
Hills, E. C. 92, 139

Hispanic America 36, 42–43, 58, 64, 68, 73, 116, 351
  US scholarship on 10, 62–63, 139–40, 220–22
  see also South America; Latin America
Hispanic Anthology 138, 361, 363
Hispanic Society of America 16, 19, 281, 328
  Rubén Darío at 92
  Juan Ramón Jiménez at 144, 146
  and Salomón de la Selva 138, 264, 285
  see also Huntington, Archer M.
hispanidad 57
hispanismo 43, 68
hispanoamericanismo 129
Home Book of Verse, The 242
Holmes, John Haynes 299
Honduras 249, 259, 335, 337
Hooley, Arthur 122, 123
Hoover, J. Edgar 277
Hopper, Edward 20, 112
Hostos, Eugenio María de 12, 107, 118
Hotel America 15, 83, 283
Hotel Astor 85, 86, 88, 131, 315
Hotel Gonfarone 1, 305–06
  the dinner at Gonfarone's 1, 4, 291, 303–07
Hotel McAlpin 149, 283
Hotel Waldorf-Astoria 278, 321, 329
Howells, William Dean 21, 229, 338
Hoyt, Helen 192, 200, 220
Huerta, Victoriano 131, 149, 153, 154, 204, 283, 310
Humboldt, Alexander von 34, 128
Huntington, Archer M. 283n15, 358
  and Rubén Darío 88, 92, 94, 97
  family background 16–18
  founding of Hispanic Society of America 18–19
  and Juan Ramón Jiménez 148
  and Spanish studies at Columbia 140
  see also De la Selva, Salomón, and Archer M. Huntington
Huntington, Helen Gates 137–38

Iberoamerica/Íbero-América 43, 64
Icaza, Javier 110
Inman, Samuel G. 217, 325
Inter-America/Inter-América 212, 218–19, 223–24, 280, 320
International American Conferences *see* Pan-American Conferences
International Council of Women 321
Ivanovitch, Dmitri 283n16, 303, 304, 308n69, 309
   'La ventana' 311–12

Jamaica 13, 291, 301
Jeffers, Robinson 20
Jefferson, Thomas 34, 128, 324
Jiménez, Juan Ramón 358
   Diario de un poeta reciencasado 143–49
   in Madrid 130
   and *modernismo* 29
   in New York 141–49
   see also De la Selva, Salomón, and Juan Ramón Jiménez
Joel's Bohemian Refreshery 16, 25
John Lane Company 201, 209, 228, 238, 246, 267, 343
Johns, Orrick 239
Johnson, James Weldon 229
Joint Committee of the Literary Arts 181, 297
Jones, Thomas S., Jr 330
Joyce, James 208, 237
Juegos Florales 281–82, 284

Keats, John 137, 242
Kemp, Harry 306, 307, 358
Kennerley, Mitchell 23, 122n134
Kerfoot, John 191
Keynes, John Maynard 111–12
Kilmer, Aline 190, 330, 359
   at dinner at Gonfarone's 307
   at the Poetry Society of America 24, 25
Kilmer, Joyce 330, 359
   at the Poetry Society of America 24, 25, 90

   translated into Spanish 137, 229, 232
   'The White Ships and the Red' 106
   see also De la Selva, Salomón, and Joyce Kilmer
Kinney, Margaret 112, 116, 359
Kinney, Troy 112, 116, 151, 359
Kipling, Rudyard 53, 75
Knapp, Harry S. 167, 323
Knox, Philander 56, 62, 249, 250
Kreymborg, Alfred 75, 220, 287, 288, 359

Land of Joy, The 209
Lars, Claudia *see* Brannon Vega, Margarita del Carmen
Lastra, Juan Julián 231
Latin America
   identity 60–64, 129, 231, 347
   Latin Americans in New York 198, 217, 222, 279, 283, 303, 321
   literature 5–7, 27
   origins of term 36–43
   poets and poetry 139, 205, 222, 224, 225, 226, 227, 240
   see also Hispanic America; South America
League of Nations 212, 214, 328
Lee, Joseph 233
Lee, Muna 190, 330, 352, 359
   at dinner at Gonfarone's 303
   marriage to Luis Muñoz Marín 289, 316, 318
   translated into Spanish 225, 232
   see also De la Selva, Salomón, and Muna Lee
Liberal Club 20, 90, 109, 137, 291
Lindsay, Vachel 20, 125, 225, 330
Little Review 204, 208, 221, 278
Lloyd, Avenarius F. *see* Cravan, Arthur
Lombardo Toledano, Isabel 116
Longfellow, Henry Wadsworth 10, 322
López, Narciso 11, 36

Lopokova, Lydia 73, 111–12
Lowell, Amy 26, 341
   translated into Spanish 226, 227, 229, 233
   see also De la Selva, Salomón, and Amy Lowell
Loy, Mina 75, 136, 220
Lucas, Ernest F. *pseudonym of* De la Selva, Salomón
Lugones, Leopoldo 224, 226
Lusitania, sinking of 106, 112

Machado de Assis, Joaquim Maria 32, 70
McDonald, Jane *pseudonym of* De la Selva, Salomón
McKay, Claude, 'If We Must Die' 302
MacKaye, Percy 121, 125, 147, 164, 359
McKinley, William 18, 100
MacLane, Mary 199–200
Madero, Francisco 131, 149, 153, 349
Madriguera, Enric 305, 308
Madriguera, Paquita 304, 308, 359
Mahan, Capt. Alfred Thayer 50, 52, 53
Maldonado, Pedro 232
Mallén, Rafael 109
Mandujano, Graciela 303, 320, 321, 322–23, 359
Manifest Destiny 36, 49, 50
Markham, Anna Catherine 23n32, 183, 305, 306, 316–17
Markham, Edwin 27, 158–64, 183, 184, 297–98, 359
   at dinner at Gonfarone's 297–98, 303, 305, 306
   'The Man with the Hoe' 160–62
   and the Poetry Society of America 23, 25, 26
   see also De la Selva, Salomón, and Edwin Markham; Muñoz Marín, Luis, and Edwin Markham
Markham, Virgil 163–64

Martí, José
   on First Conference of American states 44, 45
   journalism 32
   and *modernismo* 28
   in New York 12, 13, 15, 83, 161
   see also Darío, Rubén, and José Martí
Masses, The 24, 109, 208
Masters, Edgar Lee 233, 234, 330
Mattonel, Hipólito *pseudonym of* De la Selva, Salomón
Mejía Sánchez, Ernesto 345
Mencken, H. L. 238, 316
Méndez Rivas, Joaquín 154, 281–82
Mexico 24, 45, 108, 116, 341
   French invasion of 42
   Mexican Revolution 12–13, 131, 149, 214
   Mexicans in New York 12–13, 48, 110, 149, 153–54
   US occupation of Veracruz 109, 212
   see also Ateneo de la Juventud; US-Mexico War
Meynell, Alice 242, 260, 275–76
Meynell, Francis 275
Milholland, Inez 350
Millay, Edna St Vincent v, 3, 20, 27, 119, 120, 205–07, 360
   Aria de Capo 295
   at dinner at Gonfarone's 297, 303, 304
   'Recuerdo' 203–04
   'Renascence' 20, 25, 118
   translated into Spanish 225, 226, 229, 232
   and W. Adolphe Roberts 294–96
   'Witch-Wife' 119, 122
   see also De la Selva, Salomón, and Edna St Vincent Millay
Millay, Kathleen 305, 360
Millay, Norma 203, 207, 305, 360
Millet, Jean-François 160
Mindell, Fania 112, 179, 362
Miranda 66, 68, 147
   see also The Tempest

Miranda, Francisco de 10
Mistral, Gabriela 281, 338
M. L. S. *pseudonym of* De la Selva, Salomón
modernism 26–32, 101, 105, 204, 220, 238, 242, 243, 254
modernismo 27–29, 65, 140, 226
modernity 9, 26–32, 67, 75, 101, 243
Moffat, Thomas P. 250
Molina Wood, Jorge 226
Monroe, Harriet 23, 73, 199, 200, 204, 251, 275
Monroe Doctrine 34, 50, 51, 54, 180–81, 182, 211, 214–15
Montenegro, Ernesto 303, 313, 360
Moore, John Bassett 48, 53
Morales Macedo, Luisa 321
Morley, S. G. 92
Morton, David H. 24, 307, 330, 360
mundonovismo 128
Muñoz Marín, Luis 236–37, 282, 316–19, 360
   and the Alfau family 113–14
   at dinner at Gonfarone's 303
   translation of 'The Man with the Hoe' (Edwin Markham) 162
   marriage to Muna Lee 289, 316, 318
   and Edwin Markham 316–17
   and *La Revista de Indias* 235–36
   see also De la Selva, Salomón, and Luis Muñoz Marín
Muñoz Rivera, Luis 236

Nación, La
   correspondents in New York 188, 205
   Rubén Darío writing for 65, 88, 95, 99
   José Martí writing for 44–45
Narodny, Ivan 163–64
National Arts Club 21, 141, 255, 297
   pan-American events at 179, 181–84, 205, 217
Nelson, Cary 30, 161

Nervo, Amado 88, 95, 130, 154
   translated into English 229, 233
New York
   Broadway
      in *Diario de un poeta reciencasado* (Jiménez) 143–44
      offices of Hispanic magazines on 150, 151, 235
   Bronx 12, 81
   Brooklyn 14, 139
   Central Park 110, 132, 151, 156, 282
   East River 12, 283
   Greenwich Village 109, 178, 180, 305
   Hamilton Heights 190
   Harlem 81, 236, 301
   Long Island 171, 341
      Walt Whitman's house on 145, 146–47
   Lower East Side 14, 109
   Staten Island
      De la Selva at school on 79
      ferry 203–04
      Edwin Markham living on 162–64, 316–17
      Luis Muñoz Marín living on 318
   Times Square
      setting for Chocano poem 133
   Upper West Side
      home to de la Selva 1915–19 81
   Wall Street
      Rubén Darío writes about 85–86
      'A Song for Wall Street' (Salomón de la Selva)
      Hispanic businessmen on 283
      see also Sousândrade, *O inferno de Wall Street*
   Washington Heights
      home to Hispanic Society of America 18
      José Santos Zelaya dies there 278

Washington Square
   home to Liberal Club 90, 109
   in *Diario de un poeta reciencasado* (Jiménez) 146
New York Call
   De la Selva works at 108
   read by Luis Muñoz Marín 318
New York Public Library
   42nd Street branch newly opened 73
   Port Richmond branch 318
New York Sun
   on New York's Latin colonies 282–84
   reports on dinner at Gonfarone's 306–07
Newcomb, John Timberman 30, 203–04
Nicaragua
   possible canal route 53, 80
   US intervention in 54–56, 210, 231, 250
   León 54–55, 82, 103, 249n111, 336
   see also Sandino, Augusto; Walker, William; De la Selva, Salomón, and Nicaragua; Darío, Rubén, in Nicaragua; Zelaya, José Santos
Nin, Anaïs 304, 308, 321
Norte Americano, El (magazine) 48, 325
North America 46–47
   see also continental theory
Norton, Allen 75, 76, 179
Novedades, Las 113, 118
   hosts Rubén Darío
   publishes Francisco Henríquez y Carvajal 165, 167
Nueva York 279–84

Ober, Frederick Albion 246
O'Connor, Eileen 282
Oliveira, Alberto de 229
Oliver, Julia Elizabeth *see* Foster, Jeanne Robert

Olney, Richard 50–51
O'Neill, Eugene 136, 326
Onís, Federico de 183, 281, 360
   on modernism 29–30
   at Columbia 140
Order of Ideal Friendship 81–82, 107
Ortiz Vargas, Alfredo 304, 312–13, 361
O'Sheel, Shaemus 360
   at the Poetry Society of America 24, 25, 26
   translated into Spanish 275
   defends George Viereck 299–300
Osorio Benítez, Miguel Ángel *see* Barba Jacob, Porfirio
Others 26, 192, 204, 220–21, 233–34, 278

Páez, Ramón 43
Page, Marjorie 305, 361
Palma, Ricardo 28, 31
Palmer, A. Mitchell 277, 318
Pan American conferences 44–45, 48, 69, 88, 139, 210, 320
Pan American Society 47–48
Pan American Union 45, 102, 166, 279, 296, 339, 350
   see also Barrett, John
Pan American Union building 46–47, 102, 351
Pan-American Federation of Labor 278
Pan-American Magazine 48, 183, 217, 228–33
Pan-American Poetry 222–35
Pan-American Review 48
Panama 14, 35, 39–40, 327, 346
Panama Canal 48, 53–54, 56, 62–63, 130, 246
Paris Peace Conference 278, 280
Partridge, William Ortway 264
Patagonians, The 76
Pater, Walter 170, 242
Peladan, Joséphin 65
Pen and Brush Club 22, 181

Pendas, Francisco 151
Peoli, Juan J. 12
Pérez de Ayala, Ramón 95, 130, 307, 309, 361
Petitpas' Restaurant 20, 253, 267, 294
Peynado, Francisco 87, 118, 361
Pezoa Veliz, Carlos 229
Picabia, Francis 20, 178
Picasso, Pablo 48, 76, 112, 295
Pierce, Franklin 36, 39
Pinochet Le-Brun, Tancredo 324–25, 361
   The Gulf of Misunderstanding 325–29
Poe, Edgar Allan
   and Hispanic writers 58, 65, 66, 104–05, 133, 148–49
   and modernism 32
Poetry (magazine) 23, 73, 204, 237
Poetry Society of America
   Hispanic writers at 90, 117, 145, 179, 193
   origins 23–26
Pombo, Rafael 11, 238
Ponce de León, Néstor 83
Porter, Katherine Anne 341, 342
Porter, Kenneth W. 224
Porter, William Sydney *see* Henry, O.
Pound, Ezra
   at the Poetry Society of America 26
   see also De la Selva, Salomón, and Ezra Pound
Prensa, La 14, 112, 218
   on pan Americanism 279
   on the dinner at Gonfarone's 303–04, 307–08
   see also Juegos Florales
Prospero 57, 66, 68
   see also The Tempest
Provincetown Theatre/Playhouse/Players 20, 109, 136–37, 179, 205
Puchaca y Moya, Galán *pseudonym of* De la Selva, Salomón
Puerto Rico 130, 236–37, 318, 352

Quesada, Gonzalo de 83
Quinn, John 253

Ramos, Miguel 269, 293
Rand School of Social Science 108–09, 300–02, 318
Ray, Man 75, 220
Red Scare 277, 318, 333
Reed, John 108, 278, 302
Renard, Rosita 321
Repertorio Americano 162, 171, 174, 337, 341
Requena Legarreta, Luz 282
Requena Legarreta, Pedro 153–54
Revista de Indias, La 235–37, 257
Revista Universal: Magazine Hispano-Americano 103, 150, 162
Reyes, Alfonso 61, 341
   translated into English 232
Rice, John Pierrepont 181, 205, 225, 229, 234, 361
Ried Silva, Alberto 205, 361
Rinaldo, Joel 16
Rittenhouse, Jessie v, 361–62
   at dinner at Gonfarone's 303
   at pan-American dinner (1917) 207
   and the Poetry Society of America 2, 20, 25, 90, 163, 222
   A Second Book of Modern Verse 330–31, 333
   translated into Spanish 229
   see also De la Selva, Salomón, and Jessie Rittenhouse
Rivas, Ángel César 116–17
Rivera, Diego 76, 137, 151, 342
Roberts, Walter Adolphe 101, 119, 279, 291–96, 304–05, 361–62
   'Pierrot Wounded' 294–95
   performed at Columbia University 294
Rodó, José Enrique 64, 73
   Ariel 57–61, 86, 118
Roeder, Ralph 108, 109, 111–12, 362
Romera Navarro, Manuel 116, 117, 362
Roosevelt, Kermit 184

Roosevelt, Theodore 216–17, 277
  his American foreign policy 49–56
  see also Rubén Darío, 'A Roosevelt'; De la Selva, Salomón, confronting Roosevelt
Root, Elihu 47, 51, 70
Rostand, Aura, 'El dolor me ha elegido' 175–76
  see also Selva Escoto, María Isabel
Rounsevell, Nelson 346
Rowe, Leo S. 88
Russian Revolution 113, 210

Salvatierra, Cristina *pseudonym of* De la Selva, Salomón
Sánchez, Fernando 78
Sánchez, Francisca 87
Sandburg, Carl 20, 199, 225, 226, 330
Sandino, Augusto 339, 346, 347–48
Sanger, Margaret 136, 179, 294
Sarmiento, Domingo F. 11, 37–38, 43
Schauffler, Bennet 189, 194–95, 198, 290–91, 307, 362
Schauffler, Charles E. 189, 190, 194–95, 285, 290
Schauffler, Goodrich 189, 194–95
Schauffler, Florence Manvel 189–93, 194–95, 201, 205–07, 237, 284–85, 290, 303, 362
  'Matrix' 192
  'Renaissance' 191
  'The Woman Speaks' 195–96
  see also De la Selva, Salomón, and Florence Schauffler
Schauffler, Robert Haven 231, 232, 362
Schomburg, Arturo 12
Scriabin, Alexander 108
Seeger, Alan 24, 153, 272, 362
self-determination 210–13, 278, 301
Selva, Buenaventura 78
Selva Escoto, María Isabel 172–77
  see also Rostand, Aura
Selva Escoto, Mélida 172–77
Selva Escoto, Rogerio 250, 348
Selva Glenton, Salomón 78, 249

Semprúm, Jesús 280–81
Serís de la Torre, Homero 116, 117
Sermolino, Anacleto 305
Sermolino, Maria 305–06
Seves, Elena de 307–08
Seves, Margarita de 307–08
Shaw, Albert 252–53
Shepard Rogers, Florence 200–01
Shepherd, William Robert 139, 183
Shores, Effie Marguerite *pseudonym of* De la Selva, Salomón
Shores, Robert J. 97–99, 362
Silva, José Asunción 221
Sloan, John 20, 179–80, 254
socialism 24, 108–09, 162, 300–01, 302, 318
Socialist Party of America 300–02
Society of Independent Artists 179
Somoza García, Anastasio 348
Somoza García, Luis 348
Sorolla, Joaquín 19, 142
Sorosis 321–22
Sousândrade, *O inferno de Wall Street* 32
South America 39–40, 43, 183–84, 217–18, 283
  see also continental theory; America, 'the two Americas'; Hispanic America; Latin America
South American, The (magazine) 48
Spain 2, 18, 33, 41, 56, 68, 230, 319
  Barcelona 83
  Madrid 130
Spanish America *see* Hispanic America
Spanish-American War (1898) 33, 52, 56, 121, 187, 236
Sparta 59, 60, 61, 167
Stead, W. T., *The Americanization of the World* 61, 65
Stedman, Edmund C. 21, 22
Stevens, Wallace 20, 75, 76, 221, 232
Stevenson, Archibald 262, 301
Storni, Alfonsina 119, 338

Stravinsky, Igor 73, 111, 169
Strong, Josiah, *Our Country* 38, 50

Tablada, José Juan 153, 154–57, 233, 282, 310–11
   Al sol y bajo la luna 154–55
   'Lawn Tennis' 151, 156–57
Taft, William 56, 213, 308
Tagore, Rabindranath 23, 153
Tarbell, Ida M. 20, 22, 181
Teasdale, Sara 231, 330
Tempest, The 57–68, 72, 147
   see also Ariel; Caliban; Miranda; Prospero
Tenney, Oswald *pseudonym of* De la Selva, Salomón
Teurbe Tolón, Miguel 11, 238
Theatre Guild 109, 256, 278, 357
Thomas, Augustus 181, 297
Thompson, Francis 242, 275
Tomb of the Unknown Soldier 343–44
Torres Caicedo, José María 39
   'Las dos Américas' 40–41
Torres Calderón de Pinillos, Carmen 303, 319–20, 321
Torres García, Joaquín 76
Torres Rioseco, Arturo 93, 304, 313–16, 363
   'Antonio de Silva' 315–16
   'Rosas de nuestra América' 313–15
Torri, Julio 341
Treaty of Versailles 278
Tresca, Carlo 109, 363
Trotsky, Leon 178, 180, 210–11
Turcios, Froylán 226
Turner, John Kenneth 292

Ugarte, Adela *pseudonym of* De la Selva, Salomón
Ugarte, Manuel 62, 73, 280
Unamuno, Miguel de 5, 27
Underhill, John Garrett, 148
Unión Benéfica Española 218
Untermeyer, Louis 2, 24, 25, 109, 122, 164, 330, 363

Urbina, Luis G. 231
Urcas, Miguel del Carmen *pseudonym of* De la Selva, Salomón
Ureña de Henríquez, Salomé 107, 114–15
Urtecho, Rafael 324
USA
   Boston 21, 22–23, 59, 76
   Chicago 23, 59, 98, 190, 198–201
   Georgia, lynching in 169
   Washington DC 46, 49, 94, 296, 322
   see also New York; Spanish-American War (1898); US–Mexico War
US–Mexico War (1846–48) 33, 36, 39, 187

Valencia, Guillermo 229, 232
Valle-Inclán, Ramón del 341
Vallejo, César 5, 27
Van Vechten, Carl 209
Varela, Félix 10
Vargas, Julián *pseudonym of* De la Selva, Salomón
Vargas Vila, José Ignacio 97
Vargas Vila, José María 83, 183, 280
Vasconcelos, José 61, 110, 153, 340, 341, 345, 349, 363
   on Pan Americanism 347
Venezuela 50–51
Venizelos, Eleutherios 213–15
Verlaine, Paul 85–86, 96
Viera, Rafael 218
Viereck, George Sylvester 23, 25, 299–300, 363
Villa, Pancho 108, 129, 131, 149, 188
Villaverde, Cirilo 12

Walker, William
   Jose Martí on 45
   in Nicaragua 36, 37, 39, 78, 248, 347–48
   see also Torres Caicedo, José María, 'Las dos Américas' 39

Walsh, Thomas 116, 181, 281, 263
  translates Rubén Darío 138
  translated by Salomón de la Selva 137
  works with Salomón de la Selva 134, 135, 225, 285
  and *Hispanic Anthology* 138
  and Juan Ramón Jiménez 145
  reviews *Tropical Town* 240–42
Wardman, Vera Gwendolen Roma 274
Washington Square Players 109, 111, 208, 278
Weeks, Raymond 232–33, 364
Westerleigh Collegiate Institute 25, 79, 81, 111
Wheeler, Edward J. 90, 163, 297, 303, 364
  in London 266
  and the Poetry Society of America 23, 25, 181, 300
Whitman, Walt 69, 83, 128, 162, 317
  celebration of 100th anniversary 317
  house on Long Island 145–47
Widdemer, Margaret 2, 22, 24, 25–26, 120, 164, 330, 364
Wilhelm I (Kaiser) 299
Wilhelm II (Kaiser) 213–15
Williams, Raquel Hélène Hoheb 219
Williams, Raymond 30
Williams, William Carlos 75, 101, 219–21, 233–34
Williams, William George 219, 221, 233–34
Williams Poetry Society, The 194
Wilson, Woodrow
  and the Dominican Republic 66, 165, 168, 323
  his idealism 180–81, 208, 280
  and Pan Americanism 210
  satirised 213–15
  and self-determination 210–13, 278
  speech to Mexican journalists 211–13, 323
  visit to Williams College 157–58
  and First World War 188, 210, 299
Wood, Clement 24, 108–09, 275, 364
Woodruff, Helen S. 22, 99–100, 275, 264
Woolf, Virginia 29–30
Woolworth, Frank B. 277
Woolworth Building 84, 143, 243–44
Wyllarde, Dolf 246

Yeats, John Butler 253, 254, 267
Yeats, W. B. 23n28

Zaturenska, Marya 197, 254, 285, 287–91, 364
  see also De la Selva, Salomón, and Marya Zaturenska
Zayas, Marius de 13, 48, 75, 76, 137, 365
Zayas Enríquez, Rafael de 13, 48, 365
Zelaya, Dr Aníbal 88, 96
Zelaya, José Santos 54–55, 249–50, 277